ASPEN COLLEGE SERIES

W9-BCX-776

THE ABCs OF DEBT

A CASE STUDY APPROACH TO DEBTOR/CREDITOR RELATIONS AND BANKRUPTCY LAW

Third Edition

S<small>TEPHEN</small> P. P<small>ARSONS</small>, J.D.

Wolters Kluwer
Law & Business

Printed in the United States of America.

1 2 3 4 5 6 7 8 9 0

ISBN 978-1-4548-2803-7

Library of Congress Cataloging-in-Publication Data

Parsons, Stephen P., 1949-
  The ABCs of debt : a case study approach to debtor/creditor relations and bankruptcy law / Stephen P. Parsons, J.D. – Third edition.
      pages cm. – (Aspen college series)
  Includes an index.
  ISBN 978-1-4548-2803-7 (alk. paper) – ISBN 1-4548-2803-X (alk. paper) 1.

  Debtor and creditor–United States. 2. Bankruptcy–United States. I. Title.

KF1501.P37 2013
346.7307'7–dc23
                                        2013027041

Certified Chain of Custody
Product Line Contains At Least
20% Certified Forest Content
www.sfiprogram.org
SFI-00756

About Wolters Kluwer Law & Business

Wolters Kluwer Law & Business is a leading global provider of intelligent information and digital solutions for legal and business professionals in key specialty areas, and respected educational resources for professors and law students. Wolters Kluwer Law & Business connects legal and business professionals as well as those in the education market with timely, specialized authoritative content and information-enabled solutions to support success through productivity, accuracy and mobility.

Serving customers worldwide, Wolters Kluwer Law & Business products include those under the Aspen Publishers, CCH, Kluwer Law International, Loislaw, ftwilliam.com and MediRegs family of products.

CCH products have been a trusted resource since 1913, and are highly regarded resources for legal, securities, antitrust and trade regulation, government contracting, banking, pension, payroll, employment and labor, and healthcare reimbursement and compliance professionals.

Aspen Publishers products provide essential information to attorneys, business professionals and law students. Written by preeminent authorities, the product line offers analytical and practical information in a range of specialty practice areas from securities law and intellectual property to mergers and acquisitions and pension/benefits. Aspen's trusted legal education resources provide professors and students with high-quality, up-to-date and effective resources for successful instruction and study in all areas of the law.

Kluwer Law International products provide the global business community with reliable international legal information in English. Legal practitioners, corporate counsel and business executives around the world rely on Kluwer Law journals, looseleafs, books, and electronic products for comprehensive information in many areas of international legal practice.

Loislaw is a comprehensive online legal research product providing legal content to law firm practitioners of various specializations. Loislaw provides attorneys with the ability to quickly and efficiently find the necessary legal information they need, when and where they need it, by facilitating access to primary law as well as state-specific law, records, forms and treatises.

ftwilliam.com offers employee benefits professionals the highest quality plan documents (retirement, welfare and non-qualified) and government forms (5500/PBGC, 1099 and IRS) software at highly competitive prices.

MediRegs products provide integrated health care compliance content and software solutions for professionals in healthcare, higher education and life sciences, including professionals in accounting, law and consulting.

Wolters Kluwer Law & Business, a division of Wolters Kluwer, is headquartered in New York. Wolters Kluwer is a market-leading global information services company focused on professionals.

This book is dedicated to the memory
of Mr. and Mrs. William H. Parsons:

Bill and Juanita
Mom and Dad

Some debts can never be repaid

Summary of Contents

Contents

Preface

Approach

There are two fundamental premises underlying this book. The first is that the specialized study of bankruptcy requires an adequate foundation in other aspects of debtor/creditor relations that are too often ignored or treated only superficially in bankruptcy texts. Grasping bankruptcy concepts and procedures is challenging enough for those who understand loans, lines of credit, installment sales, consensual security arrangements involving real and personal property, surety and guarantor arrangements, statutory and equitable liens, and the priority issues that arise in all those debtor/creditor relationships. Without that foundation, the student undertaking the study of bankruptcy is at a serious disadvantage. Debt collection is another fundamental aspect of debtor/creditor relations that deserves much more attention than it usually receives in texts for this field. This book is unique in that it comprehensively addresses the topics of how debt is created (Part A) and collected (Part B) preparatory to the in-depth study of bankruptcy law and procedure that follows (Part C).

The second fundamental premise of this book is that bankruptcy and related areas of debtor/creditor law are best taught using a realistic, **case-study** approach. While most current bankruptcy texts avoid the error of teaching too much theory, many err in utilizing a piecemeal approach, in which topics such as the automatic stay, adequate protection, turnover and avoidance powers, cramdown and impairment options, postpetition debt, the use of cash collateral, the assumption or rejection of executory contracts, etc., are presented in isolation, making it difficult for the student to understand when and how such concepts come into play in a particular bankruptcy case. This book is unique in that it uses realistic, current case studies to introduce, explain, and illustrate bankruptcy law and procedure. Students see how a bankruptcy case unfolds, from the moment a debtor makes contact with a lawyer until the case is closed. That chronological, step-by-step approach is used to study cases filed under Chapter 7, Chapter 13, and Chapter 11. This book aspires not just to teach students "about" bankruptcy, but to teach them how to "do" bankruptcy.

Organization of the Book

The text is divided into three parts:

> **Part A:** The Creation of Debt (Chapters Two through Six)
> **Part B:** The Collection of Debt (Chapters Seven through Eleven)
> **Part C:** The Discharge or Reorganization of Debt in Bankruptcy (Chapters Twelve through Twenty-Five)

Following an introductory chapter that explains the learning approach to be used and debuts the three case studies utilized throughout Parts A and B of the text, Part A begins with a general overview of the various ways debt is created. It then focuses on particular categories of contractual debt, including the traditional loan, the line of credit loan, revolving credit arrangements, consumer payday loans, installment sales, and rent-to-own transactions. Credit reports and credit reporting agencies are examined, along with key provisions of the Fair Credit Reporting Act. Surety and guaranty contracts are addressed next, followed by an in-depth look at mortgages and security interests in personal property. Finally, Part A addresses nonconsensual statutory and equitable liens.

Part B begins by considering prelitigation efforts to collect delinquent debt, including the demand letter. Comprehensive coverage of the Fair Debt Collection Practices Act, as well as tort remedies for abusive collection tactics, is included. The text then walks the student step-by-step through a collection lawsuit, from the filing of the complaint through final judgment. Coverage is given to how a default judgment is taken, common defenses, the role of formal discovery, and alternative dispute resolution. Extraordinary prejudgment remedies and fraudulent transfers are covered in depth, as is entitlement to prejudgment and postjudgment interest. Finally, Part B addresses execution on a final judgment, including the appeal process and how a stay of execution is obtained. The role of exemptions, joint property, and trust arrangements in execution is examined, along with postjudgment discovery, methods of executing on a judgment, and how to enforce a foreign judgment.

Part C begins with an overview of the Bankruptcy Code, modern bankruptcy practice, and the organization and jurisdiction of the U.S. bankruptcy courts. It then introduces three new case studies with realistic assignment memos set forth in the appendices and complete **Case Files** provided for students on the disc accompanying the text. The case studies utilized in Part C illustrate how cases under Chapters 7, 13, and 11 are handled from beginning to end. Bankruptcy concepts and procedures are addressed as they actually arise in real cases. The case files on the disc accompanying the text allow students to actually see completed petitions, schedules, statements, motions, objections, notices, and orders, all of which are routinely drafted by paralegals for review by an attorney and filed in bankruptcy cases. Though cases under all chapters of the Code are covered in Part C, detailed consideration is given to those most commonly filed: the Chapter 7 liquidation, the Chapter 13 reorganization for individuals with regular income, and the Chapter 11 business reorganization.

The disc accompanying the text also contains numerous **To Learn More** (**TLM**) activities for each chapter. The TLMs are designed to challenge and enable the student to do further research on issues raised in the text or to consult additional resources for further learning. Some of the TLMs are historical (e.g., Debtor/creditor tensions in the newly independent United States were a major factor in the decision to convene the meeting in Philadelphia that became the Constitutional Convention of 1787). Some are policy oriented (e.g., Debt collection work is increasingly being outsourced to India and countries in South America; the financial services industry spent more than $100 million lobbying for the passage of BAPCPA in the eight years it was under consideration by Congress). Most require the student to locate and apply local law or procedure to the general topics raised in the text (e.g., Does your state regulate the interest rate that can be charged by payday loan companies? What property exemptions are recognized in your state?). As every instructor knows, it is not enough for students to learn what the law is generally around the country—they need to know the law of their particular state. It is not enough for them to learn the different procedures bankruptcy courts or trustees across the nation may follow—they need to know the procedures followed by the bankruptcy courts and trustees in the federal district where they will work.

The **Instructor's Manual (IM)** contains material that the instructor can use to assign **Drafting Exercises (DE)** to students as well. There are two DEs to accompany Part A of the text relating to the creation of debt and two to accompany Part B of the text relating to the collection of debt. There are ten DEs to accompany Part C of the text relating to bankruptcy. Five of the ten bankruptcy DEs for Part C involve a Chapter 7 consumer bankruptcy case; two of the ten involve a Chapter 13 case; and three of the ten involve a Chapter 11 business reorganization case. To assist with evaluating and grading student work on the ten bankruptcy DEs, the IM also provides the instructor with **Model Grading Documents** for each of those exercises prepared with Best Case software and a suggested grading matrix for each as well.

Key Features

As noted, the book utilizes realistic, current *case studies*. The first three case studies are introduced in Chapter One and are used throughout Parts A and B. The characters in each case study are given sufficient history, personality, and context that they become real people for students, not just names on a page. Debt-related problems happen to real people in the real world, and students should be taught to see clients as real people with unique stories and circumstances. Following the same three case studies throughout Parts A and B enables students to get to know these clients and their financial circumstances. Three additional case studies with case files are utilized in Part C to illustrate bankruptcy concepts and procedures being covered in Part C. The disc accompanying the text contains exhaustive case files to accompany the bankruptcy case studies used in Part C.

Numerous **Examples** are provided throughout each chapter, along with timely and relevant **Illustrations**. In addition, a number of **Problem-Hypothetical (P-H)** activities appear throughout each chapter, presenting the student with the opportunity to immediately apply what is being read in the text. Similarly, a number of **Ethical Considerations (EC)** appear periodically, drawing the student's attention to a relevant ethical or professional challenge presented by the topic under discussion. At the end of each chapter is a **Conclusion** that serves as a bridge to the next chapter, a comprehensive **Chapter Summary**, 10 to 15 open-ended **Review Questions**, and a list of **Words and Phrases to Remember**.

In addition to the Drafting Exercises previously mentioned, the IM contains suggested approaches to teaching with the text including testing and grading, and a comprehensive test bank with answer key. The TLMs are included in the IM as well since the instructor may wish to utilize some of them for graded assignments.

The substantive content of each chapter of the text, the illustrations, the forms used in the Case Files and in the Model Documents for the Drafting Exercises, and the TLMs are updated and supplemented by the author via postings on the Author Updates and Professor Materials links to the text website at http://www.aspenparalegaled.com/books/parsons_abcdebt/default.asp.

The text is designed for use by both law students and paralegal students. Thus the comprehensive term, legal professional, is used throughout to refer to the student.

A note on the dates used in the text: To keep the dates as current as possible, the illustrations and case file documents utilize a dating system in which YR00 is always the current year. YR-1 is last year, YR-2 is two years ago, YR+1 is next year, YR+2 is two years from now, and so on. As with all the pedagogical features of this text it is hoped this will make the task of mastering debtor/creditor relations and bankruptcy law as easy as A, B, C.

New for the Third Edition

For the third edition, more than two dozen new examples and P-Hs have been added along with several new illustrations. All statistics cited regarding consumer and business indebtedness and bankruptcy filings are current through the date of publication. The bankruptcy forms accompanying the three case studies used in Part C of the text and available to the student on the bind-in CD accompanying the text have been updated, as have the model forms available in the IM for grading the drafting exercises included there. The TLM activities that accompany each chapter have been expanded and updated as well. Answers to the end-of-chapter review questions now appear in the IM.

Additional material on lender liability and predatory lending has been added to Chapter Three. References to regulations promulgated by the new and aggressive Consumer Financial Protection Bureau have been added throughout Part A of the text. The material on nonconsensual liens in Chapter Six has been expanded, as have the topics of exempt property, debt collection, and debt collection abuses such as body attachment in Part B of the text. As the U.S. Supreme Court continues to mandate the enforceability of contractual arbitration clauses over objections based on state law with decisions such as *AT&T Mobility v. Concepcion*, that and other ADR topics have been expanded in Chapter Eight and the applicability of prepetition arbitration clauses to disputes arising in a bankruptcy case is addressed in Chapter Thirteen.

The introductory bankruptcy material previously covered in Chapter Twelve has been broken down into two chapters for the third edition. Revised Chapter Twelve introduces the topic, provides a history of bankruptcy practice, and generally summarizes the chapters of the bankruptcy code. A new Chapter Thirteen discusses the central role of the U.S. bankruptcy courts and provides a detailed analysis of their subject matter and personal jurisdiction. And, in light of the hornets' nest stirred up by *Stern v. Marshall* regarding the constitutional power of a bankruptcy court to decide core proceedings in a bankruptcy case, that crucial topic is addressed in new Chapter Thirteen. The remaining chapters of Part C of the text have been renumbered owing to this revision so that the third edition now sports a total of 25 chapters rather than 24 as in the second edition.

In addition to *Concepcion* and *Stern*, two other Supreme Court decisions involving the Code since the second edition appeared are *Ransom v. FIA Card Services* and *Bullock v. BankChampaign NA*. *Ransom* deals with the availability of the expense deduction for vehicle ownership in Chapter 7 and Chapter 13 cases and is addressed in Chapters Fourteen and Twenty of the text. *Bullock* clarifies what is required to show defalcation in a fiduciary capacity in order to prohibit discharge of such a debt and is addressed in Chapter Eighteen. In addition to new Supreme Court decisions, there are numerous citations to recent lower court decisions throughout Part C of the text as questions about the 2005 BAPCPA amendments to the bankruptcy code are slowly but surely being dealt with.

Discussion of a Chapter 7 debtor's options to retain pledged property via reaffirmation or redemption after BAPCPA or via ride through or lien stripping after *Dewsnup v. Timm* has been expanded in Chapter Eighteen. Similarly, the continuing impact of *Nobleman v. American Savings Bank* on a Chapter 13 debtor's cramdown option on a principal residence receives more attention in Chapter Twenty-One. The discussion of the automatic stay and remedies for its violation has been updated and expanded in Chapter Sixteen. And a new expanded section on the Chapter 9 municipality bankruptcy now appears at the end of Chapter Twenty-Five.

The bankruptcy material in Part C of the text has been updated to reflect the annual adjustment of IRS expense standards as of 2013, as well as the April 2013 triennial adjustment of applicable dollar limits for allowed exemptions and for determining debtor qualification status under various chapters of the Code.

Textbook Resources

The companion website at www.aspenparalegaled.com/books/parsons _abcdebt/default.asp includes additional resources for students and instructors, including:

- Study aids to help students master the key concepts for this course. Visit the site to access interactive StudyMate exercises such as flash cards, matching, fill-in-the-blank, and crosswords. These activities are also available for download to an iPod or other hand-held device.
- Instructor resources to accompany the text
- Links to helpful websites and updates.

Blackboard and eCollege course materials are available to supplement this text. This online courseware is designed to streamline the teaching of the course, providing valuable resources from the book in an accessible electronic format.

Instructor resources to accompany this text include a comprehensive Instructor's Manual, Test Bank, PowerPoint slides, and sample exercises for use with Best Case bankruptcy software. All of these materials are available on a CD-ROM or for download from our companion website.

Appreciation

The author wishes to thank the law students at the Appalachian School of Law in Grundy, Virginia, and the paralegal students in the Walters State Paralegal Program in Morristown, Tennessee, for serving as the amenable guinea pigs for the development of the materials and approach used here. Appreciation is also expressed to the many clients who entrusted the author with various debtor/creditor issues over the past 30 years—especially those who paid their bill.

A special thanks to Best Case Solutions for allowing the author to utilize its excellent bankruptcy software in connection with the case file documents created for use in Part C of the text and included on the disc accompanying the text.

And, as always, love and appreciation for the patience and support of the home team: Marcia, Andrew, and Emily Grayce.

THE ABCs OF DEBT

Chapter One:

▶ Introduction to Debtor/ Creditor Law and the Case Study Approach

At daybreak I'll be off, to see the Kaukonians about a debt they owe me, an old one and no trifle.

—Homer, The Odyssey

A. ▶ The Scope of Debtor/Creditor Law

This text will cover three distinct but related topics in the following order:

Part A: The creation of debt
Part B: The collection of debt
Part C: The discharge or reorganization of debt in bankruptcy

Debt The obligation of one person, enforceable at law, to pay money, tender property, or provide services to another now or in the future.

As you can see from that list, **debt** is the central, unifying theme of this study. The word "debt" can have a variety of meanings, some legal and some only moral— look at the dedication page of this book for an example of the latter. But for our purposes, debt is the obligation of one person, enforceable at law, to pay money, tender property, or provide services to another now or in the future. Most debt involves the obligation to pay money.

A study of debt is just one aspect of the broader legal topic of **commercial law**, that is, the law of commerce or doing business. Commercial law encompasses not just the creation and management of debt but many other legal aspects of doing business that are beyond the scope of our study. Here we will focus on **debtor/ creditor law**, that is, the various laws relating to the rights and obligations existing between the person who owes a debt (the **debtor**) and the one to whom the debt is owed (the **creditor**).

Debtor Person liable for a debt.

Creditor One to whom a debt is owed.

Many lawyers specialize in debtor/creditor law while others only dabble in it. The lawyer who specializes may refer to himself as a commercial lawyer, or a collection lawyer, or a bankruptcy practitioner, or a creditor's attorney, or a debtor's attorney, depending on which aspects of debtor/creditor law he practices. But all lawyers will encounter client problems involving debtor/creditor questions no matter what kind of law they practice. And the **legal professional** who assists a lawyer in debtor/creditor law must be *knowledgeable of the law* in this area and *possess the unique skills* required to effectively assist a supervising lawyer working in this area, whether that lawyer specializes or dabbles (see Part E of this chapter).

Consumer debt Debt incurred for personal, family, or household purposes.

In the course of our study you will learn that there are numerous ways to categorize debt. For introductory purposes, let's start with one of the basic categorizations, the difference between consumer debt and commercial debt. **Consumer debt** refers generally to indebtedness incurred for personal, family, or household purposes. Such debt may include a home mortgage, an apartment lease, a car loan, credit card debt, school loans, utility bills, medical bills, insurance premiums, alimony or child support obligations, federal and state income taxes, state and local property taxes, and the like. **Commercial debt** refers generally to indebtedness incurred for business or commercial purposes. Such debt may include the lease or a mortgage on a business location as well as the business's obligations for utility bills, insurance premiums, business taxes, employee withholding and salaries, materials and equipment purchased, services provided, and so forth.

A debt may be **current**, meaning that it is owed at this moment, or it may be **future**, meaning that the obligation exists now but need not be satisfied until sometime in the future. A debt may be **liquidated**, meaning that we know its dollar value to the penny, or it may be **unliquidated**, meaning that we do not yet know its dollar value. A debt may be **fixed** or **noncontingent**, meaning that nothing else needs to happen for the obligation to exist, or it may be **contingent**, meaning that it will only exist if and when another event occurs. A debt may be **disputed** by the debtor in whole or part or it may be **undisputed**. A debt to pay money may be **unsecured**, meaning that upon default of the debtor's obligation to pay, the creditor's only resort is to seek a court judgment against the debtor, or the debt may be **secured**, which means that upon default, the creditor may be able to seize certain designated real or personal property to satisfy the obligation. We will learn much more about these various categories of debt as we proceed.

B.   Introduction to the Case Studies

Throughout our study of debtor/creditor topics we will utilize *case studies*: hypothetical cases involving realistic debtors with realistic debt problems. The three case studies we will use throughout Parts A and B of the text are introduced in this chapter. If your instructor elects to do so, these case studies may also be utilized in Part C of the text when you are assigned to prepare appropriate bankruptcy filings for one or more of the case study debtors.

The clients involved in our first case study have a number of issues arising out of consumer debt. Meet Nick and Pearl Murphy (Illustration 1-a). Throughout Parts A and B of the text, we will refer to the Murphys' file as "Case Study #1" in order to illustrate typical consumer issues in debtor/creditor law and to learn how those issues are analyzed and resolved by the competent attorney assisted by the able legal professional.

We will have much more to say about the Murphys' financial circumstances throughout the text. But be aware that their various debts are all typical consumer debts. Moreover, unexpected medical costs and improvident credit card use that we see in the case study, together with unexpected job loss and divorce, are leading causes of consumer insolvency and bankruptcy.

Illustration 1-a: CASE STUDY #1: NICHOLAS (NICK) AND PEARL MURPHY

MEMORANDUM

TO: Paralegal
FROM: Supervising attorney
RE: Nicholas and Pearl Murphy

Nick and Pearl Murphy are a married couple residing in Capitol City. They have been married for 12 years and have two children, Lynette, who is 9, and Lyndon, who is 11. By an earlier marriage, Nick has a third child, Robbie, who is 15. Nick himself is 40 years old and Pearl is 39. Nick, who dropped out of high school and later earned his GED, has a degree from State Technical School and has worked in the local office of Overland Truck Services, Inc. for five years. Effective January 1 of this year he was promoted to manager of the office making $60,000 a year. Pearl has a bachelor's degree from State University in elementary education and worked as a teacher for the Capitol City public school system, full-time, until August 1, YR-3 when she underwent an emergency appendectomy and suffered complications leaving her with chronic stomach and bowel problems. Pearl was unable to work full-time for more than a year following the surgery. She was able to work some last year as a substitute teacher and returned to work full-time in January of this year.

Nick and Pearl own their home, which they purchased ten years ago for $125,000. First Bank of Capitol City holds the mortgage on the Murphys' home, which has a current balance of $92,500. The Murphys make a monthly mortgage payment of $993 to First Bank. The couple owns two vehicles. Nick drives a five-year-old Ford F-150 Truck that has 75,000 miles on it and is paid for. Pearl drives a five-year-old Honda Accord, which the Murphys bought used three years ago. They still owe $8,900 on the Honda and make monthly payments of $310 to Friendly Finance Company. Friendly Finance holds a security interest in the car to secure payment of the obligation. The Murphys have two credit cards, a Master Card with a maximum limit of $5,000 and a Visa with a limit of $3,000. The couple has maxed out both cards and pays only the minimum balance due on the cards each month. They also have an installment sales contract (which is considered in Chapter Three) with Shears Department Store for the purchase of living room furniture on which there is a $4,592 balance owing.

Less than two months before Pearl's emergency appendectomy, the Murphys took out a home improvement loan from the Teachers Credit Union in Capitol City in the amount of $35,000 to add two new rooms to their house. The credit union took a second mortgage on the house to secure repayment of the loan. The construction had barely begun when Pearl had her surgery and was never finished. Most of the money borrowed from the credit union went to pay off expenses arising from Pearl's illness. The credit union loan is to be paid back over ten years at $406 per month. The Murphys are currently three payments in arrears to the credit union and it is threatening foreclosure on their home. Nick is obligated by court order to pay his ex-wife, Sharon Murphy, $400 per month as child support for Robbie until the boy turns 18.

The Murphys are in a financial crisis due to continuing medical expenses related to Pearl's condition and the loss of her full-time income. Pearl's insurance covered most of the expenses related to the original surgery but the costs related to the complications and continuing treatment and medications have far exceeded the insurance policy's coverage. At this point, Pearl's unpaid medical bills total $28,000 and her monthly medications cost $325 out of pocket. They used up all their savings while she was not working and now are too far behind to catch up.

P-H 1-a: How many different consumer debts do the Murphys have based on the summary in Illustration 1-a?

P-H 1-b: What follow-up questions would you want to ask at this point concerning the Murphys' financial circumstances?

EC 1-a: Is there any ethical problem presented by one lawyer representing both Mr. and Mrs. Murphy in connection with their financial woes? Would your answer change if the couple was separated or divorcing? Why?

Oftentimes clients present debtor/creditor issues involving a mix of consumer and commercial debt. Meet Abelard (Abe) Mendoza (Illustration 1-b), whose case presents such a mix. Throughout the text, we will refer to the Mendoza file as "Case Study #2" in order to illustrate typical mixed consumer/commercial issues in debtor/creditor law and to learn how those issues are analyzed and resolved by the competent attorney assisted by the able paralegal.

We will have much more to say about the Mr. Mendoza's financial circumstances throughout the text. But note that his personal and family finances are intermingled with his business concerns. He has also made a series of poor financial decisions that are all too typical of the unsophisticated small-business person. These decisions have left him vulnerable and now he needs sound legal advice.

P-H 1-c: How many different types of consumer debts does Mr. Mendoza have based on the summary in Illustration 1-b? How many types of commercial debts?

P-H 1-d: What follow-up questions would you want to ask at this point concerning Mr. Mendoza's financial circumstances?

P-H 1-e: Make a list of things Mr. Mendoza should have done differently that might have prevented his present difficulties.

EC 1-b: If your lawyer supervisor agrees to undertake representation of Mr. Mendoza and his son David later comes to the same lawyer seeking representation on the criminal charge only, can that lawyer ethically undertake David's defense? Can she ethically undertake representation of both David and Mr. Mendoza regarding their financial woes? If your lawyer supervisor had represented City County Bank in connection with a school loan to David and the later, fraudulent business loan to David, can she now undertake representation of Mr. Mendoza?

And then there are the pure commercial or business cases that sometimes present themselves to the lawyer. Let's get to know Tomorrow Today, Inc. (Illustration 1-c). Throughout the text, we will refer to the Tomorrow Today, Inc. file as "Case Study #3" in order to illustrate typical commercial issues in debtor/creditor law and to learn how those issues are analyzed and resolved by the competent attorney assisted by the able paralegal.

We will have much more to say about the TTI's financial circumstances throughout the text. But note that this is a sophisticated commercial transaction involving many millions of dollars. A lot is on the line for all the parties involved.

Illustration 1-b: CASE STUDY #2: ABE MENDOZA

MEMORANDUM

TO: Paralegal
FROM: Supervising attorney
RE: Abelard Mendoza

Abelard (Abe) Mendoza immigrated legally to the United States from Mexico 35 years ago and later became a U.S. citizen. He married and raised two daughters and a son in Capitol City. He and his wife, Maria, also built a successful construction company, known as Mendoza Construction. The business was owned by Mr. Mendoza and his wife and was never incorporated. Two years ago Mr. Mendoza lost his wife to cancer and now, at age 58, his life revolves around his children.

Mr. Mendoza's youngest child is his son, David, who is now 28. In school, David was always a good student and showed talent in the sciences. However, he has had trouble deciding exactly what he wants to do for a career. He received a bachelor's degree from State University, followed by a masters in biology from the same university. He spent 18 months in a doctoral program at UCLA before dropping out, then two more years in medical school before leaving that.

David borrowed money in connection with every phase of his higher education and his parents co-signed one promissory note and executed a separate guaranty agreement (see Illustration 4-a) promising to repay one other if David failed to do so. All those obligations are now past due and David is unable to pay them so the creditors are demanding payment from Abe. The two separate notes reflecting David's educational loans for which Mr. Mendoza is liable exceed $60,000.

A year before his wife became ill, and while their annual income from the construction company was in excess of $300,000, Mendoza and his wife purchased a new home in Capitol City. They borrowed $500,000 from Security Trust Bank in Capitol City and pledged the land and house as security for repayment. The monthly payments on that mortgage are $2,500.

Last year Mr. Mendoza decided to turn the construction business over to his son, David. Mendoza himself now works as the project manager on the City Heights Condominium project, a $200 million development along the river that flows through downtown Capitol City, under contract with the owner of the project, City Heights Limited Partnership. The project has not been going well. The owner is in constant dispute with the general contractor on the job. Scheduled cash advances have been withheld from the general contractor because of the disputes and unpaid subcontractors and suppliers are threatening to place liens on the property. Mendoza fears he will be named as a defendant in numerous lawsuits arising out of the project. Soon after turning the construction business over to David Mendoza was audited by the Internal Revenue Service for the first time ever, and the government has just issued an assessment against him for unpaid income taxes for three prior tax years, plus penalties and interest, totaling $50,000. To make matters worse, recently Mr. Mendoza discovered that the bookkeeper he had hired after his wife's death (she always kept the books for the business, as well as for the family finances) has been systematically embezzling ever since she came to work for him. It looks like she has drained more than $100,000 of cash out of the company bank account, which was used to fund ongoing business operations. Mendoza had no security bond or fidelity insurance from which to recoup the loss and the woman has disappeared along with the stolen cash.

As if matters were not already bad enough, yesterday Mendoza learned that his son David procured a loan in the amount of $350,000 last year from the City County Bank in Capitol City using false financial statements listing assets he did not actually have and omitting numerous debts he did have. Apparently David, unknown to Mr. Mendoza, invested the money in a real estate scheme with some friends. The investment failed and the money is gone. City County Bank has already sued David and is demanding that Mr. Mendoza pay the money back pursuant to the guaranty he signed in favor of City County Bank in connection with two of David's school loans. Mr. Mendoza also fears that David will be criminally prosecuted as a result of the fraudulent financial statements.

Illustration 1-c: CASE STUDY #3: TOMORROW TODAY, INC.

MEMORANDUM

TO: Paralegal
FROM: Supervising attorney
RE: Tomorrow Today, Inc.

Tomorrow Today, Inc. (TTI) is an advanced technology company, the brainchild of Rosemary Chin, Donald Brabson, and Howard Kine. The three were college classmates at Stanford. Chin holds a doctorate in physics, Brabson is a mechanical engineer, while Kine is a computer software genius. They created TTI together their first year out of college and remain the only shareholders in the corporation. For the first several years of its existence, TTI enjoyed great success with contracts for the development of computerized traffic control systems for large urban areas and high-speed mass transit systems for the government of Japan.

Five years ago TTI procured a contract with Lockland Hughes Corporation, a major weapons manufacturer for the U.S. Department of Defense and the European Union, to develop a futuristic sounding defensive military device called MIES (Mobile Infantry Energy Shield). The theory behind MIES is that soldiers in the field can carry a portable computerized device, probably located in the helmet, having the ability to detect a moving projectile headed toward the soldier and instantaneously project an energy field around the soldier sufficient to block the projectile, deflect its line of flight, or at least disperse its explosive impact sufficiently to protect the soldier. The device, if it can be proven practical, has the potential to revolutionize infantry combat, particularly in urban warfare.

TTI has invested most of its resources in the MIES contract. That contract called for delivery of a working prototype 18 months ago. Despite major advances and promising tests, the prototype was not ready then and Lockland Hughes gave TTI a contract extension that expires in 12 months. Lockland Hughes has made it clear it will not extend its contract with TTI again beyond that 12-month deadline.

But TTI has run into financing problems. Five years ago, when it procured the MIES contract, TTI obtained a $10 million line of credit from its primary lender, United Bank of America (UBA) to finance research and development. TTI, of course, pledged most of its assets as security for the loan. At the time, TTI had $5 million in cash of its own. It went through its cash and the full line of credit during the first three years of development and had to go to a second lender, Bank of Europa (BE), for an additional $7.5 million line of credit, which it has now exhausted. Like UBA, BE took a security interest in most of the assets of TTI. That security interest is second or junior to UBA's.

Under the terms of the UBA line of credit, TTI has been making interest only payments, but the entire principle amount of $10 million is now due and payable and TTI does not have it. Similarly, the entire $7.5 million principle amount of the BE line of credit becomes due and payable three months from now. TTI believes it is within six months of having a working prototype of the MIES ready to deliver to Lockland Hughes. Once it does so, its contract with Lockland Hughes calls for payment of a $30 million lump sum to TTI with the expectation of a long-term exclusive contract for mass production of MIES if Lockland Hughes can sell the idea to the U.S. government.

In order to complete its production of MIES according to this projected schedule, TTI needs more cash, at least $5 million dollars. Both UBA and BE have refused TTI's requests for further loans and UBA is demanding immediate repayment of its loan and is threatening repossession of the pledged TTI assets if payment is not forthcoming.

TTI has 20 employees at various levels, not including the three principals in the company. It leases office space in downtown Capitol City and pays $2,000 a month for that space. It also leases a 100 acre test site in Nevada and pays $5,000 a month for it. TTI is current on its office lease payments but is two months behind on its test site lease.

P-H 1-f: There is one aspect of this commercial transaction that involves the personal assets of the owners of TTI. What is that?

P-H 1-g: What follow-up questions would you want to ask at this point concerning TTI's financial circumstances?

P-H 1-h: Make a list of all the categories of natural persons and businesses whose future might be dramatically impacted by what happens with TTI.

EC 1-c: Assume that you work for an attorney whose firm represents UBA, and his firm has been instructed to declare TTI in default on its obligation to UBA and to repossess TTI assets. You are aware that your attorney supervisor has been dating Rosemary Chin. Should your attorney supervisor report that relationship to his firm? Would it matter that your attorney supervisor will not be working directly on the TTI matter?

C. ▶ Sources of Law Governing Debtor/Creditor Relations

Consider once again the three topics that this text will cover: the creation of debt, the collection of debt, and the discharge/reorganization of debt in bankruptcy. The first two of these, the creation of debt and collection of debt, are controlled primarily by **state law**, not **federal law**. As we consider those two topics in upcoming chapters we will refer to state **statutes** (legislative enactments) and **case law** (court decisions) and sometimes to state **agency rules and regulations** to determine what is permissible. And since these topics are controlled primarily by state law you must always keep in mind that the law may differ from state to state. We will see this particularly in connection with the collection of debt. The collection methods authorized by various states vary markedly.

To say that the law regarding the creation and collection of debt is primarily state law does not mean that federal law doesn't come into play there at all. It does. For example, when we consider the collection of debt in Chapter Six, we will take a close look at an important federal statute, the Fair Debt Collection Practices Act, which imposes strict regulations on those regularly involved in debt collection. And when we consider credit card debt in Chapter Three, we will discuss the Credit Card Accountability, Responsibility and Disclosure Act passed by Congress in 2009, which imposes new consumer-friendly restrictions on credit card lenders. But overall, state law is primary and federal law only supplementary in these two topics.

On the other hand, the third topic, the discharge or reorganization of debt in bankruptcy, involves the Bankruptcy Code found in Title 11 of the U.S. Code. The U.S. Bankruptcy Code regulates most types of bankruptcy filings throughout the country and restricts the administration of those filings to a specialized federal court: the United States Bankruptcy Court.

But that is not to say that all aspects of bankruptcy law are federal. We will learn for example that not all entities can take advantage of the Bankruptcy Code—a few must dissolve themselves under state liquidation laws. And we will see that in a typical case filed under the Bankruptcy Code, numerous questions arise that are controlled by state law. Just as a quick example, the Bankruptcy Code allows individual debtors to declare some property exempt from being seized and distributed to creditors. The Code allows states to elect to have state exemption laws to apply in federal bankruptcy proceedings filed in those states rather than the exemption laws set out in the Code itself, and a number of states have in fact made that election. But overall, federal bankruptcy law is primary and state law only secondary in connection with this third topic.

Sound confusing? It won't be for long.

D. ▶ The Relation of Debtor/Creditor Law to Other Areas of the Law

Debtor/creditor law is closely related to the study of the law of **contracts**. As we will see in Chapter Two, the primary source of debt is a contractual relationship between the debtor and creditor.

EXAMPLE

> If you go to the bank and borrow money to purchase a car, you will sign a promissory note (see Illustration 2-a) legally obligating yourself to repay the amount borrowed to the lender together with an agreed amount of interest. That note is a contract between you (the debtor) and the lender (the creditor).

We will not restudy the law of contracts in this course. But remember that a study of contracts teaches you the basics of 1) how contracts are negotiated, entered into, and often committed to writing by attorneys; 2) how contracts are enforced or not enforced by the courts in the event of a dispute; and 3) the kinds of remedies a court may award if it finds a breach of contract. This course is an extension of that area of law.

This course is also closely related to the law of **business organizations** because debtor/creditor issues often arise in the context of a business operation. Business owners/operators incur debt all the time: They borrow money from a bank or other lender to finance their operations or expand them; they purchase materials/supplies or receive services on credit with a promise to pay within an agreed period of time (e.g., receiving goods along with a 30-day invoice); they lease (another contract) premises in which to do business or lease vehicles or equipment with an accompanying obligation to pay the lease payments as they come due; and so forth. Businesses often become creditors, too, by selling their product or services to customers (the debtors) and agreeing to accept payment in the future. And, of course, financial services businesses (e.g., banks, savings and loans, credit unions, loan companies, credit card companies) are in the business of loaning money to their customers . . . creating and collecting debt *is* their business.

EXAMPLE

From Case Study #1 (Illustration 1-a), Nick Murphy's employer, Overland Truck Services, Inc., is a corporation. Pearl Murphy's former full-time employer is the school district, a governmental entity. She substitute teaches for a private school, likely a charitable nonprofit corporation. As a private tutor she is self-employed, or we might call her tutoring business a sole proprietorship. The law of business organizations teaches us these distinctions.

P-H 1-i: Look again at Case Study #2 (Illustration 1-b). While Mrs. Mendoza was alive, in what kind of business arrangement did she and her husband own the construction company? After she died, how did Mr. Mendoza own the business? What kind of business organization is the owner of the City Heights Condominium Project?

P-H 1-j: Look again at Case Study #3 (Illustration 1-c). What kind of business organization is TTI? Lockland Hughes? UBA? BE?

We will not restudy the law of business organizations in this course. But remember that the study of business organizations provides you with the basic understanding of how people conduct business, how those various business arrangements are created, operated, and regulated. This course is an extension of that area of the law as well.

P-H 1-k: Go through all three case studies introduced in Illustrations 1-a, 1-b, and 1-c and determine which business entities mentioned are properly identified as a creditor and as a debtor.

Debtor/creditor law is also closely related to the study of **property law**, including both **real property** and **personal property**. We will not restudy the law of real or personal property in this course but remember that your study of those subjects provides you with the basic understanding of how title to real and personal property is obtained and transferred, the rights and obligations of ownership of property, and how the courts enforce those various rights. In Chapter Four we will consider the topic of consensual liens: how security interests are created and enforced in real and personal property.

The topics we consider in this course will also, on occasion, require us to deal with some aspects of **tort law**.

EXAMPLE

Nick and Pearl Murphy from Case Study #1 (Illustration 1-a) have a medical malpractice action sounding in negligence for Pearl and in loss of consortium for Nick pending against the doctor who performed Pearl's emergency appendectomy and the hospital where the surgery was performed. This pending tort suit will become an asset of their estate if and when they file for bankruptcy relief.

The topics we consider in this course will sometimes require us to deal with some aspects of **criminal law**, too.

EXAMPLE

As was noted in Case Study #2 (Illustration 1-b), David Mendoza is in danger of being charged with criminal fraud in connection with the loan he procured from City County Bank.

EXAMPLE

As we will see when we begin our study of bankruptcy law in Part C of this text, if David Mendoza were to file for bankruptcy relief, his fraud might prevent him from discharging the debt he owes to City County Bank.

This section should enable you to appreciate that although the law is usually studied by various specialized areas, it is actually an interrelated whole. A lawyer who is handling a client matter in the debtor/creditor area, and the legal professional assisting the lawyer, must also be knowledgeable of the law in a number of related areas.

P-H 1-l: Speaking hypothetically only, if Case Study #1 (Illustration 1-a) included the fact that Nick and Pearl Murphy were in the middle of a divorce, what other area of the law would the lawyer and the assisting legal professional need to be familiar with in order to advise either of them?

P-H 1-m: Speaking hypothetically only, if the estate of Abe Martinez's deceased wife in Case Study #2 (Illustration 1-b) was still being administered, what other area of the law would the lawyer and the assisting legal professional need to be familiar with in order to advise Mr. Martinez?

P-H 1-n: Speaking hypothetically only, if TTI in Case Study #3 (Illustration 1-c) was a publicly traded company, what other area of the law would the lawyer and the assisting legal professional need to be familiar with in order to properly advise it?

E.   The Role of the Assisting Legal Professional in Debtor/Creditor Practice and the Skills Needed

Hopefully you are beginning to see that there are a number of different roles that a paralegal or associate attorney may play in a debtor/creditor scenario depending on which lawyer they are assisting. The legal professional may be assisting the creditor's lawyer by attempting to collect past-due debt from the debtor, or they may be assisting the debtor's lawyer attempting to negotiate an extension of time for the debtor to pay the debt or attempting to negotiate a

Illustration 1-d:
LEGAL PROFESSIONAL
SKILLS NEEDED TO
WORK EFFECTIVELY IN
THE DEBTOR/ CREDI-
TOR AREA INCLUDE
THE ABILITY TO

- Interview clients and witnesses;
- Conduct an asset search;
- Conduct a factual investigation;
- Draft the basic legal documents regularly used in debtor/creditor practice;
- Conduct legal research on debtor/creditor issues, both state and federal;
- Communicate effectively with clients, witnesses, opposing counsel, and court personnel; and
- Organize and maintain client files.

formal settlement of the dispute whereby the debtor pays less than is owed. The legal professional may be assisting the lawyer who files for bankruptcy relief for the debtor, or the lawyer representing a creditor in the bankruptcy case, or the bankruptcy trustee appointed by the bankruptcy court to administer the bankruptcy case. Keep in mind that as you learn more about the law of debtor/creditor relations you are also learning about more potential career opportunities in areas of legal specialty.

Whatever role the assisting legal professional plays in a debtor/creditor drama, the supervising attorney will expect that assistant to have a firm grasp of the law of debt creation, debt collection, and debt discharge or reorganization, the topics we cover in this text. But the supervising attorney will also expect the one assisting to have certain legal professional **skills** in order to assist effectively. Those skills are listed in Illustration 1-d.

As in any area of the law, the more knowledgeable the assisting legal professional is and the more skills the assistant has developed, the more job opportunities that person will encounter and the greater job security that person will enjoy.

CONCLUSION

With this introduction and background we are now ready to begin looking at the various topics involved in debtor/creditor relations. The underlying premise of the debtor/creditor relationship is that the debtor owes a debt to the creditor. So our starting point is to consider how debt is created. That's the task of Part A, which begins with the next chapter.

CHAPTER SUMMARY

The scope of debtor/creditor law includes a consideration of three distinct topics: how debt is created, how debt is collected when it goes unpaid, and how debt may be reorganized or discharged in a bankruptcy case. One primary way debt is commonly categorized is to distinguish between consumer debt and commercial or business debt. There are a number of different sources of law related to debtor/creditor issues, including primarily statutes, case law, and agency rules and regulations. The study of debtor/creditor relations overlaps with several other areas of the law related to the broad area of commercial law and there are a number of specific skills the trained legal professional must have in order to effectively assist the supervising attorney specializing in debtor/creditor issues. This chapter also introduced you to the three case studies to be used in Parts A and B.

REVIEW QUESTIONS

1. What is the distinction between consumer debt and commercial or business debt?
2. Is bankruptcy law primarily federal or state law?
3. Provide one example of how state law might come into play in a bankruptcy case.
4. Is the law controlling the creation and collection of debt primarily federal or state law?
5. Provide one example of how federal law might come into play in debt collection.
6. List three other areas of law that are involved in the study and practice of debtor/creditor relations.
7. List seven different legal professional skills that come into play in debtor/creditor law.
8. Of the legal professional skills you listed in response to question 7, are any more or less important than the others?
9. Explain the difference between statutes, case law, and agency rules and regulations, as well as the difference between state and federal law.
10. From the following list of debt obligations, indicate which would be properly categorized as consumer debt, commercial debt, or a mix of the two:
    a. Tomorrow Today, Inc. borrows money from each of its three shareholders.
    b. Abe Mendoza purchases groceries using his credit card.
    c. Nick and Pearl Murphy borrow money from a bank to consolidate their debts and grant the bank a third mortgage on their house.
    d. Rosemary Chin purchases a 70-inch, high-definition, flat-screen TV for her game room to be paid for over 36 months in equal installments.
    e. Tomorrow Today, Inc. purchases the same flat-screen TV on the same terms to place in the employee lounge in its office building.
    f. Tomorrow Today, Inc. borrows money and Rosemary Chin pledges her new flat-screen TV as security for the loan.
    g. Nick and Pearl Murphy borrow money to take the family on a vacation to Hawaii.
    h. Abe Mendoza leases his personal truck to Mendoza Construction for $200 per month.

WORDS AND PHRASES TO REMEMBER

agency regulations   case law
business organizations   case studies

commercial debt
commercial law
consumer debt
contingent debt
creditor
criminal law
current debt
debt
debtor
debtor/creditor law
disputed debt
federal law
fixed debt
future debt

legal professional
liquidated debt
noncontingent debt
paralegal skills
personal property
property law
real property
secured debt
state law
statutes
tort law
undisputed debt
unliquidated debt
unsecured debt

TO LEARN MORE: A number of TLM activities to accompany this chapter are accessible on the student disc accompanying the text and on the Author Updates link to the text Web site at http://www.aspenparalegaled.com/books/parsons_abcdebt/default.asp.

THE CREATION OF DEBT

Chapter Two:

▶ How Debt Is Created

Loans and debts make worries and frets.
—Proverb

A. ▶ By Contract

Most debt is created by **contract**. A contract is a legally enforceable agreement between two or more parties. There are many kinds of contracts that create a debtor/creditor relationship. Let's look at some of the more common ones.

1. Contracts for the Loan of Money

EXAMPLE

Promissory note A contract containing an enforceable promise by one person to pay another person a certain sum of money called the principal or principal amount owed.

Nick and Pearl Murphy borrow $110,000 from First Bank of Capitol City (FBCC) to purchase their home on Cherry Street in Capitol City. FBCC requires the Murphys to sign a **promissory note** (see Illustration 2-a) setting forth the terms under which the Murphys agree to repay the loaned amount to FBCC. The Murphys are the *borrowers* (or debtors) and FBCC is the *lender* (or creditor). Regarding the promissory note (often referred to as the *note*), the Murphys are the makers of the note (the ones who sign it and promise to pay) and FBCC is the *payee* (the one who is to be paid) on the note. The note will state the principal amount borrowed (often referred to as the *principal*) and the agreed term over which the makers promise to repay it (e.g., 5 years, 10 years, 30 years) and it will state the rate of **interest** (e.g., 5%, 7%, 10%) **per annum** (per year) the makers promise to pay on the unpaid principal. Interest is the cost of using another person's money. (See the extended discussion of interest rates in Chapter Three, Section A.)

Interest The cost of using another person's money.

Per annum Per year.

EXAMPLE

To finance its purchase of the Columbiana Mall, CCD borrows $20 million from FBCC and signs a **promissory note** agreeing to repay the loan evidenced by the note over 25 years at a stated rate of interest per annum. Debt is created.

P-H 2-a: Take a look at the promissory note set out in Illustration 2-a. Who is the borrower/maker of that note? Who is the lender/payee? What is the principal amount borrowed? What is the term? What is the stated interest rate per annum?

2. Contracts for the Extension of Credit

EXAMPLE

Nick and Pearl Murphy buy a new washer and dryer from Shears Department Store and agree to pay off the purchase price in installments over the next 24 months. Debt has been created by the extension of credit by Shears (the seller or creditor) to the Murphys (the buyers or debtors).

EXAMPLE

Abe Mendoza fills out an application for a Visa credit card to be issued by a local bank and the application is approved. The card is mailed to Mendoza along with notification that he has a $2,500 credit limit on the card. The bank issuing the Visa card has agreed to provide Mendoza with up to $2,500 credit. Debt is created when he uses the card.

EXAMPLE

TTI receives a $2 million line of credit (see Chapter Three) from FBCC to fund its operations for the next 12 months.

3. Contracts for the Sale or Lease of Real or Personal Property

EXAMPLE

Donald Brabson of Tomorrow Today, Inc. (TTI) orders a new computer from Dell at a cost of $1,000 and promises to pay the purchase price upon delivery. As soon as the computer is delivered as promised, Brabson, the buyer, owes Dell, the seller, $1,000. Debt has been created by contract. Because Brabson owes the debt, he is the **debtor** The seller, as the party to whom the debt is owed, is the **creditor**.

Debtor A person liable for a debt.

Creditor One to whom a debt is owed.

EXAMPLE

TTI executes an agreement to lease office space from Capitol City Developers (CCD) for 12 months at a rate of $1,000 per month for the leased premises. Debt is created. TTI is the debtor and CCD is the creditor.

EXAMPLE

CCD executes a real estate purchase agreement agreeing to purchase Columbiana Mall from its current owner for $20 million with the full purchase price due at closing. Debt is created. CCD is the debtor and the seller is the creditor.

Illustration 2-a: PROMISSORY NOTE

PROMISSORY NOTE

January 12, YR-10   At Capitol City, Columbiana

1. MAKERS' PROMISE TO PAY: In return for a loan in the principal amount of one hundred and fifteen thousand dollars ($115,000) that we, Nicholas W. Murphy, and wife, Pearl E. Murphy (hereinafter the "Makers"), have received from First Bank of Capitol City (hereinafter the "Lender"), the Makers do hereby promise to repay to Lender the principal amount of $115,000 plus interest as set forth in Paragraph 2.

2. INTEREST: Interest will be charged on unpaid principal until the principal amount has been paid in full. Makers will pay interest on unpaid principal at the rate of 8.00% per year from the date of the making of this Promissory Note until the date the principal is paid in full. Interest hereunder shall be computed on the basis of a three hundred sixty (360) day year. Notwithstanding anything herein to the contrary, in no event shall interest payable hereunder be in excess of the maximum rate allowed by applicable law.

3. TERM AND PAYMENT: Makers will repay the principal amount to Lender with interest as provided in Paragraph 2 by making three hundred and sixty (360) consecutive monthly payments of $843.83 each beginning February 1, YR-10 and continuing on the first day of each month thereafter until completed. Payment shall be made at 111 Broad Street, Capitol City, Columbiana, or at such other place as the Lender or its successor(s) or assign(s) shall stipulate.

4. RIGHT OF ASSIGNMENT: Lender has the express right to assign or sell this Promissory Note in which case the assignee or buyer shall, as Holder, shall have all the rights of Lender under this Promissory Note including this right of assignment. Makers are prohibited from transferring this Promissory Note or any obligations under it without the prior written consent of Lender or its successor(s) or assign(s).

5. DEFAULT: If Lender fails to receive payment from Makers of any monthly payments called for in Paragraph 3 by the tenth day of any month in which a payment is due, or if default is made in the payment of the indebtedness hereunder at maturity, or in the event of default in or breach of any of the terms, provisions or conditions of this Promissory Note or any instrument evidencing or securing the indebtedness evidenced hereby, or any other instrument evidencing indebtedness from Makers, or either of them, to Lender, Makers will then be in DEFAULT. In that event, at the option of the Lender, the entire amount of the indebtedness will become immediately due and payable. Further in that event, the whole of the unpaid principal and any accrued interest shall, to the extent permitted by law, bear interest at the highest lawful rate then in effect pursuant to applicable law, or at the rate provided herein in the event no highest applicable rate is then in effect. Furthermore in that event, Lender shall be entitled to pursue all remedies available to it at law and/or equity to collect all amounts due under this Promissory Note and Makers shall pay all costs and expenses of collection, including court costs and a reasonable attorneys' fee, incurred by or on behalf of Lender in collecting the amounts due under this Promissory Note to the extent not prohibited by applicable law. Lender's failure to declare a default due to Makers' failure to make any monthly payment as called for in this Promissory Note shall not waive or otherwise prejudice Lender's right to declare a default in connection with Makers' failure to make any other monthly payment as called for in this Promissory Note.

6. SECURED NOTE: All amounts due from Makers under the terms of this Promissory Note and all extensions, modifications, renewals or amendments thereof is secured by a Mortgage of even date with the Promissory Note on certain real property located at 3521 West Cherry Street in Capitol City, Columbiana, a more complete description of which is set forth in said Mortgage.

7. RIGHT TO PREPAY: Makers have the right to make payments on the Promissory Note before the due date as determined in Paragraph 3 without premium or other prepayment charge. All prepayments will be applied first to principal until the principal amount is paid in full.

8. WAIVERS: Makers expressly waive the right of presentment and notice of dishonor, and notice of non-payment, protest, notice of protest, bringing of suit, and diligence in taking any action to claim the amounts owing hereunder and are and shall be jointly and severally, directly and primarily liable for the amount of all sums owing and to be owing under the terms of this Promissory Note and agree that this Promissory Note, or any payment hereunder, may be extended from time to time without affecting such liability. "Presentment" means the right to require the Lender or its successor(s) or assign(s) to demand payment of amounts due. "Notice of dishonor" means the right to require Lender or its successor(s) or assign(s) to give notice to other persons that amounts due have not been paid.

9. NATURE OF REMEDIES: The remedies of the Lender as provided in this Promissory Note, or in the Mortgage securing this Promissory Note, or in any other instrument evidencing or securing this Promissory Note, shall be cumulative and concurrent, and may be pursued singularly, successively, or together, at the sole discretion of the Lender, and may be exercised as often as occasion therefor shall arise. No act or omission of the Lender, including specifically any failure to exercise any right, remedy, or recourse, shall be deemed to be a waiver or release of the same, such waiver or release to be effected only through a written document executed by the Lender and then only to the extent specifically recited therein. A waiver or release with reference to any one event shall not be construed as continuing, as a bar to, or as a waiver or release of, any subsequent right, remedy or recourse as to a subsequent event.

10. TIME OF THE ESSENCE: Time is of the essence of this Promissory Note.

11. GOVERNING LAW: This Promissory Note, the Mortgage securing this Promissory Note and any other instrument securing this Promissory Note shall be governed by and construed under the laws of the State of Columbiana.

12. CONSTRUCTION OF TERMS: Where used herein the singular shall refer to the plural, the plural to the singular, and the masculine or feminine shall refer to any gender. If Maker is composed of more than one person or entity, "Makers" as used herein shall refer to any and all persons or entities constituting Makers, as the circumstances may require.

13. TERMS BINDING ON SUCCESSORS: The provisions of this Promissory Note shall be binding upon the parties, their heirs, successors, and assigns.

14. SEVERABILITY OF TERMS: The provisions of this Promissory Note are severable such that the invalidity or unenforceability of any provision hereof shall not affect the validity or enforceability of the remaining provisions.

WITNESS OUR HANDS ON THE DATE ABOVE WRITTEN:

_____
Nicholas W. Murphy (Maker)

_____
Pearl E. Murphy (Maker)

4. Contracts for Services

EXAMPLE

> Abe Mendoza has a tooth that needs a new crown. The dentist does the work and charges him $1,000. Debt is created.

EXAMPLE

> TTI owns a Xerox copier that is not working properly and City Office Equipment Co. comes and fixes it and bills TTI for $300. Debt is created.

EXAMPLE

> You go to work for a law firm that promises to pay you $1,000 a week in salary. You work for the first week and now you expect to be paid the amount promised. Debt has been created.

The types of contracts that people and businesses may enter into that create a debtor/creditor relationship are endless. We will have much more to consider regarding debt created by contract in Chapters Three, Four, and Five, where we consider specific kinds of loans and credit agreements, contractual pledges by one person to pay the debt of another, and the contractual pledging of the debtor's real or personal property to secure repayment of the debt beyond the debtor's bare promise to repay. For now we are merely summarizing how debt is created and this is our starting point: Most debt is created by contract.

B. ▶ By Assignment of Contract Rights

The right to sue on a contract (or on a liability claim, as discussed in Section D) is sometimes referred to as a **chose in action**, a type of **intangible** (nonphysical) **property** right. As such, it may be possible to **assign** or transfer the debt represented by the contract or claim to a third person. We will consider the assignment of debt based on a liability claim in Section D, but it is common for debt created by contract between two parties (the creditor and the debtor) to be assigned by the original creditor to a third party who assumes the rights of the original creditor to collect the debt.

EXAMPLE

> Assume Howard Kine of TTI goes to First National Bank (FNB) and takes out a loan for $15,000 to make home improvements. Kine signs a promissory note promising to repay the loan plus interest to FNB in monthly installments over the next five years. Debt has been created by contract. But after making his first few monthly payments to FNB, Kine receives a letter in the mail directing him to begin making his note payments to Omaha Mortgage Company (OMC) in Omaha, Nebraska, beginning next month. What has happened is that FNB has entered into a contract with OMC, assigning its (FNB's) rights as creditor under the promissory note to OMC.

Assignment The transfer of rights under a contract from a party named in the contract to a third party.

Nonassignment clause A provision in a contract that prohibits one or both parties from assigning the contract to a third party.

Delegation The transfer of obligations under a contract from a party named in the contract to a third party.

The **assignment agreement** referenced in the last example might look something like Illustration 2-b. Can FNB legally do that? Whether it can or not will be governed by the terms of the promissory note. Unless the note contains a **nonassignment clause** prohibiting FNB from assigning, it can. And the legal consequence is that Kine as the debtor now has a legal obligation to OMC, with whom he did not contract. But the debt is real and enforceable between Kine and OMC due to assignment.

While the creditor's right to receive payment of debt can typically be assigned without violating the terms of the note, the debtor's *obligation* to pay typically cannot be assigned to another. (When the debtor's obligation is transferred we call it a **delegation** rather than an assignment.) The contract creating the debt usually has a nonassignment clause applicable to the debtor preventing him from assigning (or delegating) the duty to pay the debt to another.

P-H 2-b: Does the promissory note that Nick and Pearl Murphy signed in favor of FBCC in Illustration 2-a contain a nonassignment clause? If so, is the nonassignment clause binding on both the borrower and the lender or only on the borrower? Could First Bank assign the right to receive payments under this note to another party? Could Nick and Pearl Murphy delegate the duty to pay the amounts called for in this note to another party?

Even where the debt obligation can be delegated to a third person willing to take it on, that delegation will not relieve the original debtor from the obligation to pay the creditor if the one to whom the debt has been delegated fails to do so.

Illustration 2-b: ASSIGNMENT OF PROMISSORY NOTE

For value received, First National Bank of Capitol City, Columbiana ("Assignor") does hereby sell and assign to Omaha Mortgage Company of Omaha, Nebraska ("Assignee") and its successors and assigns, all Assignor's rights and interest in a certain Promissory Note dated May 1, YR-1, in the principal amount of fifteen thousand dollars ($15,000), executed by Howard Kine of 411 Oak Street, Capitol City, Columbiana, and payable to the order of Assignor, together with all sums of money due and to become due on said Promissory Note with interest.

This Assignment is effective as of the 30th day of September, YR-1.

First National Bank, Assignor

By: _____
      Carrie D. Nation, Vice President

Omaha Mortgage Company, Assignee

By: _____
      Jack T. Swanson, President

EXAMPLE

> Assume Rosemary Chin of TTI borrows $50 from you and promises to pay you back the first day of next month. Before that date, her brother contacts you and says he will be repaying her debt when it comes due. He doesn't. Can you still sue Rosemary Chin on the debt even though she delegated the duty to pay it to her brother? Yes, you can. The fact that Rosemary delegated her duty to pay to her brother did not relive her of the duty to pay.

The federal **Anti-Assignment Act**, 41 U.S.C. §15, prohibits the assignment of contracts to which an agency of the federal government is a party without the agency's consent.

Novation The agreement of a creditor to release one debtor from a contract and to look instead to a substituted debtor.

There is one situation in which a delegation of the duty to pay debt by the original debtor to a third-person *will* relieve the original debtor of any further obligation to pay the creditor. That is when the creditor agrees to the delegation and further agrees to release the original debtor from the obligation in exchange for the third person becoming the only debtor. We call that a **novation**.

EXAMPLE

> Assume Rosemary Chin borrows $50 from you and promises to pay you back the first day of next month. Before that date, Rosemary and her brother contact you and ask if you will agree to accept payment of the debt from the brother instead of from Rosemary. You agree. Then the brother does not pay as promised. Can you still sue Rosemary on the debt even though she delegated the duty to pay it to her brother? No, you cannot. Why? Because you agreed to release Rosemary from the obligation and to look only to her brother for payment—you agreed to a novation.

It is unusual for a creditor to agree to a novation, for an obvious reason: Why let someone obligated to you off the hook if you don't have to? You most often see novation in big-money, sophisticated financial transactions where long-term debt is transferred from one debtor to another with the consent of the creditor, perhaps as part of a corporate buy-out or restructuring. Typically the creditor consents to the novation because the deal has been sweetened in some way for it: The interest rate they are to receive on the repayments may be bumped up slightly or the creditor may receive a lump-sum dollar amount as an incentive to agree to the novation.

EXAMPLE

> ABC Conglomerate, Inc. (ABC), a large company with a dozen different divisions, is selling off one of them, its cookie division. DEF, Inc. (DEF) is interested in purchasing the cookie division from ABC, including the real property on which that division is located. ABC has an outstanding loan from FNB with a balance still owing of $5 million, which it repays on a monthly basis at 7 percent interest per annum. The loan is secured by a mortgage on the real property where the cookie division is located. The loan was taken out by ABC last year to expand its cookie division and ABC wants the buyer of that division to assume liability for the loan. DEF is willing to assume liability for the existing loan but ABC not only wants to delegate the loan liability to DEF, it wants to be released from any further liability on the loan—it wants a novation. However, the promissory note evidencing the debt contains a nonassignment clause prohibiting ABC from delegating the

obligation to pay to another party without the express written consent of FNB. So ABC and DEF approach FNB and request that FNB consent to the delegation of the loan from ABC to DEF and that FNB further release ABC from any further liability on the debt. FNB balks at doing that until DEF offers to repay the balance of the loan at 7.25 percent rather than 7 percent. With the prospect of making more interest off the loan with the increased interest rate, FNB consents to the delegation and the novation. That consent might look something like Illustration 2-c.

P-H 2-c: In the last example, why didn't DEF just go out and borrow enough money to pay off the loan to FNB instead of accepting a delegation of that existing obligation at the increased interest rate? Would it help in answering the question to know that DEF could not borrow money at the time in question for less than 8 percent interest per annum? Do you see why that matters? If DEF could borrow money at the time for 6 percent interest per annum, its decision to accept the delegation and pay the higher interest rate looks like a poor business decision, don't you agree?

Illustration 2-c: CONSENT TO ASSIGNMENT/DELEGATION AND NOVATION

CONSENT TO ASSIGNMENT AND DELEGATION OF MORTGAGE
AND PROMISSORY NOTE AND NOVATION

In consideration of the promises made in the separate Assumption Agreement between the undersigned, First National Bank of Capitol City, Columbiana ("FNB") and DEF, Inc. of Kansas City, Missouri ("DEF") of even date herewith (the "Assumption Agreement"), and for other valuable consideration, FNB, as mortgagee under that certain mortgage dated May 1, YR-2 and executed by ABC, Inc. of Chicago, Illinois ("ABC") as mortgagor, and recorded in Mortgage Book 106, Page 543 in the Register's Office of Capitol County, Columbiana (the "Mortgage"), hereby consents to the assignment of the rights and delegation of the obligations of ABC under said Mortgage to DEF.

FNB further consents to the assignment of the rights and delegation of the obligations of ABC under that certain Promissory Note described in and secured by the Mortgage in the principal sum of seven million and five hundred thousand dollars ($7,500,000) and the current balance on which is five million dollars ($5,000,000) (the "Promissory Note") to DEF.

FNB further agrees to release and discharge ABC from all further and future liability to FNB on the Mortgage and Promissory Note and to look only to DEF for such liability pursuant to the terms of the Mortgage, Promissory Note, and Assumption Agreement.

This instrument shall be effective as of the 1st day of September, YR-1.

First National Bank

By: _____
Carrie D. Harris, Vice President

C. ▶ By Law

State and local governments and the federal government have various legislative enactments or **statutes** (**ordinances** in the case of local governments) and various **agency rules and regulations** that will operate to create debt **as a matter of law** (without consent of the debtor or court action). The tax laws are a prime example. If you have income taxable by the federal or state governments, or if you own real property subject to state or local property taxes, debt is created without your consent. If you don't pay those taxes as they become due, the government entity that assessed the taxes will take legal action to collect them from you. We will learn how that happens when we consider tax liens in Chapter Five and reducing a debt claim to a final enforceable judgment in Part B. At this point we are only considering how debt is created.

Other examples of debt created by law arise from the fact that many federal, state, and local agencies and departments given oversight over commercial and public activities are empowered to create debt by assessing **fines and penalties** pursuant to statute or agency rule or regulation.

EXAMPLE

Contingent debt A debt claim the enforceability of which depends on the happening of an uncertain future event.

> You are late for work and so you drive faster than you should. A city police officer stops you and gives you a speeding ticket or citation for violating the relevant city ordinance setting the speed limit on the street where you were stopped. That citation from the city government creates debt. At this point, since you might be able to contest liability in court, we would say that the citation represents **contingent debt**.

EXAMPLE

> The Environmental Protection Agency (EPA) inspects the paper mill in your city and finds that the mill is violating the Clean Air Act and EPA regulations promulgated under it. A $500-a-day fine is assessed by the EPA against the mill until the violation stops. The mill may be able to contest its liability or the reasonableness of the fine, but contingent debt has been created.

Why do the last two examples refer to the debts created as *contingent debt*? Because either debt might be successfully challenged in court and, if successfully challenged, the debt will cease to exist. Once the debt in either example is established in court by entry of a final judgment, it is no longer contingent but is **noncontingent.**

Noncontingent debt A claim that is not subject to any future contingency.

Another way to express this is to say that these debts may be disputed by the debtor and are therefore contingent on the outcome of the dispute. A **disputed debt** is a debt that the creditor claims is owed but that a debtor contends is not owed. A debt may be disputed in whole or part.

EXAMPLE

> If the mill disputes the fine assessed by the EPA, contending it was not in violation of the Clean Air Act or the regulations, the fine is a disputed debt. If the mill concedes the violation and the propriety of the fine, it is an **undisputed debt**. If the mill concedes the violation but contends the amount of the fine is too high, the debt is partially disputed.

If the debt is disputed in whole or part, the debt will be considered contingent until resolution of the dispute, a subject we will consider in detail in Chapters Eight and Nine.

Some debt is contingent for reasons other than a dispute over the debt's validity.

EXAMPLE

Assume the EPA assesses the $500-per-day fine against the paper mill but says that the fine will be forgiven if the mill installs new air filters on their equipment within 30 days of the fine. The mill does not dispute the violation or the fine. Now we have a debt created by the assessment of a fine but during the 30 days it will be considered contingent. But it is not contingent upon its validity; the mill concedes that. It is contingent upon whether the mill installs the filters within the 30 days.

EXAMPLE

Assume that an employment contract between the employer and a clothing salesman provides for the salesman to be paid $50,000 a year plus 2 percent of all clothing sales the salesman makes during the calendar year that are not returned within three months of the close of the calendar year. At the end of the year our salesman has made $200,000 in sales. At that point he now has a claim against his employer for 2 percent of that amount or $4,000 but the salesman's claim (or the employer's debt to the salesman, if you will) is contingent on whether or not any of the clothing sold is returned within three months of the close of the calendar year. There is no dispute, but there is a contingency.

Many debt claims are noncontingent. They are not disputed and there is no other contingency that must occur in order for the debt to be due and payable.

EXAMPLE

If the EPA assesses that $500-per-day fine against the paper mill and the mill does not dispute it, it will be treated as an *undisputed, noncontingent debt*.

EXAMPLE

Assume you borrow money from a bank to buy a car. Once the money has been advanced by the lender and you have signed the promissory note promising to repay the principal borrowed with interest, there would be no reason to consider your debt contingent.

D. ▶ By Court Judgment

Claim A right to payment that may be secured or unsecured, disputed or undisputed, fixed or contingent, liquidated or unliquidated.

You will recall that Nick and Pearl Murphy (Illustration 1-a, Case Study #1) have a professional malpractice claim for Pearl and a loss of consortium for Nick pending against the doctor who performed Pearl's appendectomy and the hospital where that surgery was performed. The Murphys are asking for a total of $1.5 million in damages from the two defendants in their tort suit. While the lawsuit is pending, the Murphys only have a **liability claim** against the defendants; they do not yet have a fixed or noncontingent debt. Both defendants have filed an answer to the Murphys' complaint denying any liability. We do not know yet if the Murphys will recover anything from this lawsuit. Thus, their claim in the lawsuit is properly categorized as a *contingent claim*: a claim contingent on prevailing in the lawsuit.

The Murphys' liability claim against the doctor and hospital is a cause of action sounding in the tort of negligence: it alleges breach of a duty of care owed to Pearl. But liability claims can arise not only in tort (negligence, intentional torts, and strict liability) but also under many other theories arising from other areas of the law such as property law (e.g., allegation of trespass to real or personal property) or the law of business organizations (e.g., claim by partnership that one partner breached a duty of loyalty by taking a business for himself). Unlike debt arising by contract as discussed in Section A, these liability claims will always be initially unliquidated and indeed cannot not be liquidated until a settlement is agreed to or a final court judgment is entered.

In almost all states, liability claims for personal injury and wrongful death cannot be assigned to a third person on the rationale that such claims are personal to the claimant (*actio personalis moritur cum persona*: "a personal cause of action dies with the person"), though many jurisdictions allow the assignment of the proceeds of such claims and though liability claims for harm to property can be freely assigned. (See an excellent discussion of this topic in Anthony J. Sebok, *The Inauthentic Claim*, Van. L. Rev., vol. 64:1:61 (2011).)

Final judgment An order or decree entered by a court finally resolving the issues before it.

But if the Murphys prevail in their lawsuit, the court will award them a **final judgment** against one or both defendants. That final judgment might look something like Illustration 2-d. At that point the Murphys will be considered **judgment creditors** as to the defendants against whom they obtained a judgment. Each defendant against whom the judgment is entered is considered a **judgment debtor**. Debt has been created, but note that it was not created by contract or by assignment or by law; it was created by court judgment.

Judgment creditor/ debtor Once a final judgment is entered by a court awarding a money judgment to one party, the party to whom the judgment is awarded is the judgment creditor and the one against whom it is awarded is the judgment debtor.

In Chapters Ten and Eleven we will consider how a judgment creditor can execute on a final judgment to actually obtain from the judgment defendant the amount of money awarded in the judgment. But for now, note that here is a kind of debt that was created by the judgment entered by the court. Before the final judgment (Illustration 2-d) was entered, all the Murphys had was a tort claim. Now they are judgment creditors and the defendants are judgment debtors.

Of course, the Murphys' case might settle before trial, due to negotiation or mediation, and the defendants may agree to pay the Murphys some compromised amount in settlement. If the Murphys' claim is settled, the lawsuit will be dismissed with no judgment entered for plaintiffs so we will not have debt created by court judgment. But since there would be a binding settlement agreement, we will have debt (the obligation to pay the settlement amount) created by contract, as discussed in Part A of this chapter.

Unliquidated claim A claim that has not been reduced to a dollar amount.

Liquidated claim A claim that has been reduced to a dollar amount.

But let's go back to the Murphys' pending lawsuit against the doctor and hospital to learn something else about debt. While the lawsuit is pending, and before it has gone to judgment, not only is the Murphys' claim only contingent, it is also an **unliquidated claim** at that point or, more accurately, a partially **liquidated claim**. Here's why. Just because the Murphys have asked for a $1.5 million verdict does not mean they will recover exactly that amount. Even if their case gets to a jury and the jury finds in their favor, the jury may return a verdict for a different sum. Since we don't know exactly how much the

Illustration 2-d: FINAL COURT JUDGMENT

IN THE CAPITOL COUNTY COLUMBIANA
CIRCUIT COURT

PEARL E. MURPHY and
husband, NICHOLAS W. MURPHY,   )
   Plaintiffs   )
       v.   )   DOCKET NO. 00-11111
DR. SAMUEL M. CRAFT and   )
CAPITOL CITY HOSPITAL   )
   Defendants   )

FINAL JUDGMENT

This matter came on for trial on the 18th day of December YR-1. Following the presentation of evidence the jury returned a verdict in favor of plaintiff Pearl E. Murphy against both defendants in the amount of $925,000 and in favor of plaintiff Nicholas W. Murphy against both defendants in the amount of $150,000.

Accordingly, FINAL JUDGMENT is hereby entered on the jury verdict in favor of plaintiff Pearl E. Murphy against defendants Dr. Samuel M. Croft and Capitol City Hospital jointly in the amount of $925,000 and in favor of plaintiff Nicholas W. Murphy against defendants Samuel M. Croft and Capitol City Hospital jointly in the amount of $150,000, for which execution may issue if necessary.

Court costs are assessed one-half against defendant Dr. Samuel M. Croft and one-half against defendant Capitol City Hospital for which execution may issue if necessary.

ENTER this 20th day of December, YR-1.

_____
Wilma N. Best, Circuit Judge

Murphys are going to recover on their claim until the jury speaks, their claim is *unliquidated*. A debt claim is liquidated when we know exactly, to the penny, how much it is. It is *unliquidated* if we do not.

EXAMPLE

We also know (from Illustration 1-a) that the Murphys owe FBCC the exact balance of $78,500 on the loan they took to purchase their home evidenced by the promissory note in Illustration 2-a. If the Murphys default on the note at this time, FBCC may file suit against them to recover *exactly* that amount, plus all interest and costs allowed by the promissory note. That is a **liquidated debt**. We know exactly, to the penny, how much the claim is for. It is also a *noncontingent* debt so far as we know since the Murphys do not dispute it. So we would say that the debt owed by the Murphys to FBCC is a *liquidated, noncontingent debt*. But the claim of the Murphys against the doctor and hospital, until it goes to judgment, is both *contingent* (the Murphys could lose and receive nothing) and **unliquidated** (even if they win we don't yet know how much they will be awarded on the claim).

That last example should suggest something to you that is generally true: many claims for breach of contract are liquidated even before a collection suit is initiated. We can tell from the terms of the contract exactly how much is claimed, as in the example. But claims based on torts, like the Murphys' claim against the doctor and hospital, are almost always unliquidated until they go to judgment. That is true concerning most tort claims because of the kinds of damages a plaintiff can seek in those cases, particularly in personal injury cases.

EXAMPLE

> Depending on the controlling state law, Pearl Murphy, in her negligence suit against the doctor and the hospital, can likely seek to recover for past and future pain and suffering and lost enjoyment of life. In his loss of consortium claim, Nick Murphy is seeking the lost companionship with his wife, Pearl. What is the value or dollar amount of any of those damages? We won't know until the jury brings back a verdict and tells us how much is awarded for those categories of damage. The jury might award Pearl $50,000 for her past pain and suffering or might award her $500,000 for it. These claims are *unliquidated* until the jury (or a judge in a bench trial) makes its decision.

The fact that tort claims are generally unliquidated does not mean they can never be liquidated. In fact, tort claims can be liquidated prior to a final judgment being entered.

EXAMPLE

> Assume you are involved in a car accident caused by the other driver. Fortunately you suffer no personal injury but your car is totaled. Your car was worth $12,000 at the time it was totaled. Your tort claim against the other driver is based on negligence but you only have one category of damage, damage to your personal property because your car was totaled. Do we know the value of your claim prior to judgment? Sure. We can calculate the value of your car at the moment before the accident, which will be the measure of your loss. Although your claim is *liquidated*, of course, it is still *contingent* upon your winning the case or the case settling in your favor.

It is also true that portions of a tort claim can be liquidated while other portions are unliquidated. In that situation we would characterize the plaintiff's claim as partially liquidated. In fact, this is what the Murphys' tort claim is.

EXAMPLE

> In addition to suing to recover for past and future pain and suffering and lost enjoyment of life, unliquidated damages at this point, Pearl Murphy is seeking to recover $47,983.21 in past medical expenses, $197,385 in future anticipated medical expenses, $33,289.50 in past lost income, and $275,500 in lost future income. These amounts are liquidated; we can calculate them to the penny based on bills or receipts in the case of the medical expenses and based on known past salary amounts versus current earnings in the case of lost income. Even in tort cases, some damages forming the basis of the claim (and of the debt when the case is settled or goes to judgment) may be liquidated. If some damages are liquidated and some are not, we would properly say that the tort claim is partially liquidated.

CONCLUSION

Understanding generally how debt is created is the starting point for mastering the complex subject of debtor/creditor relations. But we need to look at several of these methods of debt creation in more detail, and that is what we will do in the remaining chapters of Part A. We will begin by focusing on loans and credit arrangements, the subject of the next chapter.

CHAPTER SUMMARY

This chapter dealt generally with how debt is created. Most debt is created by various kinds of contracts, including contracts for the sale or lease of property, to provide services, to loan money, or to extend credit. When debt is created by the loan of money or extension of credit, the debtor will sign a promissory note containing the terms of repayment. Rights created by contract are deemed a chose in action, an intangible property right. The right to receive the payment of a contractual debt can usually be assigned but the obligation to pay debt rarely can be unless the creditor consents to a novation. A claim for damage to property is assignable but not a claim for personal injury or wrongful death. Debt can also be created as a matter of law as by federal or state statutes or local ordinances or by entry of a money judgment by a court of law. Debt may be disputed or undisputed, liquidated or unliquidated, contingent or noncontingent.

REVIEW QUESTIONS

1. What is a contract?
2. List four different types of contracts that create debt.
3. Define "debtor" and "creditor" and explain the difference between the two.
4. What is a novation?
5. List five different provisions typically found in a promissory note relating to the terms of payment of the debt evidenced by the note.
6. Explain the difference between contingent and noncontingent debt.
7. Explain the difference between liquidated and unliquidated debt.
8. Explain the difference between disputed and undisputed debt.
9. When does a creditor become a judgment creditor? When does a debtor become a judgment debtor?
10. For each of the following scenarios, identify i) the way this debt was created (by contract, assignment, law, or judgment); ii) whether the debt or claim is liquidated, unliquidated, or partially liquidated; and iii) whether the debt is contingent on noncontingent.
    a. John Client has been audited by the IRS and assessed $50,000 in back income taxes. The IRS disallowed almost all of his business deductions taken over the past three tax years. Client insists the deductions are all proper.
    b. Sally Client has pled guilty to the crime of shoplifting and has been ordered by the court to pay $500 in restitution to the merchant from

whom she stole. Client is relieved she got no jail time and plans no appeal.

c. Richard Client bought a car from Honest Jack's Used Cars for $15,000. Later, he learned that Honest Jack had run back the mileage odometer on the car before selling it to him. The car showed only 60,000 miles when Client bought it, but it actually had 160,000 miles on it. The car that he paid $15,000 for is actually worth only $5,000. Client sues, asking for the difference in the value of the car plus punitive damages.

d. Mary Client agreed to paint Fred's house for $1,000. She finished the job and Fred was happy with it but said he had no money to pay her.

e. JoAnne is a make-up artist. One of her clients is the famous TV anchorwoman, Wendy City. JoAnne got sick yesterday and was unable to be at the studio yesterday evening to do Wendy's makeup. But JoAnne called her friend, Phyllis, who agreed to do Wendy's makeup that evening. However, Phyllis forgot and didn't show. Wendy went on the air with no makeup and is now furious. Wendy sues Phyllis asking for $1 million for harm to her reputation as a result of having to do the broadcast without makeup. Phyllis admits she is liable for not showing up but denies that Wendy has suffered any harm.

WORDS AND PHRASES TO REMEMBER

agency rules and regulations
alternative dispute resolution
Anti-Assignment Act
assignee
assignment
assignment agreement
agency regulations
binding (nonbinding) arbitration
borrower
buyer
chose in action
claim
contingent debt (or claim)
creditor
debtor
delegation (of contractual duty)
disputed debt
final judgment
fines and penalties
intangible property

interest
lender
liquidated debt
maker
nonassignment clause
noncontingent debt (or claim)
nondisputed debt
note
ordinance
payee
per annum
police powers
principal
promissory note
rate of interest
seller
statute
undisputed debt
unliquidated debt

TO LEARN MORE: A number of TLM activities to accompany this chapter are accessible on the student disc accompanying this text and on the Author Updates link to the text Web site at http://www.aspenparalegaled.com/ books/parsons_ abcdebt/default.asp.

Chapter Three:

▶ # Loans, Credit Arrangements, and Credit Reporting Practices

I don't care too much for money, money can't buy me love.
—The Beatles

▶ ## Introduction

In Chapter Two we considered the fundamental point that most debt is created by contract. This chapter is an extension of that idea as we consider in more detail the most common ways that consumer and commercial debt is created contractually: traditional loans, line of credit loans, consumer payday loans, installment sales, and credit card arrangements. We also consider the role of credit reporting agencies and the Fair Credit Reporting Act.

A. ## The Traditional Loan

The traditional loan involves a debt created when a lender loans money to a borrower in exchange for the borrower's promise to repay the loan at some designated time in the future or in installments over some period of time, together with some agreed rate of interest on the principal amount loaned and pursuant to other agreed terms. The lender becomes the creditor and the borrower becomes the debtor and the **loan agreement** controls their legal rights and obligations.

In Chapter One we noted the distinction between **consumer debt** and **commercial debt**. We will make that distinction throughout our study of debtor/creditor law. In this section we will distinguish between a **consumer loan**, which is a loan made to one or more individuals for personal, family, or home purposes, and a **commercial loan**, which is a loan made to a business or business person for business or commercial purposes. Examples of consumer loans include an individual or couple borrowing money to purchase a home, car, boat, or major appliance; to fund a college education or a vacation; or to consolidate debt. Examples of commercial loans include a long-term loan for the purchase of a new business; a short-term loan to fund operations of an ongoing business; or a loan to fund business expansion or the purchase of additional business equipment, inventory, or other property.

Loan agreement The contract setting forth the terms of a loan transaction.

Consumer debt Debt incurred for personal, family, or household purposes.

Commercial debt Debt incurred for business or commercial purposes.

Illustration 3-a:
SUMMARY OF THE
LOAN PROCESS

- Loan application
- Credit and financial information check
- Inspection and appraisal of property to be pledged as security
- Loan approval
- Loan closing

Whether the loan is for consumer or commercial purposes, the process involved is basically the same. Illustration 3-a is a summary of the steps involved in the making of a traditional loan.

1. Loan Application

The first step in the loan process is that the borrower completes the borrower's **loan application** form. That application will typically require the borrower to disclose all sources and amounts of income for the last several years, all assets, and all liabilities. The application may inquire into the borrower's debt repayment history, including any history of bankruptcy or debt collection lawsuits. The borrower may be required to produce relevant documentation, including, for the consumer borrower: proof of identification, recent pay stubs or other verification of employment, and divorce records. For all borrowers, the requested documentation may include tax returns, bank statements, recent financial statements, contracts related to the requested loan, and any other financial information the lender may request. If the borrower is going to grant the lender a **security interest** (discussed in detail in Chapters Four and Five) in real or personal property to secure repayment of the loan, the loan application will include identification of the property to be pledged as security and proof of ownership.

Security interest An interest granted to a creditor in property of the debtor or a third party authorizing the creditor to seize and sell the pledged property to satisfy the debt obligation of the debtor in the event of a default.

Illustration 3-b sets out the borrower information portions of the Uniform Residential Loan Application (URLA) form currently used by the **Federal National Mortgage Association (Fannie Mae)** and the **Federal Home Mortgage Association (Freddie Mac)** in making loans to borrowers purchasing a residence. The Fannie Mae/Freddie Mac URLA is utilized by many other all-purpose lenders.

The loan application process can have a number of unintended consequences for the borrower and the lender. If the borrower knowingly falsifies a loan application or a financial statement given in connection with a loan application, the falsified application or statement may become a basis later for criminal prosecution of the borrower. Or if that borrower later seeks bankruptcy relief, it may become a basis to deny the borrower's request to discharge the debt created by the loan or to deny the borrower any bankruptcy relief at all.

EXAMPLE

Recall from Illustration 1-b that David Mendoza, Abe's son, has been accused of obtaining a loan from City County Bank (CCB) using false financial statements. Specifically, it is alleged that he listed assets he did not own on the statement and failed to disclose certain obligations as well. We've already noted that David is facing possible criminal prosecution based on the false financials. And as we will learn in Chapter Eighteen, there's more trouble ahead for David if he ever attempts to discharge this debt in bankruptcy.

2. Credit and Financial Information Check

Once the borrower has the completed loan application and provided the lender with the requested supporting documentation, the lender will check the **credit history** of the borrower to determine the borrower's history of timely debt repayment and credit worthiness. We will consider this important process in more detail in Section F of this chapter but, for now, understand that this credit check involves the lender contacting one or more credit reporting agencies that collect financial and debt repayment information on consumers and businesses and provide a credit-worthiness rating for them as well. If questions are raised by this credit check, the lender will require an explanation from the borrower before proceeding with the loan process.

Credit history The record of an individual's or business's history of paying debts on time.

EXAMPLE

If CCB, in the process of checking the credit history of Abe and Maria Mendoza, learns that Abe had made two late payments on a car loan he had five years ago, the bank might require a written explanation from Abe as to why those two payments were made late. And this explanation might be demanded even though Abe ultimately made those payments and paid off the entire car loan.

In addition to the credit check, the lender will verify the employment, income, and asset and debt information provided by the borrower as part of the loan application. This may involve phone calls to current or past employers but more often involves written verification utilizing standard forms, such as the Verification of Employment (VOE) requested from the consumer borrower's employer and Verification of Deposit (VOD) requested from financial institutions maintaining accounts for the borrower.

3. Property Inspection and Appraisal

If the purpose of the loan is to enable the borrower to purchase real or personal property, the lender may require that the property be inspected by its designated agent before the loan is approved. If the lender intends to require the borrower to grant the lender a **security interest** in personal property to secure repayment of the loan or a mortgage in real property to secure repayment, the lender will typically require that the property to be pledged as security for the loan be **appraised** (its current market value determined) to ensure that its value exceeds the amount of the loan. Appraisals are usually performed by state licensed (or state registered) **appraisers**.

EXAMPLE

When Abe and Maria Mendoza borrowed $500,000 from Security Trust Bank in Capitol City (see Illustration 1-b) to purchase their home, the lending bank took back a mortgage in the property as improved (the land and the house) to secure repayment of the loan. Before the bank approved the loan it had the property appraised to make sure it was worth at least $550,000. The bank's lending standards required that the property appraise for at least 10 percent more than the amount loaned.

Illustration 3-b: BORROWER INFORMATION PORTIONS OF THE UNIFORM RESIDENTIAL LOAN APPLICATION FORM USED BY FANNIE MAE AND FREDDIE MAC

Uniform Residential Loan Application

This application is designed to be completed by the applicant(s) with the Lender's assistance. Applicants should complete this form as "Borrower" or "Co-Borrower," as applicable. Co-Borrower information must also be provided (and the appropriate box checked) when ☐ the income or assets of a person other than the Borrower (including the Borrower's spouse) will be used as a basis for loan qualification or ☐ the income or assets of the Borrower's spouse or other person who has community property rights pursuant to state law will not be used as a basis for loan qualification, but his or her liabilities must be considered because the spouse or other person has community property rights pursuant to applicable law and Borrower resides in a community property state, the security property is located in a community property state, or the Borrower is relying on other property located in a community property state as a basis for repayment of the loan.

If this is an application for joint credit, Borrower and Co-Borrower each agree that we intend to apply for joint credit (sign below):

Borrower _____   Co-Borrower _____

I. TYPE OF MORTGAGE AND TERMS OF LOAN

Mortgage Applied for:	☐ VA ☐ FHA	☐ Conventional ☐ USDA/Rural Housing Service	☐ Other (explain):	Agency Case Number	Lender Case Number

Amount $	Interest Rate %	No. of Months	Amortization Type:	☐ Fixed Rate ☐ GPM	☐ Other (explain): ☐ ARM (type):

II. PROPERTY INFORMATION AND PURPOSE OF LOAN

Subject Property Address (street, city, state & ZIP)	No. of Units

Legal Description of Subject Property (attach description if necessary)	Year Built

Purpose of Loan	☐ Purchase ☐ Construction ☐ Other (explain): ☐ Refinance ☐ Construction-Permanent	Property will be: ☐ Primary Residence ☐ Secondary Residence ☐ Investment

Complete this line if construction or construction-permanent loan.

Year Lot Acquired	Original Cost $	Amount Existing Liens $	(a) Present Value of Lot $	(b) Cost of Improvements $	Total (a + b) $ 0.00

Complete this line if this is a refinance loan.

Year Acquired	Original Cost $	Amount Existing Liens $	Purpose of Refinance	Describe Improvements ☐ made ☐ to be made Cost: $

Title will be held in what Name(s)	Manner in which Title will be held	Estate will be held in: ☐ Fee Simple ☐ Leasehold (show expiration date)

Source of Down Payment, Settlement Charges, and/or Subordinate Financing (explain)

III. BORROWER INFORMATION

Borrower	Co-Borrower

Borrower's Name (include Jr. or Sr. if applicable)	Co-Borrower's Name (include Jr. or Sr. if applicable)

Social Security Number	Home Phone (incl. area code)	DOB (mm/dd/yyyy)	Yrs. School	Social Security Number	Home Phone (incl. area code)	DOB (mm/dd/yyyy)	Yrs. School

☐ Married ☐ Unmarried (include ☐ Separated single, divorced, widowed)	Dependents (not listed by Co-Borrower) no. ages	☐ Married ☐ Unmarried (include ☐ Separated single, divorced, widowed)	Dependents (not listed by Borrower) no. ages

Present Address (street, city, state, ZIP) ☐ Own ☐ Rent ___ No. Yrs.	Present Address (street, city, state, ZIP) ☐ Own ☐ Rent ___ No. Yrs.

Mailing Address, if different from Present Address	Mailing Address, if different from Present Address

If residing at present address for less than two years, complete the following:

Former Address (street, city, state, ZIP) ☐ Own ☐ Rent ___ No. Yrs.	Former Address (street, city, state, ZIP) ☐ Own ☐ Rent ___ No. Yrs.

IV. EMPLOYMENT INFORMATION

Borrower	Co-Borrower

Name & Address of Employer	☐ Self Employed	Yrs. on this job	Name & Address of Employer	☐ Self Employed	Yrs. on this job
		Yrs. employed in this line of work/profession			Yrs. employed in this line of work/profession

Position/Title/Type of Business	Business Phone (incl. area code)	Position/Title/Type of Business	Business Phone (incl. area code)

If employed in current position for less than two years or if currently employed in more than one position, complete the following:

Borrower		IV. EMPLOYMENT INFORMATION (cont'd)	Co-Borrower	
Name & Address of Employer	☐ Self Employed	Dates (from – to)	Name & Address of Employer	☐ Self Employed	Dates (from – to)

		Monthly Income $			Monthly Income $
Position/Title/Type of Business		Business Phone (incl. area code)	Position/Title/Type of Business		Business Phone (incl. area code)

Name & Address of Employer	☐ Self Employed	Dates (from – to)	Name & Address of Employer	☐ Self Employed	Dates (from – to)
		Monthly Income $			Monthly Income $
Position/Title/Type of Business		Business Phone (incl. area code)	Position/Title/Type of Business		Business Phone (incl. area code)

V. MONTHLY INCOME AND COMBINED HOUSING EXPENSE INFORMATION

Gross Monthly Income	Borrower	Co-Borrower	Total	Combined Monthly Housing Expense	Present	Proposed
Base Empl. Income*	$	$	$ 0.00	Rent	$	
Overtime			0.00	First Mortgage (P&I)		$
Bonuses			0.00	Other Financing (P&I)		
Commissions			0.00	Hazard Insurance		
Dividends/Interest			0.00	Real Estate Taxes		
Net Rental Income			0.00	Mortgage Insurance		
Other (before completing, see the notice in "describe other income," below)			0.00	Homeowner Assn. Dues		
				Other:		
Total	$ 0.00	$ 0.00	$ 0.00	Total	$ 0.00	$ 0.00

* Self Employed Borrower(s) may be required to provide additional documentation such as tax returns and financial statements.

Describe Other Income   *Notice:* Alimony, child support, or separate maintenance income need not be revealed if the Borrower (B) or Co-Borrower (C) does not choose to have it considered for repaying this loan.

B/C		Monthly Amount
		$

VI. ASSETS AND LIABILITIES

This Statement and any applicable supporting schedules may be completed jointly by both married and unmarried Co-Borrowers if their assets and liabilities are sufficiently joined so that the Statement can be meaningfully and fairly presented on a combined basis; otherwise, separate Statements and Schedules are required. If the Co-Borrower section was completed about a non-applicant spouse or other person, this Statement and supporting schedules must be completed about that spouse or other person also.

Completed ☐ Jointly ☐ Not Jointly

ASSETS Description	Cash or Market Value	Liabilities and Pledged Assets. List the creditor's name, address, and account number for all outstanding debts, including automobile loans, revolving charge accounts, real estate loans, alimony, child support, stock pledges, etc. Use continuation sheet, if necessary. Indicate by (*) those liabilities, which will be satisfied upon sale of real estate owned or upon refinancing of the subject property.		
Cash deposit toward purchase held by:	$			
List checking and savings accounts below		**LIABILITIES**	Monthly Payment & Months Left to Pay	Unpaid Balance
Name and address of Bank, S&L, or Credit Union		Name and address of Company	$ Payment/Months	$
Acct. no. $		Acct. no.		
Name and address of Bank, S&L, or Credit Union		Name and address of Company	$ Payment/Months	$
Acct. no. $		Acct. no.		
Name and address of Bank, S&L, or Credit Union		Name and address of Company	$ Payment/Months	$
Acct. no. $		Acct. no.		

VI. ASSETS AND LIABILITIES (cont'd)

Name and address of Bank, S&L, or Credit Union	Name and address of Company	$ Payment/Months	$
Acct. no. $	Acct. no.		
Stocks & Bonds (Company name/ number & description) $	Name and address of Company	$ Payment/Months	$
	Acct. no.		
Life insurance net cash value $	Name and address of Company	$ Payment/Months	$
Face amount: $			
Subtotal Liquid Assets $ 0.00			
Real estate owned (enter market value from schedule of real estate owned) $			
Vested interest in retirement fund $			
Net worth of business(es) owned (attach financial statement) $	Acct. no.		
Automobiles owned (make and year) $	Alimony/Child Support/Separate Maintenance Payments Owed to: $		
Other Assets (itemize) $	Job-Related Expense (child care, union dues, etc.) $		
	Total Monthly Payments $		
Total Assets a. $ 0.00	Net Worth (a minus b) ► $ 0.00	**Total Liabilities b.** $ 0.00	

Schedule of Real Estate Owned (If additional properties are owned, use continuation sheet.)

Property Address (enter S if sold, PS if pending sale or R if rental being held for income) ▼	Type of Property	Present Market Value	Amount of Mortgages & Liens	Gross Rental Income	Mortgage Payments	Insurance, Maintenance, Taxes & Misc.	Net Rental Income
		$	$	$	$	$	$
	Totals	0.00 $	0.00 $	0.00 $	0.00 $	0.00 $	$

List any additional names under which credit has previously been received and indicate appropriate creditor name(s) and account number(s):

Alternate Name	Creditor Name	Account Number

VII. DETAILS OF TRANSACTION / VIII. DECLARATIONS

	VII. DETAILS OF TRANSACTION		VIII. DECLARATIONS	Borrower		Co-Borrower	
			If you answer "Yes" to any questions a through i, please use continuation sheet for explanation.	Yes	No	Yes	No
a.	Purchase price	$					
b.	Alterations, improvements, repairs		a. Are there any outstanding judgments against you?	☐	☐	☐	☐
c.	Land (if acquired separately)		b. Have you been declared bankrupt within the past 7 years?	☐	☐	☐	☐
d.	Refinance (incl. debts to be paid off)		c. Have you had property foreclosed upon or given title or deed in lieu thereof in the last 7 years?	☐	☐	☐	☐
e.	Estimated prepaid items		d. Are you a party to a lawsuit?	☐	☐	☐	☐
f.	Estimated closing costs		e. Have you directly or indirectly been obligated on any loan which resulted in foreclosure, transfer of title in lieu of foreclosure, or judgment?	☐	☐	☐	☐
g.	PMI, MIP, Funding Fee		(This would include such loans as home mortgage loans, SBA loans, home improvement loans, educational loans, manufactured (mobile) home loans, any mortgage, financial obligation, bond, or loan guarantee. If "Yes," provide details, including date, name, and address of Lender, FHA or VA case number, if any, and reasons for the action.)				
h.	Discount (if Borrower will pay)						
i.	Total costs (add items a through h)	0.00					

VII. DETAILS OF TRANSACTION			VIII. DECLARATIONS					
					Borrower		Co-Borrower	
			If you answer "Yes" to any question a through i, please use continuation sheet for explanation.		Yes	No	Yes	No
j.	Subordinate financing		f. Are you presently delinquent or in default on any Federal debt or any other loan, mortgage, financial obligation, bond, or loan guarantee?		☐	☐	☐	☐
k.	Borrower's closing costs paid by Seller		g. Are you obligated to pay alimony, child support, or separate maintenance?		☐	☐	☐	☐
l.	Other Credits (explain)		h. Is any part of the down payment borrowed?		☐	☐	☐	☐
			i. Are you a co-maker or endorser on a note?		☐	☐	☐	☐
m.	Loan amount (exclude PMI, MIP, Funding Fee financed)		------------------------------------					
			j. Are you a U.S. citizen?		☐	☐	☐	☐
n.	PMI, MIP, Funding Fee financed		k. Are you a permanent resident alien?		☐	☐	☐	☐
o.	Loan amount (add m & n)	0.00	l. **Do you intend to occupy the property as your primary residence?**		☐	☐	☐	☐
			If Yes," complete question m below.					
p.	Cash from/to Borrower (subtract j, k, l & o from i)		m. Have you had an ownership interest in a property in the last three years?		☐	☐	☐	☐
			(1) What type of property did you own—principal residence (PR), second home (SH), or investment property (IP)?		____		____	
			(2) How did you hold title to the home— by yourself (S), jointly with your spouse (SP), or jointly with another person (O)?		____		____	

IX. ACKNOWLEDGEMENT AND AGREEMENT

Each of the undersigned specifically represents to Lender and to Lender's actual or potential agents, brokers, processors, attorneys, insurers, servicers, successors and assigns and agrees and acknowledges that: (1) the information provided in this application is true and correct as of the date set forth opposite my signature and that any intentional or negligent misrepresentation of this information contained in this application may result in civil liability, including monetary damages, to any person who may suffer any loss due to reliance upon any misrepresentation that I have made on this application, and/or in criminal penalties including, but not limited to, fine or imprisonment or both under the provisions of Title 18, United States Code, Sec. 1001, et seq.; (2) the loan requested pursuant to this application (the "Loan") will be secured by a mortgage or deed of trust on the property described in this application; (3) the property will not be used for any illegal or prohibited purpose or use; (4) all statements made in this application are made for the purpose of obtaining a residential mortgage loan; (5) the property will be occupied as indicated in this application; (6) the Lender, its servicers, successors or assigns may retain the original and/or an electronic record of this application, whether or not the Loan is approved; (7) the Lender and its agents, brokers, insurers, servicers, successors, and assigns may continuously rely on the information contained in the application, and I am obligated to amend and/or supplement the information provided in this application if any of the material facts that I have represented herein should change prior to closing of the Loan; (8) in the event that my payments on the Loan become delinquent, the Lender, its servicers, successors or assigns may, in addition to any other rights and remedies that it may have relating to such delinquency, report my name and account information to one or more consumer reporting agencies; (9) ownership of the Loan and/or administration of the Loan account may be transferred with such notice as may be required by law; (10) neither Lender nor its agents, brokers, insurers, servicers, successors or assigns has made any representation or warranty, express or implied, to me regarding the property or the condition or value of the property; and (11) my transmission of this application as an "electronic record" containing my "electronic signature," as those terms are defined in applicable federal and/or state laws (excluding audio and video recordings), or my facsimile transmission of this application containing a facsimile of my signature, shall be as effective, enforceable and valid as if a paper version of this application were delivered containing my original written signature.

Acknowledgement. Each of the undersigned hereby acknowledges that any owner of the Loan, its servicers, successors and assigns, may verify or reverify any information contained in this application or obtain any information or data relating to the Loan, for any legitimate business purpose through any source, including a source named in this application or a consumer reporting agency.

Borrower's Signature X	Date	Co-Borrower's Signature X	Date

If real property is being mortgaged to secure repayment of the loan, the lender will also require that the property be surveyed to determine its precise dimensions and will require a **title search** to affirm that the borrower has or will receive **good and marketable title** to the property and, consequently, can give the lender good title in the mortgage. If personal property is being pledged to secure repayment, the lender may request proof of ownership from the borrower or the seller from whom the borrower expects to take title.

4. Loan Approval

Loan commitment Official statement from the lender advising that the loan is approved and funds will be distributed if and when the rest of the transaction is completed.

Once the loan has been processed through the first three steps described above, the lender will submit for review and approval or rejection the application and all supporting documentation that has been produced in the process. There may be more than one stage of approval required. The loan officer for the lender may make the initial approval determination subject to further review by the lender's chief executive officer or, more commonly, by the lender's **loan committee**.

Approval may be final or tentative. If the loan committee has remaining questions about some aspect of the loan, it may give conditional approval: approval subject to certain further questions being answered or certain other steps being taken.

Oftentimes, the loan approval is just one step in a more complex financial transaction and the lender is asked to issue a **loan commitment**. A loan commitment is the lender's statement that the loan is approved and will be issued if and when the rest of the transaction is completed.

EXAMPLE

Assume we have a consumer transaction in which the borrower is seeking to buy a home. The contract of sale signed by the seller and the buyer/borrower makes the buyer's ability to obtain suitable financing of the purchase price a condition precedent to closing on the transaction. If the buyer is unable to obtain a loan commitment, the deal falls through right there. But assume that the contract says that once the buyer has obtained a loan commitment the seller then agrees to 1) fix several things wrong with the house prior to closing, 2) obtain a no-pest letter, and 3) obtain a certification of sufficiently low radon gas levels in the house. In this case, there are three more things to be done *after* the loan is approved. These obligations may get done but also may not, which would cause the transaction to fall through. So all the buyer/borrower wants at this point is a loan commitment, not a loan. If the seller fails to fulfill its further obligations under the contract, the buyer/borrower will not want the loan at all.

EXAMPLE

Look again at Illustration 2-c in which First National Bank (FNB) consented to the assignment/delegation of the promissory note and mortgage from ABC to DEF and for the novation of DEF in the place of ABC on those debt obligations. Obtaining the bank's approval for that assignment/delegation and novation was only one of many other steps to be taken in the sale of the cookie division of ABC to DEF. Before the bank executed that final consent, it would have given tentative consent or a commitment to consent to the assignment/delegation and novation. And once ABC and DEF had that tentative consent or commitment to consent, they could then proceed with the other parts of their sale agreement.

P-H 3-a: What other obligations might ABC have in connection with the sale of its cookie division to DEF once FNB gives its tentative consent or commitment to consent to the assignment/delegation and novation? What other obligations might DEF have at that point?

Loan closing The meeting at which a loan transaction is finalized.

Promissory note A contract containing an enforceable promise by one person to pay another person a certain sum of money, the principal.

5. Loan Closing

After the loan has been approved and all other conditions of the transaction of which the loan may be a part are finalized, the loan will be consummated or will **close**. At the **loan closing** the funds being borrowed are actually transferred from the lender to the borrower or to whomever the borrower designates (e.g., the seller in a real estate transaction). In exchange for the transfer of funds from the lender, the borrower will be asked to execute a **promissory note**.

It is the promissory note (often called just "the note") that contains the legally binding promise of the borrower to repay the loan along with the various terms of repayment to which the borrower has consented. In connection with the overall transaction, there may well be many other documents executed that add to the terms of the agreement. And if the borrower has agreed to pledge real or personal property as further security to the lender for the borrower's promise to repay, there will be important documentation executed regarding that pledge, which we will examine in Chapter Four. But here, let's focus on the promissory note.

In Illustration 2-a, we saw the promissory note signed by Nick and Pearl Murphy from Case Study #1 when they borrowed $115,000 from First Bank of Capitol City (FBCC) to purchase their home. Let's walk through that note paragraph by paragraph.

Paragraph 1: This paragraph identifies the persons obligating themselves on the note by signing it. We call each such person a **maker** or **payor** on the note. They also become a debtor by obligating themselves on the note. This paragraph also identifies the person to be paid by the maker. We call this person the **lender** if they are actually making the loan or, alternatively, the **payee** since they are the one to be paid. This paragraph also states the **principal** amount of the obligation being taken on by the makers.

Interest The cost of using another person's money.

Paragraph 2: This paragraph states the amount of **interest** the maker will pay on the principal. As we have already noted, interest is the charge made by a creditor for the use of the creditor's money; it is the cost of using another person's money. The interest rate is typically expressed as an annual percentage of the principal. Thus, in this note, the Murphys have obligated themselves to pay interest at the rate of 8 percent per year (per annum) on the remaining balance of principal. Though the balance of the principal owed by the Murphys will decline as they make their monthly payments, note that the interest rate they have agreed to pay is fixed at 8 percent throughout the 30-year term of the note (see Paragraph 3). Thus, we would call this a **fixed rate note**.

But the interest rate specified in the note could be variable, that is, it could change periodically based upon some agreed formula. **Variable rate notes** (also called "adjustable rate notes") are very common in both consumer and commercial transactions. The amount of change in the **interest** rate is usually based on changes in an agreed index, such as U.S. Treasury Bill rates or the **prime rate** (the interest rate that commercial banks charge their best customers). If the Murphys had opted for a variable rate loan from FBCC, Paragraph 2 of their note might read like Illustration 3-c.

Prime rate The interest rate that commercial banks charge their best customers.

Illustration 3-c: VARIABLE RATE LOAN LANGUAGE

Interest on the outstanding principal balance shall accrue from the date hereof at an annual rate of eight percent (8%) per annum, provided, said interest rate shall be adjusted on the adjustment dates follows. On June 30, YR+3, and on that date every three (3) years thereafter, the interest rate accruing on the outstanding principal balance hereunder shall be adjusted to an annual rate equal to three percentage points (3%) in excess of the weekly average yield on United States Treasury securities adjusted to a constant maturity of three (3) years, as made available by the Federal Reserve Board (the "Index") as of the date forty-five (45) days in advance of each such adjustment date. The new interest rate at each such adjustment date shall be rounded to the nearest one-eighth of one percentage point (0.125%).

P-H 3-b: Assume a lender advertises a home mortgage loan with a variable interest rate and an added attractive feature that works like this: Three times a year, the borrower, making monthly payments, can reduce his payment by paying *interest only* (no principal) that month. So, for example, if the borrower's monthly payments of principal and interest total $1,200 and next month $650 of that payment will go to interest and $550 to reduce the principal balance, for that month, the borrower may make a payment of only $650 and not be in default! He does not have to make the $550 payment on principal that month. And he can do this up to three times a year at his option. Why would that option be facially appealing to a borrower? Why would it likely be unwise for the borrower to exercise that option?

Usury Charging an illegal rate of interest for a loan.

Punitive damages Damages intended to punish the wrongdoer in order to deter similar conduct in the future.

Generally speaking, the rate of interest charged on a loan can be whatever the parties agree. But many states have criminal statutes that set the maximum legal rate of interest that can be charged in different types of financial transactions. If the creditor attempts to charge in excess of the statutory rate, it is considered **usury** and can be prosecuted criminally. A usurious loan may also form the basis of a civil action in which the victimized debtor seeks an **injunction** from the court, preventing the lender from enforcing the loan, as well as an award of money damages for any overpayments and, possibly, **punitive damages** (damages intended to punish the wrongdoer in order to deter similar conduct in the future). Note the last sentence of Paragraph 2 of the promissory note in Illustration 2-a, where the lender seeks to protect itself from mistakenly charging a usurious rate of interest and from a possible subsequent change in the law making the rate stated in the note usurious even though it was not at the time the note was executed.

Maximum interest rates are set in the first instance by state law and different rates are often set for different types of lenders, different sizes of loans, or different types of transactions. However, there are some federal rules that control the lawful interest rate that **federally chartered banks** can charge and other federal rules that control certain types of **federally insured loans**.

In the course of our study we will have several occasions to address the issue of interest rates. Here we are considering interest rates agreed to as part of a standard loan transaction, but the subject of interest has many more applications in debtor/creditor law.

Paragraph 3: This paragraph states the *term* of the note, that is, the length of time over which the obligation reflected in the note is to be paid. The term of the Murphys' note is 30 years, or 360 months. That is a common term for notes reflecting money borrowed for the purchase of a home.

P-H 3-c: What monetary advantage would there be to a home purchaser choosing a repayment term of 25, 20, or 15 years rather than 30 years?

Different types of notes have different terms.

EXAMPLE

> If a business borrows money in January of each year to fund its operations until the end of the year, when it anticipates having sufficient collections to pay off the note, it is likely to have a note with a one-year term: money borrowed on January 1 will be due and payable on December 31 of the same year. Many small businesses function like this.

EXAMPLE

> A consumer home improvement loan is often to be repaid over five to ten years.

EXAMPLE

> A commercial loan taken out by a business to fund the purchase of new equipment is often to be repaid over a term no longer than the anticipated useful life of the equipment.

P-H 3-d: Recall that Tomorrow Today, Inc. (TTI) from Case Study #3 (Illustration 1-c) needs to borrow an additional $5 million in order to finish the prototype of the MIES. Based on the information given to you about TTI and the MIES project in Illustration 1-c, over what term should TTI seek to repay this $5 million dollar loan, if it is able to locate a willing lender? Why did you choose the term you did?

Amortized Payments calculated on an installment note so that each installment payment of principal and interest is equal despite the declining principal balance.

Paragraph 3 also states *when* and *where* the payments under the note are to be made. In this case the Murphys are agreeing to make installment payments on a monthly basis over the 360-month term. Thus, we would call this an **installment note**. Each month when the Murphys make an installment payment on the note, a portion of that monthly payment will be applied to principal, thus reducing the balance of principal owed. And a portion of that monthly payment will be for interest charged on the previous principal balance. The next month's payment will require slightly less interest to be paid because the principal balance will be slightly less than it was in the previous month. But note that each of the 360 installment payments is required to be the same amount. How can this be if the principal balance is changing from month to month as it is paid down? What's happened is that the payments due under the note have been **amortized** over the 360-month term. That means they have been calculated in a way to make them equal in total amount over the 360 months of the term even though each individual installment includes a differing amount of principal and interest. Illustration 3-d shows a portion of the amortization schedule for the Murphys' loan.

P-H 3-e: Why is the amount of principal to be paid each month under the amortization schedule in Illustration 3-d increasing? Why is the amount of interest to be paid each month under that schedule decreasing? Over the life of the loan, how much interest are the Murphys paying for the use of the lender's money? How could they reduce that cost utilizing Paragraph 7 of the note?

In a loan secured by the borrower's residence, the monthly payments often include more than just the amortized interest and principal payments. The mortgage instrument in which the borrower pledges the residence being purchased as security for repayment of the amount borrowed (discussed in Chapter Four, Section D) typically obligates the borrower to not only make the principal and interest payments called for under the note but also to include monthly payments to an **escrow account** maintained by the lender to cover annual charges for real estate taxes and insurance on the property. The lender then holds these escrow payments and pays insurance premiums and taxes on the pledged property as they come due (see Paragraphs 4(a), (b), (d), (e), and (f) of the mortgage instrument in Illustration 4-b).

Escrow account An account established by a lender in which payments by the borrower are placed until it is time to pay certain obligations such as property taxes or insurance.

EXAMPLE

Since the loan amortized in Illustration 3-d is for the purchase of a residence, the Murphys, as borrowers, will be making total monthly payments to the lender of more than the amortized principal and interest payments of $843.83. If the annual premium for homeowner's insurance on the property is $600, the monthly payment will include an additional $50 to be held in escrow by the lender until the insurance premium is due, at which time the lender will pay it. Similarly, if the property taxes on the property are $1,200 per year, the monthly payment will include an additional $100 to be held in escrow until the taxes are due, at which time the lender will pay them. Thus the Murphy's total monthly payment will be $993.83.

Illustration 3-d: PART OF THE AMORTIZATION SCHEDULE FOR THE MURPHYS' $115,000 LOAN FOR 30 YEARS AT 8 percent PER ANNUM

Loan Overview				
Principal	Payment	APR	Total Interest	Total Loan Value
$115,000	$843.83	8%	$188,788	$303,778.80

Amortization Table				
Monthly Payment #	Payment Amount	Interest	Principal	Principal Balance
1	$843.83	$766.67	$77.16	$114,922.84
2	$843.83	$766.15	$77.68	$114,845.16
3	$843.83	$765.63	$78.20	$114,688.25
. . .				
358	$843.83	$16.65	$827.18	$1,669.84
359	$843.83	$11.13	$832.70	$837.15
360	$843.83	$6.68	$837.15	$0.00

P-H 3-f: Do you see why the lender requires this escrow arrangement and pays the tax and insurance obligations itself? What would happen to the lender's security interest in the residence if it burned to the ground and there was no insurance to cover the loss? Or, what would result if taxes were not paid on the residence and the state or local taxing authority placed a lien on the property for the back taxes?

The installment payments called for in a note need not be monthly. The parties could agree to quarterly, semiannual, or annual installments. And the note need not call for installment payments at all. Many commercial notes are what we call **balloon notes**. In a balloon note, the full amount of principal and interest may become due on a stated day in the future, rather than being repaid in installments. Or, the note may call for payment of interest with only the full principal balance falling due on a stated future date.

EXAMPLE

> A business purchases land that it expects to hold for resale. It expects to resell the purchased land within a year. If the purchase price is $100,000, it may sign a note calling for no repayments during that year but requiring full repayment with interest one year after the loan is made. Why? Because it expects to sell the land for a profit during that year and use the proceeds of the resale to pay off the note with interest on or before the due date. Or a business establishes a line of credit (discussed in Section B, below) to draw down on for the next 12 months for business expenses. The note may call for monthly interest payments only on the amount of the line of credit drawn down, with the full amount of principal due on the first anniversary of the loan.

Some notes are a combination installment and balloon; they call for low installment payments over some period of time with the remaining balance becoming due (ballooning) on a stated day.

EXAMPLE

> In the last example, the company purchasing the land for resale might sign a note calling for monthly payments of interest only during the year, with the principal balance due in full at the end of the year.

Further, some notes call for neither installment nor balloon payments. Instead they are **demand notes**, payable in full with interest at any time the payee or holder of the note (see Paragraph 4) presents it for payment.

Paragraph 4: This paragraph specifically authorizes the lender/payee to transfer the note to another party, who is then designated as the **holder** of the note. Technically, anyone in legal possession of a promissory note and entitled to demand payment under its terms is a holder. This paragraph specifically forbids the makers from transferring any of their rights or duties under the note. This is a typical **nonassignment clause**.

Paragraph 5: The first sentence of this paragraph defines what constitutes **default** by the maker under the terms of the note. A default means the maker is in breach of its obligations under the note and that the lender has certain legal rights as a result of that default. Take notice of the broad definition of what constitutes a

Nonassignment clause A provision in a contract that prohibits one or both parties from assigning the contract to a third party.

default. Remember, we said that a transaction may involve more documentation than just the promissory note, especially where the note is secured by the maker's pledge of real or personal property to secure repayment. Here, in the definition of default, you see a reflection of that and its importance.

Mortgage The pledging of real property as security for a debt.

P-H 3-g: The Murphys have pledged the real property they purchased with this loan as security for repayment of the note (see Paragraph 6). We call that a **mortgage** on the real property (discussed in more detail in Chapter Four). Assume that the mortgage agreement requires the Murphys to maintain insurance against fire, flood, wind damage, and the like on the house they are purchasing. If the Murphys violate that provision of the mortgage agreement, are they also in default on the note? Why?

Acceleration clause A common provision in a promissory note and other installment contracts making all future installments immediately due and payable upon the debtor's default.

The second sentence of Paragraph 5 of the note contains what is called an **acceleration clause**. It provides that if the maker of the note misses even one installment payment called for in the note or otherwise breaches her obligations under the note or under any agreement securing its payment, the lender can then declare the maker to be in default under the note and require immediate payment of *all* remaining amounts of principal owed under the note as well as any unpaid interest that has become due.

EXAMPLE

Assume the Murphys are late making their 10th monthly installment payment on the note. When that happens, they are not late with the 11th through 360th payments because those aren't due yet. But, due to the acceleration clause, the lender/payee/holder can accelerate all those future and not-yet-due payments to make them immediately due and payable!

The third sentence of Paragraph 5 authorizes the lender, following acceleration, to begin charging a different and likely higher interest rate on the total balance now due. The fourth sentence of Paragraph 5 authorizes the lender to undertake collection action for the entire amount owing, which may include a collection lawsuit (see Chapters Eight and Nine) and requires makers to pay all expenses and costs incurred by the lender in collecting the amount owed, including a reasonable attorney's fee incurred by the lender and court costs if a collection lawsuit is filed.

The last sentence of Paragraph 5 protects the lender from a claim by the makers that the lender has waived its right to declare default by previously accepting late payments.

EXAMPLE

Assume the Murphys are late making the monthly payment called for in the note in the 10th, 11th, and 15th months of the term but the lender accepts the late payments and does not declare default. Then the Murphys are late with payment in the 16th month and the lender declares default and activates the acceleration clause. Without this nonwaiver clause, the Murphys could assert that the lender has waived its right to now declare them in default because it accepted late payments three times previously. This clause effectively deprives the makers of this defense to a claim of default.

Paragraph 6: This paragraph makes it clear that the makers' promise to pay the obligation undertaken in the promissory note is further secured by the pledge of the referenced real property. Thus, this is a **secured note**. A secured note is secured not just by the maker's promise to pay but by the pledge of the maker's real or personal property as well. We will consider the creation of such security arrangements in more detail in Chapters Four and Five.

Paragraph 7: This paragraph authorizes the makers to make early payments under the note—that is, to make them before they are due and to do so without having to pay a fee or penalty. A note can prohibit the maker from making early payments or can impose a fee or monetary penalty for doing so.

P-H 3-h: Can you think of a reason why a lender would prohibit the maker from making early payments or would impose a fee or penalty on the maker for doing so?

Paragraph 8: This paragraph effectively waives rights that the makers would otherwise have to require the lender to go through certain formalities following a default by the makers before undertaking collection efforts. We will not concern ourselves here with those formalities because they are almost universally waived by inclusion of this language in both consumer and commercial notes.

Paragraph 9: The effect of this paragraph is to authorize the lender, upon default, to exercise any and all remedies it may have at law or equity to collect the amount due. Again, there are technicalities involved here we need not concern ourselves with beyond that basic idea.

Time is of the essence clause Contract provision meaning that the parties agree that all time deadlines set out in the contract will be strictly enforced.

Paragraph 10: This is a **time is of the essence clause** and its inclusion in a note means that the parties agree that all time deadlines set out in the note (e.g., the time for making the required payments) will be strictly enforced. The makers must make all payments by the due date or be at risk of being declared in default.

Paragraph 11: This is a **choice-of-law clause** pursuant to which the parties agree that the law of the designated state will control the note's interpretation and enforcement in the event of a dispute. Even if the lawsuit over the note is filed in another state, the law of the designated state will control the outcome of the lawsuit.

Choice-of-law clause Contract provision designating the law of a particular state to control disputes over the contract.

Paragraph 12: This paragraph seeks to avoid technical defenses that might be raised based on the tense or gender of a noun.

Paragraph 13: This paragraph makes it clear that if the lender making the loan changes its legal identity (e.g., changes its name, merges with another financial institution, goes into dissolution, etc.), the changed or succeeding identity will not affect its rights and obligations under the note. And the same is true with the makers of the note: If one of them dies, their estate will be bound by the obligation. If one of them files bankruptcy, the lender can assert their rights against the maker's trustee in bankruptcy, and so forth.

Paragraph 14: This paragraph takes care of another technical problem that could otherwise arise: What happens to the note if a court should, at some point, decide that one sentence or one paragraph is invalid for some reason? Is just that paragraph to be voided or the entire note? This paragraph states that in that event, it to be the intent of the parties for the rest of the note to be enforced, if possible.

B. ▶ The Line of Credit Loan

Line of credit A loan in which the borrowed funds are not immediately advanced to the borrower but are put at the disposal of the borrower to draw down on as needed.

A specialized type of loan used often in both consumer and commercial lending is the **line of credit** loan. In this type of loan, the lender approves the loan in a stated amount using the same process as outlined in Section A1 of this chapter. But unlike a traditional loan, once it is approved, the funds are not immediately advanced to the borrower. Instead the borrower is granted the right to draw down on the funds on an as-needed basis, all at once, or in small amounts over some agreed period of time. And, of course, repayment is not required unless and until the borrower draws down on the funds. Likewise, no interest is due and payable unless and until the borrower draws down on the funds.

EXAMPLE

Recall that five years ago, when it began work on the MIES project, TTI obtained a $10 million line of credit from United Bank of America. And we are told TTI went through that line of credit over a three-year period. What that means is that TTI drew funds from the approved $10 million line of credit, not all at once, but as needed from time to time. It might have drawn a $500,000 at the beginning of its work on the MIES project, then $250,000 six months later, and so on. That's how a line of credit works.

Revolving credit A credit arrangement whereby funds are borrowed only when the borrower chooses up to the limits of the approved credit limits.

A line of credit loan is a type of **revolving credit**, meaning the credit extended by the lender (the loan) is taken by the borrower only if and when and in the amount the borrower chooses (up to the total of the approved loan of course). That is in contrast to a traditional loan where the funds are advanced in full, following approval, and then paid back, usually, in installments. We call this traditional arrangement **installment credit**.

As with a traditional loan, the indebtedness created by a line of credit loan is reflected in a promissory note. Most of the terms of the line of credit note will be identical to what we have seen using the promissory note in Illustration 2-a. But because of the revolving nature of the credit extended, the operative language of the line of credit note regarding advancement of funds and repayment must be different. Consequently, the first three paragraphs of TTI's line of credit note with UBA might read like what is shown in Illustration 3-e.

P-H 3-i: Compare the paragraphs from the TTI note in Illustration 3-e with what we learned about the Murphys' note in Illustration 2-a. What is the term of the TTI note with UBA? Are repayments of principal and interest under the TTI note amortized? Under the TTI note, is interest owed to be paid in installments? If so, beginning when? Under its note, is principal borrowed by TTI to be repaid in installments? Does the TTI note contain a fixed interest rate or a variable rate? What do these differences between the two notes indicate concerning the flexibility the law allows in the creation of debt? What do these differences indicate concerning the ability required of attorneys and assisting legal professionals working in debtor/creditor law to be able to read and understand financial instruments?

Home equity loan A loan in which the borrower pledges the *equity* in his home as security for repayment.

Equity An ownership interest in property unencumbered by any security interest or lien.

A common line of credit loan in consumer lending is the **home equity loan**. **Equity** is the homeowner's ownership interest in the home measured by the difference between the appraised market value of the home and the balance of any outstanding mortgage on the home. It is sometimes referred to as "owner's equity."

Illustration 3-e: OPERATIVE LANGUAGE IN A LINE OF CREDIT NOTE

LINE OF CREDIT PROMISSORY NOTE

1. BORROWER's PROMISE TO PAY: For value received, the undersigned, Tomorrow Today, Inc., a Columbiana corporation ("Borrower"), promises to pay to the order of United Bank of America ("Lender"), in lawful currency of the United States of America, at its principal office in Capitol City, Columbiana, or at such other place as the holder from time to time may designate in writing, the principal sum of ten million dollars ($10,000,000), or so much thereof as may be advanced hereunder from time to time, with interest thereon as set forth in Paragraph 2.

2. INTEREST: Interest shall be computed on the unpaid principal balance from the date of initial advance at the annual rate of one and one-half percent (1.5%) over Lender's Base Rate of interest. The "Base Rate" is that rate of interest established from time to time and determined by Lender as its "Base Rate," such rate being an index used by Lender for establishing interest rates on loans. Said rate shall be adjusted (increased or decreased) on and as of the date of any change in Lender's Base Rate, as such rate of interest may change from time to time.

3. TERM AND PAYMENT: This Note shall be due and payable on demand, but if no demand is made, this Note shall be due and payable as follows:

(a) Accrued interest on the outstanding principal balance shall be due and payable monthly, beginning two years from the date of this Promissory Note and on the first day of each and every succeeding month thereafter until all unpaid principal and accrued interest is paid in full; and

(b) The entire unpaid principal and all accrued interest and other charges shall be due and payable five years from the date of this Promissory Note.

EXAMPLE

We saw in Illustration 1-a that Nick and Pearl Murphy bought their home ten years ago for $125,000 and they still owe First Bank of Capitol City $92,500 on the first mortgage. Three years ago, shortly before Pearl's botched appendectomy, the appraised value of the house had increased to $140,000 and the balance on mortgage to FBCC had been reduced to $99,000 leaving them about $41,000 of equity in the home, the difference between its value and the amount owed on the mortgage against it. At that time the Murphys decided to add two rooms onto the house and arranged a $35,000 line of credit home equity loan from Teacher's Credit Union. TCU took a second mortgage on the house to secure repayment of the loan. TCU was willing to do so because the appraised value of the house ($140,000) was sufficient to cover the balance then owed to FBCC ($99,000) plus the amount of its loan ($35,000).

Home equity loans need not be line of credit loans, of course. They can be traditional loans where the entire amount of the loan is advanced at once to the borrower and is repaid in installments.

P-H 3-j: In the past 30 years there has emerged a body of law loosely called **lender liability** that involves claims for breach of contract, fraud, or breach of fiduciary duty by a borrower against a lender. Most commonly asserted in connection with commercial transactions but available in consumer transactions as well, lender liability claims usually arise when a lender makes oral promises during negotiations for the loan, but then changes the terms in the written contract documents; wrongfully fails to honor a loan commitment; wrongfully refuses to renew a loan or to extend credit previously promised; or becomes a business advisor to the customer or even takes control of the customer's business to keep it from defaulting on the loan. Read *Siegner v. Interstate Production Credit Association of Spokane, PCA*, 820 P.2d 20 (Or. App. 1991); *Waddell v. Dewey County Bank*, 471 N.W.2d 951 (So. Dak. 1991); and *Scott v. Dime Saving Bank*, 101 F.3d 107 (2d Cir. 1996). What was the lender liability issue in each case? What was the holding of the court in each case?

C. ▶ The Consumer Payday Loan, Car Title Loans, and Other Predatory Lending

Payday loan High interest, short-term loan in which the borrower typically gives the lender a post-dated check for the amount borrowed plus interest and fees. If the amount borrowed is not repaid by the date of the check, the lender will cash it in payment.

The **payday loan**—also called variously a *cash advance, check advance, post-dated check loan, deferred deposit check loan*, or *deferred presentment loan*—has become a major source of debt, primarily for low-income consumers. Aggressively marketed by financial services companies that describe themselves as providing *check cashing services* or *check advance services*, the payday loan is a short-term loan for a small amount under terms that charge the borrower an astronomically high interest rate, sometimes camouflaged as a **transaction fee** or **finance charge**.

 EXAMPLE

> Marta Rinaldi Carlson is an employee of TTI (we will learn more about her in Chapter Fourteen). Marta needs $100 cash right now but her checking account is empty and she doesn't get paid again until the end of the month, 14 days away. She goes to a check cashing business and writes a check payable to the company for $115 and receives a cash loan of $100. She is told to postdate the check to the last day of the month and the company promises to hold and not cash the $115 check until that date, when Marta's next paycheck will, presumably, be deposited. Fourteen days later the company cashes the $115 check. The check pays them back the $100 they loaned Marta plus $15, which they receive as "interest" or "fees" or "finance charges."

Does the payday loan described in the last example sound like a good deal for Marta? She just paid $15 to borrow $100 for 14 days. That's a full 15 percent charge for using someone else's money for only two weeks. Annualized, Marta is paying 391 percent per annum interest for that loan. And, if Marta extends or rolls over her loan for another 10- or 14-day term, the same charge is imposed a second time.

EXAMPLE

> If Marta asks for another 14 days to pay back the $100 she borrowed, the charge will be an additional $15 for a total of $30 paid in interest and fees to borrow $100 for 28 days. That's a full 30 percent charge to use someone else's money for less than a month. If she rolls over the loan a second time, for an additional 14 days, the finance charge goes to 45 percent of the amount borrowed, and so on. The loan shark in the alley could do no better.

Payday lenders have also come under criticism in some states for using aggressive "body attachment" procedures in debt collection, as discussed in Section A of Chapter Eleven (see P-H 11-b).

Closely related to the payday loan is the **car title loan** where the consumer signs title to his vehicle over to the lender to secure a similar short-term loan at a triple-digit rate of annualized interest.

What about state usury statutes limiting the interest a lender can legally charge a borrower? What has happened is that many states have enacted legislation specifically exempting payday loan and car title loan companies from state usury statutes, which would otherwise control small loans and limit them to the lower double-digit range (e.g., 25% per annum). These statutory or regulatory exemptions are called **safe-harbor provisions** for the benefit of the financial services companies operating these businesses.

Safe-harbor provisions A provision in a statute or regulation that exempts a person from liability for certain conduct.

In the mid-1990s there were only a few hundred payday and car title loan companies scattered around the country. Today there are more than 20,000 locations (roughly the number of McDonald's and Burger King locations combined), most commonly in low-income neighborhoods and, until recently, around military bases. In the 2007 Defense Authorization Act, Congress capped rates on such loans made to military personnel at 36 percent per annum, resulting in a migration of payday and title loan companies away from military bases. In addition, the Servicemembers Civil Relief Act (SCRA), U.S.C.A. App. §501 et seq., as revised in 2003, authorizes military personnel going on active duty to reduce interest due on pre–active duty monetary obligations to 6 percent per annum if active duty would materially affect their ability to pay a higher interest rate (see P-H 8-h).

Though the typical payday/car title borrower is low income, a 2010 investigation by National Public Radio's *Planet Money* ("Inside a Payday Loan Shop" at www.npr.org/blogs/money/2010/05/the_tuesday_podcast_payday_len.html) revealed that a significant number of regular users of payday loan shops are solidly middle class. Payday and car title loans are often justified by the financial services industry as providing a quick, convenient, short-term loan source. However, 80 percent of payday and car title loan customers renew or **roll over** their loan once or more. In fact, the average payday/car title loan customer takes out a loan nine times per year. Sixty percent of the income of these companies is estimated to come from repeat customers.

Payday and car title loans are, needless to say, controversial. Consumer advocates consider them **predatory lending** that takes advantage of unsophisticated and sometimes desperate, lower-income consumers. Business advocates consider them a fair lending practice, subject, like other loans, to provisions of the federal **Truth in Lending Act (TILA)** and **Regulation Z** (12 CFR Part 226) promulgated under TILA, requiring lenders to disclose in writing the finance charge (a dollar amount) and the annual percentage rate (APR) to the consumer. But there is a real question whether, realistically, most payday loan customers bother to read such disclosures or understand them if they do.

A number of states have enacted legislation regulating payday and car title loan companies to some extent, capping the interest rate that can be charged and/or limiting the number of rollovers per customer per year.

EXAMPLE

> Virginia's Payday Loan Reform Act took effect on January 1, 2009. The bill caps interest rates lenders may charge at 36 percent per annum. Lenders must give borrowers two pay periods to repay a loan. Lenders are limited to making one loan at a time to borrowers, who must wait one day after repaying a loan to take out another. Borrowers who take out at least five loans in a six-month period must either wait 45 days before getting another loan or extend the payment term on the fifth loan to two months or more. Anyone taking a two-month extension option has to wait another two months before getting a new loan. An extended payment plan is available once a year, followed by a three-month cooling off period. Lenders that falsely threaten criminal prosecution for failure to make good on the check used to obtain the loan are subject to a fine three times the cost of the loan. The **Consumer Federation of America** (www.consumerfed.org/) and **Center for Responsible Lending** (www.responsiblelending.org/) are nonprofits that provide excellent resources regarding predatory lending.

Many payday and car title loan shops are subsidiaries of banks, including some of the largest banking systems in the nation. Efforts of reform-minded states to reign in predatory lending by subsidiaries of federally chartered banks were dealt a significant setback by the Supreme Court in *Watters v. Wachovia Bank*, 550 U.S. 1 (2007). *Watters* held that state rules purporting to regulate banks subject to the **National Bank Act (NBA)**, 12 U.S.C. §1 et seq., and regulations promulgated by the **Office of the Comptroller of the Currency (OCC)**, which enforces the NBA, are preempted by the NBA and OCC regulations and that such preemption applies to subsidiaries of the national banks. Finally, in the **Dodd-Frank Wall Street Reform and Consumer Protection Act of 2010 (the Dodd-Frank Act)**, Congress created the **Consumer Financial Protection Bureau** within the Federal Reserve and authorized it to promulgate regulations for most consumer financial transactions, which will include payday loans and car title loans transactions. Specifically exempted from the reach of the new bureau are automobile loans initiated by auto dealerships, many of which have also been accused of predatory lending practices such as slipping unapproved charges and fees into the small print of loan documents, doubling or tripling the income figure of the customer to qualify them for unaffordable loans, and forging signatures on financing paperwork.

P-H 3-k: The Consumer Financial Protection Bureau began its regulatory work in July 2011. Go to its Web site at www.consumerfinance.gov/ and see if you can locate any regulations it has issued to date impacting on the payday loan industry or other areas of consumer debt mentioned in this chapter or in Chapter Four, which covers real estate transactions.

P-H 3-l: With increased state regulation and with the prospect of federal regulation looming, many payday lenders have relocated to offshore, nonregulated havens in the Caribbean and elsewhere and continue to make loans in the United States via the Internet. Of course, such lenders must rely increasingly on domestic banks to seize past due payments (including interest calculated at as much as 500 percent per annum as well as exorbitant fees) from borrowers' checking and savings accounts in those domestic banks. Should U.S. banks be complicit in this predatory lending scheme? See the *New York Times* exposé at www.nytimes.com/2013/02/24/business/major-banks-aid-in-payday-loans-banned-by-states.html?nl=todaysheadlines&emc=edit_th_20130224&_r=0. Should U.S. banks adopt internal policies prohibiting this lending practice, even though it is technically legal? Should government regulation prohibit this enabling?

Payday and car title loans are the best known examples of predatory consumer lending, but there are many others. In a **pawn shop loan**, somewhat similar to the car title loan, the consumer takes out a short-term loan (usually 30 days) and pledges some kind of personal property (e.g., jewelry, gun, computer, appliance, antique) as security for repayment of the loan. The property so pledged is left in the physical possession of the pawn shop lender. The loan is made in an amount equal to a reduced value of the property pledged (usually 30–50%). If the borrower does not repay the loan by the due date, the pawn shop can sell the property for its full value and keep it. If the loan plus accrued interest and other charges (e.g., storage and transaction fees) is paid, the borrower can recover possession of the property pledged. Like other short-term consumer loans, pawn shop loans are often renewed or extended indefinitely with payment of accrued interest. Because of the danger of pawn shops being used to fence stolen goods, states impose more regulation on them, including a requirement that all transactions be reported to the police, but few regulate the terms of the transaction itself.

Buy Here Pay Here used car transactions are often subject to predatory credit terms and questionable business practices. Catering to low-income Americans who cannot qualify for a conventional car loan, these used car dealers offer the convenience of financing a car purchase through the dealer. This may seem like a good deal, except that the interest rate charged is often a multiple of the current rates of conventional loans, often 30 percent per annum or more. And many consumers who have dealt with this industry have some sad tales to tell about their treatment at the hands of these creditors.

P-H 3-m: In 2011 the *Los Angeles Times* ran a series of articles by Ken Bensinger on the Buy Here Pay Here car industry (www.latimes.com/business/buy-here-pay-here/la-fi-buy-here-pay-here-part1-storyb,0,5689256.story). After reading that series, answer the following questions. Should there be more regulation of this industry or is this simply supply meeting demand? Should the law provide protection of consumers not only regarding terms of the transaction itself, but also regarding collection/repossession methods used by these creditors?

Same As Cash financing offers, seen often in ads for the purchase of furniture, appliances, and other consumer goods, may contain hidden dangers for unsophisticated buyers. Seeming to offer an extended term for payment of the purchase price with no interest charged ("No interest for 24 months! Same as cash!"), the transaction may actually be a deferred interest trap containing a nasty surprise for the consumer. Typically in these transactions, if full payment is not made within the free term, then an interest rate much higher than conventional rates (40% per annum is not unusual) is assessed on the entire purchase price (even though a portion of the price has been paid) and the interest due is calculated over the entire period since purchase, including what the consumer thought was the interest-free period. These deals are often criticized as well for not making it clear what the length of the free term actually is and for not disclosing in advance the interest rate to be charged.

> ### D.   Installment Sales and Rent-to-Own Transactions

Consumers and businesses often purchase merchandise on credit from the seller. They don't borrow money from a lender to purchase the merchandise; they don't sign a promissory note evidencing a loan. Instead, the seller of the merchandise allows the buyer to take immediate possession of the property in exchange for the buyer's promise to pay the purchase price in installments over time. This is called an **installment sale contract** (see Illustration 5-a). The installment sale contract sets out the terms of the repayment schedule, just as a promissory note does, and the seller typically retains a security interest in the merchandise sold so that it can repossess the merchandise in the event the buyer defaults on the installment payments.

Rent-to-own agreement A contract in which the buyer leases the property until the final payment, at which time the seller/lessee conveys title to him.

A contract can provide that title to the property remains with seller until the buyer makes the final installment payment. When seller retains title to the property, the contract may be called a **rent-to-own contract**. The "buyer" is actually treated as a lessee of the property until the final payment called for in the agreement is made, at which time the owner/lessor conveys title to the lessee/buyer.

P-H 3-n: We will have more to say about installment sale contracts in Chapter Five, when we consider security interests in detail. But go ahead and examine Illustration 5-a, the installment sale and security agreement between Shears Department Store and Nick and Pearl Murphy for the purchase of the Murphys' living room furniture. Did the Murphys take title to the furniture at the time they signed this contract or is title retained by Shears? Did Shears retain a security interest in the furniture? Did the Murphys borrow any money from Shears?

Installment sale and rent-to-own contracts are also used in real estate transactions where the owner/seller allows the tenant/buyer to take possession of the realty but not obtain title to it until the final installment or rent payment is made. An upfront deposit or earnest money payment equal to a percentage (e.g., 1–5%) of the final purchase price is often required in addition to the rental payments. Such contracts may also be called **rent-to-own, lease option, lease-purchase, contract for deed**, or simply **land contract**. Whatever they are called, such **delayed title contracts** can be risky for the lessee/buyer since the installment or rental payments may not be creating any equity in the property for the tenant/buyer until they are completed and title passes. If the tenant/buyer breaches such a contract prior to completing all the payments or is unable to qualify for a traditional residential loan when the time comes to exercise the purchase option, payments made prior to that time will not have given the tenant/buyer any equity position in the property and are essentially forfeited. With the collapse in the housing and credit markets since 2008, such delayed title contracts have become more popular in this country. They can also be convenient tools for scam artists, as when an unscrupulous lessor/seller woos a tenant/buyer into the deal then looks for any excuse to claim breach. *Caveat emptor* (buyer beware).

E. ▶ Credit Card Debt

Credit card debt is a significant aspect of debtor/creditor law because of the massive amount of such debt, both consumer and commercial, that exists in our economy. As we will see in Part C of the text, the inability of many consumers to effectively manage their credit card debt is a major cause of bankruptcy filings. Each year the credit industry sends out more than 5 billion credit card solicitations. Approximately 176 million Americans have credit cards and we average 3.5 cards per person at any given time, meaning there are more than half a billion cards in use. In 2012 Americans collectively carried about $858 billion in credit card debt, an amount exceeded only by the collective amount owed on home loans ($8.15 trillion) and student loans ($914 billion). That's an average of more than $7,000 in credit card debt per American household. And for the 47 percent of households that carry a credit card balance from month to month instead of paying off the balance each month, the average balance per household is over $15,000. Globally, annual credit card spending has quadrupled since 2000 to more than $5 billion. Credit card use now represents 11 percent of worldwide gross domestic product.

P-H 3-o: As a result of the Great Recession, credit card indebtedness actually fell in this country from a high of $975.5 billion in 2008 to about $800 billion at the end of 2011, before beginning to track upward again in 2012. The Federal Reserve Bank of New York (www.newyorkfed.org/index.html) issues a quarterly Household Debt and Credit Report. Check that or some other reliable source and determine the current balances of credit card debt in the nation and in your state. Are the trends up or down? What is the average credit card debt per household? How do the current totals and averages compare to current student loan indebtedness?

Many businesses use credit cards as well, and one major effect of the continuing financial crisis that began in 2007 (sometimes referred to as the **Great Recession** due to certain similarities to the **Great Depression** of the 1930s; it technically ended in 2010 but effects are still being felt) has been unprecedented defaults by struggling businesses on their credit card debt. As a result of massive recession-related defaults by both consumer and commercial customers, credit card issuers have found it necessary to reduce credit limits for card holders and to be much more selective in approving card applications.

As a result of mergers and consolidation among companies issuing credit cards, the top seven card companies now carry about 80 percent of all outstanding credit card debt. Those seven card companies are Citigroup, Inc.; Capital One Financial Corp.; Bank of America Corp.; Discover Financial Services, LLC; JP Morgan Chase & Co.; American Express Co.; and HSBC Holdings.

Credit card arrangements are similar to the line of credit loan already considered: The bank, credit union, or other financial services company issuing the card establishes a credit limit for the card customer. The credit limit is the maximum amount of money the issuer is willing to lend the customer for card purchases, cash advances, or balance transfers from another card. If the customer does exceed the credit limit, the contract typically authorizes the issuer to charge the customer an over-the-credit-limit fee.

Some credit cards require the customer to pay off the entire balance owed on the card on a periodic (usually monthly) basis. These types of cards are more properly called **charge cards**.

Also to be distinguished from the true credit card is the **debit card**, which, when used, authorizes the direct withdrawal of funds from the debit card owner's bank account. Thus, a debit card is a sort of electronic check or a substitute for cash and not a true credit instrument. But debit card use is soaring: American consumers now make about one-third of their in-store purchases with debit cards. That popularity, combined with the potential for debit card purchases to trigger an **overdraft** in the owner's checking account, contributes to the debt problems of many consumers. An overdraft occurs when the owner of a checking account withdraws more from his or her account than is there on deposit. The withdrawal creating the overdraft can be the result of a check being written on the account, or a cash withdrawal from an **automated teller machine** (ATM) or a debit card purchase. It has long been the practice of banks, credit unions, and other financial institutions to honor the overdraft in a customer's account by effectively loaning the customer the amount of the overdraft. Called **courtesy overdraft protection**, what has actually happened is that the bank has loaned the customer the amount of the overdraft. And the bank will charge the customer an **overdraft fee** for each overdraft event. Overdraft fees may run as high as $35 and the fee may be charged periodically until the overdraft loan is repaid. Since the customer may not be aware of the first overdraft for some days, the danger of multiple overdrafts and the charging of multiple overdraft fees is high. Because of the frequency of overdrafts resulting from debit card use and ATM withdrawals, the **Federal Reserve Board**, which administers the **Electronic Fund Transfer Act**, 15 U.S.C. §1693, amended its **Regulation E** at 12 CFR Part 205, which implements that Act in the summer of 2010 to require financial institutions to obtain customer consent to overdraft protection for each account the customer has with the institution if the institution intends to charge a fee for the service. The new rule applies to overdrafts created by ATM withdrawals and debit card use but not to checks. If a customer does not consent to overdraft protection, the ATM withdrawal or debit purchase will simply not be honored to the extent it creates an overdraft.

A true credit card does not require the customer to pay off the entire balance at all so long as the card is still effective. Instead, it utilizes a **revolving credit** arrangement, whereby the customer is required to make only a *minimum payment* on the balance owed each month and is allowed to carry the remaining credit card balance over to the following month where it is added to the total of new purchases, cash advances, or balance transfers.

Of course, the issuer charges the customer interest on card balances carried over from month to month and those interest charges are themselves added to the account balance. Interest charges on a credit card are usually referred to in the contract between the issuer and the customer as the **annual percentage rate**, or APR. And the contract may call for the imposition of a number of different APRs.

Overdraft Created when the owner of a checking account authorizes the payment of more funds from his account than he has on deposit by writing a check, making an ATM withdrawal, or using a debit card.

Revolving credit A credit arrangement whereby funds are borrowed only when the borrower chooses up to the limits of the approved credit limits.

Annual percentage rate (APR) The annualized rate of interest charged periodically by lenders on the balance of a debt account such as a credit card balance.

Illustration 3-f: DIFFERENT APRs THAT MAY BE CHARGED BY A SINGLE CREDIT CARD

- *One APR for purchases, another for cash advances, and yet another for balance transfers.* The APRs for cash advances and balance transfers often are higher than the APR for purchases (e.g., 14% for purchases, 18% for cash advances, and 19% for balance transfers).
- *Tiered APRs.* Different rates are applied to different levels of the outstanding balance (e.g., 16% on balances of $1-$500 and 17% on balances greater than $500).
- *A penalty APR.* The APR may increase if you are late in making payments. For example, your card agreement may say, "If your payment arrives more than ten days late two times within a six-month period, the penalty rate will apply."
- *An introductory APR.* A different rate will apply after the introductory rate expires.
- *A delayed APR.* A different rate will apply in the future. For example, a card may advertise that there is "no interest until next March." Look for the APR that will be in effect after March.

(Source: Federal Reserve Board credit card information site: www.federalreserve.gov/Pubs/shop/#limit)

Illustration 3-f summarizes the various APRs that a single card may charge. In 2010 the average APR advertised on new credit card offers was 14.23 percent while the average APR on cards carrying a balance was 14.67 percent.

There has been an issue regarding limits on the amount of interest credit card issuers may charge. If an issuer issues a card from a state whose usury laws allow interest on such transactions to be charged up to 24 percent per annum but the card is issued to a customer residing in and using the card in another state with a 18 percent per annum limit, can the issuer charge the 24 percent without violating the usury statutes of the customer's state? The U.S. Supreme Court answered that question in *Marquette National Bank of Minneapolis v. First of Omaha Service Corp.*, 439 U.S. 239 (1978), where it held that language in the National Bank Act, 12 U.S.C. §85, allowing any national banking association "to charge on any loan" interest at the rate allowed by the laws of the state "where the bank is located," effectively preempts the usury statutes of the customers' states and allows the issuer to charge rates legal in the issuer's home state regardless of where the customer resides or in what state charges are made. *Smiley v. Citibank*, 517 U.S. 735 (1996), later held the same as to finance fees and charges.

In addition to interest charges, credit cards also charge a number of different fees to their customers. Illustration 3-g summarizes the various fees that a single credit card may charge.

Numerous individual consumers and some businesses encounter severe financial problems by failing to manage credit card debt responsibly. There are many reasons for this, including: the ease of obtaining a credit card; the ease of using the card for purchases and cash advances without being aware of the growing balance; the failure to pay off the balance on a monthly basis; the lack of awareness of the high APR rates; unnoticed increases in the APR rates; the lack of awareness of the various fees imposed by the issuer; the use of multiple cards; the use of the card to pay for long-term obligations; the use of the card to pay a large, unanticipated expense such as medical/hospital bills while already carrying a large balance; and the lack of financial or budgetary sophistication by so many credit card users. As a result, credit card debt often grows like an aggressive, unseen cancer, and once the card holder finally recognizes how deeply in debt he is, it is often too late.

Illustration 3-g: FEES THAT MAY BE CHARGED ON A SINGLE CREDIT CARD

- *Annual fee* (sometimes billed monthly): charged for having the card
- *Cash advance fee:* charged each time you use the card to obtain a cash advance; may be a flat fee (e.g., $3.00) or a percentage of the cash advance (e.g., 3%)
- *Balance-transfer fee:* charged when you transfer a balance from another credit card (Your credit card company may send you "checks" to pay off the other card. The balance is transferred when you use one of these checks to pay the amount due on the other card.)
- *Late-payment fee:* charged if your payment is received after the due date
- *Over-the-credit-limit fee:* charged if you go over your credit limit
- *Credit-limit-increase fee:* charged if you ask for an increase in your credit limit
- *Set-up fee:* charged when a new credit card account is opened
- *Returned-item fee:* charged if you pay your bill by check and the check is returned for insufficient funds (that is, your check bounces)
- *Other fees:* some credit card companies charge a fee to cover the costs of reporting to credit bureaus, reviewing your account, or providing other customer services (Read the information in your credit card agreement to see if there are other fees and charges.)

(Source: Federal Reserve Board credit card information site: www.federalreserve.gov/Pubs/shop/#limit)

P-H 3-p: Recall that Nick and Pearl Murphy from Case Study #1 (Illustration 1-a) have "maxed out" both their Master Card and Visa. Illustration 3-h shows you the Murphys' Visa bill from last August. Look it over and determine what APRs they were charged and what fees they were assessed on this statement. How was the finance charge on this bill calculated? What was their minimum payment on the preceding month's bill? What is the minimum payment on this month's bill? If the Murphys make no new charges on this card after receiving this bill and continue to make only the minimum payment each month, can you calculate approximately how long it will take them to pay off the entire balance owed?

On May 22, 2009, President Obama signed into law the **Credit Card Accountability, Responsibility and Disclosure Act** (also known as the **Credit Card Act of 2009**), Public Law 111-24, 123 Stat. 1734-1766 amending TILA and other federal statutes. Most of the changes went into effect in February 2010. The Act imposes historical restrictions on the credit card industry and is a major piece of consumer legislation. Highlights of the Act are set forth in Illustration 3-i.

Unfortunately, between the time the Credit Card Act of 2009 was passed and the date most of its provisions went into effect in 2010, including the protections against sudden hikes in interest rates, many credit card companies dramatically raised the interest rates they charge card customers. In response, the Federal Reserve adopted new rules effective in August 2010 amending Regulation Z of TILA requiring card issuers to reevaluate interest increases going back to the beginning of 2009 and to reduce those rates if the reasons justifying the changes can no longer be justified. The August 2010 amendments to Regulation Z also:

- Prohibit credit card issuers from charging a penalty fee of more than $25 for paying late or otherwise violating the account's terms unless the consumer

Illustration 3-h: NICK AND PEARL MURPHYS' VISA BILL FROM LAST AUGUST

Neopolitan Community Bank
1211 Main St.
Capitol City, Columbiana

Visa Account #xxx5678xxx1234
Nicholas W. Murphy & Pearl E. Murphy
3521 West Cherry St.
Capitol City, Columbiana

Transactions for this Month:
04 August   Citizens Cable Co.....................$59.95
08 August   WeLuvYourPet Kennel..............25.00
15 August   Action Theatres......................32.50
20 August   Bookzone.............................27.50
24 August   Metazoid Dep't Store................114.97

At your service

To call Customer Relations or to report a lost card:
1-800-888-8888

Send payments to:
Attn: Remittance Processing
Neopolitan Community Bank
1211 Main St.
Capitol City, Columbiana

Account Summary
Total Credit Line: $3,000
Total Credit Available: 0

Previous Balance.............................$3,072.50
Payments & Credits............................$100.00
Finance Charges*................................$48.38
Over the Credit Limit Fee.....................$25.00
Current Transactions..........................$259.92

New Balance....................................$3,305.80
Minimum Amount Due....................$165.00
Payment Due Date.........................09/15/20XX

*Finance Charges:	Periodic Rate	Corresponding APR	Finance Charge
Balance rate applied to $2,972.50	.05425%	19.80%	$48.38

---

has engaged in repeated violations or the issuer can show that a higher fee represents a reasonable proportion of the costs it incurs as a result of violations.

- Prohibit credit card issuers from charging penalty fees that exceed the dollar amount associated with the consumer's violation. For example, card issuers will no longer be permitted to charge a $39 fee when a consumer is late making a $20 minimum payment. Instead, the fee cannot exceed $20.
- Ban "inactivity" fees, such as fees based on the consumer's failure to use the account to make new purchases.

Illustration 3-i: HIGHLIGHTS OF THE CREDIT CARD ACT OF 2009

- Interest rates cannot be raised during the first year of an account. Historically, companies have baited customers into using a card by offering low interest rates and then increased those rates once the customer begins using the card.
- Customers must be notified 45 days in advance of any change in interest rates and of any other significant change such as increasing any fee or finance charge. This provision bans the common industry practice of arbitrarily raising interest rates/fees without prior notice. All such notifications must include a statement of the customer's right to cancel the card and such cancellation may not be treated as a default by the consumer and the card issuer may not declare all balances immediately due and payable.
- Fine print terms are eliminated. Credit card agreements now must disclose all terms in clear language including any rights reserved by the issuer to change those terms. Agreements must also be posted on the Internet where customers can review them at any time.
- The practice of **universal default**, which allowed companies to dramatically raise interest rates on a credit card if the consumer was more than 30 days late on any other debt obligation (e.g., house or car payment) is now banned.
- Bills may be paid online or over the phone and no "processing" or other fee may be charged to the customer who does so.
- A customer must be over 60 days late on payments before his or her interest rate may be raised on existing balances. If the rate is raised, it must revert to the lower rate if the customer makes the minimum payment on time for six months in a row. Congress rejected proposals that the law ban all retroactive interest rate increases.
- **Over limit fees** (see Illustration 3-g) may not be charged unless the cardholder is told that the purchase will put him or her over the limit and he or she authorizes it to go through anyway.
- If a card has more than one interest rate on existing balances, payments must be applied first to the balance carrying the highest interest rate.
- **Gift cards** may not expire for five years, and issuers may not charge dormancy fees for unused amounts left on the gift card. Gift cards remain a real risk to consumers because of the danger of store closings (making use of the card impractical) and retailer bankruptcies.
- Credit card statements must be mailed out at least 21 days before payment is due. This provision eliminates "late bill creep" where credit card companies, without notice, shortened the due date for payments, increasing the likelihood of late payment and the corresponding assessment of late fees.
- Credit cards may not be issued to individuals under 21 years of age unless 1) there is a co-signer on the card agreement, or 2) the issuer can verify that the person under 21 has **independent financial means** to make payments on the credit extended. This provision is a modest step toward dealing with the problem of credit card companies targeting teenagers and young adults inexperienced and unsophisticated in personal finance, not to mention shorter on cash than older adults, and thus more likely to overcharge and carry over balances from month to month enabling the credit card company to charge and collect more in interest and fees. For years many colleges and universities permitted credit card companies to actively solicit their students on campus and even sold student contact information to card companies.

- Prevent issuers from charging multiple penalty fees based on a single late payment or other violation of the account terms.

The Consumer Financial Protection Bureau, created by Congress in 2010 as part of the Dodd-Frank Act referenced earlier is expected to develop additional consumer protection rules in connection with credit cards (see P-H 3-k).

F. The Rise of the Debt Settlement Industry and Credit Counseling Agencies

One consequence of Americans having taken on such great amounts of credit card debt in the last generation and the current Great Recession has been the explosion of the **debt settlement industry** in the guise of **credit counseling agencies** (CCAs) (sometimes called **debt management, debt relief, debt settlement, debt negotiation,** or **credit repair companies**) that offer to assist debt-strapped individuals or businesses to avoid bankruptcy by negotiating a **debt management plan** (DMP) with the client's credit card companies or other creditors. Ideally the DMP will lower the client's required payments by extending the time for repayment, eliminate or reduce late fees and interest rates, and, in rare cases, even reduce the principal amount owed. The CCAs also provided clients **financial literacy and budget counseling**.

At the end of the twentieth century, there were approximately 200 CCAs around the country, most of which were legitimate businesses assisting consumers and small businesses on a **not-for-profit** basis and charging minimal fees. A decade later, more than a thousand CCAs exist, many of which are for-profit, and though many of them are still perfectly legitimate, the industry is now rife with complaints of false and deceptive promises regarding results to be obtained, charging excessive fees (often in advance and regardless of results obtained), charging undisclosed fees, and simply failing to provide promised services.

Since 2003, the **Federal Trade Commission** (FTC) has instituted at least six administrative actions against CCAs, including one of the largest, AmeriDebt, Inc., under the auspices of the **Telemarketing and Consumer Fraud and Abuse Prevention Act** of 1994 (15 U.S.C. §6101, et seq.) for various violations of that Act. (CCAs often market their services via telephone solicitation.) The FTC's **Telemarketing Sales Rule** (TSR), 16 CFR Part 310, was recently amended to add new restrictions aimed at curbing CCA abuse (see, e.g., the FTC's news release at www.ftc.gov/opa/2012/11/robocalls.shtm announcing the filing of complaints against A+ Financial Center, LLC, and four other companies allegedly using deceptive "This is Rachel from cardholder services" robocalls falsely promising to reduce the consumer's credit card debt). The attorneys general in a number of states have brought suit against CCAs using their state consumer protection acts and antifraud laws. A number of states have legislated licensing and/or disclosure requirements on CCAs or prohibitions on up-front fees, and four states (Connecticut, Louisiana, Wyoming, and North Dakota) prohibit for-profit CCAs entirely. In 2003 the **IRS** began to crack down on for-profit CCAs masquerading as not-for-profit and in 2006 Congress amended the **Internal Revenue Code** (IRC) to add what is now 26 U.S.C. §501(q) imposing a number of requirements on CCAs wishing to receive **tax-exempt status** as non-profit businesses, including a dictate that fees be reasonable and prohibiting fees based on a percentage of a client's debt or DMP payments unless state law expressly permits.

P-H 3-q: One of the leading trade associations for CCAs is the United States Organizations for Bankruptcy Alternatives (www.usoba.org/). Visit the USOBA site and see if you can determine the association's general position on industry regulation. What are their requirements for CCA membership in their association?

G. Credit Reports and Credit Reporting Agencies

1. For the Individual Consumer

Credit report A compilation of the debt history and bill-paying record of a consumer.

Credit reporting agencies companies in the business of compiling credit reports and providing them to creditors and other authorized persons as allowed under the *Fair Credit Reporting Act.*

Credit score Under FICO, a score ranging from a low of 300 to a high of 850 calculated by credit reporting agencies to rate the credit worthiness of a consumer. The higher the score, the more favorable the rating.

A **credit report** is a compilation of the debt history and bill-payment record of a consumer. Credit reports are compiled by businesses known as **credit reporting agencies (CRAs)** or **credit bureaus** using information supplied by a consumer's creditors (e.g., credit card issuers, mortgage holders, auto financing companies, landlords), debt collection agencies (see Chapter Six), and public records including court records (e.g., bankruptcy filings and collection suits). The reports are compiled and sold by the credit reporting agency to persons and businesses authorized to investigate the credit worthiness or financial responsibility of the consumer. CRAs and the contents of credit reports, access to them, use of them, and correction of errors in them is governed by the **Fair Credit Reporting Act** (**FCRA**), 15 U.S.C. §1681 et seq., and its implementing regulation, Regulation V (12 CFR Part 222). Many states supplement the provisions of the FCRA with their own statutes or regulations. Separate from the credit report itself, credit reporting agencies calculate and make available for purchase a **credit score** for the consumer. There are a number of different credit scoring models but the most popular one is the **FICO** credit-risk score developed by **Fair Isaac Corporation** of San Rafael, California. FICO scores range between 300 and 850: the higher the score, the greater the perceived credit worthiness of the consumer. The score is calculated based on a statistical analysis of the relevant data in the consumer's credit report (e.g., length of credit history; types of loans or credit obtained; timeliness of payments; on revolving credit accounts, the ratio of balance owed to credit limits; credit or loan applications denied; collection actions and court judgments; tax or other involuntary liens; bankruptcies filed). Currently the median FICO score is 723.

The data contained in the credit report, and the credit score in particular, are used by those authorized to access the data to make decisions such as whether to make a loan or extend credit to the consumer, whether to lease a house or apartment to them, whether to issue a policy of insurance and the amount of the premium (consumers with higher credit scores often get lower premiums), and even whether to hire them for a job. The consumer's credit score may not only determine whether a loan will be made or credit extended, but the size of loan or amount of credit the lender is willing to extend to the consumer and even the interest rate to be charged. Consumers who present safer credit risks to lenders often receive more generous loans or higher credit limits at lower interest rates and even lower premium rates on insurance.

Approximately 3 billion consumer credit reports are issued by credit reporting agencies each year in the United States and more than 36 billion updates are made to credit reports annually.

EC 3-a: It is increasingly common for employers to perform routine credit checks on job applicants. A 2008 study by the Society for Human Resource Management found that approximately 43 percent of American employers do so, up from 36 percent in 2004. Is it right for a well-qualified person in need of a job to be eliminated from consideration solely because of a poor credit history? Is this a modern form of the old debtor's prison? Is this issue a greater concern in a time of economic stress and high unemployment? Should we have more controls on the circumstances under which an employer can check a worker's credit history? Should we have more controls over the use that an inquiring employer can make of that information? There are proposals pending in several state legislatures and in Congress to restrict the use of a credit report/score in making employment decisions unless one's credit risk is specifically relevant to the position. The EEOC is considering proposing regulations restricting the practice. What do you think?

The Federal Reserve Board's Regulation B, 12 CFR Part 202, implementing the Equal Credit Opportunity Act, requires that any scoring model used to calculate a credit score be "empirically derived, demonstrably and statistically sound." A lender cannot use any credit score that was calculated on a scoring model using prohibited factors such as gender, race, color, religion, national origin, marital status, that all or part of the applicant's income derives from public assistance, or that the applicant is or is likely to become a parent. The age of an applicant cannot be used as a negative factor by the scoring model though it can be considered as a relevant predictive variable. When credit is denied to an applicant, the applicant is entitled to be notified in writing of the adverse action and, upon request made within 60 days following the notification, be given *specific* reasons for the denial. General statements that the application did not meet the lender's minimum requirements or that the applicant's credit score was too low are insufficient. The Dodd-Frank Act, referenced earlier in connection with payday loans, now requires the lender to provide the borrower with his or her credit score any time that score was a factor in the decision to deny a loan or credit application. See P-H 3-k.

EXAMPLE

> If a consumer applies for a car loan and is turned down, it is insufficient for the lender to explain the denial by saying, "Your credit score wasn't high enough." The lender must advise the consumer in writing of the denial and, if the applicant timely requests an explanation, say something like, "According to your credit report you made several late payments on your last car loan," or "You're carrying too much credit card debt from month to month for us to feel confident that you can handle these payments." Anytime the credit score was a reason for the denial the lender must also tell the borrower what their credit score was.

There are 30-some-odd true CRAs around the country but only three nationally recognized agencies:

- Experian (www.experian.com)
- Equifax (www.equifax.com) and
- TransUnion (www.transunion.com)

These three CRAs maintain records on more than 200 million Americans compiled from more than 10,000 information providers.

Personal information that appears in a consumer's credit report includes full name—including maiden name and known variations used (e.g., Bob for Robert, Beth for Elizabeth)—nicknames, current and recent addresses, Social Security number, driver's license by state of issue and number, date of birth, and current and previous employers.

Financial/credit information appearing in the report includes a list of accounts opened in the consumer's name or that list the consumer as an authorized user (e.g., as on a spouse's account); account details, including date the account was opened and type of account (e.g., revolving credit or installment loan); loan or credit limit; payment terms; balances; and payment history, including late payments. Closed or inactive accounts may stay on the report for several years after the last activity in them. Unpaid child support obligations and overdrawn checking accounts may also be reported and shown.

Information acquired from public records and made part of the report may include bankruptcy filings (see Part C of the text), collection suits and judgments (see Chapters Eight and Nine), foreclosure actions and repossessions (see Chapter Four), involuntary liens (see Chapter Six), prejudgment attachments (see Chapter Nine), and writs of execution and wage garnishments (see Chapter Eleven). Most public record information remains on the report for seven years.

Information that *cannot* be included in a credit report includes checking or savings accounts, bankruptcies that are more than ten years old, charged-off debts or debts placed for collection that are more than seven years old, gender, ethnicity, religion, political affiliation, medical history, or criminal convictions more than seven years old.

The FCRA carefully regulates who can access a consumer's credit report. Illustration 3-j lists the persons and entities entitled to access a consumer's credit report and score.

Lawyers and those assisting them in collection efforts on behalf of clients must use great caution before attempting to access a debtor's credit report without the debtor's written consent. 41 U.S.C. §1681q provides as follows:

Any person who knowingly and willfully obtains information on a consumer from a consumer reporting agency under false pretenses shall be fined under Title 18, imprisoned for not more than two years, or both.

Illustration 3-j: PERSONS ENTITLED TO ACCESS A CONSUMER'S CREDIT REPORT

- Potential lenders or extenders of credit
- Potential landlords
- Current creditors making inquiry to determine whether the consumer continues to meet the terms of an account
- Insurance companies to whom the creditor has made application
- Employers and potential employers (usually only with the consumer's written consent)
- Companies the consumer allows to monitor their account for signs of identity theft
- Agencies considering the consumer's application for a government license or benefit
- A state or local child support enforcement agency
- Any government agency (although they may be allowed to view only certain portions)
- Someone using the report to provide a product or service the consumer has requested
- Anyone having written authorization from the consumer
- The consumer himself

EC 3-b: Jim is a legal professional working for the attorney who represents Carroll Properties, Inc., a real estate leasing company. Carroll Properties has leased a house to a couple, Mike and Shirley Dunbar, for the past year. The lease is up and the Dunbars would like to renew but they made a couple of late payments near the end of the year's lease term. Carroll Properties hasn't decided whether to re-lease the space to them. The client has asked its lawyer to check the Dunbars' credit report and the lawyer has assigned that task to Jim. Can Jim legally and ethically go ahead and access the Dunbars' credit report without more?

EC 3-c: Jim's supervising attorney has also been retained by Kimberly Chang to file a negligence lawsuit against William Dupree. Chang was involved in a car accident in which Dupree was the other driver, and Chang alleges that Dupree was at fault. Jim's supervising attorney directs him to access Dupree's credit report to see what assets and liabilities it might disclose. Can Jim legally and ethically access Dupree's credit report without more? Would it be okay for Jim to contact the credit reporting agency and identify himself as a bank officer considering a loan to Dupree in order to obtain the credit report? Why or why not?

Major issues that arise in connection with credit reports are the frequency of errors contained in them and the difficulty consumers have historically encountered in getting errors removed or corrected. A study released by the California Public Interest Research Group in June 2004 (http://calpirg.org/report) found that 79 percent of the consumer credit reports surveyed contained some kind of error or mistake. Partially in response to this problem and partially in response to the growing problem of identity theft, Congress passed the **Fair and Accurate Credit Transactions Act of 2003 (FACTA)**. FACTA amended the FCRA to allow consumers to obtain a free copy of their credit report once every 12 months from each of the three leading CRAs (Equifax, Experian, and TransUnion). In cooperation with the Federal Trade Commission, the three companies operate the Web site www.annualcreditreport.com where consumers may request their report. The free report mandated by FACTA is a summary only and does not include the consumer's credit score. The consumer must pay a small fee to receive his or her credit score unless he or she has been denied a loan or credit based on the score, in which case the lender denying the application must disclose the score to the consumer.

Under FCRA, both the CRA and the information provider are responsible to correct inaccurate or incomplete information in a credit report. When the consumer notifies the CRA of a dispute concerning an inaccurate or incomplete entry, the agency must investigate the dispute within 30 days of receipt unless it deems the complaint frivolous and respond in writing to the consumer when the investigation is complete. The agency must also contact the information provider, who must investigate and respond to the credit agency. If one credit reporting agency confirms an inaccuracy and corrects it, it must also notify the other two national agencies so those records can be corrected as well. Illustration 3-k shows a consumer dispute letter form.

Illustration 3-k: CONSUMER DISPUTE LETTER REGARDING ALLEGED CREDIT REPORT ERROR

Date
Your Name
Your Address, City, State, Zip Code
Complaint Department
Name of Company
Address
City, State, Zip Code

Dear Sir or Madam:

I am writing to dispute the following information in my file. I have circled the items I dispute on the attached copy of the report I received.

This item (identify item(s) disputed by name of source, such as creditors or tax court, and identify type of item, such as credit account, judgment, etc.) is (inaccurate or incomplete) because (describe what is inaccurate or incomplete and why). I am requesting that the item be removed (or request another specific change) to correct the information.

Enclosed are copies of (use this sentence if applicable and describe any enclosed documentation, such as payment records, court documents) supporting my position. Please reinvestigate this (these) matter(s) and (delete or correct) the disputed item(s) as soon as possible.

Sincerely,

Your name

Enclosures: (List what you are enclosing.)

(Source: Federal Trade Commission Consumer Protection Web site: www.ftc.gov/bcp/edu/pubs/consumer/credit/cre21.shtms)

FACTA also contains provisions intended to help reduce identity theft, including authorizing consumers to place alerts on their credit histories if identity theft is suspected or if deploying overseas in the military, thereby making fraudulent applications for credit more difficult. Under FACTA, mortgage lenders must now provide consumer borrowers with a Credit Disclosure Notice that includes their credit scores, range of scores, credit bureaus, scoring models, and factors affecting their scores.

Notwithstanding these attempts at regulation, the number of errors found in consumer credit reports remains high and many "investigations" into complaints of errors amount to nothing more than reconfirming inaccurate information provided by creditors. Effective September 1, 2012, the new Consumer Financial Protection Bureau assumed direct oversight of the 30 largest credit reporting agencies, which together make up about 94 percent of the industry. There are high hopes among consumer advocates that the CFPB will finally put real teeth in regulating credit reporting agencies and the creditors who submit information to them.

P-H 3-r: In a study released in early 2013, the FTC reported that 26 percent of the participants surveyed cite at least one major error in their credit history as maintained by one of the big four CRAs. Most errors are caused by inaccurate data provided to CRAs by lenders and other creditors. For 5.2 percent of the survey participants, the error in their credit history produced a quantifiable negative result, which made it more costly for them to acquire a loan or insurance. Consumers successfully dispute an error and achieve a correction to their credit report that results in an upward adjustment of their credit score about 13 percent of the time, according to the study. See a summary of the study at www.ftc.gov/opa/2013/02/creditreport.shtm. What other findings of the study are interesting to you? For the industry's happy face response to the FTC report, see the press release of the Consumer Data Industry Association at www.cdiaonline.org/files/PDFs/FTC_Accuracy_Study_release_letterhead%20v021113.pdf.

P-H 3-s: Look at the CFPB site (www.consumerfinance.gov/) and determine 1) what reports the CFPB has issued since September 1, 2012, regarding CRAs, and 2) what regulations for CRAs it has proposed or implemented.

2. For a Business Entity

When a loan is made or credit extended to a business entity, it is usually referred to as a **trade credit transaction**. There are a number of **business credit reporting agencies** that collect trade credit information on corporations including limited liability companies and some other types of business, rather than consumers, using the business's name and **employer identification number (EIN)** assigned by the IRS. Some of the leading business credit bureaus (not to be confused with companies that provide ratings for corporate bonds) are Dun & Bradstreet, Experian Business, Equifax Business, and Business Credit, USA.

In addition to a credit report, these business credit bureaus calculate a credit score for businesses, usually using a scoring model producing a score range of 0 to 100 with 75 or better being good to excellent. The information in the credit report and the business credit score is made available to subscribing members of the credit bureau for a fee. Business credit bureaus are subject to the provisions of the Equal Credit Opportunity Act and Federal Reserve Board Regulation B to the extent applicable. They are not subject to the provisions of FCRA except to the extent that they may collect consumer data.

Credit reports and scores can become confusing for **sole proprietorships** (an unincorporated business having a single owner) and **partnerships** (an unincorporated for-profit business owned by more than one person) that engage in business depending on the credit worthiness of their individual owners. The credit report for such a business may contain a mix of personal as well as business data and the credit score may be based on both personal and business transactions and circumstances.

CONCLUSION

Loans and credit arrangements make up a large percentage of the debtor/creditor relationships and disputes that lawyers and assisting legal professionals work with every day. But a related topic of great importance is secured debt: debt for which the debtor or a third person has pledged his real or personal property to guarantee repayment of the debt or for which a third person has made himself liable for the obligation of the debtor. Secured debt is the topic of the next three chapters and we begin by looking at sureties, guarantors, and mortgages in real property in the next chapter.

CHAPTER SUMMARY

This chapter has considered the most common ways that debt is created by contract. The traditional loan process involves the consumer or commercial lender submitting a loan application to the lender, a credit and financial check, property inspection and appraisal, formal loan approval, and the loan closing. In a line of credit loan, also common in both consumer and commercial settings, the funds are not immediately advanced to the borrower. Instead the borrower is allowed to draw down on the funds as needed. For both traditional and line of credit loans, the borrower is asked to sign a promissory note containing the promise to repay and all the terms and conditions relating to repayment. The payday loan is a short-term loan to a consumer, who typically provides the lender with a postdated check that will be cashed only when the borrower receives her next pay check. Payday loans are marketed among low income consumers and are characterized by extraordinarily high interest rates. In an installment sale or rent-to-own transaction the buyer takes immediate possession of the property in exchange for her promise to pay the purchase price in installments over time. Credit card agreements involve a revolving credit arrangement whereby the customer/borrower is required to make a minimum payment on the balance owed each month and the unpaid balance is carried over. Credit cards may be subject to a number of APRs and fees. The Credit Card Act of 2009 has imposed some significant restrictions on the right of credit card companies to unilaterally change APRs and on how payments must be credited. Credit reporting agencies compile information regarding a consumer's debt history and bill-payment record into a credit report and supply that report to potential lenders, lessors, employers, and others authorized to access the consumer's financial history and credit worthiness. The Fair Credit Reporting Act and some state statutes regulate credit reporting agencies, the contents of the credit report, and who can access credit reports.

REVIEW QUESTIONS

1. Explain the difference between a fixed rate note and a variable rate note.
2. What is the prime rate?
3. Name two bad things that can result if a borrower lies on a loan application.
4. Define a "usurious" loan.
5. What is the difference between an installment note and a balloon note?
6. What is an escrow account?
7. Explain the difference between a traditional loan and a credit arrangement.
8. Explain amortization of an installment loan, including why the amount of interest and principal varies from payment to payment even though the total amount of the payment remains the same.

9. Under the Credit Card Act of 2009, how long must an introductory APR on a new card remain unchanged? How much notice must be given of an increase in the APR? Under what circumstances may the APR on existing balances be increased? What is "universal default" and is it still viable? When can over-limit fees be charged? Under what circumstances may a credit card be issued to one under 21 years of age?

10. What kinds of information might be included in a consumer's credit report? List as many persons as you can remember who are entitled to access a consumer's credit report.

WORDS AND PHRASES TO REMEMBER

acceleration clause
adjustable rate note
annual percentage rate (APR)
appraisal
automated teller machine (ATM)
balance transfer
balloon note
business credit
business credit reporting agency
    (or bureau)
car title loan
cash advance
charge card
check advance service
check cashing service
commercial debt
consumer debt
Consumer Financial Protection
    Bureau
contract for deed
courtesy overdraft protection
credit card
Credit Card Accountability,
    Responsibility and Disclosure Act
    (also known as the Credit Card
    Act of 2009)
credit bureau
credit counseling agency
credit reporting agency
credit history
credit limit
credit score
credit worthiness
debit card
debt collection agency
default

deferred deposit check loan
deferred presentment loan
delayed title contracts
demand note
escrow account
Electronic Fund Transfer Act
Equifax
equity
Experian
Fair and Accurate Credit
    Transactions Act of 2003
    (FACTA)
Fair Credit Reporting Act
Federal Home Mortgage
    Association (Freddie Mac)
Fair Isaac Corporation
Federal National Mortgage
    Association (Fannie Mae)
federally chartered banks
FICO score
fixed rate note
gift card
good and marketable title
Great Depression
Great Recession
holder
home equity loan
independent financial means
injunctive relief
installment credit
installment note
installment sale contracts
land contracts
lease-option contracts
lease-purchase contracts
lender

line of credit
loan agreement
loan application
loan closing
loan commitment
loan committee
maker
minimum payment
mortgage
nonassignment clause
overdraft
over-the-credit-limit fee
pawn shop loan
payday loan
payee
payor
preemption
postdated check loan
predatory lending
prime rate
principal
promissory note
punitive damages
rate of interest

Regulation E
Regulation Z
rent-to-own contracts
revolving credit
safe-harbor provision
secured note
security interest
survey
term
time is of the essence clause
title search
trade credit
trade credit transaction
TransUnion
Truth in Lending Act
universal default
U.S. Treasury Bills
usury
variable rate note
waiver
Wall Street Reform and
    Consumer Protection Act
    of 2010

TO LEARN MORE: A number of TLM activities to accompany this chapter
are accessible along with chapter updates on the Author Updates link to
the text Web site at http://www.aspenparalegaled.com/books/parsons_
abcdebt/default.asp.

Chapter Four:

 # Sureties, Guarantors, and Mortgages in Real Property

You load 16 tons, what do you get? Another day older and deeper in debt.
St. Peter, don't you call me 'cause I can't go. I owe my soul to the company store.
—Merle Travis

A. Introduction to Secured Transactions and Terminology

A debt supported by nothing more than the debtor's bare promise to pay is called an **unsecured debt**. We have already mentioned the possibility that a creditor, in making a loan or extending credit to a debtor, may require more than the debtor's promise. The creditor wants additional **security** for the repayment of the debt.

That security can take a number of different forms. It can be the promise of a **co-signer** of the promissory note to be liable for the debt along with the principal debtor. We will see that a co-signor is a form of **surety**. It can be the promise of a **guarantor** to pay the debt if the principal debtor cannot. Or, it can be the requirement that the debtor pledge his real or personal property as security for the debt such that, if the debtor defaults, the creditor can seize the pledged property and sell it to satisfy the debt obligation.

When **real property** is pledged as security for the obligation it creates a **mortgage** on the real property. When **personal property** is pledged as security for the obligation it creates a **security interest** in the personalty in favor of the creditor. Practitioners refer to the personalty so pledged as the **collateral** or as the **secured property** or as the **pledged property**. When real or personal property has been pledged as security for an obligation we may also say that there is a **lien** against the pledged property.

What all of these forms of additional security have in common is that they are *consensual*. A surety or guarantor has promised to stand good for the debt in addition to the principal. Or the debtor has granted the creditor a mortgage in his or her real property to secure payment of the debt. Or the debtor has granted the creditor a security interest in his or her personal property for that purpose. In this chapter we will consider the first three forms of consensual security for a debt: the surety arrangement, the guaranty arrangement, and the mortgage granted in real property owned by the debtor. In the next chapter we will consider the fourth: the security interest granted in the debtor's personal property.

Co-signer One who signs a promissory note as a form of security for the lender making himself primarily liable for the debt of another.

Guarantor One who guarantees the debt of another.

Guarantee As a noun, the guaranty agreement itself or the one to whom a guaranty is made.

Mortgage The pledging of real property as security for a debt.

Security interest An interest granted by a debtor to a creditor in property of the debtor authorizing the creditor to seize and sell the pledged property to satisfy the debt obligation in the event of a default.

B. ▶ The Co-signer or Surety

It is by no means unusual for a person to make himself liable on a debt even though he derives no direct benefit from the transaction.

EXAMPLE

> Recall that Abe Mendoza in Case Study #2 (Illustration 1-b) co-signed a promissory note with his son, David, in connection with money borrowed for David's education. The money loaned in that transaction did not go directly to Abe and was not used to his direct benefit.

Surety One who makes himself primarily liable for the debt of another as by co-signing a promissory note or executing a surety agreement or surety bond.

Primarily liable Being liable for a debt without regard to whether the lender pursues collection from the principal debtor first.

Secondarily liable One is liable only if the lender first pursues collection from the other.

Co-signing a promissory note creates a form of *surety*. A **surety agreement** is where one person agrees to make himself **primarily liable** for the debt of another. In the example just above, the loan was made for the benefit of David Mendoza, but his father, Abe, agreed to make himself primarily liable, along with David, on the note by co-signing it. We would say that David was the **principal debtor** on the note, while Abe is the surety. Both are primarily liable on the note.

To say that the surety is primarily liable on a debt along with the principal debtor means that the creditor can look to the surety for payment of the debt whether or not the principal debtor is able to pay and whether or not the creditor first seeks to collect the debt from the principal debtor. If the surety were only **secondarily liable** on the debt, the creditor would have to seek collection first from the principal debtor and only then could the creditor seek collection from the surety. But the nature of a surety is that he is primarily liable on the debt along with the principal debtor.

EXAMPLE

> Assume that on the note co-signed by his father, David Mendoza fails to repay when the note comes due. The holder of the note is not required to pursue collection from David before pursuing collection from Abe even though David is the principal debtor on the note. It is no defense to the holder's collection action against Abe that David is able to pay but didn't. Nor is it a defense that the holder did not pursue David at all on the obligation before commencing collection against Abe. Abe is a surety.

Co-signing a note is only one way to create a surety arrangement on a debt. Another way is for the surety to execute a separate surety agreement, or **surety bond**, promising to be primarily responsible on the debt.

EXAMPLE

> Recall from Case Study #2 (Illustration 1-b) that Abe Mendoza is the project manager for City Heights Limited Partnership, on the City Heights Condominium project. The general contractor on the project is Adams Construction Company. The contract between CHLP as owner and ACC as general contractor requires ACC to obtain and furnish a surety bond issued by an insurance company or other bonding agent. The surety bond for the project was issued by Trustus Insurance Company. The bond provides that Trustus will be liable to the owner for any damages to the owner resulting from a failure of the general contractor to perform on the project as promised. By issuing the surety bond, Trustus made itself primarily liable to the owner for any debt or liability that might arise due to ACC's failure to perform.

Notice that with the suretyship, we have introduced yet another way that debt can be created by contract. This one is a little different from what we've seen before, though, because in a surety arrangement, the surety makes itself liable for the debt of another.

C. ▶ The Guarantor

Another type of contract in which a party makes herself liable for the debt of another is the **guaranty agreement**. By executing a guaranty agreement, the guarantor makes herself *secondarily liable* for the debt of the principal debtor (see Illustration 4-a).

EXAMPLE

> Recall that Abe Mendoza in Case Study #2 (Illustration 1-b) not only co-signed the promissory note with his son, David, in connection with money borrowed for David's education, but he signed a separate guaranty agreement for another educational loan to David. As to that loan, Abe is a guarantor of David's obligations, not a surety.

The guaranty arrangement is similar to a suretyship in that it is also an obligation to pay the debt of another. But it differs from a suretyship in that the guarantor is only *secondarily* liable, not *primarily* liable.

EXAMPLE

> Assume David Mendoza fails to repay the note that his father guaranteed but did not co-sign. The holder of the note is required to pursue collection from David as the principal debtor before pursuing collection from Abe, who only promised to pay the guaranteed debt in the event that David defaulted on it. The holder of the note must prove the default by David as a condition precedent to collecting from Abe as guarantor.

Because both surety and guaranty arrangements involve one person (the surety or guarantor) agreeing to pay the debt of another (the principal debtor), issues often arise in actions brought against the surety or guarantor as to whether those defendants can raise defenses to liability that the principal debtor could have raised.

EXAMPLE

> Assume that David Mendoza defaults on repayment of the promissory note that his father guaranteed. David files bankruptcy and discharges his legal obligation for the note, but had he been sued by the lender he was prepared to show by way of defense that he never received the funds from the lender. We would call that defense a failure of consideration. When the lender sues Abe Mendoza on his guaranty, can Abe raise that defense? David's discharge of the note obligation in bankruptcy will also be a defense for him if the lender ever sues David on it. Is David's discharge in bankruptcy also a defense to Abe? If David were only 17 years old when he signed the note and could raise incapacity due to age if sued on it, could Abe raise that defense when sued as guarantor?

Illustration 4-a: GUARANTY AGREEMENT

THIS GUARANTY, is made this June 1, YR-3, by Abelard Mendoza and wife, Maria Mendoza (the "Guarantors"), to City County Bank of Capitol City, Columbiana (the "Lender").

WHEREAS Lender is the owner and holder of that certain Promissory Note (the "Note") dated June 1, YR-3 in the original principal amount of $10,000 executed by David Mendoza, (the "Borrower");

WHEREAS to induce Lender to enter into the loan transaction evidenced by the Note (the "Loan"), Guarantor has agreed to guaranty the obligations of Borrower; and

WHEREAS Lender is unwilling to enter into the Loan unless Guarantor guarantees the payment thereof;

NOW THEREFORE, as a material inducement to Lender to enter into the Loan, Guarantor agrees with Lender as follows:

1. The above recitals are true and correct and are incorporated herein.

2. To induce Lender to enter into the Loan, Guarantors guarantee and promise to pay to Lender or order, on demand, in lawful money of the United States any and all indebtedness of Borrower to Lender associated with the Loan and any other obligation, indebtedness or liability of every kind and description, direct or indirect, absolute or contingent, due or to become due, now existing or hereafter arising that Borrower may owe to Lender in accordance with the terms of this Guaranty.

3. The obligations of Guarantors hereunder are contingent on Borrower's default on the obligations to Lender for which payment is sought from Guarantors and on Lender's inability to collect said obligation from Borrower, as default and collection may be defined from time to time by the laws of Columbiana. However, once such default has been established, the obligations of Guarantors on such obligations will be deemed independent of the obligations of Borrower, and a separate action or actions may be brought and be prosecuted against Guarantors and Guarantors waive the benefit of any statute of limitations affecting their liability hereunder or the enforcement thereof.

4. Guarantors authorize Lender, without notice or demand and without affecting its liability hereunder, from time to time to (a) renew, compromise, extend, accelerate or otherwise change the time for payment or otherwise change the terms of the indebtedness or any part thereof, including increase or decrease of the rate of interest thereon; (b) take and hold security for the payment of this Guaranty or the indebtedness guaranteed, and exchange, enforce, waive, and release any such security; (c) apply such security and direct the order or manner of sale thereof as Lender in its discretion may determine; and (d) release or substitute any one or more guarantors. Lender may assign this guaranty in whole or in part.

5. Guarantors waive any defense arising by reason of any disability or other defense of Borrower except for defenses based on Lender's default or by reason of the cessation from any cause whatsoever of the liability of Borrower. Guarantors waive all notice of acceptance of this Guaranty, notice of maturity, payment or default of any indebtedness, and any other requirement or notice necessary to bind Guarantors hereunder, including but not limited to presentment, notice of dishonor and protest.

6. Guarantors acknowledge that the Loan herein guaranteed may be assigned or transferred (in whole or in part), or made subject to a participation agreement with other lenders or persons. Guarantors agree that the rights and benefits hereof shall be fully exercisable by Lender's assignees, transferees, or participants in such loans or indebtedness, or any portion thereof, and that no assignment, transfer, or participation shall invalidate or diminish Guarantors' duties and obligations hereunder.

7. Guarantors agree to pay reasonable attorneys' fees (including attorneys' fees on appeal) and all other costs and expenses which may be incurred by Lender in the enforcement of this Guaranty.

8. This Guaranty shall be interpreted, construed and enforced according to the laws of the State of Columbiana.

IN WITNESS WHEREOF, the undersigned Guarantors have executed this Guaranty the day and year first above written.

_____/s/_____
Abelard Mendoza, Guarantor

_____/s/_____
Maria Mendoza, Guarantor

Generally, a surety or guarantor can raise any defense to liability that the principal debtor could raise, including failure of consideration, fraud, duress, breach of contract, breach of warranty, and so on. However, the surety or guarantor *cannot* raise **personal defenses** available to the principal debtor. A personal defense is a defense unique to the circumstances of the principal debtor that do not go to the merits of the underlying transaction. Personal defenses would include discharge in bankruptcy or lack of capacity to contract due to age or disability, and the like.

Personal defenses Defenses to liability unique to the circumstances of the principal debtor; do not go to the merits of the underlying transaction.

P-H 4-a: Use the information just provided to answer the questions raised in the previous example.

Another important principal of surety/guaranty law is that if the creditor and principal debtor agree to make any material change in the terms of the original obligation for which the surety/guarantor is potentially liable, and do so without obtaining the prior consent of the surety/guarantor to that material change, the obligation of the surety/guarantor will be discharged by operation of law (automatically). Why? Because the material change alters the risk that the surety/guarantor agreed to assume.

EXAMPLE

Assume the note that Abe has guaranteed is due but David cannot pay. David and the lender agree that David will have six months more time to pay than the note allows but will pay a 0.25 percent higher rate of interest in exchange for the extension. No one advises Abe of this alteration in the obligation or obtains his consent. David defaults on the obligation even with the extension and the lender seeks collection from Abe. On these facts, Abe is likely discharged from any liability on his guaranty due to the **material change**.

Some states make a distinction between an **accommodation surety** and a **compensated surety** in applying this doctrine of discharge by material change. An accommodation surety is one who receives no compensation for serving as surety; he does so gratuitously. A compensated surety is one that receives a fee or other compensation for agreeing to serve as surety or guarantor.

EXAMPLE

> Abe co-signing one of David's notes and signing the guaranty for another is an example of an accommodation surety. He did this to help his son, not for compensation. Trustus Insurance Company is an example of a compensated surety since it charged and collected a fee for issuing the surety bond for Adams Construction Company.

In those states that make this distinction, an accommodation surety will be relieved from its obligation whether the material change in the obligation puts it at greater risk or not, but a compensated surety will be relieved only if the material change causes it harm or puts it at demonstrably greater risk.

P-H 4-b: The lender on the note guaranteed by Abe agrees to give David an additional six months to pay the note but does not alter the interest rate. Abe is not notified of the extension. Does merely giving David more time to pay harm Abe as guarantor or put him at increased risk? Does that matter in deciding whether the time extension is a material change that relieves Abe of his duty to guaranty the debt? Would it matter if Abe were a compensated guarantor?

D.   The Mortgage in Real Property

When a buyer purchases real property, whether residential or commercial, the buyer rarely has the cash available to pay the full purchase price, so the buyer obtains a loan to fund the purchase. The buyer will go through the loan application and approval process described in Chapter Three, Section A. At the closing, the buyer will sign a promissory note, promising to repay the amount borrowed over a stated period of time and at an agreed interest rate (see Illustration 2-a). But the lender is not satisfied with just the buyer's promise to repay the loan. As a condition to making the loan, the lender will require the buyer to convey to the lender, or to someone on behalf of the lender, an interest in the real property being purchased, which will allow the lender or the lender's agent, in the event of a default on the note by the buyer, to take possession of the property, sell it, and apply the proceeds to the satisfaction of the debt.

The security interest in the real property that the buyer conveys to the lender or the lender's agent is called a **right of foreclosure** or **power of sale** (the distinction is discussed below). We say that the owner has mortgaged the property or created a **mortgage** in the property. The owner is the **mortgagor** (the one creating the mortgage) and the lender is the **mortgagee** (the one receiving the benefit of the mortgage). In most states it is understood that the mortgagor maintains **legal title** to the property, while the mortgagee holds **equitable title** to it—that is, the right to take possession of and sell the property in the event of default.

1. Creation of a Mortgage

The legal document by which the power of sale is conveyed by the owner to the lender or lender's agent is called a **mortgage** or **mortgage deed** or, in some states, a **deed of trust** or **security deed**. Illustration 4-b shows the mortgage executed by Nick and Pearl Murphy of Case Study #1 (Illustration 1-a) to secure the loan from First Bank of Capitol City (FBCC) to buy their residence on West Cherry Street in Capitol City, Columbiana.

The mortgage in Illustration 4-b secures the promissory note, seen in Illustration 2-a. In some jurisdictions, a note securing a mortgage will be called a **mortgage note** rather than simply a promissory note. If the Murphys default on their obligations under the note, the lender, FBCC, can exercise its rights under the mortgage.

P-H 4-c: Use the Murphys' note in Illustration 2-a and the mortgage in Illustration 4-b to answer the following questions and identify the specific provisions of the note and/or mortgage that answer each question:

- If the Murphys add a sunroom onto the house on West Cherry Street after having signed the note and mortgage, is that part of the house also pledged to FBCC as security?
- If the Murphys fail to pay their state property taxes on the West Cherry Street property, can the mortgagee pay those taxes itself? Why do you think a mortgagee might want to do this? If the mortgagee does pay the taxes, how does it recoup those payments from the Murphys?
- If the Murphys make a monthly payment five days late (on the fifth day of the month instead of the first day of the month), are they in default under the note and mortgage?
- If the Murphys begin using the house on West Cherry Street as a gambling casino in violation of state law and local zoning ordinances, are they in default under the note and mortgage?
- If the mortgagee accepts two late payments from the Murphys instead of declaring them in default, can the mortgagee declare them in default when they make a third late payment?
- Seven years after signing the note and mortgage in favor of FBCC, the Murphys borrow money from Teacher's Credit Union and pledge the property on West Cherry Street to secure that second loan. They do not advise FBCC that they are doing so. Are the Murphys in default on the mortgage to FBCC?

The lender who provides the funds for the purchase and is named the mortgagee in the mortgage documents is also called the **mortgage originator**. That original lender, whether it be a **bank**, **credit union**, **savings and loan company**, or other **financial services company**, may also be referred to as a **mortgage banker** to be distinguished from a **mortgage broker**. Whereas mortgage bankers originate loans using their own funds, mortgage brokers are companies that facilitate mortgages by bringing borrowers and originators together.

Illustration 4-b: MORTGAGE

THIS MORTGAGE is made on the 12th day of January, YR-10 between Nicholas W. Murphy and wife, Pearl E. Murphy, who reside at 3521 West Cherry Street, Capitol City, Columbiana, hereinafter referred to collectively as "Borrower", and First Bank of Capitol City, located at 1111 Main Street, Capitol City, Columbiana, the original lender. The word "Lender" means the original Lender and anyone else who takes this Mortgage by transfer, sale, or assignment.

1. The debt secured: The debt secured by this Mortgage is evidenced by Borrower's promissory note dated the same date as this Mortgage, hereinafter referred to as Note, which provides for payments over 360 months in principal plus interest at 8% per annum in monthly payments of $843.83 in accordance with the terms of the Note. All terms of the Note are hereby made part of this Mortgage. This Mortgage secures to Lender: (a) the repayment of the debt evidenced by the Note, with interest, and all renewals, extensions, and modifications; (b) the payment of all other sums, with interest, advanced under Section Seven hereof to protect the security of this Mortgage; and (c) the performance of Borrower's covenants and agreements under this Mortgage and the Note. This Mortgage also secures any other indebtedness now or hereafter owing from Borrower to Lender, however or whenever created.

2. The property mortgaged: For the purposes set forth in Paragraph 1, Borrower irrevocably grants and conveys to Lender the interest and rights described in Paragraph 3 in the following described property located in Capitol County, Columbiana: [legal description omitted from illustration] . . . which has the address of 3521 West Cherry Street, Capitol City, Columbiana, and is hereinafter referred to as the "Property Address", together with all the improvements now or hereafter erected on the property, and all easements, rights, appurtenances, rents, royalties, mineral, oil and gas rights and profits, water rights and stock and all fixtures now or hereafter a part of the property. All replacements and additions shall also be covered by this Mortgage. All of the foregoing is referred to in this Mortgage as the "Property." This Mortgage covers property which is or may become so affixed to real property as to become fixtures and also constitutes a fixture filing under the laws of Columbiana.

3. Rights given to Lender: Borrower mortgages the Property to Lender and gives Lender the rights stated in this Mortgage and also those rights the applicable law does or in the future may give to lenders who hold mortgages on real property in Columbiana. When Borrower pays all amounts due to the Lender under the Note and this Mortgage, the Lender's rights under this Mortgage will end. The Lender will then cancel and release this Mortgage at Borrower's expense.

4. Borrower's covenants: Borrower covenants, promises, and warrants as follows:

a. Note and Mortgage. Borrower will comply with all the terms of the Note and this Mortgage.

b. Payment. Borrower will pay all amounts required by the Note and this Mortgage.

c. Ownership. Borrower is lawfully seized of the estate in the Property hereby conveyed and has the right to grant and convey the Property and that the Property is unencumbered, except for encumbrances of record, and that Borrower warrants and will defend generally the title to the Property against all claims and demands, subject to any encumbrances of record.

d. Taxes. Borrower will pay all taxes, assessments, and other government charges made against the Property when due. That Borrower will not claim any deduction from the taxable value of the Property because of this Mortgage. The Borrower will not claim any credit against the principal and interest payable under the Note and this Mortgage for any taxes paid on the Property.

e. Insurance. Borrower will keep the improvements now existing or hereafter erected on the Property insured against loss by fire, hazards included within the term "extended coverage" and any other hazards for which Lender requires insurance. This insurance shall be maintained in the amounts and for the periods that Lender requires. The insurance carrier providing the insurance shall be chosen by Borrower subject to Lender's approval which shall not be withheld unreasonably. All insurance policies and renewals shall be acceptable to Lender and shall include a standard mortgage clause. Lender shall have the right to hold the policies and renewals. If Lender requires, Borrower shall promptly give to Lender all receipts of paid premiums and renewal notices. In the event of loss, Borrower shall give prompt notice to the insurance carrier and Lender. Lender may make proof of loss if not made promptly by Borrower. Unless Lender and Borrower otherwise agree in writing, insurance proceeds shall be applied to restoration or repair of the Property damaged, if the restoration or repair is economically feasible and Lender's security is not lessened. If the restoration or repair is not economically feasible or Lender's security would be lessened, the insurance proceeds shall be applied to the sums secured by this Mortgage, whether or not then due, with any excess paid to Borrower. If Borrower abandons the Property, or does not answer within 30 days a notice from Lender that the insurance carrier has offered to settle a claim, then Lender may collect the insurance proceeds. Lender may use the proceeds to repair or restore the Property or to pay sums secured by this Mortgage, whether or not then due. The 30-day period will begin when the notice is given.

f. Tax and Insurance Escrow. Subject to applicable law or to a written waiver by Lender, Borrower shall pay to Lender on the day monthly payments are due under the Note and this Mortgage, until the Note is paid in full, a sum ("Funds") equal to one-twelfth of: (a) yearly taxes and assessments that may attain priority over this Mortgage; (b) yearly leasehold payments or ground rents on the Property, if any; (c) yearly hazard insurance premiums; and (d) yearly mortgage insurance premiums, if any. These items are called "escrow items." Lender shall give to Borrower, without charge, an annual accounting of the Funds showing credits and debits to the Funds and the purpose for which each debit to the Funds was made. The Funds are pledged as additional security for the sums secured by this Mortgage. If the amount of the Funds held by Lender is not sufficient to pay the escrow items when due, Borrower shall pay to Lender any amount necessary to make up the deficiency in one or more payments as required by Lender. Upon payment in full of all sums secured by this Mortgage, Lender shall promptly refund to Borrower any Funds held by Lender.

g. Repairs. Borrower will keep the Property in good repair, neither damaging nor abandoning it. Borrower will allow Lender or Lender's agent to inspect the Property upon reasonable notice.

h. Lawful use. Borrower will use the Property in compliance with all laws, ordinances and other requirements of any governmental authority.

i. Rent. Borrower will not rent the Property without the prior written consent of Lender and, in the event of such consent, will not accept any rent from any tenant for more than one month in advance.

j. Other liens. Borrower will not mortgage or otherwise pledge the Property as security for any other obligation without the prior written consent of Lender. Borrower will not take any action that could foreseeably result in any nonconsensual lien or claim being made against the Property.

5. Application of payments: Unless applicable law provides otherwise, all payments received by Lender shall be applied: first, to late charges due under the Note; second, to prepayment charges due under the Note; third, to any other amounts payable under Paragraph 4 of this Mortgage; fourth, to interest due; and last, to principal due.

6. Condemnation: If all or part of the Property is taken for public use, all compensation for such taking shall be paid to Lender. The Lender may use such compensation to repair or restore the Property or to reduce the amount owed on the Note and this Mortgage which application will not delay or postpone any other or further payment due from Borrower under the Note and this Mortgage.

7. Payments made for Borrower: If Borrower fails to keep the property insured, or to pay taxes or other assessments against the property as promised or to keep the property in good repair or to make other payments as promised in the Note and this Mortgage, Lender may make such payments for Borrower in which event said payments will be added to the principal due under the Note and will bear interest at the same rate provided in the Note and will be secured by the terms of this Mortgage and Borrower will repay Lender such amounts upon demand.

8. Default: The Lender may declare the Borrower to be in default on the Note and this Mortgage if a) Borrower fails to make any payment required by the Note or this Mortgage within ten (10) days after it is due; b) Borrower fails to comply with any other covenant or obligation under the terms of the Note or this Mortgage; c) the ownership of the Property is changed for any reason without the prior written consent of Lender; the holder of any lien, whether consensual or nonconsensual, initiates foreclosure proceedings; or d) bankruptcy, insolvency or receivership proceedings are begun by or against any Borrower.

9. Payments due upon default: Upon default, all amounts due under the Note and this Mortgage will become immediately due and payable and Borrower will pay the full amount of all unpaid principal, interest and other amounts due under the Note and this Mortgage. Borrower will also pay Lender all Lender's costs of collection, including court costs and reasonable attorney's fees.

10. Lender's rights upon default: Upon default, Lender will have all rights given by law now or at the time of default or as set forth in the Note and this Mortgage, including the right to do one or more of the following: a) take possession of the Property, including the collection of rents and profits; b) have a court appoint a receiver to accept rent for the Property to which Borrower expressly consents; c) institute a foreclosure action which will result in sale of the Property to reduce Borrower's obligations under the Note and this Mortgage; and 4) file suit against Borrower for any balance owed by Borrower to Lender.

11. No waiver by Lender: Extension of the time for payment or modification of amortization of the sums secured by this Mortgage granted by Lender to Borrower or any successor in interest of Borrower shall not operate to release the liability of the original Borrower or Borrower's successors in interest. Any forbearance by Lender in exercising any right or remedy under the Note or this Mortgage shall not be a waiver of or preclude the exercise of any right or remedy.

12. Successors and assigns bound: The covenants and agreements of the Note and this Mortgage shall bind and benefit the successors and assigns of Lender and Borrower.

13. Each Borrower liable: Borrower's covenants and agreements shall be joint and several.

14. Notices: All notices must be given in writing and personally delivered or sent by certified mail, return receipt requested, to the address given in this Mortgage. Address changes may be given by notice to the other party.

15. No oral changes: This Mortgage can only be changed by a subsequent agreement in writing singed by both all Borrowers and the Lender.

16. Signatures: By their signatures below, Borrower and Lender evidence their acceptance of and agreement to the terms of this Mortgage effective the date above written.

EXAMPLE

An individual or business wishing to buy real estate may not know which lender to approach for a loan. Instead they may work with a mortgage broker who will, for a fee, take the buyer's loan application and then locate and refer the buyer to the mortgage banker who will give the buyer the best deal given the buyer's particular circumstances. Mortgage brokers are especially valuable in complex commercial transactions, where the buyer has credit problems or other special considerations, or where the property involved is located in an area unfamiliar to the buyer.

However it happens, the coming together of a buyer and a lender to create a mortgage is referred to as the **primary mortgage market**. A variation on the traditional mortgage is the **reverse mortgage** in which a homeowner aged 62 or older borrows against the **equity** built up in the residence (the value of the property in excess of the balance owed on it) and receives that equity from the lender in either a lump sum or in installment payments. The loan is repaid when the homeowner dies or no longer lives in the home and the home is sold.

In the typical land sale transaction, the buyer who cannot pay cash for the property will borrow all or part of the purchase price from a lender and grant the lender a mortgage interest in the property to secure repayment of the loan. Sometimes, however, the seller will **self-finance** or **owner finance** the transaction by conveying title to the buyer, allowing the buyer to take immediate possession, and agreeing to accept payment of all or a portion of the purchase price over some agreed period of time. In a self-financing transaction, the buyer will execute a promissory note in favor of the seller for the balance owed and grant the seller a mortgage in the property to secure the future payments. This type of mortgage is usually called a **purchase money mortgage**.

EXAMPLE

Assume you have an owner of real property very eager to sell it—hardly an unusual circumstance following the crash of the real estate market that precipitated the Great Recession. The owner has found a buyer, but the buyer is unable to qualify for a traditional mortgage loan from any lender owing to poor credit or questions about whether the buyer's projected income flow is sufficient. If the owner is willing to assume the risk that the lenders will not, then the owner may agree to self-finance this purchase by the buyer.

2. Assignment of a Mortgage

As we considered in Chapter Two, contract rights may be assignable. In Illustration 2-b we saw an **assignment agreement** involving a promissory note. Likewise entire mortgages are freely assignable by the mortgagee. The mortgage originator/mortgagee is often not the party who will service the mortgage. Instead of adding the new mortgage to its own portfolio and servicing the mortgage over its term, the originator will instead sell and assign the mortgage to a **mortgage servicer**, who will then service the mortgage by accepting and crediting payments, giving proper notices, instituting foreclosure if necessary. Many mortgages are sold numerous times during their terms. If FBCC chose to sell and assign the mortgage it holds on the Murphys' West Cherry Street property, the assignment agreement might look like Illustration 4-c.

Mortgage brokers, in addition to bringing buyers and originators together, also purchase mortgage loans from originators to hold in their own portfolios and service them. Or the mortgage broker acts as a middleman, purchasing mortgages from originators and then immediately selling them to other servicing companies. Some mortgage brokers purchase mortgages in order to bundle them into **investment securities**, which are then marketed to investors. A security made up of mortgage loans may be variously called a **mortgage-backed security (MBS)**, **asset-backed security (ABS)**, **collateralized debt obligation (CDO)**, or **collateralized mortgage obligation (CMO)**. When a mortgage is

Illustration 4-c: ASSIGNMENT OF MORTGAGE

For value received, First Bank of Capitol City located in Capitol City, Columbiana ("Assignor") does hereby transfer assign and convey to West Coast Finance Company, located in Sacramento, California, ("Assignee") and its successors and assigns, all Assignor's right, title, interest, powers and options in, to and under that certain mortgage dated the 12th day of January, YR-10 between Nicholas W. Murphy and wife, Pearl E. Murphy and First Bank of Capitol City covering certain real property located at 3521 West Cherry Street, Capitol City, Columbiana, more particularly described in Exhibit A, attached, and Assignor does further hereby transfer, assign, and convey to Assignee and its successors and assigns, all Assignor's right, title, interest, powers, and options in, to, and under that certain Promissory Note dated the 12th day of January, YR-10 in the principal amount of $115,000 executed by Nicholas W. Murphy and wife, Pearl E. Murphy, and payable to Assignor together will all sums of money due and to become due on said Promissory Note with interest.

This Assignment is effective as of the 30th day of September, YR-10.

First Bank of Capitol City, Assignor
By: _____

Alexis W. Brown, Vice President

West Coast Finance Company, Assignee
By: _____
Russell A. Banks, President

sold by the originator into the mortgage servicing market or is bundled into a security to be marketed, it has entered the **secondary mortgage market**.

The securitization of so many subprime mortgages in the late 1990s and early 2000s played a key role in the current mortgage foreclosure crisis to be considered further in Section E of this chapter.

3. Assumption of a Mortgage

As we further considered in Chapter Two, contractual obligations of one debtor may be **delegated** to and **assumed** by another debtor. In Illustration 2-c, we saw a mortgagee consent to the assignment and delegation of an existing mortgage from the original mortgagor to a new debtor. In that transaction, the mortgagee also consented to a novation, releasing the original mortgagee from further liability on the debt represented by the mortgage in exchange for an increase in the interest rate to be paid on the balance of the debt by the new debtor. Go back and review the Consent to Assignment in Illustration 2-c and the example preceding it. The contract between ABC and DEF in which ABC agreed to sell its cookie division to DEF would contain a **mortgage assumption clause** making the transaction contingent on DEF's successful assumption of the obligations of the ABC mortgage with First National Bank (FNB). That mortgage assumption clause might look something like what you see in Illustration 4-d.

The final part of this transaction would involve an **assumption agreement** between FNB and DEF, whereby DEF would expressly assume the mortgage between ABC and FNB and would agree, as part of that assumption, to pay an interest rate of 7.25 percent on the balance rather than the original 7 percent.

Illustration 4-d: MORTGAGE ASSUMPTION CLAUSE

ABC as seller and DEF as buyer expressly agree that consummation of this transaction is contingent upon DEF's assumption of ABC's existing mortgage in favor of FNB as mortgagee including the promissory note referenced therein (the "Mortgage"). The Mortgage has an outstanding balance of $5 million and bears interest at the rate of 7% per annum, with monthly payments of principal and interest in the amount of $47,000. ABC shall take any and all steps required or reasonably necessary to enable DEF to assume the mortgage. Upon settlement of this transaction, DEF expressly assumes and agrees, as part of the consideration for this transaction, to pay said mortgage in accordance with the terms and conditions thereof as they may be amended by subsequent agreement between DEF and FNB. DEF agrees to pay all costs associated with the assumption of the Mortgage. ABC and DEF further agree that consummation of this transaction is contingent upon FNB's agreement to consent to a novation regarding ABC's obligations under the Mortgage, whereby FNB will release and discharge ABC from any further obligations under the Mortgage in exchange for the assumption of the obligations of the Mortgage by DEF.

You will recall that it was the increased interest rate that served as the inducement for FNB to agree to the novation. The operative part of the assumption agreement between DEF and FNB might look like Illustration 4-e.

When the purchaser of property assumes an existing mortgage on the property instead of taking out a new loan to pay off the balance of the existing mortgage, this is sometimes called a **wrap-around mortgage** and is usually accompanied by a small increase in the original interest rate to serve as an inducement to the mortgagee to agree to the assumption.

4. Priority Among Mortgages

It is common for real property to be subject to more than one mortgage simultaneously. The first mortgage on the property is called just that, the first mortgage. That first mortgage may prohibit the property owner from pledging the property as security for any other debt. But if it does not prohibit subsequent pledge of the property, or if the mortgagee consents to a subsequent pledge notwithstanding the prohibition (as in the ABC/DEF/FNB transaction), the owner may pledge the property as security for a second or third debt, thus creating a second mortgage or a third mortgage on the property. Often the first mortgage is referred to as the **senior mortgage**, or **senior lien**, and the subsequent ones as the **junior mortgage**, or **junior lien**.

Illustration 4-e: ASSUMPTION AGREEMENT (PARTIAL)

In consideration of the conveyance to DEF of the real property described in that certain mortgage dated May 1, YR-1 and executed by ABC, Inc. of Chicago, Illinois ("ABC") as mortgagor, and recorded in Mortgage Book 106, Page 543 in the Register's Office of Capitol County, Columbiana (the "Mortgage"), DEF hereby assumes and agrees to pay the obligations secured by the Mortgage and the promissory note referenced therein and to be bound to FNB, or its assignees or successors, by all its conditions and covenants. DEF further agrees that the controlling interest rate in the Mortgage and promissory note referenced therein shall be 7.25% per annum as of the effective date of this Agreement.

But the mortgage on real property created first in time is not necessarily first in priority. When there are multiple mortgages on property, which mortgage has priority?

EXAMPLE

> Homeowner borrows money from Bank 1 and mortgages the home to secure repayment of that loan. Before the loan from Bank 1 is paid off, Homeowner borrows money from Bank 2 and pledges the same home to secure repayment of that loan, too. Homeowner then defaults on both loans. Between Bank 1 and Bank 2, which has first claim to proceeds from foreclosure on the home? What additional information will you need to answer that question?

Recording statute State law controlling how mortgages are perfected thus determining the priority among mortgages or liens on the property.

Priority between plural mortgages is determined by which kind of **recording statute** is in effect in the state where the property lies. Most states have **race-notice statutes**, whereby priority is created by being the first to **record** a mortgage in the public office responsible for maintaining land records (in different jurisdictions that may be the office of the Registrar of Deeds, Register of Deeds, Recorder, or the city or county clerk) while having no **actual notice** of any prior unrecorded claim to the property. The recording of the mortgage serves as **constructive notice** to the world of the recording mortgagee's claim. A few states have pure **notice statutes**, which give priority to a prior unrecorded mortgage so long as subsequent mortgagees have actual notice of the prior unrecorded mortgage. A very few states have **race statutes**, which give priority to the first mortgage recorded regardless of actual notice. For the purpose of our further discussion of multiple mortgages in this chapter, we will assume that each mortgage is recorded promptly after execution and has priority as of that date.

Why would a second or third lender be willing to take a junior mortgage position on real property? Because there is sufficient owner's equity in the property to make the lender feel adequately secured in that position. Go back and review the discussion of the home equity loan in Chapter Three, Section B. Though we discussed the topic of owner's equity there in the context of a home equity loan, second and third mortgages are common in commercial transactions as well, and the owner's equity is also a relevant consideration to the commercial lender in those transactions. Of course, if a lender is being asked to take a junior mortgage position on real property, that lender might ask that, in addition to the mortgage, the owner provide a personal guaranty for the loan (see Section B of this chapter) or that the owner pledge personal property as additional security for the loan (see Section D of this chapter). Commercial loans in particular are often secured in more than one way.

P-H 4-d: A significant development during the real estate bubble and subprime lending frenzy of the late 1990s and early 2000s, together with the largely unregulated and irresponsible bundling of millions of subprime mortgages into collateralized mortgage obligations (CMOs) during that time, was the creation by lenders of the **Mortgage Electronic Registration System (MERS)** (www.mersinc. org/). MERS is a mostly private electronic registry system for land records that allows banks to avoid public filing of land records in county recording offices, thereby avoiding payment of the public recording fee. By the time the foreclosure crisis began in 2007, more than 60 percent of home mortgages in the United States were not traceable in the U.S. public land record system because of the use of MERS. And when the crisis hit, tracing and proving the multiple assignments and current ownership of individual mortgages through MERS proved next to impossible, usually because the underlying promissory note had not been assigned with the mortgage instrument. See, e.g., *Landmark Nat'l Bank v. Kesler*, 216 P.3d 158, 166-67 (Kan. 2009) and *Jackson v. MERS, Inc.*, 770 N.W.2d 487 (Minn. 2009). Those mortgages had been split, bundled into securities, sold, and resold on the global market. The difficulty of proving ownership of a particular distressed mortgage has gummed up both the foreclosure and private sale processes and is contributing to the prolonged effect of the Great Recession. See if the courts of your state have decided cases regarding the sufficiency of MERS recording to prove transfer and ownership of title to properties that were part of this fiasco.

5. Release of a Mortgage

When the owner of real property decides to sell it and there is still a balance remaining on the mortgage a portion of the purchase price paid by the buyer will go to satisfy that balance and the old mortgage placed on the property by the seller, having been paid off, will be released. A **release of mortgage** will be recorded in the public office where land records are recorded to give notice of the mortgage having been satisfied and released. In some states, a **deed of reconveyance** is required and in others the operative release document is a **satisfaction of mortgage**.

EXAMPLE

If DEF, instead of assuming ABC's mortgage with FNB, had taken out a new loan to finance its purchase of the cookie division of ABC, a portion of that DEF loan would have gone to FNB to pay off ABC's obligation and FNB would then have released its mortgage. That release might look something like Illustration 4-f.

Illustration 4-f: RELEASE OF MORTGAGE

The undersigned, First National Bank of Capitol City, Columbiana ("Mortgagee") does hereby certify that that certain mortgage dated May 1, YR-1 and executed by ABC, Inc. of Chicago, Illinois ("ABC") as mortgagor, and recorded in Mortgage Book 106, Page 543 in the Register's Office of Capitol County, Columbiana in favor of Mortgagee, is, with the promissory note accompanying it, fully paid, satisfied, released, and discharged and by this instrument Mortgagee does cancel and release the above-described mortgage.

First National Bank of Capitol City

By: _____

Herman Doright, President

P-H 4-e: What does your state require to be executed and recorded in order to release a mortgage interest? A release of mortgage? A deed of reconveyance? A satisfaction of mortgage? Something different?

6. Purchase Subject to a Mortgage

For a buyer of real estate, an alternative to paying off a preexisting mortgage (as in Illustration 4-f) or assuming it (as in Illustrations 4-d and 4-e) is to purchase the property from the seller subject to the preexisting mortgage. A purchaser who buys property *subject to* a preexisting mortgage but who does not assume the preexisting mortgage must make sure the payments are made on the preexisting mortgage (otherwise the mortgagee can foreclose). However, the purchaser does not automatically become liable for the underlying debt secured by the mortgage. The seller of the property remains liable for that underlying debt because the seller's obligation has not been paid off by a new loan, nor has the mortgagee agreed to any novation that would release seller from liability. Of course, if the original promissory note or the mortgage contains a **due on sale clause** prohibiting the owner from selling the property without the consent of the mortgagee and making all amounts due if an unauthorized sale occurs, the sale without an express assumption of the mortgage by the buyer may be an act of default by the seller authorizing the mortgagee to foreclose.

Due on sale clause Mortgage or security agreement provision providing that if the debtor sells the property pledged as security without the creditor's consent, a default has occurred and the entire amount becomes immediately due and payable.

P-H 4-f: Does the mortgage between the Murphys and FBCC in Illustration 4-b contain a due on sale clause?

P-H 4-g: Assume that DEF purchases ABC's cookie division, including the real property, but it neither takes out a new loan to pay off the existing mortgage in favor of FNB nor assumes liability for the debt underlying that existing mortgage. Instead, it takes possession of the property and begins making payments on the debt instead of ABC. If DEF stops making the required note payments to FNB and ABC does not make them either, can FNB institute foreclosure proceedings against ABC even though ABC is no longer in possession of the property? Can FNB sue ABC for any remaining balance owing after foreclosure? Can FNB sue DEF for any remaining balance owing after foreclosure?

7. Foreclosure on a Mortgage

The main idea behind a mortgage is that if the mortgagor defaults on the underlying debt, the mortgagee can take possession of the mortgaged property, sell it, and apply the proceeds to the satisfaction of the debt. We call this process **foreclosure**. Recall that the promissory note secured by the mortgage will contain an acceleration of indebtedness clause authorizing the mortgage holder to declare all amounts due from the mortgagor immediately due and payable. Thus, the

Foreclosure Process by which the holder of a mortgage in real property takes possession of the property following default by the mortgagor.

foreclosure can proceed to produce funds sufficient to pay off the entire indebtedness and other charges and expenses authorized by the note and mortgage.

Various states have authorized two different procedures for foreclosure: **power of sale foreclosure** and **judicial foreclosure**. Illustration 4-g sets out a state foreclosure laws comparison table. Almost all states that authorize a power of sale foreclosure permit judicial foreclosure as an alternative. But almost half the states mandate judicial foreclosure and permit no alternative.

P-H 4-h: Because of the foreclosure crisis discussed in the following section, the foreclosure procedure laws of many states are in flux. Check the laws of your state to see if they have been amended to speed up the foreclosure process, for example, by shortening the waiting period between default and foreclosure or trimming the public notice requirements or waiting periods. See if your state has added a judicial review requirement or otherwise expanded judicial review of the process. A handy summary of the foreclosure laws of all 50 states is accessible at www.biggerpockets.com/foreclosurelaw/index.html.

---

a. Power of Sale Foreclosure

A slight majority of the states allows mortgage instruments to convey a *power of sale* to the mortgagee. States allowing a power of sale use either a *deed of trust* or a *security deed* form of mortgage (see Section D).

EXAMPLE

> If the Murphys had executed a deed of trust with power of sale in connection with their loan from FBCC, the deed of trust would have conveyed the mortgage interest to a named trustee for the lender, rather than to the lender itself. And the language contained in the first sentence of paragraph 2 of Illustration 4-b would read as follows:
>
> > For the purposes set forth in Paragraph 1, Borrower irrevocably grants and conveys to Trustee, in trust, with power of sale, the following described property described property located in Capitol County, Columbiana. . . .

Upon default of an instrument granting a power of sale, the trustee (or substitute trustee, often appointed to carry out the foreclosure) for the mortgagee may institute foreclosure proceedings without first having to obtain any judicial or administrative approval. The trustee must be careful to comply with statutes governing the power of sale foreclosure. These statutes typically require the trustee to prepare a **notice of sale**, containing details of the intended public sale of the property (e.g., description of the property, time and place of the sale) and to provide the notice of sale to the mortgagor, any junior mortgage holders, and any other parties known to have an interest in the property (e.g., guarantors of the underlying debt). In addition to sending the notice of sale to designated interested parties, the trustee is typically required either to post the notice in a public place for some designated period of time before the sale (usually four to six weeks) or to run for a designated number weeks prior to sale an advertisement in the classified section of a newspaper of general circulation in the

Illustration 4-g: STATE FORECLOSURE LAWS COMPARISON TABLE

State	Security Instrument	Foreclosure Type	Initial Step	Time Line in Months	Right of Redemption (Months)	Deficiency	Timeline + Redemption (Months)
ALABAMA	Mortgage	Nonjudicial	Publication	1	12	Allowed	13.00
ALASKA	Trust Deed	Nonjudicial	Notice of Default	3	0	Allowed	3.00
ARIZONA	Trust Deed	Nonjudicial	Notice of Sale	3	0	Allowed	3.00
ARKANSAS	Mortgage	Judicial	Complaint	4	0	Allowed	4.00
CALIFORNIA	Trust Deed	Nonjudicial	Notice of Default	4	0	Prohibited	4.00
COLORADO	Trust Deed	Nonjudicial	Notice of Default	2	2.5	Allowed	4.50
CONNECTICUT	Mortgage	Strict	Complaint	5	0	Allowed	??
DELAWARE	Mortgage	Judicial	Complaint	3	0	Allowed	3.00
D.C.	Trust Deed	Nonjudicial	Notice of Default	2	0	Allowed	2.00
FLORIDA	Mortgage	Judicial	Complaint	5	0	Allowed	5.00
GEORGIA	Security Deed	Nonjudicial	Publication	2	0	Allowed	??
HAWAII	Mortgage	Nonjudicial	Publication	3	0	Allowed	3.00
IDAHO	Trust Deed	Nonjudicial	Notice of Default	5	0	Allowed	5.00
ILLINOIS	Mortgage	Judicial	Complaint	7	0	Allowed	7.00
INDIANA	Mortgage	Judicial	Complaint	5	3	Allowed	8.00
IOWA	Mortgage	Judicial	Petition	5	6	Allowed	11.00
KANSAS	Mortgage	Judicial	Complaint	4	12	Allowed	16.00
KENTUCKY	Mortgage	Judicial	Complaint	6	0	Allowed	6.00
LOUISIANA	Mortgage	Exec. Process	Petition	2	0	Allowed	??
MAINE	Mortgage	Judicial	Complaint	6	0	Allowed	6.00
MARYLAND	Trust Deed	Nonjudicial	Notice	2	0	Allowed	2.00
MASSACHU-SETTS	Mortgage	Judicial	Complaint	3	0	Allowed	3.00
MICHIGAN	Mortgage	Nonjudicial	Publication	2	6	Allowed	8.00
MINNESOTA	Mortgage	Nonjudicial	Publication	2	6	Prohibited	8.00
MISSISSIPPI	Trust Deed	Nonjudicial	Publication	2	0	Prohibited	2.00
MISSOURI	Trust Deed	Nonjudicial	Publication	2	0	Allowed	2.00
MONTANA	Trust Deed	Nonjudicial	Notice	5	0	Prohibited	5.00
NEBRASKA	Mortgage	Judicial	Petition	5	0	Allowed	5.00
NEVADA	Trust Deed	Nonjudicial	Notice of Default	4	0	Allowed	4.00
NEW HAMPSHIRE	Mortgage	Nonjudicial	Notice of Sale	2	0	Allowed	2.00
NEW JERSEY	Mortgage	Judicial	Complaint	3	0.25	Allowed	3.25
NEW MEXICO	Mortgage	Judicial	Complaint	4	0	Allowed	4.00
NEW YORK	Mortgage	Judicial	Complaint	4	0	Allowed	4.00

NORTH CAROLINA	Trust Deed	Nonjudicial	Notice Hearing	2	0	Allowed	2.00
NORTH DAKOTA	Mortgage	Judicial	Complaint	3	1	Prohibited	4.00
OHIO	Mortgage	Judicial	Complaint	5	0	Allowed	5.00
OKLAHOMA	Mortgage	Judicial	Complaint	4	0	Allowed	4.00
OREGON	Trust Deed	Nonjudicial	Notice of Default	5	0	Allowed	5.00
PENNSYLVANIA	Mortgage	Judicial	Complaint	3	0	Allowed	3.00
RHODE ISLAND	Mortgage	Nonjudicial	Publication	2	0	Allowed	2.00
SOUTH CAROLINA	Mortgage	Judicial	Complaint	6	0	Allowed	6.00
SOUTH DAKOTA	Mortgage	Judicial	Complaint	3	6	Allowed	9.00
TENNESSEE	Trust Deed	Nonjudicial	Publication	2	0	Allowed	2.00
TEXAS	Trust Deed	Nonjudicial	Publication	2	0	Allowed	2.00
UTAH	Trust Deed	Nonjudicial	Notice of Default	4	0	Allowed	4.00
VERMONT	Mortgage	Judicial	Complaint	7	0	Allowed	7.00
VIRGINIA	Trust Deed	Nonjudicial	Publication	2	0	Allowed	2.00
WASHINGTON	Trust Deed	Nonjudicial	Notice of Default	4	0	Allowed	4.00
WEST VIRGINIA	Trust Deed	Nonjudicial	Publication	2	0	Prohibited	2.00
WISCONSIN	Mortgage	Judicial	Complaint	Varies	0	Allowed	12.00
WYOMING	Mortgage	Nonjudicial	Publication	2	3	Allowed	5.00

(Original source of table: http://www.foreclosureforum.com/basics.html)

county where the land to be sold lies. If the Murphys had conveyed a power of sale to a trustee for FBCC per the last example and then defaulted on their payments, the trustee may have initiated a power of sale foreclosure using the notice of foreclosure sale set forth in Illustration 4-h.

Following the foreclosure sale in a power of sale foreclosure, title to the property is conveyed to the new owner through a **trustee's deed**. Proceeds of the sale will be applied first to satisfy the costs of the sale (e.g., advertising, site preparation, and auctioneer's fee), second to pay any taxes or special assessments still owed on the property, and third to pay the balance owed senior and junior mortgage holders. Finally, any balance left goes to the borrower. The minimum bid set at a foreclosure sale is normally equal to the amount owed to the foreclosing mortgagee. If no third-party bid on the property at the foreclosure sale exceeds that minimum amount, the foreclosing mortgagee is entitled to (and in some states required to) enter a bid on the property itself in an amount equal to the amount owed, a common practice known as **bidding in** or **credit-bidding**, which means the creditor takes absolute title to the property in exchange for extinguishment of the indebtedness and for no additional payment. If there is equity in the property (it is worth more than the balance owed to the mortgagee), then the purchasing mortgagee captures the equity.

Illustration 4-h: NOTICE OF FORECLOSURE SALE

WHEREAS, Nicholas W. Murphy and wife, Pearl E. Murphy, by Deed of Trust (the "Deed of Trust") dated January 12, YR-10, of record in Mortgage Book 99, Page 077 in the Register's Office of Capitol County, Columbiana, conveyed to Howard J. Sands, Trustee, the hereinafter described real property to secure the payment of a certain Promissory Note (the "Note") described in the Deed of Trust, which Note was payable to First Bank of Capital City;

WHEREAS, default has been made in the payment of the Note; and

WHEREAS, the owner and holder of the Note has demanded that the hereinafter described real property be advertised and sold in satisfaction of indebtedness and costs of foreclosure in accordance with the terms and provisions of the Note and Deed of Trust.

NOW, THEREFORE, notice is hereby given that Trustee, pursuant to the power, duty and authority vested in and conferred upon me, by the Deed of Trust, will on May 1, YR00 at 9 A.M. at the front door of the Capitol County Courthouse in Capitol City, Columbiana, Tennessee, offer for sale to the highest bidder for cash, and free from all legal, equitable and statutory rights of redemption, exemptions of homestead, rights by virtue of marriage, and all other exemptions of every kind, all of which have been waived in the Deed of Trust, certain real property located in Capitol County, Columbiana, described as follows: [property description deleted from illustration]. . . . Being the same property conveyed to Nicholas W. Murphy and wife, Pearl E. Murphy, by deed from Francis H. Harmon, of record in Deed Book 813, Page 908 in the Register's Office for Capitol County, Columbiana; and further conveyed by the Deed of Trust to the Trustee, of record in Mortgage Book 99, Page 077 in the Register's Office for said County.

The address of the above-described property is 3521 West Cherry Street, Capitol City, Columbiana.

DATED this February 1, YR00.

Francis H. Harmon, Trustee

P-H 4-i: There is quite a bit of variation among the states regarding how proceeds of a foreclosure sale are to be distributed. In some states, after the balance owed to the foreclosing mortgagee has been paid, excess proceeds must go to other creditors of the mortgagor/debtor before any are paid to him. Some states allow the mortgagee to credit-bid at an amount less than the total amount owed on the property, although this may raise questions of good faith or unconscionability if the mortgagee is allowed to (see discussion of arrearages, below) and does then pursue the debtor for any balance remaining on the account. Many states authorize a special court proceeding wherein disputes over distribution of sales proceeds can be resolved within some designated time period following the sale (e.g., six months or one year). See if you can find a summary of how your state regulates distribution of foreclosure sale proceeds.

Equity of redemption A mortgagor's right to prevent the sale of real property in foreclosure by paying the entire indebtedness owed prior to the foreclosure sale.

Until the foreclosure sale occurs, all states recognize an **equity of redemption** in the mortgagor. That is, the right of the mortgagor to redeem the property from foreclosure by paying all amounts due to the mortgagee. On the designated day and time, if the mortgagor has not exercised his equity of redemption, the trustee or a public official (e.g., the county sheriff) will conduct the foreclosure sale. The property will be sold to the highest bidder. The mortgagee is allowed to bid in the amount of the debt owed to it as the purchase price.

If holders of junior mortgages were given proper notice of the foreclosure sale, their mortgage interests in the real property are extinguished by the foreclosure sale under the laws of most states such that the purchaser at foreclosure will take title free and clear of those claims. If the proceeds of the sale produced an excess (there was more than enough money made on the sale to pay all the debts and expenses owed to the foreclosing mortgagee), that excess will go to the junior interests or to the mortgagor. The foreclosing mortgagee holding excess funds often initiates a civil lawsuit called an **impleader action**, naming the junior interest holders and the mortgagor as parties, pays the excess funds into the clerk of the court where the impleader action is filed, and requests the court to determine who is entitled to what share of those excess funds.

Impleader action A civil lawsuit in which one holding funds that more than one party may be entitled to pays the funds into court and asks the court to designate the appropriate payee.

P-H 4-j: Why do you think the foreclosing mortgagee handles the excess funds this way? What problems is the mortgagee trying to avoid by filing this impleader action?

In addition to the mortgagor's equity of redemption right, already discussed, some states provide the mortgagor with a **statutory right of redemption**. Such statutes authorize the mortgagor, for a period of six to twelve months after the foreclosure sale, to buy back the property for the foreclosure sale price. Some of the states that recognize the right of statutory redemption permit the mortgagor to waive that right in the mortgage document.

b. Judicial Foreclosure

Judicial foreclosure is initiated by the mortgagee filing a lawsuit alleging default in a debt properly secured by the mortgage and the right to foreclose and asking the court to issue an order that the property be sold to pay the indebtedness secured. Judicial foreclosure is mandated in states that do not recognize a power of sale foreclosure and is an option available to the mortgagee in states that do.

The mortgagee initiating the judicial foreclosure will name the mortgagor, junior mortgage holders, and others with an interest in the property as parties so that all alleged claims and defenses can be fully litigated in the action. If the court finds for the mortgagee and orders the property sold, required notice will be given, the property levied on or seized by the sheriff or other public official, and the sale conducted publicly by auction (**a sheriff's sale** or **referee's sale**). Title to the new owner is then conveyed by a **sheriff's deed** or **referee's deed**. Distribution of proceeds from a judicial sale will be strictly governed by statute, but generally follows the scheme discussed in connection with power of sale foreclosure.

Sheriff's sale The sale by public auction or private negotiation of property of a debtor levied on pursuant to a writ of execution.

P-H 4-k: Locate your state's judicial foreclosure statute or regulation. What is the mandated order or distribution of proceeds of foreclosure sale? If your state allows power of sale foreclosure, are there any differences in how proceeds of sale are distributed?

Many attorneys prefer the judicial foreclosure over the power of sale foreclosure, even in states authorizing the latter, because of the finality of the court decision. In a nonjudicial power of sale foreclosure, there is always the possibility the mortgagor will file suit contesting the right of the mortgagee to proceed or contesting the propriety of a foreclosure sale already conducted. All those issues should be resolved by the court in the judicial foreclosure prior to the sale. The rights and priorities of junior mortgage holders will be resolved there, too, negating the need for a subsequent impleader action.

Another consideration in choosing between a judicial foreclosure and a power of sale foreclosure is the possibility that the property sold at foreclosure may not bring enough to satisfy the full amount owed—there is a **deficiency balance**. In a judicial foreclosure, the court in most instances can enter a judgment against the mortgagor for the deficiency (a **deficiency judgment**) without a separate lawsuit being filed. In a power of sale foreclosure, however, the mortgagee must file a lawsuit following the foreclosure sale in order to obtain a deficiency judgment. And some states recognize an **election of remedies** doctrine, prohibiting the mortgagee from obtaining a deficiency judgment following a power of sale foreclosure. The mortgagee is held to have elected its sole remedy by proceeding with the foreclosure and cannot bring a deficiency action if the price received on foreclosure did not fully satisfy the debt.

Deficiency judgment The amount of a debt that remains owing after the property securing the debt has been liquidated.

Election of remedies Requires a secured creditor to choose between exercising a right of foreclosure on secured property or suing the debtor for a judgment, but disallowing both.

P-H 4-l: Another source of controversy over a deficiency balance can arise when the foreclosing mortgagee enters a credit-bid on the property at the foreclosure sale for less than the total amount owed and then seeks a judgment against the debtor for the deficiency balance in jurisdictions where that is allowed. The issue in such cases is whether the value of the property exceeded the amount of the credit-bid entered by the mortgagee. If you live in a state that allows post-foreclosure suits for deficiency balance, see if you can locate cases in your jurisdiction dealing with this issue.

A further consideration in electing between a judicial foreclosure and a power of sale foreclosure is that purchasers of the property at sale often have more confidence in the title they receive to the property by **foreclosure deed** when the sale is the result of a court order. The downside to judicial foreclosure is the delay involved in the mortgagee gaining access to the property for foreclosure sale by having to file the lawsuit, effect service of process on the mortgagee, and await a hearing date.

Finally, if the underlying promissory note is **nonrecourse**, that means the creditor agreed to look only to the secured property upon default and cannot pursue a deficiency judgment against the mortgagor. A **nonrecourse secured note** bars the creditor from pursuing a deficiency judgment regardless of whether a judicial or power of sale foreclosure was authorized.

Nonrecourse secured note A promissory note providing that the debtor has no liability beyond the value of the property securing the debt. No deficiency judgment may be brought after foreclosure or repossession.

P-H 4-m: The **Servicemembers Civil Relief Act (SCRA)**, U.S.C.A. App. §501 et seq., as revised in 2003, restricts foreclosure of properties owned by active-duty members of the military. Check the Web site of the U.S. Department of Housing and Urban Development for a summary of the protections from foreclosure provided to our active-duty service people: http://portal.hud.gov/hudportal/HUD?src=/program_offices/housing/sfh/nsc/qasscra1.

8. Alternatives to Foreclosure

Foreclosure is not a happy solution for anyone, including the foreclosing creditor. Unless the real estate market is hot, the foreclosed property may sit empty for months or years with the attendant risks of deterioration in value and vandalism. Taxes still have to be paid and insurance maintained on the property. There are always costs associated with the foreclosure sale, reducing the take of the creditor and increasing the potential liability of the debtor. Foreclosure is often devastating to the credit rating of the debtor. For these and other reasons, the debtor and creditor may agree to any one of several alternatives to foreclosure.

a. Temporary Forbearance

The creditor may agree to temporarily lower or suspend mortgage payments without declaring default and foreclosing. The homeowner debtor may be able to negotiate such forbearance directly with the creditor. Or the debtor may use the services of a private **mortgage assistance relief service** that will negotiate with the creditor on behalf of the debtor.

b. Mortgage Modification

The creditor may agree to modify the mortgage terms by extending the term of repayment and thus reducing the amount of the periodic payments or by reducing the interest rate, or even by forgiving a portion of the principal. Again, the debtor may be able to negotiate such a modification directly with the lender or use the services of a mortgage assistance relief service.

Sadly, one result of the mortgage foreclosure crisis in this country (discussed in detail in the next section) has been the appearance of private mortgage assistance relief services that run scams on home owners who are already trying to deal with looming foreclosure. In late 2010, the Federal Trade Commission issued a **Mortgage Assistance Relief Services Rule**, 16 C.F.R. Part 322, (the **MARS Rule**), recodified as Mortgage Assistance Relief Services, 12 C.F.R. Part 1015 (collectively, **Regulation O**), prohibiting these services from taking a fee from the customer unless and until an actual offer of forbearance or modification by the creditor was in hand. Notice requirements were also imposed on these services. Regulation O is now enforced by the new **Consumer Financial Protection Bureau (CFPB)** created by the **Dodd-Frank Wall Street Reform and Consumer Protection Act of 2010** (the **Dodd-Frank Act**), which is empowered to obtain ex parte (without the other party being present) temporary restraining orders against offenders, freeze their assets pending final judgment, and have a receiver temporarily appointed to oversee the operations of offending companies.

P-H 4-n: See the FTC's press release summarizing the MARS Rule at www.tba2.org/tbatoday/news/2010/ftc_mortgage_relief_scam_111910.pdf. What other requirements does the rule impose on these services? In July 2012, the CFPB demonstrated its commitment to strict enforcement of Regulation O by moving against the Gordon Law Firm in California for alleged violations. See a summary of that action at http://legaltimes.typepad.com/blt/2012/07/consumer-financial-agency-files-first-civil-enforcement-action-in-court.html. Does it appear that the CFPB means to live up to its name?

---

c. State and Federal Mortgage Assistance Programs

A number of states, such as Pennsylvania (www.phfa.org/consumers/home-owners/hemap.aspx), have established programs to assist qualifying home-owners in making their house payments or by offering incentivized forbearance or modification proposals to lenders. Similarly, the federal government has established its Making Home Affordable Program, discussed in detail in the next section. For FHA-insured loans only, the creditor may be able to obtain a one-time payment from the FHA insurance fund to be applied to delinquent payments through the Department of Housing and Urban Development's (HUD) Partial Claim fund.

d. Short Sale

In a short sale, the creditor allows the homeowner time to sell the property and agrees to accept the net proceeds of the sale in full satisfaction of the indebtedness even though the sale may not bring enough to cover the entire indebtedness and even if the underlying note is not nonrecourse. The advantages to the creditor are that the property remains occupied and the debtor/homeowner has an incentive to keep the property up in the interim. The advantages to the debtor are that he gets to remain in the property pending sale, foreclosure and consequent harm to his credit history are avoided, and, of course, he avoids any potential liability for any deficiency.

e. Deed in Lieu of Foreclosure

In a deed-in-lieu of arrangement, the debtor agrees voluntarily to transfer title to the property to the creditor in exchange for cancelling the mortgage loan. The creditor may also agree to forgive any deficiency balance remaining when the property is finally resold.

f. Filing for Bankruptcy Protection

As we will learn in Part C of the text, filing for some kinds of bankruptcy reorganization relief may enable a defaulting debtor to delay and even avoid foreclosure.

E. ▶ The Mortgage Foreclosure Crisis and the Federal Response

By now we've all heard of the **real estate bubble** that developed in this country in the late 1990s and early 2000s and then burst so spectacularly beginning in 2007. A real estate bubble is an economic phenomenon in which real estate values rise more rapidly than fundamentals such as market demand and income levels can justify. At some point, the inflated values become unsustainable and the bubble bursts.

Real estate bubbles are hardly rare and, although the bursting is always painful for those who forget that what goes up must come down, they need not result in widespread financial disaster. But this one has. Unfortunately, our bubble was accompanied by and to some extent fueled by **subprime lending**, the practice of making loans to **high risk borrowers**, meaning borrowers who have been historically excluded from the conventional or prime loan market due to low income, poor credit histories, or spotty job records. To introduce more home buyers into the market and thus keep driving up prices (and to keep generating transaction fees for the loan originators), many lenders targeted high risk and other borrowers with offers of easy credit that, in retrospect, should have been seen as too good to be true. In 2006, for example, the year before the bubble burst, the National Association of Realtors reported that 45 percent of first-time home buyers put zero money down for the purchase. In the same year, the median first-time buyer was able to finance 98 percent of the purchase price. Historically, a 10–20 percent down payment is considered prudent so that equity is immediately created in the property. Moreover, people were being approved for home loans in a dollar amount equal to eight to ten times their total annual income. Historically, it has been considered prudent to limit mortgage debt to an amount no more than three times the borrower's annual income. Not only were home buyers able to obtain these advantageous-sounding deals, existing home owners who had seen their home values more than double in the preceding decade (the typical American home increased 124 percent in value between 1997 and 2006) were able to borrow the full dollar amount of the inflated equity through **home equity loans**, often with little or no closing costs.

Exacerbating the problem of lending exorbitant amounts based on inflated values, many lenders lowered their **mortgage qualifications standards** essentially to "having a pulse." A stated income, verified assets (**SIVA**) standard was used requiring no proof of income from mortgage applicants; they had only to state their income and show that they had some money in the bank. Some lenders used no income, verified assets (**NIVA**) where no income or proof of employment was required, only a balance in the bank. Finally, there was the **NINA** (sometimes called **NINJA**) standard, no income, no assets. The applicant had only to produce a credit score to qualify.

Lenders also put new borrowers and refinancing borrowers into **adjustable rate mortgages** (ARMs) or **graduated payment mortgages** (GPMs) or **interest-only mortgages** (IOMs). In an ARM, the interest rate paid by the borrower may be adjusted during the term of the mortgage based on some agreed indices, such as the change in rates paid on U.S. treasuries, or a local or regional **cost of funds index** (COFI) (measuring the change in what it costs the lender to obtain the money loaned to the borrower). Typically the initial rate on an ARM is low and attractive to the borrower (thus called a **teaser** rate). But in an ARM arrangement, the borrower assumes the risk that the interest rate on the loan may increase beyond what the borrower can afford to pay. It is estimated that 80 percent of the subprime mortgages granted in the years leading up to the crash were ARMs.

In a GPM, the monthly payments made by the borrower are kept artificially low at the beginning of the payment schedule and then gradually increase over the life of the loan. They are ideal for young borrowers who expect their earnings to increase in line with the increased payment schedule, but lethal if that does not happen. And if the artificially low monthly payments are less than the interest that would normally be due for that period, that results in **negative amortization** (NegAm) because the unpaid interest for that period will be added to the principal amount owed and subject to additional interest charges.

An IOM allows the borrower the option to make interest-only payments some number of times (e.g., three months of each calendar year) without being in default. The problem with that, of course, is that the borrower is not reducing the principal amount owed while making interest-only payments and is instead extending both the life of the loan and the total cost to the borrower.

By March 2007, fully 20 percent of all outstanding home mortgages in the United States were classified as subprime, with a total face value of $1.3 trillion. Millions of those subprime home mortgage loans had by then been sold by the original mortgagees and bundled into securities known, among other things, as **collateral mortgage obligations** (CMOs), which were traded globally and collectively formed a significant portion of the asset base of many of the world's largest investment banks. When the real estate bubble burst, triggering the Great Recession, property values fell sharply, leaving millions of mortgages **underwater** or **upside down** (more was owed on the mortgage than the property securing it was worth), a circumstance formally known as **negative equity**. Debtors on a large percentage of those mortgages began to default and the true value of the CMOs consisting of those subprime loans was exposed as being far less than the value given for them by international banks. The world financial system has not yet recovered from the debacle. Worse still, many of those subprime mortgages had been recorded in the MERS electronic registry system rather than in county public recording offices, and that situation has produced chaos because of the difficulty in tracing assignments and true ownership of mortgages registered only in the MERS system (see P-H 4-d).

Caught in the middle of this fiasco were two key players: the **Federal Home Loan Mortgage Corporation (Freddie Mac)** and the **Federal National Mortgage Association (Fannie Mae)**. Fannie Mae was created in 1938 as part of President Franklin Roosevelt's New Deal legislation. So many banks had failed during the Great Depression that surviving lenders were reluctant to invest in home loans. Roosevelt and Congress created Fannie Mae to provide banks with federal money that the banks in turn agreed to loan to home buyers at lower, affordable rates. Thus, Fannie Mae insured liquidity in the home mortgage market by providing funds to be loaned and guarantying the loan against default.

Fannie Mae was privatized by Congress in 1968 and today operates as a **government sponsored enterprise (GSE)** along with Freddie Mac, created in 1970 to spur competition with Fannie Mae. Being GSEs means that even though they are now privately owned for-profit corporations, Fannie Mae and Freddie Mac enjoy certain privileges, including exemption from state and local income taxes and the ability to access credit directly from the U.S. Treasury. Both GSEs play a critical role in the mortgage market as mortgage brokers by purchasing or guaranteeing mortgage loans from approved mortgage originators or other mortgage brokers and by securitizing groups of mortgages and marketing them along with a guaranty to purchasers that payment of the principal and interest on the loans within the security will be paid.

When the subprime lending bubble burst so spectacularly in 2007, Fannie Mae and Freddie Mac were holding or had guaranteed approximately one-half of the $12 trillion in outstanding home mortgages in this country. Although both GSEs technically had relatively high **underwriting standards** for the loans they purchased or guaranteed, they had in fact become involved in the subprime market themselves beginning in the late 1990s and had been under continuous pressure from private lenders to ease their standards. Whether the GSEs were more a cause or a victim of the subprime mess will be debated for years. But either way, when the wave of defaults and foreclosure began in 2007, the viability of both companies became imperiled as they faced billions of dollars in potential losses, endangering not just their own profitability, but the stability and safety of the entire home mortgage industry in this country. In the months leading up to the crash, the GSEs were effectively funding 70 percent of all home loans being made. Not only was the fundamental structure of the mortgage industry threatened by the GSEs' problems, so was the solvency of a number of banks around the country that held significant quantities of stocks and bonds issued by them. In September 2008 the federal government put Fannie Mae and Freddie Mac into a conservatorship under the Federal Housing Finance Agency (FHFA).

There is plenty of blame to go around for the subprime lending/refinancing/ home equity fiasco. Many borrowers should have known better than to take such foolish risks. Lenders shouldn't have encouraged and enabled such risk taking for the sake of short-term profits and government shouldn't have allowed them. Lenders who targeted vulnerable, unsophisticated borrowers who could not understand the risk they were undertaking or lenders who knowingly advertised one rate of interest and then switched it to another at closing without explaining the consequences to the borrower (just Google or Bing Countrywide Financial Corporation) should face the full civil and criminal consequences for their actions. The fallout from the subprime lending mess and the collapse of the real estate bubble has been widespread and horrific. Even prime borrowers who had chosen to refinance or borrow against the inflated value of their property through home equity loans found themselves owing far more than the now-deflated value of their homes (having negative equity). As of March 2008, 10.8 percent of all American homeowners had negative equity in their homes. That percentage ballooned during the following years of the crisis. By mid-2012, almost 27 percent of home mortgages were rated as negative or near-negative (less than 5% equity). The numbers have improved somewhat since then, but still remain dangerously high.

A homeowner facing negative equity realizes quickly that she cannot sell her home without incurring a loss. It may seriously impair the owner's credit rating and certainly restricts her ability to obtain new credit. If that consumer's mortgage note is nonrecourse, the consumer has tremendous incentive to walk away from the mortgage, having no fear of personal liability for any balance owing on the mortgage beyond the value of the property.

Additional fallout involved the drying up of the **credit markets** for consumers and businesses because of the actual or potential losses now sitting on the balance sheets of so many lenders. Both the commercial and residential real estate markets were essentially frozen. New construction came to a screeching halt in most parts of the country. CDOs or MBSs that contained or were even suspected of containing tainted subprime mortgages (and after the bundling it was almost impossible to categorize each mortgage included in a single security) dropped to next to nothing in market value, seriously impairing the solvency of investment companies holding those securities. This development played a huge role in the government's decision to bail out many of those financial institutions through the **Troubled Asset Relief Program** (TARP) approved in late 2008. TARP authorized the U.S. Department of the Treasury to spend up to

$700 billion to purchase or insure "troubled assets" of endangered companies in order to shore up the nation's financial sector, which was in danger of collapsing completely—an event many believe would have triggered a worldwide depression.

In addition to the takeovers of Freddie Mac and Sallie Mae, the TARP bailouts, and various criminal investigations, the federal government has responded in other ways to the mortgage foreclosure crisis. On March 4, 2009 the U.S. Treasury Department announced its **Home Affordable Mortgage Program**, more commonly referred to as the **Making Home Affordable Program (MHA)**, which was broadened by the **Helping Families Save Their Homes Act of 2009**. MHA has several elements. One is a refinancing program targeting 4 to 5 million borrowers who have a Freddie Mac or Fannie Mae mortgage executed before January 1, 2009, on their principal residence and a solid payment history. Those borrowers are allowed to refinance their mortgage at today's low rates with less than the usual required 20 percent equity in their residences.

Another MHA strategy is targeted at 3–4 million higher risk homeowners and provides a mechanism for them to work with their lenders through various government agencies to temporarily (five years maximum) reduce their mortgage payments to as little as 38 percent of their income and, in some instances, with government assistance, to as little as 31 percent. Incentives are provided to lenders to encourage their agreement to **a trial mortgage modification**. If the trial modification fails, there are further incentives to encourage the lender to agree to a short sale or deed in lieu of foreclosure. To incentivize the homeowner where modification fails, the program provides up to $3,000 in relocation costs for a homeowner vacating under a short sale or deed-in-lieu arrangement.

The MHA program got off to a disappointingly slow start and, as of this writing, is still struggling. Too few homeowners have applied to participate and lenders have proven reluctant to agree to mortgage modifications.

More successful has been the federal government's **Financial Fraud Enforcement Task Force** established by President Obama in November 2009 (http://www.stopfraud.gov/index.html) as part of the **Fraud Enforcement and Recovery Act of 2009**. Spearheaded by the U.S. Department of Justice, the task force combines the resources of 20 federal agencies and works in partnership with state and local agencies to identify, investigate, and prosecute all sorts of financial crimes. One notable success in the context of the mortgage foreclosure crisis was the June 2010 consent decree entered into in the litigation between the U.S. Trustee's Program (USTP) and Countrywide Home Loans, Inc. The USTP had alleged that Countrywide had systematically filed false and inflated claims as a creditor in connection with numerous bankruptcies filed by homeowners whose mortgages were serviced by Countrywide and that Countrywide had both failed to give homeowners proper credits on their mortgage balances and had added extra charges on those balances with no notice to the homeowners. Under the consent decree, Countrywide agreed to make compensation to wronged homeowners and to revise its mortgage servicing procedures to avoid future abuses with compliance to be verified by an independent third party.

One provision of the **Helping Families Save Their Homes Act of 2009** that has proved successful is the **Protecting Tenants at Foreclosure Act (PTFA)**. What happens to a tenant if the property he leases is foreclosed on owing to a default by the landlord? In most states, the tenant's lease is terminated by the terms of the preexisting mortgage on the premises and the tenant (who is not in default himself) will have to vacate. Given the potential fallout of the mortgage foreclosure crisis on innocent tenants, Congress enacted PTFA to provide that cases in which a house or apartment under lease as a residence is foreclosed on, the "immediate successor in interest" to the defaulting owner (that successor will be the foreclosing creditor) takes title to the property subject to the rights of a **"bona fide tenant"** (**BFT**) (definition excludes tenant who is child, spouse, or parent of landlord or tenant paying less than fair market value rent). Any such BFT is entitled to a notice to vacate 90 days before the effective date on which the premises must be vacated. Thus, the tenant is given time to find substitute housing. Moreover, the BFT must be allowed to stay in possession of the leased premises for the entire term of the lease unless the property is sold after foreclosure to an owner who intends to occupy the premises as a primary residence. As initially passed, PTFA was to expire at the end of 2012, but the Dodd-Frank Act extended it through 2014.

P-H 4-o: If you are reading this after December 2014, see if Congress has further extended PTFA or if it has expired. See if your state gives statutory or regulatory protection to residential tenants when a creditor forecloses on the landlord. Interesting issues can arise under PTFA or analogous state laws. Who is a "bona fide" tenant? What is fair market rent? If PTFA notice provisions conflict with analogous state provisions, which are in control? See if the state or federal courts of your state have decided any cases under PTFA or any analogous state law.

In the summer of 2010, Congress passed the Dodd-Frank Act, referenced in Section D above, which imposes significant new regulation on mortgage brokers and lenders including:

- The commonsense requirement that the lender request and confirm the income and assets that the borrower lists in the loan application
- Banning prepayment penalties on adjustable rate mortgages
- Forbidding bonuses to loan officers based on the kind of loan they arrange for the borrower (e.g., the higher the interest rate, the greater the bonus)
- Capping mortgage origination fees at 3 percent of the loan amount, with exceptions for FHA mortgages and points paid by a borrower for a lower interest rate.

More help is on the way. The CFPB, created by the Dodd-Frank Act, has promulgated regulations amending **Regulation X**, which implements the **Real Estate Settlement Procedures Act of 1974** and **Regulation Z**, which implements the **Truth in Lending Act** with regard to the making and servicing of consumer home mortgages. The new regulations, scheduled to go into effect January 2014, include the following key points:

- Loan makers must collect and verify information sufficient to show the borrower has the financial ability to repay the loan applied for.
- Total loan payments, including principal, interest, taxes, and insurance, cannot exceed 43 percent of the borrower's gross income.
- Negative amortization options are banned.

- Loan makers cannot steer borrowers to options more financially favorable to the loan maker.
- Loan servicers must provide the borrower "continuity of contact" with personnel who have full access to borrower's case file.
- Borrowers who fall two payments behind must be advised of available help programs to avoid foreclosure, and foreclosure proceedings cannot begin until borrower is 120 days in arrears.
- When a borrower seeks a loan modification, servicers must acknowledge receipt of the modification application within five days, advising whether the application is complete and indicating further information needed.
- No **dual tracking** is allowed, that is, the practice of pursuing foreclosure proceedings while a loan modification application is pending.

Dual tracking The practice of proceeding with a mortgage foreclosure against a borrower while simultaneously processing the borrower's loan modification application.

P-H 4-p: What do you think are the reasons for each of the new CFPB regulations summarized above? Locate the new regulations from the CFPB Web site at www.consumerfinance.gov/ and see what other provisions are included.

Additionally, proposals have been introduced in both houses of Congress to amend the Bankruptcy Code to allow homeowners faced with negative equity who file for Chapter 13 relief to modify or **cram down** the secured balance of their home mortgage to the market value of the property, or extend the term of a home mortgage or reduce the contractual interest rate. At this writing these proposals do not look likely to pass. As we will learn in Part C of the text, the cram-down option is available to Chapter 13 debtors for all kinds of property pledged as security for debt except the mortgage on the debtor's principal residence. Consumer advocates have long contended this prohibition discriminates unfairly against the nonwealthy since the cram-down option is available on second homes. And others contend that the cram-down option on the debtor's principal residence should be allowed temporarily as a means of dealing with the ongoing mortgage foreclosure crisis.

P-H 4-q: Check the current status of the cram-down proposals in Congress. A creative but controversial alternative idea being suggested to cities and counties by Mortgage Resolution Partners (http://mortgageresolution.com/) is to use the government's power of **eminent domain** to condemn and purchase local underwater mortgages or securities in which such mortgages are bundled for the current market value of the underlying property (the crammed down value) and then to refinance the loans based on those current values. See the idea discussed at http://blogs.reuters.com/unstructuredfinance/tag/mortgage-resolution-partners/ or in more detail in the article "Home Economics: Can an Entrepreneur's Audacious Plan Fix the Mortgage Mess?" in *The New Yorker*, February 4, 2013, p. 26. Determine if any city or county is pursuing this idea.

CONCLUSION

You can see from this chapter that there are a number of ways that debt can be secured and that securing debt has significant legal consequences for the property pledged as security and for the person or company that agrees to serve as surety or guarantor. But there is another important aspect to secured debt that we have yet to address: the pledging of personal property to secure debt. That is the topic of the next chapter.

CHAPTER SUMMARY

This chapter considered various ways that debt is consensually secured. A surety is one who makes herself primarily liable for the debt of another. Surety agreements or bonds are routinely required in some commercial transactions like construction contracts. One who co-signs the promissory note of another is a surety as to that debt. A guaranty agreement renders the guarantor secondarily liable for the debt of another. A surety or guarantor can raise any defense to liability that the principal debtor can except she cannot raise personal defenses unique to the principal debtor that do not go to the merits of the underlying debt. A material change in circumstances surrounding the debt to which the surety or guarantor does not consent may discharge the surety or guarantor as a matter of law. A consensual lien granted to the creditor in the debtor's real property is called a mortgage. The mortgage grants the creditor/mortgagee the right of foreclosure or power of sale in the real property. Mortgages are typically assignable by the mortgagee, and sometimes existing mortgage obligations are assumed by new debtors who knowingly purchase the real property subject to the mortgage. The priority among multiple mortgages on a single piece of realty is controlled by the recording statute of the state where the land lies. Most mortgage notes contain a due on sale clause requiring a pay-off of the underlying debt if the debtor sells the mortgaged property. Upon default by the debtor on the underlying debt obligation, the mortgagee or a trustee acting for the mortgagee will foreclose on and sell the property then apply the proceeds of sale to the underlying debt and expenses of foreclosure. A foreclosure sale is subject to the debtor's equitable or statutory right of redemption. If the foreclosure sale does not bring enough to pay off the debt, the creditor may file a lawsuit to obtain a judgment for the deficiency amount unless state law prohibits such a suit under the election of remedies doctrine. There are a number of alternatives to foreclosure. We are still living through the mortgage foreclosure crisis, triggered by the decade-long real estate bubble acerbated by runaway subprime lending, easy credit, and greed by all concerned.

REVIEW QUESTIONS

1. Explain the difference between being primarily and secondarily liable for a debt.
2. Provide two examples of a personal defense that a principal debtor might have available to him that would not be available to a surety or guarantor.
3. What is the rationale for the rule that a material change in circumstances surrounding a debt to which a surety or guarantor does not consent operates to discharge the surety or guarantor? Provide an example of such a material change of circumstances.

4. What is the difference between an accommodation surety and a compensated surety and why does the distinction matter in some states?

5. Explain the difference between legal title and equitable title in mortgaged property.

6. Explain the difference between the power of sale and the power of foreclosure.

7. Explain the difference between assigning a mortgage and assuming a mortgage. Why might the purchaser of real estate be eager to assume an existing mortgage on the property?

8. Explain the difference between race, notice, and race-notice recording statutes.

9. Explain what "owner's equity" is. Explain what an owner's equitable or statutory right of redemption is. Explain the election of remedies doctrine followed in some states. List five possible alternatives to foreclosure.

10. Explain the meaning of the following terms: subprime lending, ARM, negative amortization, negative equity, mortgage modification, cram down.

WORDS AND PHRASES TO REMEMBER

accommodation surety
assumption
auction sale
bidding in
bona fide tenant
collateral
collateral mortgage obligation
    (CMO)
compensated surety
consensual lien
constructive notice
Consumer Financial Protection
    Bureau
co-signer
cost of funds index
cram down
credit-bidding
deed in lieu of foreclosure
deed of reconveyance
deed of trust
Dodd-Frank Wall Street Reform
    and Consumer Protection
    Act of 2010
dual tracking
election of remedies
eminent domain
equitable title
equity
equity of redemption

Financial Fraud Enforcement
    Task Force
first mortgage
foreclosure
foreclosure deed
Fraud Enforcement and
    Recovery Act of 2009
government sponsored
    enterprise (GSE)
guarantor
guaranty agreement
Helping Families Save
    Their Homes Act of 2009
Home Affordable Mortgage
    Program
home equity loan
impleader action
judicial foreclosure
junior mortgage
legal title
lien
Making Home Affordable
    Program (MHA)
MERS
mortgage
Mortgage Assistance Relief
    Services Rule (MARS Rule)
mortgage assumption clause
mortgage deed

negative amortization
  (NegAm)
negative equity
mortgage qualifications
  standards
nonconsensual lien
nonrecourse secured note
notice of sale
notice statute
owner finance
personal defenses
pledged property
power of sale
power of sale foreclosure
primarily liable
principal debtor
Protecting Tenants at Foreclosure
  Act (PTFA)
purchase money mortgage
race-notice statute
race statute
Real Estate Settlement Procedures
  Act of 1974
recording statute
redemption (right to redeem)
referee's deed
referee's sale
Regulation O

Regulation X
Regulation Z
reverse mortgage
Servicemembers Civil
  Relief Act (SCRA)
satisfaction of mortgage
second mortgage
secondarily liable
security deed
self-finance
senior mortgage
sheriff's deed
sheriff's sale
short sale
statutory right of redemption
subprime lending
surety
surety agreement
surety bond
trial mortgage modification
Troubled Asset Relief
  Program (TARP)
trustee's deed
Truth in Lending Act
underwater mortgage
upside down mortgage
wrap-around mortgage

TO LEARN MORE: A number of TLM activities to accompany this chapter are accessible on the student disc accompanying the text and on the Author Updates link to the text Web site at http://www.aspenparalegaled.com/ books/parsons_ abcdebt/default.asp.

Chapter Five:

▶ # Security Interests in Personal Property

Five figure living on four figure pay
At least until they took my attaché.
— *White Collar Drifter, The Swimming Pool Qs*

A. ▶ Introduction to UCC Article 9

Uniform Commercial Code (UCC) A uniform code adopted in whole or part in all states covering contracts for the sale or lease of goods, negotiable instruments, security interests in personal property and other commercial transactions.

Creditors often require debtors to pledge their **personal property** to secure a loan or other financial obligation. The creation and enforcement of a security interest in personal property is governed by Article 9 of the **Uniform Commercial Code (UCC)**, which has been adopted in slightly differing versions by all 50 states.

We call the pledging of a security interest in personal property a **secured transaction**. When personal property is pledged to secure debt, it is referred to as the **collateral** or the **secured property** or the **pledged property**. The creditor to whom the collateral is pledged is called a **secured creditor** or the **secured party** and the debt itself may be referred to as a **secured debt**.

The various rules laid out in Article 9 do *not* control other ways of securing a debt that we considered in Chapter Four: personal guaranties, surety obligations, or the mortgaging of real property. Article 9 does *not* control nonconsensual statutory liens that may be declared in property, which we will consider in Chapter Six. It *does* control the consensual pledge of most kinds of personal property to secure both consumer and commercial debt.

EXAMPLE

> When Nick and Pearl Murphy bought their living room furniture from Shears and arranged to pay for it over 48 months, Shears retained a security interest in the furniture to secure payment of the purchase price (see Illustration 5-a). The living room furniture is considered consumer goods since it is for personal, family, or household use. This is a secured consumer debt and the security interest retained by Shears is controlled by Article 9.

EXAMPLE

> You will recall that Tomorrow Today, Inc. (TTI) from Case Study #3 (Illustration 1-c) took out a $7.5 million line of credit loan with Bank of Europa (BE) in connection with the MIES project. To obtain the loan TTI was required to pledge most of the corporate assets, including *equipment, inventory, furnishings, cash on hand, bank accounts, and accounts receivable*. This is a secured commercial debt and the security interest retained by BE in the personal property mentioned is controlled by Article 9.

P-H 5-a: Do you understand why security arrangements like surety arrangements, personal guarantees, and mortgages are not controlled by Article 9? Do you understand that, although they are not controlled by Article 9, sureties, personal guaranties, and mortgages are still ways of securing repayment of debt? Do you understand why we consider TTI's debt to BE to be a secured commercial debt and the Murphy's debt to Shears to be secured consumer debt?

B. Creating a Security Interest in Personal Property

In order to create a security interest in personal property, Article 9 requires the following:

- that the debtor have *ownership rights* in the collateral that he can legally pledge to the secured party

EXAMPLE

> Each of the TTI shareholders can pledge their own shares of stock to the BE to secure the line of credit granted TTI, but none of them could pledge the shares of another shareholder; they have no ownership rights in the others' stock.

- that the secured party give *something of value* (consideration, as in contract law) to the debtor in exchange for the security interest

EXAMPLE

> Aunt Shirley promises her nephew that she will pay for his college education and wants to grant him a security interest in her antique collection to secure the promise. Sorry, Aunt Shirley. This is a gift promise and the recipient, her nephew, who would be the secured party, is not being asked to give anything of value in exchange for the promise. It won't work.

- that there be a *written security agreement signed by the debtor* that contains a *description of the collateral* sufficient to reasonably identify it.

Security agreements and debtor signatures stored in an electronic medium (e.g., an e-mail message or word processing file) that can be *authenticated* (established as genuine) are also enforceable.

P-H 5-b: Which part of the security agreement in Illustration 5-a describes the collateral? Is the description there sufficient to reasonably identify the collateral? Which part of Illustration 5-a actually grants the security interest in the collateral to Shears? Would the court enforce the security interest pledged by Nick and Pearl Murphy in Illustration 5-a if Shears did not sign the security agreement?

As an alternative to the third requirement—that there be a written or authenticated security agreement signed by the debtor and describing the collateral—Article 9 allows the creation of a security interest by verbal agreement, but only as to collateral held in the possession of the secured party.

EXAMPLE

> Assume that when TTI's line of credit with BE is fully disbursed, TTI cannot repay it. BE then verbally agrees to extend the repayment time if the three shareholders of TTI will pledge their TTI stock as further security for the debt. The shareholders verbally agree and deliver the stock certificates representing their shareholder interests in TTI to BE. Once the stock certificates are in the possession of BE, an effective security interest in the stock has been created.

P-H 5-c: In the last example, what value (the second requirement discussed above) did BE give to the TTI shareholders to support the pledge of the stock as collateral? Though the courts will enforce a verbal security agreement when the collateral is in the possession of the secured party, can you think of reasons why it would be preferable for that agreement to be reduced to writing anyway?

When a security interest is properly created in the collateral, we say that the secured interest *attaches* to the collateral. The security agreement between Shears Department Store and Nick and Pearl Murphy is shown in Illustration 5-a.

C. ▶ The Scope of a Security Interest in Personal Property: The Floating Lien

1. Proceeds

Article 9 provides that the security interest granted in collateral extends not only to the named collateral itself, but also to the **proceeds** of that collateral.

EXAMPLE

> In the security agreement between TTI and BE, TTI pledges all its equipment to BE as collateral for the line of credit loan. TTI later sells a piece of equipment pledged to BE and receives money for that sold equipment. If TTI then defaults on repayment and BE seizes the pledged collateral, can it seize the money received for the sold equipment? Yes, because the money is proceeds of the pledged equipment and also subject to BE's security interest. Another way to say this is that the security interest of BE **attached** to the money as soon as it was in the possession of TTI as the proceeds of the sold equipment.

Illustration 5-a: SECURITY AGREEMENT BETWEEN NICK AND PEARL MURPHY AND SHEARS

Installment Sale and Security Agreement

This Agreement is made and entered into this 10th day of May, YR-1, by and between Shears Department Store (Seller) and Nicholas W. Murphy and wife, Pearl E. Murphy (Buyers) who reside at 3521 West Cherry Street, Capitol City, Columbiana. The Seller agrees to sell and the Buyers agree to buy the following, here-inafter referred to as the Merchandise, on the terms set forth in this Agreement:

> 1 Comfort Tone couch ($2,499); 2 Comfort Tone Spread Eagle Chairs @$550 each ($1,100); 1 Comfort Tone Loveseat ($950); 1 American Federal Coffee Table ($350); 2 American Federal End Tables @$200 each ($400).

1. **Price and Payment**. The total net purchase price of the Merchandise is $5,299. Buyers, having elected to pay for the Merchandise in installments as set forth in this Agreement, agree to pay Seller or its assigns the time price of the Merchandise which is $6,122.40 in 48 equal monthly installments at Seller's offices at P.O. Box 22234 Atlanta, GA. 404456 or at any other address which Seller may direct in writing delivered to Buyers. The time price of the Merchandise represents the net purchase price paid over 48 monthly installments at an annual percentage rate of 7%.

Payable in 48 consecutive monthly installments of $127.55 each, except the last installment shall be the balance due.

First installment due June 1, YR-1 and each subsequent installment due on the first day of the following month.

2. **Warranties**. No representations or statements have been made by Seller concerning the Merchandise except as stated in this Agreement, and no warranty, express or implied, by Seller, arises apart from this writing. Buyers warrant that the Merchandise is purchased for use primarily for personal, family, or household purposes.

3. **Retention of security interest**. Until all installment payments, and all other amounts due under this Agreement, have been paid, Seller shall retain a security interest in the Merchandise and any and all equipment, parts, accessories, attachments, additions, and other Merchandise, and all replacements of them, installed in, affixed to, or used in connection with the Merchandise and, if Buyers sell or otherwise dispose of the Merchandise or any portion of it in violation of the terms of this Agreement, in the proceeds of such sale or disposition.

4. **Events of default**. The occurrence of any of the following shall constitute a default under this Agreement: (1) failure of Buyers to perform any obligation or Agreement specified in this Agreement, or if any warranty or representation made under this Agreement by Buyers should prove to be materially incorrect; (2) the sale or other transfer of title to the Merchandise by Buyers including the granting of any security interest in the Merchandise by Buyers without the prior written consent of Seller; (3) the institution of any proceeding in bankruptcy, receivership or insolvency against Buyers; (4) the issuance of execution process against any property of Buyers or the entry of any judgment against Buyers or any assignment for benefit of creditors; (5) when Seller shall in good faith and upon reasonable grounds believe that the prospect of performance of any obligation of Buyers under this Agreement, or of performance or payment of any obligation secured by this Agreement, by Buyers is materially diminished.

5. **Remedies on default**. In the event of a default, or if Seller or Seller's assignee shall consider the payment of the balance of the installment payments insecure, Seller shall have the right to: (1) obtain judgment for the amount of the installments delinquent under the Agreement plus interest at 6% on such delinquent payments

from due date and reasonable attorney's fees without prejudicing Seller's right to subsequently obtain judgment for additional, or the balance of, the installments or to exercise other rights contained in this Agreement or at its option, declare all unpaid installments and other moneys due or to become due under this Agreement immediately due and payable and to obtain judgment for the total amount of unpaid installments due plus interest of 6% on delinquent payments from due date and reasonable attorney's fees; (2) enter any premises and without breach of the peace take possession of the Merchandise; and (3) exercise the rights on default of a secured party under the Uniform Commercial Code. Seller shall have the right to take immediate possession of the Merchandise wherever found, with or without legal process, and to sell or otherwise dispose of the Merchandise. Unless the Merchandise is perishable or threatens to decline speedily in value or is of a type customarily sold on a recognized market, Seller will give Buyers at least five days notice by mail of the time and place of any public sale of the Merchandise or the time after which any private sale or other intended disposition is to be made. The requirements of reasonable notice shall be met if such notice is mailed, postage prepaid, to the address of the Buyers shown at the beginning of this Agreement or such other address of Buyers as may from time to time be shown on Seller's records, at least five days prior to such action. Buyers will pay any deficiency that may remain after exercise of such rights plus expenses of retaking, holding, preparing for sale, selling, or the like, including Seller's reasonable attorney's fees. All of Seller's rights under this Agreement are cumulative and no waiver of any default shall affect any later default.

6. **Miscellaneous terms and provisions**. (1) Loss or damage to the Merchandise will not release Buyers. (2) Repairs to the Merchandise and equipment or accessories placed on the Merchandise shall be at Buyers' expense and shall constitute component parts of the Merchandise, subject to the terms of this Agreement. (3) If any part of this Agreement is adjudged invalid, the remainder will not be invalidated by this. (4) Seller may assign this Agreement but Buyers shall not. Seller's assignee shall have all of the rights, powers and remedies of Seller but shall be subject to none of Seller's obligations. (5) Buyers will not assert against any assignee of this Agreement any defense which Buyers may have against Seller. (6) If there be more than one signer of this Agreement, their obligations shall be joint and several and each specifically waive presentment or demand and agree that any extension or extensions of time of payment of this Agreement or any installment or part installment may be made before, at or after maturity by Agreement with any one or more of the parties, and they waive any right which they may have to require the holder to proceed against any person. (7) This Agreement will be governed by the laws of the State of Columbiana, and all obligations of Buyers shall bind their heirs, executor, administrator or successors.

7. **Exclusive statement of Agreement**. This writing contains the full, final, and exclusive statement of the Agreement between the parties and no Agreement or warranty shall be binding on the Seller unless expressly contained in it.

_____

Nicholas W. Murphy

_____

Pearl E. Murphy

Shears Department Store, Inc.

By: _____

Wally Cousins, V-P

EXAMPLE

> What if TTI swaps the equipment pledged as collateral to BE for new equipment instead of receiving money for the pledged equipment? Does BE's security interest attach to the new equipment? Yes, because the new equipment will be considered proceeds of the pledged equipment. Proceeds do not have to be money.

Although the security agreement often specifies that the proceeds of pledged collateral are also subject to the creditor's security interest, it doesn't have to. Article 9 provides for the **automatic attachment** of the security interest to proceeds whether that is stated in the security agreement or not.

2. After-acquired Property

After-acquired property is property the debtor acquires *after* the security agreement has been executed. Article 9 authorizes the security agreement to provide that the creditor's security interest will attach to **after acquired property** as soon as the debtor acquires an interest in it, and no new or additional security agreement needs to be executed to accomplish that attachment.

EXAMPLE

> Assume the security agreement between TTI and BE contains the language you see in Illustration 5-b. Now assume that after executing the security agreement, TTI purchases a brand new piece of equipment to use in its business. The new piece of equipment is not the proceeds of any previously pledged property. Is the new piece of equipment subject to BE's security interest? Yes, because of the "hereafter" phrases in the security agreement in Illustration 5-b.

Article 9 allows a security interest to cover after-acquired property of the debtor, *only if* the security agreement specifically provides for it. It is not an automatic attachment as in the case of proceeds.

3. Future Advances

Article 9 allows a security agreement to secure debt other than the debt existing at the time the agreement is entered into—that is, to **future advances** of credit.

Illustration 5-b: AFTER-ACQUIRED PROPERTY LANGUAGE IN A SECURITY AGREEMENT

---

2. Debtor (TTI) grants to Secured Party (BE) a security interest in all inventory, equipment, appliances, furnishings, and fixtures now or hereafter placed upon any business premises utilized by Debtor or used in connection with Debtor's business and in which Debtor now has or hereafter acquires any ownership interest.

EXAMPLE

> When TTI took out its line of credit with BE and signed the security agreement pledging various personal property as collateral to secure the line of credit, it had not yet drawn down on the line of credit. In other words, it hadn't actually borrowed a penny from BE at the time it signed the security agreement. Yet the contemplation of the agreement was that TTI would, *in the future*, draw down on the line of credit and so the security interest previously given would then be effective to secure repayment.

EXAMPLE

> Assume that the security agreement between TTI and BE contains the paragraph shown in Illustration 5-c. Assume further that TTI pays off its borrowings under the line of credit with BE. Five years later, BE merges with Bank of North America (BNA). A year after that TTI takes out a $10 million loan from BNA secured, TTI thinks, only by a mortgage TTI gives BNA. TTI then defaults on the debt to BNA and is surprised when BNA acts to repossess all the personal property TTI pledged to BE all those years ago. Can BNA do that? You bet. It is the "successor" to BE, and the security agreement between BE and TTI effectively pledged the personal property as security—not just for the BE line of credit, but all future debts TTI might ever owe to BE or its successors.

Like after-acquired property clauses, **future advances clauses** must be specifically set out in the security agreement to be effective. Future advances clauses are common and very dangerous to the unsuspecting, unsophisticated borrower. Moreover, future advances clauses are commonly used, not just in security agreements, but in other contracts evidencing debt, such as promissory notes, mortgages, and guaranty agreements.

P-H 5-d: Assume the Murphys pay off their debt to Shears for the purchase of the living room furniture that is secured by that furniture. But later they run up other unsecured charges to Shears and are unable to pay. Shears wants to repossess the furniture in satisfaction of those later debts. Look at paragraph 3 of Illustration 5-a. Does that security agreement contain a future advances clause? Can Shears repossess the furniture now?

Illustration 5-c: FUTURE ADVANCES CLAUSE IN A SECURITY AGREEMENT

> 3. The security interest granted by Debtor (TTI) to Secured Party (BE) in Paragraph 2 of this Agreement shall secure all advances made by Secured Party under the line of credit referenced herein and any and all other indebtedness that Debtor now owes or shall ever owe to Secured Party, its successors, and assigns, directly or as guarantor or co-signer, and any and all other liability that Debtor now has or shall ever have to Secured Party, its successors, and assigns.

P-H 5-e: Assume that David Mendoza pays off the loan he took from City County Bank (CCB) (the loan for which his parents signed the personal guaranty in Illustration 4-a). Ten years after paying off that loan, David takes another loan from CCB, this one in the amount of $1 million, and fails to repay that second loan. His parents do not sign a new guaranty for the second loan but, nonetheless, CCB sues them on the guaranty for the first, paid-off loan. Look at paragraph 2 of the personal guaranty in Illustration 4-a and decide if CCB can do that.

P-H 5-f: Does either the promissory note signed by the Murphys to borrow money to buy their house (Illustration 2-a) or the mortgage they gave on the house to secure that note (Illustration 4-b) contain a future advances clause?

The concept of a security interest in collateral extending to proceeds of the collateral, to after-acquired property, or to future advances is sometimes referred to as the *floating lien* concept of security law. In each situation, the security interest granted moves or floats from one item of property to another or from one debt to another.

D. ▶ Perfecting a Security Interest in Personal Property: Priority Issues

In Chapter Four we addressed the question of plural mortgages and which of two or more mortgagees had *priority* when foreclosure on the mortgaged realty occurred. The same question arises in connection with security interests in personal property. It is very common for more than one creditor to hold a security interest in personal property.

EXAMPLE

> Recall from Illustration 1-c that TTI borrowed twice against its personal property. It obtained a $10 million dollar line of credit from its primary lender, United Bank of America (UBA), pledging most of its assets as security for the loan. After exhausting that line of credit as well as all its cash, TTI obtained a $7.5 million line of credit from BE and pledged the same assets as security for that loan as well.

We have assumed that BE's security interest in TTI's personal property is *second* or *junior* to the security interest of UBA because UBA's security interest was created first in time. If that is true, then when TTI defaults on both obligations, UBA, holding the first or senior security interest position in the collateral, will be able to repossess the collateral, sell it, and apply all the proceeds to satisfy the debt owed to it, plus expenses. Only if the proceeds of the sale are adequate to satisfy all of TTI's obligations to UBA will the balance be applied to satisfy TTI's debt to BE.

But as with mortgages in real estate, the first creditor to take a security interest in personal property is not necessarily first in priority. To determine if UBA's

Illustration 5-d: ARTICLE 9 RULES OF PRIORITY BETWEEN COMPETING SECURED CLAIMS

- If neither of the security interests is perfected, the first security interest to attach (be created) will have priority.
- If one security interest is perfected and the other is not, the perfected security interest has priority over the unperfected security interest, regardless of which was the first to attach.
- If both security interests are perfected, the first to perfect has priority regardless of the first to attach.

Perfected Making a security interest in property enforceable against and superior to the claims of other creditors to the property.

security interest is in fact senior to BE's we have to determine if either security interest was **perfected** and, if both were, which was perfected first. Illustration 5-d sets out the Article 9 rules for priority between competing secured claims in the same property.

Be careful not to confuse the concept of *attachment* with the concept of *perfection* when considering security interests in personal property. Attachment has to do with whether a security interest is properly created under Article 9. If so, the creditor's security claim attaches to the collateral at that point in time. But as the Article 9 priority rules (Illustration 5-d) indicate, when a security interest attaches is not the final word as to whether it has priority over other security interests in the property. To determine priority of the attached claims, we ask which security interest was first to perfect.

1. Perfection by Filing a Financing Statement

Financing statement A document filed in a designated public office to perfect a security interest in personal property under Article 9 of the UCC.

The most common method of perfecting a security interest in personal property is by the filing of a **financing statement** (also called a **UCC-1** because the financing statement form is suggested by the drafters of the UCC and identified by them as the first suggested form). You can see a financing statement form in Illustration 5-e.

Article 9 requires that the financing statement provide the name of both the debtor and the creditor and describe the collateral pledged in the security agreement. Once completed, the financing statement is *filed* in the appropriate government office (either *centrally*, with a state official such as a secretary of state, or *locally*, with a county official such as the registrar of deeds). Filing can be done by paper form or electronically. Once the financing statement is properly completed and filed, the creditor's secured claim in the named collateral is perfected.

Financing statements are indexed in the name of the debtor by the government office where they are filed and, as public records, can be seen by subsequent searchers submitting a **search request** to the office. A financing statement is usually valid for five years from the date of filing and can be renewed by the filing of a **continuation statement** within six months preceding the expiration of the five year term. If a continuation statement is not timely filed, the perfection (and priority) obtained by the original filing of the financing statement is lost, but that does not affect the attachment of the security interest to the collateral.

Illustration 5-e: A FINANCING STATEMENT (UCC-1)

UCC FINANCING STATEMENT
FOLLOW INSTRUCTIONS (front and back) CAREFULLY

A. NAME & PHONE OF CONTACT AT FILER [optional]

B. SEND ACKNOWLEDGMENT TO: (Name and Address)

THE ABOVE SPACE IS FOR FILING OFFICE USE ONLY

1. DEBTOR'S EXACT FULL LEGAL NAME - insert only <u>one</u> debtor name (1a or 1b) - do not abbreviate or combine names

1a. ORGANIZATION'S NAME			

OR

1b. INDIVIDUAL'S LAST NAME	FIRST NAME	MIDDLE NAME	SUFFIX

1c. MAILING ADDRESS	CITY	STATE	POSTAL CODE	COUNTRY

1d. <u>SEE INSTRUCTIONS</u>	ADD'L INFO RE ORGANIZATION DEBTOR	1e. TYPE OF ORGANIZATION	1f. JURISDICTION OF ORGANIZATION	1g. ORGANIZATIONAL ID #, if any	☐ NONE

2. ADDITIONAL DEBTOR'S EXACT FULL LEGAL NAME - insert only <u>one</u> debtor name (2a or 2b) - do not abbreviate or combine names

2a. ORGANIZATION'S NAME			

OR

2b. INDIVIDUAL'S LAST NAME	FIRST NAME	MIDDLE NAME	SUFFIX

2c. MAILING ADDRESS	CITY	STATE	POSTAL CODE	COUNTRY

2d. <u>SEE INSTRUCTIONS</u>	ADD'L INFO RE ORGANIZATION DEBTOR	2e. TYPE OF ORGANIZATION	2f. JURISDICTION OF ORGANIZATION	2g. ORGANIZATIONAL ID #, if any	☐ NONE

3. SECURED PARTY'S NAME (or NAME of TOTAL ASSIGNEE of ASSIGNOR S/P) - insert only <u>one</u> secured party name (3a or 3b)

3a. ORGANIZATION'S NAME			

OR

3b. INDIVIDUAL'S LAST NAME	FIRST NAME	MIDDLE NAME	SUFFIX

3c. MAILING ADDRESS	CITY	STATE	POSTAL CODE	COUNTRY

4. This FINANCING STATEMENT covers the following collateral:

5. ALTERNATIVE DESIGNATION [if applicable]: ☐ LESSEE/LESSOR ☐ CONSIGNEE/CONSIGNOR ☐ BAILEE/BAILOR ☐ SELLER/BUYER ☐ AG. LIEN ☐ NON-UCC FILING

6. ☐ This FINANCING STATEMENT is to be filed [for record] (or recorded) in the REAL ESTATE RECORDS.   Attach Addendum   [if applicable]
7. Check to REQUEST SEARCH REPORT(S) on Debtor(s) [ADDITIONAL FEE]   [optional]   ☐ All Debtors ☐ Debtor 1 ☐ Debtor 2

8. OPTIONAL FILER REFERENCE DATA

FILING OFFICE COPY — UCC FINANCING STATEMENT (FORM UCC1) (REV. 05/22/02)   International Association of Commercial Administrators (IACA)

2. Perfection by Creditor Possession

Article 9 provides that a security interest in collateral kept in the possession of the creditor is automatically perfected without the need of filing a financing statement covering such collateral. We have already seen that a security interest can be created (attach) by creditor possession; now we see that such a security interest can further be perfected by creditor possession.

EXAMPLE

> Assume that when TTI obtained the $10 million line of credit from UBA five years ago UBA required the three shareholders to pledge their stock in TTI as additional security for the line of credit. Assume that when the shareholders made that pledge to UBA, UBA took possession of the stock certificates and no mention was made of them in the financing statement that UBA filed covering the remaining collateral. Later, when TTI obtained the second line of credit from BE, BE also required that the shares of stock be pledged and specifically mentioned them in the financing statement it filed though it did not have possession of them. When TTI defaults on both obligations, which bank has first claim to the shares of stock? UBA does because it was perfected in the stock by possession prior to BE's perfection by filing the financing statement.

P-H 5-g: Stock certificates are a good example of the kind of property that can be pledged as collateral and left with the creditor. Business inventory is an example of property that would almost never be left with the creditor because the business needs it to operate. What other kinds of property can you think of in which a debtor might grant a security interest but leave in the possession of the creditor?

3. Automatic Perfection by Attachment Only: The Purchase Money Security Interest (PMSI) in Consumer Goods

For a very few kinds of property, Article 9 provides that the secured creditor's interest in the collateral will be perfected at the same moment that it attaches; nothing further needs to be done to perfect the interest. The most important example of this automatic perfection by attachment only is the **purchase money security interest (PMSI)** in **consumer goods**.

Purchase money security interest (PMSI) A security interest in personal property created by loaning or extending credit to a debtor for the express purpose of purchasing the property.

Consumer goods are those purchased primarily for personal, family, or household use. A purchase-money security interest in consumer goods is recognized where the creditor has either 1) sold the debtor the consumer goods on credit or 2) loaned the debtor the funds to purchase the consumer goods. If the agreement between the parties is that the creditor is to have a security interest in the consumer goods to secure payment of the credit granted or repayment of the loan made, the creditor is **automatically perfected** in those goods at the time they are purchased. No financing statement is needed, no recording or filing is made, and there is no possession by the creditor.

EXAMPLE

Look again at the installment sale and security agreement between the Murphys and Shears Department Store in Illustration 5-a. In that transaction, what is being purchased is living room furniture. Those will be consumer goods because they were purchased for personal, family, and household use. Shears was the seller of the goods and is extending the Murphys credit over 48 months to pay for consumer goods purchased. This is a classic PMSI in consumer goods. The result is that the security interest that Shears is retaining in the furniture to secure payment of the extended credit will be automatically perfected when the Murphys sign the agreement, which is the same moment when the security interest is created or attaches. And Shears need not file a financing statement or take possession of the furniture to perfect its security interest in the furniture.

EXAMPLE

If the Murphys went to Friendly Finance Company (FFC) and took out a loan to purchase the Shears living room furniture and FFC retained a security interest in the furniture purchased with its loan to secure repayment that would also be an example of a PMSI in consumer goods. FFC would be secured and its security interest in the furniture perfected as soon as the loan agreement is made and the furniture is purchased from Shears by the Murphys.

4. Perfecting a Security Interest in Titled Vehicles

Most states have special statutes outside of Article 9 dealing with the creation and perfection of security interests in titled vehicles (e.g., automobiles, trucks, boats, motorcycles, and, in some states, trailers, and farm vehicles, such as tractors and hay bailers). When vehicles that have a **document of title** issued by the state reflecting ownership are pledged as collateral for a debt, the security interest of the creditor is *noted on the title* itself. Illustration 5-f shows the title of a vehicle owned by Nick and Pearl Murphy, which is pledged as collateral to Friendly Finance Company (FFC) to secure repayment of a loan the Murphys secured to purchase the vehicle.

The creditor holding the security interest in a titled vehicle will typically retain possession of the title until the secured debt is paid in full. Then the creditor will note the satisfaction of the debt and release of the security interest on the title before returning the title to the owner. At that point, the owner of the vehicle has free and clear title to it.

Electronic vehicle titling (E-Title) System for registering vehicles with the state electronically pursuant to which no paper title issued unless requested.

Many states are now adopting **electronic vehicle titling** (usually called **E-Title**) systems where no paper title is issued unless requested. The record of title ownership, as well as lien records (**Electronic Lien Title** or **ELT**), is maintained electronically by the state division of motor vehicles or other licensing agency.

EXAMPLE

Florida has been a leader in the movement to electronic vehicle titling. Take a look at its Web site detailing the program at www.hsmv.state.fl.us/html/emt.htm, and then determine if your state has adopted electronic vehicle titling.

Illustration 5-f: DOCUMENT OF TITLE FOR AUTOMOBILE REFLECTING THE SECURITY INTEREST OF CREDITOR

STATE OF COLUMBIANA

CERTIFICATE OF TITLE

Vehicle Identification Number	Year	Make	Model	Body Type	Title Number
1HC44XXXXWA222X	YR-5	Honda	Accord	4D	656XX421

New/Used/Demo	Previous Title No.	Prev. State	Sale or Use Tax	County	Odometer
X	637YY809	None	$47.50	CC	25,397

Date Title Issued: 8-10-YR-3
Date Vehicle Acquired: 8-07-YR-3
Owner: Nicholas W. Murphy and wife, Pearl E. Murphy,
   JT's w/right survivorship
   3521West Cherry Street
   Capitol City, CM 55512

SATISFACTORY PROOF OF OWNERSHIP HAVING BEEN SUBMITTED UNDER COMLUMBIANA CODE §55-3-101, TITLE TO THE MOTOR VEHICLE DESCRIBED ABOVE IS VESTED IN THE OWNER'S NAME HEREIN SUBJECT TO ANY LIEN NOTED BELOW. THIS OFFICIAL CERTIFICATE OF TITLE IS ISSUED FOR SAID VEHICLE.

NOTATION OF LIEN

The vehicle described above is subject to a lien in favor of Friendly Finance Company ("lienholder"), of 114 Commerce Drive, Capitol City, Columbiana as of the 1st day of July, YR-3 to satisfy an indebtedness in the amount of $12,500. Columbiana Statutory Code §55-3-104 provides that upon satisfaction of a lien, the lienholder will within seventy-two (72) hours complete the space provided on this certificate for satisfaction of lien, detach and mail the certificate with completed satisfaction of lien to the Columbiana Department of Safety, Title and Registration Division, 44 Capitol Plaza, Suite 111, Columbiana, CM 55589.

SATISFACTION AND RELEASE OF LIEN

Lienholder, _____, pursuant to Columbiana Statutory Code §55-3-104, hereby gives notice of the satisfaction in full of the indebtedness for which a lien was granted on the vehicle described above. Lienholder hereby releases said lien effective the _____ day of _____, YR _____.

_____
Lienholder

E. ► The Right of a Debtor to Dispose of Secured Property

Commonly, the promissory note, mortgage agreement regarding real property, or security agreement covering personal property will forbid the debtor from selling any property subject to the mortgage or security interest without the prior, written consent of the creditor.

EXAMPLE

Look at paragraph 4 of the Installment Sale and Security Agreement between the Murphys and Shears Department Store in Illustration 5-a. Can the Murphys sell, pledge, or give away the furniture without Shears's consent? Look at paragraph 8 of the Mortgage between the Murphys and FBCC (Illustration 4-b). Can the Murphys sell their house or take a second mortgage on it without the mortgagee's consent?

If the debtor does sell the property in violation of the note, mortgage, or security agreement, an issue arises as to whether the buyer of the property from the debtor has taken the property **free and clear** of the mortgage or security interest or whether the property is taken still **subject to** the mortgage or security interest in the hands of the buyer.

EXAMPLE

If the Murphys sell to you the furniture pledged to Shears and then default on the payments to Shears, can Shears repossess the furniture from you even though you owe no debt to Shears? Did you buy the property from the Murphys subject to the security interest of Shears or free and clear of it? If the Murphys sell their house to you and then default on the mortgage payments to FBCC, can the bank foreclose on the house and put you out? Did you buy the house subject to the mortgage or free and clear of it?

The first question to ask in such situations is whether the security interest at issue was *perfected by filing* at the time of the sale by the debtor. If we are talking about the sale of real property and the mortgage was properly filed according to the state's recording statute, any subsequent buyer is charged with **constructive notice** of the mortgage interest and buys the property subject to it. If we are talking about personal property and perfection was achieved by the proper filing of a financing statement, the result is the same: the buyer is charged with constructive notice of the security interest and buys subject to it. There is, however, one important exception to this result, and that is where the buyer purchases the property in the **ordinary course of business** of the debtor/seller.

Ordinary course of business In general, following the typical usual practices engaged in by a business.

EXAMPLE

Assume a retail shoe store purchases pairs of shoes on credit from a supplier and grants the supplier a security interest in its inventory (the shoes) and that security interest is perfected by filing. The shoe store will, in the ordinary course of its business, sell shoes to customers. Under Article 9, the customers purchase the shoes free and clear of the supplier's perfected security interest in the shoes and that would be true even if the buyers had actual and not just constructive notice of the perfected security interest of the supplier.

Why the ordinary course of business exception? Because everyone involved in the transaction understands and foresees that inventories will be sold. The security agreement between the shoe store and the supplier will not prohibit the resale of the shoes by the shoe store because resale is foreseeable and anticipated.

Buyers of consumer goods from debtors who have pledged those goods as collateral will also take free and clear of the secured party's claim when the secured party is unperfected or where the perfection is by attachment only, as in the case of a PMSI. To do so, the buyer must:

- give value (pay something for the goods as opposed to receiving them as a gift),
- in good faith have no actual knowledge of the security interest in the goods, and
- purchase the goods for consumer use (personal, family, or household).

EXAMPLE

Assume that Shears does not file a financing statement in connection with the Murphys' pledge of the furniture to Shears. As we have already noted, since the furniture is consumer goods, Shears is perfected in the furniture by PMSI attachment only. But now assume that the Murphys sell the furniture to you in good faith and you have no actual knowledge of Shears' security interest. If you bought the furniture for consumer use yourself, you bought it free and clear of Shears' interest. Even if the Murphys now default, Shears cannot repossess from you.

This consumer goods rule allows a freer transfer of consumer goods. However, even with regard to consumer goods, if the secured party has perfected its security interest in the goods by filing, the resulting constructive notice will mean the buyer takes the property subject to the creditor's continuing security interest in it.

EXAMPLE

If Shears does file a financing statement in connection with the Murphys' pledge of the furniture and you then purchase the furniture from the Murphys, you will take the property, subject to Shears's right to repossess from you upon default by the Murphys.

F. ▶ Rights of the Secured Party on Default

What happens when a debtor who has pledged personal property as security for a debt defaults on the obligation?

1. Repossession of the Collateral

The security agreement will typically give the creditor the right to **repossess** the collateral upon default. That means the creditor can come and take possession of the property and may do so without filing any lawsuit or obtaining a judgment against the debtor. The debtor has consented to this repossession in the security agreement.

EXAMPLE

> Look at paragraph 5 of the Installment Sale and Security Agreement between the Murphys and Shears Department Store in Illustration 5-a.

Because the debtor has consented to the creditor coming and taking the pledged property, this right is sometimes called the right to **self-help repossession**. Of course, the secured party can only repossess property that was pledged in the security agreement. No other assets of the debtor are subject to the security interest.

EXAMPLE

> If the Murphys default on the note to FFC secured by the pledged vehicle (Illustration 5-f), FFC can repossess the vehicle by self-help but has no right to seize other assets of the Murphys.

Don't confuse the secured creditor's right to repossess pledged collateral with the unsecured creditor's right to sue the debtor, obtain a final court judgment, and then execute on the debtor's property, which we will consider. And as we learned in Chapter Four with regard to mortgages in real property, if the repossession and sale of pledged personal property leaves a deficiency still owing to the secured creditor, that creditor can also sue and obtain a judgment for the deficiency, then execute on other assets of the debtor to satisfy the judgment.

EXAMPLE

> If FFC repossesses the vehicle pledged as security for the Murphys' loan and the vehicle does not bring enough at sale to cover the debt, CCB might sue the Murphys for the deficiency, obtain a judgment, and then execute on the judgment against other assets of the Murphys.

There are some limits on the creditor's right to effect self-help repossession. The creditor cannot break and enter the debtor's home or business to seize the property; that would be a criminal act. The creditor can, however, come on the debtor's property in a legal fashion to take the property and is not guilty of civil or criminal trespassing to do so.

EXAMPLE

> If the Murphys default in payment of their loan from FFC secured by the automobile as in Illustration 5-f, FFC may send agents to go on the Murphys' property in the middle of the night, start the car, and drive it off. However, if the Murphys have placed the car in a locked garage, the agents probably could not break the lock or break down the door to get the car without being liable in tort for the property damage done, and they could possibly be prosecuted for criminal trespass or breaking and entering.

EXAMPLE

> If TTI defaults on its line of credit loan with UBA for repayment of which it has pledged most of its business assets, UBA may essentially lock up the TTI offices as a means of seizing the assets inside. The door to the business premises may be chained, for example, and a notice posted that the goods inside are in the legal possession of the creditor and not to be moved without the creditor's permission. UBA would have to allow removal of any assets not pledged to it.

The secured creditor is also prohibited from committing or threatening a **breach of the peace** in the course of repossession.

EXAMPLE

> If agents of FFC come to repossess the Murphys' vehicle and Nick Murphy is standing in front of it with a baseball bat telling them they'll take the car over his dead body, the FFC's agents cannot overwhelm and restrain him or threaten the use of any force at all. They must retreat.

If the secured creditor is unable to peacefully repossess the collateral from the debtor's possession, the creditor will file a lawsuit asking for a judgment in their favor as to their rights under the security agreement and for a court order, usually called a **writ of possession**, directing the sheriff to enforce the writ by taking possession of the collateral. Illustration 5-g shows a writ of possession form. If the debtor unlawfully resists the sheriff in the execution of the writ, she will be arrested and prosecuted. When the secured creditor resorts to the assistance of the court in enforcing its rights in the collateral, the creditor is utilizing **judicial repossession** rather than self-help repossession.

2. Disposition of the Repossessed Collateral

Once the creditor has repossessed the collateral, it can either keep the property in satisfaction of the obligation or sell it and apply to proceeds to the debt. Most frequently the creditor elects to sell the property and may do so by **public sale** or **private sale**.

A public sale will typically be conducted by **auction**, advertised in advance. Often the advertisement will appear in the classified ad section of local newspapers and will be described as a **repossession sale** or **judicial sale** or **sheriff's sale**, if judicial repossession was utilized. Parties involved in a repossession sale may refer to it as a **distress sale** because the goods often bring in less because of the circumstances in which they are being offered for sale and the repossessing seller's eagerness to dispose of them. Goods sold at such a sale are referred to as **distressed goods**.

In a private sale, the creditor locates one or more private buyers and negotiates a purchase price with them. The public is not notified and the sale is not advertised, though the debtor and creditors holding junior liens in the collateral must be notified, as discussed in the next subsection.

A repossessing creditor who decides to keep the property in satisfaction of the debt cannot arbitrarily attach any value it wants to the collateral.

Distress sale The sale of property in an emergency or time-pressured context as where a financially strapped debtor sells to raise cash to pay debts or where a secured creditor repossesses collateral and sells it quickly to compensate himself.

Distressed goods Goods sold at a distress sale.

Illustration 5-g: WRIT OF POSSESSION FORM FOR USE IN A JUDICIAL REPOSSESSION ACTION

IN THE CIRCUIT COURT
FOR CAPITOL COUNTY, COLUMBIANA

_____   )
Plaintiff(s)   )
)
     v.   )   Docket No._____
)
)
_____   )
Defendant(s)   )

WRIT OF POSSESSION

TO THE SHERIFF OF SAID COUNTY:

Pursuant to the Order entered by the Honorable _____, Judge of the _____ Court on the _____ day of _____, YR00, you are commanded to take with you the force of the County, if necessary, and take possession from _____

located at

_____

and give to

_____

peaceable possession of the following described property:

_____
_____
_____

and make immediate return to the Court as to how, where and when you have executed this Writ.

ISSUED: _____, YR-1

BY: _____

Clerk of the Court

SHERIFF'S RETURN

Came to hand same day issued and executed as commanded on

_____

by

_____

at

_____

This _____ day of _____, YR-1.

_____
Deputy Sheriff

> When FFC repossesses the Murphys' vehicle, it may decide to keep the car for corporate use in satisfaction of the debt. But what if the vehicle is worth $10,000 and the total debt owed is only $3,000? The law will not permit such a windfall to a creditor.

Nor can the repossessing secured creditor sell the property for any price it wants.

> When FFC repossess the Murphys' vehicle, it may decide to sell it. But what if FFC sells the car to the bank president's son for $1,000, when it is worth $10,000, and then sues the Murphys for the difference in the $1,000 sale price and the $3,000 owed? The law will not permit that injustice.

Commercially reasonable manner The standard governing the creditor's sale of repossessed property.

Article 9 provides that the repossessing creditor choosing to sell the collateral must dispose of it in a **commercially reasonable manner**. That doesn't mean that the creditor must sell the property for the absolutely highest price that can be obtained, but it does mean the creditor must make a good faith effort to sell the property at a reasonable price under the circumstances. Whether the creditor has disposed of the collateral in a commercially reasonable manner is often contested by the debtor when the creditor sues him to collect the alleged deficiency, as discussed below. Proof regarding whether the creditor complied with the commercially reasonable requirement often comes from experts who buy and sell such goods every day.

In calculating the total amount of indebtedness to be paid in a repossession proceeding, Article 9 authorizes the repossessing creditor to add the expenses of repossession, storage, and sale (e.g., advertising and auctioneer charges) to the amount of the original indebtedness.

> If FFC pays $250 to the agents who repossess the car for the bank, $200 for storage costs before it can be sold, and a 10 percent auctioneer's fee to the auction company that sells it for them, FFC will be allowed to add all those expenses to the balance of the debt itself and to recoup the total amount from the proceeds of the sale of the collateral.

When the property is sold, proceeds are applied first to reimburse the creditor for those expenses, second to the balance of the original indebtedness, and third to other secured creditors holding junior secured positions in the collateral who have submitted written or electronically authenticated demands. Any surplus remaining after those payments (a very unusual circumstance) is paid to the debtor.

> If the Murphys owe a total of $5,000 to FFC on the original debt secured by the vehicle (Illustration 5-f) plus repossession expenses and the vehicle brings $7,000 in a commercially reasonable sale following repossession, the Murphys will be entitled to the $2,000 excess.

3. Notice Requirements

The repossessing creditor is required to give the debtor, guarantors of the debt, and other creditors—those holding junior lien positions in the collateral—notice of what the creditor intends to do with the repossessed collateral (e.g., keep it or sell it by public or private sale). Unless there are exceptional circumstances (e.g., the collateral is fresh fruit that will spoil and thus must be disposed of quickly), the creditor must give the required notice several days in advance of the sale (many states require ten days' notice). In order to participate in the distribution of proceeds from the sale, a junior lien holder must, upon receiving notice, submit a written or electronically authenticated demand to the repossessing creditor.

P-H 5-h: Why do you think a guarantor of the debt would be entitled to notice of the intended sale following repossession? What policy is involved in this requirement?

---

4. Right to Redeem

Right to redeem Right of a debtor to buy back repossessed property by paying all amounts owed to the creditor.

One reason for the notice requirement is that the debtor usually has a statutory **right to redeem** the collateral. That means the debtor can get the property back from the creditor by paying off the full amount owed to the creditor (the balance of the debt plus expenses of repossession, etc.) prior to the sale. The debtor's right to redeem expires upon the sale of the collateral by the creditor and the buyer takes title to it free and clear.

5. Suit to Obtain Deficiency Judgment

Deficiency The amount of a debt that remains owing after the property securing the debt has been liquidated.

One important reason the creditor is required to dispose of the repossessed property in a commercially reasonable manner is that Article 9 allows the creditor to sue the debtor for any difference between the price for which the property is sold (or the property's valuation, if kept) and the total indebtedness owed (unless the underlying promissory note is nonrecourse as discussed in Chapter Four, Section D). This is the **deficiency**. The creditor can bring suit to obtain a judgment for the deficiency and then execute on other unpledged property of the debtor to satisfy that judgment, as we will consider in Part B of the text.

EXAMPLE

If the Murphys owe $5,000 on the debt to FFC secured by the vehicle and the vehicle brings only $3,000 in a commercially reasonable sale following repossession, FFC may file suit against the Murphys for the $2,000 deficiency. Upon obtaining a judgment for the deficiency, FFC may execute on other assets of the Murphys to satisfy the judgment.

6. Suit for Judgment in Lieu of Repossession

Sometimes the creditor does not want to repossess the collateral. It may have little or no remaining value (e.g., a car that was pledged but has been wrecked) or it may be so costly to store and sell (e.g., cattle that are diseased) that it isn't worth it. In that event, the creditor can release that collateral and bring suit against the debtor for the indebtedness. (Subject, again, to the limitations of a non-recourse note.)

CONCLUSION

You can see that the law controlling the pledging of personal property as security for debt is quite different from that controlling the mortgage of real property and the liabilities of sureties and guarantors that we considered in Chapter Four. But one thing that all these ways of securing debt have in common is that they are voluntary or consensual. With that in mind, there is one more significant aspect to secured debt and that is the involuntary or nonconsensual lien that may secure debt and that is the topic of our next chapter.

CHAPTER SUMMARY

This chapter considered the pledging of personal property as security for debt under Article 9 of the Uniform Commercial Code. A debtor may pledge personal property in which he has an ownership interest to a creditor as security for repayment of the debt if the creditor gives value for the pledge and if there is a written security agreement or, for property to be kept in the possession of the creditor, at least a verbal security interest. As part of the "floating lien" concept of Article 9, the security interest granted in personal property extends automatically to the proceeds of such property and to after-acquired property of the debtor as well if the security agreement so provides. The security interest may also attach to other or future indebtedness of the debtor to the creditor if the security agreement so provides.

Article 9 distinguishes between a security interest merely attaching to pledged property and being perfected. To be assured of a priority claim to the pledged property over subsequent creditors of the debtor, the secured creditor must perfect its security interest in the property. For most kinds of property, the secured creditor will perfect its secured interest by filing a financing statement. Perfection can also be achieved by the secured creditor retaining possession of the pledged property. A purchase money security interest in consumer goods is perfected upon attachment. And a security interest in titled vehicles is normally perfected by notation of the security interest on the title itself. The filing of a financing statement provides constructive notice to the world of a creditor's security interest in the pledged property. The purchaser of goods subject to a perfected security interest takes title subject to the security interest unless the goods were sold in the ordinary course of the debtor's business or were consumer goods subject to a PMSI.

If the debtor defaults on the underlying debt, the secured party has the right to exercise self-help repossession of the pledged property except that the creditor cannot break and enter or cause or threaten a breach of the peace while repossessing. Alternatively, the creditor can seek a writ of possession from a court. Upon repossession of the collateral, it may be disposed of by the creditor at public or private sale, subject to notice requirements. The debtor has a right to redeem the property prior to sale by paying all amounts due including the costs of repossession. The goods must be sold in a commercially reasonable manner. If the sale fails to produce sufficient funds to pay the expenses of repossession, the sale, and the balance of the underlying debt, the creditor may file a civil lawsuit against the debtor to obtain a judgment for the deficiency amount.

REVIEW QUESTIONS

1. List the requirements for an enforceable security agreement.
2. Explain the "floating lien" concept as it applies to after-acquired property.
3. Explain what a "future advances" clause is in a security agreement and how it operates.
4. What is the difference between a security interest in personal property attaching and being perfected?
5. What are consumer goods? What is a purchase money security interest in consumer goods? What kinds of personal property might be subject to a security interest perfected by possession by the creditor?
6. What is *constructive notice* as that term is used in Article 9 of the UCC? What is the ordinary course of business exception to the effect of constructive notice?
7. Explain the difference between self-help repossession and judicial repossession.
8. Explain the debtor's right to redeem. What time limits exist on that right?
9. What is a deficiency judgment? Under what circumstances might a secured creditor entitled to seek a deficiency judgment elect not to do so?
10. Debtor obtains a commercial loan from Bank A and grants it a security interest in all of Debtor's personal property used by Debtor in its business. Bank A does not file a financing statement. Six months later Debtor obtains a commercial loan from Bank B and grants it a security interest in the same personal property. Bank B files a financing statement. Debtor then defaults on both loans. Which bank has first priority in repossessing and selling Debtor's assets? Why? Did Article 9 rules for a PMSI affect your answer? Why or why not? Did Article 9 rules regarding perfection by possession affect your answer? Why or why not?

WORDS AND PHRASES TO REMEMBER

actual notice
auction sale
automatic perfection
breach of the peace
collateral
commercially reasonable manner
consensual lien
constructive notice
deficiency
deficiency judgment
distressed goods

distress sale
document of title
electronic lien title (ELT)
electronic vehicle titling (EVT)
financing statement (UCC-1)
judicial repossession
judicial sale
lien
nonconsensual lien
notation of lien
notice of sale

notice statute
ordinary course of business
pledged property
private sale
public sale
purchase money security interest
   (PMSI)
redemption (right to redeem)
repossession

repossession sale
self-help repossession
sheriff's sale
taking free and clear
taking subject to
UCC-1
writ of possession

TO LEARN MORE: A number of TLM activities to accompany this chapter are accessible on the student disc accompanying the text and on the Author Updates link to the text Web site at http://www.aspenparalegaled.com/ books/parsons_ abcdebt/default.asp.

Chapter Six:

Nonconsensual Liens (Statutory and Common Law Liens)

She's got a mortgage on my body now, a lien on my soul.
—*Robert Johnson, Traveling Riverside Blues*

Introduction

In Chapters Four and Five we considered consensual or voluntary liens: mortgages in real property and security interests in personal property granted by the voluntary act of the owner. But there are a number of situations in which the law allows a creditor to assert a lien on property of another *without the owner's consent.* Thus, we speak here of **nonconsensual** or **involuntary liens.**

If you think about it, granting one person a security interest in a second person's property without his consent is a substantial intrusion upon that second person's rights in his property. It is an extraordinary thing to do. Some nonconsensual liens arise from a recognized **social policy.** The mechanic's lien, for example, is premised on the idea that one who provides services that increase the value of another's property and who is not paid for those services should be allowed assert a lien against the property of the other up to the value of the services rendered. Others, such as tax liens, arise solely from the nature of the government's **sovereign power** and the perceived priority of its claims.

Whatever the rationale, the liens we examine in this chapter are recognized in most states today by statutes passed by the state legislatures and, in the case of federal tax liens (see Section E), by Congress. Consequently, most nonconsensual liens are referred to as **statutory liens.** A few states recognize these nonconsensual liens only by **common law** (court decisions), in which case they may be referred to either as **common law liens** or **equitable liens.** In some states, a nonconsensual lien has been made statutory but the common law lien survives as well.

Some nonconsensual liens are **possessory liens,** which means the **lien holder** must have possession of the property in which the lien is claimed (a form of **bailment** in which the **bailee** asserting the lien has legal possession of the property of the owner who is the **bailor**). Others are **nonpossessory liens,** which means that the lien holder need not have possession of the property in order to assert the lien.

Statutory liens A lien created by statute rather than by contract or court order.

Equitable lien A lien created by court rulings rather than by statute.

Possessory lien A lien that depends on the lien holder having possession of the property.

Lien holder The one who holds a lien.

Nonpossessory lien A lien that arises even though the lien holder does not have possession of the property.

There are a large number of nonconsensual liens recognized by the various states. We will focus on nonconsensual liens that are recognized in all or almost all states and that are commonly dealt with by debtor/creditor attorneys.

 ## A.   Mechanic's and Materialman's Liens on Real Property

Mechanic's lien A
statutory lien on realty
available to a party who
has supplied labor for the
improvement of the realty.

Materialman's lien A
statutory lien on realty
available to a party who
has supplied materials for
the improvement of the
realty.

A **mechanic's lien** (sometimes called a **construction lien**) is a nonpossessory lien on *real property* to secure payment for *labor* provided to improve the real property burdened with the lien. The lien cannot be asserted against real property other than that improved. The lien can also be asserted by one who provides *materials* for the improvement of the property in which case it is called a **materialman's lien** or **supplier's lien**. (For convenience, we will hereafter refer primarily to the mechanic's lien, but the procedures are similar for both liens.) The mechanic's lien is typically asserted by contractors (including both general contractors and subcontractors), laborers, and suppliers of materials for the job. In some states, surveyors, architects, and engineers who have worked on the project may also be entitled to lien protection. Read through Illustration 6-a, which presents a common dispute scenario giving rise to the filing of a mechanic's lien.

What's going to happen here? RCS could go ahead and file a lawsuit against ACC to collect its unpaid invoices. Under the state's mechanic's lien statute, RCS may have more leverage than just a threatened lawsuit. It may be in a position to assert a lien against the property for the amount of its claim for material supplied (the concrete) and labor performed (pouring the concrete pads). Of course, the owner of the property, City Heights Limited Partnership, would not consent to such a lien being filed and would likely be horrified to see it filed. That's why it is a

Illustration 6-a: MECHANIC'S LIEN SCENARIO

Ray's Concrete Services (RCS), a sole proprietorship owned by Raymond Floyd, contracted with Adams Construction Company (ACC) to supply concrete and pour some of the concrete slabs for the City Heights Condominium Project on which ACC is the general contractor. The construction subcontract between RCS and ACC called for RCS to make daily deliveries of certain quantities of concrete to the job site over a 60-day period, to pour 20 separate pads of uniform 4″ thickness during that time frame, to reinforce each pad with rebar, and then to cure and finish each pad. All of RCS's work was to be done to written job specifications, which were made part of the subcontract. RCS's invoices for its material and labor were to be presented on a weekly basis to ACC and to be paid within 30 days following completion of all the work.

RCS completed its work within the contractual 60-day period, although there were some concerns expressed to ACC by Abe Mendoza, the project manager on the job and other subcontractors concerning whether the concrete supplied by RCS was of appropriate quality and whether the pads poured by RCS were achieving uniform 4″ thickness required by the subcontract. The invoices for material and labor presented to ACC by RCS total $150,000. More than 30 days has passed since RCS completed its work but Abe Mendoza has advised ACC that some of the pad work may have to be redone. Consequently, ACC has refused to pay the invoices of RCS. Raymond Floyd has called ACC several times demanding payment.

nonconsensual lien; the owner does *not* consent to it. But the law allows this type of lien in certain situations to benefit the unpaid laborer or material supplier whose labor or material has improved the property.

P-H 6-a: ACC is not the owner of the real property on which the City Heights Condominium Project is being built and on which RCS would file its lien; it is only the general contractor. So why should ACC be particularly concerned about the lien being filed? As you think about this question, consider what the contract between ACC and the owner of the property probably says about the obligation of ACC to pay all subcontractors. Might ACC be in breach of its contract with the owner if RCS files this lien? And recall our consideration of surety bonds in Chapter Four and the surety bond that ACC acquired from Trustus Insurance Company covering its obligations on the project. If the owner becomes liable to pay RCS as a result of this mechanic's lien, it will make a claim for compensation against Trustus, who will then seek reimbursement from ACC. What other negative consequences can you think of for ACC if RCS files a mechanic's lien on the property?

---

1. Creating and Enforcing the Mechanic's Lien

The procedure for creating and enforcing a mechanic's (or materialman's) lien is somewhat detailed, involves a number of time deadlines, and varies considerably from state to state. The contractor or supplier asserting the lien must be very careful to follow the statutory procedure and to meet all deadlines or the lien will fail. Consequently, the lawyer representing any of the parties involved in a dispute giving rise to a mechanic's lien, and the assisting legal professional, must be well versed in the controlling procedures.

In most states, the contractor or supplier wishing to assert the lien must send a written **notice of nonpayment** to the owner of the property and the general contractor (unless the general contractor is the one asserting the lien) within some specified time frame. Let's assume the law of Columbiana, where the City Heights Condominium Project is located, requires the formal notice of nonpayment to be sent "within 90 days of the last day of the month when the goods or services were supplied," a typical provision.

Let's further assume that RCS signed its subcontract with ACC on January 30, YR-1; made its first delivery of concrete to the project site on March 1, YR-1; and finished its work there on April 30, YR-1. The notice of nonpayment sent by RCS to ACC as general contractor and to City Heights Limited Partnership is shown in Illustration 6-b.

Next, the contractor or supplier must file (the statute may say "record" or "register") his **notice of lien** or **abstract of lien** in a designated public records office (often the office where land records are recorded or filed) and send a copy of it (usually by registered or certified mail) to the owner and general contractor. The law of Columbiana provides that the notice of lien or abstract of lien must be filed, "within 90 days after work on the project has been substantially completed or the contract terminated." The notice of lien registered by RCS is shown in Illustration 6-c.

Illustration 6-b: NOTICE OF NONPAYMENT

NOTICE OF NONPAYMENT

TO: City Heights Limited Partnership, Owner
         [Address omitted from illustration.]
         Adams Construction Company, General Contractor
         [Address omitted from illustration.]
         Trustus Insurance Company, Surety
         [Address omitted from illustration.]

FROM: Ray's Concrete Service, Claimant
         [Address omitted from illustration.]

Pursuant to Columbiana Statutory Code §66-11-101, et seq., claimant hereby gives notice that it provided labor and materials for the improvement of real property is known as City Heights Condominiums as described in the instrument of record in Book 897, Page 455, Register's Office for Capitol County, Columbiana and more particularly described as follows: [Property description omitted from illustration.]

The labor and material provided were as described in the subcontract between claimant and Adams Construction Company dated January 30, YR-1, and consisted of the delivery of concrete to the construction site located on the property and the construction of 20 concrete pads on the property. The claim of claimant for the labor and material provided totals $150,000. The claim of claimant for the labor and material provided remains unpaid.

The last day that claimant performed labor or provided materials was April 30, YR-1.

Dated this _____ day of June, YR-1

Ray's Concrete Service

By: _____
Raymond Floyd, Owner

P-H 6-b: Given the controlling time periods in the Columbiana statutory code, has RCS sent its notice of nonpayment timely? Has it filed and sent its notice of lien timely? If the applicable Columbiana notice of lien statute required filing and notice to others, "within 60 days after the claimant has completed its last work on the project," would RCS have filed and sent its notice timely? What is the critical difference between the two alternative readings of the notice of lien statute? Why do we refer to RCS "sending" its notice of nonpayment but "filed and sending" its notice of lien?

Substantial completion The date that construction on real property is substantially done.

Assume again that the Columbiana notice of lien statute requires filing and notice to others "within 90 days after the project has been substantially completed or the contract terminated," a common requirement. *When* work on a project has reached **substantial completion** can be a contested issue in mechanic's lien cases.

Illustration 6-c: NOTICE OF LIEN

NOTICE OF LIEN

Ray's Concrete Service ("RCS"), a sole proprietorship owned by Raymond Floyd of Capitol City, Columbiana, having furnished labor and materials to improve the real property described herein pursuant to a contract with Adams Construction Company ("ACC"), for the purpose of giving notice of and/or perfecting a lien on real property and improvements to secure the amount of its claim pursuant to Columbiana Statutory Code §66-11-101, et seq., through its duly authorized officer or representative, states:

That RCS claims a lien upon all interests to which it is entitled under law in the following property situated in Capitol County, Columbiana, to-wit: [Property description omitted from illustration.]

This property is known as City Heights Condominiums and is described in the instrument of record in Book 897, Page 455, Register's Office for Capitol County, Columbiana.

That, based on information and belief, the owner of the above-described property is City Heights Limited Partnership.

That, to the extent allowable under law, a lien is hereby claimed to secure an indebtedness of $150,000 for labor and materials furnished relative to the above-described real property and improvements thereon and/or owed under RCS's contract with ACC. This amount includes amounts owed under the original subcontract between RCS and ACC. This lien is also claimed to secure any other allowable interest or service charges, as well as expenses relating to the recording of this Notice in the Register's Office for Capitol County, Columbiana. The last day which RCS supplied labor or materials under its contract with ACC relative to this property was April 30, YR-1.

RCS rzeserves the right to amend this notice and lien.

Registered this 1st day of June, YR-1

RAY'S CONCRETE SERVICE

By: _____
Raymond Floyd, Owner
[Notarization omitted from illustration.]

E X A M P L E

Assume that as the Capitol Heights Condominium construction project moves to a conclusion, the owner and ACC fear there may be more liens coming from other unpaid subcontractors and suppliers. Some condos in the project are now being offered for sale, but others are still in the *punch-list* phase: the contractor is completing a punch-list of minor finishing tasks. The owner will want to go ahead and record a *notice of completion* (Illustration 6-d) in the office of county land records that will serve as *constructive notice to the world* of substantial completion and set the 90-day clock ticking for the filing of additional liens. Illustration 6-d shows how the notice of substantial completion on this project might look.

Illustration 6-d: NOTICE OF COMPLETION

NOTICE OF COMPLETION

1. Name of owner of the land: City Heights Limited Partnership

2. Name of person, firm or organization contracted with for the entire job or improvement or demolition: Adams Construction Company, General Contractor and Fitzhugh Architects, LLC.

3. Location and description of the property: City Heights Condominiums [property description omitted from illustration].

4. Date of completion of the structure, improvement or demolition: December 1, YR-1.

5. A transfer of ownership of all or a part of the real property or an interest therein and encumbrance thereon or a settlement of the claims of parties entitled to the benefits of Columbiana Statutory Code §66-11-101, et seq., will take place not earlier than thirty days from the date of the filing of this notice of completion.

6. The name and address of the person, firm or organization to which parties entitled to the benefits of the said law may send notice of claims are as follows: City Heights Limited Partnership, c/o Andrea C. Collins, Attorney at Law, 111 City Tower, Capitol City, Columbiana 55677.

DATED the 1st day of December, YR-1

City Heights Limited Partnership, Owner

By: _____

Fred W. Troutman, General Partner

[Notarization omitted from illustration.]

P-H 6-c: Assume that Raymond Floyd, the owner of RCS, comes into the law office where you work on June 1, YR-1, at the beginning of his dispute with ACC over nonpayment of the RCS invoices. He's there to consult concerning his remedies for nonpayment of his invoices. What questions are you or the supervising lawyer going to need to ask him to see if he has the right to file a mechanics or materialman's lien? Which public records will you need to check to see what has or has not been recorded there?

Once the notice of lien has been duly filed it is only good for a certain number of days. In many states, a mechanic's lien created by a subcontractor is good for only 90 days. The same lien created by a general contractor may be good for a longer period, up to a year. What that means is that the party who has created the lien must *file suit to enforce the lien* before it expires. And the suit to enforce the lien, like the judicial foreclosure considered in Chapter Four, asks the court for an order directing the sale of the property and distribution of proceeds in order of priority to the various creditors.

EXAMPLE

If the law of Columbiana provides that the lien created by RCS is good for 90 days after it is filed; RCS must initiate suit to enforce the lien within that 90 days or lose the right to do so. RCS registered its lien on June 1, YR-1. It will have 90 days after that to file suit to enforce it.

2. Perfection of a Mechanic's Lien: Priority Issues

In Chapter Four, we considered how mortgages in real property are perfected to give the creditor holding the mortgage a priority position in the pledged property over later claimants. In Chapter Five, we considered how a creditor granted a security interest in personal property of the debtor perfects that security interest to give the creditor a priority position over later claimants to the pledged property. How then is a nonconsensual mechanic's lien perfected to give the contractor or supplier a priority position over other parties claiming consensual or nonconsensual liens on the same real property?

EXAMPLE

> What if RCS is one of 20 subcontractors and suppliers who did work or supplied materials on the City Heights construction project at different times under different contracts and each of them has given the requisite notice of nonpayment and filed the required notice of lien at different times? The question of priority among the 20 holders of a mechanic's lien on the real property involved in the project is a question of who was first to **perfect** their mechanic's lien. And what if there are one or more consensual mortgages existing on the real property when RCS and the other subcontractors and suppliers assert and perfect their mechanic's liens on the property? Can a mechanic's lien on real property ever have priority over a previously granted consensual mortgage on that property? Does it matter if the consensual mortgage is perfected? These are questions of priority among perfected consensual mortgages and nonconsensual perfected mechanic's liens on real property.

As with security interests in personal property (Chapter Five) and consensual mortgages on real property (Chapter Four), a mechanic's lien must be created (i.e., it must attach to the real property) before it can be perfected. When is a mechanic's lien deemed to exist; when does it attach to the property? There is wide variation among the states as to the answer to this question. In some states, the lien comes into existence and attaches as soon as the contract for services or materials is executed. In other states, it comes into existence the moment services are actually provided or materials delivered to the real property. In some other states, the lien comes into existence only when the contractor or supplier asserting the lien gives the owner and contractor (if it is a subcontractor asserting the lien) formal notice of nonpayment. And in still other states, the lien does not arise until the contractor or supplier files (registers or records) the required notice of lien in the county or city land records office (or other designated local or state office) where the improved property is located and gives formal notice to the owner and other appropriate parties of the filing.

EXAMPLE

> Assume the contract between RCS and ACC from P-H 6-a was entered into on January 30, YR-1. The first delivery of concrete to the job site by RCS occurred on March 1, YR-1, and the last on April 30, YR-1. When RCS has not been paid by June 1, YR-1, it gives notice of nonpayment to ACC and City Heights Limited Partnership, the owner on that day. Ten days later, June 10, YR-1, ACC files a notice of lien in the register of deeds office of the county where the real property is located. Do you see how the date the lien came into existence might vary, depending on how the statute of the state reads?

Once a mechanic's lien is deemed to exist, how is it perfected? Again, there is considerable variation among the states as to how a mechanic's lien is perfected. In most states, the lien is deemed perfected when the notice of lien is properly filed (recorded or registered) in the proper county or city office of land records and served on the owner and other appropriate parties. However, if the holder of the lien does not thereafter file suit to enforce the lien within the statutorily allowed time after filing (e.g., 90 days for a subcontractor or supplier, one year for a general contractor), the lien will have no priority at all and be unenforceable for any purpose—both the creation and perfection are forfeited. In a minority of states, the holder of the lien must actually file the lawsuit to enforce the lien in order for it to be deemed perfected.

EXAMPLE

> If RCS has done everything mentioned in the last Example, its mechanic's lien may or may not be perfected depending on whether the controlling statute requires that suit to enforce that the lien be filed in order to achieve perfection. If a dispute breaks out between RCS and the other 19 suppliers and contractors that have "liened the job," the questions of whose lien is properly created and perfected under state law will be paramount.

P-H 6-d: How is a mechanic's lien created and enforced under the laws of your state? When is it deemed to exist? How is it perfected?

What priority does a properly created and perfected mechanic's lien have against an existing consensual mortgage on the liened property?

EXAMPLE

> Assume the owner of the property, City Heights Limited Partnership, borrowed money from United Lenders (UL) on April 1, YR-1, and pledged the real property as security for the loan in a properly executed mortgage agreement that was properly recorded in the land records' office that same day, perfecting it. When RCS files its notice of lien on June 10, YR-1, and files suit to enforce it within the statutory time allowed, common sense might suggest that its lien on the property will be junior to the previously created and perfected mortgage in favor of UL, in which case proceeds of sale would go to UL to pay its claim in full before there is any distribution to RCS. But that is not necessarily the outcome here. It depends on the language of the controlling statute.

Mechanic's lien statutes commonly provide that such a lien, once created, "relates back to the date when the services or materials were first supplied." If that is the case, then the mechanic's lien of RCS in the preceding example will be treated as having attached and been perfected not on June 10 when the notice of lien was filed or on the date the lawsuit to enforce the lien was filed, but on March 1 when RCS first delivered concrete to the site—a full month before the UL mortgage was recorded.

Relation back The retrospective effect given to some liens giving them priority from a date prior to their perfection.

This **relation back** feature of a mechanic's lien is not recognized in all states, and where it is not, the mechanic's lien will only have priority from the date it is perfected. In other states the relation-back feature is present but cannot attain priority over a previously perfected **construction loan**. If that were the rule in

Columbiana in the preceding example, we would need to find out if the loan to the partnership by UL was to be used for construction on the premises. If so, it would maintain its priority. If not, it would lose its priority to the mechanic's lien of RCS.

In other states, the relation-back feature is present and goes all the way back, not to the date the contractor first performed work on the site, but to "the effective date of the lienor's contract" or "to the visible commencement of [any] operations" on the site. But usually these generous relation-back features are available only for general contractors or architects, not subcontractors or suppliers.

P-H 6-e: If the law of Columbiana provided that the mechanic's lien of RCS related back to the date of its contract, when does it attain priority status?

In any state, whatever date the mechanic's lien is deemed to be effective and perfected, it will defeat a prior **unperfected** mortgage or other unsecured claim to the property. In any event, the relation-back feature of statutory liens can create some dramatic priority clashes.

P-H 6-f: If you worked in the loan division of UL when the partnership applied for its loan, what public records would you need to check to verify that title to the property to be pledged as security for the loan is not already encumbered by any mechanic's liens? And how could UL protect itself from a later-filed mechanic's lien that relates back to a date preceding the UL loan and mortgage?

Real property owned by the federal, state, or local government is normally not subject to attachment by mechanic's lien—a **sovereign immunity** concept. And state statutory liens cannot be asserted in federally funded construction projects. To protect subcontractors and suppliers on federal projects, where the contract price exceeds $100,000, the **Miller Act**, 40 U.S.C. §3131, requires general contractors performing public works projects to provide a **performance bond** (sometimes called a **performance and payment bond**) guaranteeing the faithful performance of the job and payment of all labor and materials obligations to subcontractors and suppliers on the project. Many state and municipal governments similarly require contractors on public works projects to be bonded.

B. ▶ Possessory Liens on Personal Property

1. The Artisan's Lien

Artisan's lien The right of one who performs work on the personal property of another to retain possession of the property as security for payment and to sell the property and apply the proceeds to the amount due if necessary.

The **artisan's lien** applies to personal property, not real property. Originally a common law lien, most states now regulate it by statute (though in some states it may be both statutory and common law, a significant fact as we will see when we discuss the priority question below). The artisan's lien is a type of *possessory lien* in that it only works in favor of one lawfully in possession of tangible personal property, to secure payment of reasonable charges for services rendered and materials supplied. A typical artisan's lien statute defines artisans to include "Persons with whom are left goods or products to be repaired, developed, processed, or

Illustration 6-e: KINDS OF BUSINESSES THAT MAY ASSERT AN ARTISAN'S LIEN

Vehicle/small engine repairers	jewelers	shoe repairers
tailors	picture framers	dry cleaners
printers and bookbinders	pet groomers	computer repair technicians
aircraft maintenance technicians	upholsterers	textile processors
appliance repairers	metal fabricators	cotton ginners

improved." And such persons are declared to have a lien on goods that have been left with them for repair or improvement to the extent of the artisan's charges related to the goods.

There are any number of businesses that may be entitled to assert an artisan's lien. Illustration 6-e sets out a sampling.

Some states cover all such businesses under a single artisan's lien statute, whereas others have a variety of business-specific lien statutes (e.g., a vehicle repair lien and a separate launderer's lien).

P-H 6-g: Determine what the wording of your state's artisan's lien statute is. Does your state have a single artisan's lien statute or separate ones for the kinds of businesses in the preceding list? Are other types of "artisans" covered under statutes in your state?

EXAMPLE

> Assume Nick and Pearl Murphy take the living room couch that is pledged to Shears Department Store and have it recovered by Martha's Fabric Service. When the Murphys arrive to pick up their recovered couch, a dispute arises over the charge for recovering the couch. The Murphys refuse to pay and Martha refuses to return their couch unless they do. She intends to sell the couch if the Murphys don't pay. Martha is asserting an artisan's lien in the couch.

P-H 6-h: Assume Columbiana has a statutory definition of "artisan" that is identical to the one given in the first paragraph of this section B. On the facts given, does Martha's Fabric Service qualify as an artisan under the statute?

P-H 6-i: Assume Nick Murphy is buying gas for his car at a local gas station. When he is finished pumping the gas, the station owner asks Nick to pay a nickel per gallon more than the posted price because he was getting ready to change the price anyway. Nick refuses to pay the extra nickel per gallon and the station operator won't let him drive the car off until he pays. He says he's claiming an artisan's lien in the car. Does the station owner appear to qualify as an "artisan" under the statutory language?

a. Enforcing the Artisan's Lien

Normally, the artisan retains possession of the property hoping the owner will pay the bill owed or negotiate a settlement of it. But if that does not happen, the artisan, after some statutory period time (e.g., 90 days or six months) can enforce the lien by selling the property in satisfaction of the debt. To enforce the lien, the artisan must give *written notice* to the owner and anyone else she determines claims an interest in the property (e.g., if she knows of a co-owner or a secured party in the property). The purpose of the notice is to enable the owner, or other person having an interest, to pay the debt and recover the property prior to sale.

EXAMPLE

> If Martha's Fabric Service is aware of the Shears Department Store security interest in the couch, Shears must be given the statutory notice.

The notice typically must describe the property, itemize the services performed by the artisan, state the amount owed, and demand payment by a stated date from the date of the notice. Illustration 6-f shows the artisan's lien notice sent to the Murphys regarding the couch.

In some states, the artisan must also advertise, for some statutory number of times (e.g., twice for two consecutive weeks), the intended sale of the item in a **newspaper of general circulation** in the county where the sale is to be held. In most states, the sale can be public or private. In some states, judicial foreclosure action is required to authorize the sale, and, in others, self-help foreclosure and sale is allowed if the statutory notice requirements have been satisfied. The proceeds of sale are applied first to cover the costs of the notice and any advertisement, then the claim of any other lien holder in the property over which the

Illustration 6-f: NOTICE OF ARTISAN LIENOR'S INTENT TO SELL

Notice of Artisan Lienor's Intent to Sell

TO: Nick and Pearl Murphy [Address]

For the past three months I have retained possession of your Shears 10' living room couch (the property) as I am empowered to do under Columbiana Statutory Code §66-11-205 (the statute) to secure my charges, amounting to $225, due as a reasonable, customary, and usual compensation for the recovering service that I provided in connection with the couch.

You are hereby notified to come forward and pay these charges. On your failure to do so within ten (10) days after this notice has been given to you, I shall sell the property at public sale and apply the proceeds to the payment of such charges, paying over the balance, if any, to you or to the person entitled to it, or holding you liable for any deficiency.

Dated: June 1, YR-1

Martha's Fabric Services, Lienor
By: _____
Martha S. Fillers, Owner

---

artisan's lien does not have priority, and then to the amount owed the artisan. Any surplus proceeds are returned to the owner.

b. Priority of the Artisan's Lien

Article 9 of the **Uniform Commercial Code** (UCC), which we considered in some detail in Chapter Five, provides in §9-333 (9-310 before the latest revision of Article 9) that "a possessory lien on goods has priority over a security interest in the goods unless the lien is created by a statute that expressly provides otherwise." Most statutory artisan's liens do in fact provide expressly that the artisan's lien will *not* attain priority over preexisting and properly perfected mortgages, security interests, or other liens on the property unless notice is given to the creditors holding such preexisting claims *and* they consent in writing. Thus we say that the artisan's lien is **subordinate** to the prior security interest in the goods.

EXAMPLE

> A typical priority artisan's statute may read, "A lien under this section shall be subject to all prior liens of record, unless notice is given to all lien holders of record and written consent is obtained from all lien holders of record to the making, repairing, improving, or enhancing the value of any personal property and in this event the lien created under this section shall be prior to liens of record."

P-H 6-j: Between Martha's Fabric Service, asserting an artisan's lien in the couch, and Shears Department Store, asserting a consensual security interest in the couch, who has the priority position under the statutory language in the preceding example? Might the result turn on whether the security interest of Shears is a lien "of record"? If Shears filed a financing statement to perfect its security interest in the couch, it is of record. But if Shears did not file a financing statement and is depending on perfection by way of a purchase money security interest in consumer goods, as discussed in Chapter Four, Martha's artisan's lien may be deemed senior. Determine what the result of this dispute would be under the laws of your state.

In the last Example, the reference to "liens of record" means a prior lien that is properly perfected, a subject covered in Section D of Chapter Five. If the prior security interest is not perfected, the artisan's lien may well have priority over it. And remember that §9-333 says the artisan's lien will have priority "unless the lien is created by statute. . . ." If you live in a state that still recognizes the artisan's lien at common law, that common law lien may have priority over the prior security interest when the statutory lien would not.

2. The Warehouseman's Lien

Another possessory lien and one closely related to the artisan's lien is the **warehouseman's lien**, which recognizes the right of a party who has transported or stored a commodity (e.g., oil or corn), an animal, or other personal property that belongs to another to declare a lien on such commodity or goods still in the warehouse's possession to secure payment for unpaid transportation or warehousing charges.

EXAMPLE

> An oil refinery in Texas may purchase oil from an international seller. The oil is shipped and delivered to a storage facility that takes possession of and then stores the oil until the buyer can pick it up. Or, a garage keeper may agree to let the owner of a vehicle store his vehicle in the garage keeper's facility. Or, a self-service storage business may lease storage units to customers in which to store their property. Or, a pet hotel may keep an owner's pet while the owner is on vacation. Or, a shipping company transports goods on behalf of a seller. In any of these situations, if the agreed fee for transport or storage is not paid when due, then the party transporting or storing the other's property may refuse to turn over the property to the party demanding possession, assert the lien in the property, and retain it until payment is made.

The warehouseman's lien existed at common law and the common law lien is still recognized in many states. However, it has been made statutory in §7-209 of the UCC. And §7-210 controls the procedure for enforcing the lien and requires notice to all parties having an interest in the goods.

P-H 6-k: Locate your state's version of §7-210. What information does the required notice have to contain? How long must the warehouse wait after notice is given before the goods can be sold? Can the sale be executed by either public (auction) or private sale? Must the goods be sold by the warehouse at their absolute best price or is a commercially reasonable price good enough?

Regarding the priority of a warehouse lien over a prior security interest granted in the goods, we have already seen in conjunction with the artisan's lien that §9-333 (9-310 before the latest revision of Article 9) declares any possessory lien to have priority over a prior security interest in the goods unless the lien "is created by a statute that expressly provides otherwise." And §7-209, the statute that creates the warehouseman's lien, does have a "provides otherwise" clause right there in §7-209(c). Although the language of §7-209(c) is difficult to decipher, it basically says that the warehouseman's lien will not have priority over a prior properly perfected security interest *unless* the holder of that security interest expressly or impliedly approved the debtor's submitting the goods to another's lien claim as by shipment or storage of the goods.

EXAMPLE

> Compare *In re Sierra Publishers Associates*, 149 B.R. 359 (Bankr. S.D.N.Y. 1993) (debtor book wholesaler outsourced its inventory storage to warehouse without permission of its secured creditor; lien claim of warehouse held subordinate to secured creditor's prior perfected claim in inventory) with *In re Sharon Steel Corp.*, 176 B.R. 384 (Bankr. W.D. Pa. 1995) (debtor stored its inventory in several warehouses but security agreement with debtor's secured creditor expressly permitted such storage; warehouse liens given priority over prior perfected security interest). And recall that §9-333 does not reference a common law warehouseman's lien. Therefore, in states where the lien is still recognized by common law as well as statutorily under §7-209, the common law lien may be given priority over the prior perfected security interest in the goods.

See, e.g., *Charter One Auto Finance v. Inkas Coffee Distributors Realty*, 57 UCC Rep.Serv.2d 672, 39 Conn. L. Rptr. 110 (Conn. Super. Ct. 2005) (auto parking lot operator asserted common law lien in debtor's auto for unpaid storage fees; lien held superior to prior perfected security interest in auto because it was not created by §7-209 and thus not controlled by §9-310 (now §9-333)).

In states that still recognize the warehouseman's lien at common law, it may apply only to those that store goods and not to those that transport them. But those states will likely recognize a separate common law lien for those that transport goods, usually called a **carrier's lien**, and it will work the same way as the common law warehouseman's lien.

P-H 6-l: Determine if your state still recognizes any possessory liens at common law. If so, see if you have a case, like the Charter One case cited in the text, dealing with priority disputes between the holder of a prior perfected security interest in goods and one asserting a common law warehouseman's or carrier's lien in those goods. If so, who prevailed and why?

P-H 6-m: UCC §2-711(3) creates a warehouseman's lien in favor of a buyer in a transaction for the sale of goods. It arises wherein a buyer of goods who receives shipment of the goods from the seller and who then properly rejects the goods or properly revokes his acceptance of the goods is authorized to declare a nonconsensual security interest in goods in his possession until the seller reimburses him for any down payment made to seller for the goods and any expenses incurred in inspection, transportation, care, and custody of the goods. This buyer can refuse to return the goods to the seller until those obligations are paid, and if the seller refuses to pay then the buyer can sell the goods to recover the costs. Locate your state's version of §2-711(3). What is the procedure for a buyer in this situation to follow when he wants to sell the goods in which the lien is asserted?

3. Other Possessory Liens

There are other possessory liens recognized in many states either by statute or common law. The state may recognize an **attorney's** or **accountant's retaining lien** (or benefiting other licensed professionals) authorizing the professional to retain possession of a client's books, papers, securities, money, or other property (but not to dispose of as by sale, because it is a "passive" or "retention" lien only (see, e.g., *Brauer v. Hotel Associates, Inc.*, 192 A.2d 831, 833-834 (N.J. 1963)) until the client pays his bill or posts adequate security to cover it. A **banker's lien** may authorize a bank or other financial institution to assert the lien in a customer's property in the bank's possession (e.g., cash on deposit or certificates of deposit) and to take it to satisfy debts owed the bank. The state may recognize a **hotel operator's lien** imposed on a guest's personal property stored on the hotel premises, including automobiles and baggage, to secure reasonable room rents. The state may recognize a **landlord's lien** on the property of the tenant for unpaid rent if the tenant has abandoned the premises. Absent proof of abandonment, most states require express consent in the lease or the granting of an Article 9 security interest to the landlord before the landlord can seize a tenant's property for nonpayment of rent. The court will issue what is often called a **warrant of distress** (from the old common law action for distress or distrain), authorizing the seizure and sale of a tenant's property. Many states recognize a **vendor's lien** in favor of a party that sells personal property but retains possession of it until the full purchase price is paid (sometimes called a **layaway** or **layby** arrangement), usually enforceable as if an Article 9 consensual security interest had been granted by the buyer to the seller in the goods (see Chapter Five). Because these are possessory liens, priority disputes that arise in them will likely be determined in the same way we have already seen.

P-H 6-n: See if your state recognizes by common law or statute any of these other possessory liens and determine how they work in terms of notice to be given, time frames for asserting, the right to sell the property in which the lien is asserted where that is allowed, and the need, if any, for court action. How are priority disputes between the lien holder and holders of prior security interest in the goods determined?

C. ▶ The Attorney's Charging Lien

In contrast to the attorney's retaining lien mentioned in the previous section, which authorizes an attorney to retain possession of, but not sell, a client's books, papers, or other properties until the attorney is paid, most states recognize a separate lien, called the **attorney's charging lien** either by statute, common law, or both (for a good discussion of the distinction between the two liens, see *Starks v. Browning*, 20 S.W.3d 645, 650 (Tenn. Ct. App. 1999)). The charging lien is a *nonpossessory* lien imposed on any judgment rendered in the client's favor or on settlement proceeds due to the client in which the attorney has an interest (e.g., an undistributed contingency fee).

To enforce the lien in most states, the attorney must give written notice of the lien, record a notice of lien in the designated public records office, and file suit against the client to enforce the lien. Often the attorney's retainer agreement with the client will include a notice of the lien, using language similar to Illustration 6-g.

Illustration 6-g: NOTICE OF ATTORNEY'S CHARGING LIEN IN RETAINER AGREEMENT

The parties agree that the attorney hereby claims a lien on any and all property of the client that is or may come into the possession of the attorney in connection with this representation and on any judgment or settlement amount that is or may become payable to the client as a result of this representation.

D. ▶ The Healthcare Services Lien

Most states authorize a **healthcare services lien** to be asserted by a wide range of licensed healthcare professionals (e.g., physicians, dentists, optometrists, therapists) and providers (e.g., hospitals, clinics, EMS services, rehabilitation services) against any claim or cause of action that the patient may have against a third party who may be liable to the patient for injuries related to the healthcare service provided. The lien goes by various names in different states: medical lien, hospital lien, personal injury lien, to name a few. The lien is satisfied out of the proceeds of any judgment, award (as by arbitration), or settlement that the patient receives from the third party. Typically, a limit is imposed on the percentage of the patient's recovery that the lienholders as a class can take (e.g., 40%).

Though the procedures for enforcing the healthcare services lien vary considerably among the states, the claimant is typically required to file or record a verified (sworn) statement setting forth the name and address of the patient, the name and address of the operator of the claimant; the dates of the patient's treatment or admission and discharge; the amount claimed to be due for the healthcare or hospital care provided; and to the best of the claimant's knowledge, the names and addresses of those claimed by such patient to be liable for damages arising from the patient's illness or injuries. The statement must be filed or recorded in a designated public office (e.g., the county recorder's office or the county trustee's office for the county in which the services were provided) within a designated period of time (e.g., no later than 30 days after the services were provided).

Notice of the lien must then be given to each person believed to be liable on account of the illness or injury, and to the patient or the patient's attorney, usually by providing them with a copy of the sworn statement asserting the lien. Such notice can be mailed by certified or registered mail or hand delivered. At this point, the lien has been properly created and perfected. Thereafter, no settlement, judgment, or award resulting from the patient's claim against the responsible third party is free of the lien unless the lien holder joins in the settlement or executes a release of the lien.

If the healthcare professional or provider fails to file the lien in a timely manner or otherwise fails to follow the prescribed procedures to create and perfect it, that entity will be deemed to have waived the rights to the lien for the amounts it/he could have asserted in it (but not for charges for future services). Of course, a healthcare services lien can be granted by the patient by contract at any time, in which case a waiver will not be an issue.

EXAMPLE

Assume a person is involved in a car accident and receives medical services from the local hospital at a total cost of $10,000. The patient plans to file suit against the other driver. If the hospital for some reason fails to file and perfect its lien in a timely manner, it has waived the statutory or common law lien. However, the hospital may include the lien in the contract that the patient signs as part of the patient services rendered. Or, after waiver has occurred, the hospital may negotiate a **contractual lien** with the patient. The patient may do this to keep the hospital from filing suit against him to collect the amount owed while the suit against the other driver is still pending.

If the patient accepts any payment on the claim against the third party without obtaining a release or satisfaction of the healthcare services lien, the lien holder is entitled to enforce the lien by judicial action (filing suit). In most states, that suit may be against the patient, the patient's attorney, or any other creditor of the patient who received proceeds impressed with the lien.

EXAMPLE

Assume that, following her botched appendectomy, Pearl Murphy (from Illustration 1-a) is treated at Mercy Hospital in Capitol City (not the hospital she sued; that was Capitol City Hospital [CCH]) and incurs there a bill of $2,500, which insurance does not cover and which she and Nick have been unable to pay. Mercy Hospital properly files and gives notice of a hospital lien for that amount by sending copies of its verified statement to the Murphys and their attorney. Then the Murphys agree to a settlement of their lawsuit against CCH and Dr. Craft in the amount of $300,000. Once those settlement funds are in the hands of the Murphys' attorney for distribution, they are impressed with the hospital lien of Mercy Hospital. The Murphys' attorney must be careful to pay Mercy Hospital out of those funds. If she fails to do so, the hospital is entitled to enforce its lien by suing the Murphys and their attorney to collect the amount of the lien wrongfully denied it.

As the previous example shows, attorneys handling claims for plaintiffs must make arrangements to either satisfy or compromise a healthcare services lien before distributing funds paid in judgment or settlement.

EXAMPLE

Assume that an injured person has incurred $10,000 in hospital bills and the hospital properly creates and perfects a lien in that amount. His lawyer, who has taken the patient's case against a responsible third party on a one-third contingency basis, negotiates with the attorney for that party, but there are potentially valid defenses to his client's claim and the best the lawyer can settle the claim for is $15,000. Paying the hospital's lien in full would leave only $5,000 to be distributed to the client and the attorney and the attorney was expecting one-third of any settlement, which would eat up the remaining $5,000. Of course, the attorney and his client could simply reject the settlement offer and take their chances at trial. But what if the attorney is convinced that they will likely lose at trial and, even in a best-case scenario, recover no more than the $15,000 being offered. The attorney for the patient may negotiate with the hospital to accept 50 percent of its lien amount and release the rest. If the hospital agrees, the lien will be released and the funds will be distributed, $5,000 to the hospital, about $5,000 to the attorney, and the balance to the patient. What would be the incentive for the hospital to agree to compromise its lien claim in that situation?

P-H 6-o: The healthcare services lien is intended to be asserted against a third party that is liable to the patient for the injuries received that mandated the medical services. Is an insurance company that provides medical benefit payments to the patient as a policy beneficiary (e.g., health insurance or disability policies) such a third party? Courts disagree. Compare *Progressive Specialty Insurance Co. v. University of Alabama Hospital*, 953 So.2d 413 (Ala. Ct. App.

2006) (lien attached to proceeds of medical benefit policy where insurance company had constructive notice of lien; claims subject to lien not limited to tort claims against third parties) with *Shelby County Health Care Corp. v. Globe American Casualty Co.*, 638 F. Supp. 2d 882 (W.D. Tenn. 2008) (lien did not attach to medical benefits payment where insurance company paid proceeds of policy to creditor and not directly to patient) and with *Shelby County Healthcare Corp. v. Nationwide Mutual Ins. Co.*, 325 S.W.3d 88 (Tenn. 2010) (statute limiting lien to "causes of action for damages" does not extend to claims for medical benefit payments under contracts such as insurance policies).

E. ▶ Tax Liens

A **tax lien** is one imposed by law on the property of the delinquent taxpayer in favor of the *governmental taxing authority* to secure payment of the taxes owed as well as **interest** and **penalties** assessed on the delinquent tax. Tax liens operate in favor of the federal, state, and local governments.

1. The Federal Tax Lien

A federal tax lien can be imposed for nonpayment of *income, estate, gift, excise,* or other taxes owed to the federal government. The Federal Tax Lien Statute is found at 26 U.S.C. §§6321-6323. Section 6321 states:

> If any person liable to pay any tax neglects or refuses to pay the same after demand, the amount (including any interest, additional amount, addition to tax, or assessable penalty, together with any costs that may accrue in addition thereto) shall be a lien in favor of the United States upon all property and rights to property, whether real or personal, belonging to such person.

a. Creating the Federal Tax Lien

The tax lien does not arise until an *assessment* is made by the IRS (§6201), sometimes following an *audit* of the taxpayer's tax return. Once the tax liability has been assessed, the IRS sends the taxpayer a **Notice and Demand for Payment**, essentially a formal bill telling the taxpayer how much tax is owed. The notice will advise the taxpayer that he has ten days within which to pay the assessment. If the taxpayer fails to pay within the ten-day period, the tax lien attaches automatically to *all real and personal property* owned by the taxpayer and to all the taxpayer's "rights to property" (e.g., accounts receivables, or salary). The date of attachment is retroactive to the *date of the assessment*. Internal Revenue Code section 6322 (26 U.S.C. §6322) provides:

> Unless another date is specifically fixed by law, the lien imposed by section 6321 shall arise at the time the assessment is made and shall continue until the liability for the amount so assessed (or a judgment against the taxpayer arising out of such liability) is satisfied or becomes unenforceable by reason of lapse of time.

The U.S. Supreme Court, in *Glass City Bank v. United States*, 326 U.S. 265 (1945), held that the federal tax lien applies not only to property owned by the taxpayer at the time of the assessment, but to all property acquired by the taxpayer during the life of the lien. This is the important **after-acquired property** scope of a federal tax lien. A federal tax lien has an effective term of ten years and can be renewed for another ten-year term during a period of up to 30 days following expiration of the original term (26 U.S.C. §6323).

EXAMPLE

> Recall from Illustration 1-a that Abe Mendoza was audited by the IRS and has been assessed taxes, interest, and penalties totaling $50,000. Assume that the assessment against Mendoza is made by the IRS on January 5 of this year. Assume further that the IRS sends out its Notice and Demand for Payment to Mendoza on January 10 advising him that he has ten days from the date of the notice, or until January 20, to pay the assessment. He is unable to pay. The federal tax lien comes into being on January 21, following the expiration of the ten days, but it will be retroactive to January 5, the date of the assessment. The lien attaches to all of Mendoza's property, both real and personal. If Mendoza buys a new car on February 28, or if Mendoza Construction buys a new backhoe on March 30, the federal lien will automatically attach to both of those items per *Glass City Bank*. If it is not paid or settled, the federal lien against Mendoza will be effective for ten years from the date of assessment. The government may also report the lien to credit bureaus, significantly damaging Mendoza's ability to borrow money or obtain credit.

b. Perfecting the Federal Tax Lien

As between the federal government and the taxpayer, the lien is effective as of the date of attachment. However, to perfect the tax lien and thus attain priority status over other subsequent claimants to the taxpayer's property, the federal government must properly file a **Notice of Federal Tax Lien (NFTL).** 26 U.S.C. §6323 allows states to designate the public office where the NFTL is to be filed and many states have adopted the **Revised Uniform Federal Tax Lien Registration Act** or the more recent **Uniform Federal Lien Registration Act** which make such designations (e.g., NFTLs on personal property of corporations, partnerships, and trusts to be filed in the Office of the Secretary of State; NFTLs on real property to be filed in the public office for filing land records for the county in which the property is located). Absent designation by the state of a specific public office for filing a NFTL, it is to be filed with the U.S. District Court for the federal district in which the property is located.

Illustration 6-h shows the NFTL sent to Abe Mendoza.

The filing of the NFTL **perfects** the lien of the federal government in the taxpayer's property. As we have learned in connection with filing a mortgage instrument in Chapter Four or a financing statement in Chapter Five, filing the NFTL gives **constructive notice** to the world of the government's secured position in the taxpayer's assets and will give the government priority over earlier unsecured or secured but unperfected claims to the taxpayer's property and, with

Illustration 6-h: NOTICE OF FEDERAL TAX LIEN

Notice of Federal Tax Lien

District: Eastern District of Columbiana   Serial No. 919654312X

As provided by sections 6321, 6322, and 6323 of the Internal Revenue Code, we are giving a notice that taxes (including interest and penalties) have been assessed against the following-named tax-payer as of January 5, YR00. We have made a demand for payment of this liability, but it remains unpaid. Therefore, there is a lien in favor of the United States on all property and rights to property belonging to this taxpayer for the amount of these taxes, and additional penalties, interest, and costs that may accrue.

Name of Tax Payer: Abelard Mendoza

Residence: 8865 Shady Lane

        Capitol City, Columbiana

IMPORTANT RELEASE INFORMATION: For each assessment listed below, unless notice of lien is refiled by the date given in column (d), this notice shall, on the day following such date, operate as a certificate of release as defined in IRC 6325(a).

Kind of Tax (a)	Tax Period (b)	Date of Assessment (c)	Last Day for Refiling (d)	Balance of Assessment (e)
1040	12/31/YR-4	1/05/YR00	9/26/YR-3	$15,000
1040	12/31/YR-3	1/05/YR00	9/26/YR-2	$17,000
1040	12/31/YR-2	1/05/YR00	9/26/YR-1	$18,000

Total: $50,000

Place of Filing: County Auditor
        Capitol County
        Capitol City, Columbiana
This notice was prepared and signed at Capitol City, Columbiana
this 10th day of January, YR00 and is filed as of that date.

Signature: _____

John R. Colby
Revenue Officer, 91-0987

---

a few exceptions, over later claims to that property, whether secured and perfected or not.

P-H 6-p: Look at the NFTL in Illustration 6-h. Can you locate the part of the notice that indicates that the assessment arises out of unpaid income taxes? The part that indicates the tax years upon which the assessment was based? The part that indicates when the tax lien expires? The part that indicates the amount of assessment made for each tax year? The part that indicates the date the notice was filed?

> **P-H 6-q:**   What have you learned previously that helps you understand why the federal tax lien takes precedence over later claims to Mendoza's property whether secured and perfected or not?

It is important to understand that although the effective date of attachment of a federal tax lien is retroactive to the date of the assessment, the effective date of perfection of the lien will be the date the notice of lien is properly filed, not the date of assessment.

> **P-H 6-r:**   Using the dates and timing mentioned in the previous example, assume that on March 1, Abe Mendoza borrows $10,000 from a local bank and secures repayment of the loan with a second mortgage in his home on Shady Lane. Assume further that the bank properly records the mortgage that same day, perfecting its claim. Another bank holds the first mortgage on the property from several years ago and that first mortgage is properly recorded and perfected. Once the government files its NFTL in Illustration 6-h, what is the order of priority of the claims to the real property as between the first mortgage holder, the second mortgage holder, and the federal government holding the tax lien?

If the taxpayer wishes to sell property subject to a federal tax lien, he can apply to the IRS for a *discharge* of tax lien on that property so the buyer can take free and clear of the lien. Obviously the IRS is not going to agree to that unless the taxpayer/seller agrees that the IRS will receive all or some agreed part of the proceeds of sale. A **discharge certificate** is also issued when the taxpayer pays off the indebtedness (26 U.S.C. §6325). The IRS can also agree to withdraw a lien from property if the taxpayer consents to pay the indebtedness in agreed-upon installments. The IRS can also agree to **subordinate** its tax lien in certain property to another creditor.

EXAMPLE

> Assume that in his negotiations with the IRS over his tax assessment, Abe Mendoza convinces the IRS that if he can obtain a debt consolidation loan, he can turn his financial fortunes around and make enough money to pay off all his debts, including the tax assessment. But the lender will not consent to this new loan unless it gets a first secured position in all Mendoza's assets. The IRS, if convinced this plan has potential to succeed, may consent to a subordination of its lien to the new lenders in hopes of increasing the likelihood of ultimate payment. In December 2008 the IRS eased and expedited the process of subordinating a federal tax lien to a private mortgage if the agency concludes that doing so may ultimately assist in collecting the tax debt. A policy resulting from the current mortgage foreclosure crisis discussed in Chapter Four, the idea is to consider subordinating a tax lien to enable refinancing of the private mortgage or a sale of the house.

c. Levying on the Federal Tax Lien

Levy Seizing or taking control of a debtor's property pursuant to a lien or writ of execution.

The federal government may **levy** (rhymes with *heavy* and means to seize or execute) on its tax lien without court action by issuing a **Notice of Intent to Levy** to the taxpayer. The notice of intent to levy must be provided to the taxpayer at least 30 days before the levy occurs (26 U.S.C. §6331). The federal tax levy can also include a *garnishment* or *wage attachment*, which we will consider in more detail in Chapter Eleven.

2. State and Local Tax Liens

State and local governments may also assert tax liens on property of a taxpayer for the failure to pay state income taxes or state or local property taxes on real or personal property. Probably the most common scenario giving rise to a state or local tax lien is a property owner's failure to pay the **property tax** on real estate. In most states the procedure for creating and perfecting the lien is similar to that used in federal tax liens. The government entity asserting the lien must give notice to the taxpayer of the delinquency, identify the property in question, state the amount owed, provide a due date, and state the intent to subject the real property in question to a tax lien. The notice must also go to any mortgage holder of record in the property since its interest may be affected by a foreclosure on the tax lien. If the debt is not paid by the due date, the government must then file a notice of lien with the appropriate public office, perfecting the lien.

In many states, the state tax lien is given **superpriority** status over not just subsequent claims against the property but also over preexisting, perfected security interests, whether consensual or nonconsensual. And 26 U.S.C. §6323(b) allows states to assert priority of a state or local tax lien over a previously existing federal tax lien. In states electing to exercise that priority, a statute such as the one shown in Illustration 6-i is common.

P-H 6-s: Assume you work for the mortgage department of City Bank and Trust (CBT). Your office receives a formal notice that the state has assessed back taxes in the amount of $10,000 against the owner of a parcel of real property in which CBT holds a first mortgage. Thereafter, the state properly files a notice of tax lien on the property. The owner of the parcel is current on his payments to the bank and there is only $5,000 of equity in the property. The property's appraised value is $150,000 and the owner still owes the bank $145,000. Why does the bank have good reason to be very concerned about this tax lien? What different courses of action might the bank take to prevent foreclosure on the tax lien?

If payment is not made after the required notice has been given to the debtor and the notice of tax lien filed, the state or local government may foreclose or execute on its lien. In some states, the government entity is permitted to proceed with nonjudicial **self-help foreclosure** or **seizure** of the burdened property. In others, a **judicial foreclosure** is required, which, we have learned, means the

Illustration 6-i: TYPICAL STATE STATUTE CLAIMING SUPERPRIORITY STATUS FOR TAX LIEN

> The taxes assessed by the state of Columbiana, a county, or municipality, taxing district, or other local governmental entity, upon any property of whatever kind, and all penalties, interest, and costs accruing thereon, shall become and remain a first lien upon such property from January 1 of the year for which such taxes are assessed.

government must file a lawsuit and obtain a court order allowing sale. There usually is a statutory **right of redemption** in favor of the taxpayer either up until the time of sale or, in some states, for a designated period after the sale (e.g., one year).

F. ► Lien *Lis Pendens*

Lis pendens Public notice that a lawsuit is pending regarding title, possession, or other rights to real property.

A lien *lis pendens* (lien pending the suit) is a statutory lien that may be created in favor of one having a claim against a particular parcel of real property. The purpose of the lien is to put potential purchasers of the property and creditors on formal notice of the lien holder's claim against the property until such time as a lawsuit regarding that claim can be litigated in court. This lien is not available against personal property.

In most states, to create a lien *lis pendens*, the claimant must file an **abstract** (or **notice**) **of lien *lis pendens*** in the designated public office (usually the county office where land records are filed or recorded). The abstract typically must contain the names of the parties to the suit, a description of the real estate affected, its ownership, and a brief statement of the nature of the claim and the amount of the lien sought to be fixed. The lawsuit regarding the claim is normally filed simultaneously with the abstract so that the abstract can reference the pending suit. Some states require the lawsuit to be filed before the abstract; others require the suit to be filed within a stated number of days after the abstract is filed (e.g., five days).

The filing or recording of the abstract or notice puts the world on *constructive notice* of the lien holder's claim to the property and has the practical effect of creating a cloud on the title to the property, preventing its sale or further encumbrance, until a lawsuit to enforce the lien can be filed and litigated.

A lien *lis pendens* can *only* be filed when the lien holder has a claim to an interest in the property encumbered with the lien. It *cannot* be filed against any real property owned by the person with whom the lien holder has a dispute just because there is a dispute, and it cannot be used to secure property in a contract or tort action in which the property is not in dispute.

EXAMPLE

Recall from Illustration 1-b that Abe Mendoza discovered last month that his bookkeeper has been embezzling from his business. She is believed to have stolen more than $100,000. Mendoza certainly has legal standing to sue the bookkeeper to recover the stolen money but he cannot file a lien *lis pendens* against real property she may own just because she owes him money. However, if the facts were that the bookkeeper had used all or a portion of the stolen money to purchase the real property that she owns, then Mendoza could ask the court to declare a **constructive trust** in the real property since the property is, in whole or part, the proceeds of his stolen money.

Constructive trust An equitable remedy pursuant to which one who has wrongfully obtained title to or possession of real or personal property is deemed to hold that property in trust for the benefit of the true owner.

Assertion of a constructive trust in real property as a result of theft or fraud is a common basis for filing a lien *lis pendens*. A constructive trust is an involuntary trust declared by a court to exist in (real or personal) property owned or controlled by one person who must then hold it for the benefit of another in order to prevent an injustice. Other common grounds for assertion of a lien *lis pendens* are a genuine dispute over ownership, fraudulent conveyance, and enforcement of an equitable vendor's lien (see Section H). If Abe Mendoza does claim a constructive trust in real property owned by his former bookkeeper and files suit to collect the debt and have the constructive trust declared in that property, his lawyer may simultaneously file a lien *lis pendens* against the property. The abstract of lien *lis pendens* will look like Illustration 6-j.

The holder of a lien *lis pendens* has no right per se to foreclose on the lien. The claimant's rights in the property will be litigated in the lawsuit filed and are subject to the court's ruling. The owner of the property may sell or encumber the property after the lien *lis pendens* is created and before the lawsuit is over, unless the court issues a restraining order or a prejudgment attachment (discussed in Chapter Nine), freezing title to the property pending the suit. However, any purchaser or mortgagee will take title subject to the senior claim of the lien holder in the property.

Illustration 6-j: ABSTRACT OF LIEN *LIS PENDENS*

IN THE CAPITOL COUNTY COLUMBIANA CIRCUIT COURT

ABELARD MENDOZA, d/b/a	)	
MENDOZA CONSTRUCTION	)	
Plaintiff	)	
v.	)	DOCKET NO. 08-98777
HILDA MONTGOMERY	)	
Defendant	)	

ABSTRACT OF LIEN LIS PENDENS

Pursuant to Columbiana Statutory Code §66-10-212, notice is hereby given of a suit filed in the Circuit Court for Capitol County, Columbiana, bearing Case No.08-98777, where Abelard Mendoza, d/b/a/ Mendoza Construction is the Plaintiff, and Hilda Montgomery is the Defendant (the "Lawsuit"). A certified copy of the complaint in the Lawsuit is attached to this Abstract.

The Lawsuit is a complaint on behalf of Plaintiff alleging embezzlement and theft of funds which Plaintiff alleges were wrongfully used by Defendant to purchase the real property described below entitling Plaintiff to have a constructive trust declared in that real property for the amount of his funds used to purchase it.

The real property that is the subject of the Lawsuit is located at 765 Western Heights Blvd. in Capitol City, Columbiana and is more particularly described as follows: [Legal description of property omitted from illustration.]

Plaintiff is asserting a lien lis pendens upon the property in the amount of its claim against Defendant totaling $100,000 plus any prejudgment interest that may be awarded in the Lawsuit.

Respectfully submitted,

_____

Carlton W. Fisk,
Attorney for Plaintiff

G. ▶ The Lien for Unpaid Child Support

As part of the **Personal Responsibility and Work Opportunity Reconciliation Act of 1996 (PRWORA)**, Congress required the states, as a condition to receiving federal funding for job training and other programs intended to reform public assistance programs in this country, to establish new procedures for enforcing child support orders. The statute (42 U.S.C. §666(a)(4)) now requires all states to have laws or procedures pursuant to which child support arrearages become liens, by operation of law, against all real and personal property owned by an obligor who either resides or owns property in that state.

The manner of creating, perfecting, and enforcing the child support lien varies somewhat among the states, but Illustration 6-k contains the text of a portion of the North Carolina child support lien statute, which reflects procedures that are common among the states.

P-H 6-t: Recall from Illustration 1-a that Nick Murphy has a son, Robbie, by a first marriage, which ended in divorce. Nick is obligated to pay his ex-wife, Sharon Murphy, Robbie's mother, $400 per month in child support. Assume that Columbiana, where Nick lives, has the same child support lien statute as in Illustration 6-k. And assume that Nick is now four months behind in his child support payments to Sharon. Nick pays his child support obligation directly to Sharon and no Title IV-D agency is involved in collecting that obligation.

- Can Sharon assert a child support lien against Nick's property in Columbiana?
- Will the lien be valid against both real and personal property owned by Nick in the state?
- What is the first step that Sharon should take in order to create the child support lien?
- Where is the required verified statement to be filed?
- What does the notice to Nick, as the obligor, have to contain?
- How is the child support lien on personal property perfected in a non-Title IV-D case? On real property in a non-Title IV-D case?
- When does the child support lien attach to personal property of the obligor? To real property of the obligor?
- What priority does a properly perfected child support lien have against subsequent liens on the same property? Does it have any priority over previously created and perfected liens on the same property?
- Can a child support lien created in another state be enforced in Columbiana?
- If you instructor directs, draft a verified statement of child support delinquency and a notice to obligor on behalf of Sharon Murphy in connection with his delinquent obligation.

Illustration 6-k: NORTH CAROLINA CHILD SUPPORT LIEN STATUTE (N.C. GEN. STAT. §44-86)

LIENS FOR OVERDUE CHILD SUPPORT

§44-86. Lien on real and personal property of person owing past-due child support; definitions; filing required; discharge.

(b) Lien Created.—There is created a general lien upon the real and personal property of any person who is delinquent in the payment of court-ordered child support. For purposes of this section, an obligor is delinquent when arrears under a court-ordered child support obligation equals three months of payments or three thousand dollars ($3,000), whichever occurs first. The amount of the lien shall be determined by a verified statement of child support delinquency prepared in accordance with subsection (c) of this section.

(c) Contents of Statement; Verification.—A verified statement of child support delinquency shall contain the following information:

(1) The caption and file docket number of the case in which child support was ordered;
(2) The date of the order of support;
(3) The amount of the child support obligation established by the order; and
(4) The amount of the arrearage as of the date of the statement.

The statement shall be verified by the designated representative in a IV-D case and by the obligee in a non-IV-D case.

(d) Filing and Perfection of Lien.—The verified statement shall be filed in the office of the clerk of superior court in the county in which the child support was ordered. At the time of filing the verified statement, the designated representative in a IV-D case and the obligee in a non-IV-D case shall serve notice on the obligor that the statement has been filed. The notice shall be served and the return of service filed with the clerk of court in accordance with Rule 4 of the North Carolina Rules of Civil Procedure. The notice shall specify the manners in which the lien may be discharged. Upon perfection of the lien, as set forth herein, the clerk shall docket and index the statement on the judgment docket. The clerk shall issue a transcript of the docketed statement to the clerk of any other county as requested by the designated representative in a IV-D case or the obligee in a non-IV-D case. The clerk receiving the transcript shall docket and index the transcript. A lien on personal property attaches when the property is seized by the sheriff. A lien on real property attaches when the perfected lien is docketed and indexed on the judgment docket.

(1) IV-D Cases.—In IV-D cases, the filing of a verified statement with the clerk of court by the designated representative shall perfect the lien. The obligor may contest the lien by motion in the cause.

(2) Non-IV-D Cases.—In a non-IV-D case, the notice to the obligor of the filing of the verified statement shall state that the obligor has 30 days from the date of service to request a hearing before a district court judge to contest the validity of the lien. If the obligor fails to contest the lien after 30 days from the time of service, the obligee may make application to the clerk, and the clerk shall record and index the lien on the judgment docket. If the obligee files a petition contesting the validity of the lien, a hearing shall be held before a district court judge to determine whether the lien is valid and proper. In contested cases, the clerk of court shall record and index the lien on the judgment docket only by order of the judge. The docketing of a verified statement in a non-IV-D case shall perfect the lien when duly recorded and indexed.

(e) Lien Superior to Subsequent Liens.—Except as otherwise provided by law, a lien established in accordance with this section shall take priority over all other liens subsequently acquired and shall continue from the date of filing until discharged in accordance with G.S. 44-87.

(f) Execution on the Lien.—A designated representative in a IV-D case, after 30 days from the docketing of the perfected lien, or an obligee in a non-IV-D case, after docketing the perfected lien, may enforce the lien in the same manner as for a civil judgment.

(g) Liens Arising Out-of-State.—This State shall accord full faith and credit to child support liens arising in another state when the child support enforcement agency, party, or other entity seeking to enforce the lien complies with the requirements relating to recording and serving child support liens as set forth in this Article and with the requirements relating to the enforcement of foreign judgments as set forth in Chapter 1C of the General Statutes.

H. The Vendor's Lien on Real Property

Vendor's lien An equitable lien afforded to sellers of property on the real property sold to assure payment of the purchase price.

Equitable lien A lien created by court rulings rather than by statute.

A **vendor's lien** (also called a **mortgage lien**), a lien recognized in some states by statute or common law or both, is afforded to sellers of real property on the real property sold in the event the buyer fails to make payment when due. It is referred to as an **equitable lien** or **special lien** and is not dependent on the seller retaining possession of the property.

This lien scenario arises most commonly where the seller of land self-financed the sale by agreeing to accept direct payment(s) from the buyer rather than requiring the buyer to obtain financing to pay the seller in full at closing, but failed to have the buyer convey a consensual mortgage in the property to the seller to secure payment (a purchase money mortgage) (see Chapter Four). It might also arise where an owner of land agreed to convey a mortgage in the land to a creditor and then refused to cooperate in finalizing the mortgage. Or it might arise when one in possession of property and believing herself to be the owner makes permanent improvements to property enhancing its value and then is dispossessed by the true owner.

Where it is recognized, the lien authorizes the holder to pursue recovery of the real property in the hands not only of the buyer but also of anyone who has purchased the property from the buyer with actual or constructive notice that the purchase price to the seller has not been paid. The lien is typically created by recording the contract of sale or other documentation establishing the transaction and obligation in the county office where land records are to be filed.

EXAMPLE

Assume you have an owner of real property very eager to sell it—hardly an unusual circumstance following the crash of the real estate market that precipitated the Great Recession. The owner has found a buyer, but the buyer is unable to qualify for a traditional mortgage loan from any lender owing to poor credit or questions about whether the buyer's projected income flow is sufficient. The owner decides to assume the risk that the lenders will not and agrees to self-finance this purchase by the buyer. However, the owner fails to require the buyer to grant the owner a **purchase money mortgage** (see the discussion in Section D of Chapter Four). If the buyer defaults, then the owner may be able to assert the equitable vendor's lien to retake possession of the property notwithstanding the absence of a mortgage. If the buyer has not only defaulted but also transferred an interest in the property to someone else (e.g., has resold it or granted a security interest in it to a third-party), the owner may be able nonetheless to assert the lien against the property in the hands of that third-party if the owner can show that the third-party knew or should have known that a balance was still owed to the owner on the initial sale at the time it received an interest in the property.

In the personal property context, equitable liens are essentially identical to constructive trusts discussed earlier in this chapter and arise under the same circumstances.

CONCLUSION

This chapter concludes our consideration of how debt is created and secured, the topics of Part A. We are ready now to consider how debt is collected when it is not paid as promised. Collection of debt is the subject of Part B. You may think that to collect past due debt the creditor automatically files suit to obtain a judgment for what is owed, but that usually is not the case. More often, the creditor initiates prelitigation collection efforts, which is what we consider in the next chapter.

CHAPTER SUMMARY

In this chapter we have considered nonconsensual or involuntary liens, also known as statutory liens because they are created by state or federal statute. A mechanic's lien is one that attaches to real property for the improvement of which the lien holder has supplied labor or materials. The procedure for creating a mechanic's lien typically involves sending a notice of nonpayment to the obligor within the statutory time frame and then filing a notice (or abstract) of lien in the proper public office. Statutory time periods for filing and notice may run from the last date labor or materials were supplied, the date the contract ended, or the date of substantial completion of the construction project. To enforce the mechanic's lien, a lawsuit must then be filed by the lien holder within another statutory period or the lien will expire. Once properly noticed and filed, a mechanic's line will be deemed perfected and will have priority over any unperfected secured claim to the same real property. And if the state statute contains a relation-back feature, the mechanic's lien may enjoy priority over prior perfected security interests in the property as well.

The artisan's lien is a possessory lien that attaches to personal property to secure payment due for repair or improvement of the personal property. An artisan's lien is typically enforced by giving written notice of intent to sell to the owner, and to anyone else known to claim an interest in the property, within the statutory time period and complying with any public notice requirement. The artisan's lien normally has no priority over prior secured claims of record, absent notice to and consent by the prior lien holder.

The attorney's charging lien is a nonpossessory lien imposed on any judgment or settlement amount due a client for amounts due the attorney and is enforced by providing and recording written notice of lien and filing suit to enforce it. Healthcare liens may be asserted by insurance companies that have paid policy benefits or medical practitioners or hospitals that have provided medical services against third parties who may owe or be liable to the insured/patient in connection with the medical condition. Such liens are created by verified statement of the provider properly recorded in the designated public records office and are typically enforced by lawsuit.

A tax lien may be imposed by the governmental taxing authority on the real and personal property of a delinquent tax payer. The tax lien attaches automatically some number of days following the statutory notice and demand for payment and is normally retroactive to the date of assessment. A federal tax lien is perfected by filing a notice of federal tax lien in the appropriate public records office. State and local tax liens are usually created and perfected similarly to the federal tax lien. However, many states give state tax liens superpriority status over even prior perfected claims to debtor's property.

A lien *lis pendens* may be asserted by one having a contested claim to real property and is created by filing a notice (or abstract) of lien *lis pendens* in the appropriate public records office and is enforced by a lawsuit. By federal statute, states must provide that child support arrearages become liens, by operation of law, against all real and personal property owned by an obligor who either resides or owns property in the state. A vendor's (or mortgage) lien is an equitable afforded to sellers of real property on the real property sold in the event the buyer fails to make payment when due.

REVIEW QUESTIONS

1. Explain the difference between a statutory lien that is possessory and one that is nonpossessory.
2. What do we mean by the "date of substantial completion" and why is that a frequent subject of dispute in construction contracts?
3. Explain the relation-back feature of some state mechanic's lien statutes. What difference might it make whether the lien holder is a general contractor or a subcontractor or a supplier on the project?
4. Who is and is not an artisan for purposes of the artisan's lien? Give examples of the kinds of businesses likely to be able to assert an artisan's lien in personal property.
5. Name at least five other types of possessory liens in addition to the artisan's lien.
6. Why must an attorney representing an injured plaintiff be careful to ascertain outstanding medical and hospital bills before settling the client's claim?
7. Explain why the date a federal tax lien attaches to a debtor's property is not the same as the date the tax lien is deemed perfected.
8. Why is it a good idea for lenders taking a mortgage on a debtor's property to secure repayment to require that the debtor fund an escrow account from which the lender can pay state taxes on the property?
9. Can a lien *lis pendens* be filed against the real property of any debtor who owes money to a creditor? Why or why not? Can a lien *lis pendens* be filed against personal property?
10. What is the difference between an equitable lien and a statutory lien? What is a constructive trust?

WORDS AND PHRASES TO REMEMBER

abstract of lien *lis pendens*	audit
accountant's retaining lien	banker's lien
artisan's lien	carrier's lien
assessment	child support lien
attachment	common law
attorney's charging lien	common law lien
attorney's retaining lien	consensual lien

construction lien
constructive notice
constructive trust
contractual lien
cotton ginner's lien
discharge certificate
discharge of tax lien
equitable lien
garage keeper's lien
healthcare services lien
hospital lien
hotel operator's lien
involuntary lien
landlord's lien
launderer's lien
layaway
layby
levy
lien holder
lien *lis pendens*
materialman's lien
mechanic's lien
Miller Act
newspaper of general circulation
nonconsensual lien
notice and demand for payment
notice of completion
notice of federal tax lien

notice of intent to levy
notice of lien
notice of lien *lis pendens*
notice of nonpayment
nonpossessory lien
performance bond
printer's lien
property tax
possessory lien
purchase money mortgage
Revised Uniform Federal Tax
    Lien Registration Act
sovereign immunity
statutory lien
substantial completion
supplier's lien
tax lien
Uniform Federal Lien
    Registration Act
unperfected
vehicle repairer's lien
vendor's lien in personal
    property
vendor's lien in real property
voluntary lien
warrant of distress

TO LEARN MORE: A number of TLM activities to accompany this chapter are accessible on the student disc accompanying the text and on the Author Updates link to the text Web site at http://www.aspenparalegaled.com/ books/parsons_ abcdebt/default.asp.

THE COLLECTION OF DEBT

Introduction

Many lawyers specialize in **debt collection**; it is what they do every day. Many more attorneys do it only occasionally. There are two distinct stages to debt collection. The first is the prelitigation effort to collect the debt, which is the subject of Chapter Seven. In this first stage, the collection lawyer will typically make contact with the debtor by means of a demand letter. The demand letter may result in payment being made. Or it may induce negotiations leading to an agreed payment schedule or the compromise of disputed debt. There are also **debt collection companies**, private businesses involved in prelitigation debt collection activities on behalf of creditors, usually for a percentage of what is collected.

Anyone engaged in prelitigation debt collection must be thoroughly familiar with the legal guidelines that govern collection activities. Debtors today have substantial legal protections from certain collection tactics. And attorneys or debt collection companies who violate those protections while attempting to collect debt for a client can suffer severe consequences, including being sued for monetary damages by the debtor, being fined by government agencies regulating these activities, and, for the attorney, being subject to disciplinary action.

If prelitigation collection efforts fail, the creditor may decide to simply write off the unpaid obligation as a **bad debt**. Or the creditor may authorize the collection lawyer to file a lawsuit seeking a final court judgment against the debtor for the amount owed. The collection lawsuit is the second stage of debt collection. We will consider the process of reducing a claim to judgment and executing on that judgment in Chapters Eight through Eleven.

Debt collection companies Private businesses involved in prelitigation debt collection activities on behalf of creditors, usually for a percentage of what is collected.

Bad debt An uncollectible debt. May be written off as a loss.

Chapter Seven:

▶ # Prelitigation Efforts to Collect Delinquent Debt

If your debtor be in straights, grant him a delay until he can discharge his debt;
but if you waive the sum as alms it will be better for you, if you but knew it.
—*The Koran (Chapter 7)*

▶ ## Introduction to Part B: The Collection of Debt

According to the Consumer Financial Protection Bureau, in the aftermath of the housing crises and Great Recession, approximately 30 million Americans (about 1 in 10) are being pursued by a debt collector today for debt that averages $1,500 per debtor. And that statistic does not include nonconsumer debt in arrears at any given time.

The debt collection business, which has been around as long as there has been debt to collect, is booming in America today. In the five chapters that make up this part of the text, we will consider the debt collection process thoroughly, beginning with routine prelitigation efforts to collect delinquent debt, then moving on to the when and how of a typical collection lawsuit, and concluding with a comprehensive examination of how a final judgment is executed on and satisfied.

A. The Fair Debt Collection Practices Act

Today, lawyers and the legal professionals who assist them are heavily involved in prelitigation debt collection activities. And it is the assisting legal professional who often has the most direct and frequent contact with the debtor. Debt collection companies commonly hire nonlawyers with paralegal training. Alternatively, one with paralegal training may find herself working in a nontraditional paralegal setting for a company that generates **accounts receivables** and chooses to undertake **in-house debt collection**, putting her at the forefront of those efforts. In any of those employment contexts the trained legal professional must be aware of the limitations imposed by the law on prelitigation debt collection activities.

Fair Debt Collection Practices Act (FDCPA) 15 USC §1601, et seq. Federal statute regulating *debt collectors.*

The place to start understanding those limitations is, beyond question, the **Fair Debt Collection Practices Act (FDCPA).** Debt collection practices have historically been subject to a great deal of abuse. Before such practices were prohibited, it was common for creditors or their representatives to harass, embarrass, and humiliate debtors until a bill was paid. Insulting letters were common.

Threats to sue, to commit violence, to get the debtor fired, to pursue the debtor for the rest of his life were made. Profanity, browbeating, insults, and name calling (deadbeat, bum, cheat, thief, liar, etc.) were common both in correspondence and conversations. Telephone calls could be made as frequently as the debt collector wished and at any time, night or day. Personal visits to the debtor's house or workplace to demand payment could be made at any time, night or day. Relatives, neighbors, friends, employers, and coworkers of the debtor could be contacted and told of the debt, embarrassing the debtor and putting pressure on the debtor to pay. Creditors could undertake these debt collection efforts themselves or hire a business that specialized in debt collection. Or they could hire an attorney to do it for them.

In 1977, because of the growing amount of debt in our consumer society and the growing awareness of excessive debt collection practices by creditors and the debt collection industry, Congress passed the FDCPA found at 15 U.S.C. §1601, et seq. The FDCPA regulates the debt collection industry by prohibiting abusive collection practices and providing redress for the debtor who is victimized by them. In most states it is the single most important source of debt collection practices regulation. A number of states have passed their own debt collection practices regulations, usually enforced by a state agency charged with consumer protection or by the state attorney general (www.naag.org/). In other states, there is no specific debt collection regulation but relief may be had by debtors under the state's generic **consumer protection act**, which provides remedies for any unfair or deceptive trade practice directed at a consumer. Most states enacting specific debt collection regulation closely track the federal law concerning what constitutes a violation and remedies. In a few such states, however, the regulation of debt collection activity is even more stringent than the federal FDCPA, or state law imposes more substantial penalties than the FDCPA.

EXAMPLE

California's Fair Debt Collection Practices Act (California Civil Code §1788, et seq.), known generally as the Rosenthal Act, regulates creditors collecting their own debt, which the FDCPA does not, as we will see in Section 1. The California act also places more limitations than the FDCPA does on a debt collector contacting the debtor's employer, a topic discussed in Section 2. Many states also require debt collectors to be licensed or registered by the state, a level of regulation not imposed by the FDCPA.

P-H 7-a: The **Privacy Rights Clearinghouse** maintains a Web site with links to state debt collection laws at www.privacyrights.org/fs/fs27plus.htm. Is your state listed there? If so, what agency or government department enforces your state law? Is there a private right of action allowed for violation of your state law (see discussion in Section 4)? Must debt collectors be licensed in your state? Does your statute appear to impose more stringent limitations on debt collectors than do those in the FDCPA, summarized below? If your state attorney general's office enforces your state debt collection law, locate that office from the Web site of the National Association of Attorneys General (www.naag.org/). Does your attorney general's Web site mention abusive debt collection practices? Does it provide a convenient way to file a complaint regarding such practices?

1. Whom the FDCPA Regulates

Debt collectors Businesses where the principal purpose is to collect debts owed to consumers and individuals who regularly collect or attempt to collect such debt.

The primary regulation of debt collection activities by the FDCPA is aimed at those defined by the statute (§803(6)) as **debt collectors**. Persons acting for businesses, *"the principal purpose of which"* is to collect debts owed to another, are included, as is any individual who *"regularly collects or attempts to collect"* debts owed to another. This can include **third-party collection agencies** retained by the creditor to collect debt owed to the creditor by the debtor. It can also include **asset buyers** (also called **debt buyers**), which purchase delinquent or charged-off accounts from a creditor for a fraction of the face value of the debt and then seek to collect it themselves. Most asset buyers follow a **collection cycle** (e.g., 90 days or 6 months) in which they will attempt to collect the debt they have purchased and, failing that, will then sell the account to another asset buyer for an even more steeply discounted price from its original face value. In the business, it is not unusual for a debt account to be sold and resold numerous times. We will encounter asset buyers again in Part C of the text when we consider the bankruptcy process.

P-H 7-b: The history of the asset buyer industry is interesting. There has always been some market for debts that a creditor has given up on and is considering writing off as uncollectible. But the industry boomed as a result of the **Savings and Loan crisis of the 1980s** when 118 state and federally insured savings and loan (S&L) institutions holding $43 billion in assets failed in a 2-year period. The **Federal Deposit Insurance Corporation (FDIC)**, which insured deposits in those institutions, took over those failing S&Ls and made good all amounts on deposit at the expense of the taxpayers. The **Resolution Trade Corporation (RTC)** was then formed by the FDIC and began to actively seek buyers willing to purchase the assets of closed S&Ls, including both current and delinquent accounts. Auctions were held around the country at which performing and nonperforming accounts were bundled and sold to the highest bidder with no opportunity by the bidder to evaluate the specific accounts in the bundle purchased. Thus was birthed the modern asset buying industry.

P-H 7-c: You can read a thorough history of the S&L crisis of the 1980s at www.fdic.gov/bank/historical/history/167_188.pdf. You will see startling comparisons between that crisis and the subprime lending and mortgage foreclosure crisis of our day described in detail in Chapter Four. Both financial crises requiring bailouts by the American taxpayer were triggered by congressional deregulation of the relevant financial markets. Feel free to ask yourself the following question: When will we ever learn that greed and the inevitable human impulse to do stupid and illegal things in search of the almighty dollar must be regulated?

Interestingly, the statute excludes creditors themselves from the definition of debt collector since the creditor would be attempting to collect his own debt and not debt owed to another. However, the creditor himself can qualify as a debt collector under the statute if he "uses any name other than his own which would indicate that a third person is collecting or attempting to collect such debts" (§803(6)). And even where a creditor may not be regulated by FDCPA, he must be aware of potential tort liability that can arise in connection with debt collection activities, as discussed in Section C, below.

EXAMPLE

Recall that Nick and Pearl Murphy are obligated to Shears Department Store on the Installment Sale and Security Agreement in Illustration 5-a. If Shears collects its debts in its own name, it is not considered a debt collector within the meaning of the FDCPA. But if Shears sets up a subsidiary to collect its account receivables and calls it Credit Collectors, Inc., that subsidiary will be a regulated debt collector under the FDCPA even though it only collects debt owed to Shears. But before you conclude that Shears can engage in any collection tactic it wants in collecting its own debt under its own name, you will want to check to see 1) if state law imposes more stringent statutory regulation on collection activities than the FDCPA and 2) if tort theories recognized by relevant state law limit certain collection activities (see Section C).

EC 7-a: Although creditors can undertake their own prelitigation debt collection efforts, they may not be able to represent themselves in a civil lawsuit based on the debt (see Chapters Eight and Nine). Generally, individuals can represent themselves in court. When a person chooses to represent himself and not have a lawyer do it, we call that appearing before the court *pro se*. However, a corporation or other entity that is a party to a lawsuit cannot appear pro se and must be represented by counsel. Why? Because someone must come into the courtroom and speak for the entity (an officer or other employee of a corporation, for example). In doing so, that someone is technically practicing law because they are representing another (the entity) in a legal matter without a law license And that constitutes the unauthorized practice of law. As a result, entity creditors, while they can engage in prelitigation collection efforts without counsel, cannot file a collection lawsuit without one. An individual debtor on the other hand, including a sole proprietor who is not considered a separate entity from his business, can both engage in prelitigation collection efforts without counsel and appear **pro se** (in his own behalf) in a collection lawsuit.

What about attorneys who are hired by a client to engage in prelitigation debt collection efforts? Are they debt collectors for purposes of the statute's regulation? The statute does not expressly include attorneys hired by creditors in the definition of debt collectors and for many years after it was passed no one thought attorneys were regulated by the statute. However, the U.S. Supreme Court in *Heintz v. Jenkins*, 514 U.S. 291 (1995), held that any attorney who "regularly attempts" to obtain payment of consumer debts for clients through legal proceedings falls within the definition and regulation of debt collectors in the statute.

How frequently does an attorney have to undertake collection work before she will be deemed to be one who "regularly attempts" to obtain payment for clients? Once in a career? Unlikely. Once a year? Twice a year? Once a month? The Supreme Court didn't make it clear in *Heintz*, and no one can be sure. Consequently, lawyers who choose to undertake debt collection for clients are well advised to comply with the requirements of the Act. And legal professionals working for them must know those requirements and comply with them as well.

2. Activities Regulated by the FDCPA

The FDCPA regulates attempts to collect debt from "any *natural person* obligated or allegedly obligated to pay any debt" (§803(3)) (emphasis added). Thus, the FDCPA does *not* regulate attempts to collect debt from a debtor who is not a natural person, such as a corporate debtor. It only regulates attempts to collect debts from natural persons who are called *consumers* under the statute. Illustration 7-a lists the five categories of collection activity regulated by the FDCPA.

You should read closely for yourself the five sections of the FDCPA referenced in Illustration 7-a. The FDCPA is accessible online at a number of Web sites, including the Federal Trade Commission site (www.ftc.gov/bcp/edu/pubs/con-sumer/credit/cre27.pdf). The following subsections summarize the important provisions in each section.

a. Locating the Consumer

Pursuant to §804 of the FDCPA, a debt collector contacting someone other than the consumer himself in order to locate the consumer must properly identify himself but avoid stating that he works for a debt collection company unless specifically asked. The debt collector must state that he is looking for information to help him locate the consumer but cannot mention that the consumer owes a debt. The debt collector must not contact the same person more than once unless that person invites a subsequent contact or unless the debt collector reasonably believes the person previously contacted now has more correct information. Communications from the debt collector seeking contact information for the debtor that are placed in writing must not be by postcard (where anyone handling the card can read the message) and nothing on the envelope or in the contents of the message can disclose that the sender is a debt collector or that the debtor owes a debt.

P-H 7-d: What do you think is the policy at work behind these limitations? Are these limitations fair to the debt collector? Should there be more stringent prohibitions of the debt collector making location contacts?

Illustration 7-a: CATEGORIES OF COLLECTION ACTIVITY REGULATED BY THE FDCPA

- Acquiring information regarding the location of the consumer (see §804)
- Communications with the consumer (see §805)
- Harassment or abuse of the consumer (see §806)
- Making false or misleading representations to the consumer (see §807)
- Utilizing unfair or unconscionable means to collect a debt (see §808)

EC 7-b: Can you think of ways the unscrupulous debt collector might abuse the spirit of this prohibition without violating the letter of it?

---

b. Communications with the Consumer

Pursuant to §805 of the FDCPA, the debt collector cannot make contact with the consumer at any unusual time or place or at any time and place the creditor knows or should know would be inconvenient to the consumer. Absent information to the contrary, the debt collector is to assume that a convenient time for contacting the consumer is between 8 A.M. and 9 P.M.

If the debt collector knows that the consumer is represented by an attorney, contact must be with that attorney unless the consumer's attorney will not respond or consents to direct contact with the consumer. Contacting a consumer at work is prohibited if the debt collector knows the employer disallows such contacts.

Contacting third persons regarding the consumer's obligation is strictly limited. The debt collector is allowed to contact only the consumer himself, the consumer's attorney, the creditor, the creditor's attorney, the debt collector's attorney, or credit reporting agencies, if otherwise permitted. Note carefully the definition of consumer in §805(d). For purposes of restrictions on contacting the consumer himself, *consumer* is defined to include not just the individual who owes the debt, but his spouse, parent (if he is a minor), guardian, executor, or administrator.

P-H 7-e: Assume that one of the medical bills incurred by Pearl Murphy (Illustration 1-a) since her botched appendectomy is from Capitol City Medical Equipment (CCME) in the amount of $1,200. A debt collector hired to collect the bill, which is owed by Pearl but not by Nick, calls the Murphy home at 7:30 P.M. Nick Murphy answers and advises the caller that his wife is not at home. Can the debt collector say whatever she has to say to Nick Murphy as the spouse of the debtor without violating the statute? What specific provisions of the FDCPA tell you the answer? Now, assume it is not Nick Murphy who answers, but the Murphys' 11-year-old son, Lyndon. Can the debt collector say whatever she has to say to the son without violating the statute? What specific provisions of the FDCPA tell you the answer?

Finally, if the consumer advises the debt collector verbally or in writing that he refuses to pay the debt or does not want to be contacted any further, the contact must stop, other than the limited right of the debt collector to confirm that contact will cease or that other remedies may be or are going to be pursued (such as a collection lawsuit, to be discussed in Chapters Eight and Nine).

c. Harassment or Abuse of the Consumer

Pursuant to §806 of the statute, the debt collector cannot use or threaten to use violence or other criminal means to harm the person, reputation, or property of the consumer or anyone else. The debt collector cannot use profanity or obscene language, cannot include the consumer's name on any published a list of persons who haven't paid their debts, cannot disclose the debt by publicly advertising its sale or assignment, and cannot make anonymous phone calls or continuous phone calls intended to harass.

P-H 7-f: Assume the debt collector contacting Pearl Murphy on the debt she owes CCME contacts Pearl by phone at home at 6 P.M. but becomes angry when Pearl will not commit to pay the debt. The debt collector says if payment isn't forthcoming, she will ruin Pearl in the community and embarrass her children at their schools. When Pearl hangs up on the debt collector, she calls Pearl right back and keeps calling back every ten minutes until 9 P.M. How many violations of the FDCPA do you see?

EC 7-c: If the caller in P-H 7-f was a paralegal in your state and she was acting with the approval of her supervising attorney, how many ethical violations would have been committed by the supervising attorney? How many violations by the paralegal of paralegal ethics promulgated by the National Association of Legal Assistants (NALA) or by the National Federation of Paralegal Associations (NFPA) or by your state? If this paralegal was certified by NALA or NFPA or by your state, could this behavior threaten her certification?

---

d. False or Misleading Representations

Pursuant to §807 of the FDCPA, a debt collector cannot use "any false, deceptive, or misleading representation or means" in collecting a debt. The statute gives a number of nonexclusive examples of such prohibited acts, including

- the use of any language, clothing, or symbols that would suggest that the debt collector is affiliated with a governmental entity or a credit reporting agency, or that he is an attorney when he is not;
- saying anything false about the debt or the amount owed;
- suggesting that nonpayment of the debt is a crime or that it will result in anyone being arrested or imprisoned;
- suggesting that nonpayment will result in their property taken other than as the law allows; or
- using any false name or false paperwork.

P-H 7-g: Assume that the debt collector contacting Pearl Murphy is not an attorney. She calls the Murphys' house during permitted hours and talks with Nick Murphy, who tells the debt collector that Pearl is out of town. The debt collector hears whispering in the background and believes that Pearl is actually there at home. The debt collector calls several times over the next week and receives the same response and continues to believe that Pearl is in fact there, listening in on Nick's end of the conversation. Finally the debt collector calls the Murphy house and, when Nick answers, the caller disguises her voice and identifies herself as a police officer calling Pearl to talk with her about a crime that has been committed about which she may have knowledge. Pearl comes immediately to the phone. How many violations of §807 do you recognize?

e. Unfair or Unconscionable Means

Pursuant to §808 of the FDCPA, the debt collector "may not use unfair or unconscionable means" to collect a debt. The statute gives a number of nonexclusive examples of such practices, including

- collecting any amount not actually owed, or communicating with the consumer by postcard;
- using an envelope for communication with the consumer that identifies the sender as a debt collector;
- accepting a postdated check and then depositing or threatening to deposit it early; or
- soliciting a postdated check for the very purpose of attempting to cash it before funds are available in order to allege a criminal act by the consumer.

P-H 7-h: What other unfair or unconscionable actions can you think of that the unscrupulous debt collector might use to get the debt paid or to punish the debtor for not paying?

Though the statute does not expressly require it, a number of federal circuits have determined that Sections 804-808 of the FDCPA are to be applied using the **least sophisticated consumer standard** rather than a **reasonable consumer standard**. See, e.g., *Smith v. Consumer Credit, Inc.*, 167 F.3d 1052, 1054 (6th Cir. 1999), *Swanson v. Southern Oregon Credit Service, Inc.*, 869 F.2d 1222, 1225 (9th Cir. 1988), and *Jeter v. Credit Bureau, Inc.*, 760 F.2d 1168, 1179 (11th Cir. 1985). The least sophisticated standard is intended to protect even naïve or overly trusting consumers from deceptive debt collection practices. However, even the least sophisticated standard is applied objectively to protect debt collectors from liability for bizarre or idiosyncratic allegations from debtors. See *Arteaga v. Asset Acceptance, LLC*, 733 F. Supp.2d 1218, 1230 (E.D. Cal. 2010).

P-H 7-i: See if your federal circuit has adopted the least sophisticated consumer standard for interpreting the abuse provisions of the FDCPA. If not, does your circuit follow the reasonable consumer standard or some other standard that it has articulated? If your state regulates debt collection practices, what standard has your state courts adopted for applying the state act?

3. The "Initial Communication" and Section 809 Demand Letter

Section 809(a) of the FDCPA provides that within *five days* following the **initial communication** between the debt collector and the debtor, the debt collector *must* send to the debtor a *written communication* that contains the following

- the amount of the debt [809(a)(1)]
- the name of the creditor owed [809(a)(2)]
- a statement that the debt will be assumed valid unless the debtor disputes the debt within 30 days of receipt of the written communication [809(a)(3)]
- a statement that if the debtor, within the 30-day period, notifies the debt collector *in writing* that the debt is disputed in whole or part, the debt collector will then obtain verification of the debt (including a copy of any judgment upon which the debt is based) and mail it to the debtor [809(a)(4)]
- a statement that if the debtor, within the 30-day period, requests *in writing* the name of the original creditor, the debt collector will provide that name if it is different from the current creditor. [809(a)(5)]

Section 809(b) provides that if the debtor does, in a timely writing, either dispute the debt or request the name of the original creditor in writing, debt collection activities must cease until verification of the debt and/or name of the original creditor has been mailed to the debtor. Section 809(c) provides that the failure of a debtor to dispute a debt *cannot* be used against him as an admission of liability for the debt in a subsequent collection lawsuit.

The scheme contemplated by §809 is that the initial communication between the debtor and the debt collector will be verbal (e.g., by phone call). Then within five days of that verbal communication the §809 letter must be sent.

EXAMPLE

If the initial communication between the debt collector for CCME and Pearl Murphy is a phone call, the debt collector must send the §809 letter within five days following the phone call.

Section 809 permits the initial communication with the debtor to be in writing so long as that writing complies with the requirements of that section. If the initial communication is in writing and complies with §809, no additional written communication within five days is required. In many law offices doing collection work and at some debt collection agencies, the initial communication is indeed in writing and lawyers typically refer to that first writing as the **demand letter**. Consequently, it is important that the demand letter comply with the requirements of §809. Illustration 7-b is a demand letter from an attorney for CCME to Pearl Murphy seeking to collect the $1,200 debt she owes CCME.

Keep in mind that demand letters or other communications sent by debt collectors must comply with the general provisions of the statute relating to communications that we covered earlier in this chapter as well as the provisions of §809.

Illustration 7-b: DEMAND LETTER

TIGER AND ASSOCIATES
Attorneys and Counselors at Law
115 Commerce Street
Capitol City, Columbiana
(555) 961-9087

July 1, YR-1

Ms. Pearl E. Murphy
3521 West Cherry Street
Capitol City, Columbiana

In re: Indebtedness of $1,200 to Capitol City Medical Equipment

Dear Ms. Murphy:

Your name has been brought to our attention to collect from you the entire balance of a debt you owed Capitol City Medical Equipment (CCME) in the amount of $1,200 under the terms of that certain Medical Equipment Rental Agreement (the Agreement) that you executed on February 1, YR-1. A bill for the $1,200 that you owe CCME under the terms of the Agreement was sent to you on May 15, YR-1, and CCME advises us that you have failed and refused to pay any portion of that amount within 30 days of receipt of the bill as you are obligated to do under the terms of the Agreement.

If you want to resolve this matter without a lawsuit, you must, within 30 days of the date of this letter, either pay the entire amount owed or call the undersigned at the number shown above and work out arrangements for payment with us. If you do neither of these things, we have been authorized to file suit on behalf of CCME for the collection of this debt.

Federal law gives you thirty (30) days after you receive this letter to dispute the validity of the debt or any part of it. If you do not dispute it within that period, we will assume that it is valid. If you do dispute it by notifying us in writing to that effect we will, as required by the law, obtain and mail to you proof of the debt. And if, within the same period, you request in writing the name and address of your original creditor, if the original creditor is different from the current creditor CCME, we will furnish you that information also. The law does not require us to wait until the end of the 30-day period before suing you to collect this debt. If, however, you request proof of the debt or the name and address of the original creditor within the 30-day period that begins with your receipt of this letter, the law requires us to suspend our efforts until we have mailed information to you.

Please make arrangements immediately to pay this debt. I trust you will give this matter priority attention.

Sincerely,

_____
B.A. Tiger, Attorney at Law

Section 809 is primarily concerned with giving the debtor the opportunity to *validate* or *dispute* the debt and its provisions can be a bit tricky. Note that §809(a)(3) advises the debtor that the debt will be assumed valid unless the debtor disputes it within 30 days, but it does *not* expressly require the debtor to dispute the debt *in writing* to avoid that assumption. On the other hand, §809(a)(4),

Validation notice Required language in communication from a debt collector governed by the FDCPA to a debtor regarding the debtor's right to demand verification of the debt.

referred to as the **validation notice**, provides that if the debtor *does* dispute the debt *in writing* within 30 days, the debt collector will obtain verification of the debt and provide it to the debtor. And 809(b) requires that collection efforts stop until the verification has been mailed to the debtor.

The reference to a writing in the §809(a)(4) validation notice requirement but its absence in the §809(a)(3) right to dispute provision has led to confusion among the courts. If the debtor wishes to dispute the debt, *must* he put his dispute in writing or is that only an option? Even if the debtor is not required to state his dispute of the debt in writing, can a §809 letter *require* him to do so in order to avoid the assumption that the debt is valid? There is a split of authority among the federal circuits as to whether a §809 demand letter *does requires* or *can require* the debtor to dispute the debt in writing to avoid the assumption of validity. Compare *Graziano v. Harrison*, 950 F.2d 107, 112 (3d Cir. 1991) (debtor *must* dispute debt in writing) with *Camacho v. Bridgeport Financial, Inc.*, 430 F.3d 1078, 1080-1082 (9th Cir. 2005) (§809 does *not* impose a writing requirement on debtors).

Regardless of whether §809(a)(3) requires or can be used to require the debtor to provide written dispute of the debt, it is clear that the obligation of the debt collector to provide the debtor with verification of the debt under §809(a)(4) is triggered only by receiving **written notice** from the debtor sent within the 30-day window that the debt is disputed in whole or part. Neither verbal notice nor dispute nor untimely notice of dispute will trigger that obligation.

Section 809(a)(5) requires inclusion of a statement in the demand letter that, upon the debtor's written request within the 30-day period, the debt collector will provide the debtor with the name and address of the original creditor, if different from the current creditor. Remember, as we considered in Chapter Two and again in Chapter Four, contracts creating debt are often assigned by one creditor to another. So the creditor identified in the demand letter as the creditor to whom the debt is owed may not be the original creditor with whom the debtor dealt in creating the debt. Section 809(a)(5) provides the debtor with a means of contacting the original creditor.

EXAMPLE

Assume that Pearl Murphy has made a number of small payments to CCME on the debt she owes. She receives a demand letter written by a debt collector on behalf of AAA Finance Company (AAA) advising that AAA is now the creditor to whom the debt is owed and that she should pay the balance of $950 to AAA to satisfy the claim. Pearl thinks she only owes $800 on the bill and attempts to contact CCME, only to find that it has changed its phone number and apparently its name, too, because she can't find it in the phone book. Pearl may want to exercise her rights under §809(a)(5) to learn how to contact CCME if it is still in business.

Notwithstanding the language required to be included in a demand letter, nothing in the FDCPA requires a creditor to wait 30 days after sending the demand letter to file suit to collect the debt. Theoretically, the creditor could cause the demand letter to be sent today and file suit tomorrow without violating the FDCPA. One exception to that is §809(b). Under that provision, if the debtor does exercise his right under §809(a)(4) to timely notify the debt collector in writing that the debt is disputed in whole or part, or under §809(a)(5) to request the name and address of the original creditor, collection efforts must stop . . . but only until the information requested by the debtor has been mailed to him. Then, collection efforts, including the filing of a lawsuit, can resume.

EXAMPLE

> Assume that AAA causes the demand letter to be sent to Pearl as in the preceding example. Pearl receives the letter today. A week later, AAA decides to file suit and authorizes its attorney to do so. The next day, however, Pearl's letter requesting the name and address of the original creditor arrives. Filing the suit or any other collection action must be delayed until Pearl's request is complied with. Once it is, the suit may then be filed. What if the attorney for AAA filed the lawsuit the day before Pearl's letter arrived? In that case, there is no violation of the FDCPA by filing the suit because they did not know Pearl's letter was coming. But the collection lawsuit must not move forward (e.g., proceeding with discovery or seeking a default judgment; see Chapter Eight) until the response is in the mail.

P-H 7-j: Look at the demand letter in Illustration 7-b. Compare the letter with §§809(a)(1)-(5) of the FDCPA and identify the exact language in the letter that complies with each of the provisions of §§809(a)(1)-(5).

P-H 7-k: Redraft the letter in Illustration 7-b to make it comply with any additional or different requirements on collection letters imposed by the law of your state.

4. Penalties for Violating the FDCPA

Private right of action The right granted by a regulatory statute for the injured party to bring a civil lawsuit for damages or other relief apart from governmental regulatory action.

The FDCPA authorizes a **private right of action** on behalf of the consumer debtor for any violations of its provisions. A private right of action is the right to bring a civil lawsuit in the debtor's own name and for his own benefit rather than relying solely on government sanctions that may be imposed on the offending creditor. Pursuant to §813 of the FDCPA, a debt collector found to have violated these provisions may be civilly liable to the consumer/debtor for the debtor's **actual damages**, plus a **statutory penalty** of up to $1,000, plus the **attorney's fee** incurred by the debtor, and **court costs**. The debtor has one year from the date of the alleged violation to initiate the civil lawsuit in state or federal court to recover such private damages.

It is a defense to the debt collector in the debtor's suit if she can show by a **preponderance of the evidence** (more likely than not) that the violation "was not intentional and resulted from a *bona fide error* notwithstanding the maintenance of procedures reasonably adapted to avoid any such error" (§813(c) (emphasis supplied)). In *Jerman v. Carlisle, McNellie, Rini, Kramer & Ulrich, LPA*, 130 S. Ct. 1605 (2010), the U.S. Supreme Court held that the

bona fide error defense of the FDCPA does *not* include mistakes of law regarding the requirements of the statute. The defendant law firm in *Jerman*, seeking to collect a debt for a client, demanded that the debtor dispute the validity of the debt in writing. When the debtor sued, the trial court, affirmed by the Sixth Circuit, chose to follow the *Camacho* view that held that §809(a)(3) does *not* impose a writing requirement on debtors and ruled that the defendant's demand that he do so was a violation of the FDCPA. The defendant law firm asserted the bona fide error defense on the grounds that it had mistakenly but in good faith construed §809 to require that the debtor dispute the debt in writing. Although the Supreme Court rejected defendant's mistake of law as being within the bona fide error defense of §813(c), it did not resolve the lingering question of whether §809(a)(3) should be interpreted to require a debtor to put his dispute of the debt in writing since that precise issue was not raised in the appeal. See *Jerman*, supra, at 1610.

The FDCPA is administered in the first instance by the **Federal Trade Commission (FTC)**, and any violation can be deemed by the FTC to be an **unfair or deceptive act or practice** by the debt collector under the **Federal Trade Commission Act (FTCA)**. Such a finding authorizes the FTC to enforce compliance with the FDCPA on debt collectors and to assess fines and penalties for noncompliance. In an extreme case, the FTC could order a debt collector to stop doing business. The FTC maintains a helpful information site regarding the FDCPA at www.ftc.gov/bcp/edu/pubs/consumer/credit/cre18.shtm.

> **Unfair or deceptive act or practice** Prohibited conduct by debt collectors under the FDCPA.

Significantly, the new **Consumer Financial Protection Bureau (CFPB)** created by the Dodd-Frank Wall Street Reform Act of 2010 has been granted supervisory and enforcement authority over large collectors of consumer debt. Effective January 2013, the CFPB was authorized to supervise and regulate debt collection firms with receipts of more than $10 million per year in debt collection activities. That includes about 175 debt collection companies, which collectively account for more than 60 percent of the consumer debt collection business.

P-H 7-l: In October 2012 the CFPB issued its **Debt Collection Examination Procedures Manual** (http://files.consumerfinance.gov/f/201210_cfpb_debt-collection-examination-procedures.pdf) to alert debt collectors to the procedures and standards that the CFPB will use to determine if regulated debt collectors are following the law. Look at the Background section of the manual on pages 1–3. What federal statutes other than the FDCPA impact the activities of debt collectors? Look at Module 7 of the manual. What kinds of abusive litigation practices does the CFPB seem to be concerned about? What kinds of abusive repossession practices? What concerns does it seem to have about collecting time barred debt?

P-H 7-m: Go to the CFPB Web site at www.consumerfinance.gov/ and use the search feature there to 1) locate recent press releases by the bureau regarding consumer debt collection and 2) determine if the bureau has promulgated any specific regulations governing the debt collection industry.

B. Tort, Criminal, and Ethical Considerations in Collecting a Debt

Attorneys engaging in debt collection work, debt collection companies, and creditors themselves (even if not regulated by the FDCPA), must also beware of several **tort theories** that debtors may assert against them in order to recover damages for wrongful conduct arising out of collection practices. Some behavior that is tortious may also be considered **criminal**. Such tort liability or criminal exposure can exist whether or not the collection practice complained of violated the FDCPA and without regard to whether the debtor actually owes the debt or not.

1. Intentional Infliction of Emotional Distress

The tort of **intentional infliction of emotional distress (IIED)**, also known as **outrageous conduct**, is sometimes alleged by debtors based on grossly unreasonable collection activities.

In most states, a cause of action for IIED requires a plaintiff to prove that a defendant engaged in intentional conduct so egregious that a reasonable person would consider it outrageous and intolerable by society and that such conduct was the actual and proximate cause of severe emotional distress suffered by the plaintiff.

P-H 7-n: Locate and read *Perk v. Worden*, 475 F. Supp. 2d 565 (E.D. Va. 2007), then answer the following questions: 1) Which state's law controlled the IIED issue raised in this case? 2) Who was the defendant in the case? 3) How did plaintiff's use of a corporate credit card involve a consumer debt? 4) What had defendant allegedly done that amounted to IIED? 5) Would this court find that abusive language by itself could amount to IIED? For other interesting cases dealing with the tort of outrageous conduct in the debt collection context, see *Burdett v. Harrah's Kansas Casino Corp.*, 294 F. Supp. 2d 1215 (D. Kan. 2003); *Symonds v. Mercury Savings & Loan Assn.*, 225 Cal. App. 3d 1458, 275 Cal. Rptr. 871 (1990); and *Moorhead v. J.C. Penney*, 555 S.W.2d 713 (Tenn. 1977).

---

2. Defamation

Another tort that is sometimes alleged by the debtor in the collection context is **defamation**. Spoken defamation is **slander** and written defamation is **libel**. The tort of defamation requires proof by the plaintiff that the defendant made a false statement about the plaintiff published to persons other than the plaintiff and that the publication of the false statement caused the plaintiff harm. The harm alleged is usually to the reputation of the plaintiff and often involves claims of emotional distress as well.

Defamation does require proof that the statement made was false. And it is a defense if the defendant can show that the statement made was not false. Nonetheless, the creditor, attorney, or other debt collector must be careful not to make false statements about the debtor to third persons that could injure the debtor's reputation.

EXAMPLE

> Patty Paralegal, paralegal for B.A. Tiger, is directed by her supervising attorney to contact Pearl Murphy in order to inquire if she will voluntarily repay the debt to CCME. When Patty cannot reach Pearl, she calls Nick Murphy at Overland Truck Services, where he is employed as manager. Overland Truck does not have a policy prohibiting such calls to the workplace. Patty calls and gets the receptionist. When she asks to speak with Nick Murphy, the receptionist asks what matter she is calling about and Patty says she is calling on behalf of the law office to confirm a debt owed by Mr. and Mrs. Murphy to a client. Word that Nick doesn't pay his bills spreads from the receptionist to every nook and cranny of the business, and eventually to the regional supervisor who is Nick's boss. The regional supervisor asks Nick what is going on and why he isn't paying his bills. Nick explains that the debt is his wife's and not his and the circumstances of Pearl's condition. Nick is furious and may sue Patty, her attorney, and the client for slander to recover for the harm to his reputation at work and the resulting distress. Is it a defense if Patty misunderstood who owed the debt and thought the statement she made was true? No. Defamation is an intentional tort but the only intent required when the plaintiff is not a public figure is the intent to make the statement, which she had. (When the plaintiff in a defamation action is a public figure or public official he must prove the defendant made the defamatory statement knowing it was false or with reckless disregard for its truth or falsity.)

P-H 7-o: Patty's behavior also violates at least one provision of the FDCPA, assuming her attorney is considered a debt collector for purposes of that statute. What provision has been violated?

3. Invasion of Privacy

The tort of **invasion of privacy** (the **public disclosure of private facts** variety) may arise where the creditor or debt collector discloses the indebtedness to persons who have no business knowing that information. If you have studied torts, you will recall that a cause of action for invasion of privacy may be maintained even though the information disseminated about the plaintiff is true.

EXAMPLE

> Assume that Pearl Murphy writes a check to the local food store to pay for the week's groceries. The check bounces (payment is refused on presentment to the drawee bank due to insufficient funds) because Pearl made an error in balancing her check book. The food store owner posts the check on the checkout counter where everyone passing through can clearly see the name of both Nick and Pearl Murphy printed on the check and the "Insufficient Funds" bank stamp on the face of it. That may be cathartic to the store owner but she may be handing the Murphys a basis to sue her for invasion of privacy by the public disclosure of these very private facts.

EXAMPLE

> Patty Paralegal's disclosure to the receptionist at Overland Truck Services that she was calling to confirm a debt may constitute actionable invasion of privacy, as well as being a violation of the FDCPA.

P-H 7-p: What should Patty Paralegal have said when the Overland Truck receptionist asked why she was calling Nick?

P-H 7-q: Locate and read *Kuhn v. Account Control Technology*, 865 F. Supp. 1443 (D. Nev. 1994), and then answer the following questions: 1) What were the actions of the debt collection agency that plaintiff alleged invaded her privacy? 2) Why did the court dismiss her complaint on that theory? 3) How do the facts in *Kuhn* differ from the facts in the example of Patty Paralegal's disclosures to the receptionist at Overland Truck Services? 4) Do you think Nick Murphy could recover from Patty Paralegal and her employer on an invasion of privacy theory?

4. Harassment

Systematic campaigns of debtor harassment undertaken by a debt collector may be treated as tortious invasions of privacy by some courts. (See, e.g., *Sofka v. Thal*, 662 S.W.2d 502 (Mo. 1983), and *Chlanda v. Wymard*, LEXIS 14394 (S.D. Ohio 1995).) Other states, however, recognize an independent tort for **malicious harassment** and that conduct can be criminal as well.

P-H 7-r: Locate and read *Sams v. State*, 271 Ga. App. 617, 610 S.E.2d 592 (2005), and then answer the following questions: 1) What crime was the defendant charged with? 2) What actions of the defendant were alleged to be criminal? 3) Did it matter to the conviction whether the debt was actually owed? 4) What should the defendant have done differently in collecting the debt to avoid criminal liability?

5. Assault/Battery

Creditors and debt collectors of course have to be careful not to use physical force in connection with debt collection activities. They could face a civil tort suit for **assault/battery** or even criminal charges arising out of such conduct.

EXAMPLE

> Assume the owner of CCME sees Nick and Pearl Murphy shopping at the mall. He approaches them and begins to demand his money. Nick steps in front of his frightened wife, and the owner pushes Nick out of the way and points his finger in Pearl's face so close to her that she flinches. He calls her a deadbeat and walks away. The CCME owner may be facing both civil suit and criminal charges for assault and battery against Nick and for assault against Pearl.

P-H 7-s: If the owner of CCME is sued by the Murphys or arrested and charged with crimes arising out of his conduct in the preceding example, will it be a defense to him that he was attempting to collect his own debt and is not a debt collector within the meaning of the FDCPA?

6. Conversion/Theft

Creditors and debt collectors cannot take the debtor's property in satisfaction of the debt unless that property has been pledged as collateral as part of a secured transaction, as we considered in Part A of the text. If the creditor files a lawsuit to collect the debt and obtains a final judgment against the debtor then certain property of the debtor may be seized to satisfy the judgment as we will learn in upcoming chapters. But absent one of these circumstances, it is wrongful for a creditor or debt collector to take possession of the debtor's property and doing so could result in a civil tort suit for **conversion** or **trespass to chattel** or in a criminal prosecution for **theft**.

EXAMPLE

> Assume that the owner of CCME becomes frustrated that Pearl Murphy is not paying her bill. When the demand letter doesn't get any result and his lawyer, B.A. Tiger, tells him the Murphys may be judgment proof (see Chapter Eight), he takes matters into his own hands. He spies on the Murphys and waits until they are both inside the house, then sneaks on the property, hotwires their car, and drives it away. He leaves a note saying he will sell the car to pay their debt. Hopefully B.A. Tiger knows a good criminal defense lawyer because his client is going to need one.

P-H 7-t: Locate and read *Darcars Motors of Silver Springs, Inc. v. Borzym*, 379 Md. 249, 841 A.2d 828 (2004), and then answer the following questions: 1) What were the actions of the creditor that plaintiff alleged constituted conversion of her property? 2) What damages did the court allow plaintiff to recover? 3) What should the creditor have done differently to avoid liability?

7. Extortion/Blackmail

Creditors and debt collectors also must be careful not to make threats against debtors as part of the effort to collect. It is permissible to say in a demand letter that a civil collection suit will be filed if in fact the creditor has or decide to do. But a debt collector must *never* verbally or in writing threaten to harm a debtor's credit rating if he won't pay up, or threaten criminal action against him, even if the debtor may have been guilty of a crime. Why not? Because making such threats could be construed as civil or even criminal **extortion** or **blackmail**.

EXAMPLE

> Assume that the Murphys finally write a check to CCME to pay off Pearl's debt there. Unfortunately, the check bounces. The owner of CCME calls Pearl and demands immediate payment in cash or he will have her arrested for passing a bad check. The CCME owner has a right to institute criminal prosecution against Pearl, but must not threaten to do so in order to induce the debtor to pay the debt. And that is true even if Pearl is guilty of the crime of passing a bad check.

8. Ethical Considerations

Debt collection activities found to be a violation of FDCPA or culpable under state tort or criminal law may also be a ground for disciplinary action against the attorney involved as a violation of *legal ethics*.

EXAMPLE

> Rule 4.4 of the American Bar Association Rules of Professional Conduct prohibits an attorney from threatening criminal prosecution in order to induce payment to a client. Such conduct could therefore not only be construed as civil or criminal extortion or blackmail as discussed in the last section, it could result in disciplinary action against the attorney. Rule 4.4 states:
>
> In representing a client, a lawyer shall not:
>
>   . . .
>
>   (b) threaten to present a criminal charge, or to offer or to agree to refrain from filing such a charge, for the purpose of obtaining an advantage in a civil matter.
>
> Likewise, paralegals certified by the state in which they work or by paralegal organizations such as NALA or NFPA may lose their certification as a result of engaging in such conduct.

EC 7-d: Review the NALA Code of Ethics (www.nala.org/code.htm) and the NFPA Model Code of Ethics and Professional Responsibility (www.paralegals.org/displaycommon.cfm?an = 1&subarticlenbr = 133) and determine the various provisions of such codes that might be violated by a paralegal involved in conduct prohibited by the FDCPA or that is tortious or criminal as described in this chapter.

After considering so many abuses of debt collection activity, it is good to remind ourselves that debt collection is an honest way to make a living—a necessary and honorable trade. As always, it is the bad apples that give the barrel that sour smell. There are a number of organizations made up of members of the debt collection community who are all dedicated to the ethical and professional practice of their trade. Illustration 7-c lists a number of the more prominent ones.

Illustration 7-c: PROMINENT DEBT COLLECTION ORGANIZATIONS

1. ACA International, the Association of Credit and Collection Professionals (http://www.acainternational.org/)
2. Commercial Collection Agency Association (CCAA) (www.ccascollect.com/)
3. International Association of Commercial Collectors, Inc. (IACC) (www.commercialcollector.com/iacc/main/)
4. The Equipment Leasing and Finance Association (ELFA) (www.elfaonline.org/)
5. The Finance, Credit, and International Business Association (FCIB) (www.fcibglobal.com/)

P-H 7-u: Check the Web site of ACA International, the Association of Credit and Collection Professionals, at www.acainternational.org/. Based in Minneapolis, ACA International is one of the largest organizations of those involved in the debt collection industry: creditors, third-party collection agencies, asset buyers, and attorneys involved in debt collection. Check out the organization's Code of Ethics posted on the site. Do you see concern in the code about complying with FDCPA provisions and otherwise behaving honorably? Check the sites of other organizations listed in Illustration 7-c. Do you see references anywhere to coming regulation by the CFPB?

CONCLUSION

It is essential that one engaged in prelitigation debt collection be familiar with the provisions of the FDCPA and comply with them where applicable. That person must also be sensitive to tort liability and criminal culpability, either of which can arise from wrongful collection activities, and must always strive to comply with ethical and professional obligations when working in this area.

If prelitigation debt collection efforts do not succeed, the creditor has the option of writing off the debt or pursuing litigation against the debtor. The collection lawsuit is the subject of the next two chapters.

CHAPTER SUMMARY

In this chapter we have considered prelitigation debt collection activities. Such activities are governed primarily by the Fair Debt Collection Practices Act (FDCPA), though many states have enacted their own debt collection regulation, which may be more stringent. The FDCPA regulates the activities of debt collectors engaged in collecting debt from consumer debtors. Under the statute, debt collectors include persons acting for businesses, the principal purpose of which is to collect debts owed to another, as well as individuals who regularly collect or attempt to collect debts owed to another. Attorneys may be considered debt collectors under the FDCPA if they regularly attempt to collect debts for their clients.

The FDCPA regulates the extent to which a debt collector can gather information regarding the location of a debtor or have communications with a debtor and prohibits harassment or abuse of a debtor or the making of false or misleading representations to a debtor or utilizing other unfair or unconscionable means to collect debt. The FDCPA creates a private right of action for the consumer debtor against the debt collector violating its provisions in which the debtor can obtain his actual damages plus a statutory penalty of $1,000 as well as attorney's fees.

The Federal Trade Commission administers the FDCPA and is authorized to impose certain fines and penalties on violators and to order them to stop doing business in extreme cases. Within five days following the initial communication between the debt collector and the debtor, the debt collector must send a written communication to the debtor containing a number of provisions including the identity of the creditor, the amount owed, and a validation notice. It is essential that demand letters used by attorneys, who may be debt collectors under the FDCPA, comply with these statutory requirements. Whether or not regulated by the FDCPA, those involved in collection work must beware various tort liability that may result from inappropriate collection activities. Viable tort theories in the debt collection area include the intentional infliction of emotional distress (outrageous conduct), defamation, invasion of privacy, assault, battery, and conversion. There may be criminal culpability as well, including criminal assault and battery, fraud, theft, or extortion (blackmail). Conduct that might render one engaged in debt collection criminally culpable or civilly liable may constitute an ethical violation as well.

REVIEW QUESTIONS

1. What are the two distinct stages of debt collection? Name three different kinds of employers for whom a paralegal involved in prelitigation debt collection might work.
2. Who is a "debt collector" under the FDCPA? Under what circumstances will an attorney be considered a debt collector under the FDCPA?
3. How does the FDCPA define who is a consumer debtor for purposes of making contact with that debtor? What restrictions does the FDCPA place on a debt collector in contacting that debtor?
4. What restrictions does the FDCPA impose on a debt collector needing to contact persons to determine the location of the debtor?
5. What kinds of conduct does the FDCPA consider to be harassing or abusive by the debt collector?
6. Provide as many examples as you can of what might constitute false or misleading representations by a debt collector seeking to collect a debt.
7. Provide as many examples as you can of what might constitute unfair or unconscionable means of collecting debt.

8. What federal agency administers the FDCPA and what are the governmentally imposed penalties for its violation? What is a private right of action? What damages might a debtor recover from a debt collector who has violated the FDCPA in a private right of action?

9. Summarize the requirements imposed on debt collectors following the "initial communication" with the debtor. Why do these requirements apply so readily to the demand letter?

10. Under what tort theories might a debt collector or creditor be liable to a debtor separate and apart from the FDCPA? Of what crimes might a debt collector be guilty in connection with wrongful collection activities?

WORDS AND PHRASES TO REMEMBER

accounts receivable
assault
asset buyers
attorney's fee
bad debt
battery
blackmail
bona fide error defense
cause of action
collection cycle
consumer
Consumer Financial Protection
    Bureau
consumer protection act
conversion
court costs
debt buyers
debt collection
debt collectors
debt collection companies
Debt Collection Procedures Manual
defamation
demand letter
extortion
Fair Debt Collection Practices
    Act (FDCPA)
Fair Trade Act
Federal Deposit Insurance
    Corporation (FDIC)

Federal Trade Commission (FTC)
Federal Trade Commission Act
in-house debt collection
initial communication
intentional infliction of emotional
    distress
invasion of privacy
least sophisticated consumer
    standard
legal ethics
libel
malicious harassment
outrageous conduct
preponderance of the evidence
private right of action
reasonable consumer standard
Resolution Trust Corporation
    (RTC)
Savings and Loan crisis of
    the 1980s
slander
statutory penalty
theft
third-party collection agencies
tort theories
trespass to chattel
unfair or deceptive act or practice
validation notice

TO LEARN MORE: A number of TLM activities to accompany this chapter are accessible on the student disc accompanying the text and on the Author Updates link to the text Web site at http://www.aspenparalegaled.com/books/parsons_abcdebt/default.asp.

Chapter Eight:

Reducing a Debt or Claim to Settlement or Final Judgment—Part 1

It is very iniquitous to make me pay my debts.
You have no idea the pain it causes me.
                    —Lord Byron

A. The Decision to File a Lawsuit to Collect a Debt or Enforce a Claim

Final judgment An order or decree entered by a court finally resolving the issues before it.

Collection lawsuit A lawsuit to collect a pre-existing debt.

Liability lawsuit A civil lawsuit based on claim of liability based on tortious or other wrongful conduct.

When the various prelitigation collection efforts described in Chapter Seven fail, the creditor may file a civil lawsuit seeking to obtain a **final judgment** from a court. Where the lawsuit is based on a preexisting debt, we often call it a **collection lawsuit**. Where the lawsuit is based on a claim of liability in tort, we often call it a **liability lawsuit**. Once a final judgment is rendered in favor of the creditor in a collection suit or the claimant in a liability suit, we refer to the prevailing party as the **judgment creditor** and the person against whom the judgment is entered as the **judgment debtor**. The judgment creditor can then execute on certain assets of the judgment debtor to satisfy the judgment (as we will discuss in Chapters Ten and Eleven).

EXAMPLE

Judgment creditor/ debtor The party to whom the judgment is awarded is the judgment creditor, and the one against whom it is awarded is the judgment debtor.

> If Capitol City Medical Equipment (CCME) files suit against Pearl Murphy to collect on the debt she allegedly owes under the medical equipment lease (Illustration 7-b and P-H 7-b), that would be properly called a collection lawsuit. On the other hand, the malpractice claim brought by Pearl and Nick Murphy against Dr. Samuel Craft and Capitol City Hospital (CCH) based on alleged negligence (Illustration 1-a) would be properly called a liability lawsuit.

However, a creditor or claimant may not necessarily decide to file a lawsuit if prelitigation efforts fail. There are a number of considerations that go into a decision to initiate litigation based on the nature of the debt or claim and the particular circumstances of the parties. Let's examine some of those considerations for particular creditors.

1. The Creditor Holding a Consensual Security Interest or Mortgage

If the creditor is secured in either the real or personal property of the debtor, the creditor may have the right of self-help repossession or power of sale foreclosure as we considered in Chapters Four and Five, and the property seized and sold may satisfy the indebtedness. Only if there is a significant balance owing after disposition of the property (a **deficiency balance**) will a collection suit likely be filed to obtain a judgment for the deficiency (called a **deficiency judgment**) (subject to the election of remedies doctrine, if applicable, and whether the underlying note is nonrecourse, as considered in Chapter Four).

EXAMPLE

If Nick and Pearl Murphy default on the loan from First Bank of Capitol City (FBCC) secured by a mortgage in their home (see Illustrations 2-a and 4-b), FBCC is likely to use its right of self-help foreclosure before instituting a collection suit. If the sale of the home leaves a significant deficiency owing, FBCC may institute a collection suit against the Murphys for that deficiency. If the deficiency owing is small, FBCC is likely to just write it off. However, if the jurisdiction recognizes the election of remedies doctrine, FBCC must choose between foreclosure and filing a collection lawsuit for the entire amount owed; it cannot do both. And if the underlying promissory note is nonrecourse, FBCC's only remedy is foreclosure.

If the agreement of the parties or the law of the jurisdiction requires judicial foreclosure or repossession, then a foreclosure or repossession lawsuit must be instituted by the creditor.

What if the creditor is secured but the property to which the security interest attaches has little or no value? Is the secured creditor obligated to repossess or foreclose on the pledged property before filing a collection suit? The answer is usually no. The agreement between the debtor and secured creditor will normally give the creditor the *option* to repossess or foreclose but not the *duty* to do so. So if the creditor determines that it would be wasteful to take possession of some or all of the pledged property, the creditor may elect to forgo that option and simply file the collection suit to obtain a final judgment against the debtor. Then the creditor, as a judgment creditor, can proceed to execute on other more valuable property of the debtor that was not pledged as security for the debt.

EXAMPLE

Assume that Nick and Pearl Murphy default on their indebtedness to Shears Department Store, for which they pledged the living room furniture as collateral (see Illustration 5-a). Shears considers exercising its right to self-help repossession of the furniture but concludes that it is likely in poor condition with little or no resale value. Thus, going to the time and expense of repossessing and attempting to sell the furniture does not seem to be a good business decision to Shears. However, Shears learns that the Murphys own real property in which there is currently considerable owner's equity (see the discussion of owner's equity in Chapter Four, Section D). Of course, Shears does not hold a mortgage in the real property to secure the debt owed to it, so it cannot foreclose on the real property. However, if Shears can obtain a final judgment against the Murphys in a collection suit, it can then execute on its judgment against other property of the Murphys, including the real property containing the equity. Shears therefore elects to forego repossession of the furniture and institute a collection suit instead.

2. The Creditor Whose Debt Is Guaranteed or Subject to a Surety Agreement

In Chapter Four, Sections B and C, we discussed co-signers and other surety arrangements and guarantees. If the principal debtor fails to pay the obligation when due, the creditor may make demand on the co-signer of the promissory note, a surety, or a guarantor and file a collection suit against those parties if they fail to pay as promised. The *timing* of such a collection suit will be impacted by whether the target of the suit is *primarily* or *secondarily* liable for the debt, as we considered in Chapter Four, Section C.

3. The Creditor Holding a Nonconsensual Statutory or Equitable Lien

In Chapter Six we considered a broad range of nonconsensual liens (statutory and equitable) that can attach to a debtor's property in favor of a creditor. Whether the creditor must institute a lawsuit to enforce the nonconsensual lien depends on what kind of lien it is.

In the case of a mechanic's lien or a lien *lis pendens*, a lawsuit *must* be filed to enforce the lien, either at the time the lien is created (often a requirement to enforce a lien *lis pendens*) or within some statutory time frame following the creation of the lien (a typical requirement to enforce a mechanic's lien).

On the other hand, tax liens can typically be executed on by the taxing authority without court action. Of course, the debtor may institute a lawsuit himself to contest the underlying debt or the validity of the lien.

In most states the artisan's lien and other possessory liens do not require judicial action and are enforceable by self-help after the expiration of some statutory time period (e.g., 30 days) following satisfaction of the notice and advertisement requirements, if any. In a minority of states, judicial action is required to enforce such liens.

The same divergence of procedure among the states is seen in the enforcement of nonpossessory liens, such as the attorney's charging lien, hospital and health-care liens, and child support liens. Some states require a formal lawsuit to authorize enforcement, while others, like those utilizing a procedure similar to that set forth in the North Carolina statute we examined in Illustration 6-j, permit enforcement by execution following filing of a verified statement or notice of lien in a designated court.

4. The Unsecured Creditor or Claimant

If the indebtedness owed a creditor is not secured by any real or personal property of the debtor and there is no additional security in the form of a co-signer, surety, or guarantor, the debt is *unsecured*.

EXAMPLE

Recall the debt owed by Pearl Murphy to CCME (P-H 7-b and Illustration 7-b) for medical equipment she leased from CCME. Pearl signed the medical equipment lease and promised to pay the rental charges. But she gave no security for her promise to pay. She did not pledge any personal property as collateral for the obligation. She did not mortgage the house to secure it. Nick was not asked to co-sign or guarantee the obligation. And there is no surety for it. CCME is an unsecured creditor as to this obligation.

The only way for a creditor to collect an unsecured debt if the debtor will not voluntarily pay is to file a collection lawsuit and obtain a final judgment. If the debtor does not pay the judgment at that point, the creditor can execute on certain assets of the debtor in order to satisfy the judgment, as we will consider in Chapters Ten and Eleven. Secured creditors will use the same procedure to collect a deficiency remaining after repossession or foreclosure or to collect the entire indebtedness if the pledged property is not repossessed or foreclosed on. But the unsecured creditor normally has no right to seize and take possession of any property of the debtor prior to obtaining a final judgment in a collection suit and executing on it. (See the discussion in Chapter Nine, Section A, of prejudgment attachment, which gives creditors a limited right to attach or freeze assets of a debtor prior to the outcome of a collection suit.)

5. The Claimant Asserting an Unliquidated Claim

In Chapter Two, Section D, we observed that some debt doesn't exist until there is a court judgment; the court judgment creates the indebtedness. This is the case in most liability lawsuits. Prior to the court judgment there is only a *claim* of some liability, usually a *contingent unliquidated* claim. In order to turn the claim into a fixed obligation that can be collected, the claimant must file a civil lawsuit and obtain a final judgment. The final judgment will state the liquidated amount of the claim, and because the final judgment establishes the indebtedness, it is no longer contingent.

EXAMPLE

Recall from Illustration 1-a and Chapter Two, Section D, that Nick and Pearl Murphy have filed a lawsuit against Dr. Samuel M. Craft and CCH based on their *claim* of negligence by those defendants in connection with Pearl's botched appendectomy. In their complaint, the Murphys sought to recover $1.5 million from the defendants. That was the amount of their claim. But the final judgment entered in Illustration 2-d was for a different amount. Once the final judgment is entered, there is a debt owed, liquidated in amount, by the judgment debtors (the defendants in the lawsuit) to the judgment creditors (the plaintiffs in the lawsuit). As we will learn in Chapters Ten and Eleven, once a final judgment has been entered by a court for some number of days, and if execution on it has not been stayed (suspended) pending appeal of the final judgment, the judgment creditors can execute on the judgment by seizing certain assets of the debtor.

EXAMPLE

> Compare the previous example with the debt owed by Pearl Murphy to CCME. That debt was created when Pearl Murphy signed the medical equipment lease and used the leased equipment of CCME. It is a debt created by contract, not by court judgment. It is also a liquidated debt since the amount owed ($1,200) has been established before any lawsuit is filed against Pearl Murphy to collect the amount owed. If Pearl does not pay the debt, CCME may indeed file a collection lawsuit because, as an unsecured creditor, obtaining a final judgment is the only way CCME can put itself in a position to execute on the assets of the debtor to satisfy the indebtedness.

P-H 8-a: Assume that Pearl Murphy did indeed rent the equipment from CCME, for which it has charged her $1,200. However, she has not paid the indebtedness to CCME for two reasons: Some of the medical equipment leased by her from CCME did not function properly and the rest of it was not the exact equipment her treating physician prescribed for her medical condition. When CCME files its collection suit against Pearl to collect the $1,200 owed under the medical equipment lease, Pearl raises these defenses. Would we still say the debt is liquidated? Would we say the debt is contingent or noncontingent at that point?

6. The Judgment-Proof Debtor

Regardless of the kind of debt or claim under consideration, an important factor in the decision of whether or not to file a collection suit to obtain a money judgment against a debtor is whether the debtor has or is likely to have any assets or insurance that will be available to satisfy the judgment once it is entered by the court. Of course, a secured creditor may still choose to repossess or foreclose on pledged property, but in deciding whether to sue for a deficiency judgment, this creditor too must weigh the time and expense involved in obtaining the judgment against the likelihood that the debtor has any other property that can be executed on to satisfy the judgment. A debtor who is determined to not have any assets that can be successfully executed on is considered **judgment proof**. Many creditors will write off what such a debtor owes as a bad debt and many claimants will let the claim against a judgment-proof target go without filing suit.

Judgment proof Condition of a debtor who has no assets that might be seized to satisfy a final judgment.

EXAMPLE

> We learned in Illustration 1-b that City County Bank (CCB) has filed suit against David Mendoza, Abe's son, to collect a $250,000 loan David obtained from the bank last year and on which he has since defaulted. If CCB determined before filing suit that David has lost all the borrowed money in risky investments that didn't pan out, has no assets whatsoever, is unemployed, homeless, and in very poor health due to a heroin addiction, it might have concluded that he is judgment proof and not filed the collection suit.

Of course, just because a debtor is judgment proof as to his personal assets doesn't mean there might not be liability insurance available to pay a claim against him.

EXAMPLE

> Assume David Mendoza drives his car negligently and causes a car accident inflicting property damage and personal injury on the other driver. Though David himself may have no assets from which a judgment against him could be satisfied, if he carries a policy of liability insurance that covers his fault in the accident, he is not judgment proof to the extent of that coverage. The liability insurance policy is a form of suretyship.

And just because a debtor is judgment proof at the moment doesn't mean that he always will be.

EXAMPLE

> Counsel for CCB in the preceding example might recommend that the bank go ahead and sue, obtain a final judgment against David, and keep the judgment enforceable into the future (to be considered in Chapter Eleven) on the chance that David might one day come into assets that can then be seized.

P-H 8-b: What difference might it make in the bank's decision to sue, notwithstanding David being judgment proof, that David is only 28 years old? That he has completed significant higher education work? That he is in treatment for his heroin addiction?

Other extraneous factors may impact the decision whether to pursue a collection suit against a judgment-proof debtor.

P-H 8-c: What difference might it make in the bank's decision to sue David that the bank holds a guaranty from his father? That the loan was federally insured? That David has expressed a willingness to convey to the bank stock he bought in a small start-up biomedical company that currently has no real value but that might in the future in exchange for canceling the debt?

How does a creditor or claimant know that a debtor is judgment proof anyway? No creditor is likely to just take the word of the debtor for it. Later in this chapter, we consider discovery that can be conducted in a collection suit but, generally, that discovery cannot delve into the defendant's assets until judgment has been entered and execution begun. Frequently, the creditor or claimant will need to conduct a **factual investigation** into the assets or lack of assets of the debtor or target. Recall from our study of how debt is created (Part A of the text) how frequently various documents evidencing contractual debt (e.g., mortgages on land and financing statements for personal property) must be filed in a public office. Those records are public and accessible to the investigator who understands how debt works and where to go to locate the records. And private records of debt transactions (e.g., unrecorded leases and promissory notes) can often be obtained by asking persons likely to have them or who know their contents.

P-H 8-d: Assume you work for the attorney representing CCB in its attempts to collect the debt from David Mendoza. You know nothing about David except that he is 28 years old, claims to have lost the borrowed money in a risky real estate scheme, and claims not to have any other assets. Your supervising attorney assigns you the task of investigating David to see if the bank should file a collection suit. Make a detailed list of information you would seek in such an investigation and the public and private sources from which you would try to locate that information.

Insolvent The inability to pay debts as they come due or the state of having total liabilities in excess of total assets.

One aspect of determining whether a debtor is judgment proof is the question of **insolvency**. That a debtor is determined to be insolvent may be an important factor in the larger determination that he is judgment proof. But, of course, just because a debtor is insolvent today doesn't mean he will be one year or ten years from today. We will have more to say about insolvency in Chapter Nine.

B. Resolution of a Disputed Debt or Liability Claim by Alternative Dispute Resolution (ADR)

Regardless of the kind of debt or claim under consideration and even if the defendant is fully solvent, the creditor may want to attempt **alternative dispute resolution** (ADR)—i.e., alternative to litigation in a court of law—before proceeding to file a lawsuit. Litigation can be time-consuming, expensive, and stressful. It often produces unexpected results because of the specialized and (to the layperson) often quirky rules of procedure and evidence that govern it.

The most common forms of ADR are privately negotiated settlement, mediated settlement, and arbitration.

1. Privately Negotiated Settlement

Negotiation Dialogue between parties or their representatives, with or without the aid of a mediator, aimed at reaching an agreed compromise of a dispute.

The parties to a disputed debt or liability claim may **negotiate** a settlement of the dispute. The negotiation may occur between the parties themselves or between the respective attorneys for the parties. If the negotiations are successful, a written **settlement agreement** will typically be executed by the parties and the obligations of that agreement may displace the terms of the original contract or the liability claim.

EXAMPLE

In their malpractice claim against Dr. Croft and Capitol City Hospital (CCH), Pearl and Nick Murphy may be prepared to file a lawsuit seeking the recovery of $1.5 million. But they may be able to successfully negotiate a settlement of the claim of the lump sum payment of $500,000. That obligation and the timing of the payment will be set forth in a signed settlement agreement. The obligation of Dr. Croft and CCH to pay the Murphys $500,000 as set forth in the settlement agreement will displace the claim of the Murphys against either the doctor or CCH. In the settlement agreement, the Murphys will surrender and release all such claims in exchange for the settlement amount.

EXAMPLE

Capitol City Medical Equipment Company (CCMEC) is prepared to file suit against Pearl Murphy on the Medical Equipment Lease Agreement she signed seeking to recover $1,200 plus interest and attorney's fees. Before suit is filed, the attorneys may negotiate a settlement whereby Pearl agrees to pay $600 in six monthly installments. A settlement agreement will be signed by the parties that may displace the obligations of the original lease agreement—Pearl will promise to make the monthly payments and CCMEC will promise to release its claim for breach of the lease agreement. However, because payment of the settlement amount is going to be delayed under this agreement, CCMEC will probably insist that its claim will not be released unless and until Pearl makes all of the agreed settlement payments, and if she defaults on any payment she is promising to make in the settlement agreement, then her obligations under the original lease agreement will survive and authorize CCMEC to sue her for any balance owed under it. That settlement agreement might look like Illustration 8-a.

A disputed debt or liability claim can be settled at any time, even after a lawsuit has been filed over the dispute. In fact, trial judges will frequently inquire of the parties to a pending suit whether settlement negotiations have taken place and encourage the parties to attempt them. Of course, the judge cannot order parties to settle. However, FRCP 26(f) now authorizes the U.S. district courts to require the parties to meet and discuss a number of things about the case, including "the possibilities for promptly settling or resolving the case." This procedure is frequently used in the federal courts and in many state courts.

If the parties settle a pending lawsuit, the settlement will still be reduced to a written settlement agreement, as seen in Illustration 8-a, and a release executed by any party seeking judgment against another. But something must be done as well with the pending lawsuit. If the settlement calls for one party to make a lump sum payment to the other, then the settlement agreement will typically call for execution of the release and dismissal of the pending lawsuit by the plaintiff with prejudice (meaning it can never be refiled) upon receipt of the lump sum payment. Where the settlement agreement calls for future settlement payments to be made by a reliable third party, such as an insurance company under the terms of an annuity, the settlement agreement will typically call for the dismissal of the pending lawsuit with prejudice and execution of the release upon the execution of the settlement agreement. But what if the settlement agreement calls for one party to the pending lawsuit to make future payments to the other? Is the party who is to receive the future payments expected to dismiss its lawsuit with prejudice and trust the other party to make the payments? No. In that situation, execution of the release and dismissal of the pending lawsuit will be delayed until the final payment is made.

EXAMPLE

If CCMEC files suit against Pearl Murphy using the complaint seen in Illustration 8-b and the case is then settled, the settlement agreement, instead of reciting that no lawsuit is pending between the parties, will say something like, "There is now pending, based on the claim of CCMEC against Murphy based on the Lease Agreement, Case No. 00-7799 in the Circuit Court for Capitol County, Columbiana ("the Case"). And in addition to promising to execute the release when Pearl finishes with the settlement payments, CCMEC will promise, as well, "to file a dismissal with prejudice of the Case."

Illustration 8-a: SETTLEMENT AGREEMENT WITH RELEASE

This Compromise and Settlement Agreement ("the Settlement Agreement") is made by and between Capitol City Medical Equipment Company ("CCMEC") and Pearl E. Murphy ("Murphy"). On February 2, YR-1, Murphy entered into a Medical Equipment Lease Agreement (the "Lease Agreement") with CCMEC pursuant to which CCMEC leased and provided to defendant certain items of medical equipment set out in the Lease Agreement. CCMEC alleges that Murphy has breached her obligations under the Lease Agreement and now owes CCMEC $1,200 under the terms of the Lease Agreement plus interest and attorney's fees. Murphy disputes that she has breached her obligations under the terms of the Lease Agreement or that she owes any amount to CCMEC under the terms of the Lease Agreement.

No lawsuit is presently pending between the parties. The parties to this Settlement Agreement wish to reach a full and final settlement of all claims and defenses arising out of the facts recited above and the various disputes between the parties arising out of the Lease Agreement.

The parties to this Settlement Agreement, in consideration of the mutual covenants and agreements to be performed, as set forth below, agree as follows:

1. Murphy agrees to pay CCMEC the sum of $600 in six equal monthly installments of $100 each. Payments are to be made on the first day of each month for six consecutive months beginning September 1, YR-1.
2. Upon receipt of the sixth and final payment referenced in Paragraph 1 of the Settlement Agreement, CCMEC will execute the release attached as Exhibit 1 to this Settlement Agreement. However, if Murphy fails to make the payments referenced in Paragraph 1 of this Settlement Agreement in the amounts and at the times designated, the parties agree that the obligations of Murphy under the Lease Agreement shall remain in full force and effect and shall then be fully enforceable by CCMEC and this Settlement Agreement shall not be any bar to the right of CCMEC to seek all available legal and equitable relief for Murphy's alleged breach of that Lease Agreement.
3. The parties agree that the terms of this Settlement Agreement bind the parties and their respective heirs, executors, administrators, successors, and assigns.

Dated: _____.

_____
Pearl E. Murphy
Capitol City Medical Equipment Company

By: _____

Exhibit 1 to Compromise and Settlement Agreement

Release of Claims

Capitol City Medical Equipment Company ("CCMEC"), having confirmed that Pearl E. Murphy ("Murphy") has fulfilled all her obligations under that certain Compromise and Settlement Agreement entered into between CCMEC and Murphy on the _____ day of _____, YR-1, does hereby voluntarily and knowingly execute this Release of Claims ("Release") with the express intention of effecting the extinguishment of obligations, as designated in this Release. CCMEC with the intention of binding itself, its successors, and assigns, does hereby release and discharge Pearl E. Murphy, her heirs, executors, administrators, and assigns, from all claims, demands, actions, judgments, and executions that the CCMEC ever had, or now has, or may have, against Pearl E. Murphy created by or arising out of, that certain Medical Equipment Lease Agreement (the "Lease Agreement") dated February 2, YR-1.

Dated: _____.

Capitol City Medical Equipment Company
By: _____

Alternatively, a party who agrees to accept future payments or performance from the other party may ask that the paying party consent to the entry of a **consent decree** (also referred to as a **final judgment by consent** or an **agreed final judgment**) in the pending lawsuit (see Illustration 9-i). The basis of the obligation between the parties then becomes that final court judgment. We will consider the enforcement of final judgments in Chapters Ten and Eleven.

P-H 8-e: What would happen if Pearl and Nick settled their malpractice lawsuit against defendant Dr. Croft and accepted an agreed amount of money from him in that settlement but continued their lawsuit against co-defendant Capitol City Hospital? And what if the settlement agreement between Croft and Nick and Pearl provided that Croft was "loaning" some or all of the settlement funds to the couple to use in their continuing lawsuit against CCH, and that if there were any recovery by them against CCH then the loan would have to be repaid? Such agreements are called **loan receipt agreements** or **Mary Carter agreements** from *Booth v. Mary Carter Paint Co.*, 202 So.2d 8 (Fl. App. 1967). For a good discussion of how they work, read *Banovz v. Rantanen*, 649 N.E.2d 977 (Ill. App. 1995) and then determine if your state allows such agreements in personal injury or tort litigation. If so, must the settlement agreement be disclosed to the remaining defendants? Can those defendants offer proof of the Mary Carter agreement into evidence if one of the settling parties testifies in order to impeach that witness by showing an interest in the outcome of the case?

---

2. Mediated Settlement

Mediation A form of alternative dispute resolution in which an impartial person serving as mediator uses back and forth dialogue with the disputing parties to assist them in reaching a settlement.

The parties may employ the services of a **mediator** to assist them in reaching a negotiated settlement. **Mediation** is a form of ADR in which the mediator, a neutral third party to the dispute, seeks to facilitate a negotiated settlement between disputing parties. The mediator will listen to both sides, serve as a communication link between the disputing parties, and will encourage both sides to be reasonable and move toward a realistic settlement. The mediator has no authority to compel a settlement or to make any ruling in the favor of either party, nor does the mediator report the content of the discussions to the judge.

Mediation has become a popular and successful ADR tool. States now give trial judges the authority to order the parties to engage in good faith mediation and to select the mediator from a list of **court approved mediators**. Many federal district courts have adopted similar procedures by local rule, and some state appellate courts and federal circuit courts of appeals have mediation procedures for cases on appeal (see, e.g., **mediation conference** procedures for the Sixth Circuit at www.ca6.uscourts.gov/internet/mediation/aboutmediationconferences. htm).

If a case is successfully mediated, the mediated agreement will be reduced to a written settlement agreement, as already discussed.

3. Arbitration

Arbitration A form of ADR in which the disputing parties agree that a third-person arbitrator, or panel of arbitrators, may hear the dispute informally and render a decision. May be binding or non-binding.

Federal Arbitration Act Federal statute governing arbitration in cases affecting interstate commerce or maritime issues.

Arbitration is a different form of ADR in which the disputing parties agree that a third-person **arbitrator**, or **panel of arbitrators**, will hear the dispute and render a decision (the **arbitrator's award**). Like mediation, arbitration is considered to be a less-expensive and less time-consuming method of resolving disputes than formal litigation.

The **Federal Arbitration Act** (**FAA**), 9 U.S.C. §1 et seq., governs the procedures and enforcement of arbitration awards involving **interstate commerce** or **maritime issues**. Most contracts containing mandatory binding arbitration clauses *do* involve interstate commerce and thus are subject to the FAA. Contracts with arbitration clauses that affect *only* **intrastate commerce** are not governed by the FAA and state law controls them. Nonetheless, 35 states have adopted some version of the FAA and 14 other states have adopted similar procedures by miscellaneous statutory and regulatory enactments.

Arbitration can be *binding* or *nonbinding* under the FAA and similar state statutes. **Nonbinding arbitration**, as the phrase suggests, means that either party dissatisfied with the arbitration award can still resort to formal litigation to resolve the dispute. **Binding arbitration** means that neither party dissatisfied with the arbitration award can thereafter resort to formal litigation to resolve the dispute. A binding arbitration award can only be attacked subsequently in court if the arbitration process itself was flawed or corrupted in some way, as by the arbitrators failing to follow the rules of the arbitration process or by proof of **partiality** or **bias** on the part of the arbitrators.

Parties to a dispute can elect to arbitrate their dispute at any time. More typically, though, arbitration is mandated by the contract between the parties that gave rise to the dispute. It is increasingly common for both commercial and consumer contracts to contain mandatory binding arbitration clauses such as that seen in Illustration 8-b.

EXAMPLE

Assume that the Medical Equipment Lease Agreement between Pearl Murphy and CCME seen as an exhibit to the complaint in Illustration 8-c contains the arbitration clause shown in Illustration 8-b. The arbitration panel finds in favor of CCME and awards it $1,500. Because the contract clause said the arbitration was binding, and assuming the arbitration clause itself is enforceable in the state, Pearl's only judicial recourse now will be to challenge the integrity of the arbitration process, not the underlying indebtedness.

The FAA *mandates* a presumption that an award arising out of the arbitration is valid and enforceable as a final judgment of a court unless the other party, within 90 days, files an action challenging the integrity of the arbitration process (e.g., fraud or prejudice) or seeks to vacate or modify the award based on some material

Illustration 8-b: CONTRACTUAL ARBITRATION CLAUSE

In the event of a dispute between the parties over the interpretation of this Agreement or any purported performance or failure to perform by either party, the parties agree, in lieu of litigation, to submit said dispute to binding arbitration pursuant to the rules of the American Arbitration Association.

error (e.g., an obvious miscalculation of figures). We will have more to say about final judgments in Chapter Nine.

Beginning with *Southland Corp. v. Keating*, 465 U.S. 1 (1984), the U.S. Supreme Court (SCOTUS) has construed the FAA to preempt state rules that might prohibit or limit the scope of a contractual arbitration clause.

P-H 8-f: Read *Hall Street Associates, L.L.C. v. Mattel, Inc.*, 552 U.S. 576 (2008). Can a contract containing an arbitration clause also grant a court discretion to engage in a broader review of the arbitration award than discussed in the text? Read *Doctor's Assocs. v. Cassarotto*, 517 U.S. 681 (1996). Can a state require that a contract containing an arbitration clause also contain special notice requirements to ensure that the clause is conspicuous and clear? Read *AT&T Mobility v. Concepcion*, 131 S.Ct. 1740 (2011). Can a state common law doctrine of unconscionability be used to strike down a clause in a consumer contract requiring binding arbitration but prohibiting class action arbitration? Read *American Exp. Co. v. Italian Colors Restaurant*, 570 U.S. __ (2013 WL 3064410). What is the "effective vindication rule" and why did the majority reject it?

Notwithstanding the FAA and its broad construction by SCOTUS, a few federal statutes specifically restrict the use of mandatory binding arbitration clauses in predispute contracts. Those include:

- The Motor Vehicle Franchise Contract Arbitration Fairness Act, 15 U.S.C. §1226, prohibits automobile manufacturers from requiring their franchisees to agree to binding arbitration on a predispute basis.
- The John Warner National Defense Authorization Act for Fiscal Year 2007, Subtitle F §670, 10 U.S.C. §987, prohibits creditors from requiring military personnel and dependents to arbitrate consumer credit disputes.
- The Farm Bill of 2008, 7 U.S.C. §97(c), requires that growers and producers of livestock or poultry be provided an opportunity to decline to be bound by arbitration provisions on predispute basis.
- The Department of Defense Appropriations Act of 2009 amended USC §1303 by including the "Franken Amendment," detailed in 48 C.F.R. §§222.7400-7405, restricts the use of mandatory arbitration agreements by prohibiting defense contractors from requiring employees or independent contractors to agree to arbitrate claims for violation of civil rights or for sexual assault or harassment.
- The Dodd-Frank Wall Street Reform and Consumer Protection Act provides the new Bureau of Consumer Financial Protection authority to study and regulate mandatory predispute arbitration with respect to consumers' use of financial products or services.
- Dodd-Frank grants the Securities Exchange Commission authority to issue rules prohibiting or limiting the use of predispute agreements with respect to securities claims brought by customers or clients of brokers or dealers and rules prohibiting or limiting the use of predispute agreements with respect to securities claims brought by customers or clients of investment advisors.
- Dodd-Frank prohibits lenders from imposing mandatory arbitration in residential mortgages or home equity loans.

- Dodd-Frank restricts the enforcement of provisions waving rights or requiring arbitration in civil cases alleging retaliation by a government agency wherein fraud is reported.

> **P-H 8-g:** Go to the Web site of the Consumer Financial Protection Bureau at www.consumerfinance.gov/ and see if the CFPB has promulgated any regulations regarding mandatory arbitration clauses in consumer financial contracts.

If no private or mediated settlement is reached in a dispute, and if no enforceable arbitration clause is present, the creditor may file a civil lawsuit against the debtor asking the court to resolve the dispute by entering a final judgment in favor of the creditor against the debtor.

C. Filing the Lawsuit: Default and Contested Cases

1. The Complaint

Complaint The pleading that initiates a civil suit to collect a debt.

A lawsuit brought to obtain a final judgment on a preexisting debt or a claim begins with the filing of a **complaint** in a court of law. Such suits overwhelmingly are brought in *state court* rather than *federal court*. However, the plaintiff's lawyer may choose to file in federal court if the dispute happens to involve a federal statute that gives federal courts **jurisdiction** (power to hear the case) under 28 U.S.C. §1331, or if the plaintiff and defendant are residents of different states (called **diversity of citizenship**) and the amount in controversy exceeds $75,000, which gives federal courts jurisdiction under 28 U.S.C. §1332.

The contents of the complaint in a collection suit may vary with particular state pleading requirements, but all will contain the same basic allegations:

- the identity of the plaintiff and defendant;
- the relevant law controlling the suit;
- the factual circumstances giving rise to the debt or claim;
- the balance allegedly owing or damages claimed; and
- the **prayer for relief** (request for judgment) in favor of the plaintiff against the defendant in the amount owed or claimed.

Prayer for relief The part of a civil complaint that states the relief sought from the court.

If CCME files suit against Pearl Murphy to collect the $1,200 it alleges that she owes on the medical equipment lease, the complaint will look something like what is shown in Illustration 8-c.

Answer The pleading a defendant must file to a complaint filed against him to avoid a default judgment.

2. The Uncontested Case: Default Judgment

Default judgment A final judgment rendered against a defendant in a civil suit who fails to file an answer to the complaint or to otherwise defend.

Once the complaint is served on the defendant, the defendant will have some number of days determined by state law (or federal rules of procedure if the case is filed in federal court) to file an **answer** to the complaint or an appropriate **motion** (e.g., to dismiss the complaint on some ground) in response to it. If the defendant fails to file a timely answer or a responsive motion, the plaintiff will be entitled to request a **default judgment** against the defendant. Defendants to a collection

Illustration 8-c: COMPLAINT OF CCME IN COLLECTION LAWSUIT AGAINST PEARL MURPHY

IN THE CAPITOL COUNTY COLUMBIANA
CIRCUIT COURT

CAPITOL CITY MEDICAL EQUIPMENT COMPANY, Plaintiff	)))	
v.	)	DOCKET NO. 00-77991
PEARL E. MURPHY, Defendant	)))	

COMPLAINT

Plaintiff, Capitol City Medical Equipment Company, for its cause of action against defendant, Pearl E. Murphy, alleges as follows:

1. Plaintiff is a corporation organized and existing under the laws of Columbiana and has its primary place of business in Capitol City, Columbiana. Defendant, Pearl E. Murphy, resides at 3521 West Cherry Street in Capitol City, Columbiana.

2. On February 2, YR-1, defendant entered into a Medical Equipment Lease Agreement (the "Agreement") with plaintiff pursuant to which defendant leased and provided to defendant certain items of medical equipment set out in the Agreement. A true and genuine copy of the Agreement is attached to this complaint as Exhibit 1 and its terms are hereby incorporated into this complaint by reference.

3. Pursuant to the terms of the Agreement defendant promised and agreed to pay plaintiff the rental amounts due under the Agreement within thirty (30) days of receiving a bill from plaintiff for said rental amounts. On May 15, YR-1, plaintiff prepared and mailed to defendant a bill for rental amounts due under the Agreement in the amount of $1,200 (the "Bill"). A true and genuine copy of the Bill is attached to this complaint as Exhibit 2 and its terms are incorporated into this complaint by reference.

4. Defendant has failed to pay any portion of the rental amount due to plaintiff within 30 days of receipt of the Bill in material breach and violation of her duties under the Agreement. Plaintiff is entitled to judgment against defendant for the principal balance of $1,200 plus interest at the rate of 15% per annum on such principal balance since the date payment was first due under the terms of the Agreement. Plaintiff is further entitled to judgment against the defendant for its reasonable attorney's fee incurred in connection with the collection of this indebtedness.

WHEREFORE, plaintiff prays as follows:

a. For final judgment against defendant in the amount of $1,200 representing the principal balance due under the terms of the Agreement;

b. For final judgment against defendant for interest on the principal balance due under the terms of the Agreement from the date payment was first due until the date judgment is entered at the rate of 15% per annum;

c. For final judgment against defendant for plaintiff's reasonable attorney's fee incurred in connection with the collection of this indebtedness in an amount to be shown to the court at trial; and

d. For general relief.

This August 5, YR-1

_____

B.A. Tiger, Attorney at Law
Counsel for Capitol City Medical
Equipment Company
101 East Broadway
Capitol City, Columbiana
(555) 213-1234

Exhibit 1 to Complaint

MEDICAL EQUIPMENT LEASE AGREEMENT

This Agreement is made this 2nd day of February, YR-1, between Capitol City Medical Equipment Company ("Company") and the undersigned Customer.

1. Company agrees to lease to Customer the medical equipment set forth on Exhibit A to this Agreement for a term not exceeding 90 days from the date of this Agreement.

2. Customer agrees to pay Company the daily rental amount for each item of medical equipment as set forth on Exhibit A no later than 30 days following the date of billing to Customer.

3. Company will bill Customer upon the return of the medical equipment leased to Customer pursuant to this Agreement or at the end of the lease term which ever occurs sooner.

4. In the event Customer fails to pay the billing referenced in Paragraphs 2 and 3 in full, Customer shall be liable to Company for interest on the unpaid balance at the rate of 15% per annum until said balance is paid in full.

5. In the event Company finds it necessary to undertake legal action to recover possession of any item of medical equipment leased to Customer pursuant to this Agreement or to undertake collection efforts with regard to any unpaid balance of the billing referenced in Paragraphs 2 and 3, Customer shall be liable to Company for all costs incurred by Company is such repossession or collection effort, including court costs and a reasonable attorney's fee.

Capitol City Medical Equipment Company
By:_____/s/_____

Mark Andrews, Manager
Pearl E. Murphy_____/s/_____
Customer

Exhibit 2 to Complaint

CAPITOL CITY MEDICAL EQUIPMENT COMPANY
413 Richardson Avenue
Capitol City, Columbiana
(555) 214-8765

TO: Pearl E. Murphy
RE: Invoice for February 2, YR-1, Agreement
DATE: May 15, YR-1

Balance due per terms of lease agreement: $1,200 for medical equipment leased pursuant.

BALANCE IS DUE in full no later than 30 days from the date of this invoice.

suit often have no legitimate defense to the creditor's complaint and consequently do not answer or otherwise respond to it. Thus, default judgments are very common in collection lawsuits.

The procedure for seeking a default judgment will vary in detail from state to state. However there are basic similarities and Illustration 8-d sets out a typical state rule of procedure for taking a default judgment.

Assume that the rule you see in Illustration 8-d is the controlling rule in Columbiana and that Pearl Murphy fails to file a timely answer or other response to the complaint of CCME. The attorney for CCME will immediately file an **application for default judgment** (which may be called a "motion" or "petition" in other states) as shown in Illustration 8-e.

Note that the rule set out in Illustration 8-d requires that the defendant be given *notice* of the application for default. This is done, like service or process at the beginning of a lawsuit, to comply with the dictates of **due process** or fundamental fairness to the defendant (the Fourteenth Amendment to the U.S. Constitution provides that, "no state shall deprive any person of life, liberty, or property without due process of law"). The **notice of application for default judgment** provided by Capitol City Medical Equipment Company to Pearl Murphy might look like Illustration 8-f.

In ruling on an application for default judgment, an actual trial or evidentiary hearing may or may not be necessary. If the amount sought in the collection suit is liquidated (i.e., known or can be calculated to the penny based on a preexisting contract or other known information), then proof of the indebtedness is often allowed by **affidavit** without any evidentiary hearing. An affidavit is a signed statement made under oath subject to penalties of perjury. (Affidavits are called **declarations** in some jurisdictions.) The affidavit is typically signed in the presence of a notary public, who then notarizes the signature of the **affiant**.

This is the procedure being used by CCME. Note that the application for default in Illustration 8-e references two affidavits submitted in support of the application. The affidavit of Mark Andrews, the CCME manager, will provide sworn testimony regarding the factual allegations of the indebtedness as recited

Due process Fundamental fairness mandated by the Fifth and Fourteenth Amendments to the U.S. Constitution.

Illustration 8-d: TYPICAL STATE RULE FOR TAKING A DEFAULT JUDGMENT

When a party against whom a judgment for affirmative relief is sought has failed to plead or otherwise defend as provided by these rules and that fact is made to appear by affidavit or otherwise, judgment by default may be entered as follows:

The party entitled to a judgment by default shall apply to the court. All parties against whom a default judgment is sought shall be served with a written notice of the application for judgment at least five days before the hearing on the application, regardless of whether the party has made an appearance in the action. No judgment by default shall be entered against an infant or incompetent person unless represented in the action by a general guardian, committee, conservator, or other such representative who has appeared therein. If, in order to enable the court to enter judgment or to carry it into effect, it is necessary to take an account or to determine the amount of damages or to establish the truth of any averment by evidence or to make an investigation of any other matter the court may conduct such hearings or order such references as it deems necessary and proper and shall accord a right of trial by jury to the parties when and as required by any statute.

Illustration 8-e: APPLICATION FOR DEFAULT JUDGMENT IN A COLLECTION LAWSUIT [STYLE OF CASE OMITTED FROM ILLUSTRATION]

APPLICATION FOR DEFAULT JUDGMENT

Plaintiff, Capitol City Medical Equipment Company, applies to the court pursuant to Rule 55 of the Columbiana Rules of Civil Procedure for default judgment in its favor in the principal amount of $1,200 plus prejudgment interest at the rate of 15% per annum calculated from June 16, YR-1, through the date judgment is entered plus $1,000 in attorney's fees.

In support of this application plaintiff would show that the court file establishes that defendant Pearl E. Murphy was served with process in this case on August 7, YR-1, and that defendant failed to file an answer or responsive motion to the complaint within thirty (30) days as required by CRCP 12. Accordingly, pursuant to CRCP 55, plaintiff is entitled to a judgment by default in its favor as to all allegations of liability contained in the complaint.

In further support of this application, plaintiff submits the affidavits of Mark Andrews, plaintiff's manager and attorney B.A. Tiger, counsel for plaintiff, attached hereto as Exhibits 1 and 2, respectively. Those affidavits together establish that plaintiff is entitled to judgment against defendant for $1,200 as unpaid rent due under the terms of the Medical Equipment Rental Agreement referenced in the complaint, and for prejudgment interest at the rate of 15% per annum from June 16, YR-1, through the date of judgment and for attorney's fees in the amount of $1,000 for expenses incurred in collecting this debt from defendant. Plaintiff also asks that court costs be assessed against defendant.

This September 9, YR-1
[Attorney's signature and certificate of service omitted from illustration.]

Illustration 8-f: NOTICE OF APPLICATION FOR DEFAULT JUDGMENT [STYLE OF CASE OMITTED FROM ILLUSTRATION]

NOTICE OF APPLICATION FOR DEFAULT JUDGMENT

TO: Pearl E. Murphy
3521 West Cherry Street
Capitol City, Columbiana

NOTICE is hereby given, pursuant to CRCP 55, that plaintiff, Capitol City Medical Equipment Company, has filed an application for default judgment in this case. A copy of the application for default judgment is attached.

The court will conduct a hearing on the application on September 15, YR-1, at 9 A.M.

Dated: September 9, YR-1
[Attorney's signature and certificate of service omitted from illustration.]

---

in the complaint and will properly **authenticate** (prove the genuineness of) the Medical Equipment Rental Agreement and the Bill referenced in the complaint, from which the calculations of the exact amount owed on the debt can be made. The affidavit of the attorney, B.A. Tiger, will establish the amount of attorney's fees incurred by CCME and that they are reasonable. Illustration 8-g and 8-h set forth the affidavits of plaintiff's two affiants.

Illustration 8-g: AFFIDAVIT OF MARK ANDREWS IN THE CCME v. PEARL MURPHY CASE [STYLE OF CASE OMITTED FROM ILLUSTRATION]

AFFIDAVIT OF MARK ANDREWS

STATE OF COLUMBIANA   )
COUNTY OF CAPITOL   )

Affiant, Mark Andrews, after first being duly sworn according to law, deposes and states as follows:

1. I am the manager of Capitol City Medical Equipment Company of Capitol City, Columbiana, the plaintiff in this case (CCME).
2. I have personal knowledge of the matters contained in this affidavit. This affidavit is submitted in support of the application for default judgment filed by CCME.
3. On February 2, YR-1, I witnessed defendant Pearl E. Murphy sign the Medical Equipment Lease Agreement that is attached to the complaint in this case as Exhibit 1 (the "Agreement"). I also signed the Agreement on that date in my capacity as manager of CCME. The medical equipment described in Exhibit A to the Agreement was delivered to defendant on February 3, YR-1, and returned by her within 90 days of the date of the Agreement.
4. The rental fee for the medical equipment leased by defendant from CCME pursuant to the Agreement totaled $1,200. On May 15, YR-1, I caused to be prepared and mailed to defendant the Bill, a copy of which is attached as Exhibit B to the complaint in this case, in the amount of $1,200 representing the rental fee due from defendant under the terms of the Agreement. Defendant has never paid any portion of the $1,200 owed to CCME. Pursuant to paragraph 2 of the Agreement, payment in full was due from defendant no later than June 15, YR-1.
5. Pursuant to Paragraph 4 of the Agreement, CCME is entitled to receive interest on the amount due from defendant at the rate of 15% per annum from June 16, YR-1, through the date of judgment.
6. Pursuant to Paragraph 5 of the Agreement, CCME is entitled to recover from defendant its expenses in connection with collecting the indebtedness owed including a reasonable attorney's fee. CCME has incurred attorney's fees totaling $1,000 to date in connection with its efforts to collect this debt from defendant. More specifically, on or about July 1, YR-1, CCME authorized attorney B.A. Tiger to write a demand letter to defendant in connection with this debt. When defendant failed to respond to the demand letter of Mr. Tiger CCME authorized Mr. Tiger to file this lawsuit and obtain a judgment against defendant.
7. In all my dealings with defendant as manager of CCME I never received any information suggesting that defendant was or is in military service and, on such information and belief, she is not.

FURTHER AFFIANT SAYETH NOT.

_____
Mark Andrews

[Notarization omitted from illustration.]

If B.A. Tiger has sent his client a written bill for the legal services rendered he may attach that bill to his affidavit and authenticate it in the affidavit as Mark Andrews did the agreement and bill that went to Pearl Murphy. Both of the affidavits you see in Illustrations 8-g and 8-h would be attached to the application for default judgment as referenced in Illustration 8-e. If the judge found the affidavits sufficient and the total amount due could be calculated from the

Illustration 8-h: AFFIDAVIT OF B.A. TIGER IN CCME v. PEARL MURPHY CASE [STYLE OF CASE OMITTED FROM ILLUSTRATION]

AFFIDAVIT OF B.A. TIGER

STATE OF COLUMBIANA   )
COUNTY OF CAPITOL   )

Affiant, B.A. Tiger, after first being duly sworn according to law, deposes and states as follows:

1. I am an attorney licensed to practice law in the state of Columbiana.
2. I have personal knowledge of the matters contained in this affidavit. This affidavit is submitted in support of plaintiff's application for default judgment.
3. On July 1, YR-1, I was retained by plaintiff Capitol City Medical Equipment Company (CCME) to represent it in collecting the amounts due to it from defendant Pearl E. Murphy pursuant to the terms of the Medical Equipment Lease Agreement referenced in the complaint. On July 1, YR-1, I prepared and mailed a demand letter to defendant on behalf of CCME. A copy of my July 1, YR-1, letter is attached to this affidavit as Exhibit 1. When defendant failed to respond to my demand letter CCME authorized me to prepare and file the complaint in this case and, subsequently, the application for default judgment and supporting documents.
4. I have expended 4.0 hours on this matter on behalf of plaintiff in connection with the collection of the debt owed to it by defendant. My billing rate is $250 per hour. Consequently my fees chargeable to plaintiff for my work on this matter total $1,000. I have 21 years of experience as an attorney and have done substantial collection work. I consider my fee in this case to be reasonable in light of my experience, the nature and amount of the debt, and the work done to obtain a judgment for CCME.

FURTHER AFFIANT SAYETH NOT.

_____
B.A. Tiger

[Notarization omitted from illustration.]

---

evidence provided by affidavit, final judgment by default would be entered based on the affidavits (see Illustration 8-i).

Sometimes though, proof of indebtedness by affidavit is not sufficient and a trial or evidentiary hearing where witnesses are called and testify in court is necessary. Note the last sentence in the rule set forth in Illustration 8-d. The most common situation giving rise to an evidentiary hearing in a default context is where the amount sued for by the plaintiff is *unliquidated* and must be determined by a finder of fact (a jury or the judge if no jury has been demanded) based on sworn testimony.

EXAMPLE

Assume that in Nick and Pearl Murphys' lawsuit against Dr. Samuel M. Craft and Capitol City Hospital (Illustration 1-a), Dr. Craft fails to file a timely answer or otherwise respond to the complaint and the Murphys file an application for default judgment against him. The court may grant default judgment as to the fact of **liability** without an evidentiary hearing, but a trial or other evidentiary hearing will be necessary regarding **damages** because the Murphys' damages

Illustration 8-i: FINAL JUDGMENT BY DEFAULT IN CCME v. PEARL MURPHY [STYLE OF CASE OMITTED FROM ILLUSTRATION]

FINAL JUDGMENT BY DEFAULT

This action was commenced on August 5, YR-1. Defendant Pearl E. Murphy was served with process on August 7, YR-1, and has filed no answer or other response to the complaint in the time allowed by law. Plaintiff has filed an application for default judgment pursuant to CRCP 55 supported by affidavits establishing its right to recover for all amounts sought in the complaint. It is therefore,

ORDERED, that a final judgment by default should be and hereby is entered in favor of Plaintiff Capitol City Medical Equipment Company against Defendant Pearl E. Murphy in the amount of $2,247.70 calculated as follows:

$1,200 as unpaid rent due under the terms of the Medical Equipment Lease Agreement referenced in the complaint;

$47.70 as prejudgment interest on the unpaid rent at the rate of 15% per annum from June 16, YR-1, through the date of this judgment; and

$1,000 in attorney's fees as expenses incurred in collecting this debt from defendant. And it is further

ORDERED, that court costs in this matter are taxed to Defendant Pearl E. Murphy for which execution shall issue if necessary.

ENTER this 20th day of September YR-1

_____

Juanita A. McBride, Circuit Judge

---

claims are unliquidated. They've asked for a specific amount in their complaint, $1.5 million, but there is no existing evidentiary basis to conclude that they are entitled to that amount as there is in the case of a preexisting contract or promissory note. For example, part of Pearl's claim is for pain and suffering. What is the dollar value of that? Only a finder of fact can determine that, after hearing and weighing the evidence. If she asks for hedonic damages (loss of enjoyment of life) due to her injuries, only a fact finder can decide from hearing and weighing the evidence how much that is worth in dollars. The same is true as to Nick's claim for lost consortium with his wife due to her injuries.

P-H 8-h: Assume that Nick and Pearl Murphy default on the loan from First Bank of Capitol City (FBCC) secured by a mortgage in their home (see Illustrations 2-a and 4-b). FBCC repossesses the home, sells it, then institutes a collection suit against the Murphys for the deficiency. The Murphys do not respond to the complaint and FBCC applies for a default judgment. Can that default be finalized by affidavits or will an evidentiary hearing be necessary? What about Abe Mendoza's suit to enforce a lien *lis pendens* and have a constructive trust declared in real property owned by his former bookkeeper (see Illustrations 1-b and 6-i) in the event she fails to respond to the complaint?

Assume that when CCME files suit against Pearl Murphy, she does not respond and a default judgment is entered against her. That default judgment will look something like what is shown in Illustration 8-i.

Confession to a judgment A debtor's waiver of the right to contest liability and authorization of the creditor to enter a consent judgment on his behalf.

It is possible for a debtor to agree to a **confession to judgment** (sometimes called a **cognovit** or a **warrant of attorney**) at the time the debt is incurred. In those jurisdictions that still recognize it, the effect of the confession is to authorize the creditor to act as the debtor's agent in consenting to a final judgment in the event of default. The debtor has effectively waived the right to defend against the collection suit. Because of their harshness, many jurisdictions have abolished such confessions to judgment as a matter of public policy, at least in connection with consumer transactions.

P-H 8-i: Special requirements are imposed when default judgment is sought against one who is a member of the armed forces on active duty, including reservists and members of the National Guard. The **Servicemembers Civil Relief Act (SCRA)**, U.S.C.A. App. §501 et seq., requires that an affidavit in support of the application for default state whether the defendant is a member of the military (see paragraph 7 of the Mark Andrews affidavit in Illustration 8-g) and provides that default judgment cannot be entered against an individual who is, until the court has appointed an attorney to represent his interests, as by attempting to give him notice of the proceeding against him. If a default is entered against him during his active duty or within 60 days following his release from active duty, the judgment must be set aside and the case reopened upon application of the service member. The SCRA gives considerable other protections to active-duty service members. Read the summary found at http://usmilitary.about.com/cs/sscra/a/scra2.htm and summarize other provisions that may impact on a service member's obligation for personal debt.

---

3. The Contested Case: Defenses, the Answer, and the Counterclaims

If the defendant in a collection suit intends to contest it, he will file an answer to the complaint or a motion asking for summary relief. Assume that Pearl Murphy contends that the medical equipment she leased from CCME either didn't work properly or was not the correct equipment her treating physician prescribed for her medical needs. Her answer might look like what is shown in Illustration 8-j.

There are any number of defenses that a defendant/creditor may have to liability, all of which will depend on the specific facts of the case. The debtor may deny that she agreed to pay the obligation alleged. Or, if she did agree, the debtor may deny, as Pearl Murphy does, that the creditor itself performed as promised and, therefore, is not entitled to recover. The debtor may agree that she owes some of the debt alleged against her but not all. The debtor may contend as a defense that the dispute over the debt has been previously compromised and settled, which would act as a defense to further liability. If the collection suit is one brought by a secured creditor to collect a deficiency remaining after real or personal property has been foreclosed on or repossessed and sold by the creditor, the debtor may raise as a defense in the suit to collect the deficiency that the repossession or foreclosure sale was not done in a reasonably commercial manner and if properly done would have satisfied all or more of the deficiency. In Chapter Four, Section C, we considered defense of *material change* that may be available to a surety or guarantor who is named a defendant in a collection action. As we will

Illustration 8-j: ANSWER TO COMPLAINT IN COLLECTION LAWSUIT [STYLE OF CASE OMITTED FROM ILLUSTRATION]

ANSWER

Defendant, Pearl E. Murphy, for her answer to the complaint filed against her in this cause, would show the court as follows:

1. The allegations contained in Paragraphs 1-3 of the complaint are admitted.

2. As to the allegations contained in Paragraph 4 of the complaint, defendant admits that she has not paid any portion of the bill sent to her by plaintiff but alleges affirmatively that she is not in breach or violation of the agreement between the parties due to failure of consideration in that the medical equipment provided to defendant by plaintiff either did not function properly or was not the correct equipment prescribed by defendant's treating physician for her medical condition. None of the medical equipment provided to defendant by plaintiff was of any value to defendant and defendant affirmatively alleges that she is not obligated to plaintiff for any amount under the terms of the agreement between the parties.

3. For the reasons set forth in Paragraph 2 of this answer, defendant alleges affirmatively that it is plaintiff that has breached and violated the agreement between the parties and said breach and violation constitutes a bar on plaintiff's right to recover any amounts from defendant.

WHEREFORE, defendant pays as follows:

a. That the complaint be dismissed with prejudice;
b. That court costs be taxed to plaintiff; and
c. For general relief.

This August 20, YR-1

_____

N.O. Way, Attorney at Law
Counsel for Pearl E. Murphy
201 West Broadway
Capitol City, Columbiana
(555) 213-5678

---

see in Part C of the text, if the debtor has filed a bankruptcy petition, that filing may operate to *automatically stay* (suspend) the collection suit, at least temporarily. If the bankruptcy filing has resulted in the debt being *discharged in bankruptcy*, that discharge may operate as an absolute defense against further liability on the debt.

Statute of limitation A statutory time limitation placed on the right to bring a lawsuit on a particular theory of liability.

Every state has **statutes of limitation** establishing strict periods of time within which a lawsuit must be filed in order to collect a preexisting debt or to assert a claim that could result in a debt obligation (as in the Murphys' malpractice claim against Dr. Craft and Capitol City Hospital). If the creditor/claimant's collection suit is filed after the applicable statute of limitations has expired, that may give rise to an affirmative defense on behalf of the debtor even though the debt is actually owed or the claim is valid.

EXAMPLE

Assume that Columbiana has a one-year statute of limitation on medical malpractice lawsuits. The Murphys file their lawsuit against Dr. Craft and Capitol City Hospital (CCH) 13 months after Pearl's surgery. Subject to state law on the possible tolling (suspending) of statutes of limitations for the reasonable failure of the patient to discover the malpractice within the statutory period or fraud by the defendant, effectively hiding the malpractice from the plaintiff, the defendants may have a valid defense to the Murphys' lawsuit even though the malpractice was real and provable.

EXAMPLE

Assume that Columbiana has a two-year statute of limitations on filing suit to collect contractual debt. Suit must be filed within two years after the alleged breach. If CCME files suit on the alleged breach by Pearl Murphy of the Medical Equipment Lease Agreement 25 months after the breach, she may have a valid defense to the lawsuit even though she owes the debt.

P-H 8-j: If the contract between Pearl Murphy and CCME had been entered into and breached by Pearl in your state, what would be the controlling statute of limitations for CCME to file suit to collect? Your state may have different statutes of limitation for different kinds of contractual debt. For example, look at your state's version of UCC 2-725, which may provide for a four-year statute to sue for alleged breach of a contract for sale of goods. What statute in your state would control in a suit to recover on a bank's home purchase loan? On a bank's commercial loan? On a suit by a plumber or a lawyer to recover amounts owed for services rendered? On a landlord's claim for unpaid rent?

Counterclaim A claim for relief against the plaintiff brought by a defendant in a civil lawsuit.

Occasionally the defendant in a collection suit will not only deny liability on the alleged obligation but will **counterclaim** for affirmative relief himself against the creditor or claimant.

P-H 8-k: Assume Pearl Murphy alleges that her recovery was delayed or her medical condition worsened by the failure of CCME to provide her with the correct equipment or with equipment that worked properly. Assume further that she alleges that she had to procure the correct equipment from another source and paid $500 more than she would have paid to CCME for the correct, properly functioning equipment. Draft her counterclaim, which would be included in the answer to CCME's complaint.

P-H 8-l: Recall our discussion of the judgment-proof debtor earlier in this chapter and the importance of the creditor or claimant performing a factual investigation prior to filing the collection lawsuit. What does the possibility of the defendant/debtor having a counterclaim against the creditor/claimant tell you about the extent of the factual investigation to be performed before the creditor files suit? There have been many creditors who filed suit to collect a debt without investigating and later regretted it.

4. The Contested Case: Pretrial Discovery

If the collection suit is contested, then the parties will prepare for trial. The rules of civil procedure in all 50 states and the Federal Rules of Civil Procedure authorize the five methods of **formal discovery** set out in Illustration 8-k.

EXAMPLE

If Pearl Murphy contests the complaint filed against her by CCME, there is a great deal of relevant information CCME may seek from her in discovery. But there is no basis for CCME to use discovery to determine what assets Pearl may have out of which a final judgment in CCME's favor might be satisfied.

As we will see in Chapter Eleven, once a final money judgment has been entered in favor of the creditor, the judgment creditor may use **postjudgment discovery** for the express purpose of discovering assets of the judgment debtor out of which the judgment may be satisfied. There are unusual situations where state law may allow discovery of assets prior to final judgment. For example, where the plaintiff is asking for **punitive damages**—damages intended to punish the wrongdoer for intentional or fraudulent behavior (to be contrasted with **compensatory damages**, which are intended to compensate the wronged party)—as part of its relief, discovery can normally be had into the assets of the defendant because that information is deemed relevant to what an appropriate punitive award might be. And where the creditor seeks a prejudgment attachment of the debtor's assets (see Chapter Nine, Section A), discovery may be allowed to determine the existence, location, or value of debtor's assets being wrongfully concealed or disposed of to defeat the creditor's future efforts to seize them in satisfaction of an anticipated judgment.

In CCME's lawsuit against Pearl Murphy, CCME might use written **interrogatories**, such as those shown in Illustration 8-l, and **requests for production of documents and things**, such as those shown in Illustration 8-m, to obtain information and documents relevant to defenses Pearl has raised in her answer.

Punitive damages Damages intended to punish the wrongdoer in order to deter similar conduct in the future.

Illustration 8-k: FIVE METHODS OF FORMAL PRETRIAL DISCOVERY

- Written interrogatories
- Requests for production of documents, records, and things
- Depositions
- Request for physical or mental examination
- Request for admissions

In general, these discovery methods can be used by the parties to the litigation to obtain information *relevant* to the issues raised in the lawsuit or information reasonably calculated to lead to relevant admissible evidence. That normally does *not* include information about the assets of the defendant/debtor. Why? Because the enforceability of any judgment rendered in plaintiff's favor is not yet an issue in the case, only whether the defendant is liable to plaintiff and, if so, for how much.

Illustration 8-l: INTERROGATORIES FROM CCME TO PEARL MURPHY [STYLE OF CASE OMITTED FROM ILLUSTRATION]

PLAINTIFF'S FIRST INTERROGATORIES TO DEFENDANT

Plaintiff, Capitol City Medical Equipment Company, submits the following interrogatories to defendant Pearl E. Murphy, to be answered under oath within 30 days of service pursuant to Rule 33 of the Columbiana Rules of Civil Procedure.

    1. Identify each item of medical equipment you rented from plaintiff pursuant to the February 2, YR-1, Medical Equipment Lease Agreement (the "Agreement") between you and plaintiff and which you contend did not work properly and, for each one identified, state in detail how the equipment did not work properly.

    2. Identify each item of medical equipment you rented from plaintiff pursuant to the Agreement between you and plaintiff and which you contend was not the correct equipment prescribed for you by your treating physician(s) and, for each one identified, state in detail how the equipment failed to comply with what your treating physician(s) prescribed.

    3. Identify by name, address and phone number each and every treating physician you refer to in Paragraph 2 of your answer.

    4. Identify by name, address and phone number each and every person having unprivileged knowledge of the medical equipment you identified in response to Interrogatory No. 1 not working properly and every person having unprivileged knowledge how each item of equipment you identified in response to Interrogatory No. 3 failed to comply with what your treating physician(s) prescribed.

This October 1, YR-1

[Attorney's name and certificate of service omitted from illustration.]

Illustration 8-m: DOCUMENT REQUESTS FROM CCME TO PEARL MURPHY [STYLE OF CASE OMITTED FROM ILLUSTRATION]

PLAINTIFF'S FIRST REQUEST
FOR PRODUCTION OF DOCUMENTS TO DEFENDANT

    Plaintiff, Capitol City Medical Equipment Company, pursuant to Rule 34 of the Columbiana Rules of Civil Procedure, requests that defendant produce for inspection and copying by plaintiff the following documents, records and things. Plaintiff requests that said production be made at the offices of plaintiff's counsel on the 2nd day of November, YR-1, or at such other place and time as the parties, through counsel, may agree.

    1. All documents or records of any kind, including correspondence, whether in paper or electronic format, that in any way tend to support or refute your contention that any item of medical equipment leased to you by plaintiff pursuant to the February 2, YR-1, Medical Equipment Lease Agreement (the "Agreement") did not work properly or was not the correct equipment prescribed for you by your treating physician(s).

    2. Each and every written prescription from a treating physician that you rely on to support your allegation that any item of medical equipment leased to you by plaintiff pursuant to the Agreement was not the correct equipment prescribed for you by your treating physician(s).

This October 1, YR-1

[Attorney's name and certificate of service omitted from illustration.]

P-H 8-m: What other questions should CCME ask Pearl Murphy in its interrogatories to her? If she had filed the counterclaim you drafted for her in P-H 8-h, what additional questions might CCME want to ask in its interrogatories to her? Draft additional interrogatories to be included in Illustration 8-l asking these additional questions.

P-H 8-n: What other documents or things should CCME ask Pearl Murphy to produce? If she had filed the counterclaim you drafted for her in P-H 8-j, what additional documents or things might CCME want to request from her? Draft additional document requests to be included in Illustration 8-m seeking to have her produce these documents and things.

The parties in a contested collection suit will also use **depositions** to obtain sworn pretrial answers from opposing parties and from witnesses they anticipate will testify at trial. The person examined in a deposition is the **deponent**. Upon the request of the attorney taking the deposition, the court reporter will prepare a written transcript of the deposition and provide it to the attorneys for all parties. The **deposition transcript** is then used by the attorneys to prepare questions to be asked of the deponent at trial. They will also use the deposition transcript to *impeach* the deponent when he testifies at trial if the deponent gives a different answer to a question at trial than he gave to the same question in the deposition.

P-H 8-o: Based on what you know about the CCME v. Pearl Murphy case at this point, make a list of the persons CCME's attorney might want to depose before trial of this case. Make a list of the persons Pearl's attorney might want to depose before trial. If you were the attorney for CCME deposing Pearl Murphy herself, what would your first ten questions to her be, not including biographical data? If you were the attorney for Pearl Murphy deposing CCME manager Mark Andrews, what would your first ten questions to him be, not including biographical data?

Requests for physical or mental examination are rarely used in the discovery phase of a collection lawsuit because the physical or mental condition of a debtor is not normally a legally sufficient excuse for nonpayment and is thus irrelevant to the liability of the defendant. However, if a debtor was contending as a defense to liability that he was mentally incompetent to enter the contract sued upon or was so disabled as to not be acting knowingly or voluntarily, then it might be relevant for the creditor to ask that he submit to a physical or mental examination by a doctor or other medical professional of the creditor's choosing.

Requests for admissions are commonly used in collection suits. The idea behind the request for admissions is that if the opposing party will admit the truth of certain facts or will admit the authenticity of certain documents prior to trial, the party seeking the admission will not need to prove those facts or authenticate those documents with witnesses at trial. The trial will be expedited and expenses likely reduced by the admissions.

Illustration 8-n: REQUEST FOR ADMISSIONS FROM PEARL MURPHY TO CCME [STYLE OF CASE OMITTED FROM ILLUSTRATION]

DEFENDANT'S REQUEST FOR ADMISSIONS TO PLAINTIFF

Defendant, Pearl E. Murphy, pursuant to Rule 36 of the Columbiana Rules of Civil Procedure, requests that defendant admit the truth of the following:

1. That on February 2, YR-1, defendant Pearl E. Murphy left in the possession of CCME agents a written order from Dr. Lucille McElhaney specifying five different items of medical equipment to be leased to defendant by CCME (the "Doctor's Order").
2. That after defendant had left the Doctor's Order with CCME agents, said agents misplaced and lost the Doctor's Order and failed to contact defendant or Dr. McElhaney to obtain another copy of the Doctor's Order.
3. That on February 3, YR-1, Mark Andrews, in his capacity of manager of CCME was advised of the events described in No.'s 1 and 2 and in response wrote in his own handwriting the note a true and genuine copy of which is attached to this request for admissions as Exhibit A and left said note for the CCME employee charged with selecting the medical equipment to be supplied to defendant pursuant to the Agreement.

This December 10, YR-1

[Attorney's name and certificate of service omitted from illustration.]

EXAMPLE

Assume that in the course of discovery in the CCME v. Pearl Murphy case, Pearl's attorney discovers by deposing three different employees of CCME that on the day that Pearl Murphy signed the Medical Equipment Lease Agreement, CCME misplaced the doctor's order she had left with CCME detailing the specific medical equipment to be provided to her. And assume further that Pearl's attorney has discovered through a document request, a handwritten note authored by Mark Andrews, the CCME manager, directing an employee to "make your best guess" as to what equipment she needed. Prior to trial, Pearl's attorney may prepare and serve on CCME's attorney the request for admissions shown in Illustration 8-m.

5. The Contested Case: Trial Preparation

Once discovery is completed, both sides will prepare for trial. That preparation will typically involve the following:

- Deposition transcripts will be indexed or summarized for ease of use at trial.
- Documents, photos, and other records to be offered as exhibits at trial will be copied as needed, pre-marked for identification, and arranged in the anticipated order in which they will be offered; the parties may or may not stipulate in advance to their admissibility.
- A **trial notebook** will be prepared by each lawyer containing copies of relevant pleadings and discovery; deposition summaries for use in examining

witnesses; questions for witnesses; notes for use in **voir dire** (jury selection if the case is to be tried to a jury), opening and closing statements; legal citations for use in arguing anticipated motions or objections during trial; proposed jury charges for the trial judge to consider if the case is to be tried to a jury.

- Witnesses will be subpoenaed to assure their presence at trial.
- The client and cooperating witnesses, including expert witnesses, will be prepped for their testimony on direct examination and any anticipated cross-examination.

6. The Contested Case: Trial

At trial the offering and admissibility of evidence will be governed by the applicable **rules of evidence** for the court in which the case is tried (e.g., Federal Rules of Evidence for cases in federal court and the state rules of evidence for cases tried in state court). The applicable **rules of civil procedure** (again Federal Rules of Civil Procedure in federal court, state rules of civil procedure in state court) will control procedural, non-evidentiary aspects of the trial. A detailed study of the rules of evidence and civil procedure are beyond the scope of our study but it should be kept in mind that a debt collection lawsuit is a civil action and is governed by the same rules and procedures as any civil lawsuit.

P-H 8-p: Litigating a civil case through filing, service, discovery, trial preparation, and trial can be time consuming and expensive. That is why ADR has become so favored in the modern era. Another alternative available to speed up the decision making process and keep costs down is what was originally known as the **summary jury trial**, today more commonly called **short, summary, and expedited civil action**. Essentially, this is a procedure whereby the parties consent, not to remove the case from the litigation process, but to shorten and expedite the process as by shortening the time period of discovery, limiting the scope of discovery, limiting the kinds of objections that can be made at trial to testimony and exhibits, Several states have adopted pilot programs in certain counties where the SSE civil action is being experimented with. Read about this alternative and those pilot programs at www.ncsc-jurystudies.org/What-We-Do//media/Microsites/Files/CJS/Jury%20News/12-IAALS-118_Expedited-Trials-FINAL-WEB%20pdf.ashx and www.ncsc.org//media/Files/PDF/Information-tion%20and%20Resources/Civil%20cover%20sheets/ShortSummaryExpedited-online%20rev.ashx. Determine if the courts of your state are utilizing or considering utilizing the SSE civil action alternative.

P-H 8-q: So great is the pressure being exerted on attorneys today to resolve civil disputes using ADR that a backlash has arisen. There is a feeling among many attorneys that a significant number of clients who want their day in court are being unduly pressured by attorneys or by the court to utilize ADR when they would really rather not, resulting in increasing dissatisfaction with the system. And there is growing discussion that some civil cases that need to be put to public trial in order to expose to the public and to hopefully deter wide spread or particularly egregious practices (e.g., the making and distribution of dangerous products, dishonest business practices) are instead being railroaded into ADR processes that result in confidential settlements the terms of which are unknown to the public and to lawmakers and thus spark no public outrage leading to change and produce no deterrent effect on the wrongdoer. Locate and read Abraham Wickelgren and Ezra Friedman, *No Free Lunch: How Settlement Can Reduce the Legal System's Ability to Induce Efficient Behavior*, 61 SMU Law Review 1355 (2008) and Joseph F. Anderson, Jr., *Where Have You Gone, Spot Mozingo? A Trial Judge's Lament over the Demise of the Civil Jury Trial*, 4 Fed. Cts. L. Rev. 90 (2010) available online at www.fclr.org/fclr/articles/html/2010/Where%20 have%20you%20gone.pdf. Do you agree with the conclusions of these researchers? Should we pull the reigns in on the rush to ADR in all civil cases? How might we do that?

CONCLUSION

The collection lawsuit may settle or be otherwise resolved during discovery or at any time prior to trial. The parties may negotiate a settlement with or without the aid of mediation, as discussed in Chapter Two, or they may submit the dispute to binding arbitration, also considered in Chapter Two. But if not, the trial will be scheduled, prepared for by both sides, and conducted according to the rules of civil procedure and evidence. In the next chapter we will examine the process of taking a final judgment in a collection suit. And we will also look at the creditor's right, in certain situations, to obtain some sort of relief even before a final judgment is entered, relief we call *prejudgment remedies*.

CHAPTER SUMMARY

In this chapter we have considered the collection lawsuit from its filing through the discovery stage. If prelitigation collection efforts fail, the creditor must decide whether to file a lawsuit to collect the debt. A number of factors may influence the creditor's decision of whether or not to file: whether the debt is liquidated; whether it is contested; the size of the debt; whether the debtor targeted is primarily or secondarily liable for the debt; the cost and duration of litigation; and whether the debtor is judgment proof or insolvent. A dispute over a debt may be resolved without litigation either by privately negotiated settlement or settlement produced through mediation. If the contract contains a mandatory binding arbitration clause, the dispute may have to be arbitrated rather than litigated in the courts. The collection lawsuit is a civil action instituted by filing a complaint, usually in state court. If the defendant fails to file a timely answer or motion in response to the complaint, the plaintiff will file an application for default judgment. Upon applying for default and if the amount of the debt is liquidated, default will normally be entered on the basis of a sworn complaint or affidavit proving the amount. If the amount of the debt is unliquidated, an evidentiary hearing may be necessary to prove the amount owed. If the defendant in the collection suit chooses to contest it, she will file an answer to the complaint setting forth her denial, if any, and any affirmative defenses she may have, such as compromise and settlement, running of the statute of limitations, or discharge in bankruptcy. If the defendant has an affirmative claim back against the plaintiff, he will file a counterclaim in the collection lawsuit. Once the parties have filed their pleadings in a contested case, it enters the discovery stage. The rules of civil procedure normally allow discovery to be had using written interrogatories; requests for production of documents, records, and things; depositions; requests for physical or mental examination; and requests for admissions.

REVIEW QUESTIONS

1. List some reasons why a creditor unable to collect a debt by prelitigation collection efforts may decide not to file a collection lawsuit.
2. Is there any difference between a debtor who is judgment proof and one who is insolvent? If so, what are those differences?
3. Explain why a creditor holding a lien *lis pendens* or a mechanic's lien has no choice as to whether to file suit if he wishes to enforce his lien.
4. Under what circumstances might a collection suit be filed in federal court rather than state court?
5. List five different types of information included in a complaint filed in a collection suit.
6. Describe the typical procedure for obtaining a default judgment where the debt is liquidated. Do the same where the debt is not liquidated.
7. What is an affidavit or declaration and how are they used in collection cases?
8. What are the five types of formal discovery permitted in a civil lawsuit?
9. What method of discovery might best be used to obtain documents from an opposing party relevant to the issues in the lawsuit?
10. What method of discovery results in the preparation of a transcript that is later used at trial in the examination of the deponent?

WORDS AND PHRASES TO REMEMBER

affidavit
agreed final judgment
application for default
authenticate
automatic stay
civil lawsuit
collection lawsuit
compensatory damages
complaint
consent decree
counterclaim
court approved mediators
court ordered mediation
damages
declarations

default judgment
deficiency balance
deficiency judgment
deponent
deposition
deposition transcript
discharge in bankruptcy
discovery (formal; pretrial)
diversity of citizenship
due process (clause)
factual investigation
federal court
final judgment
insolvent
interrogatories

judgment by default
judgment creditor
judgment debtor
judgment proof
jurisdiction
liability
loan receipt agreements
Mary Carter agreements
mediated settlement
mediation
mediator
motion
negotiate
postjudgment discovery
prayer for relief

punitive damages
release
relevant
request for admissions
request for physical or mental exam
request for production of documents
   or things
Servicemembers Civil Relief Act
   (SCRA)
settlement
settlement agreement
state court
statutes of limitation
write off (bad debt)

TO LEARN MORE: A number of TLM activities to accompany this chapter are accessible on the student disc accompanying this text and on the Author Updates link to the text Web site at http://www.aspenparalegaled.com/books/parsons_ abcdebt/default.asp.

Chapter Nine

Reducing a Debt or Claim to Settlement or Final Judgment—Part 2

Do not accustom yourself to think of debt as only an inconvenience; you will find it a calamity.

—*Samuel Johnson*

 A. ## Prejudgment Remedies

An **unsecured creditor** has no legal right to seize and sell property of the debtor to pay the debt unless and until the creditor obtains a final, enforceable judgment from a court. As we saw in Chapters Four and Five, a **secured creditor** may be able to seize and sell the property the debtor pledged as security. But if the secured creditor then sues to recover a **deficiency judgment** it, too, must await a final court judgment before seizing unpledged property of the debtor. Likewise, a claimant pursuing a tort liability claim against a defendant has no right to seize the defendant's property to satisfy the claim until a final judgment has been entered for that claimant. We will consider how final judgments are executed on in Chapters Ten and Eleven.

Allowing a creditor to take possession of the debtor's unpledged property prior to the entry of a final judgment would normally violate the debtor's right to **due process** under the Fourteenth Amendment to the U.S. Constitution. There are, however, a number of **prejudgment remedies** that creditors and liability claimants are allowed to pursue under certain exceptional conditions. A prejudgment remedy is one that is available at the beginning of or during the lawsuit and before final judgment is entered. And because they are exceptions to the usual rule of not seizing unpledged property prior to final judgment, they are considered **extraordinary remedies**.

1. Prejudgment Attachment

Under certain exceptional circumstances, the trial court can order a defendant's **nonexempt property** (see Chapter Ten, Section D) to be attached before entering a final judgment that declares the defendant's liability to the plaintiff. When the judge orders an **attachment** (sometimes called a **sequestration**) of defendant's property, that property is seized and held by the sheriff, the clerk

Deficiency judgment The amount of a debt that remains owing after the property securing the debt has been liquidated.

Prejudgment remedies Extraordinary relief available to plaintiffs during a civil lawsuit to prevent removal, loss, or dissipation of the defendant's property pending final judgment and execution.

Execution The satisfaction of a final judgment by the seizure and sale of non-exempt property of the debtor.

Judgment creditor Once a final judgment is entered by a court awarding a money judgment to one party, the party to whom the judgment is awarded.

of the court, or some other officer pending the outcome of the litigation. If a judgment is subsequently entered against the defendant, the property is then available for **execution** by the **judgment creditor**. If the defendant prevails at trial, the property will be returned to him. Illustration 9-a sets out a typical pre-judgment attachment statute, which enumerates such exceptional circumstances.

A prejudgment attachment can be sought any time during the litigation or after a final judgment is entered only if the plaintiff can show that one of the statutory grounds exist. That relief is usually sought by motion (or petition or application). What is sought is usually called a **writ of attachment**. (A **writ** is another word for a court order or mandate.) Typically the motion for writ of attachment must be sworn to under penalties of perjury or be supported by sworn testimony in the form of live witnesses or **affidavits** or **declarations** (written statements that are sworn to and signed by the witness).

EXAMPLE

Assume that while the Murphys' negligence action against Dr. Craft and Capitol City Hospital is still pending (no judgment has yet been entered) the Murphys' attorney learns that Dr. Craft believes he is going to lose at trial and, because he doesn't have enough malpractice insurance to cover the anticipated judgment, is planning to sell off a parcel of land he owns to a relative at a price well below what the land is worth. The Murphys' attorney may file a motion for writ of attachment like the one shown in Illustration 9-b.

The party seeking the prejudgment attachment will be required to post a **bond**, which is a type of surety contract considered in Chapter Four. A typical bond statute is shown in Illustration 9-c.

The judge issuing the writ will determine the dollar amount of the bond required of the plaintiff. The amount is normally a reasonable calculation of likely harm to the defendant if the attachment ultimately proves to be wrongful or if defendant ultimately prevails in the lawsuit. It is a way of compensating the defendant for the lost use and possible lost value of his property by reason of the attachment.

Illustration 9-a: A TYPICAL PREJUDGMENT ATTACHMENT STATUTE

Any person having a debt or demand due at the commencement of an action, or a plaintiff after action for any cause has been brought, and either before or after judgment, may sue out an attachment at law or in equity, against the property of a debtor or defendant, in the following cases:

1. Where the debtor or defendant resides out of the state;
2. Where he is about to remove, or has removed, himself or property from the state;
3. Where he has removed, or is removing, himself out of the county privately;
4. Where he conceals himself, so that the ordinary process of law cannot be served upon him;
5. Where he absconds, or is absconding or concealing himself or property;
6. Where he has fraudulently disposed of, or is about fraudulently to dispose of, his property;
7. Where any person liable for any debt or demand, residing out of the state, dies, leaving property in the state; or
8. Where the debtor or defendant is a foreign corporation which has no agent in this state upon whom process may be served by any person bringing suit against such corporation; provided, however, that the plaintiff or complainant need only make oath of the justness of his claim, that the debtor or defendant is a foreign corporation and that it has no agent in the county where the property sought to be attached is situated upon whom process can be served.

Illustration 9-b: MOTION FOR WRIT OF ATTACHMENT IN MURPHY v. CRAFT, ET AL. [STYLE OF CASE OMITTED FROM ILLUSTRATION]

MOTION FOR WRIT OF ATTACHMENT

Plaintiffs hereby move the Court for the issuance of a writ of attachment against a 4-acre parcel of real property in which defendant Samuel M. Craft has an ownership interest more particularly described as follows: [Property description omitted from illustration.]

As grounds therefore plaintiffs would and show the Court as follows:

1. As established by the affidavit of Marvin Jones attached to this motion as Exhibit A, there is a reasonable probability that cause exists under Columbiana Statutory Code §29-6-101(6) for the issuance of a writ of attachment in that defendant Craft has made statements to Marvin Jones that defendant Craft believes that a verdict is likely to be entered against him in this cause in excess of his professional liability insurance limits and that defendant Craft is planning to transfer title to the real property to a relative at a price substantially less than the market value of such property.

2. Attached as Exhibit B to this motion is an unsigned quit-claim deed prepared for the signature of defendant and dated six months after this lawsuit was filed purporting to convey defendant's interest in the real property to his brother, Rodney L. Craft, and reciting consideration paid of only $10.

3. Attached as Exhibit C to this motion is the affidavit of Carla Brewer, a registered notary public in Columbiana who states that she was asked to notarize the signature of defendant Craft on the quitclaim deed to Rodney L. Craft and that she overheard defendant Craft and Rodney L. Craft discuss the purchase price of the four-acre parcel. In that conversation, Carla Brewer states that she heard defendant Craft tell Rodney L. Craft that he didn't need to pay defendant Craft anything for the property now and to just hold on to the property until "this damned lawsuit" is over. Carla Brewer further states that Rodney L. Craft then told defendant Craft the he (Rodney L. Craft) could not go through with the plan and that, consequently, defendant Craft did not sign the quit-claim deed, a copy of which is attached as Exhibit B, but defendant Craft did then say, "Okay, I'll find someone else who can."

4. Attached as Exhibit D to this motion is the affidavit of William J. Hurst, a certified appraiser in the state of Columbiana, who states that in his professional opinion the real property in question has a current market value of at least $200,000.

5. Cause for the issuance of a writ of attachment exists under Columbiana Statutory Code §29-6-101(6) as plaintiff believes that defendant Craft is preparing to fraudulently convey, transfer, or assign the real property in which defendant Craft holds an ownership interest with the intent of hindering or delaying plaintiffs as prospective creditors, or to render process of execution unavailing if judgment is obtained against defendant Craft by plaintiffs.

WHEREFORE, plaintiff prays that this Court issue a writ of attachment to the Sheriff of Capitol County, Columbiana, directing the Sheriff forthwith to sequester and attach the real property described above, and to hold the same as provided by law for the satisfaction of any judgment recoverable by plaintiff.

[Attorney's signature and referenced affidavits omitted from illustration.]

Illustration 9-c: A TYPICAL ATTACHMENT BOND STATUTE

As a condition to issuance of the writ of attachment, the plaintiff shall post a bond with sufficient security, payable to the defendant, and conditioned that the plaintiff will prosecute the attachment with effect, or, in case of failure, pay the defendant all costs that may be adjudged against him, and, also, all such damages as he may sustain by the wrongful suing out of the attachment.

EXAMPLE

> Assume the court grants the Murphys' motion for prejudgment attachment as to the four-acre parcel, which Dr. Craft attempted to convey to his brother and which has been appraised at $200,000. The court requires the Murphys to post a bond in the amount of $25,000, which is shown in Illustration 9-d.

P-H 9-a: Why would the court order the Murphys to post a bond for only $25,000 to attach real property worth $200,000? Consider how much longer this case might last until the Murphys' claim is resolved and the potential loss to Dr. Craft by having this parcel tied up until then so that he cannot lease or sell it.

Ex parte An appearance before a court seeking relief without notice to or presence of other parties.

A hearing must be held on the motion for prejudgment attachment. In most states, the writ of attachment can be issued *ex parte* (only the movant being present) if irreparable harm will be done before a hearing can be held. But in that event, the hearing must be held quickly after the writ is issued *ex parte* (e.g., within five days). In many states, as a further condition to issuing the writ, the applicant must convince the court that she is likely to prevail when the case finally goes to trial. The writ issued by the judge against defendant Craft's four-acre parcel is shown in Illustration 9-e.

The prejudgment writ of attachment can apply to personal as well as real property.

EXAMPLE

> If Dr. Craft owned a valuable antique car collection and was discovered to be giving the cars away as gifts to avoid they're being executed on by the Murphys, a writ of attachment could issue allowing the sheriff or other official to take possession of the cars pending final judgment.

Illustration 9-d: BOND SUPPORTING PREJUDGMENT WRIT OF ATTACHMENT [STYLE OF CASE OMITTED FROM ILLUSTRATION]

BOND

   We, Nicholas W. Murphy and Pearl E. Murphy, as principals, and Capitol City Insurance Company, as surety, are held and firmly bound to Samuel M. Craft ("Craft") in the sum of $25,000 for the payment of which we do jointly and severally bind ourselves, our heirs, executors, successors, and assigns.

   The condition of the above obligation is as follows: Principals are plaintiffs are seeking a judgment in this action against Craft in the amount of $1.5 million by reason of alleged medical malpractice (professional negligence), and have asked that a writ of attachment be issued against certain real property owned by Craft. The property to be attached is: [Legal description of real property omitted from this illustration.]

   If principals shall pay Craft all damages that Craft may sustain by reason of any wrongful suing out of this attachment, then this obligation shall be void and of no effect; but otherwise it shall remain in full force and effect.

   [Signatures of principals and surety omitted from this illustration.]

Illustration 9-e: WRIT OF ATTACHMENT [STYLE OF CASE OMITTED FROM ILLUSTRATION]

WRIT OF ATTACHMENT

State of Columbiana,
To the Sheriff of Capitol County, greeting:

Whereas, Nicholas W. Murphy and Pearl E. Murphy, plaintiffs, have filed suit against defendant Samuel M. Craft in this court alleging that said defendant is liable to them in tort for $1.5 million and whereas plaintiffs have complained on oath established by affidavits that said defendant has attempted to fraudulently convey, transfer, or assign his interest in a certain four-acre parcel of real property with the intent of hindering or delaying plaintiffs as prospective creditors, or to render process of execution unavailing if judgment is obtained against defendant Craft by plaintiffs, and bond having been given as required by law in attachment cases, you are hereby COMMANDED to attach the real property described below so to secure that the same may be liable to further proceedings thereon in this matter. Further, you are directed to appear before this court at 9 A.M. on December 17, YR-1, when and where you will make known how you have executed this writ. The property to be attached is more fully described as: [Description of real property omitted from illustration.]
     ISSUED this 11th day of December, YR-1

_____
                                                                         Judge

---

P-H 9-b: Assume the Murphy v. Craft and CCH case is pending in a state court in your state and the Murphys want to attach Craft's real property based on the facts given. Determine whether your state allows a plaintiff in a lawsuit involving a tort claim to obtain a prejudgment attachment. If so, what are the grounds for doing so? What is the procedure to be followed to obtain the attachment?

2. Receivership

Receivership Proceeding in which a person is appointed to take control of a debtor's property and manage it under court supervision.

Sometimes it is not feasible for the sheriff, clerk, or other public officer to retain possession of attached assets. In that event, the court ordering the attachment may also appoint a **receiver** to hold the assets and preserve them for trial. A receiver is a person, disinterested in the outcome of the litigation, who, for a fee, agrees to hold and preserve property pursuant to the court order. When property is held by a receiver it is said to be in **receivership**. The motion seeking such relief would properly be titled *motion for prejudgment attachment and for receivership*.

EXAMPLE

Assume that Dr. Craft owns an antiques store managed by his wife. The Murphys are able to prove that Dr. Craft, with the cooperation of his wife, is systematically selling off the inventory and other assets of the business for less than fair market value in order to deprive the Murphys of those assets when the judgment is entered. The Murphys may file a motion asking the court to attach all the assets of the business and to appoint a receiver to take possession of the business and to continue to operate it to avoid loss of value. For obvious reasons, neither the sheriff nor the court clerk nor other public officer would have the time or probably the expertise to operate the business—thus the need for a qualified receiver.

3. Injunction

Injunction A court order directing a party to do or to cease doing something on pain of contempt.

Sometimes it is sufficient for the court to merely order a defendant to do something or to refrain from doing something that would be harmful to the value of the property on pain of a court-imposed fine or jail sentence for contempt. Such a court order is called an **injunction**. An injunction does not deprive the defendant of possession of the property, it only directs him to use it or stop using it in some way.

EXAMPLE

Rather than dispossessing Dr. Craft of the antique automobiles by means of a writ of attachment, the court might simply enjoin (to order something by way of injunction) Dr. Craft to stop giving them away and to preserve them for the duration of the litigation. Because Dr. Craft is still in possession of the automobiles, there has not been an attachment, but he is enjoined by court order and subject to being fined or found in contempt of that order if he disobeys it. And if he does disobey it, the court may then also order the automobiles attached.

An injunction is obtained in much the same way as a writ of attachment. A verified motion or motion supported by sworn testimony, affidavits, or declarations must establish the facts alleged by the movant. Notice and an opportunity for a hearing must be had and a bond is usually required for the same reasons as pertain when attachment is ordered. The standard for granting injunctive relief in most jurisdictions is that the movant must show that irreparable harm will be done to his interests in the property unless the injunction is granted.

4. Prejudgment Garnishment

Garnishment A court order pursuant to which property of the debtor in the hands of a third person or a debt owed by a third person to the debtor is levied on.

An order (or writ) of **garnishment** is an order of the court directed not to the defendant, but to a third party in possession of property or wages of the defendant or who owes the defendant a debt. The garnishment instructs that third party (called the **garnishee**) to hold the property, wages, or other amount owed the defendant until further order of the court. Although garnishment is available as a prejudgment remedy, it is most commonly used as a postjudgment collection method and it is in that context that we consider it in more detail in Chapter Eleven, Section B.

When used as a prejudgment remedy, the plaintiff must normally show the court that one of the grounds supporting a prejudgment attachment (see Illustration 9-a) is present to support issuance of the garnishment.

EXAMPLE

> Assume that while Nick and Pearl Murphys' malpractice liability suit against Dr. Craft is still pending, they learn that on June 30 Craft will receive a semiannual partner's distribution from his medical practice, expected to be in the $200,000 range. Because no final judgment has been entered in their favor yet, the Murphys normally have no legal basis to seize the distribution owed to Dr. Craft. But assume they can show that, upon receipt, he intends to send the cash offshore to a bank in the Caymen Islands in order to deny the Murphys access to it should they prevail in the lawsuit. On those facts, the Murphys may seek an order of garnishment directed to the medical practice as garnishee, ordering it to hold on to the money due Dr. Craft pending further orders of the court.

When granted as a prejudgment remedy, a bond is typically required in an amount equal to the defendant's lost use of the property in the event it is later determined that the garnishment was unwarranted.

5. Replevin

Replevin A civil action for the recovery or provisional possession of specific personal property.

A motion for an order (or writ) of **replevin** asks the trial court to order the return to the moving party of property that belongs to that party. Replevin can be the basis for a separate lawsuit where the return of the property is all that is at issue between the parties. In that event, the plaintiff would file a complaint for replevin and the order of replevin would be in the nature of a final judgment. However, if there are other issues to be decided between the parties the order of replevin would be a prejudgment remedy.

EXAMPLE

> Recall from Illustrations 1-b and 6-i that Abe Mendoza's bookkeeper, Hilda Montgomery, has embezzled more than $100,000 and stolen some company records as well. In the lawsuit that Abe files against her, there may be many issues to be resolved by the final judgment, especially if she has used the embezzled proceeds to purchase real property (see Illustration 6-i). But if, during the suit, Abe's lawyer discovers that the bookkeeper did in fact steal the company records and still has them, he may file a motion for replevin to have those records returned while the case is still pending. And if he discovers that the bookkeeper has given those records to her son, who is starting up his own construction company using that information, the attorney may institute a separate lawsuit against the son using a complaint for replevin.

6. Lien *Lis Pendens*

We considered the **lien *lis pendens*** in Chapter Six, Section F, in the context of nonconsensual statutory liens. But it should also be understood as a type of prejudgment remedy because it is a statutorily allowed method for a plaintiff to effectively place a cloud on real property owned by the defendant pending final resolution of the issues.

7. *Ne Exeat* (Arrest)

Ne exeat A prejudgment writ preventing a party from leaving the court's jurisdiction.

In a number of states a **writ *ne exeat*** (from *ne exeat regno*, "let him not go out of the kingdom"), also called a **writ of arrest**, is obtainable to prevent a defendant from leaving the state or the jurisdiction of the court, where it can be shown that the defendant is fleeing to avoid judgment or execution on a future judgment. The writ typically operates much like an injunction, simply ordering the defendant not to flee. But it will contain penalties, including fines and incarceration, for its violation, and if the defendant does flee in violation of the writ, he may be taken into custody.

In the modern era, this writ is most commonly used in domestic disputes, for example, to stop one parent from fleeing the jurisdiction with a child before the court rules on custody. It is seldom sought or issued in nondomestic debtor/creditor cases and may be subject to constitutional challenge in that instance, as smacking too much of the old debtor's prison system.

P-H 9-c: How many of the prejudgment remedies discussed in this section are authorized by the laws of your state? Compare the procedure for enforcing any such remedies with the procedure described in this chapter and note differences.

B. ▶ Recovering Fraudulent Transfers: The Uniform Fraudulent Transfer Act

An action to recover a prior transfer of the debtor's property to a third-party transferee can be brought as a prejudgment action like those we've been considering, or as part of postjudgment collection efforts. What distinguishes a **fraudulent transfer** action from the other remedies considered here is that title to the property has been previously transferred or conveyed to someone other than the debtor. The transferee is therefore a proper and necessary party to the action to set aside the transfer.

EXAMPLE

In Illustration 9-b the Murphys sought an attachment remedy against the four-acre parcel owned by Dr. Craft because he still owned it. He had attempted to convey title to the parcel to his brother but the conveyance had not yet occurred. If title had been conveyed and the Murphys could prove it was a fraudulent conveyance, they would seek relief to both set aside the fraudulent conveyance and to attach the property: fraudulent conveyance to reverse the conveyance and put title to the property back in Dr. Craft, and then attachment to have it attached once title was back in Dr. Craft. Because, in the fraudulent conveyance portion of that action, the Murphys would be asking the court to take action against property then titled in Dr. Craft's brother, the brother would have to be made a party to the fraudulent conveyance action.

Uniform Fraudulent Transfer Act A uniform act regulating the recovery of fraudulent transfers.

In more than 40 states, fraudulent transfer law and procedure is governed by the **Uniform Fraudulent Transfer Act of 1984 (UFTA)**. Under the UFTA, a transfer of the transferor's property may be fraudulent as to a creditor if the creditor can show *either* **intentional fraud** or **constructive fraud** in connection with the transfer.

1. Transfers Made with Intent to Defraud

The UFTA provides the creditor with relief if it can be shown that the transfer was made with the "intent to defraud, hinder or delay" the creditor. With regard to what constitutes a *transfer of property*, §1(12) of the UFTA defines transfer as "every mode, direct or indirect, absolute or conditional, voluntary or involuntary, of disposing of or parting with an asset or an interest in an asset, and includes payment of money, release, lease, and creation of a lien or other encumbrance."

EXAMPLE

> Under this broad definition, a fraudulent transfer could include not just selling property for less than it is worth, as Dr. Craft attempted in Illustration 9-b, but also 1) making a gift of property, 2) changing of beneficiary designation on an insurance policy, 3) renouncing an inheritance in a decedent's estate, 4) pledging the property as collateral to secure a debt to another creditor, or 5) allowing foreclosure or repossession of pledged property.

Of course, just because a defendant in a collection or liability suit transfers property does not make the transfer fraudulent. The fraudulent intent must be proven by the plaintiff. Proving fraudulent intent is difficult. Who knows the intent of a person in his own mind and heart?

P-H 9-d: Assume that Dr. Craft did in fact transfer the four-acre parcel to his brother and the Murphys sue them both to set aside the transfer alleging a fraudulent transfer. Make a list of legitimate reasons he and the brother might give for the transfer to defend against a charge of fraudulent intent.

Badges of fraud In the law of fraudulent transfer, certain recognized circumstances from which the inference may fairly be drawn that a transfer was made with intent to defraud creditors.

Because of the difficulty of proving fraudulent intent, the courts, beginning with the venerable *Twyne's Case*, 3 Coke 80, 76 Eng. Rep. 809 (1601), developed what came to be called **badges of fraud**, circumstances or indicia surrounding the transfer that were relevant and provable as tending to show the fraudulent intent. Those badges of fraud have now been incorporated into the UFTA and are set forth in Illustration 9-f.

P-H 9-e: Again, assume that Dr. Craft did in fact convey the four-acre parcel to his brother. When the Murphys sue the brothers alleging fraudulent transfer, how many of the indicia of fraud from Illustration 9-f can they argue are present to prove fraudulent intent?

2. Transfers Made with Constructive Fraud

As an alternative to proving fraudulent intent, §4(a)(2) of the UFTA allows a court to find a fraudulent transfer has occurred 1) if the debtor transfers the property without receiving **reasonably equivalent value** in exchange for the

Illustration 9-f: THE BADGES OF FRAUD AS THEY NOW APPEAR IN §4(b) OF THE UFTA

- The transfer or obligation was to an insider.
- The transferor retained possession or control of the property transferred after the transfer.
- The transfer or obligation was disclosed or concealed.
- Before the transfer was made or obligation was incurred, the transferor had been sued or threatened with suit.
- The transfer was of substantially all the transferor's assets.
- The transferor absconded.
- The transferor removed or concealed assets.
- The value of the consideration received by the transferor was not reasonably equivalent to the value of the asset transferred or the amount of the obligation incurred.
- The transferor was insolvent or became insolvent shortly after the transfer was made or the obligation was incurred.
- The transfer occurred shortly before or shortly after a substantial debt was incurred.
- The transferor transferred the essential assets of the business to a lienor who transferred the assets to an insider of the transferor.

Constructive fraud A means of finding fraud based on inference from circumstances rather than proof of actual intent.

transfer *and* 2) the debtor is insolvent at the time of the transfer or becomes insolvent as a result of the transfer or is left with unreasonably small capital to continue in business as a result of the transfer. This is **constructive fraud** (sometimes called **presumed fraud**). Unlike the intentional fraudulent transfer, no intent to defraud need be proven.

Note the "and" in the definition of constructive fraud under §4(a)(2) of the UFTA. There are two mandatory findings required to apply the constructive fraud theory. Whether the debtor receives reasonably equivalent value for a transfer is a question of fact based on the circumstances of the case.

Fair market value The price at which property would change hands between a willing buyer and a willing seller.

Reasonably equivalent value is normally determined using the **fair market value** of the property involved as of the date of the transfer. Fair market value is generally considered to be the price at which the property would change hands between a willing buyer and a willing seller, neither being under any compulsion to buy or to sell and both having reasonable knowledge of relevant facts. See *United States v. Cartwright*, 411 U.S. 546, 551 (1973).

P-H 9-f: Which of the following scenarios raise a genuine issue in your mind as to whether Dr. Craft received reasonably equivalent value for his property?

1. He sells the four-acre parcel appraised at $200,000 for $195,000 to avoid having to advertise it for sale or list it with a realtor, who will charge a fee for selling it.

2. He sells the four-acre parcel appraised at $200,000 for $150,000 to avoid having to advertise it for sale or list it with a realtor, who will charge a fee for selling it.

3. Dr. Craft, who is 49 years old and in good health, conveys the four-acre parcel to his 20-year-old daughter in exchange for her verbal promise to take care of him in his old age.

4. Dr. Craft consolidates his existing debts totaling $225,000 with one creditor and secures the consolidated debt by pledging the four-acre parcel to that creditor.
5. Dr. Craft negotiates a line of credit loan with a lender in an amount to be decided later and pledges the four-acre as parcel as security for that loan.
6. Dr. Craft makes a gift of the four-acre parcel to his medical school in the name of his professor/mentor there from 20 years ago. Dr. Craft says he owes the school and his mentor for his guidance and has always wanted to do something to show his appreciation.

Insolvency The inability to pay debts as they come due or the state of having total liabilities in excess of total assets.

Balance sheet test of insolvency A test of *insolvency* whereby a debtor's liabilities exceed his assets.

Equity test of insolvency When the debtor is not paying his or her debts as they become due.

Under §§2(a)(b) of the UFTA, **insolvency**, the second requirement of constructive fraud, can be established by using either the **balance sheet test of insolvency** (the sum of the debtor's debts is greater than all of the debtor's assets, at a fair valuation) or the **equity test of insolvency** (the debtor is not paying his debts as they become due).

P-H 9-g: Assume that, while their lawsuit against Dr. Craft is pending, the Murphys learn that Craft has conveyed the four-acre parcel to his medical school, as suggested in scenario 6 in P-H 9-f. The Murphys believe a fraudulent conveyance has occurred. Outline the questions their lawyer would want to ask Craft and identify the documents she would want to obtain from Craft to establish the insolvency part of constructive fraud.

We will revisit fraudulent transfer and the issue of what constitutes reasonably equivalent value in Part C of the text in the context of a bankruptcy case in which a debtor has made a prepetition fraudulent transfer of property (see Chapter Seventeen, Section E).

3. Remedies for Fraudulent Transfer

In a fraudulent transfer action, the most common remedy sought by the plaintiff is to have the court void or set aside the fraudulent transfer and order that title to the property be returned to the debtor. If the fraudulent transfer claim is made in a prejudgment context, the plaintiff may also seek to attach the property, pending final resolution of the suit. If the fraudulent transfer claim is being made in a postjudgment context, the plaintiff/judgment creditor likely is seeking to execute on the property once it is returned to the debtor in order to satisfy the judgment.

Section 7 of the UFTA provides a number of different remedies that the court can impose once it finds a fraudulent transfer has occurred. A list of those remedies is provided in Illustration 9-g.

P-H 9-h: Has your state adopted the UFTA? If so, compare the wording of your state's UFTA with the definitions, procedures, and remedies discussed in the chapter. Are there material differences? How would the examples and scenarios presented in the P-Hs in this section be decided under the laws of your state? If your state has not adopted the UFTA, research the statutory or case law that exists on fraudulent transfer and answer those questions.

Illustration 9-g: REMEDIES AVAILABLE UNDER §7 OF THE UFTA

- Avoid the transfer or obligation to the extent necessary to satisfy the creditor's claim.
- Attach the asset transferred or other property of the transferee.
- Obtain an injunction against further disposition by the debtor or a transferee, or both, of the asset transferred or of other property.
- Obtain the appointment of a receiver to take charge of the asset transferred or of other property of the transferee.
- Obtain any other relief the circumstances may require.
- If the creditor has already obtained a judgment against the debtor, levy execution on the asset transferred or its proceeds.

C. Entitlement to Prejudgment Interest

In paragraph 4 of its complaint against Pearl Murphy (Illustration 8-a) CCME asks for not only the $1,200 in lease payments it claims are due but also interest on that amount at 15 percent from the date payment was first due to the date judgment is entered. This is a request for **prejudgment interest**. Trial courts are authorized to award a prevailing creditor prejudgment interest in certain situations. Illustration 9-h shows a typical state statute regarding prejudgment interest.

The statute posits two different situations where the court may award prejudgment interest. One is where the parties have a contract expressly providing for it. Take a look at paragraph 4 of the Medical Equipment Lease Agreement between Pearl Murphy and CCME attached as Exhibit 1 to the complaint in Illustration 8-a. This contractual provision is the source of CCME's request for prejudgment interest at the contractual rate, not the 10 percent statutory rate.

The other circumstance where prejudgment interest may be awarded is where there is no contractual provision dealing with it but where **principles of equity** allow it. The most typical equitable situation is where the amount owed by the debtor was established and known (liquidated) prior to the lawsuit being filed. Once the creditor's entitlement to payment is established, it is deemed equitable to charge the defendant/debtor with interest on the amount it should have paid the creditor earlier. The creditor has lost the use of the money since the day it was due, so the equities favor this award.

Illustration 9-h: TYPICAL PREJUDGMENT INTEREST STATUTE

Prejudgment interest, i.e., interest as an element of, or in the nature of, damages may be awarded by courts or juries in accordance with the principles of equity at any rate not in excess of a maximum effective rate of ten percent (10%) per annum. In addition, contracts may expressly provide for the imposition of the same or a different rate of interest to be paid after breach or default within the limits set by [other applicable provisions].

EXAMPLE

> Assume that the Medical Equipment Lease Agreement makes no mention of interest, but a court finds that in fact Pearl Murphy owed CCME $1,200 under the agreement and should have paid it within 30 days of the billing. The court likely will award prejudgment interest on equitable principles on those facts, notwithstanding the absence of any contractual provision regarding interest.

On the other hand, where the amount of a debt or claim is unliquidated and contingent prior to the lawsuit, most courts deem it inequitable to award prejudgment interest even though the claimant ultimately prevails.

EXAMPLE

> If Nick and Pearl Murphy prevail in their negligence action against Dr. Craft and Capitol City Hospital (Illustrations 1-a and 2-d) they may request prejudgment interest be awarded on the jury verdict from the date of the negligence. But a court is very unlikely to grant such a request because neither the basis for liability nor the amount of the judgment was established prior to the entry of judgment.

D. ▶ The Final Judgment

When the collection or liability suit is finally decided, the trial judge will enter a **final judgment** (which may also be called a **final decree** or **final order**). As that phrase suggests, the final judgment resolves and decides all pending issues in the case: in a collection suit whether the defendant owes the debt and in what amount, and in a liability suit whether the defendant is liable on the claim made against him and in what amount.

As we have seen, the final judgment may be entered as a result of 1) a *default* by the defendant (see Illustration 8-i) or 2) at the conclusion of a *trial on the merits* when the debt is contested (see Illustration 2-d). A third possibility is that the lawsuit is contested but settled prior to trial, in which case the creditor will likely require that the *settlement* amount be established in a **consent judgment** (also referred to as a **consent decree** or an **agreed final judgment**) entered by the court.

Consent decree A final judgment entered by agreement of the parties.

EXAMPLE

> When CCME sues Pearl Murphy and she contests liability, a settlement may be negotiated by the attorneys for the parties or through **mediation**. If the parties negotiate a settlement pursuant to which Pearl agrees to pay $900 in 12 monthly installments of $75 each in full satisfaction of CCME's claim, CCME may require, as a condition to settlement, that Pearl agree to entry of a consent judgment in the amount of $900 rather than merely signing a settlement agreement. The consent judgment will specify the terms of payment of the settlement amount and will protect the creditor by allowing immediate execution on the judgment in the event of default. No new lawsuit will be needed.

Assume that Pearl Murphy and CCME agree to mediate their dispute (see the discussion of mediation in Chapter Two, Section C) and, as a result, they agree that 1) Pearl will pay a total of $900 to satisfy the entire indebtedness; and 2) that she will pay the agreed amount in installments of $75 per month for the next 12 months; and 3) that if she fails to do so, final judgment will be for $1,900, on which CCME can commence execution immediately. Illustration 9-i sets forth the final judgment by consent entered based on the mediated settlement.

P-H 9-i: Why would a creditor such as CCME insist that a settlement be reflected in a consent judgment and not just a settlement agreement? Think it through: If there is only a settlement agreement and no final judgment by consent, what will happen if Pearl breaches the settlement agreement by failing to make the promised payments? What will happen if the judgment debtor defaults on the terms of the consent judgment?

A fourth possibility is that the final judgment may be entered to enforce a binding arbitration award (see the discussion of arbitration in Chapter Eight, Section B). The arbitrator(s) will hear all parties to the dispute and their witnesses in a proceeding more informal than a civil trial and will then enter a decision called an **award** in the dispute. To enforce the arbitration award, the prevailing party will file an **application to enforce arbitration award** in a court having jurisdiction over the parties and subject matter. The court order granting the application will then be treated for all purposes as a final judgment of that court.

Illustration 9-i: CONSENT JUDGMENT IN CCME v. PEARL MURPHY [STYLE OF CASE OMITTED FROM ILLUSTRATION]

CONSENT JUDGMENT

The parties having announced to the court, through counsel, that all matters in dispute have been resolved and settled and that defendant, Pearl E. Murphy, consent to final judgment being entered against her on the terms set forth in this judgment, it is hereby

ORDERED AND DECREED that judgment in favor of plaintiff, Capitol City Medical Equipment Company, should be and hereby is entered against defendant, Pearl E. Murphy, in the amount of $900; and it is further

ORDERED AND DECREED that defendant shall pay the amount of said judgment in twelve successive monthly installments of $75 beginning October 1, YR-1; and it is further

ORDERED AND DECREED that if defendant shall fail to make any of the 12 monthly installments that the judgment amount shall be $1,900 on which plaintiff can commence execution without further delay after giving defendant credit for all amounts paid to that date; and it is further

ORDERED AND DECREED that court costs in this matter are taxed to Defendant Pearl E. Murphy for which execution shall issue if necessary.

ENTER this 20th day of September YR-1

Juanita A. McBride, Circuit Judge

Illustration 9-j: TYPICAL POSTJUDGMENT INTEREST STATUTE

> Interest on judgments, including decrees, shall be computed at a rate equal to 1% plus the average interest rate paid at auctions of 5-year United States treasury notes during the 6 months immediately preceding July 1 and January 1, as certified by the state; treasurer, and compounded annually provided, that where a judgment is based on a note, contract, or other writing fixing a rate of interest within the limits provided in [other applicable provisions] for that particular category of transaction, the judgment shall bear interest at the rate so fixed.

E. ▶ Postjudgment Interest

Postjudgment interest Statutory interest that runs on a final judgment from the date entered until paid.

In many states **postjudgment interest** begins to run, at a statutory rate, on money judgments as a matter of law. A typical postjudgment statute is shown in Illustration 9-j.

Because the right to postjudgment interest is statutory, a creditor does not have to ask for it in the complaint. Once the judgment is final and can be executed on (see Chapter Eleven), postjudgment interest can be collected, calculated at the statutory rate, from the date of the judgment until payment. Further, as the statute in Illustration 9-j suggests, many states allow parties to agree by contract to a rate of postjudgment interest different from the statutory rate, so long as the agreed rate does not violate the state's usury laws.

P-H 9-j: Locate your state's statutes, regulations, or court rulings regarding prejudgment and postjudgment interest. Under what circumstances will prejudgment interest be allowed and in what amount? Will your state enforce contractual provisions for prejudgment interest and are there any legal or public policy limitations on such provisions? Is postjudgment interest automatically collectible following entry of a final judgment in your state? Is the rate of postjudgment interest set by law or up to the discretion of the judge?

CONCLUSION

Once a creditor has obtained a final judgment against a debtor his next concern is to obtain payment from the debtor for the amount of the judgment. Sometimes payment is made promptly. Sometimes the debtor chooses to delay payment while he appeals the final judgment to a court of appeals. And sometimes the debtor just ignores the final judgment, leaving the creditor to pursue postjudgment collection efforts against the assets of the debtor. All this is the subject of Chapters Ten and Eleven.

CHAPTER SUMMARY

There are a number of prejudgment remedies that may be available to a creditor under extraordinary circumstances. A writ of attachment or sequestration may be issued prejudgment, ordering that the property of the defendant be seized by the sheriff, clerk, or other public officer, pending outcome of the litigation. Statutory grounds justifying the attachment must be proven by the creditor, which typically involves a real danger that the defendant will conceal, destroy, or abscond with the property prior to final judgment. The creditor must normally post a bond to cover harm that may accrue to the defendant if the attachment is later proven wrongful. In some instances the court may order that the property attached be held by a receiver, in which case the property is in receivership. It may be sufficient for the judge to simply order or enjoin a defendant from removing or disposing of her property, pending the final outcome of a case, and such order is an injunction. A writ of garnishment may be issued prejudgment, directing a third party in possession of property or wages of the defendant or who owes the defendant a debt to hold the property until further order of the court. A writ of replevin orders the person to whom it is directed to return property that belongs to the moving party to the moving party. A writ of arrest or writ *ne exeat* forbids a defendant to leave the jurisdiction of the court if it can be shown that he is fleeing or intends to flee to avoid judgment or execution on a future judgment.

This chapter also considered a creditor's right to recover property of the debtor, the title to which was previously transferred to a third party. Most states have enacted the Uniform Fraudulent Transfer Act (UFTA), under which the creditor must show that the transfer of the property was made with intent to defraud, hinder, or delay the creditor. Either intentional or constructive fraud may normally be proven and the "badges of fraud" are frequently used as evidence of intentional fraud. Constructive or presumed fraud may be established by showing that the debtor transferred the property without receiving "reasonably equivalent value" in exchange for the transfer and that the debtor was insolvent at the time of the transfer or was rendered insolvent by the transfer. Insolvency can be established using either the balance sheet test or the equity test. Prejudgment interest on the amount owed may be awarded to a creditor if there is a contract between the debtor and creditor authorizing its payment or as a matter of equity where the amount owed was liquidated prior to suit.

If the court finds for the creditor plaintiff in a collection suit, a final judgment will be entered in the creditor's favor. If the judgment was entered by default, it may be called a default judgment. If it was entered by consent of the parties following a negotiated settlement, it may be called a consent judgment. If the dispute was submitted to binding arbitration rather than litigation, the award can be enforced as a final judgment in most states by filing the award in the appropriate court and awaiting the expiration of time allowed the losing party to dispute the fairness of the arbitration process. In many states postjudgment interest begins to run on the final judgment at a statutory rate from the date of entry.

REVIEW QUESTIONS

1. Explain why an unsecured creditor must normally wait until final judgment is entered in its collection suit to take possession of the debtor's property. Under what circumstances must a secured creditor do the same?

2. Name as many of the usual grounds for the issuance of a prejudgment attachment as you can.
3. Explain what an *ex parte* hearing is and under what circumstances it is allowed.
4. What is a bond in the context of a writ of attachment and how does the judge determine the proper amount of such bond in a given case?
5. Explain the difference between an order of attachment, an order of receivership, and an injunction.
6. To whom is a writ of garnishment directed? Give examples of persons or institutions that are common targets of writs of garnishment.
7. What is the difference between a writ of replevin and a writ of arrest? Give examples of circumstances that might give rise to a motion for such writs.
8. Give four examples of what might constitute a "transfer" of property for purposes of the UFTA.
9. What is the difference between intentional and constructive fraud for purposes of the UFTA? Explain what is meant by "badges of fraud" in connection with a fraudulent transfer and name as many of them as you can. How is fraud proven constructively in a fraudulent transfer action? Explain the difference between the balance sheet test of insolvency and the equity test.
10. Explain the difference between prejudgment and postjudgment interest and the circumstances under which either can be awarded.

WORDS AND PHRASES TO REMEMBER

affidavits
alternative dispute resolution
application (for writ or order)
application for enforcement of arbitration award
arbitration
arbitration award
arrest (writ or order of)
attachment (writ or order of)
award (arbitrator's)
balance sheet test of insolvency
bias
bond
consent judgment(decree)
constructive fraud
declarations
debtor's prison
default judgment
equity test of insolvency
execution
ex parte

extraordinary remedy
Federal Arbitration Act (FAA)
final judgment
final judgment by consent
fraudulent intent
fraudulent transfer
garnishee
garnishment (writ or order of)
injunction
insolvent
irreparable harm
judgment creditor
mediation
mediator
motion
nonexempt property
partiality
petition (for writ or order)
prejudgment attachment
prejudgment interest
prejudgment remedies
presumed (constructive) fraud

principles of equity
reasonably equivalent value
replevin (writ or order of)
settlement
sequestration (writ or order of)

Uniform Arbitration Act (UAA)
Uniform Fraudulent Transfer
  Act (UFTA)
writ (order)
writ *ne exeat* (writ of arrest)

TO LEARN MORE: A number of TLM activities to accompany this chapter are accessible on the student disc accompanying the text and on the Author Updates link to the text Web site at http://www.aspenparalegaled.com/ books/parsons_ abcdebt/default.asp.

Chapter Ten:

► Executing on a Final Judgment—Part 1

Some people use half of their ingenuity to get into debt
and the other half to avoid paying it.
—George D. Prentice

A. ► The Postjudgment Execution Grace Period

Execution grace period The time between the date a final judgment is entered and the date execution on the judgment can begin.

Stay of execution A halt or freeze on the judgment creditor's right to execute on a final judgment.

When a final money judgment has been entered in a lawsuit, the prevailing party is thereafter known as the **judgment creditor** and the party against whom the judgment is entered is known as the **judgment debtor**. If the judgment debtor does not pay the amount of the judgment entered against him, the judgment creditor can **execute** on certain assets of the debtor to satisfy the judgment. However, the judgment creditor cannot normally begin execution immediately after entry of the judgment. State and federal rules grant the judgment debtor an **execution grace period** to decide whether to pay the judgment, file certain postjudgment motions to gain relief from the final judgment, or to appeal the judgment to a court of appeals. During this grace period there is a **stay of execution**, i.e., a halt or freeze on the judgment debtor's right to execute on a final judgment. A typical state grace period rule is shown in Illustration 10-a.

EXAMPLE

According to Illustration 8-i, the final judgment by default in favor of Capitol City Medical Equipment (CCME) was entered against Pearl Murphy on September 20, YR-1. CCME cannot execute on Pearl's assets to satisfy the judgment until October 21, YR-1, if the rule in Illustration 10-a is controlling. But note the second sentence of that rule. If CCME has provable information that Pearl, as the judgment debtor, is fraudulently disposing of her property to defeat execution, CCME can act before the 30-day grace period has run. How? By filing a motion with the trial court requesting either an attachment of her assets, as in a prejudgment attachment (see Chapter Nine, Section A), or by requesting permission to go ahead and execute. The decision will be up to the trial judge ruling on the motion.

P-H 10-a: Check Rule 62(a) of the Federal Rules of Civil Procedure and determine how the federal grace period delaying execution on final judgments in federal court compares to the statute in Illustration 10-a and to the grace period rule in your state.

Illustration 10-a: TYPICAL STATE GRACE PERIOD RULE

> Except as otherwise provided in this Rule, no execution shall issue upon a judgment, nor shall proceedings be taken for its enforcement until the expiration of 30 days after its entry. The party in whose favor judgment is entered may also obtain execution or take proceedings to enforce the judgment prior to expiration of the 30-day period if the party against whom judgment is entered is about fraudulently to dispose of, conceal, or remove his or her property, thereby endangering satisfaction of the judgment.

Even during the execution grace period the attorney for the judgment creditor can do a number of things to prepare for execution if the attorney has reason to believe that payment of the judgment will not be forthcoming. Those preparatory activities include the following:

- Review the file for information on debtor that may expedite execution when it begins: jobs, addresses, banks, copies of checks with account numbers, credit applications, realty and personal assets mentioned in pretrial discovery or in trial testimony.
- Ask the client what information he may have regarding the judgment debtor, his assets that may be seized, or debts owed to him that may be garnisheed (see Chapter Eleven).
- Perform a public records search in the land records office to see if the judgment debtor owns an interest in realty that may be attached or seized, a search with the secretary of state to see what corporations or partnerships the judgment debtor might own an interest in, and a search with the state department of vehicles to see if he owns vehicles in which there might be equity.
- While performing those public records searches, look for transfers out by the judgment debtor of real or personal property that might constitute fraudulent conveyances (discussed in Chapter Nine).
- Perform online searches, including on social network sites, for references to or postings by the judgment debtor that may contain information regarding potential assets.
- Order a certified copy of the final judgment from the clerk of the court in which the judgment was entered to use for creating a judgment lien (see Chapter Eleven) when the grace period expires.
- With the client's consent, negotiate with the debtor or his counsel for an installment payment of the judgment amount or even a lump sum settlement.

Many states also allow a judgment creditor to request **accelerated execution** during the grace period upon a showing by affidavit or sworn testimony that the judgment debtor is or is about to fraudulently dispose of, conceal, or remove his property to prevent execution on it by the judgment creditor. This option is very similar to the prejudgment attachment remedy discussed in Chapter Nine.

B. The Effect of Postjudgment Motions on the Right to Execute

Postjudgment motions Motions the losing party may file in the trial court seeking to invalidate or amend a final judgment or for a new trial.

Under the rules of civil procedure controlling in both state and federal actions, a defendant against whom a judgment has been entered by a trial court has the option of filing one or more **postjudgment motions** in an effort to convince the trial judge to reverse or modify the judgment or to grant a new trial. A list of typical postjudgment motions allowed in most state jurisdictions and under the federal rules is shown in Illustration 10-b.

There is variation among the states as to the kinds of postjudgment motions allowed, the time frame for filing them, and the effect of such motions on the judgment creditor's right to begin executing on the judgment. Under the prevailing rule in many states, filing one of these postjudgment motions will further stay execution on the final judgment until the motion is ruled on by the trial judge and often for some number of days after that ruling. The rule set out in Illustration 10-c is typical.

> **P-H 10-b:** In the preceding example, we determined that if the final judgment by default in favor of CCME was entered against Pearl Murphy on September 20, YR-1 (Illustration 8-i), CCME cannot execute on Pearl's assets to satisfy the judgment until October 21, YR-1, if the rule in Illustration 10-a is controlling. Assume that the rule in Illustration 10-c is also controlling in the case and that on October 19, YR-1, an attorney for Pearl Murphy makes a belated appearance in the case (remember the judgment in Illustration 8-i went down against her by default) and files a motion to set aside the default judgment and to grant a new trial. The trial court conducts a hearing on those motions and denies them on November 1. What is the earliest date that CCME can begin execution on its judgment granted back on September 20, YR-1?

Illustration 10-b: COMMON POSTJUDGMENT MOTIONS ALLOWED

- Motion for new trial
- Motion to alter or amend judgment
- Motion to make additional findings (in a bench trial only)
- Motion for relief from judgment or order
- Motion for judgment notwithstanding the verdict (directed verdict; in a jury trial only)

Illustration 10-c: PROCEDURE FOR POSTJUDGMENT MOTIONS USED IN SOME STATES

The execution of or any proceedings to enforce a judgment shall also be stayed pending and for 30 days after entry of any of the following orders made upon timely motion: (1) granting or denying a motion for judgment in accordance with a motion for a directed verdict; (2) granting or denying a motion to amend or make additional findings of fact; (3) granting or denying a motion to alter or amend the judgment; and (4) denying a motion for a new trial.

Illustration 10-d: FRCP 62(b)

On appropriate terms for the opposing party's security, the court may stay the execution of a judgment—or any proceedings to enforce it—pending disposition of any of the following motions:

- under Rule 50, for judgment as a matter of law;
- under Rule 52(b), to amend the findings or for additional findings;
- under Rule 59, for a new trial or to alter or amend a judgment; or
- under Rule 60, for relief from a judgment or order.

P-H 10-c: What would be your answer to the last problem if Pearl Murphy's attorney had filed a motion on October 19, YR-1, to set aside the default judgment but did not file a motion for a new trial? Read the rule in Illustration 10-c again carefully before you answer.

In other state jurisdictions, and under the federal rules, the filing of a post-judgment motion will *not* automatically stay execution on the judgment. Instead, to stay execution pending the court's ruling on the motion, the judgment debtor must also ask the court to *order* a stay of execution until the postjudgment motion is decided. Federal Rule of Civil Procedure 62(b), set forth in Illustration 10-d, suggests how this procedure works in federal court actions and in state actions following the same procedure.

P-H 10-d: Assume the same facts as set out in P-H 10-b except that the state rule controlling is identical to FRCP 62(b) in Illustration 10-d. If Pearl Murphy's attorney does not file an additional motion asking for stay of the execution pending resolution of the other motions, can CCME begin execution before those motions are ruled on? If Pearl Murphy's attorney does file a motion asking for stay of the execution pending resolution of the other motions, is the trial judge obligated to grant that motion to stay?

In the next section, we look at a motion to stay execution and consider the posting of a bond for "the other party's security" as a condition to granting a motion to stay execution.

 C.

The Effect of an Appeal on the Right to Execute: The Stay Bond

A defendant against whom a final judgment has been entered may also file an **appeal** of the judgment to the appropriate state court of appeals or, if it is a federal court judgment, to the appropriate U.S. Circuit Court of Appeals. The normal sequence of events following entry of a final judgment is that the party against whom the judgment is entered first attempts to obtain relief through one or more of the postjudgment motions considered in Section B and, failing that, then initiates an appeal.

Again, there is variation among the states as to the time frame and procedure for appealing a final judgment and as to the effect of an appeal on the judgment creditor's right to begin executing on the judgment. In most states the appeal is initiated by the filing of a **notice of appeal** within a designated time period following entry of the final judgment. Illustration 10-e shows a typical state statute.

What if the judgment debtor files one of the postjudgment motions we looked at in Section B? Does that affect the timing for filing the notice of appeal? Yes. Illustration 10-f sets out a typical state rule explaining how.

P-H 10-e: Assume the same facts as in P-H 10-b and that Pearl Murphy's motion for new trial is denied by the trial court on November 1, YR-1. Assume that the appeal of the judgment against Pearl is controlled by the rules set out in Illustrations 10-e and 10-f. What is the last date on which Pearl's attorney can file a notice of appeal?

P-H 10-f: Locate Federal Rules of Appellate Procedure 3(a)(1) and 4(a)(1) and (4). Do the federal rules utilize a different time frame or procedure than the typical state rules, set out in Illustrations 10-e and 10-f? Do they utilize a different time frame or procedure than the controlling rules in your state?

Whether postjudgment motions are filed or not, if the notice of appeal is not filed within the time period designated by the rules just considered, the court of appeals lacks **jurisdiction** over the appeal and it will be disallowed. That means the final judgment entered by the trial court is final and can be executed on by the judgment creditor.

But what if the party against whom the judgment is entered does file a timely appeal? Can the judgment creditor execute on the judgment if a timely appeal has been filed? It is important to know that merely filing of a timely notice of appeal does *not* prevent the judgment creditor from executing on the judgment. The

Illustration 10-e: TYPICAL STATE STATUTE REGARDING PROCEDURE AND TIMING OF APPEAL

> In an appeal as of right to the court of appeals, the notice of appeal required by these rules shall be filed with and received by the clerk of the trial court within 30 days after the date of entry of the judgment appealed from.

Illustration 10-f: TYPICAL STATE RULE REGARDING IMPACT OF A POSTJUDGMENT MOTION ON TIMING OF THE NOTICE OF APPEAL

> If a timely motion under the Rules of Civil Procedure is filed in the trial court by any party: (1) for judgment in accordance with a motion for a directed verdict; (2) to amend or make additional findings of fact; (3) for a new trial; (4) to alter or amend the judgment; the time for appeal for all parties shall run from the entry of the order denying a new trial or granting or denying any other such motion.

judgment debtor, in addition to filing the notice of appeal, must ask the trial judge to **stay the execution pending the appeal**. Illustration 10-g sets out a typical state rule.

P-H 10-g: Locate Federal Rules of Civil Procedure 62(a) and (d). How does the procedure controlling in the appeal of a federal court judgment differ from the procedure dictated by the rule you see in Illustration 10-g? How does it differ from the procedure under the rules of your state?

Be sure you understand what is at stake in a court's decision to stay execution on a judgment pending appeal. The judgment creditor stands in the position of a party who has prevailed at trial. That party has a court judgment in its favor. The appeal may take months or even years. Most appeals result in the trial court judgment being upheld. If the judgment creditor is forced to wait until the conclusion of the appeal to execute, the financial circumstances of the judgment debtor may deteriorate, making it more difficult for the creditor to locate and seize assets to satisfy the judgment. The judgment creditor therefore has a strong argument that it is not fair to delay execution on its judgment pending the appeal. In response, the judgment debtor can argue that he might prevail on appeal, negating the creditor's judgment. The judgment creditor has the benefit of postjudgment interest running on the judgment amount (see Chapter Nine, Section E) to compensate him for the delay. If we allow the creditor to seize his property now, before the appeal is decided, and the debtor later prevails on appeal, then the debtor is in the unenviable position of having to go back against the creditor to recover his property, which of course may no longer be available. How do we accommodate these legitimate competing interests?

The compromise is to allow a judgment debtor to obtain a stay of execution pending appeal, but only if that debtor is able to provide adequate *security* for payment of the debt. That security assures the creditor that if the appeal is not successful, assets will be available from the debtor's property or from a *surety* to satisfy the judgment. Accordingly, the usual condition imposed by the court on the judgment debtor's motion to stay execution pending appeal is that the debtor provide a **stay bond** (sometimes called a **supersedeas bond** or **appeal bond**) to provide the judgment creditor that security. Illustration 10-h sets out a typical state rule regarding this procedure.

Recall that in Section B of this chapter (see Illustration 10-d) we learned that, in some states and under the federal rules, a motion to stay execution and providing "appropriate terms for the other party's security" is required to stay execution pending the court's decision on postjudgment motions as well as

Stay bond Cash, property or surety contract sufficient to cover the amount of a judgment plus accrued interests during the appeal posted by a party seeking to stay execution as a condition to obtaining such stay.

Illustration 10-g: TYPICAL STATE RULE REGARDING STAYING EXECUTION PENDING APPEAL

When an appeal is taken from a final judgment, the court in its discretion may stay execution, suspend relief, or grant whatever additional or modified relief is deemed appropriate during the pendency of the appeal and upon such terms as to bond or otherwise as it deems proper to secure the other party.

Illustration 10-h: TYPICAL STATE RULE REQUIRING BOND TO OBTAIN A STAY OF EXECUTION ON APPEAL

> When an appeal is taken, the appellant by giving a bond may obtain a stay. The bond may be given at or after the time of filing the notice of appeal. The stay is effective when the bond is approved by the court.
>
> A bond for stay shall have sufficient surety and (1) if an appeal is from a judgment directing the payment of money, the bond shall be conditioned to secure the payment of the judgment in full, interest, damages for delay, and costs on appeal; in cases involving judgments payable in periodic installments, bond shall be fixed in such a manner as the court shall deem sufficient; (2) if an appeal is from a judgment ordering the assignment, sale, delivery, or possession of personal or real property, the bond shall be conditioned to secure obedience of the judgment and payment for the use, occupancy, detention, and damage or waste of the property from the time of appeal until delivery of possession of the property and costs on appeal.
>
> If the appellant places personal property in the custody of an officer designated by the court, such fact shall be considered by the court in fixing the amount of the bond.

pending appeal. In those states, the procedure for posting a bond and obtaining a stay pending the court's decision on postjudgment motions will be governed by a rule similar to that seen in Illustration 10-h. There are a number of different ways that the judgment debtor (the **appellant** in the appeal) may satisfy the bond requirement and obtain the stay of execution.

1. Cash or Personal Property Bond

The bond may be cash or other personal property delivered to the clerk of the court or other person designated by the court to hold until the appeal is over. In that event, the clerk will hold the property, invest it safely if it is cash, and pay it over to whichever party the court directs at the end of the appellate process.

EXAMPLE

Assume that Pearl Murphy wishes to appeal the judgment against her in favor of CCME but she and Nick lack the means to post any kind of appeal bond using their own property or credit. To avoid the judgment being executed on pending the appeal, Pearl's mother agrees to give Pearl the necessary cash to post the stay bond. The money will be delivered to the clerk of the court who, with the judge's permission, will invest the cash in short-term FDIC insured certificates of deposit or in U.S. Treasury Bills.

2. Real Property Bond

The judgment debtor/appellant may post his owner's equity in real property as a bond. To convey real property to the clerk as a stay bond, the debtor will execute a mortgage or deed of trust to the trustee (see Chapter Four), spelling out the clerk's right to convey the debtor's interest in the property to the party designated by the court later.

> Assume Nick and Pearl lack the cash to post a cash bond and no family member is able to help. The only thing they do have is equity in their home. With the court's approval, they may convey a portion of that equity in their real property to the clerk of the court with the understanding that if the appeal is lost the clerk can convey it to CCME, who can foreclose and sell.

3. Surety Bond

Surety bond A contract pursuant to which a surety makes itself primarily liable to a named principal for a debt owed to the principal by a named obligee.

The most common method of posting a stay bond is by providing a **surety bond**. A surety is one who makes himself primarily liable for the debt of another. As we learned in Chapter Four, Section B, a surety bond is a contract in which the surety promises to the judgment creditor that if the judgment debtor loses the appeal, the surety will pay the full judgment amount plus interest that has accrued during the appeal. The **surety** must be a person or business that can demonstrate that it has sufficient assets to pay the amount assured. Usually the surety is an *insurance company* that, for a fee to be paid by the debtor, will issue the surety bond in favor of the creditor. Of course, if the surety does have to pay the bonded amount to the judgment creditor, it has a contractual right to seek reimbursement from the judgment debtor.

What is the appropriate amount of a bond to stay execution? Practice varies among the states, but typically, the required bond amount will be set at 120 percent to 150 percent of the judgment amount to account for the postjudgment interest that will have accrued on that amount while the appeal was ongoing. But how can we know at the beginning of the appellate process how much postjudgment interest will accrue before it is over? We can't know for sure, but the trial court will order postjudgment interest calculated at the likely length of time that the appeal will last.

EXAMPLE

> If Pearl Murphy files a notice of appeal from the final judgment entered against her in favor of CCME and files a motion to stay execution, the trial court will require her to post a bond equal to the full amount of the judgment ($2,247.70, per Illustration 8-i) and will add an amount equal to postjudgment interest for as long as the appeal is likely to take. If appeals normally take 12 months to move through the system, the court may order 12 months of postjudgment interest to be added. If the controlling postjudgment interest rate is 10 percent per annum per the statute in Illustration 9-j, that means an additional $224.77 must be added to the principal judgment amount and the total stay bond posted by Pearl must be in the amount of $2,472.47.

A handful of states have imposed statutory limits on the size of stay bond that a court can require from an appellant. And courts do retain discretion to order a lesser bond amount based on exceptional circumstances. Illustration 10-i sets forth a typical state rule regarding such discretion.

If the trial court rejects the judgment debtor's motion for stay of execution pending appeal, the debtor can renew his motion with the court of appeals. Illustration 10-j sets forth a typical state rule regarding such power in the court of appeals.

Illustration 10-i: TYPICAL STATE RULE GRANTING JUDGE DISCRETION IN SETTING BOND AMOUNT

> Upon motion submitted to the trial court and for good cause shown, the bond for stay may be set in an amount less than that called for in the first section of this rule. In ruling on such a motion, the trial court may consider all appropriate factors including, but not limited to, the appealing party's financial condition and the amount of the appealing party's insurance coverage, if any. Nothing in this Rule shall be construed to limit the power of the court in exceptional cases to stay proceedings on any other terms or conditions as the court deems proper.

Illustration 10-j: TYPICAL STATE RULE REGARDING COURT OF APPEALS POWER TO GRANT STAY

> Nothing in this Rule shall be construed to limit the power of an appellate court or a judge thereof to stay proceedings or to suspend relief or grant whatever additional or modified relief is deemed appropriate during the pendency of an appeal or to make any order appropriate to preserve the status quo or the effectiveness of any judgment that may subsequently be entered.

Illustration 10-k: NOTICE OF APPEAL [STYLE OF CASE OMITTED FROM ILLUSTRATION]

> <u>NOTICE OF APPEAL</u>
>
> Notice is hereby given pursuant to Columbiana Rule of Appellate Procedure 3(a), that defendant, Pearl E. Murphy, hereby appeals to the Columbiana Court of Appeals from the Final Judgment by Default Dismissal entered against her in this action on September 20, YR-1, by the Circuit Court for Capitol County, Columbiana and from the Order of that court entered November 1, YR-1, denying defendant's Motion to Set Aside Default Judgment and for New Trial.
> Dated this 10th day of November, YR-1
>
> [Attorney signature and certificate of service omitted from illustration.]

Assume that Pearl Murphy does file an appeal of the final judgment against her and the refusal of the court to grant her postjudgment motion to set aside the default and grant her a new trial. Her notice of appeal is set out in Illustration 10-k.

Pearl wishes to stay execution of the judgment against her while the appeal is pending so she files a motion to stay execution. Her lawyer knows that a stay bond will be required, so the motion includes a request to approve bond for stay. Pearl's motion is shown in Illustration 10-l.

P-H 10-h: Assume that the final judgment in Illustration 2-d is entered in favor of Nick and Pearl Murphy against Dr. Samuel Craft and Capitol City Hospital (CCH) in the amount of $925,000 and that defendants wish to appeal the judgment. What bond amount will likely be required of those defendants in order to stay execution pending appeal? What bond amount would be required under the rules of your state?

Illustration 10-l: MOTION TO STAY EXECUTION AND TO APPROVE BOND FOR STAY [STYLE OF CASE OMITTED FROM ILLUSTRATION]

<u>MOTION TO STAY EXECUTION AND TO APPROVE BOND FOR STAY</u>

Defendant, Pearl E. Murphy, pursuant to Rule 62 of the Columbiana Rules of Civil Procedure, moves the court to stay execution on the Final Judgment by Default entered against her in this cause on September 1, YR-1, pending the outcome of the appeal of said judgment initiated by defendant by filing a notice of appeal on November 10, YR-1. Defendant further moves the court to approve the surety bond attached as Exhibit A to this motion issued by Capitol City Insurance Company in favor of plaintiff Capitol City Medical Equipment in the amount of $2,472.47 representing the principal amount of the judgment entered against defendant plus postjudgment interest for 12 months. Said bond is conditioned on approval by this court and on the affirmation of the judgment in favor of plaintiff by the court of appeals.

Dated this 11th day of November, YR-1

[Attorney signature and certificate of service omitted from illustration.]

Exhibit A

<u>Surety Bond</u>

Date: November 11, YR-1 Bond No. XX-9876

KNOW ALL MEN BY THESE PRESENTS, that we, Pearl E. Murphy of Capitol City, Columbiana (Principal) and Capitol City Insurance Company of Capitol City, Columbiana (Surety) are held and firmly bound unto Capitol City Medical Equipment (CCME) in the sum of $2,472.47 to be paid to CCME, its certain attorneys or assigns, to which payment well and truly to be made we bind ourselves, our heirs, executors, administrators, successors and assigns jointly and severally firmly by these presents.

WHEREAS, the above bound Principal is the defendant in a civil action in the Circuit Court for Capitol County, Columbiana bearing docket number 008-7791 (the Civil Action) and has filed a notice of appeal to the Columbiana Court of Appeals from a judgment entered against Principal in the Civil Action; and

WHEREAS, this bond is filed with the Circuit Court for Capitol County, Columbiana to obtain a stay of execution against Principal for the judgment rendered against Principal in the Civil Action. This bond shall be effective as of the date it is approved by the Circuit Court of Capitol County, Columbiana, as condition to a stay of execution being granted Principal against execution of the judgment rendered in the Civil Action and shall remain in force and effect until a final order is rendered in the appeal of the Civil Action or until the Surety is released from liability by the written order of a court. Such release shall not affect any liability incurred or accrued hereunder prior to said release.

NOW, THEREFORE, the condition of this obligation is such that if the above bound Principal shall prevail in Principal's appeal of the judgment rendered against Principal in the Civil Action then this obligation shall be void; otherwise it shall be and remain in full force and effect.

IN WITNESS WHEREOF, this instrument has been duly executed by the above named Principal and Surety the day and year written.

[Signatures of principal and surety omitted from illustration.]

Assume that the trial court hears Pearl's motion on November 20, YR-1, and grants the motion to stay execution. The court's order may look like what you see in Illustration 10-m.

Illustration 10-m: ORDER GRANTING STAY OF EXECUTION AND APPROVING BOND [STYLE OF CASE OMITTED FROM ILLUSTRATION]

ORDER APPROVING STAY OF EXECUTION AND STAY BOND

This matter came on for hearing on November 20, YR-1, on the motion of defendant, Pearl E. Murphy, pursuant to Rule 62 of the Columbiana Rules of Civil Procedure, to stay execution of the Final Judgment by Default rendered against her in this action on September 20, YR-1, pending the outcome of defendant's appeal of the final judgment. It appearing to the court that defendant has initiated an appeal of the final judgment to the Columbiana Court of Appeals on November 10, YR-1, and it further appearing to the court that defendant has provided sufficient security to plaintiff by posting a surety bond in the full amount of the judgment plus postjudgment interest on that amount for 12 months, it is

ORDERED that execution on the judgment rendered against defendant Pearl E. Murphy should be and hereby is stayed pending resolution of the appeal of that judgment or further order of this court. And it is further

ORDERED that the surety bond dated November 11, YR-1 issued by Pearl E. Murphy as principal and Capitol City Insurance Company as surety in favor of plaintiff in the amount of $2,472.47 is hereby approved.

ENTER this 20th day of November, YR-1

Juanita A. McBride, Circuit Judge

P-H 10-i: Capitol City Insurance Company will charge a fee (or premium) for agreeing to serve as surety on the stay bond shown in Illustration 10-l. Usually the fee is a percentage of the amount to be assured and must be paid by the principal up front. Go to www.suretybondservices.com/courtbondcalc.htm and calculate the premium Pearl Murphy would have to pay to obtain a surety bond to stay execution on appeal. Then calculate the premium Dr. Craft and CCH would have to pay to stay execution on the judgment in the malpractice action.

D. ▶ Property Exempt from Execution

Every state declares some property owned by the judgment debtor **exempt** from execution (and from prejudgment attachment or garnishment discussed in Chapter Nine, Section A). Such exemptions are established by statute or constitutional fiat.

When we say property is "exempt from execution" we mean that the judgment creditor cannot seize and sell that property to satisfy the judgment. The judgment creditor can only seize and sell **nonexempt property**. States allow debtors to exempt property from execution as a matter of **public policy**; states do not want to leave a debtor penniless. That destitute person would likely become a ward of the state and that is not in the state's interest.

1. Controlling Law on Exemption Issues

State property exemption laws apply generally to executions undertaken to enforce both state and federal court judgments, though, as we will see, federal law mandates that states exempt some kinds of property from execution.

EXAMPLE

Assume that a creditor in New York files suit against a Florida resident in a U.S. District Court in New York based on diversity of citizenship (see Chapter Eight, Section H) and takes a judgment against that defendant. When the judgment creditor seeks to execute on property owned by the judgment debtor in New York, it will be New York state law that controls the property exemption issue. (The singular exception to this rule is where the federal government is enforcing a federal tax lien. See that discussion later in this section).

When a final judgment is entered in one state and the debtor owns property in another state, the law of the state where the property is located will control the exemption issue.

EXAMPLE

If a judgment creditor holding a final judgment issued by a New York state court (or U.S. District Court in New York) seeks to execute on property owned by the judgment debtor in Florida, the Florida exemption laws will control the disposition of that Florida property, not New York exemption laws.

Federal law provides that various types of federal government benefits are exempt from execution on final judgments rendered in either state or federal court. A summary of those exempt federal benefits is set out in Illustration 10-n.

There are exceptions. The federal benefits listed in Illustration 10-n may be seized to pay delinquent federal taxes or student loans or to satisfy state child support or spousal support (alimony) obligations (see 42 U.S.C. §407 and 20 CFR 404.970).

Where you are dealing with a federal tax lien (discussed in Chapter Six, Section E) or other lien created by federal law (e.g., to collect unpaid federal or federally guaranteed student loans) state exemption laws will not protect a debtor's property from the reach of such federal liens; state exemption laws are

Illustration 10-n: FEDERAL GOVERNMENT BENEFITS EXEMPT FROM EXECUTION

- Social Security benefits
- Supplemental Security Income (SSI) benefits
- Veterans' benefits
- Civil service and federal retirement and disability benefits
- Service members' pay
- Military annuities and survivors' benefits
- Student assistance
- Railroad retirement benefits
- Merchant seamen's wages
- Longshoremen's and harbor workers' death and disability benefits
- Foreign service retirement and Disability benefits
- Compensation for injury, death, or detention of employees of U.S. contractors outside the United States
- Federal Emergency Management Agency Federal disaster assistance

preempted by federal law authorizing the lien (see *United States v. Bess*, 357 U.S. 51 (1958) and *Commissioner v. Stern*, 357 U.S. 39 (1958)). You must look to federal exemption law in such situations (see, e.g., property exempted from federal tax lien by 26 U.S.C. §6334).

State law varies considerably regarding the kinds of state benefits (e.g., income from state unemployment or public assistance programs, state or local government sponsored retirement plans for government workers, etc.) that are exempt from execution.

Federal law also mandates that states exempt certain property other than the federal benefits listed in Illustration 10-n.

EXAMPLE

> Section 206(d) of the Employee Retirement Income Security Act of 1974 (ERISA) mandates that states exempt qualified pension, profit-sharing, SEP, and 401-k plans with exceptions for Qualified Domestic Relations Orders, tax levies, and payment of criminal fines and penalties. (IRAs and private annuities do not receive such federal protection, though states may choose to exempt them.) Section 525 of the Internal Revenue Code mandates the exemption of proceeds in college savings plans up to a maximum of $25,000.

2. The Homestead Exemption

Homestead exemption The exemption available to a debtor to protect the equity in his primary residence.

Forty-six of the 50 states currently recognize a **homestead exemption**, allowing the debtor to retain some or all owner's equity in the family home or domicile (the primary home or domicile when the debtor owns more than one). There is, however, tremendous variation among the states in the dollar amount of the allowed exemption. In Texas, for example, the constitutional homestead exemption is unlimited in dollar amount, though subject to certain acreage limits, while in Tennessee, by statute, the homestead exemption is limited to owner's equity of $5,000 for an individual owner and $7,500 (total) for a married couple unless the owner has a minor child, in which case the exemption is $25,000. Minnesota, on the other hand, falls somewhere in the middle of those extremes, allowing a $200,000 statutory homestead exemption for urban property and $500,000 for rural property, subject to acreage limits and subject to adjustment for inflation every other year. Quite a difference.

P-H 10-j: Assume that Nick and Pearl Murphy execute on the judgment in their favor against Dr. Samuel Craft (Illustration 2-d). Dr. Craft is single and owns his home. He purchased the home five years ago for $1.2 million and has a mortgage on it in favor of Capitol City Bank (CCB), with a current balance owed of $900,000. The home is appraised today at $1.5 million. If Dr. Craft's real property is in Texas, how much will the Murphys be able to realize out of it if they execute? What if the property is in Tennessee? In Minnesota? In your state? Check the Asset Protection Book's State Information site at www.creditorexemption.com/ and figure out Dr. Craft's homestead exemption status in other states.

If a debtor's equity in the homestead exceeds the applicable homestead exemption, the executing creditor can force the property sold, pay the debtor the homestead amount and apply the rest to the debt.

EXAMPLE

> Assume Dr. Craft's home is in a state that allows a $50,000 homestead exemption. When the Murphys execute on their judgment and the property is sold for $1.5 million, the first $900,000 will go to pay off the existing mortgage to CCB, assuming it is properly perfected giving it senior status and the first right to proceeds of the property pledged. The next $50,000 will go to Dr. Craft as his homestead exemption amount. The Murphys can then apply the balance of $650,000, minus the costs of sale, to satisfy the judgment owed them.

As the preceding example illustrates, an executing judgment creditor will not have a claim to the debtor's property that is superior to a previously secured and perfected interest (the CCB mortgage in that example). And that example also illustrates that exemptions do not apply to a creditor to whom the debtor has pledged the property as security.

EXAMPLE

> Assume that Dr. Craft owes CCB $1.5 million and the entire indebtedness is secured by a mortgage on his home. If Craft defaults on his obligation to CCB and the bank forecloses on the home and sells it for $1.5 million, all of the proceeds of sale will go to retire the indebtedness owed to CCB. What about Dr. Craft's $50,000 homestead exemption? It doesn't apply as between him and the bank since he voluntarily mortgaged the property in which he would have had the exemption. Creditors consensually secured in property that the debtor could otherwise claim as exempt are not bound by those exemptions.

In some states, the homestead exemption is inapplicable to mechanic's and materialman's liens filed against the property.

As we will see in Part C of the text, exempt property issues arise in bankruptcy proceedings as well, where individual debtors routinely exempt certain property from their creditors.

3. Personal Property/Income Source Exemptions

States also exempt various types and dollar amounts of personal property or income sources from execution (or from prejudgment attachment or garnishment, as discussed in Chapter Nine, Section A). The variation of personal property/income exemptions among the states is significant. We have already seen in Illustration 10-n and the text following that federal law mandates that states exempt some categories of personal property and income sources. Illustration 10-o sets out other commonly recognized personal property/income source exemptions.

P-H 10-k: Apply the personal property exemptions of your state to yourself or someone else with whose financial situation you are familiar. If a judgment creditor was executing on your assets (or someone else you know), what personal property could you or would you claim as exempt under the exemption laws of your state?

Illustration 10-o: COMMON PERSONAL PROPERTY AND INCOME SOURCE EXEMPTIONS

- Household furniture, up to a designated dollar amount of current value or equity (e.g., $5,000)
- Vehicles, up to a designated dollar amount of current value or equity
- Equipment or tools used by the debtor in a trade or business
- Necessary and proper clothing and personal possessions, such as the family Bible or Koran, family photographs/portraits, pets, school books.
- Livestock, up to a designated dollar amount of current value or equity
- Any personal property, up to a designated dollar amount of current value or equity (e.g., $10,000 of value and the debtor can choose the property to be exempted)
- IRAs (including Roths) and private annuities
- State or local government employee retirement funds (often including teachers, police officers, firefighters, etc.)
- Disability or unemployment payments
- Child support or alimony payments
- Life insurance policies covering the life of the debtor on which the debtor's spouse or children are the sole beneficiaries
- Proceeds of a disability policy or annuity constituting compensation of debtor for his personal injury or the personal injury or death of one upon whom the debtor was dependent

As we saw with the homestead exemption in real property, no exemption can be claimed by the debtor in personal property that has been pledged as collateral to secure debt when it is the secured creditor seeking to repossess and sell that property.

EXAMPLE

If Shears Department Store seeks to repossess the living room furniture pledged as collateral by Nick and Pearl Murphy to secure the debt they owe to Shears (Illustration 5-a), the Murphys cannot claim an exemption in the furniture. However, if the furniture belonged to Pearl only and CCME attempted to execute on it, she could likely assert an exemption in it for household furniture up to the allowed dollar amount of such exemption. Why? Because CCME, though a judgment creditor, is not a secured creditor in that furniture as Shears is.

4. Declaring Exemptions in Property

In some states, debtors have the automatic benefit of allowed exemptions and do not need to take any action to assert them. In those states, when writs of execution or garnishment are issued by the court following entry of final judgment (subjects we will cover in detail in Chapter Eleven), the writs will advise the recipients of property that is to be exempted from the execution. In other states, debtors must file a written **declaration of exemptions** (also called a **claim of exemptions**) with the clerk of the court where the judgment may be or has been entered against them or with some other designated public office. Or a motion to claim exempt property may be filed with the court (see Illustration 11-p).

As we will see in Part C of the text, individual debtors in bankruptcy are required to complete a specific form asserting claimed exemptions in property or lose the benefit of such exemptions.

5. Applicability of Property Exemptions to Government Claims

As previously noted, the federal government enforcing a federal tax lien or other obligation to the federal government (e.g., federal student loan, farm or small business loan) is *not* subject to any state property exemption law affecting real or personal property due to the **Supremacy Clause** of the U.S. Constitution (Article VI, Paragraph 2). However, in 26 U.S.C. §6334, Congress has created specific exemptions applicable to execution on a federal tax lien, which include:

- Worker's compensation benefits
- Unemployment benefits
- Necessary clothing and school books
- Furniture and personal effects up to a total value of $6,250
- Necessary books and tools of the trade up to a total value of $3,125
- Income or wages equal to the applicable standard deduction allowed the debtor for federal income tax purposes

Though 26 U.S.C. §6334 appears to also exempt social security benefits from execution on a federal tax lien, subsequent legislative enactments suggest otherwise, and the IRS has taken the position that such benefits are subject to levy (see 20 CFR 404.970).

The federal government may also offset (deduct) amounts owed to any federal agency from social security payments or income tax refunds due the debtor.

EXAMPLE

Assume an individual defaults on a federal student loan administered by the U.S. Department of Treasury or on a small business loan administered by the U.S. Small Business Administration. Either of those federal agencies could have amounts withheld from the individual's social security check (including SSI payments) or tax refund to satisfy the obligation.

The homestead exemption will not defeat a state or local tax lien arising out of unpaid property taxes on the homestead property.

E. The Effect of Concurrent Ownership of Property on Creditor Execution Efforts

Where two or more persons share ownership in a single piece of property they are said to be **concurrent owners.** Concurrent ownership raises questions regarding the right of the judgment creditor of only one of the concurrent owners to execute on the ownership interest of that owner in the property.

> Nick and Pearl Murphy concurrently own their home and there is equity in the home. CCME is a judgment creditor of Pearl, but not Nick. The issue raised is whether CCME can execute on Pearl's share of the equity in the home. Assume that Pearl and her brother Paul concurrently own a valuable antique vase. CCME has a judgment against Pearl but not Paul. The issue raised is whether CCME can execute on Pearl's ownership interest in the vase.

Of course, if the final judgment is entered against all the concurrent owners of property the judgment creditor can execute on the property.

> If CCME had a final judgment against both Nick and Pearl, it could execute on the equity in the home they concurrently own. If CCME had a final judgment against both Pearl and her brother Paul, it could execute on the vase they own concurrently.

But whether the judgment creditor holding a final judgment against only one concurrent owner of property can execute on the interest of that one owner in the property depends on what type of concurrent ownership it is. There are several.

1. Tenancy by the Entireties

Tenancy by the entireties A form of joint ownership of property between a husband and wife where each has a right of survivorship.

A **tenancy by the entireties** is a form of concurrent ownership of property that pertains to a husband and wife only. When a husband and wife hold title to property together as tenants by the entireties they each have a **right of survivorship** in the property, which means that on the death of one spouse the survivor takes the entire ownership interest as a matter of law. So long as both spouses are alive, neither can transfer their individual interest in the property (which is only the right of survivorship) as by selling, pledging, or gifting it to another, and neither can effectively convey their interest in the property by will or intestate succession. They must convey their interests together or not at all. Where a married person is the object of a judgment execution but the spouse is not, the ownership interest of the debtor spouse in assets concurrently owned in a tenancy by the entireties cannot be executed on.

> Assume that CCME executes on the default judgment in its favor against Pearl Murphy (Illustration 8-i). If Pearl and Nick own their home as tenants by the entireties, CCME, as the judgment creditor of Pearl only, cannot force the homestead to be sold as part of the execution.

2. Community Property

Community property is another form of concurrent ownership applicable to spouses only in which each spouse is deemed to own an undivided one-half interest in property acquired during the marriage. Generally speaking, property acquired prior to the marriage and property acquired by either spouse by gift or inheritance during the marriage is not considered community property. This form of concurrent ownership between spouses is recognized in only ten states and Puerto Rico. Like property held between spouses as tenants by the entirety, neither spouse can sell, pledge or gift community property during life without the consent of the other and judgment creditors of only one spouse cannot execute on community property. Unlike the tenancy by the entirety, either spouse can leave their half interest in community property to a third person by will but if either spouse dies intestate (without a will) their undivided half interest in the community property goes to the surviving spouse as a matter of law.

EXAMPLE

Assume that CCME executes on the default judgment in its favor against Pearl Murphy (Illustration 8-i). If Pearl and Nick reside in a community property state, CCME, as the judgment creditor of Pearl only, cannot force the homestead to be sold as part of the execution if it is deemed community property as it will be if title is in both their names.

In 2001, one community property state, California, recognized the right of spouses to hold title to property as **community property with a right of survivorship**. When so titled, neither spouse can leave their undivided half interest in the community property to a third person by will. The right of survivorship will mandate that the half interest of the deceased spouse go to the surviving spouse whether or not there is a will. The rule barring judgment creditors from executing on the undivided half interest of one spouse remains unchanged.

3. Tenancy in Common

Tenancy in common A form of concurrent ownership in which each owner has an undivided interest in the property. There is no right of survivorship.

A **tenancy in common** is a form of concurrent ownership in which each owner has an undivided interest in the property owned. If the judgment debtor owns property concurrently with a spouse or anyone else as tenants in common, the undivided interest of the judgment debtor in the property can be partitioned or sold as part of the execution process.

EXAMPLE

Partition action A lawsuit asking a court to segregate or divide the undivided ownership interest of one concurrent owner of property so it can be seized by that owner's creditors.

Assume that Pearl and her brother Paul own a one-acre parcel of unimproved land as tenants in common with Pearl having an undivided, one-third interest in the property and Paul an undivided two-thirds interest. CCME, as the judgment creditor of Pearl, can execute on Pearl's undivided one-third interest in the property, ask a court to *partition* (divide) it from Paul's two-thirds interest, and then sell her partitioned portion of the land and apply the proceeds in satisfaction of the judgment. A lawsuit seeking partition of property in this manner is called a **partition action**. If the parcel cannot be partitioned (perhaps the parcel only has value as a whole), the entire parcel will be sold and Pearl's share of the proceeds (one-third in this example) paid to the executing creditor. If Pearl and Paul also own the antique vase as tenants in common, it cannot be partitioned as realty can, so it will be sold and Pearl's share of the proceeds paid over to the executing creditor.

4. Joint Tenancy

Joint tenancy A form of concurrent ownership in which each owner holds an equal, undivided share and there is a right of survivorship.

In a **joint tenancy**, the concurrent owners each own an equal, undivided interest in the property and there is a right of survivorship as in a tenancy by the entireties. That means that when one joint tenant dies, the surviving joint tenants will take the decedent's interest in the property rather than it passing through her will or to her heirs by intestate succession. The joint tenancy is different from the tenancy by the entireties, however, in that, prior to death, a joint tenant may transfer her interest in the property to another by sale, pledge, or gift. The transferee of the joint tenant's interest does not become a joint tenant in the property but a tenant in common only. The joint tenancy is broken by the transfer. Significantly for our purposes, judgment creditors of a single joint tenant, like creditors of a single tenant in common, *can* execute on the joint tenant's interest in the property jointly owned.

EXAMPLE

Assume Pearl and her two brothers, Paul and Peter, concurrently own the antique vase as joint tenants. CCME, as the judgment creditor of Pearl only, can execute on Pearl's undivided interest in the vase, force it to be sold and her one-third of the proceeds paid over to it.

F. ▶ Trust Arrangements That May Defeat Creditor Execution Efforts

Trust A legal arrangement where the owner of property conveys property into the hands of a trustee charged with holding and administering the property for the benefit of named beneficiaries.

A **trust** is an arrangement whereby the owner of property (called variously the **grantor**, **trustor**, or **settlor**) conveys title in the property to a designated **trustee** to be held by the trustee for the benefit of another party, called the trust **beneficiary**. The property placed in trust is called the **trust principal** or the **trust property** or the **trust res**. There are many different kinds of trusts, but we will focus only on two that have special consequences for efforts to execute on indebtedness.

1. Spendthrift Trust

Spendthrift trust Prohibits alienation of trust property to protect the property from dissipation by the beneficiary or seizure by creditors.

A **spendthrift trust** is a trust established to provide certain benefits to a designated beneficiary from time to time that prohibits the beneficiary from selling or pledging as security any of the trust principal or any future distributions to be received from the trust. The idea behind the spendthrift trust is to protect the beneficiary from his own poor judgment by limiting his access to trust principal or interest. In most states, the spendthrift trust has the added benefit to the beneficiary of preventing his creditors from executing on assets of the trust unless and until they are distributed to the beneficiary.

EXAMPLE

Assume the one-acre parcel mentioned in the preceding two examples had been placed in a spendthrift trust by Pearl's parents, naming her as the sole beneficiary. Assume further that the land is income producing because coal is mined from beneath it. Under the spendthrift provisions of the trust, Pearl could not sell or mortgage her interest in the land or income from it while either was held in trust for her, nor could CCME seize the land or income still held in the trust to satisfy its judgment against Pearl. If and when payments of interest were made to Pearl by the trustee of the trust or if the land itself was conveyed to her at the conclusion of the trust, then those payments or the land could be seized.

EXAMPLE

The reason that qualified retirement plans are exempt from execution (as discussed in Section D of this chapter) is that Section 206(d)(1) of ERISA requires that in order to be qualified, a retirement plan must include an anti-assignment clause and prohibit alienation of plan assets by the beneficiary. This section is known as the **federal spendthrift clause** and has been construed to defeat both the claims of creditors of the beneficiary and the beneficiary's own worst instincts to spend the assets on anything other than retirement.

2. Asset Protection Trust

Asset protection trust A trust whereby the settlor can convey his own property into trust, name himself as the beneficiary to receive distributions of principal or interest as proscribed in the trust document, yet prevent his creditors from seizing trust assets not yet distributed.

An **asset protection trust** (sometimes called a **self-settled trust**) is an arrangement whereby the settlor can convey his own property into trust, name himself the beneficiary to receive distributions of principal or interest as proscribed in the trust document, and yet prevent his creditors from seizing trust assets not yet distributed. Previously available only as questionable **foreign asset protection trusts** or **offshore trusts** under the laws of other nations (typically a Caribbean island), approximately eight states have authorized asset protection trusts by statute. To obtain the protection of the trust assets from creditors of the settlor/beneficiary, the conveyance of the property into trust must be *irrevocable* (i.e., the settlor cannot ever withdraw the assets from the trust; he can only receive the distributions from the trust as a named beneficiary); and the settlor cannot also serve as trustee of the trust (although most states allow the settlor to remove a trustee and appoint someone else to serve).

With any type of trust arrangement, once a distribution of principal or interest is made to a beneficiary/debtor, the distributed property can be seized by the creditor. And any trust arrangement is subject to legal attack if the creation of the trust itself can be demonstrated to be a *fraudulent transfer* (see Chapter Nine) as to creditors.

CONCLUSION

Once a judgment is final and can be executed on, the judgment creditor must locate property of the debtor on which to execute. The creditor may use post-judgment discovery for this purpose, a topic we consider in Chapter Eleven. There, we will also examine the various methods of execution the law allows, including how a judgment entered in one state is executed on in another.

CHAPTER SUMMARY

After a final judgment has been entered, the judgment debtor will have a grace period before execution on the judgment commences to allow the debtor to pay the judgment, file a postjudgment motion, or initiate an appeal. In some jurisdictions, filing a postjudgment motion will further stay execution until the motion is decided; in others, it will not and the debtor must file a motion to stay execution along with the postjudgment motion. If the judgment debtor initiates an appeal of the final judgment, filing of the appeal does not automatically stay execution on the judgment. The debtor must request that execution be stayed pending resolution of the appeal, which normally requires the filing of a stay bond, also called a supersedeas or appeal bond, in the full amount of the judgment plus interest. A stay bond may be a cash or personal property bond, a real property bond, or a surety bond. In most states, an appeal is initiated by filing a notice of appeal within a mandated period of time following entry of the final judgment.

Every state declares some property of the debtor to be exempt from execution. Such exempt property will include some or all of the debtor's equity in his homestead, which means his primary residence, and some types of personal property up to a certain dollar amount. Exemptions are selected by the debtor by filing a claim or declaration of exemptions with the clerk of the court where the final judgment was entered. When a judgment is entered against a married person who owns property with a spouse as tenants by the entirety, the creditor cannot seize the debtor's interest in the property so held. The debtor spouse's only interest in the property is a right of survivorship. If the judgment is entered against both spouses the property owned as tenants by the entirety may be seized by the judgment creditor subject to any preexisting lien or mortgages on the property. If the judgment debtor owns property jointly with others as tenants in common, the debtor's undivided interest may be seized by her judgment creditor and the court may order a partition and sale of her undivided interest. Some states permit unmarried persons to hold property as joint tenants with a right of survivorship. In that case the judgment debtor of one joint tenant cannot be seized and partitioned, though that joint tenant may voluntarily convey his interest to another.

Certain trust arrangements may defeat a judgment creditor's attempts to execute on the property of a judgment debtor held in trust. A spendthrift trust prohibits the beneficiary from selling or pledging any trust principal or any future distributions to be received from the trust, and creditors of the beneficiary may not execute on assets held in such trust until they are actually paid to the beneficiary. An asset protection or self-settled trust, recognized in some states, allows the trustor to convey his own property into trust, name himself as the beneficiary to receive distributions of principal or interest as proscribed in the trust document, and yet prevent his creditors from seizing trust assets not yet distributed.

REVIEW QUESTIONS

1. Name five common postjudgment motions the judgment debtor may file.
2. What is the difference between a surety bond and a property bond?

3. What is the name of the document that is filed to initiate an appeal?
4. Explain the concept of exempt property. Why do states have exempt property rules? If a final judgment is entered in a federal court, do federal exemptions apply to its collection? If a final judgment is entered in the courts of one state, what exempt property laws govern property of the debtor lying in another state?
5. What is the homestead exemption and how does it vary among the states?
6. List as many types of personal property as you can that are commonly declared exempt from execution.
7. What is a declaration of exemptions and where is it filed?
8. Explain the differences between a tenancy by the entireties and a tenancy in common. Explain the differences between a tenancy by the entireties and a joint tenancy with a right of survivorship.
9. Explain what a trust is and identify the three necessary parties to a trust.
10. What is a spendthrift trust? What is an asset protection trust?

WORDS AND PHRASES TO REMEMBER

accelerated execution
appeal
appeal bond
appellant
asset protection trust
beneficiary
declaration of exemptions
execute
execution grace period
exempt property
federal spendthrift clause
foreign asset protection trust
grantor
homestead exemption
joint tenancy
judgment creditor
judgment debtor
nonexempt property
offshore trust
partition (suit)

personal property exemption
postjudgment motions
public policy
right of survivorship
self-settled trust
settlor
stay bond
stay of execution
supersedeas bond
Supremacy Clause
surety
surety bond
tenancy by the entireties
tenancy in common
trust
trustee
trustor
trust principal
trust property
trust res

TO LEARN MORE: A number of TLM activities to accompany this chapter are accessible on the student disc accompanying the text and on the Author Updates link to the text Web site at http://www.aspenparalegaled.com/ books/parsons_abcdebt/default.asp.

Chapter Eleven:

Executing on a Final Judgment—Part 2

Running into debt isn't so bad, it's running into creditors that hurts.
—*Anonymous*

A. ► Discovery in Aid of Execution: Postjudgment Asset Discovery

In Chapter Eight we observed that discovery in a collection or liability suit is limited to issues of liability and damages and cannot inquire into the defendant's assets or ability to pay any judgment rendered unless punitive damages are sought or unless such discovery is relevant to some prejudgment remedy sought by plaintiff. All that changes once final judgment has been entered and the judgment creditor is seeking to execute on it. By statute or rule of procedure, the judgment creditor seeking to execute on the judgment can utilize some or all of the formal discovery methods considered in Chapter Eight to identify and locate assets of the judgment debtor. We call this **discovery in aid of execution** or **postjudgment asset discovery**.

In most states the right to engage in postjudgment asset discovery is automatic. In others, the judgment creditor must first attempt execution (see Section B, below) and then seek court permission to engage in postjudgment discovery. In a very few states the creditor must first attempt execution and then initiate a second lawsuit by filing a **creditor's bill** alleging the failure of execution to locate sufficient assets to pay the judgment.

The most common discovery methods used in postjudgment asset discovery are **interrogatories, document requests**, and **depositions**. Of these, interrogatories are probably the most commonly used. Illustration 11-a sets forth a form for postjudgment interrogatories.

Discovery in aid of execution Formal discovery undertaken postjudgment to locate assets of the debtor available for execution in satisfaction of the judgment.

P-H 11-a: Based on the information sought by interrogatories in Illustration 11-a, what documents might the judgment creditor seek to obtain from the judgment debtor utilizing postjudgment request for production of documents? Draft a set of document requests based on your answer.

When using interrogatories, the attorney for the judgment creditor must keep in mind any limits set by statute or court rule on the number of interrogatories that can be served.

Illustration 11-a: POSTJUDGMENT INTERROGATORIES FROM CAPITOL CITY MEDICAL EQUIPMENT (CCME) TO PEARL MURPHY [STYLE OF CASE OMITTED FROM ILLUSTRATION]

INTERROGATORIES IN AID OF JUDGMENT

Because you have failed to pay the full amount of the judgment against you entered in favor of plaintiff, plaintiff has the right to attempt to enforce that judgment by execution on your assets. Plaintiff also may inquire concerning the existence and location of those assets.

Pursuant to Rules 33 and 69 of the Columbiana Rules of Civil Procedure you are required to make full and complete answers to the questions set forth below. These answers must be made in writing, under oath, within thirty (30) days after service upon you. Attach additional sheets if necessary to completely answer questions.

Should you fail to answer, the court may enter an order imposing sanctions against you. If you do not understand your duty to answer these questions, you should consult a lawyer. If you do not have or know a lawyer, then you should go to or telephone the office set forth below to find out where you can get legal help.

[Lawyer Referral Service address and telephone number omitted from Illustration.]

1. State whether you are currently employed. If so, state whether you are paid weekly, semimonthly, biweekly, monthly, or in some other fashion. If you are self-employed, state the name of your business, address, nature of your business, and annual income.
ANSWER:

2. *ACCOUNTS:* State whether or not you maintain any checking or savings accounts. If so, state the name and location of the banks or savings and loan association or building and loan association or credit union and the branch or branches thereof, the identification (account) numbers of each account, and the amount or amounts you have in each account. If you maintain any of these jointly with another person, give their name and address. Also provide the above information with respect to any such bank accounts that were maintained and were closed within the past twelve (12) months.
ANSWER:

3. *REAL ESTATE:* Do you have an ownership or interest in any real estate anywhere in the United States? If so, set forth a brief description thereof, including the lot size and type of construction; the location, including the state, county, and municipality; the volume and page number of the official record; and state further whether you own it solely or together with any other person or persons and give their full name and address. If any of the above properties are mortgaged, supply the name and address of the lender[s], the date and amount of the mortgage, where it is recorded, the monthly payments, and the balance now due.
ANSWER:

4. *DEBTS, NOTES & JUDGMENTS:* State the names and addresses of any and all persons whom you believe owe you money and set forth in detail the amount of money owed, the terms of payment, and whether or not you have written evidence of this indebtedness and, if so, the location of such writing. Also, state if the matter is in litigation and, if so, give full details. If you hold a judgment or judgments as security for any of these debts, state where and when the judgment was recorded, and the county, number, and term where the judgment is recorded. If you hold this judgment jointly with any other person or persons, give their name and address.
ANSWER:

5. *INSURANCE:* State whether or not you are the owner of any life insurance contracts. If so, state the serial or policy number or numbers of said contract, the face amount, the exact name and address of the insurance company, the named beneficiary or beneficiaries and their present address. If you own this insurance jointly with any other person or persons, give their name and address.
ANSWER:

6. *MORTGAGES:* State whether you own any mortgages against real estate owned by any other person in the United States. If so, state whether or not you own this mortgage with any other person or persons and, if so, supply their full name and address. State further the names and addresses of all borrowers and the state and county where said mortgage is recorded together with the number of the volume and the page number.
ANSWER:

7. *AGREEMENTS:* State whether you have any agreements involving the purchase of any real estate anywhere in the United States. If so, state with whom this agreement is made, and state whether or not any persons are joined with you in the agreement. Supply full names and addresses of all parties concerned. If the agreement is recorded, provide the state and county of recordation, volume and page numbers.
ANSWER:

8. *STOCKS, SHARES, OR INTERESTS:* State whether or not you own any stocks, shares, or interests in any corporation or unincorporated association or partnership, limited or general, and state the location thereof. Include the names and addresses of the organizations and include the serial numbers of the shares or stock. If you own any of the stock, shares, or interests jointly with any other person or persons, give their name and address.
ANSWER:

9. *GOVERNMENT, MUNICIPAL, OR CORPORATE BONDS:* State whether or not you own individually or jointly any corporate or governmental bonds including U.S. Savings Bonds. If so, include the face amount, serial numbers, and maturity date, and state the present location thereof. If you own any of these bonds jointly with any other person or persons, give their name and address.
ANSWER:

10. *SAFETY DEPOSIT BOXES:* State whether or not you maintain any safety deposit box or boxes. If so, include the names of the bank or banks, branch or branches, and the identification number or other designation of the box or boxes. Include a full description of the contents and also the amount of cash among those contents. If you maintain any of these jointly with any other person or persons, give their full name and address.
ANSWER:

11. *TRANSFERRED ASSETS AND GIFTS:* If, since the date this debt to *[creditor]* was first incurred, you have transferred any assets (real property, personal property, chose in action) to any person and/or, if you have given any gift of any assets, including money, to any person, set forth, in detail, a description of the property, the type of transaction, and the name and address of the transferee or recipient.
ANSWER:

12. *INHERITANCE:* State whether or not, to your knowledge, you are now or will be a beneficiary of or will inherit any money from any decedent in the United States, and state the place and date of death, the legal representative of the estate, and the location of the court where the said estate is administered or to be administered.
ANSWER:

13. *ANNUITIES:* State whether you are a beneficiary of any trust fund and, if so, state the names and addresses of the trustees and the amount of the payment and when the payment is received.
ANSWER:

14. *PERSONAL PROPERTY:* Set forth a full description of all furnishings and any other items of personal property (including jewelry) with full description, value, and present location. State also whether or not there are any encumbrances against that property and, if so, the name and address of the encumbrance holder,

the date of the encumbrance, the original amount of that encumbrance, the present balance of that encumbrance, and the transaction that gave rise to the existence of the encumbrance. If you own any personal property jointly with any other person or persons, give their name and address.
ANSWER:

15. *RENTAL INCOME:* State whether you are the recipient, directly or indirectly, of any income for the rental of any real or personal property, and, if so, state specifically the source of payment, the person from whom such payments are received, and the amount and date when those payments are received.
ANSWER:

16. *MOTOR VEHICLES:* State whether or not you own any motor vehicles. Include a full description of such motor vehicles, including color, model, title number, serial number, and registration plate number. Also show the exact name or names in which the motor vehicles are registered, the present value of those motor vehicles, and their present location and place of regular storage or parking. State also whether or not there are any liens or encumbrances against those motor vehicles and, if so, the name and address of the encumbrance, the present balance of the encumbrance, and the transaction that gave rise to the existence of the encumbrance.
ANSWER:

17. *PENSION:* State whether you are a participant in or the recipient of any pension or annuity fund and, if so, state specifically the source of payment, the person to whom such payments are made, the amount of the payments, and date when those payments are received.
ANSWER:

18. *OTHER ASSETS:* If you have any asset or assets that are not disclosed in the preceding 17 interrogatories, please set forth all details concerning those assets.
ANSWER:

[Attorney's signature and certificate of service omitted from illustration.]

Postjudgment discovery may be used to obtain information from third persons, as well as from the judgment debtor, and **subpoena** power is available to compel attendance of such third parties at depositions, and the production of documents and things that might be in their possession. Often the judgment debtor is uncooperative with postjudgment discovery requests and the attorney for the judgment creditor must seek and obtain orders from the trial court compelling cooperation on pain of **contempt**.

Contempt Power of a court to declare one subject to the court's order in violation of the order and to impose penalties.

P-H 11-b: Did you think that imprisonment for owing a private debt (**debtor's prison**) was a thing of the past? Maybe not. A recent and growing controversy has arisen from the practice of some judgment creditors noticing the judgment debtor to a postjudgment deposition and then, if the debtor fails to show, having the judge find the debtor in contempt of court for not showing and issue a **capias**, or **bench warrant**, for the arrest of the defendant (informally called a **body attachment**), pursuant to which the debtor is taken into custody until there is a court hearing or the debtor posts bond (which often they cannot do). The problem also arises when a final judgment or slow pay order (discussed in Section B in connection with garnishments) directs the judgment debtor to make the payment or appear in court to explain why it was not made. These are called **pay or appear** provisions. When the debtor fails to pay or to appear as ordered, the capias warrant issues. It appears to be a small number of highly aggressive debt collectors in urban areas using this tactic with cooperative judges. In 2012, Illinois passed the Debtors' Rights Act requiring judges to make an affirmative finding of the debtor's ability to pay out of nonexempt sources of income before using a pay or appear provision in an order and requiring proof that a debtor received actual notice of a postjudgment deposition. Is this a problem in your state? If so, has your legislature addressed the problem?

P-H 11-c: What about imprisoning a person for failing to pay a court-imposed fine? In *Bearden v. Georgia,* 461 U.S. 660 (1983), the U.S. Supreme Court ruled that it is a violation of the **Equal Protection Clause** of the 14th Amendment to incarcerate a person who is unable to pay a court-imposed fine. One who is able to pay but refuses to do so may be incarcerated. But according the October 2010 study by the American Civil Liberties Union, *In for a Penny: The Rise of America's New Debtors' Prisons* (available online at www.aclu.org/prisoners-rights-racial-justice/penny-rise-americas-new-debtors-prisons), the practice of imprisoning those unable to pay fines continues in at least five states. And read the ACLU's subsequent 2013 study, *The Outskirts of Hope: How Ohio's Debtor's Prisons Are Ruining Lives and Costing Communities* (available online at www.acluohio.org/wp-content/uploads/2013/04/TheOutskirtsOfHope2013_04.pdf). What tactics are used in these states to incarcerate those unable to pay government-imposed fines? Is this a problem in your state?

B. ▶ Methods of Executing on the Final Judgment

In this section we will consider the three most common methods of executing on a final judgment under state law. Recognize, however, that there is tremendous variation in state law regarding the specific methods of execution allowed, the procedures that must be followed, and the relevant nomenclature used for the execution process. Consequently, the material presented here is necessarily general rather than specific and, after reading this section, you should compare the information provided here with the specific methods, procedures, and nomenclature used in your state in connection with execution.

1. The Judgment Lien

Judgment lien A judicial lien created on all real property owned by a judgment debtor in the county where the final judgment is recorded or docketed.

Judicial lien A lien arising from court action rather than from contract or statutory lien.

The judgment creditor can create an *involuntary lien* on any real property owned by the judgment debtor by filing a **judgment lien**. Commonly the judgment lien is created by obtaining a **certified copy** of the final judgment from the clerk of the court that issued the judgment and then **recording**, **filing**, or **registering** that certified copy in a designated public office (e.g., the office where land records are recorded or the office where financing statements are filed or registered). Illustration 11-b sets out a typical statute dealing with the procedure for creating a judgment lien. A judgment lien is a type of **judicial lien**. A judicial

Illustration 11-b: A TYPICAL STATUTE REGARDING PROCEDURE FOR CREATING A JUDGMENT LIEN

> Judgments and decrees in any court of record and judgments in excess of five hundred dollars ($500) in any court not of record in this state shall be liens upon the debtor's land from the time a certified copy of the judgment or decree shall be registered in the lien book in the register's office of the county where the land is located. Such lien shall be valid against any person having, or later acquiring, an interest in such property who is not a party to the action wherein such judgment is issued.

lien is a lien arising from court action in contrast to a consensual security interest (see Chapters Five and Eight) or statutory lien (see Chapter Six).

The judgment lien becomes a **cloud on the title** to any real property owned by the debtor in the county where the judgment is recorded, just as a consensual mortgage would.

EXAMPLE

> Assume that Nick and Pearl Murphy obtain a certified copy of their judgment against Dr. Samuel Craft (Illustration 2-d) and record it in Capitol County, Columbiana, pursuant to the statute in Illustration 11-b. Assume also that Dr. Craft is single and owns a home in Capitol County, which he purchased five years ago for $1.2 million on which he has an existing mortgage in favor of Capitol City Bank (CCB) with a current balance owed of $900,000. As of the moment of recording their judgment, the Murphys have a lien against Dr. Craft's home in Capitol County in the amount of the final judgment plus the postjudgment interest, which is continuing to accumulate. It is just as if Dr. Craft had conveyed a second mortgage to the Murphys in that amount. Of course, if CCB has properly perfected its first mortgage, the judgment lien in favor of the Murphys will be second, or junior, to that first mortgage. But if Dr. Craft now seeks to sell his home, both the CCB mortgage and the Murphys' judgment lien are of public record, and any buyer must either pay them off or take title to the property subject to those two liens. (See the last sentence of the statute in Illustration 11-b.)

P-H 11-d: Assume Dr. Craft also owns real property in Silver County, which is another county in Columbiana. Carefully read the language of the statute in Illustration 11-b. If the Murphys record their judgment lien in Capitol County only, does that subject the Silver County property to the lien? If not, what must the Murphys do to create a judgment lien on the Silver County property owned by Dr. Craft? Since the final judgment on which the Murphys are executing was entered by a court in Capitol County, Columbiana (see Illustration 2-d), does that mean it cannot be recorded in another county to create a judgment lien on property there? What if Dr. Craft owns real property in another state? See Section C on that issue.

Not only does a judgment lien create a cloud on title to the debtor's real property effectively preventing its sale, but the judgment creditor holding the judgment lien can also **foreclose** on the lien, sell the real property subject to it, and apply the proceeds to the judgment amount owed. Since no consensual

Illustration 11-c:
TYPICAL STATUTE
AUTHORIZING
FORECLOSURE ON A
JUDGMENT LIEN

> As long as a judgment lien is effective, no levy is necessary; the judgment creditor may move for an order of sale. Otherwise a levy occurs when the sheriff exercises control over the judgment debtor's realty.

power of sale has been conveyed by the debtor to the judgment creditor, the lien holder must seek a **judicial foreclosure** (see Chapter Four, Section D) either by applying to the court for an **order of sale** or by having the sheriff seize the property by writ of attachment or writ of execution (discussed below in this section) and conducting a sheriff's sale. Illustration 11-c sets forth a typical state statute authorizing this procedure.

When the real property is sold, the proceeds will be applied first to the expenses incurred in the sale and then to the amount of the judgment, including accrued postjudgment interest. Of course, if there are other liens on the property senior to the judgment lien or if there are any exemptions, those must be satisfied in full before any proceeds are applied to the judgment amount.

E X A M P L E

> If the Murphys create a judgment lien on Dr. Craft's home in Capitol County, as posited in the preceding example, and then obtain an order of sale, proceeds of the sale will be applied first to the expenses of sale, then to pay off the balance in full of the mortgage held by CCB and only then to the Murphys. This is so because the CCB mortgage on the property is senior to the Murphys' judgment lien.

P-H 11-e: If the balance owed to CCB on its mortgage is $900,000 and the property is appraised at only $910,000, should the Murphys seek an order of sale at this time? Can you think of an alternative strategy for them to pursue that could result in them obtaining proceeds from the property later?

In most states, a judgment lien will attach to any real property the judgment debtor acquires *after* the judgment lien has been created so long as it is still in effect.

E X A M P L E

> Assume that the Murphys create their judgment lien in Capitol County today. Six months from now, Dr. Craft purchases an interest in an empty lot in a residential area of the county. The Murphys will have an automatic lien against Dr. Craft's interest in that lot without having to re-record their judgment. The judgment lien created today will attach to the property acquired in six months if it has not been satisfied in the interim.

The preceding example raises the question of how long a judgment lien is valid. States differ, but a common term of validity is ten years from the date the lien was created. And the judgment lien holder typically has the option to *revive* the judgment lien before the end of that term either by re-recording the original judgment or by obtaining an order from the court granting an extension of the

Illustration 11-d:
TYPICAL STATUTE
REGARDING TERM OF
JUDGMENT LIEN AND
REVIVAL OF LIEN

> Once a judgment lien is created by registration, it will last for the time remaining in a ten-year period from the date of final judgment entry in the court clerk's office and for any extension granted by the court. For the extension of the lien to be enforceable, the judgment creditor must register the court's order extending the judgment lien.

judgment (see discussion in Section F) and then recording (registering or filing) that **order of extension**. Illustration 11-d sets out a typical statute regarding this procedure.

If a judgment debtor pays off the indebtedness owed to the judgment creditor after a judgment lien has been created on the debtor's property (or after a lien *lis pendens* has been created on it, as discussed in Chapter Six, Section F), the now-satisfied judgment creditor will record (register or file) a **release of lien** or **termination statement**. Illustration 11-e sets out a typical state statute regarding this procedure.

Similarly, if the judgment creditor has created a judgment lien on the debtor's property and the debtor thereafter obtains a stay of execution pending appeal, the trial court may order the judgment creditor to remove the lien pending the outcome of the appeal.

In some states, the judgment lien is deemed to attach to the judgment debtor's personal property, as well as to his real property when the lien has been properly filed (or recorded or registered) in the public office responsible for UCC filings (see Chapter Five, Section D).

2. The Writ of Execution

The method of execution used to seize nonexempt personal property of the debtor from the debtor himself is the **writ of execution**, sometimes called a writ of *fieri facias*. The writ is typically applied for from the clerk of the court that rendered the final judgment. Illustration 11-f sets forth an application for writ of attachment that CCME might file once its judgment by default against Pearl Murphy (see Illustration 8-i) becomes final and executable.

The clerk will issue the writ, which is then delivered to the sheriff (or other government officer charged with executing it), and directs the sheriff to seize property of the debtor to satisfy the indebtedness. The writ of execution issued on behalf of CCME against Pearl Murphy might look like what is shown in Illustration 11-g.

Rule 69 of the Federal Rules of Civil Procedure provides that in executing on a final judgment entered in the U.S. District Court, the practice and procedure of the state in which the district court is held may be utilized. Thus, writs of

Illustration 11-e: TYPICAL STATUTE REGARDING TERMINATING AN INVOLUNTARY LIEN ON PROPERTY FOLLOWING SATISFACTION OF INDEBTEDNESS

> Upon satisfaction of the judgment, the judgment debtor may demand that the judgment creditor record in the register's office a termination statement to supersede any lien *lis pendens* or judgment lien of record. If the judgment creditor fails to register a termination statement within ten days after demand, the judgment creditor shall be liable to the judgment debtor for $100 and for any loss caused to the judgment debtor by failure to register.

Illustration 11-f: APPLICATION FOR WRIT OF EXECUTION [STYLE OF CASE OMITTED FROM ILLUSTRATION]

APPLICATION FOR WRIT OF EXECUTION

The Plaintiff hereby makes application to the Clerk of the Circuit Court to issue a writ of execution in the above styled case to satisfy a judgment against the defendant Pearl E. Murphy in the amount of $2,247.70 entered on September 20, YR-1. The balance of the judgment that remains unsatisfied after the defendant is credited with payments made on said judgment is $2,247.70 plus postjudgment interest accruing on said amount from September 20, YR-1, through the date of payment.

This 1st day of November, YR-1

[Attorney's signature omitted from illustration.]

Illustration 11-g: WRIT OF EXECUTION [STYLE OF CASE OMITTED FROM ILLUSTRATION]

WRIT OF EXECUTION

To the Sheriff of Capitol County, Columbiana:

On September 20, YR-1, a judgment was entered in the docket of this court in favor of Capitol City Medical Equipment Company as judgment creditor and against Pearl E. Murphy as judgment debtor, for $2,247.70 the full amount of which is due on the judgment as entered together with interest on the judgment amount at 10% per annum, or $.62 per day, from the date of entry of the judgment to the date of issuance of this writ, to which must be added court costs of $255 and the commissions and costs of the officer executing this writ.

You are hereby commanded to satisfy the judgment with interest, commissions, and costs as provided by law, out of the personal property of the debtor. If sufficient personal property cannot be found, then this judgment may be satisfied out of the debtor's real property or if the judgment is already a lien on real property, then out of the debtor's real property. You are to make return of this writ within not less than 10 days nor more than 60 days after satisfaction of this judgment, with what you have done endorsed on this writ.

Dated: November 1, YR-1

_____
[Clerk]

By: _____
[Deputy Clerk]

---

execution issued by the U.S. District Court Clerk can be directed to the U.S. Marshal (a federal law enforcement official) or to the county sheriff.

In some states, a writ of execution can only authorize the seizure of a debtor's personal property. In others, it can authorize the seizure of either the debtor's personal or real property. And in those latter states, there may be an order of priority in which the debtor's property can be seized. A typical mandated order of priority is that the sheriff must first attempt to satisfy the execution out of the debtor's personal property, and only if that property is insufficient can the sheriff then seize the debtor's real property. This mandatory ranking or order of priority in seizing the debtor's property is often called the **marshalling of assets**.

Marshalling of assets Requirement that a judgment creditor executing on property of the judgment debtor seize and exhaust property in a certain order.

In executing the writ, the sheriff (or U.S. Marshall in a federal case) will locate and **levy** on (take possession of) property of the debtor. This may include cash, in which case the sheriff will be careful to not only inventory the cash on the return (discussed below) but to specify how the cash was applied. When cash is taken from the cash register of a debtor, that is sometimes called a **till tap**. If personal property is seized pursuant to the writ, the sheriff will store it, and then sell it either by advertised **auction** (often called a **Sheriff's sale**) or, in some states, by a **private sale** if the sheriff concludes that will bring more money. The debtor may be able to claim some property as exempt from execution following the procedures we considered in Chapter Ten, Section D.

In most instances, the sheriff takes personal property into his possession by moving it to a storage facility. But if that is not practical, the sheriff may leave the property in place, secure it with chains and locks as needed, and post a prominent notice advising anyone reading it that the property is in the possession of the sheriff and is not to be disturbed. The same will be done when real property is seized.

Till tap The direct seizure of cash from the cash register of a business pursuant to a writ of execution.

Sheriff's sale The sale by public auction or private sale of property of a debtor levied on pursuant to a writ of execution.

EXAMPLE

> Assume a writ of execution is issued on a docked boat. The sheriff might move the boat to another facility but, if that is not feasible, the sheriff might leave the boat in the dock, disable it from being operated, chain and lock it to the dock so it cannot be towed away, and place yellow tape across the entrance to it along with a posted notice of the seizure and penalties for trespassing or tampering. If the sheriff seizes a house next to the dock, a similar procedure will be followed. The house will be securely locked, yellow tape placed across all entrances, and a written notice posted.

Nulla bona Return made by sheriff on writ of execution when no executable property found.

Lien of levy The lien existing in favor of a judgment creditor against the property of the judgment debtor seized pursuant to a writ of execution.

The sheriff executing the writ must make a **return** of the writ to the clerk of the court. That means physically returning the executed writ to the clerk, stating the date(s) it was executed, and itemizing the assets seized (sometimes called the **inventory**). If the writ was executed but no assets were found, it will be returned *nulla bona* (*with nothing found*).

Once the writ has been executed and property of the debtor has been taken into custody by the sheriff, the legal status of the judgment creditor in that property is enhanced to that of a **judicial lien creditor**, which means she has a legally recognized priority claim to the seized property to satisfy the judgment. The lien that now exists in the seized property in favor of the judgment creditor is called a **lien of levy** in some states. Illustration 11-h sets out a typical state statute

Illustration 11-h: STATE STATUTE CREATING LIEN OF LEVY

(1) Levy. A levy is effective when the sheriff with a writ of execution exercises control over the judgment debtor's personalty.
(2) Lien of Levy. A lien of levy in the judgment creditor's favor is effective when the sheriff levies on the judgment debtor's personalty. The first judgment creditor to deliver a writ of execution to the sheriff, as shown by record in the clerk's office, has priority over other judgment creditors as to the property levied upon. A lien of levy remains effective until the property is sold or otherwise released from the sheriff's control.

regarding the creation of a lien of levy. Like the judgment lien considered in the last section, the lien of levy is a type of judicial lien because it arises from judicial process.

EXAMPLE

Assume the writ of execution in Illustration 11-g is issued by the clerk on November 1, YR-1, and delivered to the sheriff of Capitol County on November 2. On November 5 the sheriff executes on the writ by seizing jewelry owned by Pearl Murphy. Under the terms of the statute in Illustration 11-h, at the moment the sheriff takes possession of the jewelry on November 5, CCME, as judgment lien creditor, enjoys a lien of levy in the jewelry.

In most states, the lien of levy will not take priority over prior, properly perfected consensual and nonconsensual liens in the property.

EXAMPLE

Assume the same facts as the preceding example except that on November 4 Pearl Murphy borrows money from First City Bank (FCB) and pledges the jewelry as collateral to secure repayment of that loan. FCB perfects its security interest in the jewelry by filing a financing statement on November 4. If the sheriff seizes the jewelry on November 5, the lien of levy in favor of CCME will be subordinate, or junior, to the consensual lien of FCB in the jewelry, and if the sheriff sells the jewelry, the proceeds will go first to repay in full FCB before they are applied to the CCME judgment. However, if FCB failed to properly perfect its lien in the jewelry before the sheriff seized it on November 5, then CCME's lien of levy will be superior to the FCB security interest in the jewelry.

P-H 11-f: If Pearl does pledge the property to secure a loan from FCB on November 4, the day before the sheriff comes around to execute on the writ of attachment, what argument might CCME make that the pledge of the jewelry to FCB should be set aside by the court (see Chapter Nine, Section B)?

The lien of levy will, however, take priority over and be senior to most consensual and nonconsensual liens in the property created or perfected *after* the lien of levy.

EXAMPLE

Assume that the sheriff seizes Pearl's jewelry on November 5, and on November 6, Pearl pledges that jewelry as security for a loan from CCB. CCB perfects its security interest in the jewelry on November 6. If Pearl fails to repay the loan from CCB as promised, CCB may seek to repossess the jewelry. But CCB's claim to it will be junior to the lien of levy in it in favor of CCME.

P-H 11-g: What happens if the sheriff executes on the jewelry on November 5 but Pearl files a petition for bankruptcy relief on November 6, before the sheriff has sold the jewelry? The bankruptcy trustee will seek possession of the jewelry for the benefit of all of Pearl's creditors. Which claim has priority? The claim of

CCME as a judicial lien creditor as of November 5 or the claim of the bankruptcy trustee as of November 6? Hold that thought. We will answer this question when we get to Part C of the text.

Competing writs of execution are typically given priority by the order in which they are delivered to the sheriff.

EXAMPLE

> Assume the writ of execution in Illustration 11-g is issued by the clerk and delivered to the sheriff on November 2. On November 3, before the sheriff has attempted execution on the writ delivered to him on November 2, a second writ of execution is delivered to the sheriff on behalf of a second judgment creditor of Pearl Murphy, directing the Sheriff to seize her assets in satisfaction of that judgment as well. When the sheriff seizes Pearl's property, which judgment creditor gets paid first? In most states, the writ delivered on November 2 will have priority and must be satisfied in full before proceeds of sale can be applied to the writ delivered on November 3. How does the statute in Illustration 11-h resolve this question?

EC 11-a: What does the preceding example suggest about the importance of the attorney for the judgment creditor being diligent about having a writ of execution issued as quickly as possible after a judgment becomes final and collectible? What ethical rule might be violated by an attorney in your state who fails to be diligent in this regard and allows another creditor to obtain a priority position over her client in assets of a debtor?

States typically require the sheriff to conduct the sheriff's sale of the property within some designated time period following levy and to give prior public notice of the sale. Some states require specific notice of the sale to the debtor. A typical statute setting forth the procedure for notice and sale is shown in Illustration 11-i.

Once the judgment debtor's assets seized pursuant to the writ are sold, the proceeds will go first to pay the sheriff's administrative expenses involved in seizing, storing, and selling the property, and then to pay court costs assessed against the judgment debtor, and then to satisfy the judgment of the levying creditor (unless another creditor has a priority position in the property), and then to satisfy any other consensual or nonconsensual lien existing in the property. Any excess proceeds go to the debtor.

Bona fide purchaser for value One who purchases property in good faith with no actual or constructive knowledge of a defect in title; takes good title to such property.

In most states, the purchaser of property at the sheriff's sale is considered a **bona fide purchaser for value** and his title cannot be disturbed, even by a late exemption claim from the owner, who is now nothing but a prior owner as to the property.

Illustration 11-i:
STATE STATUTE
SETTING FORTH
PROCEDURE FOR
NOTICE AND SALE

> The sheriff shall sell personalty by auction. At least ten days before the sale, a notice, generally describing the personalty and stating the time, place, and terms, shall be published in a newspaper of general circulation at the judgment creditor's expense, taxable as court costs. If the personalty is perishable, no notice of sale is required.

3. The Writ of Garnishment

The method of execution used to obtain nonexempt personal property that belongs to the debtor or that is owed to the debtor from a third person (rather than from the debtor herself) is the **writ of garnishment**. Typical targets of a garnishment are the employer of the judgment debtor (called a **wage garnishment**), a financial institution holding funds of the judgment debtor in a checking or savings account (a **bank garnishment**), or anyone who owes the judgment debtor money (e.g., tenants of the judgment debtor who owe him rent). Like the writ of execution, the writ of garnishment is applied for by the judgment creditor to the clerk of the court that rendered the final judgment.

EXAMPLE

Recall from Illustration 1-a that Pearl Murphy has done some substitute teaching for the public school system in Capitol City. Assume that CCME is ready to execute on its final judgment by default against Pearl (Illustration 8-g). CCME learns that Pearl has a paycheck due at the end of this month from the school district. If the attorney for CCME decides to garnish that paycheck, the application for writ of garnishment might look something like what is shown in Illustration 11-j.

The party who is served with the writ of garnishment is called the **garnishee**. In some states the writ served on the garnishee advises that party of its duty to turn over the property of the debtor in its possession, or to pay the wages or other amounts owed to the debtor, to the clerk of the court that issued the writ. The clerk will then deliver the property or pay the funds over to the judgment creditor. In other states the writ orders the garnishee to hold any funds it has in its possession payable to the judgment debtor and to await further order of the court before paying them over. The writ of garnishment served on the Capitol City Public School System pursuant to the application seen in Illustration 11-j might look something like what is shown in Illustration 11-k.

In some states, the judgment creditor may also be obligated to provide the judgment debtor with **notice of the garnishment** (sometimes called **notice of levy**). The garnishment lien attaches to the property of the debtor held by the garnishee as soon as the garnishment is served on the garnishee. Because it is created by judicial process, the garnishment lien is another example of a *judicial lien*.

As reflected in the language of Illustration 11-k, the garnishee typically has a duty to respond to a writ of garnishment by making a personal appearance in the court issuing the writ or, more commonly, by filing a written answer within some designated time period (ten days under the terms of Illustration 11-k) acknowledging that it does hold property of the judgment debtor or funds due her and describing the property or funds. Thereafter the garnishee must turn over property of the debtor or pay over the garnished funds owed to the debtor within some designated time period (30 days under the terms of Illustration 11-k) or upon receipt of further court order. If the garnishee answers the garnishment by saying

Illustration 11-j: APPLICATION FOR WRIT OF GARNISHMENT [STYLE OF CASE OMITTED FROM ILLUSTRATION]

APPLICATION FOR WRIT OF GARNISHMENT

STATE OF COLUMBIANA   )
COUNTY OF CAPITOL   )

    Capitol City Medical Equipment Company, Judgment Creditor, makes oath that the Judgment Debtor's last known address is 3521 West Cherry Street, Capitol City, Columbiana, and the Judgment Creditor's address for mailing any notice required by Columbiana Statutory Code §26-2-204 is 413 Richardson Avenue, Capitol City, Columbiana.

    The Judgment Creditor hereby makes application to the Clerk of the Circuit Court to issue a writ of garnishment in the above styled case to satisfy a judgment entered against the Defendant herein on September 20, YR-1, in the amount of $2,247.70 plus interest on the judgment amount at 10% per annum, or $.62 per day, from the date of entry of the judgment to the date of issuance of this writ, plus court costs of $255.

This 1st day of November YR-1

                                   Capitol City Medical Equipment Company

                    By: _____
                                   Mark Andrews, Manager

                           [Notarization omitted from illustration.]

Serve the garnishment execution on: Capitol City Public School system at the following address: 1211 Post Road, Capitol City, Columbiana.

---

the judgment debtor is no longer employed by the garnishee or that the garnishee no longer has funds of the judgment debtor, the judgment creditor can typically engage in discovery from the garnishee (deposition, interrogatory, or document request) to obtain more information on the location of the judgment debtor or his property.

    Each state regulates how much of a debtor's paycheck may be garnished (e.g., maximum of 25%), and that amount is typically calculated based on the debtor's **disposable income**, which is defined, generally, as after-tax income. Most states also permit the judgment debtor whose employer or other income source has been garnisheed to move the court for permission to pay the judgment amount in installments less than what the payments would be from the garnishment. When such a **motion to pay judgment in installments** (sometimes referred to informally as a **slow pay motion**) is filed, the burden is on the judgment debtor to demonstrate to the court that his income sources are insufficient to live on with the garnished amounts deducted. The judgment debtor will ask the court to set an alternative amount of payments in equity. Illustration 11-l sets out a typical statute authorizing the motion to pay judgment in installments.

Disposable income The income of a garnishee, a statutory percentage of which is subject to garnishment.

Illustration 11-k: WRIT OF GARNISHMENT [STYLE OF CASE OMITTED FROM ILLUSTRATION]

WRIT OF GARNISHMENT

TO: Capitol City Public School system,
1211 Post Road
Capitol City, Columbiana

TAKE NOTICE: The earnings of your employee, Pearl E. Murphy ("Employee"), are hereby garnisheed and attached in satisfaction of a judgment rendered in favor of plaintiff, Capitol City Medical Equipment Company, against Employee in this action on September 20, YR-1, in the amount of $2,742.70 plus interest on the judgment amount at 10% per annum, or $.62 per day, from the date of entry of the judgment to the date of issuance of this writ, plus court costs of $255. Capitol City Medical Equipment Company, Judgment Creditor, makes oath that the Judgment Debtor's last known address is 321 West Cherry Street, Capitol City, Columbiana and the Judgment Creditor's address for mailing any notice required by Columbiana Statutory Code §26-2-204 is 413 Richardson Avenue, Capitol City, Columbiana.

YOU ARE HEREBY COMMANDED to appear in person or by sworn affidavit before the Clerk of the Circuit Court of Capitol County, Columbiana (the "Clerk") within ten (10) days of your receipt of this writ and to then and thereby answer this garnishment under oath as to:

(1) Whether you are or were at the time of this garnishment was issued, indebted to the Employee; if so, how and to what amount;
(2) Whether you have in your possession or under your control any property, debts, or effects belonging to the Employee, at the time of serving this garnishment, or has at the time of answering, or has had at any time between the date of service and the time of answering; if so, the kind and amount;
(3) Whether there are, to such garnishee's knowledge and belief, any and what property, debts, and effects in the possession or under control of any other, and what, person; and
(4) Such other questions as may be put to you by the court or the judgment creditor as may tend to elicit the information sought.

YOU ARE HEREBY FURTHER COMMANDED to calculate the portion of Employee's wages that are payable to the Clerk pursuant to this garnishment as set forth in Columbiana Statutory Code §26-2-205 and to pay said amounts to the Clerk within 30 days of the date of this writ and thereafter as they become due and payable to Employee. THE MAXIMUM PART OF THE AGGREGATE DISPOSABLE EARNINGS OF AN INDIVIDUAL FOR ANY WORK WEEK WHICH IS SUBJECTED TO GARNISHMENT MAY NOT EXCEED:

(A) Twenty-five percent (25%) of his disposable earnings for that week, minus two dollars and fifty cents ($2.50) for each of her dependent children under the age of sixteen (16) who reside in the state of Columbiana as provided in §26-2-102; or
(B) The amount by which her disposable earnings for that week exceed thirty (30) times the federal minimum hourly wage at the time the earnings for any pay period become due and payable, minus two dollars and fifty cents ($2.50) for each of his dependent children under the age of sixteen (16) who reside in the state of Columbiana, whichever is less.

"Disposable earnings" means that part of the earnings of an individual remaining after the deduction from those earnings of any amounts required by law to be withheld.

BE ADVISED that, pursuant to §26-2-207, you are liable for failure to withhold the proper garnishment amount from the Employee's wages and for failure to pay these moneys to the Clerk.

[Clerk's address and signature omitted from illustration.]

Illustration 11-l: TYPICAL STATUTE AUTHORIZING MOTION TO PAY JUDGMENT IN INSTALLMENTS

After any judgment has been rendered in any court and the time to appeal therefrom has elapsed without such an appeal having been made, the judge of the court which rendered the judgment may, either before or after the issuance and service of garnishment, upon written consent of the parties or upon written motion of the judgment debtor, after due notice and after full hearing of such motion, enter an order requiring such judgment debtor to pay to the clerk of the court a certain sum of money weekly, biweekly or monthly to apply upon such judgment. The filing of such motion by the debtor shall stay the issuance, execution or return of any writ of garnishment against wages or salary due the judgment debtor or any other funds belonging to the judgment debtor sought to be substituted to the satisfaction or payment of or upon such judgment during the period that such judgment debtor complies with the order of the court. Such motion of the judgment debtor shall be supported by an affidavit stating the debtor's inability to pay such debt with funds other than those earned by the debtor as wages or salary, or received from other sources in such amounts as to necessitate or make equitable installment payments, the name and address of the debtor's employer, or other source of funds and amount of such wages or salary, and the date of payment thereof.

P-H 11-h: Note that the statute set out in Illustration 11-l allows a judgment debtor to file the motion to pay judgment in installments any time after a final judgment has been entered when no appeal has been made. The judgment debtor does not have to wait to file this motion until after execution has begun. Not all states allow this procedure. Check the statutes of your state. Does it recognize a motion to pay judgment in installments? If so, when can such motion be filed under your state's statute?

If the garnishee fails to respond to the writ of garnishment by answer or appearance or fails to pay over the property or funds as it is obligated to do, many states make the garnishee itself liable to the judgment creditor for either the value of the property that should have been delivered to the court clerk pursuant to the garnishment or for the entire amount of the debt. What happens procedurally is that, upon default by the garnishee, a **conditional judgment** against the garnishee is applied for by the attorney for the judgment creditor and issued by the court. The garnishee then has ten days to request a hearing and **show cause** why the conditional judgment should not be made final. Illustration 11-m sets out a typical statute regarding this aspect of garnishment law.

If more than one garnishment is served on a garnishee for the same debtor, the one served first in time normally will receive priority. Garnishments typically have an effective time limit on them (e.g., six months from date of issue) and may need to be renewed until the judgment is satisfied.

Illustration 11-m: STATE STATUTE REGARDING GARNISHEE'S LIABILITY

If the garnishee fails to timely answer or pay money into court, a conditional judgment may be entered against the garnishee and an order served requiring the garnishee to show cause why the judgment should not be made final. If the garnishee does not show sufficient cause within ten days of service of the order, the conditional judgment shall be made final and a writ of execution may issue against the garnishee for the entire judgment owed to the judgment creditor, plus costs.

C. Enforcing Foreign Judgments (the UEFJA)

Foreign judgment A final judgment entered in a state other than the state in which it is enforced.

What happens if the judgment debtor owns property in a state other than the one in which the final judgment was issued? Can the final judgment in one state be executed on property of the debtor located in another state? Not automatically. In order to execute on property in the other state, the judgment creditor will have to comply with the laws of that state regarding enforcement of a **foreign judgment**. The phrase *foreign judgment* refers to a judgment entered in a state other than the one where enforcement is sought.

EXAMPLE

If CCME obtained its judgment by default against Pearl Murphy in the state of New York and then sought to execute the judgment against property owned by Pearl in South Carolina, the state of South Carolina would consider the New York judgment to be a foreign judgment. To enforce the New York judgment by execution in South Carolina, CCME's attorney will have to comply with the laws of South Carolina with regard to the enforcement of a foreign judgment.

Uniform Enforcement of Foreign Judgments Act (UEFJA) State statute regulating the enforcement in one state of a final judgment entered in another.

Most states have adopted some version of the **Uniform Enforcement of Foreign Judgments Act (UEFJA)**. Those that have not will have their own statutory scheme for enforcing foreign judgments, which may be very different from the procedures of the UEFJA.

Under the UEFJA, the judgment creditor seeking to enforce the foreign judgment must petition a court in the state where enforcement is sought for permission to register the judgment in that state. Normally the court in which the **petition for permission to register foreign judgment** is filed or registered is a **court of record** (a court in which an official record is maintained of its acts and proceedings) in the county where the property to be executed on is located. The petition must be accompanied by an **authentic copy** of the final judgment (i.e., a copy of the final judgment attested to be genuine by the clerk of the court that issued it). Many states require that the petition be **verified** (i.e., sworn by the person signing the petition to allege true facts).

EXAMPLE

Assume that CCME wishes to enforce the final judgment by default taken against Pearl Murphy in the Circuit Court of Columbiana (Illustration 8-g) by executing on property owned by Pearl in another state. The petition for permission to register filed in a court in the state of enforcement might look like what is shown in Illustration 11-n.

The clerk of the court where the petition is filed will issue a summons to be served on the judgment debtor along with a copy of the petition and all exhibits. Typically, no execution can begin on the foreign judgment until the judgment debtor has been served with the summons and petition and has been given some time (e.g., 30 days following service) to file a response raising a defense to the validity of the foreign judgment. The judgment debtor cannot relitigate the underlying debt or liability claim because that was decided by the court that issued the final judgment. The judgment debtor may be in a position to attack the underlying validity of the final judgment, however, by arguing that the court

Illustration 11-n: VERIFIED PETITION FOR PERMISSION TO REGISTER A FOREIGN JUDGMENT [STYLE OF CASE OMITTED FROM ILLUSTRATION]

PETITION SEEKING REGISTRATION OF FOREIGN JUDGMENT

Capitol City Medical Equipment Company, Judgment Creditor, by undersigned counsel, hereby petitions to file a foreign judgment rendered against Judgment Debtor, Pearl E. Murphy, entered in the Circuit Court for Capitol County, State of Columbiana, on September 20, YR-1, and as grounds therefore states as follows:

1. Judgment creditor received a judgment against Judgment Debtor in the Circuit Court for Capitol County, Columbiana on September 20, YR-1, for the principal amount of $2,247.70 plus interest on the judgment amount at 10% per annum, or $.62 per day, from the date of entry of the judgment to the date of issuance of this writ, plus court costs of $255 all of which remains fully unsatisfied. A copy of the authenticated foreign judgment is attached hereto as Exhibit A.

2. The judgment rendered against Judgment Debtor is a valid and final adjudication, remaining in full force in the state of its rendition, and capable of being enforced there by final process.

3. The name and last known post office address of the Judgment Debtor is 321 West Cherry Street, Capitol City, Columbiana.

4. The name and last known post office address of the Judgment Creditor is 413 Richardson Avenue, Capitol City, Columbiana.

Acknowledgement: The statements contained in this Petition Seeking Registration of Foreign Judgment are true to the best of my knowledge, information and belief.

_____

Mark Andrews, Manager
Capitol City Medical Equipment Company

[Notarization form omitted from illustration.]

Subject matter jurisdiction A court's power to hear and decide certain types of cases.

Personal jurisdiction The requirement that it satisfy **due process** for a court to enter a final order binding on a named defendant.

that entered the final decree lacked **subject matter jurisdiction** over the case or **personal jurisdiction** over the debtor as defendant.

If the judgment debtor makes an appearance and contests the enforceability of the foreign judgment, the court will conduct a hearing and decide the dispute. In that event, no execution can begin on the judgment until the dispute is resolved. If the judgment debtor fails to make an appearance following service of the petition in the time allowed, execution normally can commence automatically with no further action by the court. Under the UEFJA, a state court can execute the judgments entered by federal courts sitting in another state as well.

 ## D. ▶ Continuing Execution on a Judgment

Often, a final judgment cannot be immediately satisfied in full by execution. The judgment debtor may not have sufficient nonexempt income or assets that can be located and taken. But, of course, that could always change in the future: The judgment debtor could become employed or better employed, acquire nonexempt assets or receive them by gift or inheritance. And that raises the question of how long the judgment creditor can continue to execute on the judgment.

Illustration 11-o: STATE STATUTE REGARDING TERM OF VIABILITY OF A FINAL JUDGMENT AND THE PROCEDURE FOR EXTENSION OR RENEWAL

Within ten years from entry of a judgment, the judgment creditor whose judgment remains unsatisfied may move the court for an order requiring the judgment debtor to show cause why the judgment should not be extended for an additional ten years. A copy of the order shall be mailed by the judgment creditor to the last known address of the judgment debtor. If sufficient cause is not shown within thirty (30) days of mailing, another order shall be entered extending the judgment for an additional ten years. The same procedure can be repeated within any additional ten-year period until the judgment is satisfied.

States differ in the term of viability granted a final judgment but, whatever the term, the term of enforceability can be renewed or extended if proper procedures are followed. Illustration 11-o sets out a typical statutory term of viability and the procedure for extension or renewal.

Compare the statutory scheme set out in Illustration 11-o with the procedure for renewing a judgment lien as discussed in connection with Illustration 11-d.

 E. ## Claiming an Exemption in Property Executed On

When a garnishment is served on a financial institution, the debtor may have funds on account with the institution that are exempt from execution as discussed in Chapter Ten (e.g., Social Security or child support payments). Or the sheriff may unknowingly seize personal property that the debtor claims as exempt (e.g., tools of the trade) when acting on a writ of execution. Or a judgment lien may attach to real property in which the judgment debtor claims a homestead exemption. The judgment debtor will need to assert his claimed exemption in such property as quickly as possible.

States have different procedures for asserting exemptions in property subject to collection. In some states, the writs of execution or garnishment issued by the court will automatically advise the recipients of property that is exempt from under execution under federal and state law. In some states, the summons with which the defendant/debtor is served at the beginning of a civil action advises the defendant to file a **declaration of exemptions** with the clerk of the court and warns that the exemptions may be waived by failing to do so. In other states the debtor has the opportunity to file the declaration as soon as the final judgment is entered. If a declaration is filed and the clerk of the court is aware of a claimed exemption at the time the writ of execution or garnishment is sought, the writ may specifically exclude the exempted property from the scope of the writ. If the judgment creditor does not agree with the claimed exemption, that creditor must file a motion with the court contesting the claimed exemption.

If no prior declaration of exemptions is allowed or required prior to the time execution is sought on a final judgment, or if the debtor could have but did not previously file a declaration and has not been deemed to have waived it, the debtor must file a **motion to claim exempt property**. At the hearing on the motion, the parties can be heard over whether the exemption is properly claimed. Illustration 11-p sets out the approved form in North Carolina for filing a motion to claim exempt property.

Illustration 11-p: NORTH CAROLINA FORM FOR MOTION TO CLAIM EXEMPT PROPERTY

(TYPE OR PRINT IN BLACK INK) **STATE OF NORTH CAROLINA** _____ County	**File No.**	**Abstract No.**
	Judgment Docket Book And Page No.	
	Date Judgment Filed	

In The General Court Of Justice
☐ District   ☐ Superior Court Division

Name Of Judgment Creditor (Plaintiff)

VERSUS

Name Of Judgment Debtor (Defendant)

**MOTION TO CLAIM
EXEMPT PROPERTY
(STATUTORY EXEMPTIONS)**
(Use if judgment filed after 1/1/06)

G.S. 1C-1603(c)

NOTE TO JUDGMENT DEBTOR: *The Clerk of Superior Court cannot fill out this form for you. If you need assistance, you should talk with an attorney.* **THERE ARE CERTAIN EXEMPTIONS UNDER STATE AND FEDERAL LAW THAT YOU ARE ENTITLED TO CLAIM IN ADDITION TO THE EXEMPTIONS LISTED BELOW.** *These exemptions may include social security, unemployment, and workers' compensation benefits and earnings for your personal services rendered within the last 60 days. There is available to you a prompt procedure for challenging an attachment or levy on your property.*
You must pay $20 to the Clerk of Superior Court to file this document. Payment can be made in cash, cashier's check or money order. If you cannot afford to pay this fee you can apply to the Clerk to file as an indigent by completing form "PETITION TO SUE/APPEAL/FILE MOTIONS" AOC-G-106.

I, the undersigned, move to set aside the property claimed below as exempt.

1. I am a citizen and resident of _____ .
2. ☐ a. I am married to _____ .
   ☐ b. I am not married.
3. My current address is _____ .
4. The following persons are dependent on me for support:

Name(s) Of Person(s) Dependent On Me	Age	Relationship

5. I wish to claim as exempt *(keep from being taken)* my interest in the following real or personal property, or in a cooperative that owns property, that I use as a residence. I also wish to claim my interest in the following burial plots for myself or my dependents. I understand that my total interest claimed in the residence and burial plots may not exceed $35,000.00 except that if I am unmarried and am 65 years of age or older, I am entitled to claim a total exemption in the residence and burial plots not to exceed $60,000.00 so long as the property was previously owned by me as a tenant by the entireties or as a joint tenant with rights of survivorship, and the former co-owner of the property is deceased.

Street Address Of Residence

County Where Property Located	*Township*	*No. By Which Tax Assessor Identifies Property*

Legal Description (Attach a copy of your deed or other instrument of conveyance or describe property in as much detail as possible. Attach additional sheets if necessary.)
☐ I am unmarried and 65 years of age or older and this property was previously owned by me as a tenant by entireties or as a joint tenant with rights of survivorship and the former co-owner of the property is deceased.

Name(s) Of Owner(s) Of Record Of Residence	*Estimated Value Of Residence (What You Think You Could Sell It For)* $

AOC-CV-415, Page 1 of 4, Rev. 8/11
© 2011 Administrative Office of the Courts

(Over)

Amount Of Lien(s) And Name(s) And Address(es) Of Lienholder(s): *(How much money is owed on the property and to whom)*	Current Amount Owed
	$
	$
Location Of Burial Plots Claimed	*Value Of Burial Plots Claimed*
	$

6. I wish to claim the following personal property consisting of household furnishings, household goods, wearing apparel, appliances, books, animals, crops or musical instruments as exempt from the claims of my creditors *(in other words, keep them from being taken from me)*. These items of personal property are held primarily for my personal, family or household use.

   I understand that I am entitled to personal property worth the sum of $5,000.00. I understand I am also entitled to an additional $1,000.00 for each person dependent upon me for support, but not to exceed $4,000.00 for dependents. I further understand that I am entitled to this amount after deducting from the value of the property the amount of any valid lien or security interest. Property purchased within ninety (90) days of this proceeding may not be exempt. *(Some examples of household goods would be TV, appliances, furniture, clothing, radios, record players.)*

Item Of Property	Fair Market Value *(What You Could Sell It For)*	Amount Of Lien Or Security Interest *(Amount Owed On Property)*	Name(s) Of Lienholder(s) *(To Whom Money Is Owed)*	Value Of Debtor's (Defendant's) Interest *(Fair Market Value Less Amount Owed)*
	$	$		$
	$	$		$
	$	$		$

7. I wish to claim my interest in the following motor vehicle as exempt from the claims of my creditors. I understand that I am entitled to my interest in one motor vehicle worth the sum of $3,500.00 after deduction of any valid liens or security interests. I understand that a motor vehicle purchased within ninety (90) days of this proceeding may not be exempt.

Make And Model	*Year*	*Name Of Title Owner Of Record*
Fair Market Value (What You Could Sell It For) $		*Name Of Lienholder(s) Of Record (Person(s) To Whom Money Is Owed)*
Amount Of Liens (Amount Owed) $		*Value Of Debtor's (Defendant's) Interest (Fair Market Value Less Amount Owed)* $

8. (This item is to claim any other property you own that you wish to exempt.) I wish to claim the following property as exempt because I claimed residential real or personal property as exempt that is worth less than $35,000.00, or I made no claim for a residential exemption under section (5) above. I understand that I am entitled to an exemption of up to $5,000.00 on any property only if I made no claim under section (5) or a claim that was less than $35,000.00 under Section (5). I understand that I am entitled to claim any unused amount that I was permitted to take under section (5) up to a maximum of $5,000.00 in any property. *(Examples: If you claim $34,000 under section (5), $1,000 allowed here; if you claim $30,000 under section (5), $5,000 allowed here; if you claim $35,000 under section (5), no claim allowed here.)* I further understand that the amount of my claim under this section is after the deduction from the value of this property of the amount of any valid lien or security interests and that tangible personal property purchased within ninety (90) days of this proceeding may not be exempt.

Item Of Personal Property Claimed	Fair Market Value	Amount Of Lien(s)	Name(s) Of Lienholder(s)	Value Of Debtor's (Defendant's) Interest
	$	$		$
	$	$		$
	$	$		$
	$	$		$

Real Property Claimed   *(I understand that if I wish to claim more than one parcel, I must attach additional pages setting forth the following information for each parcel claimed as exempt.)*

Street Address	*Estimated Value Of Property (What You Could Sell It For)* $
County Where Property Located	*Township*	*No. By Which Tax Assessor Identifies Property*

Description (Attach a copy of your deed or other instrument of conveyance or describe the property in as much detail as possible.)

AOC-CV-415, Page 2 of 4, Rev. 8/11
© 2011 Administrative Office of the Courts

VERSUS	File No.		Abstract No.
Name Of Judgment Creditor (Plaintiff)	Judgment Docket Book And Page No.		Date Judgment Filed

Name And Address Of Lienholder	Current Amount Owed $
Name And Address Of Lienholder	Current Amount Owed $

(Attach additional sheets for more lienholders.)

9. I wish to claim the following items of health care aid *(wheelchairs, hearing aids, etc.)* necessary for ☐ myself ☐ my dependents.

Item	Purpose

10. I wish to claim the following implements, professional books, or tools (not to exceed $2,000.00), of my trade or the trade of my dependent. I understand such property purchased within ninety (90) days of this proceeding may not be exempt.

Item	Estimated Value (What You Could Sell It For)	What Business Or Trade Used In
	$	
	$	
	$	

11. I wish to claim the following life insurance policies whose sole beneficiaries are my spouse and/or my children as exempt.

Name Of Insurer	Policy Number	Beneficiary(ies)

12. I wish to claim as exempt the following compensation that I received or to which I am entitled for the personal injury of myself or a person upon whom I was dependent for support, including compensation from a private disability policy or an annuity, or compensation that I received for the death of a person upon whom I was dependent for support. I understand that this compensation is not exempt from claims for funeral, legal, medical, dental, hospital or health care charges related to the accident or injury that resulted in the payment of the compensation to me. *(Add additional sheets if more than one amount of compensation.)*

Amount Of Compensation $	Method Of Payment Lump Sum Or Installments (If Installments, State Amount, Frequency And Duration Of Payments)
Location/Source Of Compensation	

13. I wish to claim my individual retirement accounts, including Roth accounts, and individual retirement annuities (IRA's) that are listed below.

Name Of Custodian Of IRA Account	Type Of Account	Account Number
Name Of Custodian Of IRA Account	Type Of Account	Account Number

14. I wish to claim the following funds I hold in a college savings plan that is qualified under section 529 of the Internal Revenue Code, not to exceed $25,000.00. I understand that the plan must be for my child and must actually be used for the child's college expenses. I understand that I may not exempt any funds I placed in this account within the preceding 12 months, except to the extent that any contributions were made in the ordinary course of my financial affairs and were consistent with my past pattern of contributions.

College Savings Plan	Account Number	Value	Name(s) Of Child(ren) Beneficiaries
		$	
		$	

(Over)

AOC-CV-415, Page 3 of 4, Rev. 8/11
© 2011 Administrative Office of the Courts

15. I wish to claim the following retirement benefits to which I am entitled under the retirement plans of other states and governmental units of other states. I understand that these benefits are exempt only to the extent these benefits are exempt under the law of the state or governmental unit under which the benefit plan was established.

State/Governmental Unit	Name of Retirement Plan	Identifying Number

16. I wish to claim as exempt any alimony, support, separate maintenance, or child support payments or funds that I have received or that I am entitled to receive. I understand that these payments are exempt only to the extent that they are reasonably necessary for my support or for the support of a person dependent on me for support.

Type Of Support	Person Paying Support	Amount Of Support	Location Of Funds
		$	
		$	

17. The following is a complete listing of my property which I do **NOT** claim as exempt.

Item	Location	Estimated Value
		$
		$
		$

18. I certify that the above statements are true.

Date	Signature Of Judgment Debtor/Attorney For Debtor (Defendant)

19. A copy of this Motion was served on the judgment creditor (plaintiff) by: ☐ delivering a copy to the judgment creditor (plaintiff) personally ☐ delivering a copy to _____ , the judgment creditor's attorney. ☐ depositing a copy of this Motion in a post-paid properly addressed envelope in a post office, addressed to the judgment creditor (plaintiff) at the address shown on the notice of rights served on me. ☐ depositing a copy of this motion in a post-paid properly addressed envelope in a post office, addressed to the judgment creditor's (plaintiff's) attorney at the following address: _____

Date	Address And Phone Number Of Attorney For Debtor (Defendant)
Signature Of Judgment Debtor/Attorney For Debtor (Defendant)	

> **P-H 11-i:**   Locate the statute or rule governing the procedure for claiming property to be exempt from execution in your state. How is it done there?

CONCLUSION

At this point, we have learned how debt is created (Part A of the text) and how debt is collected (Part B of the text). Now it is time to turn our attention to how debt is reorganized or discharged in a bankruptcy proceeding.

CHAPTER SUMMARY

Formal discovery may be utilized postjudgment to aid the judgment creditor in locating assets on which to execute in satisfaction of the judgment. Discovery in aid of execution may also be compelled from third persons using the subpoena powers of the court, ordering the third person to appear and give deposition testimony or to produce documents and things. The contempt powers of the court are available to compel compliance of the debtor and third persons with postjudgment discovery.

A final judgment may be executed on in a number of ways. A judgment lien is created by filing, registering, or recording a certified copy of the final judgment in the appropriate public office. The lien so created attaches to all the real property owned or later acquired by the debtor and located in the county where the filing occurred. The judgment lien creates a cloud on the property to which it attaches and may be enforced by judicial foreclosure. Once the underlying judgment is satisfied, a satisfaction of lien will be filed or recorded, effectively extinguishing the lien. In some states a judgment lien attaches to the personal property of the debtor as well. A writ of execution, or writ of *fieri facias*, is a court order directing the sheriff or other public official to seize and sell the personal property of the named debtor. In some states the writ also authorizes the seizure of the debtor's real property but that right may be subject to the marshalling of assets rule, which dictates the priority order in which property may be seized and sold (e.g., all nonexempt personal property must exhausted before real property may be seized). Property seized pursuant to the writ is subject to a lien of levy in favor of the judicial lien creditor, which lien will have priority over most subsequent secured claims to the property except as to prior perfected claims to it. Property levied on is sold by the sheriff at a public or private sale and proceeds are applied first to the expenses seizure and sale, then to court costs, and then to the balance of the final judgment. A writ of garnishment is a court order directed at third persons such as employers or banks holding property of the debtor and instructing the garnishee to pay over some or all such property to the clerk of the court for distribution to the judgment creditor.

Final judgments entered in one state can be enforced against the property of the debtor in another state pursuant to the Uniform Enforcement of Foreign Judgments Act (UEFJA). A motion for permission to register final judgment is filed in the appropriate court of the enforcing state, together with a certified copy of the foreign judgment. The debtor is served with a copy of the petition and has a set number of days following service to contest the validity of the judgment to be enforced or the jurisdiction of the enforcing court over the debtor but may not contest the validity of the underlying debt. If the debtor fails to contest or contests and loses, execution can then issue from the enforcing court as if it had entered the final judgment itself. Every state has procedures for extending the term of enforceability of a final judgment.

REVIEW QUESTIONS

1. What are the three most common methods of formal discovery used in aid of execution? Of the three, which one is probably most commonly used?
2. List as many different types of questions as you can recall that might be asked in interrogatories by a creditor seeking assets of a debtor on which to execute.
3. Explain what a judgment lien is. How is it obtained? How is it enforced? How is it terminated?
4. How is a writ of execution obtained? How is it executed and by whom? What property can be seized pursuant to a writ and how does the marshalling of assets doctrine affect the seizure of property?
5. What priority, if any, does a lien of levy have over other secured claims to the property levied on? What priority does it have over unsecured claims to the property levied on? If the sheriff receives two writs of execution arising from two final judgments and both writs direct her to seize the same property, which writ has priority?
6. How is a writ of garnishment obtained? Who are the two most common recipients of writs of garnishment?
7. Describe the duty of the garnishee in responding to a writ of garnishment. What risks are there for a garnishee who fails to respond to the writ of garnishment as ordered?
8. Summarize the procedure for enforcing a foreign judgment under the UEFJA.
9. What defenses might a judgment debtor be unable to raise in an action against him to enforce a final foreign judgment? What defenses might he be able to raise?
10. What is the typical procedure required to extend the enforceable life of a final judgment? Typically, how often must this be done?

WORDS AND PHRASES TO REMEMBER

authentic (or authenticated) copy
bank garnishment
bench warrant
body attachment
bona fide purchaser for value
capias
certified copy

cloud on title
conditional judgment
contempt (of court)
debtor's prison
declaration of exemptions
depositions
discovery in aid of execution

disposable income
document requests
foreclose
filing
foreign judgment
garnishee
interrogatories
involuntary lien
judicial foreclosure
judicial lien creditor
judgment lien
levy
lien of levy
marshalling of assets
motion to claim exempt property
motion to pay judgment
    in installments
nulla bona
notice of garnishment
notice of levy
order of extension
order of sale
pay or appear
personal jurisdiction

petition for permission to register
    foreign judgment
postjudgment asset
    discovery
power of sale
private sale
recording
release of lien
registering
sheriff
sheriff's sale
show cause
slow pay motion
subpoena
subject matter jurisdiction
termination statement
Uniform Enforcement of Foreign
    Judgments Act (UEFJA)
U.S. Marshall
wage garnishment
writ of execution
writ of *fieri facias*
writ of garnishment

TO LEARN MORE: A number of TLM activities to accompany this chapter are accessible on the student disc accompanying the text and on the Author Updates link to the text Web site at http://www.aspenparalegaled.com/ books/parsons_abcdebt/default.asp.

THE DISCHARGE OR REORGANIZATION OF DEBT IN BANKRUPTCY

Introduction

In the third and final part of the text we look at the U.S. Bankruptcy Code, which is found in Title 11 of the U.S. Code and which will, for the most part, be referred to as the **Bankruptcy Code** or just the **Code** (e.g., "§547 of the Code" instead of "11 U.S.C. §547"). The Code was enacted pursuant to Article I, §8, of the U.S. Constitution, which states that "Congress shall have the power to establish uniform laws on the subject of bankruptcies throughout the United States."

Discharge
Permanent relief from debt pursuant to order of the bankruptcy court.

The Bankruptcy Code should be seen as a formal system of *compulsory debt adjustment* that seeks to balance the interests of both the debtor and his creditors. The interests of the debtor seeking bankruptcy relief are 1) to stop or at least delay debt collection efforts of creditors and then 2) to obtain some form of long-term, court-sanctioned debt relief, which may take the form of either the permanent **discharge** of some or all the debt or the **reorganization** of the debt obligations to make them more manageable for the debtor. When a debtor files for bankruptcy relief, the primary concern of creditors is to obtain payment of as much of the debt as possible as quickly as possible. The Code then is best understood as a statutory scheme created by Congress to regulate and balance these competing interests and, ideally, to produce a workable result that is palatable (if only barely sometimes) to both debtors and creditors.

In Part C you will become familiar with the various players in the bankruptcy process, the different types of bankruptcy proceedings permitted by the Code, and the governing rules, procedures, and forms used in bankruptcy cases. As in Parts A and B, we will utilize realistic case studies to learn the bankruptcy process. But first let's take a brief look at how our current bankruptcy laws came to be.

Chapter Twelve:

 # Introduction to Bankruptcy

Think what you do when you run in debt;
you give to another power over your liberty.

—*Benjamin Franklin*

A. ▶ A Brief History of Debt Relief and Bankruptcy Laws

Fresh start The opportunity provided to a debtor following a discharge in bankruptcy.

A fundamental premise underlying modern American bankruptcy law is that, in certain circumstances, debtors are entitled to some form of relief from their debts that will provide them with a **fresh start**. As stated by the U.S. Supreme Court:

> [I]t gives to the honest but unfortunate debtor . . . a new opportunity in life and a clear field for future effort, unhampered by the pressure and discouragement of preexisting debt. *Local Loan Co. v. Hunt*, 292 U.S. 234, 244 (1934).

The basic human compassion in that premise is moderated by a second fundamental premise underlying our laws: One who incurs a debt ought to pay it. Striking the balance between these two premises has never been easy or simple. Not all human societies have even attempted to strike such a balance. Look through the timeline set out in Illustration 12-a to get an idea of the ebb and flow of attitudes and practices toward debt punishment/forgiveness.

Illustration 12-a: TIMELINE OF DEBT PUNISHMENT/FORGIVENESS ATTITUDES AND PRACTICES

> **1600 B.C.E.**—*Clean Slate* proclamations by kings of ancient Babylon mandate the periodic restoration of land that had been pledged as security for debt and lost for nonpayment and occasionally forgive individual private debt.
>
> **1400 B.C.E.**—Moses' law mandates a *Sabbatical Year* every seven years, when all debts are to be forgiven. At the end of every seventh Sabbatical Year (thought to be every 50th year) a *Year of Jubilee* is declared when debts are forgiven, slaves freed, and land taken for nonpayment of debt is returned to former owners or their heirs (other than the houses of laypersons within walled cities). These practices are discontinued following the Babylonian captivity in the sixth century BCE.

1000 B.C.E.—By this time, credit arrangements are firmly established as basis of commerce by and among Assyria, Babylon, and Egypt.

500 B.C.E.—Ancient Greece has no bankruptcy relief laws. Debtors, their families, or servants can be imprisoned or sold into slavery as *debt slaves*. Crises sometimes develop when a good portion of the farming class is in jail or enslaved and there aren't enough workers to tend the crops. Accordingly, some, but not all, Greek city-states limit the term of debt slavery to five years and protect them from severe abuse (*protection of life and limb*).

250 B.C.E.—In the days of the Roman Republic, debtors, or their families or servants, can be sold into slavery, imprisoned, and even killed by creditors. (It is said that in Roman times, creditors not only divided the debtor's property, but they also took him to the public plaza and bodily divided him!)

100 C.E.—Under the Caesars, the Roman Empire adopts some debt collection laws, including the appointment of a trustee to sell off a merchant debtor's assets after the merchant ceases business still owing money. The merchant's trade bench or selling counter is destroyed to publicly announce his failure, literally *banca rotta* (broken bench), which may be the source of our modern word, *bankruptcy*. The trustee is called the *curator bonorum* (caretaker) of the debtor's property for the benefit of creditors.

1285—England's *Statute of Merchants* allows imprisonment of merchant debtors.

1542—The state of being bankrupt is made an official crime in England, mandating a hearing before the chancellor, and is punishable by confiscation of property and imprisonment.

1570—Under Queen Elizabeth I of England, the first official bankruptcy law is passed by Parliament. It is exclusively a creditor's device, involuntary for the debtor. The creditor can formally declare a merchant bankrupt and seek official relief, including confiscation of property, imprisonment, and corporal punishment, the last of which could include having the debtor pilloried (a form of public humiliation by having hands and head locked in place by wooden stock) or having an ear cut off. In Padua, Italy, the bankrupt is required to appear nearly naked, in the Palace of Justice and to slap his buttocks three times against "The Rock of Shame" while loudly proclaiming, "I declare bankruptcy!"

1705—England's *Statute of Queen Anne* marks the first attempt at a humane reform of bankruptcy law. At the request of the debtor and with creditors' consent, debt can be discharged following liquidation of assets. The death penalty for the debtor is allowed for committing fraud in bankruptcy but is only known to have been enforced five times.

1788—The U.S. Constitution is ratified, including Article I, §8, which authorizes Congress "[t]o establish . . . uniform laws on the subject of bankruptcies throughout the United States." In its first session, Congress considers adopting a bankruptcy law but demurs. Without federal rules, states follow their colonial practices based on English precedent, including imprisonment and pillorying.

1800—The Panic of 1797 in America leads to the imprisonment of thousands of debtors by the states, including the "Financier of the Revolution," Robert Morris. As a result, Congress passes the first federal bankruptcy law. It allows only creditors to declare a person bankrupt. Debts can be discharged after liquidation of the debtor's assets if they have been cooperative and two-thirds of their creditors consent. Repealed in 1803.

1833—Federal imprisonment for debt is abolished in the United States by act of Congress (now 28 U.S.C. §2007). Individual states begin to follow suit.

1841—The economic depression of 1837 results in Congress passing its second bankruptcy law, which for the first time permits debtors, including non-merchants, to voluntarily file for bankruptcy relief. Due to high administrative costs, questions of constitutionality, and the discontent of creditors, the law is repealed in 1843.

1867—Following the turmoil of the Civil War, northern creditors want a system to collect from southern debtors. Congress passes a third bankruptcy law to enable them to do so, but it is repealed in 1878, again due to high administrative costs, an unwieldly bureaucracy, and little return to creditors.

Bankruptcy Act The predecessor of the current Bankruptcy Code. Enacted in 1898 and superseded in 1978.

1898—The economic panic of 1893 results in passage of the landmark Nelson Act, initiating the modern effort to balance debtor/creditor interests. The law, formally called the **Bankruptcy Act**, acknowledges the new credit economy, provides for a debtor-initiated discharge of debts, allows debtors to keep significant exempt property, and establishes the **bankruptcy referee** (predecessor of the modern bankruptcy judge) as the designated officer of the U.S. district court to administer the law.

Bankruptcy referee Office created under Bankruptcy Act of 1898. Predecessor to the modern bankruptcy judge.

1938—The Chandler Act amends the existing Bankruptcy Act to allow reorganizations in bankruptcy for both individual and business debtors (today known as Chapter 13 and Chapter 11 bankruptcies, respectively), enabling debtors with the means to repay all or a part of their debts under court supervision as an alternative to liquidation. For the first time, bankruptcy becomes a viable option to achieve economic survival rather than the failure of liquidation.

1950—The first modern or "universal" credit card, the Diners' Club card, is introduced, accelerating the expansion of consumer debt.

Bankruptcy Reform Act The 1978 statute that introduced the current Code. Also the name of the 1994 statute that amended the Code.

1978—The **Bankruptcy Reform Act** substantially rewrites the nation's bankruptcy law. Now formally known as the **Bankruptcy Code**, the law contains the current chapter numbering (Chapter 7, Chapter 13, Chapter 11, etc.), bankruptcy judges are given expanded judicial powers to administer bankruptcy cases, Chapter 11 business reorganizations are made more feasible, and states are given the option to "opt out" of the Code's property exemptions and apply their own exemption laws instead.

1982—The U.S. Supreme Court decides *Northern Pipeline Construction Co. v. Marathon Pipeline Co.*, 458 U.S. 50 (1982), declaring the Bankruptcy Reform Act of 1978 unconstitutional. The court rules that Congress had overstepped its bounds in granting bankruptcy judges, created under Article I of the Constitution, powers of Article III judges in administering the Code. The court grants Congress a grace period to amend the Bankruptcy Reform Act to cure the defect.

1984—The Bankruptcy Amendments and Federal Judgeship Act finally addresses the *Marathon* decision, reconstituting bankruptcy courts and judges as units of the U.S. district courts, with bankruptcy proceedings officially "referred" to bankruptcy courts under the standing orders of the district courts.

1986—The Code is amended to create the Chapter 12 proceeding for family farmers with regular income on a test basis and to make permanent the U.S. Trustee system to help administer bankruptcy cases, a system that had been tested on a pilot basis since 1978.

1994—The **Bankruptcy Reform Act of 1994** contains provisions to clarify when bankruptcy courts can conduct jury trials, to expedite bankruptcy proceedings, to encourage individual debtors to use Chapter 13 to reschedule their debts rather than Chapter 7 to liquidate, and to aid creditors in recovering claims against bankrupt estates.

1996—For the first time ever, one million Americans file for bankruptcy in a single year.

2005—After over a decade of study and debate, Congress passes the **Bankruptcy Abuse Prevention and Consumer Protection Act (BAPCPA)**, which is intended to reduce the number of bankruptcies and encourage repayment by making it more difficult to file for Chapter 7 liquidation relief and to force more debtors to file for Chapter 13. The Chapter 12 family farmer proceeding is made permanent and expanded to include family fishermen. The Chapter 15 proceeding is added to provide a mechanism for dealing with bankruptcy proceedings across international borders.

2011—The U.S. Supreme Court decides *Stern v. Marshall*, 131 S. Ct. 2594 (2011), reviving *Marathon* concerns over constitutional power of Article 1 bankruptcy courts to decide core proceedings.

B.   An Overview of the Bankruptcy Code and the Types of Bankruptcy Proceedings

Illustration 12-b lists and identifies the subject matter of each chapter of the Code. Three of these chapters contain definitional, administrative, and procedural types of rules (Chapters 1, 3, and 5), while six of them set forth specific types of bankruptcy cases that qualifying debtors can file (Chapters 7, 9, 11, 12, 13, and 15). We use the Code's chapter designation to identify and describe the type of bankruptcy case that a debtor files (e.g., 1 "He filed a Chapter 7 case.").

Illustration 12-b: THE CHAPTERS OF THE BANKRUPTCY CODE

Chapter 1—General Provisions
Chapter 3—Case Administration
Chapter 5—Creditors, the Debtor, and the Estate
Chapter 7—Liquidation
Chapter 9—Adjustment of Debts of a Municipality
Chapter 11—Reorganization
Chapter 12—Adjustment of Debts of a Family Farmer or Fisherman with Regular Annual Income
Chapter 13—Adjustment of Debts of an Individual with Regular Income
Chapter 15—Ancillary and Other Cross-Border Cases

EXAMPLE

> If Abe Mendoza (Case Study #2; see Illustration 1-b) found it necessary to file a liquidation type bankruptcy proceeding under Chapter 7 of the Code, we would say that he has "filed a Chapter 7" or he is "in Chapter 7." If Nick and Pearl Murphy (Case Study #1; see Illustration 1-a) elected to file a Chapter 13 case as individuals with regular income seeking, not liquidation, but merely an adjustment of their debts, we would say that they have "filed a Chapter 13" or that they are "in Chapter 13." If Tomorrow Today, Inc. (TTI) (Case Study #3; see Illustration 1-c) elected to file a Chapter 11 case seeking to reorganize its debts in bankruptcy, we would say that it "filed a Chapter 11" or it is "in Chapter 11."

Illustration 12-c sets forth a brief summary of each of the six different types of bankruptcy proceeding authorized by the Code.

The vast majority of bankruptcy cases filed today are Chapter 7 liquidations or Chapter 13 reorganizations for individuals with regular income. Next in frequency come Chapter 11 business reorganization proceedings, followed by Chapter 12 family farmer/ fisherman proceedings. Chapter 9 municipality filings are, fortunately, very rare, as are Chapter 15 cross-border cases in most jurisdictions, although those can be expected to increase over time. Consequently, the text focuses on Chapter 7, 13, and 11 cases. Because a Chapter 12 proceeding is so similar to a Chapter 13, we consider it in connection with our study of Chapter 13.

Illustration 12-d contains a brief summary of the definitional, administrative, and procedural chapters of the Code. In general, the provisions in these chapters apply to all six types of bankruptcy proceedings summarized in Illustration 12-c.

P-H 12-a: To become more familiar with the chapters of the Code dealing with definitional, administrative, and procedural matters, consult the Code and find the answers to the following questions. (If you don't have a paper copy of the Code you can access it online from Cornell Law School's Legal Information Institute at www.law.cornell.edu/uscode/html/uscode11/usc_-sup_01_11.html.) Find these answers and indicate the specific Code provision (e.g., §101(2)) that provides the answer. The table of contents at the beginning of each Code chapter might be a good place to start to locate the answers quickly.

- Consult the definitions in Chapter 1 of the Code to determine who qualifies as a "family farmer" for purposes of filing a Chapter 12 bankruptcy case.
- Consult the section in Chapter 1 of the Code controlling who can be a debtor to determine if a railroad can file for bankruptcy relief under the Code.
- Consult Chapter 3 of the Code to determine what has to be filed to commence a voluntary case.
- Consult Chapter 5 of the Code to determine whether the Code contains a prohibition of the debtor making a fraudulent transfer of property.

Illustration 12-c: BRIEF SUMMARY OF THE SIX TYPES OF BANKRUPTCY PROCEEDINGS

Liquidation proceeding The sale or other disposition of a debtor's nonexempt assets for the purpose of distribution to his creditors in exchange for a discharge of most unpaid debt.

A **Chapter 7 bankruptcy** is a **liquidation proceeding**. All of the debtor's non-exempt property is turned over to a *bankruptcy trustee* appointed by the **bankruptcy court** administering the case. The bankruptcy trustee will sell (thus the "liquidation") that property and distribute the proceeds to the various creditors of the Chapter 7 debtor based on claims they have filed with the court and which the trustee will have reviewed and verified. The debtor thus loses all her property that is nonexempt in the liquidation proceeding, but in exchange she gets a permanent **discharge** from future liability for most (but not all, as we shall see) of the debts that remain unpaid. Chapter 7 is the classic **fresh start**, or **clean slate**, bankruptcy.

Reorganization proceeding The rearrangement of a debtor's finances under a court approved plan as an alternative to liquidation.

A **Chapter 11 bankruptcy** is not a liquidation proceeding like a Chapter 7. Instead it is a **reorganization proceeding** designed for a business. In a Chapter 11, the debtor (or his creditors) will propose a **plan of reorganization** pursuant to which, if it is approved by the bankruptcy court, the debtor will restructure the debts and sometimes the assets of its business and repay some or all of its debts out of future income. Some debt may be liquidated as part of the reorganization. A Chapter 11 reorganization plan can run up to five years.

A **Chapter 13 bankruptcy** is also a reorganization proceeding, but Chapter 13 is designed not for a business, like Chapter 11, but for an "individual with regular income." The individual debtor will propose a **Chapter 13 plan** for court approval. If the plan is approved, the debtor will use income received during the plan to pay off all or part of her debts. Some debt may be liquidated as part of the reorganization.

A **Chapter 9 bankruptcy** is designed specifically for "municipalities," which are defined in §101(40) of the Code to include political subdivisions of a state such as cities, counties, towns, villages, and public agencies or instrumentalities of a state such as taxing districts, municipal districts, school districts, or public utilities. This is a highly specialized type of bankruptcy and, fortunately, one that very rarely occurs.

Ancillary proceeding A bankruptcy case filed in a bankruptcy court in the United States that is related to the primary case filed in another country.

A **Chapter 12 bankruptcy** proceeding is a reorganization proceeding designed for debtors who qualify as **family farmers** or **family fishermen**. It is very similar to a Chapter 13 proceeding but not so frequently used.

Cross-border cases A bankruptcy case involving debtors, assets, and creditors in more than one country.

A **Chapter 15 bankruptcy** proceeding is a special **ancillary proceeding** filed in a bankruptcy court in the United States after the primary proceeding has been commenced in a foreign country. It provides mechanisms for dealing with insolvency cases involving debtors, assets, and creditors in more than one country (**cross-border cases**) and allows adjudication of those interests located in the United States.

Illustration 12-d: BRIEF SUMMARY OF THE DEFINITIONAL, ADMINISTRATIVE, AND PROCEDURAL CHAPTERS OF THE CODE

- Chapter 1 of the Code contains general provisions, definitions, and rules of construction that govern the bankruptcy case.
- Chapter 3 of the Code sets out the procedures for commencing the bankruptcy case and administering it.
- Chapter 5 of the Code contains specific provisions pertaining to the rights and responsibilities of the debtor and creditors in the bankruptcy case, as well as indicating what property is to be included in the bankruptcy estate.

C. Distinguishing Between Consumer and Business Bankruptcy Cases

Debtor in bankruptcy A person who files a petition under the Code.

Business bankruptcy case A bankruptcy case in which the debtor is an entity or an individual with primarily business debts.

Consumer bankruptcy case A bankruptcy case in which the debtor is an individual with primarily *consumer debts.*

Consumer debt Debt incurred for personal, family, or household purposes.

Both individuals and business entities that file for bankruptcy relief are properly referred to as the **debtor** or the **debtor in bankruptcy** under the Code (see §§101(13) and (41)). Organizations that compile statistics regarding annual bankruptcy filings (e.g., the American Bankruptcy Institute and the Administrative Office of the Federal Courts; see Illustration 13-k) commonly distinguish between **business bankruptcy cases** and **consumer** (or *nonbusiness*) **bankruptcy cases.** There is no formal definition of these particular terms in the Code, and it is the clerks of the bankruptcy courts who subjectively designate each case filed in their courts as a business or consumer bankruptcy. In general, though, business bankruptcies include cases filed by business entities (corporations, including limited liability companies, and partnerships) or individuals engaged in business as sole proprietors, whereas consumer bankruptcies include cases filed by individuals with primarily **consumer debt** defined in Code §101(8) as "debt incurred by an individual primarily for a personal, family, or household purpose." Most business bankruptcy cases tend to be Chapter 7 liquidations or Chapter 11 reorganizations; most consumer bankruptcies tend to be Chapter 7 liquidations or Chapter 13 reorganizations. But the distinction between a business bankruptcy and a consumer bankruptcy can become cloudy.

EXAMPLE

The sole proprietor of a business may file individually for Chapter 13 or even Chapter 11 relief to manage his business debts. Should the sole proprietor's filing be designated a consumer case or a business case? Or the shareholder of a corporation may place her corporation in a Chapter 11 and then file a Chapter 7 individually to discharge business debts she has personally guaranteed. Should the individual Chapter 7 be considered a consumer case or a business case?

From the debtor's standpoint, consumer bankruptcies tend to be handled by a different set of lawyers than business bankruptcies. Chapter 7 and 13 consumer cases tend to involve relatively few assets, routine procedures, and produce low fees per case for the debtor's attorney. Consumer debtor attorneys must therefore handle a large volume of cases in order to prosper. Chapter 7 and 11 business cases tend to involve substantially more assets, more creditor claims, and more complex issues. In particular, Chapter 11 filings are more complicated and time consuming and the attorney's fees are consequently more substantial. Today, approximately 95 percent of annual filings are categorized as consumer cases. Though business bankruptcies constitute only about 5 percent of the total filings in most federal districts, they dominate a large segment of the court's time and produce substantial fees for the attorneys involved, including the debtor's attorney.

The **National Association of Consumer Bankruptcy Attorneys** caters to attorneys involved in consumer cases. The **Commercial Law League of America** caters to attorneys involved in business cases. And the **American Bankruptcy Institute** caters to everyone involved in the bankruptcy process. (See Illustration 13-k.)

EXAMPLE

In consumer cases, Code provisions regarding property exemptions are always important as the individual debtor struggles to hold on to as much property as possible, whereas they play little or no role in business cases. In contrast, the bankruptcy trustee's power to avoid prepetition property transfers and reclaim that property for the estate (a topic to be considered in detail later) is almost always critical in business cases but only rarely plays a significant role in consumer cases.

D. ▶ Who Files for Consumer Bankruptcy Relief and Why

The three leading causes of consumer bankruptcies (including Chapter 7 and 13 filings) are sudden job loss or downsizing, unexpected medical expenses, and divorce or separation. More than 90 percent of persons filing consumer bankruptcies fall into one of the three categories. People with children at home are nearly three times as likely to file bankruptcy as people with no children. A single woman raising a child alone is more than four times as likely to file bankruptcy as a single woman with no children. Divorced fathers also file with much greater frequency than men with no children. Unmanageable prescription drug expenses and other medical costs are a primary reason that older Americans file for relief. More than one-half of Chapter 7 cases filed by Americans of all ages involve excessive medical bills (see Illustration 12-e).

The easy availability of credit cards and the failure of some debtors to constrain or manage the resulting debt, even without individual or family emergencies, is a significant factor in bankruptcy filings as well. In Chapter Three we considered various forms of debt, including credit card debt and payday loans, that trap unwary consumers in perpetual debt. The substantial role of credit card debt in bankruptcy filings can be seen in Illustration 12-e, which sets forth a comprehensive profile of consumers filing for bankruptcy relief (Chapter 7 or 13). In the past 30 years, approximately 1 in 7 American households has filed for some type of bankruptcy relief. Illustration 12-f lists the 10 states with the highest per capita rate of bankruptcy filings in 2012.

Illustration 12-e: PROFILE OF CONSUMERS FILING FOR BANKRUPTCY RELIEF

- Average age: 38
- Median income: $20,172
- Total median assets: $37,000
- Homeowners: 50 percent
- Median value of homes owned by debtors who are homeowners: $90,000
- Median nonhome assets: $9,657
- Median total debt-to-income ratio: 3.04 (the median debtor owes 3.04 times more total debt than his annual income)
- Median nonmortgage debt-to-income ratio: 1.48 (the median debtor owes 1.48 times more nonmortgage debt than his annual income)
- Percentage of median nonmortgage debt represented by credit card debt: 50 percent
- Percentage of debtors who owe more than a year's income in credit card debt: 21.8 percent
- Percentage of debtors who owe more than $10,000 in credit card debt on date of filing: 56.2 percent
- Percentage of debtors who owe more than $20,000 in credit card debt on date of filing: 34.6 percent
- Married couples: 44 percent
- Single women: 30 percent
- Single men: 26 percent
- Slightly better educated than general population
- Two out of three sustained job loss or downsizing that contributed to filing
- Half have experienced a serious health problem that contributed to filing
- Fewer than 9 percent have *not* experienced a contributing medical problem, job loss, or divorce

(Source: Compiled by the author primarily from the sources listed in Illustration 13-k.)

P-H 12-b: Are you good at math? If a debtor owes 3.04 times more total debt than her annual income and her net annual income is $25,000 per year, 1) how much total debt does she owe? And, 2) assuming she has 25 percent of her net annual income available to pay off her existing debt, how long will it take her to pay it off, disregarding mounting interest charges?

Illustration 12-f: STATES WITH THE HIGHEST BANKRUPTCY FILINGS PER CAPITA (PER 1,000 RESIDENTS) IN 2012

1. Tennessee 6.86
2. Georgia 6.54
3. Nevada 6.51
4. Alabama 5.84
5. Indiana 5.53
6. Utah 5.53
7. Illinois 5.34
8. Colorado 5.14
9. Michigan 5.08
10. California 4.91

(Source: Administrative Office of the U.S. Courts.)

E. ▶ Growth of Bankruptcy Filings in the Modern Era

In 1980 there were approximately 300,000 total bankruptcy filings in the United States. The increased popularity of credit cards and the attendant rise in consumer debt caused that number to swell to more than 1 million per year by 1996. In 2005 filings exceeded 2 million for the first time ever, although that number was inflated by filings intended to beat the October 17, 2005, effective date of the **Bankruptcy Abuse Prevention and Consumer Protection Act of 2005 (BAPCPA)** (pronounced "bap-SEE-pah," and discussed in the next section), which placed new restrictions on Chapter 7 filings. After BAPCPA went into effect, filings for 2006 fell sharply to a little over 600,000 then climbed back to 850,000 in 2007 as debtor's lawyers became acquainted with the BAPCPA changes. With the onset of the **Great Recession** (see discussion in Chapter Four), both consumer and business filings surged to 1.1 million for calendar year 2008, 1.47 million for 2009, and approximately 1.6 million for 2010 before falling off to approximately 1.4 million in 2011 and 1.2 million in 2012. Illustration 12-g charts the total number of bankruptcy filings for the period 1980 to 2012.

Bankruptcy Abuse Prevention and Consumer Protection Act of 2005 (BAPCPA) The 2005 statute that amended the Code in numerous ways including introducing the means test for Chapter 7 individual filers with primarily consumer debts.

P-H 12-c: To locate the most current bankruptcy filing statistics, check the Federal Judiciary Web site at www.uscourts.gov/Statistics/BankruptcyStatistics.aspx or the bankruptcy statistics link on the American Bankruptcy Institute site at www.abiworld.org/. What were the total filings in your state for last year? So far this year? Where does your state rank on per capita filings?

F. ▶ The Bankruptcy Abuse Prevention and Consumer Protection Act of 2005

BAPCPA made sweeping changes in the Code for both consumer and business cases. Its most dramatic effect was to impose new restrictions on consumers seeking to file Chapter 7 liquidation cases, with the intended effect of forcing more to file Chapter 13 reorganization cases instead. Whether or not BAPCPA will ultimately achieve that effect to any significant degree is not yet clear.

We will refer to the numerous new Code requirements introduced by BAPCA as we proceed. But it is worth noting that the new law is not without continuing controversy. Consumer advocates and others continue to urge Congress to revisit provisions of the law that are considered onerous to consumer debtors and unfairly biased toward creditors, and to enact additional consumer protection legislation to curtail perceived abusive lending practices that cause or contribute to consumer financial problems that eventually leave those consumers no choice but to seek bankruptcy protection.

Illustration 12-g: TOTAL BANKRUPTCY FILINGS FROM 1980 TO 2012

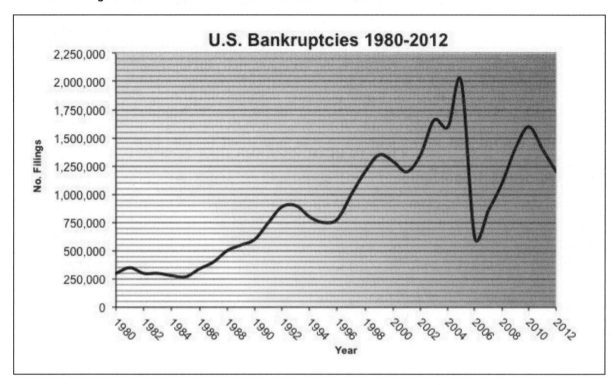

G. ▶ Important Sources of Law for Bankruptcy Practice

In addition to the Code itself, there are a number of legal sources that play a critical role in bankruptcy practice and the legal professional working in the bankruptcy field must be familiar with them.

1. The Federal Rules of Bankruptcy Procedure

In addition to the Code itself, Congress has adopted the **Federal Rules of Bankruptcy Procedure (FRBP)**. We will refer to the FRBP frequently, as they comprise the procedural rules that provide guidance and detail regarding how to comply with the Code requirements in all six types of bankruptcy cases.

Federal Rules of Bankruptcy Procedure (FRBP) The formal rules supplementing the Code and governing proceedings in bankruptcy cases.

P-H 12-d: To become more familiar with the FRBP, consult those rules and find the answers to the following questions. (If you don't have a paper copy of the FRBP you can access them online from the Federal Judiciary Web site at www.uscourts.gov/RulesAndPolicies/FederalRulemaking/Overview/BankruptcyRules.aspx.) Find these answers and indicate the specific FRBP (e.g., FRBP 1007) that provides the answer. The table of contents at the beginning of each part of the FRBP would be a good place to start to locate the answers quickly.

- Consult Part I of the FRBP to determine to whom the filing fee is paid when a bankruptcy case is commenced.
- Consult Part V of the FRBP to determine what days the bankruptcy courts and bankruptcy court clerk's offices are open.
- Consult the definitions in Part IX of the FRBP to determine whether "to mail" something pursuant to the Code means mailing by first class, second class, or something else.

2. The Official Bankruptcy Forms

In addition to the Code and the FRBP, Congress has adopted **Official Bankruptcy Forms** (OBF). The OBF are drafted by the **Administrative Office of the U.S. Courts** (www.uscourts.gov/) and that office is constantly revising the forms to comply with changes in the Code or the FRBP, new court decisions, or recommendations from judges and practitioners. FRBP 9009 provides that the official forms "shall be observed and used."

P-H 12-e: To become more familiar with the OBF, locate the particular form requested in the list below. (If you don't have a paper copy of the OBF you can access them online from the Federal Judiciary Web site at http://www.uscourts.gov/RulesAndPolicies/FederalRulemaking/Overview/BankruptcyRules.aspx.) Indicate the specific official form requested by its number and name (e.g., Official Form B5: Involuntary Petition).

1. Voluntary Petition
2. Schedule A—Real Property
3. Statement of Financial Affairs
4. Proof of Claim
5. Discharge of Debtor

3. The Federal Rules of Civil Procedure

Adversary proceedings Certain disputes defined by Bankruptcy Rule 7001 that arise in a bankruptcy case and are conducted according to procedures governing a formal civil lawsuit.

The **Federal Rules of Civil Procedure** (FRCP) control the procedure in all types of civil proceedings in bankruptcy courts. As we will see, some disputes that arise in a bankruptcy case that must be resolved by the bankruptcy judge are treated by the Code and the FRBP as mini-lawsuits, which we will learn to call **adversary proceedings**. The FRCP govern the procedure in adversary proceedings in bankruptcy court, just as they would in any civil trial before a federal judge. If you do not have a paper copy of the FRCP you can access them online at www.law.cornell.edu/rules/frcp/.

4. The Federal Rules of Evidence

The **Federal Rules of Evidence (FRE)** govern the admissibility of evidence at hearings conducted in all federal courts, including the U.S. Bankruptcy Courts. Whenever the bankruptcy judge conducts a hearing where evidence is presented (called an **evidentiary hearing**), the FRE will control the presentation of that evidence. If you do not have a paper copy of the FRE you can access them online at www.law.cornell.edu/rules/fre/.

5. Local Court Rules

Local court rules The written rules of procedure and practice that prevail in a particular court.

Each bankruptcy court around the country has its own **local court rules**. These local rules are important and will control the way that the particular court processes bankruptcy cases in accordance with the Code and FRBP.

EXAMPLE

In some bankruptcy courts, by local rule, the party filing a motion for the judge to decide is required to arrange a date for the motion to be heard and to notify the other interested parties. In other bankruptcy courts, by local rule, the party need only file the motion and the clerk of the court will arrange the date for the motion to be heard.

EXAMPLE

When a creditor files a proof of claim in a debtor's bankruptcy case in accordance with the Code and FRBP, some bankruptcy courts require by local rule that a copy of the filing be sent directly to the bankruptcy trustee by the creditor. Others require by local rule that the bankruptcy court clerk send a copy of the proof of claim to the bankruptcy trustee after it has been filed with the clerk by the creditor.

6. Miscellaneous Provisions of the U.S. Code

Although, as we have noted, the Bankruptcy Code is found in Title 11 of the U.S. Code, other provisions of the U.S. Code come into play in bankruptcy cases. Most notably, Title 28 of the U.S. Code contains provisions identifying the various federal districts where bankruptcy courts are located (§152), the procedures for the appointment of bankruptcy judges (§152), procedures for the referral of bankruptcy cases from the district court to the bankruptcy court (§159), and other details concerning their duties. Title 28 also sets out the extent of bankruptcy jurisdiction (§1334) and venue (§§1408-1412). And it contains provisions creating and regulating the U.S. Trustee system (§§581-589), discussed in more detail below.

Title 18 of the U.S. Code contains provisions regarding the offenses of bankruptcy fraud (§157), embezzlement against a bankruptcy estate (§153), false oaths and claims (§152), and other federal crimes that may arise in bankruptcy cases.

7. State Law

Though the bankruptcy code is a federal statute, state law plays a major role in the administration of a bankruptcy case. For example, whether a debt created by contract is valid and collectible will normally be determined by state law (see Chapters Two and Three). Whether a creditor is properly secured and perfected in personal property of the bankrupt debtor will be determined by the state's version of Article 9 of the UCC (see Chapter Five). Whether a creditor holds a mortgage in the debtor's real property will be determined by state law (see Chapter Four). Whether a creditor holds a valid nonconsensual lien in property of the bankrupt will be determined by state law (see Chapter Six). Even the question of where the debtor resides for purposes of deciding the proper bankruptcy court in which to file his case is a question of state law. Attorneys practicing in the bankruptcy law area and legal professionals who assist them are constantly dealing with various aspects of state law.

H. ▶ Alternatives to Filing for Bankruptcy Relief

A debtor facing the prospect of filing for bankruptcy relief may seek legal advice as to possible alternatives. There may be several, although whether they are preferable to filing for bankruptcy relief when all consequences are considered is for the debtor and his attorney to decide.

1. The Assignment for Benefit of Creditors

In an **assignment for the benefit of creditors** (commonly called an **ABC**), the debtor conveys his nonexempt property to an assignee, often a lawyer or accountant, who will liquidate the property and then distribute the proceeds pro rata to the claimants. The ABC does not discharge the balance remaining on any indebtedness, as a bankruptcy proceeding might, and so its usefulness is limited. But if the debtor has reason to believe that his creditors will not file suit to collect the deficiencies, the ABC may be a cheaper, quicker route than bankruptcy.

EXAMPLE

> If Abe Mendoza (Case Study #2; see Illustration 1-b) is in danger of being sued by his various creditors and losing his home to foreclosure, he may well be a candidate for a Chapter 7 liquidation bankruptcy. But before filing that, he might consider transferring all his nonexempt assets to a cooperating attorney as part of an ABC. This would be especially appealing if the exempt property statutes of the State of Columbiana would allow him to exempt the equity in his home and his other creditors would not likely file suit against him for any deficiencies owed after the liquidation and distribution of his other assets.

In some states, ABCs are regulated by statute and, in others, by common law decision. Once the property has been assigned by the debtor to the assignee as part of an ABC, the property is exempt from execution by individual creditors (other than those previously secured and perfected in the property). And, typically, the assignee of the ABC takes title to the property as a lien creditor with a superior claim to any prior unsecured claim to the property (see UCC Article 9, §§301(1)(b) and (3), and Revised Article 9, §§309(12) and 317). Some states allow the ABC to prefer some creditors over others in the distribution, while others forbid any such preference.

2. The Composition and Extension Agreements

Composition agreement A contract made between a debtor and his creditors pursuant to which partial payment is made and accepted in full satisfaction of claims.

A **composition agreement** is a private, voluntary arrangement between a debtor and her creditors, pursuant to which the creditors agree to take a stated partial payment in full satisfaction of their claims. The composition agreement is often accompanied by an **extension agreement**, whereby the creditors agree to give the debtor additional time to make the agreed payments. Like the ABC, the composition and extension agreements might be preferable to bankruptcy in terms of cost and time, but they are contingent on the cooperation of creditors. The agreements will typically stipulate that if the debtor defaults on any promised payment, the original debt will be revived in full.

EXAMPLE

> TTI (Case Study #3; see Illustration 1-c) might well be a candidate for an expensive, drawn-out Chapter 11 reorganization in order to stay in business. Before filing that Chapter 11, though, the attorney for TTI might contact the company's various creditors to see if a composition agreement might be reached with all of them, including an extension of time to repay scheduled debt. Some or all of the creditors might even be willing to take less than 100 cents on the dollar of debt owed in exchange for having the company avoid a Chapter 11, which will be expensive and drawn out for them as well.

Private debt consolidation is now big business. Some nine million Americans seek credit counseling each year. There are debt consolidation companies everywhere offering assistance to consumer and commercial debtors in managing their debt, often by way of a composition and extension agreements that the company negotiates with creditors on behalf of the debtor. Frequently, the company will also take an assignment of the debtor's wages and pay the debt obligations directly rather than permitting the debtor to do so. Part of the agreement between the debtor and the company often involves the debtor giving up all credit and debit cards and agreeing that he will not incur new debt without the consent of the company for the term of the agreement. Fees charged by these businesses are usually based on a percentage of indebtedness managed.

3. The Receivership

Receivership Proceeding in which a person is appointed to take control of a debtor's property and manage it under court supervision.

A **receivership** action is a lawsuit in which the court is asked to appoint a **receiver** to take legal control of the debtor's property, along with the power to manage that property. In most states, receivership actions are controlled by statute, and there are also some federal receivership laws, notably for railroads and securities businesses. Receiverships can be chosen voluntarily by qualifying debtors, but creditors can also seek the receivership for dissenting debtors. This is an important aspect of receivership law for creditors of certain debtors like churches, political committees, or other nonprofit organizations, which cannot be forced into involuntary bankruptcy. (Involuntary bankruptcy filings are considered in Chapter Fifteen.)

Like an ABC, once the assets of the debtor are place in receivership, they are immune from attachment or execution by individual creditors. The receiver will act on behalf of all the creditors to liquidate the assets and distribute the proceeds pro rata to creditors. Disputes among creditors as to the validity of their claims will be resolved by the court that ordered the receivership.

4. The Bulk Sale Transfer Act

Bulk Sale Transfer Act (BSTA) Article 6 of the *UCC* providing a non-bankruptcy procedure for the sale of all of the assets of a business outside the ordinary course of business. Repealed in most states.

A handful of states have adopted Article 6 of the **Uniform Commercial Code (UCC)**, which is known as the **Bulk Sale Transfer Act (BSTA)**. The BSTA requires a business that is selling "all or substantially all" of its assets "outside of the ordinary course of business" to give prior written notice of the sale to its creditors. A sale outside the ordinary course of business is usually defined as the sale of more than one-half of a business's assets at one time or to one buyer. In a typical BSTA statute, the notice given to creditors must advise of the assets being sold, the price, the identity of the buyer, the expected payout (i.e., "pro rata" or "share and share alike"), and must be given at least 45 days before the sale. The creditors of the seller then have six months following the date of the sale to submit claims to the buyer of the business assets. The buyer is then required to pay the creditors of the seller on some fair basis.

The BSTA became popular at the beginning of the 20th century as a means to avoid a businessperson selling all of his assets and disappearing without paying his business creditors. With the popularity of the Uniform Enforcement of Foreign Judgment Act, which we considered in Chapter Eleven, the need for the BSTA has diminished and today only a very few states still have it.

The BSTA applies primarily to the payment of unsecured creditors. Creditors secured in property of the debtor/seller will typically have the right to repossess the pledged property in the event of default so it is not available to be sold in the bulk sale.

5. Dissolution of a Business Entity Under State Law

Every state has laws under which a business entity such as a corporation, limited liability company, or partnership may simply dissolve and go out of business. Such laws contain detailed procedures for the entity to elect **dissolution**, give notice to the state and to creditors, wind up its business, and distribute its assets in an orderly fashion and according to a strict priority (e.g., creditors of a business entity being dissolved under state law are to be paid in full before any distribution of assets to owners). Creditors of a business entity may have standing to compel an **involuntary dissolution** on certain grounds such as insolvency of the entity, failure to pay its debts as they come due, or fraud by management. The state may also have authority to compel dissolution for failure of the entity to pay taxes and assessments or other grounds.

P-H 12-f: Locate the statutes in your state governing the dissolution of a corporation. Summarize the procedure that the corporation must follow to elect dissolution. What notices must be given? What are the time frames for wind up and distribution? What is the order of priority for distribution of assets? Can creditors compel an involuntary dissolution under your state laws? Can the state itself compel dissolution?

P-H 12-g: Do not confuse the right of creditors to compel a debtor corporation or partnership to dissolve under state law with the right of a creditor to sue the entity for a past due debt. And do not confuse either of those with the right of one or more shareholders of a corporation to bring a **derivative action** under state law on behalf of the corporation against the officers and directors for mismanagement. Such derivative actions are based on the **fiduciary duty** (duty of care, loyalty, and honesty) that officers and directors owe to the corporation and to its shareholders. Check the corporate act of your state and determine the procedure for the filing of a shareholder derivative action.

P-H 12-h: What about corporate creditors? Can those creditors initiate a derivative action against the officers and directors on behalf of the corporation? Most states say yes, when the corporation becomes insolvent. See, e.g., *N. Am. Catholic Educ. Programming Foundation, Inc. v. Gheewalla*, 930 A.2d 92, 101-102 (Del. 2007) (when a corporation becomes insolvent, its creditors replace the shareholders as the principal constituency injured by breaches of duty, reducing the entity's value). See if your state follows *Gheewalla* on this point either by statute or case law.

P-H 12-i: If creditors of an insolvent corporation can file a derivative action against the officers and directors on behalf of the corporation, does it follow that those officers and directors owe a fiduciary duty to each individual creditor of the corporation that would permit each such corporate creditor to sue the officers and directors for breach of that duty? The majority rule is no. See *Gheewalla*, *supra,* at 101-102 (no fiduciary duty owed by officers and directors to individual corporate debtors who are in a position to protect their interests through contract with the corporation). See if your state follows *Gheewalla* on this point.

P-H 12-j: The universal rule that when a business entity is being dissolved under state law, all creditors of the entity are to be paid in full before there is any distribution of assets to owners is known as the **trust fund doctrine**. For an interesting case discussing the doctrine, see *Sanford v. Waugh & Co., Inc.*, 328 S.W.3d 836 (Tenn. 2010). Does the trust fund doctrine apply even before dissolution begins if an entity is insolvent? Does it apply to a technically solvent corporation that chooses to dissolve? Does the doctrine allow a creditor of a corporation to gain possession of corporate property conveyed to a third party in violation of the doctrine if that third party was not a good faith purchaser for value? Does your state recognize the trust fund doctrine by case law or statute?

6. Dissolution or Reorganization of Certain Businesses Denied the Right to File for Bankruptcy Relief

The Code denies some types of businesses the right to file for bankruptcy relief—commercial banks chartered by a state or by the federal government, credit unions, savings banks, savings and loan associations, and insurance companies being notable examples per Code §109(b)(2). A railroad company can file for Chapter 11 reorganization but not for Chapter 7 liquidation per Code §§109(b)(1) and (d). So what happens when such an entity needs reorganization or liquidation and is denied the right to file under the Code? The financial institutions mentioned will be placed into involuntary receivership by the chartering authority—the state banking commissioner in the case of state-chartered institutions; the Office of the Comptroller of the Currency for national banks; and the Office of Thrift Supervision for federal savings banks, credit unions, and savings and loan associations. Insurance companies and railroads are dealt with under state law.

CONCLUSION

With this introduction and general overview of the Bankruptcy Code, we are now ready to examine more specifically the jurisdiction of the U.S. bankruptcy courts and the methods those courts use for resolving disputes that arise in cases pending before them.

CHAPTER SUMMARY

The U.S. Bankruptcy Code governs the bankruptcy options and procedures for most individuals and entities in this country. The Code authorizes six different types of bankruptcy proceedings for qualifying debtors and contains definitions and rules for case administration and procedure. Business bankruptcies are cases filed by corporations (including limited liability companies) and partnerships or by individuals with primarily business debts. Nonbusiness or consumer bankruptcies are cases filed by individuals with primarily consumer debts.

The Federal Rules of Bankruptcy Procedure (FRBC) supplement the Code and provide detailed guidance on numerous procedural aspects of a bankruptcy case. Congress has also approved Official Bankruptcy Forms (OBF) for use in bankruptcy cases across the country. Each bankruptcy court has its own local rules that further supplement the Code, the FRBC, and the OBF.

Alternatives to bankruptcy include an assignment for benefit of creditors where the debtor assigns her nonexempt property to a designated assignee, who liquidates it and distributes the proceeds to creditors pro rata. A composition agreement is a private voluntary arrangement between a debtor and her creditors pursuant to which the creditors agree to take a stated partial payment in full satisfaction of their claims. A receivership is a court proceeding in which the court is asked to appoint a receiver to take legal control of the property of the debtor along with the power to manage that property. A few states still retain the Bulk Sale Transfer Act (BSTA), Article 6 of the Uniform Commercial Code, which provides a statutory scheme for a business selling all or substantially all of its assets outside the ordinary course of business.

REVIEW QUESTIONS

1. Where are the bankruptcy laws located within the U.S. Code? What authorizes Congress to enact bankruptcy legislation? Why do we call the Bankruptcy Code a system of compulsory debt adjustment? What is meant by the phrase "fresh start" in the bankruptcy context?

2. Identify and briefly describe the six different types of bankruptcy proceedings authorized under the Code. Indicate which types are most and least commonly filed. Identify and briefly describe the contents of the other chapters of the Code.

3. Explain the difference between a business bankruptcy filing and a consumer bankruptcy filing.

4. What are the three definitions of consumer debt?

5. Approximately what percentage of bankruptcy filings nationwide are Chapter 7 liquidation cases?

6. Approximately what percentage of bankruptcy filings nationwide are business filings, as opposed to consumer filings?

7. Describe the circumstances of the typical consumer debtor who files for Chapter 7 relief.

8. What are local court rules?

9. What title of the U.S. Code contains the Bankruptcy Code? What title of the U.S. Code defines the various federal districts around the country where U.S. bankruptcy courts are located? What title of the U.S. Code contains federal criminal laws related to bankruptcy?

10. Explain the difference between an assignment for benefit of creditors and a composition agreement?

WORDS AND PHRASES TO REMEMBER

assignment for the benefit of creditors (ABC)

Bankruptcy Abuse Prevention and Consumer Protection Act of 2005 (BAPCPA)

Bankruptcy Act

Bankruptcy Amendments and Federal Judgeship Act of 1984

Bankruptcy Reform Act of 1994

Bankruptcy Appeals Panels (BAPs)

Bankruptcy Code (Code)

bankruptcy court clerk

bankruptcy judge

Bankruptcy Reform Act of 1987

Bankruptcy Reform Act of 1994

bankruptcy trustee

Bulk Sale Transfer Act (BSTA)

business (nonbusiness) bankruptcy cases

Chandler Act

Chapter 7 bankruptcy

Chapter 9 bankruptcy

Chapter 11 bankruptcy

Chapter 12 bankruptcy

Chapter 13 bankruptcy

Chapter 15 bankruptcy

clean slate

composition and extension agreements

compulsory debt adjustment

consumer bankruptcy cases

consumer debt

court-sanctioned debt relief

creditor

creditor's attorney

debt slaves

debtor

debtor's attorney

discharge

dissolution

family farmers
family fishermen
Federal Rules of Bankruptcy Procedure
    (FRBP)
Federal Rules of Civil Procedure
    (FRCP)
Federal Rules of Evidence (FRE)
fresh start
involuntary dissolution
legislative courts
local rules
liquidation

Nelson Act
Official Bankruptcy Forms
plan of reorganization
protection of life and limb
receivership
reorganization
Sabbatical Year
Statute of Merchants
Statute of Queen Anne
U.S. bankruptcy court
Year of Jubilee

TO LEARN MORE: A number of TLM activities to accompany this chapter are accessible on the student disc accompanying the text and on the Author Updates link to the text Web site at http://www.aspenparalegaled.com/ books/parsons_abcdebt/default.asp.

Chapter Thirteen:

▶ The U.S. Bankruptcy Courts: Jurisdiction, Procedures, and Important Players

A small debt produces a creditor, a large one an enemy.
—Publilius Syrus (First century, B.C.E.)

A. ▶ Number and Location of the U.S. Bankruptcy Courts

Congress has divided the United States geographically into 94 different **federal districts**. Each of those federal districts, in turn, lies within a larger **federal circuit**, over which sits one of the 13 **U.S. circuit courts of appeal**. In each of the 94 federal districts, there are one or more **district judges** presiding over a **U.S. district court**. And in each of those 94 federal districts, there is also one or more **bankruptcy judges** presiding over a **U.S. bankruptcy court**.

P-H 13-a: Go to the Web site of the Administrative Office of the Federal Courts (www.uscourts.gov/courtlinks/) and look at the map provided there showing all the federal districts Congress has created in the 50 states, the District of Columbia, Puerto Rico, and the Virgin Islands. Locate on the map the federal district in which you live and work. Then, in option 1 above the map select "Bankruptcy Court" and in option 2 type in your ZIP code or your city and state, and then hit the "Search" button. The site should bring up a list of all the bankruptcy courts in your federal district and provide you the option of linking to the Web site for each such court. Using this information, answer the following questions:

- How many different divisional offices does the bankruptcy court maintain in your federal district?
- Where is the main office located?
- What are the names of the U.S. bankruptcy judges who hold court at each office?
- Who is the chief bankruptcy judge in your federal district?
- Who is the clerk of the bankruptcy court in your federal district?
- Does the Web site provide a link to the local rules of the bankruptcy courts in your federal district?

> • Does the Web site provide a link to recent decisions of the bankruptcy courts in your federal districts?
> • Does the Web site provide a link to the Code, the FRBP, or the OBF?

On your computer, bookmark this Web site for further use.

B. ▶ Subject Matter Jurisdiction of the Bankruptcy Courts

1. Distinguishing Between Article III and Article I Courts, Public and Private Rights, and the Need for Referral Jurisdiction

As was noted in Illustration 12-a, due to the Supreme Court's 1982 decision in *Marathon* and the subsequent **1984 Bankruptcy Amendments and Federal Judgeship Act** (the 1984 Amendments Act), bankruptcy courts today, as courts created by Congress under Article I of the U.S. Constitution, serve as *units* or *adjuncts* of the U.S. district courts which are Article III courts.

The distinction between Article III and Article I courts is archaic but important in order to understand the jurisdiction of the bankruptcy courts. Article III of the Constitution mandates that "The judicial power of the United States shall be vested in one Supreme Court and in such inferior courts as the Congress may from time to time ordain and establish." The **Article III courts** are the U.S. Supreme Court, the 13 U.S. circuit courts of appeals and the 94 U.S. district courts. The judges of these courts are selected by the constitutionally mandated process of nomination by the president and confirmation by the U.S. Senate and they enjoy lifetime tenure since Article III says that they "shall hold their offices during good behaviour." It has long been understood that only these Article III courts, constituting the judicial branch of the federal government, can enter final orders that determine issues involving life, liberty, or property rights (see, e.g., *American Ins. Co. v. 356 Bales of Cotton*, 1 Pet. 511 (1828) (commonly referred to as *Canter*) and *Ex parte Bakelite Corp.*, 279 U.S. 438 (1929)).

Other specialized federal courts created by Congress are deemed **Article I courts** or **legislative courts**. Since they are created by Congress for some specialized legislative purpose they do not enjoy plenary Article III powers and the judges of those courts do not enjoy lifetime tenure. More specifically, Article I courts cannot be empowered to decide disputes between private parties controlled by state law (called actions involving **private rights**). In its most recent decision on the matter the Supreme Court described private rights claims as those involving "the liability of one individual to another under the law as defined." See *Stern v. Marshall*, 131 S.Ct. 2594, 2612 (2011). Instead, Article I courts can only decide designated disputes between the government and persons subject to its authority (called actions involving **public rights**). In *Stern* the Supreme Court defined a public right claim as one that "derives from a federal regulatory scheme, or in which resolution of the claim by an expert governmental agency is essential to a limited regulatory objective within the agency's authority." *Stern* at 2613.

The gist of *Marathon* was that the Bankruptcy Reform Act of 1978 violated the **separation of powers doctrine** of the Constitution by purporting to give bankruptcy courts the power to enter final orders determining issues regarding property in disputes between private parties controlled by state law, i.e., claims involving private rights, a power reserved by the Constitution for the Article III courts. In response to *Marathon*, the 1984 Amendments Act amended Title 28 to make it clear that it is U.S. district courts that have subject matter jurisdiction over bankruptcy matters and that U.S. bankruptcy courts are units of those Article III courts.

That is why, today, 28 U.S.C. §1334 technically bestows **subject matter jurisdiction** over bankruptcy matters to the Article III district courts. Per 28 U.S.C. §157(a) that grant of jurisdiction includes:

Subject matter jurisdiction A court's power to hear and decide certain types of cases.

- each and every case filed under the Code (see Illustration 12-c);
- all procedural matters arising out of the Code or in a case filed under any chapter of the Code (see Illustration 12-b); and
- any other matter arising in or related to such a case.

EXAMPLE

Assume a debtor files a petition for relief under Chapter 7 of the Code. That is a case filed under Title 11. To administer that case the procedures under Chapters 1, 3, 5, and 7 will be followed. But there may be other matters involved in that case. Perhaps at the time the debtor filed the petition, he was a party to a lawsuit in state court involving a dispute over the location of a property line on a parcel of land that he owns. That property line dispute is not a case under the Code and does not involve procedural matters under the Code, but it is an "other matter" arising under a case under the Code. Upon filing of the Chapter 7 petition, the U.S. district court has subject matter jurisdiction over all these matters, pursuant to 28 U.S.C. §1334. And this would be true even though the "other matter" property line dispute could not originally have been filed in the U.S. district court.

Referral jurisdiction A description of the subject matter jurisdiction of U.S. bankruptcy courts since such jurisdiction depends on referral from the U.S. district courts.

Though subject matter jurisdiction over bankruptcy matters technically resides in the Article III district courts, 28 U.S.C. §157(a) authorizes the district courts to refer bankruptcy cases to the bankruptcy courts in their districts. Consequently, the Article I bankruptcy courts obtain jurisdiction over bankruptcy cases by *referral* from the Article III district courts. They have **referral jurisdiction**. In the vast majority of federal districts, bankruptcy cases are automatically referred to the bankruptcy courts by **standing order** of the district court. However, 28 U.S.C. §157(d) authorizes the district court to **revoke the reference** at any time on its own motion or upon the motion of any party in interest for cause shown. (For an example of how the bankruptcy court's subject matter jurisdiction is properly alleged, see the Carlson case file, Document 35, Paragraph 3, on the disc provided with the text.)

Core proceedings A proceeding in a bankruptcy case involving the determination of rights under the Code or issues arising in a bankruptcy case as suggested by the list in 28 U.S.C. §157(2).

2. Core and Noncore Proceedings

Twenty-eight U.S.C. §157 distinguishes between **core** and **noncore proceedings** in bankruptcy cases referred to the bankruptcy courts. In general, core proceedings include the administration of the bankruptcy case itself and the resolution of issues related to substantive rights created by the Code or the bankruptcy case. Core proceedings are understood to involve procedures and rights that would not exist except for the Code whereas noncore proceedings involve issues and rights that would exist even if there was no bankruptcy case (even

Noncore proceedings Disputes governed by non-bankruptcy law the outcome of which may affect the administration of a bankruptcy estate.

though their resolution postpetition will impact on the bankruptcy estate). Section 157(b)(1) provides that the bankruptcy court can enter final judgment or dispositive order in all core proceedings when the case has been properly referred to it by the district court. Section 157(b)(2) enumerates a number of specific matters that regularly arise in a bankruptcy case and that are to be considered core proceedings properly decided by the bankruptcy court pursuant to the reference (see Illustration 13-a). Note that the various matters listed in §157(b)(2) are not exclusive. As stated in *In re Marshall*, 264 B.R. 609, 627 (C.D. Cal. 2001), Congress intended to confer on bankruptcy judges authority to adjudicate a broad span of actions.

If a matter to be decided is related to the bankruptcy case but is considered a noncore proceeding, then pursuant to 28 U.S.C. §157(c)(2), the bankruptcy court can enter a final judgment in the matter only if all the parties consent. Absent unanimous consent of the parties to allow the bankruptcy court to enter a final judgment in the matter, then per §157(c)(1) it can only make proposed **findings of fact** and **conclusions of law** for review **de novo** (as from the beginning with no presumption of correctness) by the district court, which will then enter the final judgment.

As a practical matter, when the matter to be decided is noncore and all the parties will not consent to the bankruptcy court entering a final judgment, one or more of the parties will file a motion with the district court asking it to revoke the reference and hear and decide the matter. After all, if the bankruptcy judge hears it, all that court can do is enter proposed findings and conclusions that will have to be reviewed by the district court anyway. So revoking the reference usually saves time and money.28 U.S.C. §157(b)(2) defines proceedings in a bankruptcy

Illustration 13-a: TYPES OF PROCEEDINGS ARISING IN A BANKRUPTCY CASE DESIGNATED AS CORE PROCEEDINGS (BASED ON 28 U.S.C. §157(b)(2))

- Matters concerning the administration of the estate
- Allowance or disallowance of claims against the estate
- Counterclaims by the estate against persons filing claims against the estate
- Exemptions of property from the estate
- Orders in respect to obtaining credit
- Orders to turn over property of the estate
- Proceedings to determine, avoid, or recover preferential transfers
- Motions to stay, annul, or modify the automatic stay
- Proceedings to determine, avoid, or recover fraudulent transfers
- Determinations as to the dischargeability of particular debts
- Objections to discharge
- Determinations as to the validity, extent, or priority of liens
- Confirmation of plans
- Orders approving the use or lease of property, including the use of cash collateral
- Orders approving the sale of property (other than property resulting from claims brought by the estate against persons who have not filed claims against the estate
- Other proceedings affecting the liquidation of assets of the estate or the adjustment of the debtor/creditor relationship or the equity security holder relationship
- Recognition of foreign proceedings and other matters under Chapter 15 of the Code

case that are considered core proceedings but there is no statutory definition of what constitutes a noncore proceeding. And we now know that the distinction is important since the bankruptcy courts are authorized to hear and enter final judgment or order in the former but in the latter only with consent of the parties. Noncore proceedings are matters that do not emanate from the Code—they are not creatures of bankruptcy law or necessary case administration. Instead they are matters that would be at issue even if there was no bankruptcy case pending and could be decided in a non-bankruptcy forum, usually, by state law.

EXAMPLE

> Domestic relations disputes over parentage, adoption, divorce, child custody, and support matters have nothing to do with bankruptcy law or procedure. But if one of the parties involved in such a dispute is a debtor in a bankruptcy case, the outcome of the domestic dispute can certainly affect the bankruptcy case. It will be deemed a noncore matter. Or if a debtor in a bankruptcy case was involved in a prepetition car accident and has a negligence lawsuit pending by or against him. That common law negligence suit has nothing to do with bankruptcy law or procedure and is governed by state common law or statutory law. But the outcome of the negligence suit could certainly affect the bankruptcy case. It will be deemed a noncore matter. The same is true of will contests and other estate and probate matters.

Contrast the examples given of noncore matters with matters that exist to be decided only because the bankruptcy case was filed: issues related to the proper filing of a bankruptcy petition and supporting schedules, the qualification and appointment of a bankruptcy trustee, the trustees right to possession of property of the estate from the debtor or third parties, whether the automatic stay has been violated by a creditor or should be lifted so a secured creditor can seize pledged property of the estate, disputes over value of estate property, whether property of the estate should be sold or abandoned, the distribution of estate assets to creditors, the terms and confirmability of plans of reorganization under Chapter 11 or Chapter 13, the validity of claimed exemptions in the debtor's property, the validity and enforceability of creditor claims, whether a particular debt should be deemed nondischargeable in bankruptcy, whether a final discharge will be granted, etc. These types of matters and many more arise because there is a bankruptcy case, they are core proceedings and bankruptcy judges may enter final judgment or order in such matters.

Note that 28 U.S.C. §157(c) does not prohibit bankruptcy courts from hearing noncore proceedings that arise in a bankruptcy case. It simply says that the bankruptcy court cannot hear the matter and enter a final judgment or order on it unless all parties consent. If all parties do not consent then the bankruptcy court can hear the matter but, instead of entering a final judgment, can only issue proposed findings of fact and conclusions of law that go to the district court for review and final determination.

Notwithstanding this procedure for bankruptcy courts to hear noncore matters that arise in a bankruptcy case, federal jurisprudence has long recognized a **domestic relations exception** to federal subject matter jurisdiction (see *Barber v. Barber*, 62 U.S. (21 How.) 582 (1858)) pursuant to which a federal court will not hear domestic relations disputes (divorce, paternity, custody, etc.) even when a federal court has technical jurisdiction to do so. Similarly, federal jurisprudence has long recognized a **probate exception** (see *Markham v. Allen*, 326 U.S. 490 (1946)) pursuant to which federal courts will not hear probate-related disputes (will validity, beneficiary qualifications, distribution priority, etc.). When such a noncore matter is related to a bankruptcy case, the bankruptcy judge will typically abstain from hearing the case as permitted by 28 U.S.C. §1334(c)(1) and allow it to be heard (or order the parties to have it heard) and decided by the appropriate state court and then apply that decision as appropriate in the bankruptcy case. And bankruptcy judges may also do this with other noncore matters such as personal injury and wrongful death claims, particularly where a lawsuit was pending in another court when the bankruptcy case was filed.

P-H 13-b: Note that while 28 U.S.C. §1334(c)(1) grants the federal court discretion to abstain from hearing the noncore matter, 28 U.S.C. §1334(c)(2) mandates abstention where a party to the dispute files a timely motion to have the matter heard and decided by a state court where the matter is already pending. When might a motion for abstention be deemed untimely? If the matter was not already pending in a state court would the lawyer seeking abstention rely in her motion on 28 U.S.C. §1334(c)(1) or (c)(2)? Note there is one other requirement for mandatory abstention. What if the matter is already pending in a state court when a timely §1334(c)(2) motion for abstention is filed but it is a matter that could have been filed in federal district court to begin with under diversity of citizenship jurisdiction? Will the §1334(c)(2) motion be granted?

---

3. The Right to a Jury Trial in Bankruptcy Court

A bankruptcy court may conduct a jury trial if demanded by a party in either a core or noncore proceeding but *only* when all parties consent and the district court specifically designates the bankruptcy court to conduct that trial (see 28 U.S.C. §157(e) added by the **Bankruptcy Reform Act of 1994**). One exception to that is a claim for wrongful death or personal injury that arises in a bankruptcy case. Pursuant to 28 U.S.C. §157(b)(5), bankruptcy courts *may not* conduct trials involving such claims regardless of whether they qualify as core proceedings and may not even make tentative findings in them as in a noncore proceeding. Section 157(b)(5) provides that the U.S. district court is to hear and decide such claims and 28 U.S.C. §1334 gives the district courts subject matter jurisdiction to hear such cases even in the absence of federal question or diversity of citizenship jurisdiction. Alternatively, the bankruptcy court or district court may allow or order claims for personal injury or wrongful death that are related to a bankruptcy case to be heard and decided by a state court having jurisdiction as permitted by 28 U.S.C. §1334(c).

C. ▶ Constitutional Limits on the Power of Bankruptcy Courts to Enter Final Judgments in Core Proceedings: Constitutional Jurisdiction

Notwithstanding the designation of certain proceedings as core in 28 U.S.C. §157(b)(2) and notwithstanding Congress's grant of power to bankruptcy courts in §157(b)(1) authorizing them to enter final judgments in core proceedings, the U.S. Supreme Court has found that the Constitution nonetheless prohibits bankruptcy courts from entering final judgments in some core proceedings. Thus, in addition to the statutory subject matter jurisdiction granted to bankruptcy courts in Title 28 of the U.S. Code, those courts must also have **constitutional jurisdiction** to finally decide disputes that come before them.

In *Granfinanciera, S.A. v. Nordberg*, 492 U.S. 33 (1989), a Chapter 11 trustee filed suit in the bankruptcy case against a defendant seeking to nullify a prepetition transfer of property by the debtor to the defendant that was fraudulent under state law. The defendant was not a creditor of the estate and thus had filed no claim against the estate. The bankruptcy judge treated the lawsuit as a core proceeding based on 28 U.S.C. §157(b)(2)(H), which specifically designates fraudulent transfer actions as core proceedings (see Illustration 13-a). The defendant demanded a jury but the trustee did not consent and the case was tried in bankruptcy court as a core proceeding without a jury. On appeal the Supreme Court held that even though §157(b)(2)(H) designates fraudulent conveyance actions as core proceedings in a bankruptcy case, that section was unconstitutional to the extent it deprived a non-creditor of a right to jury trial in a civil action as guaranteed under the Seventh Amendment. Though decided under the guise of the Seventh Amendment, at the heart of *Granfinanciera* is the separation of powers problem addressed in *Marathon*. The court was saying that it violated the Seventh Amendment right to a jury trial to allow an Article I court to decide a fraudulent transfer action that, despite its enumeration by Congress as a core proceeding, in fact was not a cause of action created exclusively by the bankruptcy law (an action involving a public right) but because it existed prepetition, was controlled by state law, did not involve determination of a creditor's bankruptcy claim, was instead an action involving a private right, the kind of private right to which Seventh Amendment protection attached and which Congress could not take away.

It was following and because of *Granfinanciera* that Congress enacted §157(e) seeking to clarify the right to jury trial in bankruptcy court by making it hinge on consent of the parties. But neither §157(e) nor any other changes made by Congress since *Granfinanciera* dealt with the underlying question of whether and when a bankruptcy court, with our without a jury, can enter a final judgment in a case involving a private right just because it arises in a bankruptcy case. Then came *Stern*.

In *Stern v. Marshall,* 131 S. Ct. 2594 (2011), a creditor asserted a claim in a Chapter 11 case alleging defamation by the debtor and filed a complaint in the bankruptcy case seeking to have the alleged debt owed to him on that basis declared non-dischargeable in bankruptcy. The debtor counterclaimed against the creditor seeking to recover from the creditor for prepetition tortious interference with the debtor's right to inherit from her spouse. The bankruptcy judge treated the counterclaim as a core proceeding based on §157(b)(2)(C), which specifically designates counterclaims filed by the estate against creditors who have asserted claims against the estate as core proceedings. On appeal the Supreme Court held that even though §157(b)(2)(C) designates such as actions as core proceedings in a bankruptcy case, it was an unconstitutional violation of the separation of powers doctrine to allow a bankruptcy court to enter a final judgment in such an action where the counterclaim involved a prepetition state law claim that was not necessary for the bankruptcy court to decide in order to determine the validity of the creditor's claim: it was an action on a private right, not a public right even though the counterdefendant was a creditor. Determination of the creditor's claim in the bankruptcy case (whether debtor had defamed creditor) was not affected by the decision on the counterclaim (whether creditor had tortuously interfered with debtor's inheritance rights), therefore no public right was involved in the counterclaim. Once again the Supreme Court emphasized, as in *Marathon*, that the prepetition state law claim was in the nature of a private right allowing and allowing an Article I bankruptcy court to enter a final judgment in such a case violated the Constitution's separation of powers doctrine.

Significantly, although *Stern* recognized that §157(c)(2) authorizes a bankruptcy court to enter a final judgment in a noncore proceeding where all parties consent, it rejected the idea that the creditor had so consented simply by filing a claim against the estate. Left open was the question of whether a party to an action in bankruptcy court can *ever* effectively consent to have the bankruptcy judge enter a final judgment on an issue properly triable by the district judge due to constitutional jurisdiction requirements or can effectively waive his argument under the Constitution that the district judge must enter the final judgment by failing to make that argument in a timely fashion before the bankruptcy judge enters final judgment (e.g., by raising the argument for the first time only on appeal.) If *Stern* should be interpreted to mean that a party can never consent to a bankruptcy judge entering final judgment in an action the Constitution requires be decided by an Article III judge and cannot waive his argument in that regard, then the consent provision of §157(c)(2) would not appear to be available for actions designated as core proceedings in §157(b)(2) but which they are constitutionally prohibited from finally deciding by reason of *Granfinanciera* and *Stern*. It's not that these actions are noncore—they are statutorily declared core in §157(b)(2)—it's that such proceedings, regardless of their designation as core by Congress, are constitutionally outside the power of the bankruptcy courts to decide; and consent of the parties or waiver by one party cannot change that. If *Stern* is to be so interpreted, there is a "gap" in the statutory jurisdiction of the bankruptcy courts.

P-H 13-c: The consent/waiver issue and its impact on §157(c)(2) (the jurisdictional gap issue) has very quickly divided the circuit courts post–*Stern*. *Waldman v Stone*, 698 F.3d 910 (6th Cir. 2012), cert. denied, 133 S. Ct. 1604 (2013), held that parties *cannot* consent to final adjudication of matters as to which the bankruptcy court lacks authority to enter a final judgment, because that constitutional grant of authority is a nonwaivable "structural principle advanced by Article III." But *In re Bellingham Ins. Agency, Inc.*, 702 F.3d 553 (9th Cir. 2012), cert. granted, June 24, 2013, No. 12-200, held that an independent judiciary "serves to protect primarily personal, rather than structural interest" and that accordingly, as a personal right (rather than a structural right, such as the nature and extent of a court's subject matter jurisdiction), the constitutional "guarantee of an impartial and independent federal adjudication is subject to waiver." See if the courts of your federal district have weighed in on this issue. The Supreme Court granted certiorari in *Bellingham* in June 2013. Determine the status of that case before the Supreme Court.

So what is the impact of *Granfinanciera* and *Stern* on the core/noncore distinction of §157(b) and the power of a bankruptcy court to enter a final judgment in either a core or noncore proceeding? First, it is clear that the proceedings identified as core by Congress in §157(b)(2) are not the equivalent of proceedings involving determination of public rights though that may have been Congress's intent. In other words, the statutory classification of actions of core/noncore is not determinative of a bankruptcy court's power to enter a final judgment. In addition to that statutory classification there is the separate constitutional question of whether the matter to be decided involves a public or private right. If it involves a public right then the bankruptcy court may enter final judgment or dispositive order. If it involves determination of a private right then the bankruptcy court may not enter final judgment or dispositive order, only the Article III district court can do that.

Second, notwithstanding §157(c)(2), if the parties to a noncore matter consent to the bankruptcy judge entering a final judgment in the matter, the bankruptcy court will be powerless to do so under the Constitution if that matter is found to involve determination of a private and not a public right. Thus in determining the power of a bankruptcy court to finally decide a matter one must be concerned with both statutory subject matter jurisdiction from Title 28 of the U.S. Code, and with constitutional jurisdiction issues arising from *Marathon*, *Granfinanciera* and *Stern*.

Third, notwithstanding §157(e), if the parties to either a core or noncore proceeding consent to a jury trial before a bankruptcy court, that court will be powerless to conduct a jury trial in the matter if it is found to involve determination of a private and not a public right.

Fourth, we do not yet know how many of the proceedings designated as core in §157(b)(2) will ultimately be found to involve determination of private and not public rights and thus be outside the power of a bankruptcy court to finally decide. One post-*Stern* decision confronting this question observed "This area of the law has a potluck quality" meaning, no one really knows at this point. It seems clear that the Constitutional jurisdiction problem is not to be limited to the specific proceedings involved in *Granfinanciera* (actions to recover prepetition fraudulent conveyances under state law) and *Stern* (claims based on state tort law against a non-creditor of the estate or against a creditor of the estate that are not dispositive of that creditor's claim). But how broadly are they to be read? If these cases are to be read broadly as treating any proceeding in a bankruptcy court based on state law as an action involving determination of a private right then most core proceedings listed in §157(b)(2) will be off limits to bankruptcy court determination as will many noncore proceedings since they almost always involve state law issues.

As you may already have concluded, *Stern* has set off a firestorm of commentary and concern about its implications for the existing bankruptcy framework. In the first 18 months after it was decided, *Stern* was cited in almost 700 bankruptcy decisions. Some courts and commentators fear the worst, that bankruptcy judges will be reduced to mere law clerks for district judges, limited to making recommendations for adoption by the Article III court in bankruptcy cases. Or to mere office administrators, empowered to do nothing more than carry out decisions of the district court in bankruptcy cases. Others choose to limit the scope of *Granfinanciera* and *Stern* to their specific holdings and trust the Supreme Court and lower courts not to disrupt the bankruptcy system further with more expansive readings. The future reality probably lies somewhere in between and we are all going to have to wait and see how it plays out. Of course, Congress could resolve the whole mess by making bankruptcy judges Article III judges and granting them lifetime tenure and plenary judicial power to decide disputes involving both public and private rights. Or it could simply hold that the 1984 Amendments Act fixed the problem following *Marathon* (as Congress likely thought that it was) by giving the district courts plenary jurisdiction over all bankruptcy cases and issues and that those Article III courts are effectively exercising that power through their designated adjunct units the bankruptcy courts. But neither of those developments is likely.

The first samplings of post-*Stern* court decisions indicate that a majority are choosing to read it very narrowly (e.g., *Miller v. Greenwich Capital Fin. Prods. (In re Am. Bus. Fin. Servs., Inc.)*, 457 B.R. 314, 319–20 (Bankr.D.Del.2011) (bankruptcy court has power after *Stern* to issue a final judgment on fraudulent transfer claim) and *In re AFY, Inc.*, 461 B.R., 541, 547-48 (8th Cir. BAP 2012) (the "Supreme Court itself has cautioned that its holding is a narrow one. . . . Unless and until the Supreme Court visits other provisions of Section 157(b)(2), we take the Supreme Court at its word and hold that the balance of the authority granted to bankruptcy judges by Congress in 28 U.S.C. §157(b)(2) is constitutional.")) but a minority are not (e.g., *In re El–Atari*, 2011 WL 5828013 (E.D.Va. Nov. 12, 2011) ("*Stern*, together with *Granfinanciera*, clearly supports the conclusion that the authority to issue a final decision in a fraudulent conveyance action is reserved for Article III courts.")). Confusion reigns.

P-H 13-d: A recent decision by the Sixth Circuit may provide a good look at the post-*Stern* world of constitutional jurisdiction of bankruptcy courts. In *Waldman v. Stone*, 698 F.3d 910 (6th Cir. 2012), cert. denied, 133 S. Ct. 1604 (2013), a Chapter 11 debtor brought an action in the bankruptcy court asking the court to disallow the claims of his major creditor based on prepetition state law fraud by the creditor in the creation of those debts (the "disallowance claims"). The debtor also asked for a judgment for damages sustained by the debtor by reason of the same prepetition fraudulent behavior of the creditor (the "money damage claims"). The bankruptcy judge treated the matter as a core proceeding under 28 U.S.C. §157(b)(2)(B) because it involved allowance or disallowance of claims against the estate and entered final judgment in favor of the debtor following a bench (non-jury) trial. In response to creditor's argument on appeal that the bankruptcy court lacked constitutional jurisdiction to decide the disputes because they involved determination of private rights, the Sixth Circuit agreed with respect to the money damage claims holding that they involved determination of pure private rights because those claims arose prepetition under state law, could have been asserted by debtor if no bankruptcy case had been filed, were not part of debtor's effort to restructure his relations with the creditor in the bankruptcy case and were relevant to the bankruptcy case only because they might increase the size of the bankruptcy estate. On the other hand, the court rejected creditor's argument that the bankruptcy court lacked constitutional authority to decide the disallowance claims. The court found the debtor's allegation that the creditor's claim in the bankruptcy case should be disallowed due to the same fraudulent acts involved in the money damage claims involved determination of public rights.

Notwithstanding the state law nature of the disallowance claims, the court said they arose under the Code as "part and parcel of the claims allowance process in bankruptcy." See if the bankruptcy or district courts of your state or the circuit court of your federal circuit have decided any post-*Stern* constitutional jurisdiction cases. Are those courts construing *Stern* narrowly or broadly? Would they likely agree or disagree with the Sixth Circuit's decision in *Waldman*?

P-H 13-e: As noted earlier, per §157(c)(1), bankruptcy courts are authorized in noncore proceedings to enter proposed findings of fact and conclusions of law that are then submitted to the district court for final determination. Does that mean they can also do so in connection with a core or noncore proceedings which they are constitutionally prohibited from finally deciding by reason of *Granfinanciera* and *Stern*? Most courts are concluding that *Stern* does not prohibit a bankruptcy court from hearing and submitting proposed findings of fact and conclusions of law to the district court in §157(b)(2) proceedings that it may not constitutionally decide finally (see, e.g., *In re Agriprocessors, Inc.*, 479 B.R. 835, 846 (Bkrtcy. N.D. Iowa 2012). But a minority interpret *Stern* to deprive bankruptcy courts of the power to hear such a case at all (see, e.g., *In re Blixseth*, 2011 WL 3274042 (Bankr. D. Mont., Aug. 1, 2011) (A bankruptcy court has no statutory authority to render findings of fact and conclusions of law for core proceedings that it may not constitutionally hear.) Have the courts of your federal circuit dealt with this post-*Stern* issue?

P-H 13-f: The debtor involved in the *Stern* case, Anna Nicole Smith, was quite a character (she died in 2007). The former model, stripper and Playboy's 1992 Playmate of the Year was 26 years old when she married 89-year-old billionaire J. Howard Marshall. Marshall passed away only 14 months following the nuptials, and his estate was admitted to probate in Texas. The young widow alleged that her late husband had promised to leave her a small fortune but had been deterred from doing so by his son, Pierce Marshall. While that squabble was going on in the Texas probate action, Anna Nicole filed a Chapter 11 bankruptcy case in California. It was in that case that Pierce Marshall filed his claim alleging defamation and his complaint seeking to have his claim treated as nondischargeable. And it was to that complaint that Anna Nicole filed her now famous counterclaim alleging tortious interference with inheritance rights. It was quite a show played out daily in American media. You can get all the titillating details of the story by reading *In re Marshall*, 253 B.R. 550, 553–56 (Bankr. C.D. Cal. 2000).

Illustration 13-b diagrams the complex and yo-yo–like jurisdiction granted to U.S. bankruptcy courts.

D. ▶ The Effect of a Prepetition Arbitration Agreement on the Bankruptcy Court's Power to Decide a Dispute

As was discussed in Chapter Eight, Section B, the U.S. Supreme Court has identified a strong congressional policy arising from the **Federal Arbitration Act (FAA)**, 9 U.S.C. §1 et seq., in favor of enforcing contractual **arbitration**

Illustration 13-b: DIAGRAM OF THE REFERRAL JURISDICTION OF U.S. BANKRUPTCY COURTS

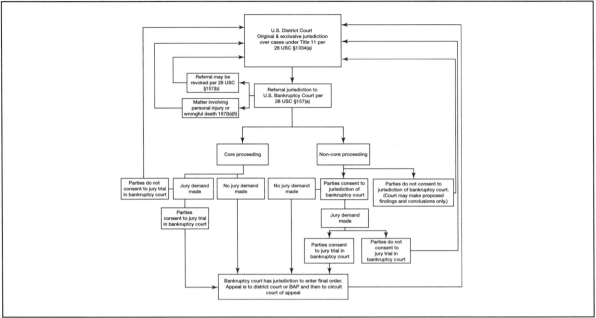

agreements (see P-H 8-f). As arbitration agreements become more common, the question arises more frequently in bankruptcy cases involving disputes between parties to a prepetition arbitration agreement as to whether the bankruptcy court can decide those disputes or must refer the matter to arbitration per the parties' prepetition agreement. The issue is typically raised when one of the parties to the dispute files a **motion to compel arbitration** with the bankruptcy court asking the court to order that the matter be referred to arbitration. Must the court order arbitration or does it have discretion to retain and decide the matter itself.

In *Shearson/American Express, Inc. v. McMahon*, 482 U.S. 220 (1987) the Supreme Court addressed the validity of arbitration clauses, not with respect to the Code, but with respect to a civil action arising under two other federal statutes, the Securities Exchange Act and the Racketeer Influenced and Corrupt Organizations Act. In holding that such claims were subject to the arbitration agreement between the disputing parties, the Supreme Court said that a party opposing application of an arbitration clause in resolving a civil dispute under federal law must demonstrate that "Congress intended to make an exception to the Arbitration Act" pursuant to the applicable statute, "an intention discernible from the text, history, or purposes of the statute." The Court instructed courts to examine whether there exists "an inherent conflict between arbitration and the statute's underlying purposes." 482 U.S. at 227.

In applying the *McMahon* test to determine whether arbitration clauses must be honored in bankruptcy cases, the courts have made a distinction between core and noncore proceedings. In noncore proceedings that involve issues and rights that would exist even without a bankruptcy case, prepetition arbitration agreements must be honored. See *Whiting-Turner Contracting Co. v. Electric Mach. Enter., Inc. (In re Electric Mach. Enter., Inc.)*, 479 F.3d 791, 796 (11th Cir. 2007) ("Applying the *McMahon* factors to the Bankruptcy Code, we find no evidence within the text or in the legislative history that Congress intended to create an exception to the FAA in the Bankruptcy Code." "In general, bankruptcy courts do not have the discretion to decline to enforce an arbitration agreement relating to a non-core proceeding.") Today it is near universally understood that prepetition arbitration agreements must be honored to resolve noncore disputes arising in bankruptcy cases. See, e.g., *In re Cooker Restaurant Corp.*, 292 B.R. 308, 311-312 (S.D. Ohio 2003). ("In non-core proceedings in which the parties do not dispute the making of an agreement to arbitrate, a bankruptcy court is without jurisdiction to deny a motion to stay the proceedings and compel arbitration.")

That does not mean that arbitration agreements can be ignored in the resolution of disputes involving core proceedings. Utilizing the McMahon test that an arbitration agreement cannot be disregarded unless an inherent conflict exists between arbitration and the statute's underlying purposes, the Fifth Circuit found in the leading case of *In the Matter of Nat'l Gypsum Co.*, 118 F.3d 1056, 1067 (5th Cir. 1997) that it would be inappropriate to adopt a position that "categorically finds arbitration of core bankruptcy proceedings inherently irreconcilable with the Bankruptcy Code . . . We refuse to find such an inherent conflict based solely on the jurisdictional nature of a bankruptcy proceeding . . . We believe that nonenforcement of an otherwise applicable arbitration provision turns on the underlying nature of the proceeding, *i.e.*, whether the proceeding derives exclusively from the provisions of the Bankruptcy Code and, if so, whether arbitration of the proceeding would conflict with the purposes of the Code." Thus today it is universally understood that, as the Second Circuit said in *Crysen/Montenay Energy Co. v. Shell Oil Co. (In re Crysen/Montenay Energy Co.)*, 226 F.3d 160, 166 (2d Cir. 2000), although core proceedings implicate more pressing bankruptcy concerns, "even a determination that a proceeding is core will not automatically give the bankruptcy court discretion to stay arbitration."

Though it is difficult to discern any bright line test from the decisions involving arbitration agreements and core proceedings, generally speaking, the more central the core proceeding dispute is to accomplishing the unique goals of the Code the more likely it is that a bankruptcy court will find that there exists a conflict between arbitration and the purposes of the Code and exercise its discretion to refuse arbitration. See, e.g., *In the Matter of Nat'l Gypsum Co.* 118 F.3d 1056, 1067 (5th Cir. 1997) (core proceeding declaratory judgment complaint deemed central to confirmation of debtor's Chapter 11 plan and involving prepetition contract issues only peripherally could be decided by the court and motion to compel arbitration denied) and *In re White Mountain Mining Co., L.L.C.*, 403 F.3d 164, 168-169 (4th Cir. 2005) (core proceeding brought to determine whether pre-petition cash advances were debt or equity need not be submitted to arbitration due to importance under the Code of centralizing resolution of disputes and determination of issues in order to effect debtor's reorganization in Chapter 11, a fundamental purpose of the Code). On the other hand, where the nature of the dispute clearly falls with the scope of the arbitration agreement and no fundamental or unique Code purpose is articulated, courts have no problem honoring the arbitration demand. See, e.g., *In re Great Spa Mfg. Co., Inc.*, 2009 WL 1457740 (Bkrtcy. E.D. Tenn., 2009 at pages 3-4) (core proceeding by debtor to establish prepetition debt owed by defendant; arbitration involved no inherent conflict with Code; motion to compel arbitration granted) and *In re Transport Assocs., Inc.*, 263 B.R. 531, 535 (Bankr. W.D. Ky. 2001) (core proceeding involving debtor's objection to creditor's claim ordered to arbitration even though issues arose through "claims allowance process; arbitration of prepetition contractual dispute creates no conflict with Code").

P-H 13-g: Locate decisions of the courts in your federal circuit to see how they have decided the issue of enforceability of prepetition arbitration agreements in bankruptcy cases.

E. ▶ Personal Jurisdiction of the Bankruptcy Courts

Whereas subject matter jurisdiction has to do with the power of a court to hear and decide a particular kind of case, **personal jurisdiction** (also called *in personam* jurisdiction) has to do with the power of a court to enter a binding order on a particular defendant.

EXAMPLE

> Assume a bankruptcy case is pending in a U.S. bankruptcy court in Delaware. One asset of the debtor in bankruptcy is an account receivable owed to the debtor by a corporation in Arizona. When the bankruptcy trustee files a lawsuit in the bankruptcy case (we will learn later to call this an adversary proceeding) to collect the debt owed to the estate by the Arizona defendant, the lawsuit is a core proceeding over which the bankruptcy court has subject matter jurisdiction. But the Arizona defendant may object to being hailed into a bankruptcy court located in the state of Delaware. The question of whether the bankruptcy court in Delaware can properly assert power over the defendant and enter orders binding on it raises the issue of personal jurisdiction.

The notion of personal jurisdiction is intertwined with the demands of **due process** required by the Fifth Amendment to the U.S. Constitution when the federal government seeks to deprive a person of life, liberty, or property (and by the Fourteenth Amendment when such action is taken by a state). In order to satisfy the dictates of due process, it must be shown that the assertion of jurisdiction over a defendant by a particular court is consistent with **traditional notions of fair play and substantial justice**. What this has come to mean generally is that both state and federal courts have personal jurisdiction over a defendant where the defendant consents to that jurisdiction or is present in the **forum state** (the state where the federal or state court sits). A nonresident defendant who does not consent must be shown to have **minimum contacts**, personal or business, with the forum state in order for the court to assert personal jurisdiction over him. (See *International Shoe Co. v. Washington*, 326 U.S. 310

(1945); *Burger King v. Rudzewicz*, 471 U.S. 462 (1985); *Asahi Metal Industry Co. v. Superior Court of California*, 480 U.S. 102 (1987); and *Burnham v. Superior Court of California*, 495 U.S. 604 (1990). Where the dispute is over real or personal property, mere ownership of the property by a nonresident of the forum state with no other minimum contacts is sufficient to give courts in that state **in rem jurisdiction** (jurisdiction over the thing, i.e., the property). With *in rem* jurisdiction courts can enter orders binding on the nonresident owner as they pertain to the property but not as to other matters unless the minimum contacts requirement is met (see *Shaffer v. Heitner*, 433 U.S. 186 (1977)). Whenever a plaintiff seeks to bring a defendant before a state or federal court in a particular forum, due process also requires that the defendant be **served with process** (formal notification of the lawsuit and the claims made in it against the defendant) in a way that satisfies FRCP 4 in federal court actions or the applicable state rule of procedure.

The preceding paragraph is a summary of the normal rules surrounding personal jurisdiction in federal and state courts. It is given so you can understand that the grant of personal jurisdiction given to bankruptcy courts administering cases under Title 11 of the U.S. Code is much broader. The provisions of 28 U.S.C. §157 together with §1334 and Federal Rule of Bankruptcy Procedure 7004(b) and (d) (authorizing nationwide service of process) have been construed to mean that a bankruptcy court administering a case can bring a defendant before it so long as the defendant has minimum contacts with the United States, not just with the particular state where the court is located. Thus the guiding standard for the personal jurisdiction of the bankruptcy courts is not minimum contacts with the forum state, it is **national contacts**. The rationale for this expanded standard is that since a bankruptcy case usually does not affect only the sovereignty of a particular state but has effects throughout the country as a whole, the assertion of personal jurisdiction satisfies the due process requirement of fairness (see *In re Tandycrafts, Inc.*, 317 B.R. 287, 289 (Bankr. D. Del. 2004) (Mexican company that transported goods into the United States and had post office box in Texas was subject to personal jurisdiction of bankruptcy court in Delaware despite lack of other contacts with forum state).

EXAMPLE

Under the national contacts standard, the bankruptcy court in Delaware can assert personal jurisdiction over the Arizona defendant in the action to collect the debt owed the debtor so long as that defendant has minimum contacts with any of the 50 states. Since it is located in and doing business in Arizona, that standard is met. It does not matter whether minimum contacts with Delaware in particular can be shown.

P-H 13-h: Two good cases to read to get a handle on the dramatic national contacts standard for bankruptcy court personal jurisdiction are *Tandycrafts* and *In re Uni-Marts, LLC*, 399 B.R. 400 (Bankr. D. Del. 2009). See if the federal courts in your circuit have decided any national contacts cases for bankruptcy courts and whether they follow the reasoning of these two cases.

F. Appeal of a Bankruptcy Court Final Order

Standard of review The standard utilized by higher courts in reviewing decisions of the bankruptcy court; normally such decision will not be reversed unless clearly erroneous.

In those instances when the bankruptcy court does enter a final order, the losing party may appeal the order to the district court from which the bankruptcy court received the referral. The **standard of review** utilized by the district court in considering whether to reverse a final order entered by the bankruptcy court is the **clearly erroneous** standard—that is, the decision will be reversed only if the district court finds it was clearly erroneous (compare the *de novo* standard mentioned earlier). A party unhappy with the decision of the district court may then appeal that ruling to the appropriate U.S. circuit court. An appeal to the U.S. circuit court is an **appeal as of right**, meaning the court of appeals must hear and decide the issues raised in the appeal. A party unhappy with the decision of the circuit court of appeals may file an **application for writ of certiorari** (pronounced sir-she-o-RARE-ee) with the U.S. Supreme Court, asking it to accept the appeal and review the circuit court's ruling. But that appeal is not "as of right" and the Supreme Court need not grant the writ.

Bankruptcy Appellate Panel (BAP) A court made up of bankruptcy judges appointed in some federal circuits to hear the appeal of rulings by other bankruptcy judges in lieu of the District Court.

In some federal circuits, appeals of final orders entered by bankruptcy courts go to a special panel of bankruptcy judges from the entire federal circuit instead of to the district court. The panels of bankruptcy judges established in these federal circuits to hear appeals from bankruptcy courts within the circuit are called **Bankruptcy Appellate Panels (BAPs)**. Decisions of the BAP are appealable directly to the circuit court, effectively bypassing the district court. Illustration 13-g outlines the appeal process from final orders entered by a bankruptcy court.

G. Procedures for Resolving Disputes in a Bankruptcy Case

In the course of administering a bankruptcy case there may be no disputes between the **parties in interest** (generally, the debtor, the bankruptcy trustee, the U.S. trustee, creditors, and other third parties whose interest in property may be impacted by the proceeding)—a petition is filed, a trustee is appointed, proofs of claim are filed, decisions about exemptions, property of the estate, and order of distribution are made and implemented, and a discharge is granted all with no objection being raised. But it is not unusual for even a routine bankruptcy case to involve some disputes that the bankruptcy judge will have to resolve. And in a significant number of cases, there may be numerous disputes that arise during administration of the case.

EXAMPLE

What if a creditor objects on the basis of improper venue to the debtor's petition being filed in the federal district chosen by debtor's lawyer? What if creditors file an involuntary petition to which the debtor objects? What if, like Marta Carlson (see Document 5 in the Carlson case file), debtor needs more time to file her supporting schedules? What if a debtor claims property as exempt and the trustee disagrees with the valuation placed on the property by debtor? What if a creditor files a proof of claim in the case by the debtor contends the claim is not valid? What if debtor contends a creditor has violated the automatic stay of §362(a)? What if a secured creditor needs the automatic

> stay lifted in order to repossess the pledged property? What if a party in interest to the case wants the bankruptcy trustee appointed in the case removed for cause? What if a third party is in possession of an item of debtor's property when the petition is filed and refuses to turn it over to the trustee?

The fact is, every aspect of a bankruptcy case can potentially give rise to a dispute that the bankruptcy judge may be asked to resolve if the parties cannot resolve it themselves. That means there are an unlimited number of potential disputes that can and do arise in any given case. Of course, the more complex a case is, the more property there is to squabble over, the more creditors there are, etc. then the more disputes there are likely to be. And a few disputes arise in so many cases they become almost predictable and routine (e.g., disputes over valuation of property for exemption purposes, disputes over the validity or amount of creditor's claims, etc.).

We call attention to potential disputes in bankruptcy cases in order to raise this important question: when a dispute does arise in administering a bankruptcy case, what is the procedure for resolving the dispute? How is the dispute brought to the attention of the bankruptcy judge and how will the judge resolve it?

Contested matter A proceeding arising in a bankruptcy case that is initiated by motion or objection or statement of intent to act.

There are actually two different procedures for resolving disputes in a bankruptcy case. The Code itself or the FRBP designate most disputes as **contested matters** but an important few are designated as **adversary proceedings**. We will consider these two procedures separately. Of course, we have not yet studied the particular kinds of disputed matters that are mentioned as examples in the following discussion, but as we come to each of those matters in the following chapters of the text we will refer to this discussion to remind the student of how the bankruptcy court will resolve it.

1. Contested Matters

A contested matter is one governed by FRBP 9014. It requires a **hearing** before the bankruptcy judge but not requiring a full trial. At the hearing on the contested matter, the bankruptcy judge may consider **written briefs** filed by the contesting parties and the **oral arguments** of counsel. If necessary, the court may also listen to the **sworn testimony** of witnesses. Any evidence offered by sworn testimony at a hearing on a contested matter will be governed by the **Federal Rules of Evidence**.

A contested matter is initiated in one of three ways:

- by filing a motion
- by filing an objection
- by filing of a notice of intended action followed by an objection

a. By Motion

A **motion** is simply a written request made to a court seeking an order from the court granting the moving party affirmative relief regarding the subject of the request. A verbal motion may be made during a hearing before the judge. FRBP 9013 governs the required content of a motion and who is to be served with a copy of it.

EXAMPLE

> In Chapter Fifteen, Section C, we will consider the time requirements for filing the various schedules, statements, and other documents that accompany the bankruptcy petition. Marta Carlson filed a motion for additional time to file her supporting schedules. (See Document 5 in the Carlson case file.) In Chapter Sixteen, Section E, we will consider the automatic stay that goes into effect on the filing of a bankruptcy petition and will see when it is possible for a secured creditor to file a motion to lift the automatic stay or for the debtor filing a motion to extend the automatic stay. These are but three examples of innumerable motions that may be filed by the various parties in interest during a bankruptcy case.

b. By Objection

An **objection** is very similar to a motion. It is a written request to a court seeking an order from the court denying another party some relief or adjusting the rights of the other party in some way in connection with the subject of the request. A verbal objection may be made during a hearing before the judge.

EXAMPLE

> In Chapter Fifteen, Section B, we will learn that a trustee or other party in interest may file an objection to an exemption claimed in the debtor's Schedule C. In Chapter Seventeen, we will consider such an objection in more detail as well as another objection frequently filed by the trustee—one to disallow the claim of a creditor.

c. By Notice of Intended Action

Notice of intended action Procedure authorized under the Code for giving parties in interest notice of the intent to take some action.

The **notice of intended action** is a procedure unique to bankruptcy practice. A notice of intended action does not seek a court order. It simply gives required notice that the party filing the notice intends to take some action unless a party in interest objects. The Code allows some actions to be taken by a debtor or trustee simply by giving the required notice of the intended action. No further approval by the court is necessary and no hearing will be held on the matter unless a party in interest files a timely objection to the intended action. If an objection is filed to the notice of intended action the matter is then treated as a contested matter and a hearing will be scheduled on it before the bankruptcy judge.

EXAMPLE

> In Marta Carlson's case, the bankruptcy trustee has filed a *notice of intent to abandon* certain property under §554 of the Code (see Document 36 in the Carlson case file). If no party in interest objects to this intended action within 14 days of the mailing of the notice per FRBP 6007(a) the property will be deemed abandoned by the trustee without any further action by the court. However, if a timely objection is filed, the matter will be treated as a FRBP 9014 contested matter and a hearing scheduled. This unique feature of a notice of intended action—that once notice is given no hearing is held and no court approval is needed for the action unless a timely objection is filed—is known, ironically, as the **"after notice and a hearing"** procedure. It is defined in §102(1) of the Code. And looking at that definition helps dispel the irony because what is contemplated by the procedure is notice and *the opportunity* for a hearing if an objection to the intended action is timely filed.

Importantly, not only are notices of intended action authorized by the Code governed by the "after notice and a hearing" procedure, a number of (but by no means all) matters properly raised by motion or objection are as well. But whereas any action authorized by the Code to be accomplished by notice of intended action will be governed by the "after notice and a hearing" procedure, only those motions and objections specifically designated as to be accomplished "after notice and a hearing" will be subject to that procedure. Thus when a notice of intended action is authorized by the Code or where the Code specifically makes a motion or objection subject to the "after notice and a hearing" procedure, that means that written notice of the intended action, motion, or objection *must* be given to parties required to receive it. However, a hearing on the matter will be conducted *only* if a party in interest objects within the time allowed to the intended action or to the relief requested in the motion or objection. If no party in interest contests the motion or objection made or no party in interest objects to the notice of intent in the time allowed for a response, the court will grant the motion or objection or the action that was the subject of the notice of intent can go forward.

Regarding the time allowed for a response, that time can vary considerably according to the subject of the motion or the noticed action. Time periods may run from as many as 30 days to as few as 7 (compare, e.g., FRBP 2002, 6004(b), and 3007). Local rules may also contain relevant time periods.

Illustration 13-c summarizes some of the common administrative actions accomplished by this curious "after notice and a hearing" procedure.

It bears repeating that the "after notice and a hearing" procedure *only* applies to matters properly raised by motion or objection when the Code specifically says that it does. If a matter is properly raised by motion or objection but is not made

Illustration 13-c: ADMINISTRATIVE ACTIONS ACCOMPLISHED BY MOTION, OBJECTION, OR NOTICE OF INTENDED ACTION THAT ARE SUBJECT TO THE "AFTER NOTICE AND A HEARING" PROCEDURE OF THE CODE

- Under §554 of the Code, the bankruptcy trustee may notice the intent to abandon property of the estate, "after notice and a hearing."
- Under §363(b) and FRBP 6004, the bankruptcy trustee may notice the intended use, sale, or lease property of the estate in other than the ordinary course of business "after notice and a hearing."
- Under §362, a motion for relief from the automatic stay may be approved "after notice and a hearing."
- Under §324(a), a motion to remove the bankruptcy trustee for cause may be approved "after notice and a hearing."
- Under FRBP 9019, a motion to compromise or settle a dispute may be approved "after notice and a hearing."
- Under §§707(a) and (b), a motion to dismiss or convert a Chapter 7 case to a case under Chapter 13 or 11 on certain grounds may be approved "after notice and a hearing."
- Under §1112(b), a motion to dismiss or to convert a Chapter 11 case to a case under Chapter 7 on certain grounds may be approved "after notice and a hearing."
- Under §§1208(c) and (d), a motion to dismiss or to convert a Chapter 12 case to a case under Chapter 7 on certain grounds may be approved "after notice and a hearing."
- Under §502(b), the objection to a claim is to be decided "after notice and a hearing."
- Under FRBP 4003(c), an objection to a claimed exemption is to be decided "after hearing on notice," which some, but not all, courts treat as after notice and a hearing.

specifically subject to the "after notice and a hearing" procedure, they will be treated automatically as contested matters and a hearing scheduled.

EXAMPLE

Look at the Motion for Additional Time to File Schedules, Statement of Affairs, etc., filed by Marta Carlson (Document 5 in the Carlson case file). This motion is authorized by §521(i)(3) and FRBP 1007(c) but it is not designated there as an "after notice and a hearing" matter. Instead, FRBP 1007(c) provides that the time to file can be extended by motion and for "cause shown." So when Marta's lawyer files this motion, it automatically will be treated as a contested matter and a hearing will be scheduled as the notice of motion indicates. Compare the Objection to Claim filed by the bankruptcy trustee in Marta's case (Document 31 in the Carlson case file). Section 502(b) designates this as an "after notice and a hearing" matter, so if the creditor, Pine Ridge Nursing Home, does not file a written response to the objection to its claim, the court may rule on the objection without a hearing. All this is explained to Pine Ridge in the notice of objection and hearing accompanying the objection.

P-H 13-i: Review the Motion for Order of Contempt for Violation of Automatic Stay fled by Marta Carlson against Pine Ridge Nursing Home and the accompanying Notice of Motion (Document 27 in the Carlson case file). Can you tell by looking at the Notice of Motion whether this motion is subject to the "after notice and a hearing" procedure?

Motion, objection, and notice of intended action practice in a bankruptcy case is summarized in Illustration 13-d.

The procedure outlined in Illustration 13-d is generic and there is great diversity among the bankruptcy courts across the land regarding the exact procedures followed in motion practice. Many courts address motion practice in their local court rules, which should always be consulted. Many courts have developed their own forms for motions and notices as well. The lawyer and assisting legal professional must become familiar with **local custom and practice.**

Local custom and practice The unwritten way things are done in a particular court.

d. Ex Parte Practice in Bankruptcy Court

The Code permits a number of actions to receive court approval based on **ex parte** (at the request of one party without the presence or input of others) motion or application to the court. No hearing is noticed or scheduled and the court may act unilaterally. If appropriate, notice of the court's action is afterwards given to parties in interest. If an objection is filed by a party in interest before or after the court enters the ex parte relief requested, the matter will be treated as a contested matter and set for hearing. Illustration 13-e sets out actions the Code allows the court to approve ex parte.

Ex parte An appearance before a court seeking relief without notice to other parties.

Note by the way that the motion for additional time filed by Marta's lawyer and the order entered (Documents 5-6 in the Carlson case file) have the same *caption* setting forth the name of the court, the title of the case, the docket number assigned to the case, and a brief description or title identifying the document. All the OBFs we have looked at provide for the entry of caption data in the form. This is in compliance with FRBP 9004(b), which requires the use of such captions for *all* documents filed with the court in a bankruptcy case.

Illustration 13-d: MOTION, OBJECTION, AND NOTICE OF INTENDED ACTION PRACTICE IN A BANKRUPTCY CASE, INCLUDING THE "AFTER NOTICE AND A HEARING" PROCEDURE

- A written motion or objection seeking a court order or a notice of intended action is filed with the clerk of the bankruptcy court, who notifies the judge of the filing and places it in the official case file.
- Copies of the motion, objection, or notice are *served* on parties in interest. A *certificate of service* included in or attached to the motion, objection, or notice certifies that service was made by listing the names and addresses of the persons and entities served, the means of service (by mail, hand delivery, or electronic attachment (e-mail)), and the date of service.
- The party filing the motion, objection, or notice includes with the copy served on parties in interest a *notice of motion (or objection)*, advising those parties of the date set for a hearing on the matter. In some bankruptcy courts, the clerk of the court or the judge's chambers assumes responsibility for serving the notice of motion.
- If the subject of the motion, objection, or notice is not controlled by the "after notice and a hearing" procedure, then it is treated as a contested matter and the hearing will be conducted as scheduled. The notice of motion may advise parties in interest to file a written response by a certain date.
- If the subject of the motion, objection, or notice is controlled by the "after notice and a hearing" procedure, the notice of motion will explain that a response is due by a certain date and that if no response is filed by that date, the motion or objection may be granted or the action authorized by the court without any hearing or any further action by the court. In some bankruptcy courts, no hearing date will be set on a matter controlled by "after notice and a hearing" unless and until a party in interest files a response. If a party in interest does file a response, the hearing will be held (or scheduled and held in those courts where no hearing date is set in the original notice).
- The bankruptcy judge, by order or local rule, may direct the parties to submit written briefs prior to the hearing date. The briefs set forth the arguments of the parties on matters related to the motion or notice and the law they rely on in connection with those arguments.
- If briefs were ordered by the trial judge, they are filed with the clerk of the court by the due date. The clerk causes the briefs to become part of the official case file.
- At the hearing, the party filing the motion, objection, or notice and other parties in interest are allowed to make an appearance and be heard by the judge by way of oral argument to supplement the written argument made in the briefs, if any. If necessary, the judge hears sworn testimony and receives any exhibits offered through that testimony.
- The judge rules on the contested matter, either at the conclusion of the hearing or shortly thereafter, either granting, denying, or modifying the relief requested in the motion or the intended action stated in the notice. The ruling is memorialized in a written *order* signed by the judge.
- The clerk of the court *enters the order* by causing it to become part of the official case file. The date of entry is noted on the order.
- Copies of the order are sent by the clerk to the movant and all parties in interest.

2. Adversary Proceedings

Adversary proceedings Certain disputes defined by Bankruptcy Rule 7001 that arise in a bankruptcy case and are resolved by the procedures governing a formal civil lawsuit.

Some disputes that arise in a bankruptcy case are treated, not as contested matters, but as more formal **adversary proceedings**. An adversary proceeding is essentially a formal **civil lawsuit** initiated *within* the bankruptcy case and involving a dispute related to the case. FRBP 7001 lists the types of disputes that *must* be presented to the court as an adversary proceeding, and they are summarized in Illustration 13-f.

In an adversary proceeding, the **Federal Rules of Civil Procedure (FRCP)** come into play and are largely incorporated by Part VII of the FRBPs (7001

Illustration 13-e: ACTIONS THE COURT MAY APPROVE EX PARTE

- Granting extensions of time to take some actions (FRBP 9006(b))
- Ordering Rule 2004 examinations (FRBP 2004)
- Deferring grant of Chapter 7 discharge (FRBP 4004(c))
- Closing or reopening a closed bankruptcy case (§350)
- Ordering the consolidation or joint administration of a case (FRBP 1015)
- Ordering conversion of a case from one chapter to another upon request of the debtor, where permitted (§§706(a), 1307(a), 1208(a), and 1112(a))

Illustration 13-f: DISPUTES THAT MUST BE RESOLVED AS ADVERSARY PROCEEDINGS

- A proceeding to bar the debtor from receiving a discharge in bankruptcy or to revoke a discharge previously granted
- A proceeding to declare a particular debt nondischargeable
- A proceeding to determine the validity, extent, or priority of a lien on property of the debtor
- A proceeding to recover money or property from a third party
- A proceeding to obtain an injunction or other equitable relief
- A proceeding to obtain approval to sell property in which both the debtor and a nondebtor have an interest
- A proceeding to subordinate a creditor's claim or interest to other claims
- A proceeding to revoke an order confirming a plan in a Chapter 11, 12, or 13 case

through 7087) formally governing adversary proceedings. The party initiating the adversary proceeding, usually the bankruptcy trustee or a creditor, does so by filing a **complaint**. (See Document 34 in the Carlson case file.) OBF 16D provides the basic form for the caption of a complaint used to initiate an adversary proceeding. **Service of process** under FRCP 4 must be accomplished on the defendant. The defendant must file an **answer** to the complaint or a **default judgment** will be entered against her. The formal rules of **pretrial discovery** found in FRCP 26 through 37 are available to the parties (interrogatories to parties, depositions, requests for production of documents and things, requests for physical or mental examination, and requests for admission). And the case, if not settled, will be scheduled for trial and tried in the bankruptcy court.

Default judgment A *final judgment* rendered against a defendant in a civil suit who fails to file an *answer* to the *complaint* or to otherwise defend.

P-H 13-j: Compare the bankruptcy trustee's objection to the claim of Pine Ridge Nursing Home (Document 31 in the Carlson case file) with the complaint filed against Evelyn Rinaldi to recover the doll collection in her possession that belongs to her sister, Marta Rinaldi Carlson (Document 35 in the Carlson case file). The former is a not an adversary matter under FRBP 7001 and can be resolved as a contested matter by motion. The latter is an adversary matter under FRBP 7001 because it is an action to recover money or property of the estate from a third person (see Illustration 13-f) under §542 (discussed in Chapter Seventeen,

Section D). Does the caption of the complaint in Document 34 comply with the required format of OBF 16D? What other differences in detail and formality do you see in the two documents? To resolve the contested matter raised by motion, the court will schedule a hearing within a few days and the parties will appear to present proof and/or make argument. They may or may not prepare prehearing briefs for the court. But in the adversary proceeding, the named defendant must be formally served with process pursuant to FRCP 4, be given time to file a formal answer to the complaint, engage in formal pretrial discovery allowed by FRCP 26 through 37, and make any pretrial motions allowed by the FRCP. The parties to the adversary proceeding may also be entitled to demand a jury for the trial of the case. Review Illustration 13-b to determine what happens if a party to an adversary proceeding demands a jury.

P-H 13-k: In the vast majority of situations the Code makes it clear whether a dispute is to be treated as a contested matter or as an adversary proceeding. But not always. See that issue raised in P-H 16-c in connection with a debtor's contention that a creditor has violated the automatic stay of §362(a). Look at Document 27 in the Carlson case file. Does the court handling the Carlson bankruptcy case treat this type of dispute as a contested matter or an adversary proceeding? How do the bankruptcy courts of your federal district treat it?

H. ▶ Other Important Players in a Bankruptcy Case

Debtor A person who files a petition under the Code.

Creditor One to whom a debt is owed.

The party that files the bankruptcy proceeding is the **debtor**. In the forms that the debtor files in connection with his bankruptcy case he will identify his **creditors** and will state whether each creditor is secured or unsecured and so forth. Beginning with the **petition in bankruptcy** the debtor files to begin the case, all documents in a bankruptcy case are filed with the **bankruptcy court clerk's** office in most federal districts, though a few require filing with the **district court clerk**. The court clerk is the administrative officer for the court in which the case is pending. The clerk's office will maintain all records regarding the case and is responsible for sending out various notices regarding actions taken or to be taken in the case (e.g., notice to listed creditors of the filing of the case, notice of the first meeting of creditors, notice of upcoming hearings on disputed matters). It is essential that the legal professional practicing in the bankruptcy area become familiar with the personnel and procedures of the clerk's office.

Most debtors hire attorneys to help them prepare and file the necessary papers and to represent them throughout the bankruptcy proceeding. These attorneys are known as **debtor's attorneys**. Creditors also often retain attorneys to assist them in processing their claim through the bankruptcy proceeding. These attorneys are known as **creditor's attorneys**.

In most bankruptcy cases (and always in Chapter 7 and 13 cases), as soon as the petition is filed beginning the case, the bankruptcy court will appoint a **bankruptcy trustee** to administer the case. As we shall see later, the bankruptcy trustee is given broad powers under the Code and is responsible to the court and to the creditors of the estate for his actions. Sometimes the bankruptcy trustee finds it

Illustration 13-g: APPEAL PROCESS FOR FINAL ORDERS ENTERED BY A BANKRUPTCY COURT

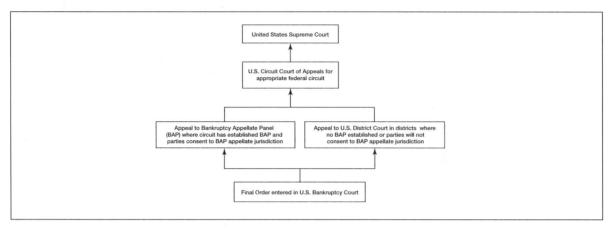

appropriate to hire an attorney to represent him in some proceeding in the case, like an adversary proceeding. The attorney the trustee hires is known as the **bankruptcy trustee's attorney.**

In most but not all federal districts, there is another government official involved in bankruptcy cases: the **U.S. Trustee** (never to be confused with the **bankruptcy trustee**). The U.S. Trustee is given responsibilities under §586 of the Code and various FRBP to perform duties such as:

- to determine who is eligible to serve as a bankruptcy trustee;
- to oversee and monitor the work of the bankruptcy trustees;
- to monitor pending cases; and
- to make recommendations to the bankruptcy judge on contested issues that arise before the bankruptcy judge.

The U.S. Trustee program is administered and overseen by the U.S. Department of Justice (www.usdoj.gov/ust). In North Carolina and Alabama, there are no U.S. Trustees, but **bankruptcy administrators** perform the same tasks in those states, overseen by the Administrative Office of the U.S. Courts (www.uscourts.gov).

In the course of administering a bankruptcy case, the services of a number of different professionals and businesspeople may be utilized by the bankruptcy trustee, the debtor, or creditors. Those may include *auctioneers, realtors, appraisers, insurance agents, bankers, economists, accountants,* and *repossession* and *storage services.*

Party in interest Generally, a person or entity having a stake in the outcome of a matter arising in a bankruptcy case.

A number of Code provisions refer to the right of a **party in interest** to take some action in a bankruptcy case. For example, §502(a) authorizes a party in interest to object to the claim filed in a case by a creditor of the debtor (discussed in Chapter Seventeen, Section A). FRBP 4003(b) authorizes a party in interest to object to a debtor's claim of exempt property (discussed in Chapter Fifteen, Section B). Curiously, neither the Code nor the FRBP define who is a party in interest leaving courts to make that determination based on the particular right to act being granted by the Code. But, generally speaking, a party in interest is a person or entity who is deemed to have standing to be heard by the court on a matter to be decided in the bankruptcy case. For most matters, the debtor, the bankruptcy trustee, the U.S. trustee or bankruptcy administrator, and creditors or other third parties (e.g., persons who are not in bankruptcy but who are jointly liable with the bankruptcy debtor on certain obligations or nondebtor owners of an entity in bankruptcy) who may be affected by the action taken will be deemed are parties in interest.

I. The Role of the Assisting Legal Professional in a Bankruptcy Case

Knowing who the various players are in a bankruptcy case helps you understand where well-trained legal professionals may find employment in this area. Illustration 13-h lists the offices or persons for which the bankruptcy legal professional may work.

Debtor's attorneys in particular make significant use of legal professionals, particularly for client interviewing and document preparation. It is not unusual for the assisting legal professional to have the first and major interaction with potential clients in those offices. Illustration 13-i lists typical duties of the legal professional assisting a debtor's attorney.

Illustration 13-h: OFFICES OR PERSONS FOR WHICH THE BANKRUPTCY LEGAL PROFESSIONAL MAY WORK

- Bankruptcy court clerk's office
- Debtor's attorney
- Creditor's attorney
- Bankruptcy trustee's office
- U.S. Trustee's office
- Attorney representing the bankruptcy trustee

Illustration 13-i: DUTIES OF A LEGAL PROFESSIONAL ASSISTING A DEBTOR'S ATTORNEY

- Interviewing prospective clients/bankruptcy debtors
- Locating and gathering financial and other information related to a client's case
- Reviewing and organizing financial information supplied by clients and prospective clients
- Preparing the bankruptcy petition and supporting financial schedules for filing with the court
- Researching legal issues arising in a debtor's case
- Drafting of motions, briefs, and orders on matters related to a client's case
- Assisting the supervising attorney in preparing for and conducting court hearings related to a client's case
- Organizing and maintaining client files
- Attending administrative hearings (like the first meeting of creditors, which we consider later) to observe and take notes for the attorney
- Monitoring filings related to client cases by creditors or the bankruptcy trustee in the clerk's office

The expansive duties often given to assisting legal professionals by busy debtor's attorneys, who often carry hundreds of cases at a time, raise the potential for unethical conduct.

EC 13-a: Mary is a paralegal for John Law, a very busy debtor's bankruptcy lawyer. Law doesn't make a lot of money from any one bankruptcy case. His fee for a simple Chapter 7 is $1,000 and not much more for a typical Chapter 13. Law has learned that, in order to prosper, he must have a lot of cases going on simultaneously. He knows he is fortunate to have Mary working for him. She is smart, experienced, and has good work habits. Over time, Law begins to delegate more and more responsibility to Mary. She handles the first meeting with potential new clients, explains the bankruptcy process to them, answers their questions about it, collects the necessary information from them, and prepares the petition and supporting schedules to file the case. He's even stopped reviewing and signing the documents himself, trusting Mary to make sure they are correct and then adding his signature. In fact, Law doesn't even meet or communicate with his clients until it's time to attend the first meeting of creditors, where his attendance is mandatory. Law wishes Mary could handle that as well. What ethical/professional conduct violations can you identify for attorney Law and for Mary the paralegal?

J. ▶ Electronic Filing in Bankruptcy Courts

Every bankruptcy court in the country now employs **electronic case filing** instead of paper filing for all or most documents. A few courts still require the petition itself to be filed in paper, but most have gone completely paperless. This means that all filings by the various parties in interest to the bankruptcy case (the petition, supporting schedules, statements and lists, motions, objections, reports, applications, etc.) are submitted electronically, the court's orders are entered electronically, and all notices and other communications from the court to case participants are distributed electronically. Needless to say, lawyers and those assisting them in the bankruptcy field must become familiar with the e-filing system utilized in bankruptcy courts.

Case Management/Electronic Case Files (CM/ECF) The current system for filing documents with a bankruptcy court electronically.

The electronic system used in all bankruptcy courts is known as **Case Management/Electronic Case Files (CM/ECF)**. The way the system works is that documents created in a lawyer's office by word processing software are saved in a portable document format (PDF). The attorney then logs in by computer to the local court's CM/ECF system using a log-in name and password provided by the court clerk, identifies the case in which the document is to be submitted, attaches the PDF file containing the document to be filed in the case, and presses a "submit" button. In the clerk's office, the CM/CEF immediately sends the lawyer's office by e-mail an **electronic receipt** confirming receipt of the document filed. The receipt can be saved or printed by the lawyer's office. The CM/ECF system allows 24-hour, 7-day-a-week filing for case participants. Once a party has made an appearance in a pending case, they then receive electronic notification of case activity (other filings, entry of orders, etc.) by means of a **Notice of Electronic Filing (NEF)**, which allows the recipient a one-time look at the document filed and the opportunity to copy or save it. The system also allows the payment of filing fees by credit card.

In order to be able to view all documents in a case (any case) at any time and as frequently as desired (rather than the one-free-look allowed by CM/ECF), lawyers must subscribe to **Public Access to Court Electronic Records (PACER)**. Members of the public may also subscribe to PACER. To avoid having to pay for access to electronic records, lawyers or members of the public may also go physically to the office of the bankruptcy court clerk and view files on screens made available there. A charge will be made, however, for documents copied.

Notices from the bankruptcy court to case participants is also done electronically through the **Electronic Bankruptcy Noticing (EBN)**, which allows attorneys and others to receive notices from the bankruptcy court by e-mail link, e-mail with PDF attachment, or fax.

P-H 13-l: Go to www.pacer.gov/ and choose one or more of the video tutorials available there explaining how the CM/ECF, PACER, and EBN systems work.

If a party in interest is entitled to notice or service of a motion or other document filed in the case but does not participate in CM/CMF, notice or service on that party must then be accomplished by sending a paper copy by first class mail or hand delivery. Typically, a party filing a motion or other document will utilize electronic filing and then examine the electronic receipt to make sure all parties entitled to notice received it by the electronic filing. If any party did not receive it electronically, they are then served with paper copy by hand delivery or first class mail. The certificate of service included on the document filed will advise that service was accomplished electronically or by hand delivery or mailing.

P-H 13-m: There has been considerable unhappiness about the cost of downloading bankruptcy documents on PACER and the lack of free or less costly access to public court records in general. That unhappiness is giving impetus to private alternatives to PACER. Check out the Recap Web site at www.recapthelaw.org/ and the Inforuptcy site at www.inforuptcy.com/. How do these sites make bankruptcy filings initially accessed for a fee on PACER available to the public for little or nothing?

K. Bankruptcy Software

Attorneys who represent bankruptcy debtors utilize **bankruptcy software** programs to expedite the preparation of the numerous schedules and

Illustration 13-j: A SAMPLING OF BANKRUPTCY SOFTWARE PROVIDERS

- BestCase (www.bestcase.com)
- New Hope (www.bankruptcysoftware.com)
- Law Firm Software (www.lawfirmsoftware.com)
- Blumberg Blankrupter (www.blumberg.com/)
- EZ Filing (www.ezfiling.com)
- LegalPro (www.legal-pro.com)
- National LawForms (http://nationallawforms.com)
- Standard Legal (www.standardlegal.com)
- Law Disks (www.lawdisks.com)

statements required in every case. A good software program can save time for the debtor's attorney and assist legal professionals by automatically filling in repetitive information, performing calculations, and formatting the documents in a way to comply with electronic filing requirements. Some programs allow for unlimited use and some are limited to one-time use. A number of bankruptcy software providers and their Web sites are listed in Illustration 13-j. A number of the Web sites provide a free online demonstration and/or permit the free download of forms that can be used for demonstration purposes.

P-H 13-n: Visit some or all of the Web sites listed in Illustration 13-j and try the online demonstrations or download and compare the free forms. Which provider seems to offer the software that is the easiest to use? Which seems to provide the most comprehensive services? Which allow unlimited use and which only one-time use? Why would an attorney choose a one-time use software package?

L. Web-Based Resources for Learning About Bankruptcy

There are a number of excellent Web sites providing free access to current news and information of interest to bankruptcy professionals, as well as bankruptcy-specific legal research. Illustration 13-k lists a number of these.

Illustration 13-k: USEFUL BANKRUPTCY INFORMATION SITES

The Bankruptcy Code, Rules, Forms, and General Information:

- Title 11 of the U.S. Code: www.law.cornell.edu/uscode/text/11 or http://codes.lp.findlaw.com/uscode/11 or http://uscode.house.gov/download/title_11.shtml
- Rules of Bankruptcy Procedure: www.uscourts.gov/uscourts/RulesAndPolicies/rules/2011%20Rules/Bankruptcy%20Procedure.pdf
- Official Bankruptcy Forms: www.uscourts.gov/FormsAndFees/Forms/BankruptcyForms.aspx
- Administrative Office of the Federal Courts' Federal Judiciary Home Page (www.uscourts.gov)
- United States Trustees Program (administered by the U.S. Department of Justice) (www.usdoj.gov/ust)
- Electronic Bankruptcy Noticing Center (www.ebnuscourts.com)
- AO site with links to all current federal rules of practice and procedure: www.uscourts.gov/RulesAndPolicies/rules/current-rules.aspx
- AO Bankruptcy Basics: www.uscourts.gov/FederalCourts/Bankruptcy/BankruptcyBasics.aspx
- Cornell University Law School's Legal Information Institute's Bankruptcy Information Page (www.law.cornell.edu/wex/index.php/Bankruptcy)
- The Internet Bankruptcy Library (http://bankrupt.com)
- FindLaw's Internet Guide to Bankruptcy Law (http://library.findlaw.com/1999/Mar/1/128347.html)
- Bernstein's Dictionary of Bankruptcy Terminology (www.bernsteinlaw.com/publications/bankdict.htm)
- NOLO Bankruptcy in Your State: http://www.thebankruptcysite.org/topics/bankruptcy-your-state

Organizations Concerned with Bankruptcy Practice:

- American Bankruptcy Institute (www.abiworld.org)
- National Association of Bankruptcy Trustees (www.nabt.com/faq.cfm)
- National Association of Chapter 13 Bankruptcy Trustees (www.nactt.com)
- National Association of Consumer Bankruptcy Attorneys (www.nacba.org)
- National Consumer Law Center (www.nclc.org)
- The Commercial Law League of America (www.clla.org)

Bankruptcy Blogs and other News and Information Sites:

- ABA Journal Blawg Directory (www.abajournal.com/blawgs/topic/bankruptcy+law)
- ABI Blog Exchange (http://blogs.abi.org/)
- Bankruptcy Attorneys on the Web (www.bestcase.com/bkattys.htm)
- Bankruptcy Law Network (www.bankruptcylawnetwork.com)
- Bankruptcy Lawyers Blog (http://blog.startfreshtoday.com)
- Bankruptcy Litigation Blog: http://www.bankruptcylitigationblog.com/
- LAW 360:Bankruptcy(www.law360.com/bankruptcy)
- Bankruptcy Preference Digest: http://www.burbageweddell.com/blog/
- Becker & Posner Blog: http://www.becker-posner-blog.com/
- BKBlog: http://www.thebklawyer.com/thebkblog/
- Credit Slips blog on Credit, Finance and Bankruptcy (www.creditslips.org/creditslips)
- Daily Bankruptcy News: http://bkinformation.com/news/dailynews.htm
- Finance and Bankruptcy Blog: http://www.bankruptcylawblog.com/
- In the Red Business Bankruptcy Blog (http://bankruptcy.cooley.com/)
- New Generation Research (NGR) (www.turnarounds.com)
- Wall Street Journal Bankruptcy Beat Blog (http://blogs.wsj.com/bankruptcy/)
- Weil Bankruptcy Blog: http://business-finance-restructuring.weil.com/

CONCLUSION

Having introduced the Bankruptcy Code in Chapter Twelve and added an understanding from this chapter regarding the issues surrounding the subject matter and personal jurisdiction of the U.S. bankruptcy courts as well as the various procedures those courts use to resolve disputes in cases pending before them, we are ready to examine the various types of bankruptcy proceedings in more detail. And we are going to use the case study method to do so. We will begin in Chapter Fourteen with the most commonly filed bankruptcy case, the Chapter 7 liquidation proceeding.

CHAPTER SUMMARY

Bankruptcy courts and judges are found in every federal district around the country and today serve as units or adjuncts of the U.S. district courts. Most U.S. district courts have formally referred bankruptcy jurisdiction to the bankruptcy courts in their districts by standing order so that new bankruptcy cases are filed in the bankruptcy court rather than the district court, though issues remain regarding exactly what matters bankruptcy courts, as Article 1 courts, have constitutional jurisdiction to decide under the separation of powers doctrine. Upon proper referral, bankruptcy courts may enter final orders in core proceedings arising in a bankruptcy case but not in noncore proceedings, unless the parties involved unanimously consent to it doing so. Absent that consent, the bankruptcy court can only enter proposed findings and conclusions in noncore proceedings; however, the district court must enter the final order. Likewise, the bankruptcy court can conduct a jury trial in a core or noncore proceeding only if all parties consent. Final orders entered by a bankruptcy court may be appealed to the U.S. district court subject to a clearly erroneous standard of review, unless the federal circuit in which the bankruptcy court lies has established a Bankruptcy Appellate Panel (BAP). Decisions of the district courts or BAP are appealable to the appropriate circuit court of appeals.

Some procedural matters in a bankruptcy case are governed by the "after notice and a hearing" procedure, pursuant to which, once proper notice of the motion or intended action is given to parties in interest, the relief requested will be granted or the action authorized unless a party contests the motion or notice, thereby making it a contested matter. Once the dispute becomes a contested matter, the court will conduct a formal hearing and take evidence if necessary before ruling on the motion. Some procedural matters in a bankruptcy case are always treated as contested matters. Other disputes that arise in a bankruptcy case are treated as adversary proceedings rather than mere contested matters and require formal compliance with most of the Federal Rules of Civil Procedure for a full civil trial.

There are a large number of people involved in a bankruptcy case, including the debtor, his creditors, the attorneys for the debtor and creditors; the bankruptcy judge; the bankruptcy court clerk; the U.S. Trustee; a bankruptcy trustee (if one is appointed); and various professionals or tradespersons that the debtor, creditors, or the bankruptcy trustee might retain for case-related services. Legal professionals may be found working for any of these players in the bankruptcy case and there are numerous skills that the assisting legal professional must possess in order to be successful working in the bankruptcy area. Bankruptcy courts now employ electronic filing of documents using Case Management/Electronic Case Files (CM/ECF), Notice of Electronic Filing (NEF), and Electronic Bankruptcy Noticing (EBN). Filings in bankruptcy cases nationwide may be accessed through Public Access to Court Electronic Records (PACER).

REVIEW QUESTIONS

1. Explain what is meant by "referral jurisdiction" of the bankruptcy courts.
2. List as many types as you can of proceedings in a bankruptcy case that would be considered core proceedings.
3. Name two types of disputes that might arise in a bankruptcy case that would not be considered core proceedings. What difference does the distinction make?
4. What is the Bankruptcy Appellate Panel? Explain the procedure for appealing a final order entered by a bankruptcy court.
5. Explain the difference between a U.S. Trustee and a bankruptcy trustee.
6. Why does the "after notice and a hearing" procedure used for resolving certain matters in a bankruptcy case not necessarily require a hearing?
7. What is the difference between the procedure used to resolve a contested matter and that used to resolve an adversary proceeding? Name at least three types of proceedings that are considered adversary proceedings.
8. List as many different types of nonlawyer professionals as you can think of who may be involved in a bankruptcy case.
9. List six different players in a bankruptcy case that an assisting legal professional might work for. List as many duties as you can think of that a legal professional assisting a debtor's attorney might be given.
10. Describe the electronic filing system used in bankruptcy courts and include an explanation of CM/ECF, NEF, EBN, and PACER.

WORDS AND PHRASES TO REMEMBER

Administrative Office of the
  U.S. Courts
administrative officer
adversary proceedings
after notice and a hearing procedure
ancillary proceeding
answer (to complaint)
appeal as of right
application for writ of certiorari
appraisers
arbitration
Article I courts
Article III courts
auctioneers

Bankruptcy Abuse Prevention
  and Consumer Protection Act
  of 2005 (BAPCPA)
bankruptcy administrators
Bankruptcy Appeals Panels (BAPs)
Bankruptcy Reform Act of 1994
Bankruptcy Code (Code)
bankruptcy court clerk
bankruptcy judge
bankruptcy referee
bankruptcy software
bankruptcy trustee
certiorari
civil lawsuit
clearly erroneous

Commercial Law League
    of America
complaint (in a civil case)
conclusions of law
constitutional jurisdiction
contested matter
core (and noncore) proceedings
creditor
creditor's attorney
de novo
debtor
debtor's attorney
default judgment
derivative action
due process
economists
Electronic Bankruptcy
    Noticing (EBN)
electronic case filing
electronic receipt
evidentiary hearing
ex parte
Federal Arbitration Act
Federal Rules of Civil Procedure
Federal Rules of Evidence
fiduciary duty
final order
findings of fact
forum state
hearing
in personam jurisdiction
in rem jurisdiction
insurance agents
legislative courts
local custom and practice
local rules
Marathon

motion to compel arbitration
National Association of Consumer
    Bankruptcy Attorneys
National Bankruptcy
    Review Commission
national contacts
notice of intended action
objection
oral argument
PACER
party in interest
personal jurisdiction
private rights
protection of life and limb
public rights
realtors
referral jurisdiction
repossession services
revoke the reference
separation of powers doctrine
service of process
standard of review
standing order
surveyors
standard of review
Stern
subject matter jurisdiction
sworn testimony
traditional notions of fair play and
    substantial justice
trust fund doctrine
U.S. bankruptcy court
U.S. circuit court
U.S. district court
U.S. Trustee
written brief

**TO LEARN MORE: A number of TLM activities to accompany this chapter are
accessible on the student disc accompanying the text and on the Author
Updates link to the text Web site at http://www.aspenparalegaled.com/
books/parsons_abcdebt/default.asp.**

Chapter Fourteen:

The Chapter 7 Case: The Means Test and Other Qualifications to File

Forgive us our debts, as we forgive our debtors.
—*Matthew 6:12, King James Bible*

Introduction

Beginning with this chapter we will examine in detail each of the three most commonly filed bankruptcy proceedings authorized by the Code: Chapter 7, Chapter 13, and Chapter 11 cases. The more rarely filed Chapter 12 case will receive summary treatment in connection with our study of the Chapter 13 bankruptcy.

Approximately 70 to 75 percent of all bankruptcy filings nationwide (see Illustration 12-g) are Chapter 7 liquidation cases and about 98 percent of those are consumer bankruptcies filed by individuals with nonbusiness debt. Chapter 7 is a liquidation proceeding in which a bankruptcy trustee is authorized to locate and take possession of the nonexempt assets of the debtor, **liquidate** (sell) those assets, and distribute the proceeds to creditors of the estate per a distribution formula established by the Code. Either an individual or an entity may be a Chapter 7 debtor but, as we will see, that is not to say that *any* individual or entity can file for the Chapter 7 fresh start.

Most debts remaining unpaid after the distribution and not formally reaffirmed by the debtor in the bankruptcy proceeding will be permanently **discharged** by order of the bankruptcy court. Thus, the basic idea in a Chapter 7 is that the debtor makes all of her nonexempt assets available to her creditors in exchange for a discharge of most of her unpaid debts. We will learn, however, that some debts cannot be discharged in a Chapter 7 and some Chapter 7 cases do not result in any discharge at all.

For our study of Chapter 7 in this and the next four chapters, we will focus on the case of an individual who in many ways fits the profile of a typical debtor whom you saw in Illustration 12-e. It's time to meet Marta Rinaldi Carlson. Go to Appendix A of the text at this time and read the Assignment Memorandum. The entire Chapter 7 file in Marta Carlson's Chapter 7 case is available on the disc accompanying this text.

> **P-H 14-a:** Using the information in the Assignment Memorandum in Appendix A, see how Marta Carlson fits into the various categories of the profile in Illustration 12-e.

A. The Basic §109 Qualifications

Section 109(a) of the Code provides that, "only a person that resides or has a domicile, a place of business, or property in the United States, or a municipality" can file as a debtor under any of the six chapters of the Code. Regarding who can file for Chapter 7 relief, §109(b) says any "person" can, and "person" is defined by §101(41) to include both individuals (natural persons) and business entities, such as corporations (including limited liability companies) and partnerships, but not governmental units. However, §109(b) specifically prohibits railroads, insurance companies, commercial banks chartered by federal or state governments, savings banks, savings and loan associations, credit unions, and some other financial institutions from filing for Chapter 7 liquidation relief. (As discussed in Section H of Chapter Twelve, such entities are liquidated under state law or specialized federal regulation, and railroads may file for Chapter 11 reorganization.)

EXAMPLE

If Abe Mendoza (Case Study #2, Illustration 1-b) decides to file for Chapter 7 relief, he will qualify under §109 because he is an individual. If Tomorrow Today, Inc. (TTI) (Case Study #3, Illustration 1-c) decides to file for Chapter 7 relief, it will qualify because it is a corporation. But if Security Trust Bank, which holds the mortgage on Abe Mendoza's home, decides to file for Chapter 7 relief it will not qualify and will have to seek relief under separate statutory authority involving both state and federal law. If the municipality of Capitol City itself decides to file for Chapter 7 relief, it will not qualify and will have to seek relief under Chapter 9 of the Code.

B. The §727(a) Prior Discharge Limitations

Pursuant to §727(a), a debtor qualified to file a Chapter 7 case under §109 cannot receive a discharge in Chapter 7 if he previously received a discharge in a Chapter 7 or Chapter 11 case within *eight years* preceding the filing of the petition or in a Chapter 13 or Chapter 12 case within *six years*.

C. The §707(b) Means Test and Presumption of Abuse Limitation for Individual Consumer Debtors

1. Introduction to the Means Test and the Presumption of Abuse

Recall that in Chapter Twelve, Section C, we distinguished between **business bankruptcy cases** and **consumer bankruptcy cases**, defining the latter as the

Consumer debt Debt incurred for personal, family, or household purposes.

Presumption of abuse The presumption of inappropriate filing of a Chapter 7 case for the debtor who fails the *means test.*

Means test A test for Chapter 7 filers introduced by BAPCPA intended to determine whether the debtor has sufficient *disposable income* to enable the debtor to repay some or all of his debts in a Chapter 13 case.

case of an individual with primarily consumer debts. And recall that §101(8) of the Code defines **consumer debt** as "debt incurred by an individual primarily for a personal, family or household purpose."

Section 707(b)(1) authorizes the court to dismiss a Chapter 7 case filed by a consumer debtor if it finds that the granting of relief would be an "abuse of the provisions of this chapter." Section 707(b)(2)(A)(i), as amended by BAPCPA, raises a **presumption of abuse** if the debtor fails a **means test** created by that section. The means test essentially compares the debtor's average monthly income to the median income of a family the size of the debtor's in the state where the debtor resides. If the debtor's income is equal to or less than the state median income figure, the debtor can file for Chapter 7 relief. If the debtor's income (calculated with the debtor's spouse if the spouse is not filing) exceeds the state median income figure, the presumption of abuse arises and the debtor cannot file for Chapter 7 relief. Debtor's income from the following sources is included in the calculation:

- Wages, salary, tips, bonuses, overtime, and commissions
- Gross income from a business, profession, or a farm
- Interest, dividends, and royalties
- Rental and real property income
- Regular child support or spousal support
- Unemployment compensation
- Pension and retirement income
- Workers' compensation
- Annuity payments
- State disability insurance

Debtor's income from the following sources is excluded from the calculation:

- Tax refunds
- Social Security retirement benefits
- Social Security Disability Insurance
- Supplemental Security Income
- Temporary Assistance for Needy Families

The object of the means test is to identify **"can-pay" debtors** and to funnel them into Chapter 13 filings, where the excess disposable income is made available to pay all or a portion of the debtor's debts.

Entity debtors and individual debtors whose debts are primarily business rather than consumer debts are not subject to the means test. Veterans suffering from a 30 percent or higher permanent disability and whose indebtedness arose primarily during active duty or while performing a homeland defense activity are expressly exempted from the means test, as are certain members of the National Guard and armed forces reserves who were called to duty for at least 90 days following September 11, 2001, pursuant to the **National Guard Reservists Debt Relief Act of 2008.**

EXAMPLE

The vast majority of Marta Carlson's debt, as described in the Assignment Memorandum in Appendix A, will qualify as consumer debt. One exception might be the indebtedness to Dreams Come True Finance Company, which was incurred to fund a business venture for her ex-husband. Since Marta is an individual consumer debtor, she will have to satisfy the means test of §707(b) in order to maintain a Chapter 7 filing.

P-H 14-b: What happens if a debtor files a petition in Chapter 13 (which requires a calculation of disposable income for purposes of a Chapter 13 plan but does not involve a means test) and then converts the case to one in Chapter 7? Will that debtor have to satisfy the means test in order to proceed in Chapter 7? There is actually a split on this question with a majority of courts following what is called the "common sense" view that the means test must still be satisfied because Congress intended all Chapter 7 debtors to do so (see, e.g., *In re Kellett*, 379 B.R. 332 (Bankr. D. Ore. 2007), but a strong minority follow the "plain language" view, saying that the debtor converting a Chapter 13 case over need not satisfy the means test because, literally read, §707(b) only requires the test in consumer cases "filed" under Chapter 7 and a converted Chapter case was not filed under Chapter 7 (see, e.g., *In re Layton*, 480 B.R. 392 (Bkrtcy. M.D. Fla. 2012)). How have the bankruptcy or district courts of your federal district or circuit decided this issue?

The means test is completed using Official Bankruptcy Form (OBF) 22A, **Statement of Current Monthly Income and Means Test Calculation** (all official bankruptcy forms are available at www.uscourts.gov/bkforms/index.html). You can see questions related to the means test exemptions in Part I of that form. You can see Marta Carlson's entire completed Form 22A in Document 21-A in the Carlson case file on the disc accompanying this text. Illustration 14-a below reproduces Parts II and III of her Form 22A for easy consultation. The means test and OBF 22A are new with BAPCPA and many questions concerning how it works remain unanswered. As we work through OBF22A using Marta Carlson's case, we will look at a number of recent cases beginning to interpret the test. Additionally, the U.S. Trustee Program has issued its own **Statement on Legal Issues Arising Under the Chapter 7 Means Test** that can be accessed at www.justice.gov/ust/eo/bapcpa/docs/ch7_line_by_line.pdf and can be consulted with profit as we venture through OBF 22A.

2. Step 1 of the Means Test: Comparing the Debtor's Annualized Monthly Income to the State Median Family Income Using Parts II & III of OBF 22A

Median family income State by state statistics compiled by the U.S. Census Bureau every ten years when a constitutionally mandated census is taken and set out by family size.

Calculating the means test is a one- or two-step process. In Step 1 we use Parts II and III of Form 22A to compare the debtor's annualized **current monthly income** to the annualized **median family income** for a similar size family in the debtor's state of residence. Section 707(b)(7) provides that if the debtor's current monthly income is equal to or less than the applicable median family income, no presumption of abuse arises and the means test is satisfied for that debtor.

The median family income numbers are published by the **U.S. Census Bureau** by state and family size and are updated annually. The Web site of the U.S. Trustee

Program (at www.usdoj.gov/ust/eo/bapcpa/meanstesting.htm) sets forth the Census Bureau's current tables for median family income.

P-H 14-c: Assume that the fictional state of Columbiana, Marta's state of residence, has the same median family numbers as the actual state of Missouri. There are three persons in Marta's family. Go to the U.S. Trustees Web site (at www.usdoj.gov/ust/eo/bapcpa/meanstesting.htm) and locate the Census Bureau's current tables for median family income for a family of three in the state of Missouri. This is the median family income figure against which we will compare Marta's annual income to see if she passes the means test. While you are there, check out the median family income for your family size in your state.

Note: The median income figures from the Census Bureau are adjusted annually. Marta's form uses the correct median income figure for Missouri as of January 2013, but that figure may be different when you read this.

Current monthly income The monthly income of a consumer debtor calculated by averaging the debtor's income from all sources for the six months preceding the filing of the petition.

To determine the debtor's annual income, we first calculate the debtor's **current monthly income** (CMI), defined in §101(10A) to include the **average monthly income from all sources** that the debtor has received during the six months preceding the filing of the petition (known as the **look back period**), regardless of whether such income is taxable as well as any amounts paid by a third party for the household expenses of the debtor. The sixth month to be included in the look back period is the month immediately preceding the date the case is filed.

EXAMPLE

> If a Chapter 7 petition is filed on September 15, the applicable look back period for calculating the debtor's CMI will be income from all sources received from March through August of that year. Income from those six months will be averaged to arrive at the current monthly income figure. So if the debtor had income totaling $26,400 during the look back period, the applicable CMI will be $4,400 ($26,400 divided by six).

Part II of OBF 22A is used to calculate the debtor's CMI (see Illustration 14-a).

P-H 14-d: Determining Marta's current monthly income is a simple calculation since she is the sole debtor and currently has only one source of income, her salary from TTI. But it's not always so simple. If a husband and wife file a joint petition, then the income of both spouses must be reported in Columns A and B of Part II respectively (see instructions in Box 2d of the form). If a married debtor files, but the spouse from whom she is legally separated does not, the debtor must check Box 2b of the form and the income of the nonfiling spouse need not be reported. But if a married debtor files and is not legally separated from her spouse, she must check Box 2c of the form and report the nonfiling spouse's income in column B of Part II. If any of the reported income of the nonfiling spouse is not available on a regular basis to help with household expenses of the debtor or the debtor's dependents, that will be reported on Line 17 in Part IV of the form, discussed below. If Marta owned and operated a business, she would include **net income** from that business on Line 4. If she was leasing a house or apartment

Illustration 14-a: PARTS II & III OF MARTA CARLSON'S FORM 22A ASSUMING ANNUAL INCOME OF $34,000

B22A (Official Form 22A) (Chapter 7) (04/13)			2

	Part II. CALCULATION OF MONTHLY INCOME FOR § 707(b)(7) EXCLUSION		
2	**Marital/filing status.** Check the box that applies and complete the balance of this part of this statement as directed. a. ☒ Unmarried. **Complete only Column A ("Debtor's Income") for Lines 3-11.** b. ☐ Married, not filing jointly, with declaration of separate households. By checking this box, debtor declares under penalty of perjury: "My spouse and I are legally separated under applicable non-bankruptcy law or my spouse and I are living apart other than for the purpose of evading the requirements of § 707(b)(2)(A) of the Bankruptcy Code." **Complete only column A ("Debtor's Income") for Lines 3-11.** c. ☐ Married, not filing jointly, without the declaration of separate households set out in Line 2.b above. **Complete both Column A ("Debtor's Income") and Column B ("Spouse's Income") for Lines 3-11.** d. ☐ Married, filing jointly. **Complete both Column A ("Debtor's Income") and Column B ("Spouse's Income") for Lines 3-11.**		

	All figures must reflect average monthly income received from all sources, derived during the six calendar months prior to filing the bankruptcy case, ending on the last day of the month before the filing. If the amount of monthly income varied during the six months, you must divide the six-month total by six, and enter the result on the appropriate line.	Column A Debtor's Income	Column B Spouse's Income
3	**Gross wages, salary, tips, bonuses, overtime, commissions.**	$ 2,833.33	$
4	**Income from the operation of a business, profession or farm.** Subtract Line b from Line a and enter the difference in the appropriate column(s) of Line 4. If you operate more than one business, profession or farm, enter aggregate numbers and provide details on an attachment. Do not enter a number less than zero. **Do not include any part of the business expenses entered on Line b as a deduction in Part V.** a. Gross receipts $ 0.00 $ b. Ordinary and necessary business expenses $ 0.00 $ c. Business income Subtract Line b from Line a	$ 0.00	$
5	**Rent and other real property income.** Subtract Line b from Line a and enter the difference in the appropriate column(s) of Line 5. Do not enter a number less than zero. **Do not include any part of the operating expenses entered on Line b as a deduction in Part V.** a. Gross receipts $ 0.00 $ b. Ordinary and necessary operating expenses $ 0.00 $ c. Rent and other real property income Subtract Line b from Line a	$ 0.00	$
6	**Interest, dividends, and royalties.**	$ 0.00	$
7	**Pension and retirement income.**	$ 0.00	$
8	**Any amounts paid by another person or entity, on a regular basis, for the household expenses of the debtor or the debtor's dependents, including child support paid for that purpose.** Do not include alimony or separate maintenance payments or amounts paid by your spouse if Column B is completed. Each regular payment should be reported in only one column; if a payment is listed in Column A, do not report that payment in Column B.	$ 0.00	$
9	**Unemployment compensation.** Enter the amount in the appropriate column(s) of Line 9. However, if you contend that unemployment compensation received by you or your spouse was a benefit under the Social Security Act, do not list the amount of such compensation in Column A or B, but instead state the amount in the space below: Unemployment compensation claimed to be a benefit under the Social Security Act Debtor $ 0.00 Spouse $	$ 0.00	$
10	**Income from all other sources.** Specify source and amount. If necessary, list additional sources on a separate page. **Do not include alimony or separate maintenance payments paid by your spouse if Column B is completed, but include all other payments of alimony or separate maintenance.** Do not include any benefits received under the Social Security Act or payments received as a victim of a war crime, crime against humanity, or as a victim of international or domestic terrorism. a. _____ $ b. _____ $ Total and enter on Line 10	$ 0.00	$
11	**Subtotal of Current Monthly Income for § 707(b)(7).** Add Lines 3 thru 10 in Column A, and, if Column B is completed, add Lines 3 through 10 in Column B. Enter the total(s).	$ 2,833.33	$

12	**Total Current Monthly Income for § 707(b)(7).** If Column B has been completed, add Line 11, Column A to Line 11, Column B, and enter the total. If Column B has not been completed, enter the amount from Line 11, Column A.	$	2.833.33

Part III. APPLICATION OF § 707(b)(7) EXCLUSION

13	**Annualized Current Monthly Income for § 707(b)(7).** Multiply the amount from Line 12 by the number 12 and enter the result.	$	34.000.00
14	**Applicable median family income.** Enter the median family income for the applicable state and household size. (This information is available by family size at www.usdoj.gov/ust/ or from the clerk of the bankruptcy court.) a. Enter debtor's state of residence: _____ CL (MO) _____ b. Enter debtor's household size: _____ 3 _____	$	58,342.00
15	**Application of Section 707(b)(7).** Check the applicable box and proceed as directed. ☒ **The amount on Line 13 is less than or equal to the amount on Line 14.** Check the box for "The presumption does not arise" at the top of page 1 of this statement, and complete Part VIII; do not complete Parts IV, V, VI or VII. ☐ **The amount on Line 13 is more than the amount on Line 14.** Complete the remaining parts of this statement.		

and had rental income, she would include net income from that rental on Line 5. If she had received interest income on a savings or checking account or other source, she would include that income on Line 6. If she had received pension or retirement income during the relevant six-month period, she would report that on Line 7. If she were receiving child support payments from her ex-husband, she would include those on Line 8. She would also include alimony or separate maintenance payments here unless she had remarried and was including her new spouse's income in Column B of the form. If she had lost her job but received unemployment compensation, she would report that on Line 9. If Marta's parents had been helping her out with occasional payments during the past six months those payments would have to be reported on Line 10. Note that Social Security payments do not have to be reported on the form. Why do you think that is?

Once the CMI itemized in Part II of the form has been totaled on Line 12, we then take that total to Part III of the form where it is **annualized** by being multiplied by 12 on Line 13 (CMI × 12).

EXAMPLE

Look at Illustration 14-a or Document 21-A in the Marta Carlson case file. Her total CMI from the past six months is $2,833.33 based on her salary from TTI, and we annualize that to get $34,000 for her annual income.

Next we determine the **median family income** figure for the debtor's state of residence from the Census Bureau's tables posted on the U.S. Trustee Program's Web site mentioned above and record that number on Line 14 of the form. Then we compare the debtor's annualized monthly income number with the median family income number. If the debtor's annual income is *equal to* or *less than* the applicable median family income for his state, he is what practitioners call a **below median debtor** and the presumption of abuse does not arise in his case. The below median debtor has passed the means test and need not go to Step 2 by completing Parts IV through VII of Form 22A. Instead, he will merely complete the verification in Part VIII of Form 22A and indicate on the first page of the form that the presumption of abuse does not arise in his case.

EXAMPLE

> Look at Illustration 14-a or Document 21-A in the Marta Carlson case file. Marta's annualized monthly income is $34,000. The median family income for a family of three living in Columbiana (remember we're using the actual state of Missouri) as of January 2013 is $58,342. Since her annualized monthly income is less than the state median income for her size family, the presumption does not arise. She is a below median debtor and has passed the means test. She will indicate on page 1 of the form that the presumption does not arise. She can skip Parts IV-VII of the form, sign the verification in Part VII, and be done. (Remember that the median income figures from the Census Bureau are adjusted annually and may be different from the illustration and document in the case file when you read this.)

3. Step 2 of the Means Test: Determining the Debtor's Disposable Monthly Income to Determine the Feasibility of Funding a Chapter 13 Plan

If the debtor's annualized CMI is greater than the applicable median family income figure, the debtor is an **above median debtor** and must go to Step 2 of the means test by completing Parts IV-VII of Form 22A. The purpose of Parts IV-VII is to determine if the debtor will have sufficient **disposable monthly income** to fund a Chapter 13 reorganization plan. Specifically, we calculate the debtor's disposable income by deducting from his current monthly income a mix of actual and standardized expenses based on the **National Standards for Allowable Living Expenses** and **Local Standards for Transportation and Housing and Utilities Expenses** published by the **Internal Revenue Service**. Section 707(b)(2)(A)(i) provides that if the debtor has sufficient disposable income to pay $12,475 over five years, or as little as $208 a month to creditors (as of March 2013; the dollar amounts will be adjusted again in March 2016 per §104), the presumption of abuse arises and the case *must* be dismissed or converted (with the debtor's consent) to a Chapter 13 case. If the debtor does not have sufficient income to pay that much to creditors, then the means test is satisfied (the presumption of abuse does not arise).

To see how Step 2 of the means test works, let's assume that Marta Carlson's salary at TTI is $76,000 a year. In that case, she is an above median debtor and will *not* satisfy the means test under Step 1. She will have to complete Parts IV-VI of Form 22A. Marta's alternative Form 22A based on the assumption of higher income is document 21-B in her case file, and Illustration 14-b sets out Parts II and III of that alternative Form 22A. (Since the median income figures are adjusted annually, if the applicable median income figure for a family of three in Missouri exceeds the $76,000 used in Document 21-B and Illustration 14-b at the time you are reading this, then raise Marta's hypothetical income to $5,000 in excess of that number.)

Let's also assume that the fictional county of Capitol County, Columbiana, where Marta Carlson resides, has the same local standards data as Boone County, Missouri. Illustration 14-c sets out Parts IV-VII of Marta Carlson's Form 22A using the applicable data for that county as of January 2013 (remember, the numbers

Illustration 14-b: PARTS II & III OF MARTA CARLSON'S FORM 22A ASSUMING ANNUAL INCOME OF $76,000

B22A (Official Form 22A) (Chapter 7) (04/13)   2

	Part II. CALCULATION OF MONTHLY INCOME FOR § 707(b)(7) EXCLUSION		
2	**Marital/filing status.** Check the box that applies and complete the balance of this part of this statement as directed. a. ☒ Unmarried. **Complete only Column A ("Debtor's Income") for Lines 3-11.** b. ☐ Married, not filing jointly, with declaration of separate households. By checking this box, debtor declares under penalty of perjury: "My spouse and I are legally separated under applicable non-bankruptcy law or my spouse and I are living apart other than for the purpose of evading the requirements of § 707(b)(2)(A) of the Bankruptcy Code." **Complete only column A ("Debtor's Income") for Lines 3-11.** c. ☐ Married, not filing jointly, without the declaration of separate households set out in Line 2.b above. **Complete both Column A ("Debtor's Income") and Column B ("Spouse's Income") for Lines 3-11.** d. ☐ Married, filing jointly. **Complete both Column A ("Debtor's Income") and Column B ("Spouse's Income") for Lines 3-11.**		

	All figures must reflect average monthly income received from all sources, derived during the six calendar months prior to filing the bankruptcy case, ending on the last day of the month before the filing. If the amount of monthly income varied during the six months, you must divide the six-month total by six, and enter the result on the appropriate line.	**Column A** Debtor's Income	**Column B** Spouse's Income
3	**Gross wages, salary, tips, bonuses, overtime, commissions.**	$ 6,333.33	$
4	**Income from the operation of a business, profession or farm.** Subtract Line b from Line a and enter the difference in the appropriate column(s) of Line 4. If you operate more than one business, profession or farm, enter aggregate numbers and provide details on an attachment. Do not enter a number less than zero. **Do not include any part of the business expenses entered on Line b as a deduction in Part V.** a. Gross receipts — Debtor $ 0.00 / Spouse $ b. Ordinary and necessary business expenses — Debtor $ 0.00 / Spouse $ c. Business income — Subtract Line b from Line a	$ 0.00	$
5	**Rent and other real property income.** Subtract Line b from Line a and enter the difference in the appropriate column(s) of Line 5. Do not enter a number less than zero. **Do not include any part of the operating expenses entered on Line b as a deduction in Part V.** a. Gross receipts — Debtor $ 0.00 / Spouse $ b. Ordinary and necessary operating expenses — Debtor $ 0.00 / Spouse $ c. Rent and other real property income — Subtract Line b from Line a	$ 0.00	$
6	**Interest, dividends, and royalties.**	$ 0.00	$
7	**Pension and retirement income.**	$ 0.00	$
8	**Any amounts paid by another person or entity, on a regular basis, for the household expenses of the debtor or the debtor's dependents, including child support paid for that purpose.** Do not include alimony or separate maintenance payments or amounts paid by your spouse if Column B is completed. Each regular payment should be reported in only one column; if a payment is listed in Column A, do not report that payment in Column B.	$ 0.00	$
9	**Unemployment compensation.** Enter the amount in the appropriate column(s) of Line 9. However, if you contend that unemployment compensation received by you or your spouse was a benefit under the Social Security Act, do not list the amount of such compensation in Column A or B, but instead state the amount in the space below: Unemployment compensation claimed to be a benefit under the Social Security Act Debtor $ 0.00 Spouse $	$ 0.00	$
10	**Income from all other sources.** Specify source and amount. If necessary, list additional sources on a separate page. **Do not include alimony or separate maintenance payments paid by your spouse if Column B is completed, but include all other payments of alimony or separate maintenance. Do not include any benefits received under the Social Security Act or payments received as a victim of a war crime, crime against humanity, or as a victim of international or domestic terrorism.** a. Debtor $ / Spouse $ b. Debtor $ / Spouse $ Total and enter on Line 10	$ 0.00	$
11	**Subtotal of Current Monthly Income for § 707(b)(7).** Add Lines 3 thru 10 in Column A, and, if Column B is completed, add Lines 3 through 10 in Column B. Enter the total(s).	$ 6,333.33	$

12	**Total Current Monthly Income for § 707(b)(7).** If Column B has been completed, add Line 11, Column A to Line 11, Column B, and enter the total. If Column B has not been completed, enter the amount from Line 11, Column A.	$	6,333.33

	Part III. APPLICATION OF § 707(b)(7) EXCLUSION		
13	**Annualized Current Monthly Income for § 707(b)(7).** Multiply the amount from Line 12 by the number 12 and enter the result.	$	**76.000.00**
14	**Applicable median family income.** Enter the median family income for the applicable state and household size. (This information is available by family size at www.usdoj.gov/ust/ or from the clerk of the bankruptcy court.) a. Enter debtor's state of residence: CL (MO) b. Enter debtor's household size: 3	$	**58,342.00**
15	**Application of Section 707(b)(7).** Check the applicable box and proceed as directed. ☐ **The amount on Line 13 is less than or equal to the amount on Line 14.** Check the box for "The presumption does not arise" at the top of page 1 of this statement, and complete Part VIII; do not complete Parts IV, V, VI or VII. ☒ **The amount on Line 13 is more than the amount on Line 14.** Complete the remaining parts of this statement.		

are adjusted annually), her listed actual expenses, and a presumed income of $76,000 from TTI (see her complete Form 22A based on these assumptions in Document 21-B in her case file).

P-H 14-e: Access the IRS's **National Standards for Allowable Living Expenses** and **Local Standards for Transportation and Housing and Utilities Expenses** that apply to Boone County, Missouri at www.justice.gov/ust/eo/bapcpa/20100315/meanstesting.htm. Some of the deductions allowed in Part V of Form 22A as seen in Illustration 14-c or Document 21-B in the Carlson case file are based on the IRS's national, regional, and local standards and some are based on the actual expenses of the debtor described in the Assignment Memo in Appendix A to the text. Use these materials as we work through Parts IV-VII of Marta's alternate Form 22A.

---

a. Part IV of OBF 22A: The Marital Adjustment

Marta does not utilize the **marital adjustment** on Line 17 in Part IV of the form because she is not married and did not check Box 2c. But recall from our earlier discussion that a married debtor who does check Box 2c must include the income of her spouse even though that spouse is not filing with her. It is on Line 17 that such a debtor can adjust her annualized monthly income figure from Parts II and III of the form by deducting as much of the nonfiling spouse's income as is not actually made available for household expenses. The reason that the nonfiling spouse's income is not available for household expenses must be stated. The most common reason is that the nonfiling spouse is required to pay spousal or child support from an earlier marriage.

P-H 14-f: The marital adjustment cannot be made as part of Step 1 of the means test even though it may result in the debtor not satisfying the test in Step 1. Is it fair that a debtor who could satisfy the means test in Step 1 by making the marital adjustment to annualized monthly income there may not do so and must complete Step 2? This is one of the many controversial features of the current means test calculation on Form 22A.

b. Part V of OBF 22A: Deductions from the Debtor's Annualized Monthly Income

Part V of the form allows the debtor to deduct a variety of expenses from his annualized monthly income computed in Part II. On Line 19A the debtor enters his deduction for food, clothing, housekeeping supplies, personal care products, and related services calculated, not from his actual expenses, but from the IRS national standards for such expenses accessible at the Web site of the U.S. Trustee Program. (Remember when comparing the current IRS national and local standard amounts that they are adjusted annually. Illustration 14-c and Document 21-B in the Marta Carlson case file reflect the applicable amounts as of January 2013.)

On Line 19B, the debtor again accesses the IRS national standards to deduct an amount for projected out-of-pocket health-care costs including medical services, prescription drugs, and medical supplies for each member of his family.

P-H 14-g: Access the U.S. Trustee Program's Web site and determine the current IRS national standard for the food and clothing, etc., deduction and for the out-of-pocket health-care expenses deduction for a family of your size.

On Lines 20A and 20B the debtor utilizes the IRS local standards for projected housing expenses, which can include mortgage or rent, property taxes, interest, insurance, maintenance, repairs, gas, electric, water, heating oil, garbage collection, telephone, and cell phone. Due to the wide variation in such expenses around the country, the IRS standards are organized by state and county as well as by family size. Those projected costs are also broken down into nonmortgage/rent expenses, entered on Line 20A, and mortgage/rent expenses entered on Line 20B. If the debtor actually owns a home and has a mortgage against it, the projected mortgage expense from the local standards entered on Line 20B must be reduced by the amount of the debtor's actual monthly mortgage payment. That may seem unfair, but the debtor will be able to receive a deduction for his future mortgage payments on Line 42 as discussed below.

If the debtor contends that the IRS local standards do not accurately reflect his real expense for housing and utility expenses (e.g. a debtor lives in a remote location and pays a premium for utility service) he can enter an adjustment to be made to such deduction (i.e., increase it) on Line 21. The bankruptcy trustee will question that entry closely so the debtor will need to document his contention.

EXAMPLE

The applicable IRS local standard for nonmortgage housing and utility expenses in Capitol County, Columbiana (Boone County, Missouri) where Marta Carlson resides is $488 (as of January 2013) so she enters that amount on Line 20A. The local standard for mortgage/rental expense is $862 so she enters that amount on Line 20B(a). But the two mortgages on her residence require her to pay a total of $1,442 per month (see the Assignment Memo in Appendix A) so she must enter that actual monthly payment total on Line 20B(b) and deduct it from the amount on Line 20B(a). Since the amount of her actual monthly payments ($1,442) exceeds the local standard for mortgage/rent ($1,028 as of January 2013), she enters zero on Line 20B. But on Line 42 she will enter and receive a deduction for her actual mortgage payments.

On Line 22A the debtor utilizes the IRS local standards for vehicle operation/public transportation to deduct an amount for the expense of operating up to two vehicles or, if the debtor does not pay operating expenses on a vehicle, for public transportation. The IRS local standards are actually arranged by region of the country and broken down into operating costs for owners of vehicles and public transportation costs for nonowners of vehicles.

Illustration 14-c: PARTS IV-VII OF MARTA CARLSON'S FORM 22A ASSUMING ANNUAL INCOME OF $76,000

	Part IV. CALCULATION OF CURRENT MONTHLY INCOME FOR § 707(b)(2)		
16	**Enter the amount from Line 12.**	$	6,333.33
17	**Marital adjustment.** If you checked the box at Line 2.c, enter on Line 17 the total of any income listed in Line 11, Column B that was NOT paid on a regular basis for the household expenses of the debtor or the debtor's dependents. Specify in the lines below the basis for excluding the Column B income (such as payment of the spouse's tax liability or the spouse's support of persons other than the debtor or the debtor's dependents) and the amount of income devoted to each purpose. If necessary, list additional adjustments on a separate page. If you did not check box at Line 2.c, enter zero. <table><tr><td>a.</td><td></td><td>$</td></tr><tr><td>b.</td><td></td><td>$</td></tr><tr><td>c.</td><td></td><td>$</td></tr><tr><td>d.</td><td></td><td>$</td></tr></table> Total and enter on Line 17	$	
18	**Current monthly income for § 707(b)(2).** Subtract Line 17 from Line 16 and enter the result.	$	6,333.33
	Part V. CALCULATION OF DEDUCTIONS FROM INCOME		
	Subpart A: Deductions under Standards of the Internal Revenue Service (IRS)		
19A	**National Standards: food, clothing and other items.** Enter in Line 19A the "Total" amount from IRS National Standards for Food, Clothing and Other Items for the applicable number of persons. (This information is available at www.usdoj.gov/ust/ or from the clerk of the bankruptcy court.) The applicable number of persons is the number that would currently be allowed as exemptions on your federal income tax return, plus the number of any additional dependents whom you support.	$	1,227
19B	**National Standards: health care.** Enter in Line a1 below the amount from IRS National Standards for Out-of-Pocket Health Care for persons under 65 years of age, and in Line a2 the IRS National Standards for Out-of-Pocket Health Care for persons 65 years of age or older. (This information is available at www.usdoj.gov/ust/ or from the clerk of the bankruptcy court.) Enter in Line b1 the applicable number of persons who are under 65 years of age, and enter in Line b2 the applicable number of persons who are 65 years of age or older. (The applicable number of persons in each age category is the number in that category that would currently be allowed as exemptions on your federal income tax return, plus the number of any additional dependents whom you support.) Multiply Line a1 by Line b1 to obtain a total amount for persons under 65, and enter the result in Line c1. Multiply Line a2 by Line b2 to obtain a total amount for persons 65 and older, and enter the result in Line c2. Add Lines c1 and c2 to obtain a total health care amount, and enter the result in Line 19B. <table><tr><td colspan="3">Persons under 65 years of age</td><td colspan="3">Persons 65 years of age or older</td></tr><tr><td>a1.</td><td>Allowance per person</td><td>60</td><td>a2.</td><td>Allowance per person</td><td></td></tr><tr><td>b1.</td><td>Number of persons</td><td></td><td>b2.</td><td>Number of persons</td><td></td></tr><tr><td>c1.</td><td>Subtotal</td><td></td><td>c2.</td><td>Subtotal</td><td></td></tr></table>	$	180
20A	**Local Standards: housing and utilities; non-mortgage expenses.** Enter the amount of the IRS Housing and Utilities Standards; non-mortgage expenses for the applicable county and family size. (This information is available at www.usdoj.gov/ust/ or from the clerk of the bankruptcy court). The applicable family size consists of the number that would currently be allowed as exemptions on your federal income tax return, plus the number of any additional dependents whom you support.	$	488

20B	**Local Standards: housing and utilities; mortgage/rent expense.** Enter, in Line a below, the amount of the IRS Housing and Utilities Standards; mortgage/rent expense for your county and family size (this information is available at www.usdoj.gov/ust/ or from the clerk of the bankruptcy court) (the applicable family size consists of the number that would currently be allowed as exemptions on your federal income tax return, plus the number of any additional dependents whom you support); enter on Line b the total of the Average Monthly Payments for any debts secured by your home, as stated in Line 42; subtract Line b from Line a and enter the result in Line 20B. **Do not enter an amount less than zero.**				
	a.	IRS Housing and Utilities Standards; mortgage/rental expense	$ 1,028		
	b.	Average Monthly Payment for any debts secured by your home, if any, as stated in Line 42	$ 1,442		
	c.	Net mortgage/rental expense	Subtract Line b from Line a.	$	0.00

| 21 | **Local Standards: housing and utilities; adjustment.** If you contend that the process set out in Lines 20A and 20B does not accurately compute the allowance to which you are entitled under the IRS Housing and Utilities Standards, enter any additional amount to which you contend you are entitled, and state the basis for your contention in the space below:

_____ | $ | 0.00 |
|---|---|---|---|

| 22A | **Local Standards: transportation; vehicle operation/public transportation expense.** You are entitled to an expense allowance in this category regardless of whether you pay the expenses of operating a vehicle and regardless of whether you use public transportation.

Check the number of vehicles for which you pay the operating expenses or for which the operating expenses are included as a contribution to your household expenses in Line 8.

☐ 0   ☒ 1   ☐ 2 or more.

If you checked 0, enter on Line 22A the "Public Transportation" amount from IRS Local Standards: Transportation. If you checked 1 or 2 or more, enter on Line 22A the "Operating Costs" amount from IRS Local Standards: Transportation for the applicable number of vehicles in the applicable Metropolitan Statistical Area or Census Region. (These amounts are available at www.usdoj.gov/ust/ or from the clerk of the bankruptcy court.) | $ | 212 |
|---|---|---|---|

22B	**Local Standards: transportation; additional public transportation expense.** If you pay the operating expenses for a vehicle and also use public transportation, and you contend that you are entitled to an additional deduction for you public transportation expenses, enter on Line 22B the "Public Transportation" amount from IRS Local Standards: Transportation. (This amount is available at www.usdoj.gov/ust/ or from the clerk of the bankruptcy court.)	$	0.00

| 23 | **Local Standards: transportation ownership/lease expense; Vehicle 1.** Check the number of vehicles for which you claim an ownership/lease expense. (You may not claim an ownership/lease expense for more than two vehicles.)

☒ 1   ☐ 2 or more.

Enter, in Line a below, the "Ownership Costs" for "One Car" from the IRS Local Standards: Transportation (available at www.usdoj.gov/ust/ or from the clerk of the bankruptcy court); enter in Line b the total of the Average Monthly Payments for any debts secured by Vehicle 1, as stated in Line 42; subtract Line b from Line a and enter the result in Line 23. **Do not enter an amount less than zero.** | | | | |
|---|---|---|---|---|---|
| | a. | IRS Transportation Standards, Ownership Costs | $ 517 | | |
| | b. | Average Monthly Payment for any debts secured by Vehicle 1, as stated in Line 42 | $ 210 | | |
| | c. | Net ownership/lease expense for Vehicle 1 | Subtract Line b from Line a. | $ | 307 |

| 24 | **Local Standards: transportation ownership/lease expense; Vehicle 2.** Complete this Line only if you checked the "2 or more" Box in Line 23.

Enter, in Line a below, the "Ownership Costs" for "One Car" from the IRS Local Standards: Transportation (available at www.usdoj.gov/ust/ or from the clerk of the bankruptcy court); enter in Line b the total of the Average Monthly Payments for any debts secured by Vehicle 2, as stated in Line 42; subtract Line b from Line a and enter the result in Line 24. **Do not enter an amount less than zero.** | | | | |
|---|---|---|---|---|---|
| | a. | IRS Transportation Standards, Ownership Costs | $ | | |
| | b. | Average Monthly Payment for any debts secured by Vehicle 2, as stated in Line 42 | $ | | |
| | c. | Net ownership/lease expense for Vehicle 2 | Subtract Line b from Line a. | $ | 0.00 |

25	**Other Necessary Expenses: taxes.** Enter the total average monthly expense that you actually incur for all federal, state and local taxes, other than real estate and sales taxes, such as income taxes, self employment taxes, social security taxes, and Medicare taxes. **Do not include real estate or sales taxes.**	$	1,083

B22A (Official Form 22A) (Chapter 7) (04/13)   5

26	**Other Necessary Expenses: involuntary deductions for employment.** Enter the total average monthly payroll deductions that are required for your employment, such as retirement contributions, union dues, and uniform costs. **Do not include discretionary amounts, such as voluntary 401(k) contributions.**	$	0.00
27	**Other Necessary Expenses: life insurance.** Enter total average monthly premiums that you actually pay for term life insurance for yourself. **Do not include premiums for insurance on your dependents, for whole life or for any other form of insurance.**	$	0.00
28	**Other Necessary Expenses: court-ordered payments.** Enter the total monthly amount that you are required to pay pursuant to the order of a court or administrative agency, such as spousal or child support payments. **Do not include payments on past due obligations included in Line 44.**	$	0.00
29	**Other Necessary Expenses: education for employment or for a physically or mentally challenged child.** Enter the total average monthly amount that you actually expend for education that is a condition of employment and for education that is required for a physically or mentally challenged dependent child for whom no public education providing similar services is available.	$	0.00
30	**Other Necessary Expenses: childcare.** Enter the total average monthly amount that you actually expend on childcare - such as baby-sitting, day care, nursery and preschool. **Do not include other educational payments.**	$	0.00
31	**Other Necessary Expenses: health care.** Enter the total average monthly amount that you actually expend on health care that is required for the health and welfare of yourself or your dependents, that is not reimbursed by insurance or paid by a health savings account, and that is in excess of the amount entered in Line 19B. **Do not include payments for health insurance or health savings accounts listed in Line 34.**	$	900
32	**Other Necessary Expenses: telecommunication services.** Enter the total average monthly amount that you actually pay for telecommunication services other than your basic home telephone and cell phone service - such as pagers, call waiting, caller id, special long distance, or internet service - to the extent necessary for your health and welfare or that of your dependents. **Do not include any amount previously deducted.**	$	0.00
33	**Total Expenses Allowed under IRS Standards.** Enter the total of Lines 19 through 32.	$	4,397

Subpart B: Additional Living Expense Deductions
Note: Do not include any expenses that you have listed in Lines 19-32

34	**Health Insurance, Disability Insurance, and Health Savings Account Expenses.** List the monthly expenses in the categories set out in lines a-c below that are reasonably necessary for yourself, your spouse, or your dependents.		

	a.	Health Insurance	$	85
	b.	Disability Insurance	$	
	c.	Health Savings Account	$	

			$	85

Total and enter on Line 34.

If you do not actually expend this total amount, state your actual total average monthly expenditures in the space below:

$_____

35	**Continued contributions to the care of household or family members.** Enter the total average actual monthly expenses that you will continue to pay for the reasonable and necessary care and support of an elderly, chronically ill, or disabled member of your household or member of your immediate family who is unable to pay for such expenses.	$	0.00
36	**Protection against family violence.** Enter the total average reasonably necessary monthly expenses that you actually incurred to maintain the safety of your family under the Family Violence Prevention and Services Act or other applicable federal law. The nature of these expenses is required to be kept confidential by the court.	$	0.00
37	**Home energy costs.** Enter the total average monthly amount, in excess of the allowance specified by IRS Local Standards for Housing and Utilities, that you actually expend for home energy costs. **You must provide your case trustee with documentation of your actual expenses, and you must demonstrate that the additional amount claimed is reasonable and necessary.**	$	0.00
38	**Education expenses for dependent children less than 18.** Enter the total average monthly expenses that you actually incur, not to exceed $156.25* per child, for attendance at a private or public elementary or secondary school by your dependent children less than 18 years of age. **You must provide your case trustee with documentation of your actual expenses, and you must explain why the amount claimed is reasonable and necessary and not already accounted for in the IRS Standards.**	$	80

* Amount subject to adjustment on 4/01/16, and every three years thereafter with respect to cases commenced on or after the date of adjustment.

39	**Additional food and clothing expense.** Enter the total average monthly amount by which your food and clothing expenses exceed the combined allowances for food and clothing (apparel and services) in the IRS National Standards, not to exceed 5% of those combined allowances. (This information is available at www.usdoj.gov/ust/ or from the clerk of the bankruptcy court.) **You must demonstrate that the additional amount claimed is reasonable and necessary.**	$ 0.00
40	**Continued charitable contributions.** Enter the amount that you will continue to contribute in the form of cash or financial instruments to a charitable organization as defined in 26 U.S.C. § 170(c)(1)-(2).	$ 0.00
41	**Total Additional Expense Deductions under § 707(b).** Enter the total of Lines 34 through 40	$ 165

Subpart C: Deductions for Debt Payment

42	**Future payments on secured claims.** For each of your debts that is secured by an interest in property that you own, list the name of the creditor, identify the property securing the debt, state the Average Monthly Payment, and check whether the payment includes taxes or insurance. The Average Monthly Payment is the total of all amounts scheduled as contractually due to each Secured Creditor in the 60 months following the filing of the bankruptcy case, divided by 60. If necessary, list additional entries on a separate page. Enter the total of the Average Monthly Payments on Line 42.	

	Name of Creditor	Property Securing the Debt	Average Monthly Payment	Does payment include taxes or insurance?	
a.	Capitol Savings Bank	Real property at 1212 Spruce St.	$ 965.00	☒yes ☐no	
b.	Dreams Come True Financing	Real property at 1212 Spruce St.	477.00	No	
c.	Automotive Financing, Inc.	YR-4 Toyota Camry	210.00	No	
			Total: Add Lines		$ 1,652.00

43	**Other payments on secured claims.** If any of debts listed in Line 42 are secured by your primary residence, a motor vehicle, or other property necessary for your support or the support of your dependents, you may include in your deduction 1/60th of any amount (the "cure amount") that you must pay the creditor in addition to the payments listed in Line 42, in order to maintain possession of the property. The cure amount would include any sums in default that must be paid in order to avoid repossession or foreclosure. List and total any such amounts in the following chart. If necessary, list additional entries on a separate page.	

	Name of Creditor	Property Securing the Debt	1/60th of the Cure Amount	
a.	Capitol Savings Bank	Real property at 1212 Spruce St.	$ 32.16	
b.	Dreams Come True Financing	Real property at 1212 Spruce St.	23.85	
c.	Automotive Financing, Inc.	YR-4 Toyota Camry	7.00	63.01
			Total: Add Lines	$

44	**Payments on prepetition priority claims.** Enter the total amount, divided by 60, of all priority claims, such as priority tax, child support and alimony claims, for which you were liable at the time of your bankruptcy filing. **Do not include current obligations, such as those set out in Line 28.**	$

45	**Chapter 13 administrative expenses.** If you are eligible to file a case under chapter 13, complete the following chart, multiply the amount in line a by the amount in line b, and enter the resulting administrative expense.	

a.	Projected average monthly chapter 13 plan payment.	$ 200.00	
b.	Current multiplier for your district as determined under schedules issued by the Executive Office for United States Trustees. (This information is available at www.usdoj.gov/ust/ or from the clerk of the bankruptcy court.)	x .042	
c.	Average monthly administrative expense of chapter 13 case	Total: Multiply Lines a and b	$ 8.40

46	**Total Deductions for Debt Payment.** Enter the total of Lines 42 through 45.	$ 1,723.41

Subpart D: Total Deductions from Income

47	**Total of all deductions allowed under § 707(b)(2).** Enter the total of Lines 33, 41, and 46.	$ 6,285.41

Part VI. DETERMINATION OF § 707(b)(2) PRESUMPTION

48	**Enter the amount from Line 18 (Current monthly income for § 707(b)(2))**	$ 6,333.33
49	**Enter the amount from Line 47 (Total of all deductions allowed under § 707(b)(2))**	$ 6,285.41
50	**Monthly disposable income under § 707(b)(2).** Subtract Line 49 from Line 48 and enter the result.	$ 47.92

B22A (Official Form 22A) (Chapter 7) (04/13)   7

51	**60-month disposable income under § 707(b)(2).** Multiply the amount in Line 50 by the number 60 and enter the result.	$	2,875.20
52	**Initial presumption determination.** Check the applicable box and proceed as directed. ☒ **The amount on Line 51 is less than $7,475**. Check the box for "The presumption does not arise" at the top of page 1 of this statement, and complete the verification in Part VIII. Do not complete the remainder of Part VI. ☐ **The amount set forth on Line 51 is more than $12,475*** Check the box for "The presumption arises" at the top of page 1 of this statement, and complete the verification in Part VIII. You may also complete Part VII. Do not complete the remainder of Part VI. ☐ **The amount on Line 51 is at least $7,475*, but not more than $12,475*.** Complete the remainder of Part VI (Lines 53 through 55).		
53	Enter the amount of your total non-priority unsecured debt	$	
54	**Threshold debt payment amount.** Multiply the amount in Line 53 by the number 0.25 and enter the result.	$	
55	**Secondary presumption determination.** Check the applicable box and proceed as directed. ☐ **The amount on Line 51 is less than the amount on Line 54.** Check the box for "The presumption does not arise" at the top of page 1 of this statement, and complete the verification in Part VIII. ☐ **The amount on Line 51 is equal to or greater than the amount on Line 54.** Check the box for "The presumption arises" at the top of page 1 of this statement, and complete the verification in Part VIII. You may also complete Part VII.		

Part VII. ADDITIONAL EXPENSE CLAIMS

56	**Other Expenses.** List and describe any monthly expenses, not otherwise stated in this form, that are required for the health and welfare of you and your family and that you contend should be an additional deduction from your current monthly income under § 707(b)(2)(A)(ii)(I). If necessary, list additional sources on a separate page. All figures should reflect your average monthly expense for each item. Total the expenses.

	Expense Description	Monthly Amount
a.		$
b.		$
c.		$
d.		$
	Total: Add Lines a, b, c, and d	$

EXAMPLE

Marta Carlson operates one vehicle and so indicates on Line 22A of her Form 22A. The IRS local standards for the Midwest region where Columbiana (Missouri) is located designate $212 for operating costs of one vehicle (as of January 2013) so that is the amount entered on her Line 22A. If she did not have a motor vehicle, she could enter $182 for public transportation costs on this line instead. If she had both operating costs for a vehicle and also used public transportation she could enter the operating costs figure on Line 22A and the public transportation figure on Line 22B. Again, a bankruptcy trustee may and will challenge such deductions, and the debtor should be prepared to corroborate both categories of expense.

On Lines 23 and 24 the debtor utilizes the IRS local standards for vehicle ownership/lease expense for up to two vehicles. However, as with the mortgage expense standard entered on Line 20B, the local standard amount for vehicle ownership/lease expense must be reduced by the actual monthly payment the debtor makes on a vehicle that is subject to a security interest. Again, that initially seems unfair, but the debtor will be able to enter and deduct future payments on the secured vehicle on Line 42.

EXAMPLE

Marta Carlson only has one vehicle and so indicates on Line 23. She enters the IRS local standard for ownership costs for one car in the Midwest region, which as of January 2013 was $517. But since she makes monthly payments totaling $210 on her car to a secured creditor, Automotive Financing, Inc. (AFI) (see the Assignment Memo in Appendix A), she must deduct the amount of that actual payment from the IRS standard figure leaving a balance of $307 entered on Line 23. However, on Line 42 she will enter and deduct the amount of her monthly payment to AFI. Line 24 is left blank on Marta's Form 22A because she does not own a second car.

P-H 14-h: May a debtor take the expense deduction for vehicle ownership allowed in Lines 23–24 if the vehicle is paid for and is subject to neither a lease nor a secured debt? That issue has arisen under BAPCPA and OBF 22A (as well as OBF 22C used in Chapter 13 cases as we will see later). Lower courts were badly split on this issue until the Supreme Court held in *Ransom v. FIA Card Services, N.A.*, 131 S. Ct. 716 (2011), that a debtor cannot use the IRS Local Standards Transportation Ownership Costs for a car that is owned free of debt or lease obligations. Although *Ransom* involved a Chapter 13 debtor and OBF 22C, the decision is controlling in Chapter 7 cases involving OBF 22A as well. There is an interesting dissent by Justice Scalia in *Ransom*. Read the majority and dissenting opinions and see who you think gets it right.

On Lines 25–32 the debtor is allowed to enter and deduct his average monthly amounts actually expended on expenses related to the IRS standards but not expressly covered by them, including taxes (other than real estate and sales taxes) (Line 25), payroll deductions for items such as retirement contributions, union dues and uniform costs (Line 26), term life insurance for policies covering the debtor's life only (Line 27), court-ordered payments such as child support or alimony (in their full amount, not averaged) (Line 28), education expenses for the debtor that are a condition of employment or for a physically or mentally challenged dependent child for whom no such public education service is available (Line 29), child care (Line 30), unreimbursed health-care expenses in excess of the amount entered on Line 19B and not including health insurance premiums (Line 31), and telecommunication expenses in excess of home phone and cell phone service but only to the extent necessary to the health and welfare of the debtor or his dependents (Line 32). These amounts are based on averages of the debtor's actual expenses and not IRS standards.

EXAMPLE

Marta Carlson's average monthly expense for income, Social Security, and Medicare taxes is $1,083, and she enters that amount on Line 25. She does not include real estate taxes because those are included in her mortgage payments that she will deduct on Line 42. Sales taxes are excluded too since they are part of the calculation of the IRS's national standards for food and clothing, etc., deducted on Line 19A and house and car standards deducted on Lines 20A, 22A and 23. She has not deducted any of her educational expenses on Line 29, concluding that they are not a "condition" of her continued employment at TTI. She is not currently incurring child care expenses so there is no deduction on

Line 30. She has incurred additional health-care expenses for her daughter (see the Assignment Memo in Appendix A) and in recent months has been paying an average of $900 a month on those obligations, even though she is in arrears on her mortgages and car payment. Thus $900 is the amount she enters on Line 31. She can expect to be challenged on such a large deduction for this item and should have documentation ready to support it.

Line 34 allows the debtor to deduct premiums paid monthly for health and disability insurance or payments into a health savings account, items that were excluded from Line 3.

EXAMPLE

On Line 31 Marta Carlson entered an amount equal to the average payment she has been making on unreimbursed health-care expenses for herself and the two children, but health insurance premiums she pays for the TTI group coverage were not included there. The monthly premium for that group coverage is included on Line 34.

Line 35 allows the debtor to enter and deduct extraordinary expenses incurred for the care and support of a member of the debtor's household or a member of the debtor's immediate family who is elderly, chronically ill, or disabled.

EXAMPLE

If Marta Carlson's elderly mother was still living and was a member of her household, Marta might be able to deduct any extra expenses incurred for her mother's upkeep here (e.g., having someone stay with her during the day). Or if her chronically ill daughter was incurring expenses other than medical costs Marta has deducted on Line 31 (e.g., expensive foods for a special diet) those could be deducted here. This is again the kind of unusual deduction a bankruptcy trustee will examine closely and the debtor must have supporting documentation.

On Line 36 a debtor who has been the victim of domestic violence or stalking and who qualifies for protection under the **Family Violence Prevention and Services Act** may deduct expenses related to keeping the family safe (e.g., home security system).

If the average monthly amount the debtor actually expends on utilities exceeds the IRS local standard for that item used on Line 20A, the debtor may deduct the excess on Line 37 but will need to provide documentation if challenged.

On Line 38 the debtor with minor children may deduct average monthly school costs actually incurred in connection with their attendance at a public or private elementary or secondary school up to a current maximum of $156.25 per child (that amount will be next adjusted in April 2016).

EXAMPLE

Marta Carlson has calculated that she spends an average of $40 a month on each of her two children for special equipment or supplies or field trips. Thus, she has deducted a total of $80 here. Such expenses must be documented and must be beyond routine costs of sending children to school (e.g., normal school clothes and supplies).

If the average monthly amount the debtor *actually* spends on food and clothing and other items exceeds the amount allowed by the IRS local standard for such items that was entered on Line 19A, a debtor may deduct the excess on Line 39 up to a maximum of 5 percent of the IRS standard but will need to provide documentation if challenged.

On Line 40 the debtor may enter and deduct charitable contributions the debtor plans to "continue" making. This wording suggests that the debtor must have a legitimate and provable history of making such contributions to justify this deduction from annualized monthly income and the amount must be reasonable.

EXAMPLE

> Per the language of the form, a debtor who has rarely if ever made charitable contributions may not enter an amount here on the grounds that he or she intends to begin making those contributions. Listed contributions must be continuing. Additionally, a dedicated member of a religious organization who has actually contributed 50 percent of his earnings to it monthly for 20 years will not be allowed to enter that great an amount here. The issue of charitable contributions to a religious organization raises First Amendment issues of the government interfering with the free exercise of religion, but, generally, such donations will be limited to the historical amount up to a maximum of 10 to 15 percent (compare §1325(b)(2)(A)(ii) for this deduction in a Chapter 13 case expressly limiting the deduction to 15 percent of gross income). The U.S. Trustee Program has taken the position that such contributions by a Chapter 7 debtor should not be allowed in excess of 15 percent (see Statement of U.S. Trustee at www.justice.gov/ust/eo/bapcpa/docs/ch7_line_by_line.pdf).

P-H 14-i: Section 707(b)(1) actually contains language saying that in making the determination of whether to dismiss a Chapter 7 case for abuse, "the court may not take into consideration whether a debtor has made, or continues to make, charitable contributions. . . ." That language could be construed to mean that the form's limitation of this deduction to continuing contributions is inappropriate and that a bankruptcy judge may not limit the amount of such deductions if they are bona fide. A form, even an official form, cannot vary the terms of a bankruptcy rule or the Code itself. FRBP 9009 states, "The forms shall be construed to be consistent with these rules and the Code." See *In re Meyer*, 355 B.R. 837, 843 n.6 (Bankr. D.N.M. 2006) ("[O]ne looks to the statute to determine what the law is, and then interprets the form in light of the statute's dictate.") There is little case law interpreting §707(b)(2) or the apparent inconsistency of the form language, probably since statistics suggest that few Chapter 7 debtors claim the charitable deduction and only about 2 percent claim a charitable deduction of more than 5 percent of their gross income.

P-H 14-j: It is worth noting the interesting fact that low-income Americans tend to give more of their income to charity than do high-income Americans. In 2011, the wealthiest 20 percent gave an average of 1.3 percent to charity (favoring colleges, universities, arts organizations, and museums), whereas the poorest 20 percent gave an average of 3.2 percent (favoring religious organizations and social services entities). Why do you think that is the case? Does having less equate to greater sensitivity to need? Is the drive to increase wealth inconsistent with favoring communal support? Do the wealthy put their self-interests above that of others? Moreover, do the wealthy have a higher propensity to engage in unethical behavior owing to a more casual attitude toward greed? See the paper *Higher Social Class Predicts Increased Unethical Behavior*, by Paul Piff, in the *Proceedings of the National Academy of Sciences*, February 2012, and discussed in a *New York* magazine article at http://nymag.com/news/features/money-brain-2012-7/; the article *Why the Rich Don't Give*, by Ken Stern, in *The Atlantic* magazine, April 2013; and *How America Gives*, a study done by the Chronicle of Philanthropy (http://philanthropy.com/) in August 2012.

On Line 42 the debtor may enter and deduct scheduled monthly payments on debt secured by the debtor's real or personal property. This entry was discussed in connection with Lines 20B and 23–24 above.

EXAMPLE

> On Line 42 of her Form 22A, Marta Carlson enters her scheduled monthly payments for both mortgages and the payment to AFI secured by her automobile. Commonly in a Chapter 13 case, the debtor will propose a plan to continue paying the mortgage debt on his house and the secure debt on at least one car in order to keep those items of property, and those continued payments are what is contemplated here. Remember, the purpose of Step 2 of the means test is to see if the debtor might have enough remaining disposable income after making such payments to fund a Chapter 13 plan. We will consider all that when we take up Chapter 13 later.

P-H 14-k: An issue has arisen under the new means test regarding whether a debtor may deduct secured payments for her home or vehicles on Line 42 of Form 22A where the debtor intends to surrender such property rather than keep it (as Marta Carlson plans to do per her Debtor's Statement of Intent, which is Document 20 in the Carlson case file). We will consider the surrender of property in more detail in the next chapter, but it essentially means that the debtor intends to stop paying for the property and relinquish possession of it to the secured creditor. Some courts have held that the debtor who intends to surrender secured property may deduct those payments on Line 42 as part of the means test determination, while other courts have held that she may not. Compare *In re Rivers*, 466 B.R. 558 (Bankr. M.D. Fla. 2012) (deduction allowed) with *In re Fredman*, 471 B.R. 540 (Bkrtcy. S.D. Ill. 2012) (not allowed). Read both cases. Which view constitutes the majority view? Which view is supported by the stronger reasoning in your opinion? Should the Supreme Court's decision in *Ransom*, discussed in P-H 14-h, be determinative on this issue? Determine if the courts of your federal district or circuit have taken a position on this issue.

We will learn in our study of a Chapter 13 bankruptcy (Chapters Nineteen through Twenty-Two) that a debtor there may propose a plan to keep secured property during the term of his plan, cure arrearages on secured debt, and continue making the future contractual payments in full. Most Chapter 13 plans run 5 years or 60 months, so the proposal to cure the arrearage may include payments made over 60 months. On Line 43 of Form 22A the debtor may include and deduct the monthly amounts of such arrearage payments as might be proposed in a Chapter 13 plan.

EXAMPLE

> At the time she files her petition, Marta Carlson is two payments in arrears on the mortgage held by Capitol Savings Bank for a total of $1,930. If she proposed a Chapter 13 plan to cure that arrearage over 60 months she would pay $32.16 a month for that purpose. She is 3 payments in arrears on the mortgage held by Dreams Come True Finance Company for a total of $1,431. Over a 60-month plan she would pay $23.85 to cure that arrearage. She is 2 payments behind to AFI on her secured car debt for a total of $420 and would need to make 60 payments of $7 per month to cure that arrearage. Those are the cure amounts she lists on Line 43.

We will learn later that there are some creditors who hold claims that enjoy a priority over others in a bankruptcy case when it comes to distributing proceeds in a Chapter 7 or making payments in a Chapter 13 or 11 reorganization. If the debtor is in arrears on such priority claims at the time a Chapter 13 petition is filed, those priority claims must be paid in full in the debtor's plan. On Line 44 the debtor enters the monthly payments that he would propose in a Chapter 13 plan to bring those priority claims current over the term of the plan (60 months).

In a Chapter 13 case, once a proposed plan is approved, the debtor will make payments, usually monthly, to a Chapter 13 trustee who will then distribute the payments among the creditors of the debtor as called for in the plan. The trustee will receive a fee for doing so that is a percentage of the payments distributed. That fee is an administrative expense of the Chapter 13 case. We will learn more about this later when we study Chapter 13 in earnest, but, for now, on Line 45 of Form 22A the Chapter 7 debtor lists a projected monthly payment he would make into a Chapter 13 plan and the projected monthly administrative expense is calculated using the appropriate multiplier, which as of January 2013 is 4.02 percent.

EXAMPLE

> Marta Carlson projects that the best she could do in funding a Chapter 13 plan would be to pay in $200 per month. Based on an applicable current multiplier of 4.02 percent this results in a projected monthly administrative expense on such a plan of $8.40.

c. Part VI of OBF 22A: Determination of the Presumption

In Part VI of Form 22A, the debtor subtracts all deductions entered in Part V of the form from the current monthly income figure entered on Line 18. (This figure is the monthly income figure calculated in Part II as modified by the marital adjustment of Part IV.) The result is entered on Line 52 and constitutes the monthly disposable income figure for the debtor; that is, the amount the debtor would have available to fund a Chapter 13 plan over the next 5 years after all projected expenses were deducted as was done in Part V of the form. On Line 51 we then multiply that number by 60, again because the typical Chapter 13 plan would run 60 months.

EXAMPLE

> Marta Carlson's deductions from Part V total $6,285.41 leaving her a monthly disposable income figure of $47.92. Over the life of a 5-year Chapter 13 plan, then, she would have a total of $2,875.20 of disposable income available with which to fund the plan ($47.92 × 60) and that is the figure entered on Line 51 of her form.

Recall that Step 2 of the means test is controlled by §707(b)(2)(A)(i), which provides that if the debtor has *more than* $12,475 (the current figure, to be adjusted again in 2016) in disposable income with which to fund a 5-year plan under Chapter 13 ($208 a month) the presumption of abuse arises and that debtor may not continue in Chapter 7. If the debtor has *less* than $12,475 in disposable income, we have to ask one more question before we can conclude that the presumption does not arise: Is the debtor's total disposable income over the projected 60 months of the plan *also less than* the greater of $7,475 (the current figure, to be adjusted again in 2016) or 25 percent of the debtor's **nonpriority unsecured debts**.

We mentioned earlier that some claims enjoy a priority in a bankruptcy case. Most debts do not. We will consider priority and nonpriority claims in more detail in Chapter Eighteen, Section B. Suffice it to say at this point that if a Chapter 7 debtor required to complete Step 2 of the means test has total disposable income of less than $7,475 the presumption will not arise in his case. That debtor will check the first box on Line 52 of the form, note on page 1 of the form that the presumption does not arise, complete the verification in Part VIII of the form, and proceed in Chapter 7. If the debtor has total disposable income of more than $7,475 but less than $12,475, that debtor must complete Lines 53–55 of Part VI of the form to determine if his disposable income is less than 25 percent of his nonpriority unsecured debts, a calculation made on Lines 53–54 of the form. If it *is* less, the presumption does not arise in his case and he will check the first box on Line 55 of the form, note on page 1 of the form that the presumption does not arise, complete the verification in Part VIII of the form, and proceed in Chapter 7. If that debtor's total disposable income is *not* less than 25 percent of his nonpriority unsecured debts as noted on Line 54 (i.e., it is equal to or more than that figure), the presumption of abuse will arise. That debtor must check the third box on Line 55 of the form, and note on page 1 of the form that the presumption does arise in his case. He may be able to show additional expenses in Part VII of the form that should be deducted from his current monthly income. A hearing before the bankruptcy judge will be necessary, however, to determine if those additional expenses should be deducted to save this debtor from the effect of the presumption of abuse.

EXAMPLE

> Marta Carlson has total disposable income over the projected five years of a Chapter 13 plan totaling $2,875.20 as noted on Line 51 of her form. Since that is less than $7,475, the presumption does not arise in her case. She has checked the first box on Line 52 of her Form 22A, noted on page 1 that the presumption does not arise in her case, and completed the verification in Part VII of the form. She is ready to proceed in Chapter 7, assuming there is no challenge by the trustee to her income stated in Part II of the form or her deductions taken in Part V.

P-H 14-l: If Marta's ex-husband had been paying her $1,000 per month in child support for the six months preceding her filing and continuing to assume she was making $76,000 per year at TTI, would the presumption of abuse arise in her case using Step 2? What if her jurisdiction disallowed the deduction from income of her mortgage payments on the house and her car payments on the YR-04 Toyota Camry on Line 42 of her form 22A since she plans to surrender the house and car to the creditors secured in those assets (see *In re Fredman*, supra)? Would the presumption of abuse then arise in her case, requiring her to file under Chapter 13 or not at all?

4. The Right to Challenge the Presumption of Abuse by Showing Special Circumstances

Special circumstances Unique financial circumstances of a Chapter 7 debtor involving additional expenses or adjustments of current monthly income for which there is no reasonable alternative which may be sufficient to rebut the presumption of abuse.

The presumption of abuse is just that—a presumption. That means that if the debtor cannot satisfy the means test under either Step 1 or Step 2 of Form 22A, the debtor may still challenge the presumption by filing a motion with the bankruptcy court and presenting proof of **special circumstances** sufficient to **rebut the presumption of abuse.** Section §707(b)(2)(B) defines special circumstances as those that "justify either additional expenses or adjustments of current monthly income for which there is no reasonable alternative" and gives examples such as a serious medical condition of the debtor or a dependent or a call to active duty in the military that is likely to impact on future income or future expenses in a way not disclosed on Form 22A.

P-H 14-m: The BAPCPA changes are still new enough that we do not know what other circumstances may or may not satisfy the special circumstances test of §707(b)(2)(B). For example, if the debtor shows she is facing the possibility of a layoff, will that suffice or would the court expect the debtor to file a Chapter 13 and then convert the case to a Chapter 7 if the layoff actually occurred and no substitute employment could be found? Research the cases in your federal district to see if issues regarding what constitutes special circumstances have been decided. Part VII of Form 22A does not appear to be directly related to the special circumstances showing of §707(b)(2)(B) but it is to be expected that a debtor hoping to show additional expenses to justify that test would list them in that part of the form and would likely be questioned closely if she did not list them there and later raised them.

5. The Right to Challenge the Debtor's Conclusion that the Presumption of Abuse Does Not Arise in His Case

Even if a debtor concludes on his Form 22A that the presumption of abuse does not arise in his case using Step 1 or Step 2, that conclusion is *not* binding on the court. The bankruptcy trustee, the U.S. Trustee, any party in interest (e.g., a creditor) or the bankruptcy court acting *sua sponte* (on its own motion) may challenge the debtor's numbers and seek dismissal of the case under §707(b)(1).

Alternatively, that section allows the case to be converted to a Chapter 13 case with the debtor's consent.

P-H 14-n: Early indications suggested that no more than 1 percent of Chapter 7 debtors failed the means test and triggered the BAPCPA presumption of abuse. See Clifford J. White III, *Making Bankruptcy Reform Work: A Progress Report in Year 2*, 26 Am. Bankr. Inst. J. 16 (June 2007), reporting that only 7.9 percent of Chapter 7 debtors have above-median incomes triggered Step 2 of the test, and of those, only 9.5 percent trigger the presumption of abuse. This study is consistent with reports of many practitioners who say that not only do the vast majority of above-median debtors using Step 2 of the test not trigger the presumption, the few that do are clients they would have steered toward a Chapter 13 filing even without the BAPCPA changes. If this is the case, it raises real questions of whether the alleged abuse at which BAPCPA is targeted was real or, as opponents of that legislation insisted at the time, only contrived by the financial services industry that lobbied heavily for its passage and even assisted members of Congress in drafting it. See if you can locate more current studies than the cited White article. See if you can determine from the U.S. Trustee's office or from one of the bankruptcy judges in your district the estimated percentage of Chapter 7 filings that trigger the presumption of abuse. What percentage triggers the presumption but rebuts it by satisfying the special circumstances test?

P-H 14-o: If the means test of BAPCPA has not accomplished its purpose of curing abuse by directing more debtors into Chapter 13, it has certainly increased the complications and expense of filing Chapter 7 cases for debtors and of administration of those cases by the courts. See the 2008 Report of the U.S. Government Accountability Office on Dollar Costs Associated with BAPCPA at www.gao.gov/new.items/d08697.pdf reporting an increase in the average cost to a debtor for filing Chapter 7 from $921 to $1,477 attributable to BAPCPA. Contact debtors' lawyers in your area to see if they confirm these increases and with the bankruptcy court clerk or U.S. trustee in your federal district to see if administrative costs have risen.

We noted earlier that the requirement to satisfy the means test to avoid the presumption of abuse is *only* imposed on the individual debtor with primarily consumer debts. It is *not* imposed on an entity debtor or an individual debtor who has primarily business debts. This disparity in the treatment of the consumer debtor is one of the major criticisms of BAPCPA. However, as we will see in Chapter Seventeen, §707 contains other abuse provisions that may be used to dismiss the case of *any* Chapter 7 debtor, whether an individual or an entity, and whether involving primarily consumer or business debts.

E-C 14-a: Recall our discussion from Chapter Twelve regarding the steep drop-off in the number of bankruptcy filings following the effective date of BAPCPA in October 2005 (see Illustration 12-g). One of the reasons for the drop-off was the concern of debtors' attorneys about compliance with the dramatically new and complicated procedures introduced by BAPCPA, especially for the means test calculation in Chapter 7 cases (and as we will see, the disposable income calculation under Chapter 13). As you wrestle with OBF 22A (and later with OBF 22C), you may appreciate why those concerns were legitimate. This dramatic change in the law and resulting confusion reaffirms the important ethical and professional guideline that lawyers and those that assist them should never undertake client representation in an area where they lack competence. As you gain knowledge and, eventually, experience in the field of debtor/creditor relations and bankruptcy law, don't forget the importance of thoroughly training and closely supervising persons who may one day assist you in this technical and complicated area of the law.

D. ▶ The Prepetition Credit Counseling Requirement for All Individual Debtors

Prepetition Events occurring before the filing of a petition for relief in bankruptcy.

Section 109(h)(1) of the Code provides that no *individual* (either individual consumer or individual business debtors, but *not* entities) may be a debtor under any chapter of the Code unless, within 180 days before filing the petition (**prepetition**), the individual receives "an individual or group briefing" (which can be by phone or Internet) from "an approved nonprofit **budget and credit counseling agency**" that outlines "the opportunities for available credit counseling" and assists the individual "in performing a related budget analysis." The court may grant an exemption to the prepetition credit counseling requirement based on the debtor's sworn statement that he needed emergency relief and did not have time to complete it prepetition, but the exemption expires 30 days *after* the petition is filed, and so the counseling must be completed by that time. The briefing is not required if the court determines that the debtor is incapacitated (mentally), disabled (physically), active military in a combat zone, or where the U.S. Trustee determines that there are insufficient approved agencies to provide the required counseling. Debtors themselves must pay any costs associated with this required counseling but the cost is not prohibitive and the counseling can often be accomplished by phone or Internet.

Fortunately, not just any credit counseling agency (CCA) can provide these required services (see the discussion of CCAs and the current problems with some of them in Chapter Three, Section F). CCAs desiring to provide these services to debtors sufficient to satisfy the §109(h)(1) requirement must be *nonprofit* and certified by the U.S. Trustee and to become and remain certified they must successfully complete in-depth preliminary and subsequent examinations by the office of the U.S. Trustee. The current list of CCAs certified by the U.S. Trustee to provide these services can be seen at www.usdoj.gov/ust/eo/bapcpa/ccde/ cc_approved.htm. The bankruptcy court clerks are also required by §111 of the Code to maintain a list of approved CCAs.

The individual debtor's compliance with the prepetition credit counseling requirement is demonstrated by the completion of Exhibit D to the petition. (See Document 1 in the Carlson case file.)

CONCLUSION

If the Chapter 7 debtor can satisfy the means test and otherwise qualifies to file for Chapter 7 relief, he is ready to proceed in Chapter 7. In the next chapter we will look at the Chapter 7 petition itself and the supporting schedules and statements that must accompany the petition.

CHAPTER SUMMARY

Chapter 7 is a liquidation proceeding in which a bankruptcy trustee appointed by the court locates and takes possession of the nonexempt assets of the debtor, liquidates those assets, and distributes the proceeds to creditors of the estate per a distribution formula established by the Code. Either an individual or an entity debtor can file for Chapter 7 relief. Individual consumer debtors must satisfy the means test introduced by BAPCPA in 2005 in order to qualify for Chapter 7 relief. The means test compares the debtor's annualized monthly income to the median family income for a similar size family in the debtor's state of residence. If the debtor's income is equal to or less than the applicable median income, no presumption of abuse arises in the case and he may proceed in Chapter 7. If the debtor's income exceeds the applicable median income but the debtor lacks sufficient projected disposable income to fund a Chapter 13 plan of reorganization, the presumption of abuse does not arise and he may proceed in Chapter 7. If, however, the debtor's income exceeds the applicable median income and the debtor does have sufficient projected income to fund a Chapter 13 plan of reorganization, the presumption of abuse arises and the case must be either converted to a Chapter 13 or dismissed, unless the debtor can show special circumstances justifying the case continuing in Chapter 7. Requirements to proceed in Chapter 7 also include completion of a prepetition credit counseling course and the absence of a prior discharge in bankruptcy within a certain number of years.

REVIEW QUESTIONS

1. Name two types of businesses that may not file for bankruptcy relief under Title 11.
2. If a debtor has received a discharge under Chapter 7, how long must he wait to file another Chapter 7 case?
3. When was the means test and presumption of abuse introduced to the Bankruptcy Code? To which Chapter 7 debtors do the test and presumption apply?
4. What is the difference between an above median debtor and a below median debtor for purposes of the means test?
5. How do we calculate current monthly income of a debtor on OBF 22A?
6. Why do we care about the state median income of the debtor in connection with the means test?
7. Who determines the median income figures for the various states and how often are they adjusted?

8. What is the marital adjustment and who may take advantage of it?
9. What is the role of IRS national and local standards for expenses in applying the means test?
10. What kind of special circumstances might a Chapter 7 debtor show to rebut the presumption of abuse in his case?
11. Who has the standing to challenge the debtor's determination that the presumption of abuse does not arise in his case?
12. What are the options of a Chapter 7 debtor in whose case the presumption of abuse arises and is not rebutted?

WORDS AND PHRASES TO REMEMBER

above median debtor
annualized monthly income
answer
automatic dismissal
Bankruptcy Abuse Prevention and Consumer Protection Act of 2005 (BAPCPA)
bankruptcy fraud
below median debtor
burden of proof
business debt
can-pay debtors
cause shown
consumer debt
codebtor
consumer debtor
debtor (debtor in bankruptcy)
debtor's annual income
default
disposable monthly income
domestic support obligation
evidentiary hearing
Family Violence Prevention and Services Act
individual business debtor
individual consumer debtor
IRS National Standards for Allowable Living Expenses and Local Standards
for Transportation and Housing and Utilities Expenses
local court rules
look back period
mandatory dismissal
means test
median family income
monthly income
motion
party in interest
prepetition
presumption of abuse
pro se
special circumstances
sua sponte
summons
under oath
U.S. Census Bureau
standing
Statement of Current Monthly Income and Means Test Calculation (OBF 22A)
Statement of the U.S. Trustee Program's Position on Legal Issues Arising Under the Chapter 7 Means Test

TO LEARN MORE: A number of TLM activities to accompany this chapter are accessible on the student disc accompanying the text and on the Author Updates link to the text Web site at http://www.aspenparalegaled.com/ books/parsons_abcdebt/default.asp.

Chapter Fifteen:

The Chapter 7 Case: The Petition, Supporting Schedules, and Statements

Some debts are fun when you are acquiring them, but none are fun when you set about retiring them.

—Ogden Nash

A. The Petition Commencing the Case

1. The Voluntary Petition

Petition The document filed to initiate a bankruptcy case under the Code.

Order for relief The formal beginning of a bankruptcy case triggered by the filing of a voluntary petition or by court order following an involuntary petition.

A bankruptcy case under any chapter is commenced by the filing of the bankruptcy **petition** per §301(a) of the Code and Federal Rules of Bankruptcy Procedure (FRBP) 1002. The voluntary petition is OBF 1. Per §301(b), the filing of the petition constitutes an **order for relief** under the Code, a term used often in the Code as we will see.

P-H 15-a: Go to www.uscourts.gov/bkforms/index.html and view the voluntary bankruptcy petition, which is OBF 1. Scroll down through the voluntary petition form and note the kinds of information that have to be provided there. Just some of the information to be provided includes:

- Not just the debtor's full name, but all other names used in the preceding eight years
- The address where the debtor's principal assets are located
- The type of debtor (individual, corporation, partnership, etc.)
- The chapter of the Code the filing is under (7, 11, 13, etc.)
- The nature of the debts (consumer or business)
- How the filing fee will be paid
- Estimates of creditors, assets, and debts
- Whether a prior case has been filed within eight years
- Whether any other case is pending

Remember that if you are assisting the debtor's attorney, you may be given responsibility for gathering all this information from the debtor and preparing the petition for the attorney's review. Which would be the better way to gather that information from the client: to develop a form for the client to complete and then transfer the information from the client form to the bankruptcy form? Or to just give the client a copy of the bankruptcy form with instructions to complete it by hand and then transfer the information to the form to be filed with the court? Law offices do it both ways.

2. The Joint Petition, Consolidation, and Joint Administration

Joint administration Where two or more related bankruptcy cases are ordered to be administered by the same trustee to save administrative costs.

A married couple may file a **joint petition** (see §302 of the Code), in which case they will identify themselves as debtor and joint debtor (with the Supreme Court having stricken down the Defense of Marriage Act in *United States v. Windsor*, 133 S.Ct. 2675 (2013), this should now include same-gender couples married under the laws of a state recognizing same-gender marriage). When a married couple file a joint petition, only one set of schedules (discussed below) is required. Other closely related debtors cannot file a joint petition, but the court may order the **joint administration** of related cases, pursuant to FRBP 1015(b). And if two or more petitions are pending in the same court involving the same debtor, the court may order those cases **consolidated** pursuant to FRBP 1015(a).

Consolidation The merging of two or more bankruptcy cases involving the same debtor into one.

> **EXAMPLE**
>
> Assume a brother and sister are partners in a business. They both decide to file for bankruptcy relief. Even though the two debtors are closely related and share the same income sources and debts they cannot file a joint petition. However, once both of them have filed individual petitions, the court may order the joint administration of their cases. If the business partnership files a separate petition, its case may be ordered jointly administered with those of the two partners. If a corporation were in bankruptcy and one of its subsidiaries filed a separate petition in the same court, the court might order joint administration if the assets and obligations of the two corporations are intertwined and creditors will not be prejudiced. If a debtor files a voluntary petition and his creditors then file an involuntary petition (discussed below) against him in the same court, the court might consolidate the two cases into one.

Marta Carlson is a divorced, single woman. Her individual voluntary petition for Chapter 7 relief is shown in Document 1 in the Carlson case file.

3. Proper Venue for Filing the Petition

Venue The appropriate bankruptcy court in which the debtor's petition should be filed.

In the next-to-last box on page 2 of the voluntary petition form (OBF 1) there are questions related to **venue** In a bankruptcy case, venue has to do with which bankruptcy court the case should be filed in or, more specifically, which federal district the case should be filed in. The general venue rule in bankruptcy cases is that the petition should be filed in the bankruptcy court in the district where the debtor has resided or had its principal place of business for the 180 days preceding filing (see 28 U.S.C. §1408). If the debtor has resided or had his primary place of business in more than one district during that time frame, then venue is proper in whichever district the debtor has had such contacts for the longer part of the past 180 days.

4. Signatures on the Petition

a. *The Debtor's Signature*

Pursuant to FRBP 1008, the debtor(s) must sign the voluntary petition **under oath** (see page 3 of OBF 1), which means the debtor is subject to penalties of **perjury** for a deliberate misstatement or omission on the petition and supporting schedules. An entity debtor must sign the petition through an authorized agent. When an entity is the debtor, OBF 2, **Declaration Under Penalty of Perjury On Behalf of a Corporation or Partnership**, must accompany the petition.

The individual debtor must also sign Exhibit D to the petition. **Individual Debtor's Statement of Compliance with Credit Counseling Requirement**, to demonstrate his compliance with that requirement. (See OBF 1, Exhibit D, and Document 1 in the Carlson case file.) This, too, the debtor signs under oath, subject to penalties of perjury. A corporate debtor whose stock is publicly traded must execute Exhibit A to the petition (see OBF 1, Exhibit A), providing information regarding shares of stock and major shareholders. And all debtors who have in their possession real or personal property that may pose an imminent threat to public health or safety must execute Exhibit C to the petition (see OBF 1, Exhibit C), describing such property and its location.

b. *The Signature and Certification of the Attorney for the Debtor*

The attorney for the debtor will sign the voluntary petition as well (see page 3 of OBF 1). Pursuant to FRBP 9011, the attorney's signature on the petition or any other document filed with the court constitutes a certification to the court that "to the best of the attorney's knowledge, information and belief formed after an inquiry reasonable under the circumstances,"

- The filing is not done for any improper purpose (e.g., to harass or delay),
- The factual allegations or denial of an opponent's factual contentions have or likely will have evidentiary support,
- And all legal contentions are warranted by existing law or a nonfrivolous argument for what the law should be.

BAPCPA, however, added a new dimension to the attorney's signature on the petition. New §707(b)(4)(D) of the Code provides as follows:

> The signature of an attorney on the petition shall constitute a certification that the attorney has no knowledge after an inquiry that the information in the schedules filed with such petition is incorrect.

This BAPCPA requirement is still too new to be sure exactly what this additional "inquiry" requires of debtor's attorneys or what penalties may be imposed on the attorney if a satisfactory inquiry is deemed not to have been made. Is the attorney being asked to guarantee the accuracy of his client's information? Is the attorney responsible if the client misstates or falsifies information that appears in the petition and schedules? Can an attorney not simply rely on the veracity and accuracy of the information his client gives him? Though the provision is too new for all these questions to be answered, one bankruptcy court construed the new inquiry requirement to mean that the attorney's inquiry need only be "a reasonable one" and suggested that courts should be careful not to impose burdens on lawyers that prove unrealistic in light of real life circumstances. See *In re Withrow*, 391 B.R. 317, 327 (Bankr. D. Mass. 2008). Another bankruptcy court characterized the new inquiry obligation as requiring debtor's attorneys to "exercise significant care as to the completeness and accuracy of all recitations on their clients' schedules after they have made a factual investigation and legal evaluation" that conforms to the existing requirements of FRBP 9011. See *In re Robertson*, 370 B.R. 804, 809 n.8 (Bankr. D. Minn. 2007). In the case of *In re Dean*, 401 B.R. 917 (Bankr. D. Idaho 2008), the debtor's attorney advised his clients to perfect a relative's security interest in their motor home before filing a bankruptcy petition, then took their word for it that it had been done. The court found that since the security filing was easily verifiable by the attorney and had not been done, the attorney had violated his duty of inquiry under §707(b)(4)(D). The court entered a **turnover order** directing him to **disgorge** (refund) the fee paid to him by debtors.

c. The Signature of a Debt Relief Agency (DRA) Providing Assistance in a Consumer Debtor Case: The Debtor's Attorney as a DRA

BAPCPA introduced the concept of a **debt relief agency** (DRA) to the Code. Section §101(12A) defines a DRA in part as one "who provides any bankruptcy assistance to an assisted person in return for the payment of money or other valuable consideration. . . ." An **assisted person** is defined in §101(3) as an individual debtor with primarily consumer debts.

Of course there are numerous private, non-attorney businesses that are engaged in providing financial advice to consumers for a fee to whom this definition applies. We have met them before in the guise of **credit counseling agencies** discussed in Section F of Chapter Three. But an immediate issue arose after BAPCPA became law as to whether debtor's attorneys would be considered DRAs in light of several new sections introduced by BAPCPA imposing restrictions and requirements on DRAs. For example, §526(a)(4) prohibits a DRA from advising an assisted person to incur more debt in contemplation of bankruptcy, something attorneys routinely do (e.g. to refinance debt at a lower rate, pay certain bills or purchase a reliable car), raising a First Amendment free speech issue. In *Milavetz, Gallop & Milavetz v. U.S.*, 559 U.S. 229 (2010) the U.S. Supreme Court held that lawyers *are* DRAs under the Code, but narrowly construed the restriction of §526(a)(4) to prohibit *only* advice to a client to load up on debt because they plan to file for bankruptcy, advice that would likely be unethical and possibly fraudulent anyway.

As another example, §528 of the Code requires that DRAs identify themselves as such in any advertising and make certain disclosures in advertising that attorneys do not normally make, also raising free speech issues. The court in *Milavetz* upheld those disclosure requirements as reasonably related to the government's interest in protecting consumers.

Further, Code §527(a)(1) requires DRAs to comply with the requirements of §342(b) by providing consumer debtors with written notice explaining all the options for filing bankruptcy (usually Chapters 7, 11, 12, and 13 for the individual debtor) and the differences between each type of filing. The written notice that must be provided to consumer debtors to comply with §342(b) can be seen in OBF 201(A). Since the Supreme Court has clarified that attorneys for consumer debtor are DRAs, that means the attorney will also sign the box labeled Exhibit B on page 2 of the voluntary petition representing that their §527(a)(1) duty has been fulfilled.

Section 342(b) seems to literally place the requirement of providing debtors with written notice of their filing options and differences between the various bankruptcy filings on the clerk of the bankruptcy court, not the DRA/debtor's attorney. So, pursuant to §527(a)(1), do both the attorney *and* the clerk have to give the debtor this notice? No. The clerk will typically provide the notice only if the debtor has no attorney (such a debtor is filing *pro se*) or if the debtor's attorney fails to sign the Exhibit B box on the petition.

d. The Signature of the Nonattorney Petition Preparer

Section 110 of the Code authorizes nonattorneys to assist debtors in preparing the petition and supporting schedules and to receive a fee for doing so. However, the **nonattorney bankruptcy petition preparer (NABPP)** is subject to numerous limitations and requirements. The NABPP is strictly prohibited from providing his client with any legal advice, including advice concerning the petition or what chapter of bankruptcy to file under, and the NABPP must disclose his limitations in writing to the client per OBF 19B. The NABPP is subject to the forfeiture of any fee deemed excessive or the entire fee collected for failure to comply with the requirements imposed on him, plus an additional $500 penalty for failure to comply with a *turnover order* (the court order to *disgorge* and refund fees received from the debtor), and possible criminal prosecution under 18 U.S.C. §156 for the knowing disregard of a bankruptcy law or rule. The NABPP must sign the voluntary petition (see page 3 of OBF 1) and separately sign under oath and file

- OBF 19, Certification and Signature of Non-Attorney Bankruptcy Petition Preparer,
- OBF 280, Disclosure of Compensation of Bankruptcy Petition Preparer, and
- OBF 201B, Certification of Notice to Consumer Debtors Under §342(b) of the Bankruptcy Code

NABPP are also considered DRAs per the definition of Code §101(12A) and must comply with those provisions as well.

Bankruptcy petition preparer Prepares a bankruptcy petition for a fee. Not an attorney or working under the supervision of an attorney.

5. The Filing Fee

Per FRBP 1006, the **filing fee** is normally paid to the clerk of the bankruptcy court at the time the petition is filed, although the Code does permit a debtor to pay the fee in installments. In that event, the debtor must file OBF 3A, **Application to Pay Filing Fee in Installments**, along with the petition. (See Documents 2 and 3 in the Carlson case file.) The number of installments is limited to four, and the debtor must make the final installment no later than 120 days after filing the petition. However, that time limit can be extended to 180 days on motion and for cause shown. In Chapter 7 cases only, the debtor may request **waiver of the fee** entirely by filing OBF 3B with the petition, but as you can see by reading OBF 3B, that remedy is only available to the very poor.

P-H 15-b: Go to www.uscourts.gov/bkforms/index.html and view OBF 3B, Application for Waiver of the Chapter 7 Filing Fee, and then answer these questions:

- What is the current filing fee for a Chapter 7 bankruptcy petition?
- How close to the poverty line does the debtor have to be in order to qualify for waiver of the fee?
- Is the application signed by the debtor under penalties of perjury?
- If the debtor is assisted in completing this form by a NABPP, does that person have to sign the application?
- What is the current official poverty line for a family of four?

6. The Involuntary Petition

The vast majority of bankruptcy cases are filed voluntarily, meaning the debtor himself makes the decision to file for relief. But §303 of the Code does permit a debtor to be forced into a Chapter 7 (or Chapter 11) bankruptcy by creditors filing an **involuntary petition**. Three creditors with unsecured claims totaling at least $10,000 may join in the petition. If the debtor has fewer than 12 unsecured creditors, then a single creditor with a claim of at least $10,000 can initiate the involuntary petition. The involuntary proceeding is available only in Chapters 7 or 11.

FRBP 1010 through 1013 provide that when an involuntary petition is filed it must be served on the debtor along with a summons, just as would happen in a civil lawsuit under the Federal Rules of Civil Procedure. Once the debtor is served with the petition and summons, he must file an **answer to the petition** within 21 days raising any defenses or objections he has to the petition. If he fails to do so, the court will enter an order for relief on the involuntary petition by **default** and the case will proceed. FRBP 1011(a) allows a nonpetitioning partner to contest an involuntary petition against the partnership but does not allow a nonpetitioning creditor or other **party in interest** to contest an involuntary petition.

Party in interest Interpreted generally to refer to any party having a stake in the outcome of a matter arising in a bankruptcy case.

P-H 15-c: Look at §101 of the Code and FRBP 9001. Is "party in interest" defined in either place? Generally, a party in interest is the debtor and any other person or entity sufficiently affected by the bankruptcy case that it is reasonable to grant him **standing** to be heard on a matter. Would that include the U.S. Trustee? The bankruptcy trustee appointed to administer the case? All the creditors of the debtor or any committees of creditors? The debtor's parents or other family members who are not creditors or business partners of the debtor? The local media? The debtor's noncreditor nosey neighbor? If the debtor is a corporation, its directors? Its officers? Its employees?

Evidentiary hearing A court hearing at which sworn testimony is taken and exhibits may be offered subject to the Federal Rules of Evidence.

If the involuntary petition is properly answered and contested, the court will then conduct an **evidentiary hearing** where live testimony is given and relevant exhibits introduced, all subject to the Federal Rules of Evidence. At the hearing, the court must decide whether to enter an *order for relief* allowing the involuntary case to proceed or to dismiss the petition. The creditors filing the involuntary petition have the **burden of proof** at the hearing to demonstrate that sufficient grounds exist to justify proceeding with the bankruptcy case over the debtor's objection. To satisfy their burden, the creditors must demonstrate that one or both of the following grounds are present:

- the debtor is not generally paying its bona fide debts as they come due; or
- within 120 days preceding the filing of the involuntary petition, a receiver, assignee, or custodian has taken possession of all or substantially all of the debtor's property.

The first ground, that the debtor is not paying his debts as they come due, is the ground most frequently asserted in an involuntary case. Consider why creditors force a debtor into bankruptcy: Because the creditors are unsecured or undersecured in specific property of the debtor, they are not being paid, and they cannot gain access to the debtor's assets without suing him and obtaining a judgment, which could take months or years. And those creditors fear that the debtor will have dissipated his assets by then, so there will be no property to execute on to satisfy the judgment when it is finally rendered. Forcing the debtor into a liquidation bankruptcy is seen as the quickest and surest way to stop the debtor from further dissipating his assets and to force a distribution of the remaining assets for the benefit of all the creditors.

Creditors must proceed with caution in filing an involuntary petition. If the petition is contested and dismissed then §303(i) of the Code permits the bankruptcy court to award court costs and attorney fees to the debtor for contesting the petition. And if the judge finds that the petition was filed in bad faith then the court may award the debtor consequential damages (e.g., lost profits to the business caused by the filing) and even punitive damages.

B. ▶ Schedules, Statements, and Other Documents That Accompany the Petition

As required by §521 of the Code and FRBP 1007, the debtor must file a number of schedules, statements, and other documents in addition to the voluntary petition and its exhibits. Section 521, as amended by BAPCPA, is dense, poorly structured, and not well worded. However, the BAPCPA changes have now been in effect long enough for bankruptcy practitioners and judges to figure out with some confidence what is required.

This section will summarize the schedules, statements, and other documents that must be prepared and filed in support of the Chapter 7 petition. Where there is an OBF for the required schedules, statements and the like, that form is referenced in the summary. Remember that the OBFs can be accessed and viewed at www.uscourts.gov/bkforms/index.html if you do not have them in paper form.

The schedules, statements and other documents filed by Marta Carlson in connection with her Chapter 7 case are set forth in the Carlson case file. As you read the description of each schedule below, compare that description to the Carlson filings in her case file. Keep in mind as you review these schedules, statements, and other documents that if you work as an assisting legal professional for the debtor's attorney, you will be preparing them for review by the supervising attorney using information supplied by the debtor/client. If you are the assisting legal professional for a creditor's attorney, the bankruptcy trustee, or the U.S. Trustee, you will be reviewing them for the accuracy of the information and to summarize them for your supervisor.

1. The List of Creditors

Section 521(a)(1) requires that the debtor file a **list of creditors**. (See Document 4 in the Carlson case file.) There is no OBF for this list, but most bankruptcy courts provide practitioners with a matrix form accessible from the court's Web site. The list will serve as a **mailing matrix** by the clerk's office to provide creditors notice of the bankruptcy filing (to be considered in Chapter Sixteen, Section D) and of other proceedings in the case.

2. Schedule A, Real Property (OBF 6A)

On this form the debtor must list, by description and location, each parcel of real property in which the debtor owns any interest, identify the interest held (fee simple, life estate, leasehold, etc.), state the estimated dollar value of the interest, and state the balance owed on any debt secured by the property. (See Document 7 in the Carlson case file.)

3. Schedule B, Personal Property (OBF 6B)

All personal property in which the debtor has an ownership interest must be identified and described here, along with a statement of its location and current value of the debtor's interest. The form utilizes 34 specific categories of personal property, as well as an "other" category. (See Document 8 in the Carlson case file.)

4. Schedule C, Exempt Property (OBF 6C)

a. How Exemptions Work

In Chapter Ten we considered exempt property in the context of a judgment creditor executing on a judgment. Similarly, the Code allows an individual bankruptcy debtor to claim certain property as exempt. Exemptions are not available to Chapter 7 entity debtors (corporations and partnerships) since they go out of business at the end of the liquidation and do not retain assets. Individual debtors are required to set forth the property they claim as exempt on Schedule C. Illustration 15-a shows Marta Carlson's Schedule C.

The Chapter 7 bankruptcy trustee cannot seize the property that is fully exempt and sell it for the benefit of the creditors. Instead the debtor will retain possession of the fully exempt property.

EXAMPLE

In her Schedule C (Illustration 15-a and Document 9 in the Carlson case file) Marta Carlson has claimed her jewelry to be fully exempt under §522(d)(4). It is worth $1,350 and that Code section currently allows her to exempt such property up to $1,550. If her valuation of the jewelry is correct, she has fully exempted it and the trustee cannot seize it.

If the debtor is unable to fully exempt property, the trustee may seize it and sell it in order to realize the equity in the property for the benefit of the estate. But the debtor is entitled to receive the exempted value following the sale.

EXAMPLE

> In her Schedule C Marta Carlson has claimed exemptions totaling $4,900 in her YR-4 Toyota Camry. But the vehicle is worth $8,500 so she is unable to fully exempt it. Once the trustee determines there is equity for the estate in that property, he will seize the car and sell it. But Marta will have to be paid her exempt amount of $4,900 from the proceeds of the sale.

If a creditor is properly secured and perfected in the property claimed as exempt, the debtor's claimed exemption normally cannot defeat that secured claim (subject to an exception for judicial liens discussed later in this section) and there is no equity for the estate in the property to the extent of the secured claim.

EXAMPLE

> Automotive Finance, Inc. (AFI) has a claim in the amount of $1,750 secured by the YR-4 Toyota Camry in which Marta also claims an exemption of $4,900. If the trustee seizes and sells the vehicle, AFI's secured claim must be paid in full first from the proceeds, then Marta's exemption claim. Only after those two superior claims are satisfied can the trustee take the balance of the proceeds of the sale into the estate for the benefit of creditors.

P-H 15-d: On her Schedule C, Marta Carlson has claimed an exemption in her home of $22,975, the maximum **homestead exemption** currently allowed under §522(d)(1). As you can see on her Schedule D (Document 10 in the Carlson case file), she has two mortgages on the property and those two secured claims together total $180,000. The home is valued by Marta on her Schedules A and D at $255,000. Assume her bankruptcy trustee seizes the home and sells it for that price and incurs no sales commission in doing so. Using the last example, in what order will the proceeds of sale be distributed? If the trustee incurs a 6% realtor's commission on the sale of the home, that expense will come out of his share of the proceeds.

---

b. The Federal Exemptions and Right of States to Opt Out

The Code contains a uniform set of federal exemptions for individual debtors set out in §522(d). In a case where husband and wife are joint debtors, §522(m) provides that each debtor may claim the stated exemption separately, a process practitioners call **doubling** or **stacking**. As mandated by §104, the dollar value of the federal exemptions is adjusted in April of every third year. The last adjustment was on April 1, 2013, and the next will be on April 1, 2016.

Illustration 15-a: MARTA CARLSON'S SCHEDULE C—PROPERTY CLAIMED AS EXEMPT

B6C (Official Form 6C) (04/13)

In re   **Marta Rinaldi Carlson** _____   Case No.   081441-CP _____
_____
Debtor(s)

SCHEDULE C - PROPERTY CLAIMED AS EXEMPT

Debtor claims the exemptions to which debtor is entitled under: ☐ Check if debtor claims a homestead exemption that exceeds
(Check one box) $155,675.*
☒ 11 U.S.C. §522(b)(2)
☐ 11 U.S.C. §522(b)(3)

Description of Property	Specify Law Providing Each Exemption	Value of Claimed Exemption	Current Value of Property Without Deducting Exemption
Other Property			
Residence at 1212 Spruce Street, Capitol City, CL	11 U.S.C. § 522(d)(1)	22,975.00	255,000.00
YR-4 Toyota Camry automobile	11 U.S.C. § 522(d)(2) & (5)	4,900.00	8,500.00
Shears washing machine	11 U.S.C. § 522(d)(3)	350.00	350.00
Shears clothes dryer	11 U.S.C. § 522(d)(3)	250.00	250.00
All other household furnishings & clothing	11 U.S.C. § 522(d)(3)	8,500.00	8,500.00
Jewelry	11 U.S.C. § 522(d)(4)	1,350.00	1,350.00
TTI 401(k)	11 U.S.C. § 522(d)(10)(E)	7,600.00	7,600.00
Child support arrearage	11 U.S.C. § 522(d)(10)(D)	15,000.00	15,000.00
Male golden retriever dog (Max)	11 U.S.C. § 522(d)(3)	50.00	50.00
	Total:	60,975.00	296,600.00

Amount subject to adjustment on 4/01/16, and every three years thereafter with respect to cases commenced on or after the date of adjustment.
Schedule of Property Claimed as Exempt consists of 1 total page(s)

Software Copyright (c) 1996-2013 CCH INCORPORATED - www.bestcase.com   Best Case Bankruptcy

EXAMPLE

> As of April 1, 2013, the federal homestead exemption allowed under §522(d)(1) is $22,975. If a husband and wife both own the homestead and they are joint bankruptcy debtors, they may each claim the full exemption amount and, together, exempt $45,950 of equity in their home.

Illustration 15-b summarizes the **federal exemptions**.

Section 522(b) allows states, acting through their legislatures, to **opt out** of using the federal exemptions set out in §522(d) and to use the state exemption laws instead. More than 30 states have opted out of the federal exemptions. In those states, bankruptcy filers must use the state exemption laws that control in executions on final judgments. In states that have not opted out of the federal exemptions, §522(b) permits the individual bankruptcy filer to choose between the federal exemptions and the applicable state exemptions. The filer in those states cannot pick and choose among the federal and state exemption provisions, however. He must use *only* the federal exemptions or *only* the state exemptions. And a husband and wife filing a joint petition in those states must *both* use the federal exemptions or *both* use the state exemptions.

P-H 15-e: In her Schedule C, Marta Carlson has utilized the federal exemptions of §522(d). What does that tell you as to whether the fictitious state of Columbiana has opted out of the federal exemptions? Go through each exemption she has claimed and be sure you understand why she is claiming each exemption listed. Has she cited the proper subsection of §522(d) in connection with each claimed exemption?

P-H 15-f: Go to www.assetprotectionbook.com/state_resources.htm or www.thebankruptcysite.org/topics/bankruptcy-your-state or directly to your state statute regarding exemptions and compare the exemptions allowed in your state with the federal exemptions set forth in §522(d) of the Code. Which appear more generous to debtors? Which appear more reasonable to you? If your state has opted out of the Code exemptions to use its own exemptions, do you think that was a good idea? If it has not, should it?

P-H 15-g: In *Rousey v. Jacoway*, 544 U.S. 320 (2005), the Court held that assets in Individual Retirement Accounts (IRAs) are protected under §522(d)(10)(E) as payments "on account of age" notwithstanding they can be accessed prior to age 59½ and are thus exempt. This decision has broad implications for the baby-boomer generation, providing millions of Americans nearing retirement with increased protection of their earnings. Read the Pew Research report on baby at www.pewresearch.org/daily-number/baby-boomers-retire/. How many baby boomers are turning 65 each day? How many will retire over the next 20 years or so?

Illustration 15-b: SUMMARY OF §522(d) FEDERAL EXEMPTIONS (ALL DOLLAR VALUES STATED ARE AS OF APRIL 1, 2013)

- $22,975 of equity in the a residence owned by the debtor and used by the debtor or a dependent (§522(d)(1))
- $3,675 of equity in one vehicle (§522(d)(2))
- $12,250 of equity (not to exceed $575 per item) in household goods and furnishings, appliances, wearing apparel, books, animals, crops, or musical instruments held for personal, family, or household use by the debtor or a dependent (§502(d)(3))
- $1,550 of equity in jewelry used by the debtor or a dependent (§502(d)(4))
- $1,225, plus up to $11,500 of any unused balance of the homestead exemption of §522(d)(1) (§522(d)(5)) (known as the **wild card exemption)**
- $2,300 of equity in implements or tools of the trade or professional books of the debtor or a dependent (§522(d)(6))
- An unlimited amount in unmatured life insurance policies owned by the debtor, excluding credit life contracts (§522(d)(7))
- $12,250 in cash value of an insurance policy (e.g., a whole life policy) (§522(d)(8))
- An unlimited amount in prescription health aids for the debtor or a dependent (§522(d)(9))
- An unlimited amount in Social Security, welfare, disability, unemployment, or veteran's benefits and in alimony, child support, or separate maintenance, to the extent reasonably necessary to support the debtor or a dependent, and in qualified pension and profit sharing plans (§522(d)(10))
- An unlimited amount as crime victim's reparation benefits and wrongful death recovery or life insurance benefits if the debtor was a dependent of the deceased, to the extent reasonably necessary for the support of the debtor or a dependent, and up to $22,975 in recovery on a personal injury claim involving the debtor or a dependent, and compensation for lost future earnings of the debtor or one of whom the debtor was a dependent, to the extent reasonably necessary for the support of the debtor or a dependent (§522(d)(11))
- An unlimited amount in any retirement fund exempted from taxation by the IRS (e.g., 401(k), 403(b), and IRA plans) (§522(d)(12))

Wild card exemption Practitioner's phrase for §522(d)(5) allowing an individual debtor a general exemption in any property up to a stated value.

EC 15-a: The right of states to opt out of the federal exemption scheme and apply their own exemptions in bankruptcy cases filed in the federal courts within that state is a striking example of variation allowed in the application of what was intended to be a uniform national bankruptcy process imposed by federal law. The exemptions a debtor in one state might enjoy are quite different from those a debtor in another state will have to settle for. Is this right in a moral/ethical sense? Does it encourage forum shopping, in the sense that a financially challenged debtor might change his state of residence in advance of a foreseeable bankruptcy filing? Is it ethical for an attorney to advise a client to do that?

Another consideration in determining what exemptions apply in a particular case is §522(b)(3)(A), which provides that it is the law of the debtor's **domicile** that will determine what exemptions apply in his case but only if he has been domiciled there 730 days (two years) prior to the date the petition is filed. If he has not been domiciled in any one state for the requisite 730 days, then the law of the state where he was domiciled for the 180 days preceding the 730-day period will determine the exemptions.

EXAMPLE

> Assume a debtor files for bankruptcy relief in a U.S. bankruptcy court in California. The debtor moved to California from Minnesota six months ago. He had lived in Minnesota five years before moving to California. Though California is now the debtor's domicile, he has not lived there 730 days preceding the filing of the petition, and so California exemption laws will not control his Schedule C exemptions. Because he lived in Minnesota for the requisite 180 days preceding the 730-day period, Minnesota exemption laws will control his Schedule C exemptions.

Applicable exemptions will control property of the debtor wherever it is located. (Compare the rule for controlling exemption law in the enforcement of final judgments, as discussed in Chapter Ten, Section D.)

EXAMPLE

> Assume the debtor from the previous example owns property in Texas. Minnesota exemption laws will control his right to exempt any such property on his Schedule C, not Texas law.

c. Limitations on the Homestead Exemption: The 1,215-Day Rule

There is an important limitation on the right of a debtor in bankruptcy to claim the homestead exemption (for the principal residence) in a state that has opted out of the federal exemptions. As we considered in Chapter Ten when studying state exemption laws in the context of a judgment debtor executing on a final judgment, some states have very generous homestead exemptions, far more generous than the federal homestead exemption, which is limited to $22,975 for a sole individual debtor or $45,950 for a husband and wife filing as joint debtors (per §522(d)(1) as of April 1, 2013).

EXAMPLE

> A bankruptcy debtor residing in a state that allows an unlimited homestead exemption and which has opted out of the federal exemptions could theoretically exempt all the equity in his principal residence just as he could exempt it from executing judgment creditors. Thus, that bankruptcy debtor could emerge from a Chapter 7 liquidation with his debts discharged and not lose his home.

1,215-day rule Rule limiting amount of homestead exemption for principal residence purchased less than 1,215 days before petition in bankruptcy filed.

However, §522(p)(1), added by BAPCPA, provides that if the bankruptcy debtor has not owned the principal residence for more than 1,215 days preceding the filing of the petition he cannot exempt more than $155,675 of equity in it (as of April 1, 2013) regardless of the applicable homestead exemption. This is the **1,215-day rule**.

EXAMPLE

Assume the debtor in the previous example bought his home 24 months before filing for bankruptcy relief and has a total of $250,000 of equity in the home. He has owned the home only 730 days. So even though the state where he resides allows him an unlimited homestead exemption, and even though that state has opted out of the federal exemptions for bankruptcy cases, he will be limited to a homestead exemption of no more than $155,675.

Section 522(p)(2)(B) does say that the limitation of §522(p)(1) does not apply to any equity the debtor has in his current principal residence that was transferred from a prior principal residence so long as the prior residence was acquired outside of the 1,215-day limit and was in the same state.

EXAMPLE

Assume the debtor in our previous example bought his first home six years (2,190 days) before filing for bankruptcy relief. Then 24 months ago he sold that first residence and used $225,000 of the equity he realized from that sale to purchase his current home. At the time he files his petition in bankruptcy, he has a total of $250,000 equity in his home. That debtor can exempt all of the $225,000 equity he transferred from his first home to his second but not the additional $25,000 of equity he has accumulated since the purchase of the second home less than 1,215 days before filing. But note that if the first home of the debtor had been located in a different state from the second home, he would not get the benefit of this exception to the 1,215-day rule.

d. Valuing Property Claimed as Exempt

Schedule C requires the debtor to state the *value of the claimed exemption* and the current *value of the property claimed as exempt without regard to the exemption*. That can be confusing.

EXAMPLE

As you can see on her Schedule C, Marta Carlson claims an exemption of $4,900 in her four-year-old Toyota Camry. To reach that exemption amount she combined the $3,675 exemption for motor vehicles authorized by §522(d)(2) with the $1,225 wildcard exemption of §522(d)(5) (both values as of April 1, 2013). However, the car is worth $8,500 so she enters $4,900 as the amount of her claimed exemptions in the car and $8,500 as the value of the property in which the exemptions are claimed without regard to the exemptions. If the claimed exemptions in the car are approved, when the bankruptcy trustee sells the car, the proceeds will be applied first to pay off the claim of Automotive Financing, Inc. (AFI), totaling $1,750, which is secured by the vehicle, and second to pay Marta $4,900 as her total exemption in the vehicle. The balance will then be used by the bankruptcy trustee for estate administration costs or distribution to creditors.

P-H 15-h: Marta has a total of $6,750 of equity in the YR-4 Toyota Camry ($8,500 value minus the $1,750 owed to AFI). She could have exempted all of that equity using §522(d)(2) and the wildcard exemption of §522(d)(5), but it would have reduced the amount of the homestead exemption she could claim under §522(d)(1). If she had chosen to do that, what would be the maximum homestead exemption she could have claimed under §522(d)(1)?

Fair market value The price that a willing buyer would pay a willing seller for an item, neither being under a compulsion to sell or buy.

Section 522(a)(2) and Schedule C require the debtor to list the **fair market value** of property claimed as exempt, "as of the date of the filing of the petition." Undefined in the Code, fair market value has been held to mean the estimated price that a willing buyer would pay to a willing seller for the item, neither being under a compulsion to sell or buy and both having reasonable knowledge of the underlying facts (see *U.S. v. Cartwright*, 411 U.S. 546 (1973)).

e. The Right to Object to a Claimed Exemption

The bankruptcy trustee appointed to administer the Chapter 7 case does not have to accept the debtor's Schedule C exemptions. FRBP 4003 authorizes the trustee or other party in interest to object to the debtor's claimed exemptions. The objection may contend that the debtor is not entitled to exempt a particular item of property listed on Schedule C or that the value assigned by the debtor to an item of property claimed as exempt is too low. (Recall the discussion in Chapter Thirteen, Section G, regarding how disputes in bankruptcy court are resolved using motions, objections, notices of intended action, or adversary proceedings.) Challenges to a debtor's claimed exemptions are common and we will consider them further in Chapter Seventeen, where we consider the various actions that a bankruptcy trustee may take to identify and take possession of property of the estate for the benefit of creditors.

EXAMPLE

In her Schedule C, Marta claims her jewelry as exempt, assigning it a value of $1,350 which is $200 below the maximum exemption amount for jewelry allowed by §522(d)(4)($1,550 as of April 2013). If that valuation is correct, she will be able to keep the jewelry because it has no value in excess of the allowed exemption. But if the bankruptcy trustee can prove that the jewelry is actually worth $5,000, he will object to Marta's valuation in that exemption and if he prevails on his objection, will take possession of it as property of the estate, sell it, give Marta $1,550 of the proceeds as her maximum exempt amount, and then use the balance for estate administration costs or distribution to creditors.

What happens if a debtor claims as exempt the full value of property having an actual value in excess of the maximum dollar amount of the exemption applicable to that property but no timely objection is filed? The U.S. Supreme Court has held that absent a timely objection, the property claimed as exempt will be excluded from the estate and retained by the debtor even if the exemption's actual value exceeds what the Code permits. See *Taylor* v. *Freeland & Kronz*, 503 U.S. 638, 642–643 (1992). (Debtor who listed expected proceeds of pending employment discrimination lawsuit as exempt on Schedule C entitled to keep all those proceeds even though the dollar amount of recovery exceeded all allowable exemption amounts where trustee failed to file timely objection to claimed exemption.)

On the other hand, what happens if a debtor assigns a specific dollar amount to property claimed as exempt thinking that is its full value but the property turns out to have a higher value than that claimed? In *Schwab v. Reilly*, 130 S. Ct. 2652 (2010) the Supreme Court held that a debtor is only entitled to the dollar amount of the exemption *actually claimed* on Schedule C, *not* the full value of the exempted property where that value turns out to be more than the claimed exempted amount even though the debtor *intended to* and *could have* exempted the full value of the property and was merely *mistaken* as to its true value. Moreover, the court held that in such situations the failure of the trustee to file a timely objection to the exemption on the basis of the incorrect value is no bar to the trustee treating the dollar value of the property in excess of the claimed exemption amount as **property of the estate** (a concept to be considered in depth in Chapter Seventeen, Section B).

> **P-H 15-i:** In a practical sense, what does the result in *Taylor* mean for the trustee examining a debtor's claimed exemptions? And what does the result in *Schwab* mean for the legal professional assisting the debtor client in filling out the debtor's Schedule C?

f. The Right to Avoid a Judicial Lien in Property Claimed as Exempt

As noted earlier in this section, if a debtor has granted a consensual **security interest** in property he could exempt in bankruptcy, the secured creditor's claim to the property will be superior to the debtor's claimed exemption in the property.

EXAMPLE

If the debtor in our series of homestead exemption examples has obtained a home equity loan for an amount equal to all his equity in the principal residence and granted the lender a mortgage interest in the residence to secure repayment, the debtor will have no equity in the home to exempt when he files a petition in bankruptcy. His right of homestead exemption will not defeat the mortgagee's secured position in the home.

The same is true as to **statutory liens** in the debtor's property (see Chapter Six). They are superior to a claimed exemption in the property that is subject to the statutory lien.

EXAMPLE

If the debtor in our series of homestead exemption examples enters into a contract to sell his principal residence but that contract subsequently falls through, the frustrated buyer who believes the debtor has breached the contract of sale may file a lien *lis pendens* on the property and file suit to enforce it. The lien *lis pendens* is a statutory lien. If the debtor then files a petition in bankruptcy, his right of homestead exemption will not defeat the claim of the holder of the lien *lis pendens*.

Judicial lien Any lien resulting from court proceedings.

Interestingly though, §522(f)(1)(A) empowers the debtor to avoid a **judicial lien** on his property to the extent that the lien impairs an exemption the debtor would otherwise have in the property. Judicial liens are defined by §101(36) as liens obtained by judgment, levy sequestration or other legal or equitable process and include those prejudgment remedies we considered in Chapter Nine and the postjudgment execution remedies we considered in Chapter Eleven. FRBP 4003(d) provides that a proceeding to avoid a judicial lien to preserve an exemption is to be initiated by motion, not adversary proceeding.

EXAMPLE

If the debtor in our series of homestead exemption examples has a judgment entered against him for $100,000 and the judgment creditor has created a judgment lien on the debtor's principal residence by recording the judgment, when the debtor files his bankruptcy petition he may avoid that judgment lien under §522(f)(1)(A) to the extent it impairs his exemption. So if the debtor has $250,000 of equity in his home, all of which state law allows him to exempt as homestead, and has owned it more than 1,215 days so that the 1,215-day rule does not limit his right to claim all his equity as exempt, he can avoid the creditor's judgment lien on the property entirely and claim his full exemption.

Domestic support obligation An obligation to pay alimony, child support, or maintenance.

Section 522(f)(1)(A) does provide, however, that a judicial lien resulting from a **domestic support obligation** (child support, alimony, or maintenance recoverable by a spouse, former spouse, or child of the debtor) cannot be avoided by the debtor.

EXAMPLE

If the creditor holding the judgment lien in the previous example is the ex-spouse of the debtor and the judgment is for unpaid child support, the debtor will be unable to avoid that lien on his principal residence.

Section 522(f)(1)(B) also authorizes the individual Chapter 7 debtor to avoid a nonpossessory, nonpurchase money security interest (defined in Chapter Five, Section D) in certain household items and tools of the trade to the extent the lien impairs an exemption. We will illustrate that section later in connection with the Chapter 13 case (see Chapter Twenty-One, Section B if you want to read about it now).

In Chapter Seventeen, Sections A, D, and E, we will consider various powers granted to the bankruptcy trustee to compel the turnover of debtor's property by third parties having custody or control of such property and to avoid (cancel or set aside) certain prepetition transfers of property from the debtor to third parties and to setoff creditor claims against certain obligations of the creditor to the debtor in order to recover the property involved for the estate. The debtor may claim an exemption in property returned to the estate as a result of the trustee's turnover or avoidance actions. Moreover, §§522(g)(h)(i) authorize the Chapter 7 debtor to initiate such turnover, avoidance, or setoff actions himself if the trustee refuses to do so in order to assert an exemption in property recovered.

P-H 15-j: If your state has opted out of using the federal exemptions, compare your state's exemptions to Marta Carlson's schedules. What property could she exempt on her Schedule C under the exemption laws of your state?

5. Schedule D, Creditors Holding Secured Claims (OBF 6D)

The debtor must list on Schedule D every creditor who claims a security position in the debtor's property, along with detailed information about any codebtors, the value of the property, the amount of the claim, whether the claim is contingent, unliquidated, or disputed, and whether there is any portion of the claim that is not secured. (See Document 10 in the Carlson case file.)

6. Schedule E, Creditors Holding Unsecured Priority Claims (OBF 6E)

When it is time for the bankruptcy trustee to distribute proceeds of the estate to the various creditors of the estate, some creditors get paid in full before others are paid anything, pursuant to §507 of the Code. Schedule E itself gives you an idea of the priority distinctions the Code makes among unsecured creditors. We will look at §507 in more detail in Chapter Seventeen, Section B, but you should recognize now that in Schedule E the debtor must identify creditors that appear to the debtor to have a priority position. (See Document 11 in the Carlson case file.)

7. Schedule F, Creditors Holding Unsecured Nonpriority Claims (OBF 6F)

The debtor must list on Schedule F all creditors who have unsecured claims that have no priority over other general creditors under §507 of the Code. The debtor must also state whether each claim is disputed or undisputed, contingent or not, and whether it is liquidated or unliquidated. It is important to note that a debtor must list a claim even if the debtor disputes all or part of it. (See Document 12 in the Carlson case file.)

As we learned in Chapter Two, a contingent claim is one that hasn't fully matured yet.

EXAMPLE

> In her Schedule F (Document 12 in the Carlson case file) Marta lists the claim of Pine Ridge Nursing Home against her in the amount of $45,290 but designates it as disputed and contingent on the outcome of the lawsuit Pine Ridge has filed against her. (See the Assignment Memorandum in Appendix A.)

As we also learned in Chapter Two, an unliquidated debt is one that has not yet been reduced to a sum certain.

EXAMPLE

> In her Schedule F (Document 12 in the Carlson case file) Marta lists the claim of Pine Ridge Nursing against her as unliquidated. Although that claim is liquidated in the sense that Pine Ridge is seeking a sum certain against Marta, she lists it as unliquidated because the exact amount that she might ultimately owe, if anything, might be less than the full amount sought. (See the Assignment Memorandum in Appendix A.)

8. Schedule G, Executory Contracts and Unexpired Leases (OBF 6G)

Executory contract A contract which has not been fully performed by either party to it.

An **executory contract** is one that is ongoing and on which both parties still owe some performance. Those ongoing contracts and unexpired leases may give rise to additional claims by the other party to the contract if the debtor intends to discharge continuing obligations under the contract in a Chapter 7. (In a reorganization case under Chapters 11, 12, or 13 of the Code they are also important to know about because the debtor's plan will have to deal with them in some way.) (See Document 13 in the Carlson case file.)

EXAMPLE

> Since Marta Carlson is not a party to any executory contract or unexpired lease, her Schedule G (Document 13 in the Carlson case file) simply lists "None." If, however, at the time she filed her petition, she had ordered a new car and was awaiting delivery before paying, that would qualify as an executory contract: Both parties would still owe performance at the time of filing.

9. Schedule H, Codebtors (OBF 6H)

Codebtor Two or more debtors liable for the same debt.

What happens if the bankruptcy debtor wants to discharge a debt on which someone else is also liable as a **codebtor?** Of course the codebtor may have also filed bankruptcy and, if the codebtor is a spouse of the debtor, the codebtor may be a joint petitioner in the same bankruptcy case. But if the codebtor has not also filed for bankruptcy relief is that codebtor still liable for the debt even though this debtor has filed for bankruptcy relief? Yes. A Chapter 7 discharge releases only the debtor from the discharged debts. The liability of a codebtor to a creditor is not affected by that discharge. (See Document 14 in the Carlson case file.)

In Chapter Sixteen, Section E, we will see that the filing of the bankruptcy petition triggers an automatic stay, prohibiting creditors of the debtor from continuing to pursue collection of the debts owed to them. In a Chapter 7 case, a codebtor does *not* benefit from the automatic stay and collection efforts can continue against him unless he is also a joint petitioner or has filed his own bankruptcy case. In Chapter Nineteen, Section C, we will learn that in a Chapter 13 case under the Code the codebtor *does* enjoy the benefit of the automatic stay.

EXAMPLE

> In her Schedule H (Document 14 in the Carlson case file) Marta identifies her ex-husband, Eugene, as a codebtor on obligations that originated during the marriage. On her Schedules D and F (Documents 10 and 12 in the Carlson case file) she notes the existence of a codebtor in listing those debts. But since this is a case under Chapter 7 and not Chapter 13, Eugene does not receive the protection of the automatic stay, and so those creditors can continue collection efforts against him. And though Marta may receive a discharge from those obligations, Eugene will not unless he files his own bankruptcy case.

10. Schedule I, Current Income of Individual Debtors (OBF 6I)

Debtors who are individuals (not entities) must complete this form whether they are consumer debtors or business debtors. (See Document 15 in the Carlson case file.)

11. Schedule J, Current Expenditures of Individual Debtors (OBF 6J)

Schedule J is a companion form to Schedule I, requiring individual debtors to list their average monthly expenses. (See Document 16 in the Carlson case file.)

12. Summary of Schedules (OBF 6-Summary)

This form requires the debtor to enter the totals from Schedules A through J and to summarize them. Individual consumer debtors (not individual business debtors or entity debtors) must provide additional information as well. (See Document 17 in the Carlson case file.)

13. Declaration Concerning Debtor's Schedules (OBF 6-Declaration)

On this form, the individual debtor will sign, declaring under penalties of perjury that the information contained on the various schedules is true and correct to the best of the debtor's knowledge, information, and belief. If the petition and schedules were prepared by a nonattorney bankruptcy petition preparer (NABPP), that person must also sign under oath, not that the information is true, but that the preparer has complied with all his obligations under the Code. (See Document 18 in the Carlson case file.)

If you are the legal professional assisting the debtor in gathering and entering all the information contained in the various schedules, you have a large responsibility in making sure the debtor's declaration is true.

14. Statement of Financial Affairs (OBF 7)

This is a comprehensive form that the debtor must complete and file along with the schedules and which is due, like the schedules, within 14 days of filing the petition, per FRBP 1007(b) and (c). This form requires disclosure of different types of financial information than was disclosed in the schedules. For example, the form inquires concerning payments to creditors in the 90-day and one-year period prior to filing the petition, lawsuits to which the debtor has been a party, as well as any garnishments, repossessions, or seizures of the debtor's property within one year preceding the filing, and gifts made within one year of filing. We will see in Chapter Seventeen, Section E that this information relates to powers given the bankruptcy trustee to cancel certain transfers of the debtor's property made within a certain number of months of the bankruptcy filing and to bring the transferred property back into the bankrupt estate. (See Document 19 in the Carlson case file.)

The statement of financial affairs also has questions regarding safety deposit boxes, closed financial accounts, current and former businesses, former spouses, the location of financial records, and so on. The bankruptcy trustee is entitled to know where all the debtor's property is or may be located and is empowered to search thoroughly for undisclosed assets of the debtor that may be in someone else's possession. As part of that task, the trustee may want to obtain and review the debtor's financial records to make sure all property and income is accounted for. We consider the Chapter 7 bankruptcy trustee's duties in more detail in Chapter Sixteen, Section B.

15. Statement of Intent by Individual Debtor (OBF B8)

If an individual Chapter 7 debtor has listed property in which a creditor has a security interest, §521(a)(2) of the Code requires the debtor to state in this form whether he intends to **surrender** the property to the secured creditor or try to **retain** it. By stating his intent to surrender the pledged property, the debtor is giving notice that he will voluntarily relinquish possession of the property to the creditor. As we will see, a Chapter 7 debtor's statement of intent to abandon is not the end of the matter, however, since the bankruptcy trustee may assert an interest in it for the benefit of the estate if the property has value in excess of the amount owed or if the trustee can avoid the lien (to be considered in Chapter Seventeen, Section E). And even if the trustee decides to formally **abandon** the pledged property to the creditor (to be considered in Chapter Eighteen, Section A) as being of no interest to the estate, the creditor must make sure the **automatic stay** of §362 (to be considered in Chapter Sixteen, Section E) has been lifted before proceeding to repossess the property. All of this in due time.

An individual Chapter 7 debtor may seek to retain property pledged as collateral if the debtor intends to avoid the lien and exempt the property as discussed above in connection with Schedule C, or if the debtor intends to either **redeem the property** or **reaffirm the debt**, topics that will be considered in Chapter Eighteen, Section C. But, for now, understand that the individual debtor must state his intent in this form. The debtor's statement of intent must be filed within 30 days after the petition is filed or before the first meeting of creditors, whichever is earliest. (See Document 20 in the Carlson case file.)

If the individual debtor is a party to an unexpired lease, he must state his intent on this form to either discharge his obligation under the lease or to reassume that obligation.

16. Statement of Current Monthly Income and Means Test Calculation (OBF 22A)

This form is required of individual consumer debtors only and was discussed in the last chapter in connection with the means test. (See Document 21-A in the Carlson case file.)

17. Statement of Social Security Number (OBF 21)

This form is required of all individual debtors (both consumer and business). (See Document 22 in the Carlson case file.) To protect the privacy of the debtors, it is filed with the bankruptcy court clerk separately from the petition, schedules, and statements and is withheld by the clerk from the publicly accessible case file.

18. Statement Disclosing Reasonably Anticipated Increase in Income or Expenditures over the 12-month Period Following the Date of Filing the Petition

This form is required of all individual debtors (both consumer and business). (See Document 23 in the Carlson case file.)

19. Statement Disclosing Compensation Paid or to be Paid to the Attorney for the Debtor (OBF 203)

This disclosure form is required of all debtors whether individuals or entities pursuant to Code §329(a). (See Document 24 in the Carlson case file.) This is not the same as requiring the **fee agreement** itself to be in writing. However, since the attorney for a consumer debtor is a DRA (see discussion of *Milavetz* in Section A, supra), §528(a)(1) effectively requires that the attorney/client fee agreement in consumer debtor cases be in writing. Otherwise the Code does not require fee agreements between debtors and attorneys to be in writing but state professional rules governing attorneys may so require. Whether required or not, having the fee agreement in writing is always a good idea for both the attorney and the client.

Furthermore, although OBF 203 requires the disclosure of attorney's fees in a Chapter 7 case, such fees need not be *approved* by the bankruptcy court, as we will learn is required in a Chapter 11, 12, or 13 case. Thus, the fee that debtor's attorneys charge their Chapter 7 clients is determined for the most part by the marketplace. However, §329(b) gives the bankruptcy court authority in any case filed under title 11, in the event a debtor or other party in interest objects to the attorney's fee, to cancel the fee agreement or to order the attorney to disgorge (refund) as much of a fee already paid that it finds excessive. The test in such a case is whether the fee charged by the attorney, "exceeds the reasonable value of any such service." And as we saw illustrated in the *In re Dean* case cited in Section A, supra, the court can order a **disgorgement of fees** by an attorney for misconduct or failure to comply with requirements of the Code.

P-H 15-k: Does your state require attorneys to place their fee agreements with clients in writing? Check the advertisements of debtor's attorneys in your local media or contact an attorney who handles Chapter 7 cases and find out what is currently the typical fee for handling a Chapter 7. How does that fee compare with what is charged in surrounding areas? In more urban or more rural areas of your state? How frequently are §329(b) challenges asserted to debtor's attorney fee agreements?

Attorneys representing debtors in Chapter 7 cases typically get their full fee in advance to eliminate the risk that their claim as a creditor for the unpaid portion of the fee will be discharged.

20. Statement Disclosing Compensation Paid or to be Paid to Nonattorney Bankruptcy Petition Preparer (OBF 280)

This form is required where the debtor uses a NABPP.

21. Copies of All Payment Advices or Other Evidence of Payment Received from Any Employer Within 60 Days Before the Filing of the Petition

This is required of all individual debtors (both consumer and business). (See Document 25 in the Carlson case file.)

22. Record of Any Ownership Interest in an Education IRA or State Tuition Program

This is required of all individual debtors (both consumer and business).

23. Copy of the Debtor's Last Federal Income Tax Return

This is required of all individual debtors (both consumer and business) and is to be provided to the bankruptcy trustee (not filed with the clerk with the petition) no later than seven days before the first meeting of creditors (to be discussed in Chapter Sixteen, Section F). In addition, a copy of all tax returns filed during the case, including tax returns for prior years that had not been filed when the case began, must be supplied. Section 521(e)(2)(B) calls for **mandatory dismissal** of the case if the debtor fails to comply with this requirement and cannot show that failure to comply was beyond his control.

24. Certification and Signature of Nonattorney Bankruptcy Petition Preparer (OBF 19)

This is required when the debtor uses a NABPP as discussed in Section A, supra.

25. Notice to Debtor by Nonattorney Bankruptcy Petition Preparer (OBF 201B)

This is required when the debtor uses a NABPP as discussed in Section A, supra. If for any reason the attorney preparer has not signed the certification on page 2 of the petition (OBF 1) regarding having given the notice to debtor, then the attorney preparer must file OBF 201B. When OBF 201B is filed, the official notice itself, OBF 201(A), should be attached to it.

P-H 15-l: OBF 200, Required Lists, Schedules, Statements and Fees, contains a convenient list of the required schedules, statements, lists, and other documents. Go to www.uscourts.gov/bkforms/index.html and view OBF 200. Review the Carlson case file and determine if Marta Carlson has filed all the necessary schedules, statements, lists, and other documents required of a consumer debtor in a Chapter 7 case.

---

26. Other Required Filings Mandated by Local Court Rules

The **local court rules** of particular bankruptcy courts may mandate other filings and should always be consulted. In addition, local court rules may mandate use of a designated form for providing some of the information mandated by §521 and FRBP 1007 but that does not have an OBF.

P-H 15-m: Check the local rules of the bankruptcy court in your district to see if they contain any information in addition to that mandated by §521 and FRBP 1007 to be provided by the debtor filing a Chapter 7 petition. If so, see if the local rules or the court's Web site provides a form for use in providing that information.

---

27. Required Filings for Entity Debtors

Our discussion thus far of the various schedules, statements, and lists to accompany the bankruptcy petition has assumed that the debtor is an individual. The filing requirements for entity debtors are somewhat different and are considered in depth in Chapter Twenty-Three of the text, where we study the filing of a Chapter 11 case by an entity debtor.

C. The Time Frame for Filing the Supporting Schedules, Statements, and Lists and FRBP 9006 for Computing Time Deadlines

The list of creditors must be filed with the petition. The required schedules and statements usually are filed then as well, but §521(a) and FRBP 1007(c) allow the schedules, statement of affairs, and most other documents to be filed within 14 days after the petition without penalty, and the statement of intent by an individual debtor may be filed within 30 days after the petition. In addition, those grace periods may be extended by *motion* filed with the bankruptcy court and **cause shown** per FRBP 1007(c). (See Document 5 in the Carlson case file.)

There is a limit to the time extension the court can grant a debtor to comply with his obligation to file the various schedules, however. Section 521(i)(1) of the Code provides that if the debtor fails to file the required schedules within 45 days following the date the petition is filed, the petition is to be "automatically dismissed effective on the 46th day after the date of the filing of the petition." This section could be read to mean that bankruptcy judges have *no discretion* to grant extensions beyond 45 days and that the failure to comply with the 45-day filing requirement cannot be forgiven or cured. To date, however, two circuits have found an ambiguity between the apparent mandate of §521(i)(l) and the arguably conflicting language of §521(a)(1)(B) directing the debtor to file the various schedules and statements "unless the court orders otherwise" and construed the sections to mean that bankruptcy courts retain discretion to waive or excuse the failure to file the required information within the 45-day window notwithstanding the automatic dismissal language (see *In re Acosta-Rivera*, 557 F.3d 8 (1st Cir. 2009) and *In re Warren*, 568 F.3d 1113 (9th Cir. 2009).

P-H 15-n: Read the two cases cited in the last paragraph. Do you agree with their interpretation of §521? Determine whether and how other circuits have decided this issue? Has your federal circuit addressed the issue? If not, where are the bankruptcy courts in your circuit coming down on it?

FRBP 9006 is the primary source for guidelines governing the computation of time periods for all actions mandated or allowed under the Code. It helps practitioners deal with issues like those raised in P-H 15-n.

P-H 15-o: What happens if the last day to file something falls on a weekend or legal holiday? Which legal holidays are recognized for purposes of extending a deadline? Does the *last day* to file something end at midnight that day or when the clerk's office closes for that day? What happens if the clerk's office is unexpectedly closed for weather or other eventuality on the day something is due?

D. The Importance of Reporting Accurate and Complete Information

It is critical to both the debtor and his attorney that all information reported in the petition, schedules, statements, and other documents filed in connection with a bankruptcy case be accurate and complete. As we will learn in Chapter Seventeen, failing to list a creditor in Schedules D, E, or F can result in that creditor's claim not being discharged. Providing inaccurate or incomplete information can result in denial of any discharge or revocation of a discharge already granted (see Illustrations 18-c and 18-d). If the debtor is found to have acted intentionally with regard to the withheld, incomplete, or inaccurate information, there could be state or federal criminal charges brought against the debtor and anyone who knowingly assisted him, including charges of **bankruptcy fraud** or making **false oaths and claims** under 18 U.S.C. §§157 or 152.

P-H 15-p: Research the criminal statutes of your state to identify crimes that might be charged arising out of a bankruptcy case. Compare what you find with the federal crimes mentioned. Do you understand why both federal and state prosecutors might file charges arising out of a bankruptcy case pending in a bankruptcy case in your state? What is the federal interest? What is the state interest?

CONCLUSION

At this point, we understand how a Chapter 7 case is filed. But like the kickoff in a football game, there is much more to come. In Chapter Sixteen, we will begin our consideration of how the case is administered and by whom.

CHAPTER SUMMARY

A Chapter 7 case is commenced by filing a voluntary petition with a bankruptcy court having proper venue. Husbands and wives may file a joint petition. The bankruptcy court may order two or more cases involving debtors with related assets and debt obligations to be jointly administered and two or more cases involving the same debtor to be consolidated. In certain circumstances, creditors of a debtor may force him into bankruptcy by filing an involuntary petition for the debtor. In addition to the petition, the debtor must file a number of supporting schedules of assets and liabilities, a statement of affairs, a list of creditors, and a number of other documents in the time required by the Code and FRBP.

The individual Chapter 7 debtor is entitled to claim certain property as exempt using federal exemptions set forth in the code or the exemptions laws of his state of residence if his state has elected to opt out. BAPCPA has placed limitations on an individual debtor's right to claim all of the equity in his principal residence as exempt if he has owned it fewer than 1,215 days before filing his petition The debtor's schedules must indicate whether creditor claims are secured or unsecured, liquidated or unliquidated, contested or uncontested, contingent or noncontingent, or entitled to any priority treatment under the code. It is essential that the information contained in the debtor's petition, schedules, and supporting statements be accurate and complete.

REVIEW QUESTIONS

1. Who may file a joint bankruptcy petition?
2. Explain the difference between the consolidation of two or more bankruptcy cases and the joint administration of two or more bankruptcy cases.
3. List at least five different kinds of information the debtor enters on her bankruptcy petition.
4. Summarize the circumstances under which creditors may force a debtor into an involuntary bankruptcy proceeding. What is the procedure followed after the filing of an involuntary petition?
5. What is venue and what bankruptcy court is the proper venue for a bankruptcy filing?
6. What or who is a debt relief agency and what is their role in a bankruptcy case?
7. What or who is a nonattorney bankruptcy petition preparer and what is his or her role in a bankruptcy case?
8. Who signs a voluntary petition in bankruptcy and which of those signatures is under oath?
9. Explain the opt-out feature of the Code for purposes of claimed exemptions. What types of property are typically made exempt and in what amounts? May a debtor claim as exempt property in which he has granted a perfected security interest? Property in which a creditor claims a statutory lien? Property in which a creditor claims a judicial lien?
10. List as many of the schedules as you can recall that a debtor must file in addition to her petition. When must these schedules be filed? When must

the statement of affairs be filed? List as many as you can of the other statements that a Chapter 7 debtor must file.

11. What is the homestead exemption? If a debtor want to claim her state's unlimited homestead exemption, what limits does the Code place on her right to do so?

12. Why is it important for the debtor and the debtor's attorney and assisting legal professional to make sure that the information contained in the petition, schedules, and statements be accurate and complete? What possible criminal liability is present?

WORDS AND PHRASES TO REMEMBER

answer

automatic dismissal

Bankruptcy Abuse Prevention and Consumer Protection Act of 2005 (BAPCPA)

bankruptcy fraud

bankruptcy petition preparer

burden of proof

cause shown

codebtor

consumer debtor

credit counseling

debtor (debtor in bankruptcy)

Declaration Concerning Debtor's Schedules (OBF 6-Declaration)

disgorgement of fees

domestic support obligation

doubling

evidentiary hearing

executory contract

exemption (federal & state)

false oath and claim

filing fee

joint petition

list of creditors

local court rules

mailing matrix

motion

nonattorney bankruptcy petition preparer (NABPP)

opt out

order for relief

party in interest

petition (voluntary and involuntary)

prepetition

pro se

Schedule A, Real Property (OBF 6A)

Schedule B, Personal Property (OBF 6B)

Schedule C, Exempt Property (OBF 6C)

Schedule D, Creditors Holding Secured Claims (OBF 6D)

Schedule E, Creditors Holding Unsecured Priority Claims (OBF 6E)

Schedule F, Creditors Holding Unsecured Nonpriority Claims (OBF 6F)

Schedule G, Executory Contracts and Unexpired Leases (OBF 6G)

Schedule H, Codebtors (OBF 6H)

Schedule I, Current Income of Individual Debtors (OBF 6I)

Schedule J, Current Expenditures of Individual Debtors (OBF 6J)

stacking

Statement Disclosing Anticipated Increase in Income or Expenditures

Statement Disclosing Compensation Paid or to be Paid (to attorney or to nonattorney bankruptcy petition preparer)

Statement of Current Monthly Income and Means Test Calculation (OBF 22A)

Statement of Financial Affairs (OBF 7)

Statement of Social Security Number (OBF 21)

Statement of the U.S. Trustee Program's Position on Legal

Issues Arising Under the   venue
Chapter 7 Means Test   waiver (of filing fee)
Summary of Schedules   1,215-day rule
   (OBF 6-Summary)

TO LEARN MORE: A number of TLM activities to accompany this chapter are accessible on the student disc accompanying the text and on the Author Updates link to the text Web site at http://www.aspenparalegaled.com/ books/parsons_abcdebt/default.asp.

Chapter Sixteen:

The Chapter 7 Case: From the Order for Relief to the First Meeting of Creditors

A man in debt is so far a slave.
—*Ralph Waldo Emerson*

Once the bankruptcy petition is filed, the case is commenced and very important consequences flow from that fact for both the debtor and his creditors. From the very moment the case is filed the provisions of the Code and the Federal Rules of Bankruptcy Procedure (FRBP) are set in motion. Filing a bankruptcy petition is somewhat like turning the ignition switch in a car. The machine roars to life as numerous systems inside begin to operate—warming up, lighting up, lubricating, rotating, inspecting themselves, preparing to perform. In this chapter, we will see how the various systems that make up the great machine of bankruptcy procedure roar to life with the filing of the Chapter 7 petition and then methodically grind forward to administer the case.

A. The Order for Relief

Petition The document filed to initiate a bankruptcy case under the Code.

Order for relief The formal beginning of a bankruptcy case triggered by the filing of a voluntary petition or by court order following an involuntary petition.

The Chapter 7 case is commenced by the filing of the bankruptcy **petition** per §301(a) of the Code and Federal Rules of Bankruptcy Procedure (FRBP) 1002. Per §301(b), the filing of the petition constitutes an **order for relief** under the Code, a term used often in the Code as we will see. The Code and a number of the Official Bankruptcy Forms (OBFs) refer to the order for relief as if it were something separate from the petition. For example, §341(a) says, "Within a reasonable time after the order for relief in a case under this title, the United States trustee shall convene and preside over a meeting of creditors." Some courts do enter a formal order for relief after the petition is filed. But in most districts the petition itself is treated as the order for relief and no separate order is entered by the court. When an **involuntary petition** is filed and granted, a separate order for relief will be entered (see OBF B253). In this chapter, we refer interchangeably to the filing of the petition, the commencement of the case, and the order for relief.

Local rules Supplemental rules of procedure and practice that prevail in a particular court.

P-H 16-a: Determine if the bankruptcy court in your federal district enters a formal order for relief upon filing of the petition or if it allows the petition itself to serve that purpose. The **local rules** of that court will probably give you the answer. If the court does utilize a separate order for relief, see if the court's Web site provides a form for that order, or obtain one from the court clerk.

B. ▶ The Chapter 7 Bankruptcy Trustee

Section 701 of the Code provides that, "promptly after the order for relief under this chapter" (i.e., Chapter 7), the **U.S. Trustee** is to appoint a person to serve as **bankruptcy trustee** in the Chapter 7 case. Section 586(a)(1) of Title 28 directs the U.S. Trustee in each federal district to, "establish, maintain, and supervise a panel of private trustees that are eligible and available to serve as trustees in cases under Chapter 7." It is from this **trustee panel** that the U.S. Trustee will select the bankruptcy trustee for each Chapter 7 case. Persons selected to serve on the panel of trustees may be lawyers, accountants, retired bankers, and other businesspeople.

Though it is rare for creditors to *not* accept the initial choice of trustee made by the U.S. Trustee, §702 authorizes them to elect someone else to serve as trustee at the first meeting of creditors (discussed in Section F). Thus, the trustee appointed by the U.S. Trustee serves only in an interim capacity until after that meeting. Section 324 of the Code authorizes the court to remove a trustee for *cause*. Though **cause for removal** is not defined in the Code and is, fortunately, a rare event, cause for removal can be anything from dishonesty to dilatoriness to inability to work with the debtor.

The creditors may form a **creditors committee** to work closely with the trustee and to represent the creditors before the court (see §705). Creditors' committees are unusual in a Chapter 7 and common in a Chapter 11, so we will consider them in detail when we study the Chapter 11 case (see Chapter Twenty-Three, Section C).

Bankruptcy trustees must be **bonded** because they are handling the property of the estate. They are responsible not only to the debtors, the creditors of the estate, and the U.S. Trustee who selects and supervises them, but also to the bankruptcy judge before whom they will appear as the representative of the estate (see §323(a)). In the notice of commencement of the case, parties are advised of the identity of the person appointed to serve as trustee. (See Document 26 in the Carlson case file.)

1. Duties of the Bankruptcy Trustee

The duties of the Chapter 7 trustee are set out in §701 of the Code. Illustration 16-a summarizes those duties. We will examine many of these duties in detail as we move work through the administration of the case.

Once a Chapter 7 case is filed, the bankruptcy trustee becomes the primary actor in the case. FRBP 2015 requires the trustee to file a complete **inventory of the property of the estate** within 30 days following his appointment, to keep

Illustration 16-a: DUTIES OF THE BANKRUPTCY TRUSTEE IN A CHAPTER 7 CASE

Property of the estate All property in which the debtor holds a legal or equitable interest at the commencement of a bankruptcy case.

- To investigate the financial affairs of the debtor
- To locate and take possession of all nonexempt property of the debtor (called **property of the estate** under the Code)
- To preserve the property of the estate and then liquidate it (in a Chapter 7) for the benefit of the creditors of the estate, or abandon it if it has no value to the estate
- To examine the exempt property claims of the debtor and challenge them if there are disputes as to the legitimacy of the claimed exemption or the value claimed by the debtor
- To examine the claims of creditors in an asset case, allow those that appear properly supported, and to challenge and disallow those that are not
- To raise objections to discharge of the debtor if grounds for such objection are present
- To distribute property of the estate in the order of priority dictated by the Code
- To prepare and file reports with the U.S. Trustee and the court, fully disclosing actions taken with regard to the debtor and the property of the estate (see FRBP 2015)

detailed records of the receipt and disposition of property of the estate, and to provide interim reports (often quarterly) regarding affairs of the estate. Section 345 of the Code requires the trustee to invest cash belonging to the estate in government insured accounts or certificates unless the court otherwise orders. All records of the trustee's handling of estate property are open to examination by the debtor, creditors, the U.S. Trustee, and the court.

Serving as a bankruptcy trustee is a challenging task. Working as a legal professional on the trustee's staff demands a high level of expertise, an honest character, and a substantial capacity for working under pressure.

2. Compensation of the Bankruptcy Trustee

Sections 326 and 330 of the Code govern the trustee's fees. In general, the trustee is entitled to reasonable compensation based on the nature of the services rendered to the estate, their market value, and the time spent. A minimum payment is allowed a trustee under §330(b), which comes in part from the filing fee. In a no-asset case (discussed in the next section), that may be the only compensation the trustee receives. Where there are assets in the estate to be distributed to creditors, the trustee also receives as compensation a percentage of the value distributed, within certain limits established by §326. The trustee's fee is considered an administrative expense and is given a significant priority in the distribution of the estate, as discussed in Chapter Eighteen, Section B.

The No-Asset Case

The first thing the newly appointed trustee will do in a Chapter 7 case is review the petition and supporting schedules to make an initial determination as to

No-asset case A Chapter 7 liquidation case in which there are no assets available for liquidation and distribution to creditors.

whether the case is an **asset case** or a **no-asset case**. A no-asset case is one in which all of the debtor's assets are either properly exempted (which means the debtor can keep the property, despite the bankruptcy proceeding) or subject to validly perfected **prepetition security interests or lien s** that give the secured creditors a priority claim to the pledged property over the claim of the bankruptcy trustee. (See discussion of the trustee's lien avoidance powers in Chapter Seventeen, Section E.) Approximately 90 percent of all Chapter 7 cases nationwide are no-asset cases.

> **NOTE ON THE MARTA CARLSON CASE STUDY:** A review of Marta Rinaldi Carlson's schedules in the Carlson case file will quickly disclose that hers is an asset case and, in that sense, her Chapter 7 case is atypical. But we use a Chapter 7 asset case study in order to illustrate various aspects of case administration that would not arise in a no-asset case. Working through a no-asset case will not teach you how to handle an asset case. Working through an asset case will teach you how to handle both.

Since bankruptcy trustees are compensated out of the filing fee paid by the debtor and a percentage of property located and sold for the benefit of creditors in the case, the trustee's compensation can be dramatically impacted by whether a case is an asset case or a no-asset case.

Before finally concluding that the case is a no-asset one, the bankruptcy trustee will question the debtor at the first meeting of creditors (discussed in Section F) and do any further investigation he deems appropriate. As suggested in the list of the trustee's duties in Illustration 16-a, that may include a close review of the debtor's claimed exemptions and the values asserted by the debtor and a close review of the claims of listed secured creditors. If the trustee concludes that the case is a no-asset one, he will file a **no-asset report** with the bankruptcy court and a **discharge in bankruptcy** will be issued promptly and the case closed (see Chapter Eighteen, Section G).

D. ▶ Notice to Creditors of Commencement of Case

Pursuant to §342 of the Code, upon the filing of the petition, the bankruptcy court clerk will issue a **notice of commencement of case** to the creditors and the U.S. Trustee. Section 342(d) provides that if the case is filed by a consumer debtor, the notice is to be given no later than ten days after the petition is filed. This notice is OBF B9 and there is a separate notice form for cases filed under Chapters 7, 11, 12, or 13. (Remember that all official bankruptcy forms are available at www.uscourts.gov/bkforms/index.html.) There are also different notice of commencement forms for Chapter 7 cases, depending on whether the debtor is an individual or an entity and on whether the case is an asset case or a no-asset case.

Marta Carlson's Chapter 7 case is by an individual with assets so the clerk has used OBF 9C (see Document 26 in the Carlson case file). Observe that the first page of the notice provides the creditor with the name, address, and phone number of the bankruptcy trustee appointed in the case. As we move through the other aspects of case administration, refer back to the notice to see how it advises creditors of the various aspects of case administration that apply to them.

E. The Automatic Stay

Automatic stay The prohibition on creditors continuing collection efforts against a debtor that arises automatically upon the debtor's filing of a bankruptcy petition.

The **automatic stay** is one of the most important events in a bankruptcy case. Section 362(a) of the Code provides that the filing of a bankruptcy petition automatically stays (stops) any action by a creditor to collect on the indebtedness owed to him by the debtor or any action by the creditor to improve his position vis-à-vis other creditors (e.g., by obtaining a postpetition security interest in the debtor's property). A stay mandates the following:

- All informal collection efforts against the debtor must stop.
- All pending collection lawsuits must stop.
- All efforts to collect on a final judgment previously entered must stop.
- All efforts to obtain a security interest must stop.
- All efforts to repossess or foreclose on the debtor's property pursuant to a consensual or nonconsensual lien must stop.

EXAMPLE

As indicated in the Assignment Memorandum in Appendix A, Pine Ridge Nursing Home has filed suit against Marta Carlson to collect on amounts allegedly owed on the personal guaranty she signed. If that case is scheduled to go to trial tomorrow, the trial must be continued (postponed). If motions are scheduled to be heard in that case tomorrow, the motions will have to be postponed. If the judge has just entered a judgment in favor of Pine Ridge Nursing Home, it must take no action to collect on the judgment lest it be found in violation of the automatic stay.

EXAMPLE

As indicated in the Assignment Memorandum in Appendix A, the Dreams Come True Financing Company has declared the loan to Marta to be in default and is preparing to foreclose on her home. With the filing of the bankruptcy petition, that foreclosure proceeding must stop.

1. Exceptions to the Automatic Stay

Section 362(b) of the Code sets out a number of exceptions to the automatic stay—collection activities that *can* continue (that are not stayed). A number of these are actions involving domestic disputes. Illustration 16-b lists various domestic disputes that, per §362(b), are *not* automatically stayed by the filing of a bankruptcy petition.

Per §362(b)(10), a landlord's eviction action against a debtor involving a **nonresidential lease** is not stayed where the eviction is based on expiration of the agreed lease term either before or after the bankruptcy petition is filed. The stay will apply to such eviction action if it is based on some other ground

Illustration 16-b: DOMESTIC ACTIONS NOT SUBJECT TO THE §362 AUTOMATIC STAY

- To establish paternity
- To establish or modify an order for domestic support obligations
- Concerning child custody or visitation
- To dissolve a marriage, except to the extent that such proceeding seeks to determine the division of property that is property of the estate
- Regarding domestic violence
- To collect a domestic support obligation from property that is not property of the estate
- To withhold income of the debtor or intercept a tax refund due the debtor in order to satisfy a domestic support obligation under state law
- To withhold or restrict a driver's license or a professional, occupational, or recreational license for non-payment of domestic obligations under state law
- To report nonpayment of a domestic obligation to a credit reporting agency

---

(e.g., nonpayment of rent). Per §§362(b)(22) and (23), a landlord's eviction action against a debtor involving a **residential lease** is not stayed where:

- The landlord has obtained a prepetition judgment of eviction;
- The landlord certifies that the basis of the eviction action is the debtor's endangerment of the property; or
- The landlord certifies that the basis of the eviction action is the debtor's illegal use of controlled substances on the property.

Per §362(b)(1), neither state nor federal criminal actions against a debtor are stayed by the filing of a petition. Per §362(b)(4), regulatory actions against a debtor by any governmental unit that involve protecting public health and safety (e.g., a state department of health acting to shut down debtor's business for violations of state fire code or state food handling regulations) are not stayed.

Though §362(a)(8) provides that tax disputes pending in U.S. Tax Court when the petition is filed are stayed, §362(b)(9) provides that state or federal government actions to audit a debtor for tax liability, to issue tax deficiency notices, to demand tax returns, or to issue a past-due tax assessment and demand payment are not stayed. Other actions to collect a tax from the debtor will be stayed, as will any other action to create, perfect, or enforce a tax lien. Section §362(b)(18) does exempt from the stay an action by a governmental unit to create or perfect a statutory tax lien arising from a property tax or special assessment on debtor's real property, but only where such tax or assessment becomes due after the petition if filed.

Though most foreclosure actions are subject to the stay, §362(b)(8) does except from the stay foreclosure actions initiated by the U.S. Department of Housing and Urban Development (HUD) on properties consisting of five or more living units.

Recall from Chapter Six, Section A, our consideration of **nonconsensual statutory liens** and how they are created and perfected and how the date on which such a lien is deemed to exist or deemed to be perfected may be impacted by the **relation back** feature of the state statutes regulating those liens. What has that got to do with the automatic stay? Well, actions by a creditor to create, perfect, or renew a security interest in the debtor's property are subject to the automatic stay of §362(a), with an important exception. Section §362(b)(3) excepts from the operation of the automatic stay the creation or perfection of a security interest where applicable state law authorizes a grace period (such as the relation back feature of nonconsensual statutory liens) for determining the effective date or date of perfection of a prepetition security interest.

EXAMPLE

> Assume a state's mechanic's lien statute provides that such a lien is created and perfected by filing of a notice of lien and giving owner of the real property written notice of the filing. The statute also provides that the lien, once created, "relates back to the date when the services or materials were first supplied." Now suppose a subcontractor provides services for the improvement of the owner's real property on March 1. Payment is not made when due, and on June 10 the subcontractor's lawyer is preparing to file the required notice of lien and to give the owner notice of the filing when she learns that the owner filed a bankruptcy petition on June 9. Does the automatic stay prevent filing and service of the notice of lien? No. Because the statute contains the relation back feature and will deem the lien created and perfected on March 1 (prepetition), §362(b)(3) allows the attorney to file and serve the notice of lien postpetition without violating the stay.

EXAMPLE

> Recall from Chapter Five, Section D1, the discussion of perfecting a security interest in personal property by filing a **financing statement (UCC-1)** pursuant to **Article 9** of a state's version of the **Uniform Commercial Code (UCC)**. We noted there that, once filed, such financing statements are valid for only a stated number of years (typically five years), but can be renewed under state law by filing a **continuation statement** within six months of the expiration of the original five-year term. What if a creditor filed a financing statement properly perfecting a security interest in personal property of the debtor four years and five months ago and is now preparing to file a continuation statement when debtor files a bankruptcy petition? Does the automatic stay bar the creditor from filing the continuation statement? No. Because the security interest existed prepetition and filing the continuation statement during the six-month grace period created by state law merely continues (relates back to) the security interest that was created prepetition. Section 362(b)(3) allows creditor to file the continuation statement postpetition without violating the stay.

In addition to recognizing state law grace periods or relation back periods impacting on when a security interest is created or perfected, §362(b)(3) creates its own relation back period for perfecting a security interest postpetition without violating the stay. By referencing §547(e)(2)(A) (a section of the Code that we will look at in more detail in the next chapter), §362(b)(3) allows a security interest to be perfected postpetition in a consensual prepetition transfer of property to the debtor so long as the perfection is completed within 30 days of the transfer.

EXAMPLE

> Assume a borrower purchases a house on June 1 and borrows money from the bank to make the purchase. At the closing on June 1, the borrower provides the bank with a mortgage on the house to secure repayment of the amount borrowed. The bank does not record the mortgage (an act required to perfect its secured position in the property, as we learned in Chapter Four) until June 3. Meanwhile, the borrower files a bankruptcy petition on June 2. Has the bank violated the automatic stay by recording the mortgage instrument on June 3? No. Per §362(b)(3), the bank has the 30 days following transfer of the property to the debtor on June 1 allowed by §547(e)(2)(A) to perfect its secured position in the property without running afoul of the statute.

P-H 16-b: Assume a debtor has filed for Chapter 7 bankruptcy relief. In his schedules he lists the following pending actions to collect indebtedness. Determine which ones are automatically stayed by §362(a):

- Lawsuit by his former business partner alleging fraud by debtor
- Criminal prosecution of debtor by the state for that fraud
- Child custody dispute with debtor's ex-wife
- Hearing on property division in divorce action in state court brought by debtor's ex-wife
- Eviction action brought by landlord of the apartment where debtor resides seeking to evict him for playing loud music; no judgment entered when petition filed
- Repossession by bank on debtor's business assets
- Foreclosure by bank on debtor's home
- Repossession by bank on car owned by debtor's ex-wife who is not in a bankruptcy proceeding herself

2. Enforcing the Automatic Stay and Sanctions for Violation

As the name implies, the automatic stay is truly automatic; the debtor does not have to ask for it nor does the bankruptcy court have to order it. It goes into effect upon the filing of the petition.

In most bankruptcy courts, the procedure for obtaining damages or other relief for violation of the automatic stay is for the debtor to file a **motion** in his bankruptcy case alleging the violation and seeking appropriate sanctions. A motion creates a **contested matter** in the bankruptcy case that the bankruptcy judge will hear and decide. In a minority of federal districts, allegations of violation of the automatic stay must be brought as formal **adversary proceedings**, essentially mini-lawsuits within the bankruptcy case. (You may want to review the distinctions in these procedures as discussed in Chapter Thirteen, Section G.)

P-H 16-c: Determine which procedure the bankruptcy courts of your federal district require that a debtor use to alleging violation of the automatic stay.

Contempt Power of a court to declare one subject to the court's order in violation of it and to assess penalties.

The typical remedies sought against a creditor accused of violating the automatic stay are for the court to **enjoin** (stop) any continuing violation by the creditor, to declare any actions taken by the creditor in violation of the stay **void** and of no effect (e.g., to cancel the repossession of a vehicle violation of the stay and order the vehicle returned to debtor), and, if the violation of the stay was done with knowledge that a bankruptcy case was pending, to declare the creditor in **contempt** of the bankruptcy court since the automatic stay is a court order that has been violated by the creditor.

EXAMPLE

> The notice of commencement of case sent to creditors specifically references the danger of proceeding with postpetition collection activities. Look at the first page of the notice in Marta Carlson's case (Document 26 in the Carlson case file) under the heading "Creditors May Not Take Certain Actions."

Punitive damages Damages intended to punish the wrongdoer in order to deter similar conduct in the future.

For any "willful violation" of the stay, §362(k)(1) provides that the court may also award the individual debtor his **actual damages** caused by the violation of the stay, **court costs, attorney's fees** incurred by the debtor, and "in appropriate circumstances" even **punitive damages** (damages intended to punish the wrongdoer).

EXAMPLE

> Pine Ridge Nursing Home filed a motion for summary judgment in its collection lawsuit after receiving notice of Marta Carlson's bankruptcy filing. Marta's attorney responded with a motion for order of contempt for violation of the automatic stay (see Document 27 in the Carlson case file). Following the hearing on the motion, the court found Pine Ridge Nursing Home in contempt and ordered it to pay Marta's attorney fee incurred in making the motion and enjoined any further violation of the stay (see Document 28 in the Carlson case file).

Not surprisingly, there is much dispute over what constitutes a "willful violation" of the stay under §362(k)(1). Courts have held that a creditor commits a willful violation if it acts intentionally with knowledge that its action violates the stay or even with knowledge that a bankruptcy case has been filed by the debtor, even if it lacks specific knowledge of the automatic stay (see, e.g., *In re Wagner*, 74 B.R. 898, 904 (Bankr. E.D. Pa. 1987)) ("knowledge of the bankruptcy filing is the legal equivalent of knowledge of the stay").

If a creditor continues with collection efforts after the filing of the petition but does not have any actual or constructive notice of the filing of a bankruptcy case by the debtor, much less the automatic stay itself, the court will not hold the creditor in contempt but will likely set aside any actions taken by the creditor after the filing of the petition. There still has been a violation of the stay; it just has not been willful.

EXAMPLE

> If Pine Ridge Nursing Home had filed its motion for summary judgment after Marta's petition was filed but before receiving notice, the judge likely would not have imposed sanctions on Pine Ridge but instead would have ordered the motion stricken until the stay is lifted, as discussed below.

Section 362(k)(2) provides a creditor accused of willfully violating the automatic stay with a defense wherein the action taken by the creditor involved personal property pledged as security and the creditor can show that it believed in **good faith** that debtor had failed to file a timely §521(a)(2) **statement of intent** (OBF 88, discussed in Chapter Fifteen, Section B) with regard to such property (see Document 20 in the Carlson case file).

P-H 16-d: Most courts limit the recovery of §362(k)(1) willful violation damages to individual debtors and disallow them to entity debtors (corporations, partnerships, etc.) since the section references "an individual injured . . ." (see, e.g. *In re Spookyworld, Inc.*, 346 F.3d 1, 6 (1st Cir. 2003)). However, a minority construe "individual" to include entity debtor (see, e.g., *Budget Service Co. v. Better Homes of Virginia, Inc.*, 804 F.2d 289, 292 (4th Cir. 1986)), finding it difficult to accept that Congress meant to give remedy for intentional violation to individual debtors only and emphasizing the important role of §362k in repairing and deterring willful violations. How do the courts of your federal district come down on this issue?

P-H 16-e: It is not just the offending creditor who may be tagged with damages and costs in a proceeding alleging willful violation of the stay. Attorneys and those assisting them who represent the creditor are at risk as well. Read *In re Repine*, 536 F. 3d 512 (5th Cir. 2008) to see a case where a creditor's attorney was held liable for punitive damages in a stay violation case. What does that case say about the standard for assessing punitive damages in such a case? Is it enough that the conduct of the creditor or his representative was willful or must there be something more to justify such damages? What kinds of "actual damages" might a debtor sustain because of a willful violation of the stay? Do actual damages have to be some kind of economic loss to the debtor or can they be emotional distress type damages? Compare what the court said about that in *In re Repine* with *Dawson v. Wash. Mut. Bank, F.A.*, 390 F.3d 1139 (9th Cir. 2004) and *Aiello v. Providian Fin. Corp.*, 239 F.3d 876 (7th Cir. 2000).

EC 16-a: **Legal professionals** assisting debtor's attorneys may be assigned the task of notifying creditors by phone immediately after the petition has been filed in order to stop a lawsuit, foreclosure, or repossession from going forward. Verbal notification provided prior to the receipt of the formal notice of filing is sufficient to put a creditor on notice of the automatic stay and trigger a contempt finding. Legal professionals working for a creditor, a collection agency, or a creditor's attorney must be careful to understand the significance of a bankruptcy filing and know to *stop* all collection efforts immediately. Otherwise that legal professional, the supervising attorney, and the client may be found in contempt of the bankruptcy court. What ethical problems might that raise for the attorney? For a certified paralegal?

The rationale behind the automatic stay provision is that once the debtor has filed the petition seeking bankruptcy relief, he is immediately entitled to the protections afforded by the Code, and his property is also immediately subject to the procedures outlined in the Code. Consequently, the automatic stay serves to freeze actions against the debtor's property at the commencement of the case so that the bankruptcy procedure can control what happens to the debtor and his property from that point on.

P-H 16-f: Section 342(g)(1), added by BAPCPA, provides that if the creditor designates a person or organizational subdivision to receive bankruptcy notices and has a reasonable procedure to deliver notices to such person or subdivision, then a notice has not been "brought to the attention" of the creditor until the designated person or subdivision receives the notice. It is unclear at this time whether this **safe harbor provision** for creditors violating the automatic stay [they cannot be held in contempt under §362(a) unless they were given notice in compliance with §342(g)(1)] is going to require something more than verbal notice. Research the decisions of the bankruptcy, district, and circuit courts in your federal circuit to see if there have been any rulings on this issue yet. This is arguably an example of the pro-creditor bias of the BAPCPA in that it may, depending on how the courts interpret and apply it, make it harder for debtors to benefit from the automatic stay and harder to have violating creditors held in contempt. Is this a fair provision in your opinion? Is it consistent with the stated rationale of the automatic stay provision in the Code?

Safe harbor provision A provision in a statute or regulation that exempts a person from liability for certain conduct.

There are some special rules added by BAPCPA pertaining to the automatic stay for the individual debtor (not the entity debtor) who has previously filed a case under Chapters 7, 11, or 13 and had it dismissed within one year preceding the filing of the current case. If an individual debtor filing today has filed a different bankruptcy case within one year preceding this filing and had the preceding filing dismissed, then the automatic stay goes into effect, but only for 30 days, pursuant to §362(c). To extend the stay, that debtor must file a **motion for extension of stay** with the court. A hearing will be conducted and the court will decide whether to extend the stay or not. The burden in such a hearing is placed on the debtor to show by **clear and convincing evidence** that this bankruptcy case has been filed in **good faith** and that the debtor is entitled to the stay per §362(c)(3).

Good faith Generally, honesty in fact and compliance with the letter and spirit of the Code.

If the individual debtor has filed *two* bankruptcy cases within the year preceding the filing of this one, whether Chapters 7, 11, or 13, and both have been dismissed, there is *no* automatic stay at all upon the filing of the third petition. In such case, the debtor must file his motion for automatic stay immediately upon filing his petition and carry his burden of showing a good faith filing by clear and convincing evidence per §362(c)(4).

EC 16-b: Remember, one purpose of BAPCPA was to stop debtor abuse of the Code. Do you see why repeated bankruptcy filings by a debtor triggering the automatic stay provision might be a tactic to unfairly delay or complicate a creditor's efforts to collect on a legitimate debt? Do you think these BAPCPA provisions are fair and reasonable? What ethical implications might there be for an attorney who cooperates with a debtor client to make repeated filings for the primary purpose of delaying collection efforts by triggering the automatic stay with no real intent to see the bankruptcy case through?

3. Lifting the Automatic Stay

The automatic stay created by §362(a) does not necessarily last for the duration of the case as against secured creditors of the debtor in a Chapter 7 liquidation. A creditor who is properly secured and perfected in property of the debtor will typically have a superior claim to it over that of the bankruptcy trustee unless the value of the secured property exceeds the amount of the creditor's claim. (See further discussion of this struggle for priority in Chapter Seventeen, Section D.)

EXAMPLE

> Recall from the Assignment Memorandum in Appendix A that Marta Carlson has two mortgages on her home, one in favor of Capitol City Savings Bank (CCSB) with a balance of $142,500, and one in favor of Dreams Come True Finance Company (DCT) with a balance of $37,500. Marta is in default on the debt owed to DCT and, prior to the bankruptcy, it declared foreclosure and initiated foreclosure proceedings. But DCT's plan to foreclose is delayed by Marta's filing of the Chapter 7 petition, triggering the automatic stay. If DCT files a motion to lift the stay, the bankruptcy trustee will object. Do you see why? Assuming the property is worth $255,000, as the realtor has estimated to Marta, if it sells for that amount, the first $142,500 would go to CCSB, holder of the first mortgage. The next $37,500 would go to DCT, holder of the second mortgage. Per §522(d)(1) of the Code, Marta would take the next $22,975 as her federal homestead exemption in the home (see Illustration 15-a). But that leaves $52,025, to which the bankruptcy trustee will be entitled, subject to expenses of sale, and the bankruptcy judge will not lift the stay and allow repossession. Instead, it will order the stay kept in place and allow the bankruptcy trustee to liquidate the property and distribute the proceeds as indicated.

If the value of the secured property is less than the amount of the debt, however, and the security interest of the creditor is properly perfected and superior to any claim the bankruptcy trustee can make to the property, then the trustee will not object to the lifting of the stay.

EXAMPLE

> As indicated in Marta's Schedule D (Document 10 in the Carlson case file), she owes $900 to Shears Department Store for a washer and dryer she purchased nine months ago. Shears is perfected in the washer and dryer for the entire amount of the indebtedness and the washer and dryer together are valued at only $600. Thus, if Marta is in default on her obligation to Shears and it seeks the lifting of the stay to repossess the washer and dryer, the bankruptcy trustee will not object. He will, of course, review the claim of Shears closely and the paperwork offered in support of its perfected security interest before conceding the superiority of Shears' claim to the property.

Section §362(d) sets out the procedure available to a creditor for lifting the automatic stay so that it can proceed against the property of the debtor. In most circumstances the creditor will file a **motion to lift stay**, per FRBP 4001. If the motion is contested, the bankruptcy judge will conduct a hearing on the motion at which the creditor has the burden of showing that one of the two grounds set forth in §362(d)(1) for lifting the stay is present. (Motion procedure is discussed in Section G, below.)

Adequate protection Must be provided by the bankrupt estate to a creditor whose interest in property is threatened by the estate's continued possession and use of the property.

The first ground for lifting the stay in §362(d)(1) is that there is lack of **adequate protection** in the collateral. That means the collateral is at risk for some reason. Maybe it is at risk because the debtor does not have it insured so that if it is damaged or stolen the creditor effectively loses its security for the debt.

EXAMPLE

Recall from the Assignment Memorandum in Appendix A that Marta Carlson owns a Toyota Camry with a book value of $8,500 and that she owes a balance on it of $1,750 to Automotive Financing, Inc. (AFI), which holds a security interest in the car. If Marta had let her insurance policy on the Toyota lapse because she could not afford the premiums, AFI would consider itself at risk (e.g., Marta could total the car leaving AFI with no security). The bankruptcy trustee will consider the interests of the estate at risk as well since there is $3,075 of equity in the car for the estate (the value of the car minus the amount owed to AFI and Marta's §522(d)(2) exemption of $3,675). Either of these parties in interest would have standing to ask that the stay be lifted so that the car could be taken into custody and protected from risk of loss until it could be sold.

We will revisit the concept of adequate protection when we study the Chapter 11 business reorganization, where it comes up not only in connection with lifting the automatic stay but also in connection with motions to use property of the estate (see Chapter Twenty-Three, Section D). In Chapter 7 liquidation cases however, the second ground for lifting the stay, set out in §362(d), is more commonly asserted:

- that the debtor has no equity in the property (more is owed on it than it is worth), and
- that the debtor does not need it for an effective reorganization.

Since Chapter 7 is a liquidation proceeding and not a reorganization as in Chapters 11, 13, and 12, the second criteria, that the debtor does not need it for an effective reorganization, is obviously satisfied. But the creditor seeking to lift the stay on this second ground must also show that there is no equity in the property.

EXAMPLE

As we saw in the example dealing with Marta's home, if the property involved has value in excess of the amount owed the creditor, the stay will not be lifted. The bankruptcy trustee will want the stay continued so that the property remains with the estate, can be sold, and the excess value (equity) made available for distribution as part of the estate. But if Shears sought to lift the stay on its repossession of the washer and dryer pledged to it, the outcome will be different. The amount owed to Shears is $900 and the value of the pledged property is only $600; thus, there is no equity in the property and the stay would be lifted.

Hearings on motions to lift stay are often hotly contested on the critical valuation/equity issue. If the stay is lifted as to the secured creditor, it will be allowed to take the property just as it would have if the debtor had not filed for bankruptcy relief.

4. Expiration of the Automatic Stay for Secured Personal Property of the Individual Chapter 7 Debtor

BAPCPA created a creditor-friendly **automatic expiration of stay** on personal property only, in Chapter 7 cases only, and involving individual debtors only. The procedure, set out in §521(a)(6), provides that the automatic stay in personal property of the individual Chapter 7 debtor automatically expires 45 days after the first meeting of creditors (discussed in the next section) unless the debtor enters into a reaffirmation agreement (see Illustration 18-b) with the creditor or redeems the property from the security interest. (We consider reaffirmation agreements and the redemption option in Chapter Eighteen, Section C.)

The effect of §521(a)(6) is to save the secured creditor the trouble and expense of having to file a motion to lift stay and of having to establish one of the grounds of §362(d)(1) in order to prevail on such motion. It effectively shifts the burden to the debtor to file a motion seeking to extend the stay and to show the court why the stay should *not* be automatically lifted. It also forces the debtor to take the initiative to file that motion within 45 days after the first meeting of creditors. Likewise, if the bankruptcy trustee believes there is equity for the Chapter 7 estate in the pledged property, he must file a motion with the court to retain the property in the estate before that deadline runs.

EXAMPLE

> Since Marta Carlson is an individual debtor in a Chapter 7, §521(a)(6) applies in her case. So if Shears wishes to repossess the washer and dryer (personal property in which it is secured), instead of filing its own motion under §362(d)(1) seeking an order lifting the stay, it can simply wait until the §521(a)(6) deadline expires and then repossess the property. The stay will have expired automatically. The Code is unclear as to whether the bankruptcy court must enter a formal order lifting the stay upon the expiration of the 45 days; in practice, some do and some don't. The attorney and the assisting legal professional must check the local rules of the court or learn the informal local practice.

5. Effect of Individual Debtor's Surrender of Pledged Property on the Automatic Stay

In Chapter Fifteen, Section B, we learned that an individual Chapter 7 debtor must file a statement of intent with regard to property pledged as collateral, indicating whether he will **surrender** that property to the secured creditor or seek to retain it. If the debtor does indicate an intent to surrender pledged property, the secured creditor must still take appropriate action to have the automatic stay lifted or await the automatic lifting of the stay before taking possession of the property. And, of course, the creditor must await the decision of the bankruptcy trustee regarding whether to **abandon** the pledged property to the creditor as being of no interest to the estate (to be considered in Chapter Eighteen, Section A) or to assert an interest in the property for the benefit of the estate as by avoiding the lien (to be considered in Chapter Seventeen, Section E) or by contending that there is **equity** in the property for the estate (i.e., it is worth more than is owed the creditor).

If an individual debtor fails to file the required statement of intent with regard to personal property pledged as collateral, §362(h)(1) provides that the automatic stay is lifted as to such property and it is no longer to be considered property of the estate. We have already seen that §362(k)(2) provides a creditor accused of willfully violating the automatic stay as to such property with a good faith defense.

6. The Automatic Stay and Utility Service

An issue that can arise in any bankruptcy case, but which is most common in consumer cases, involves a debtor who is in arrears to a public utility (water, gas, electric, etc.) at the time the petition is filed. Section 366(a) prohibits the utility from discontinuing service to the debtor postpetition, notwithstanding the arrearage. The utility may, however, demand a reasonable deposit or security as **adequate assurance** of future performance and may discontinue service after 20 days following the filing of the petition if the deposit or security is not provided per §366(b). Disputes over what is a "reasonable" deposit are resolved by the court.

F. ▷ The First Meeting of Creditors

Pursuant to §341 of the Code and FRBP 2003, the U.S. Trustee is required to call a meeting of creditors within 21 to 40 days following the order for relief in a Chapter 7 case. This **first meeting of creditors** is required in a case filed under any chapter of the Code, but the timing of the meeting varies (e.g., 21 to 40 days after the order for relief in Chapter 7s and 11s; 21 to 35 days in a Chapter 12; and 21 to 50 days in a Chapter 13). Practitioners often refer to the first meeting of creditors as the **341 meeting**.

EXAMPLE

> The notice of commencement of the case (OBF 9, see Document 26 in the Carlson case file) advises creditors of the date and time set for the 341 meeting.

The 341 meeting is conducted by the bankruptcy trustee. This is not a court hearing and the bankruptcy judge is not present. The debtor is put under oath and must answer questions regarding his assets and financial affairs. Frequently nonexempt property of the debtor is turned over to the bankruptcy trustee at this meeting: keys to cars, houses, lockboxes, and the like. There are often questions about assets or liabilities the debtor has or hasn't listed in his schedules, or issues discussed regarding the valuation of property claimed as exempt. All these matters may be inquired into at the 341. Since the debtor is under oath, it is important that he answer truthfully and candidly.

EC 16-c: The legal professional assisting the debtor's attorney may be assigned to prepare the client for the questioning the client will undergo at the first meeting of creditors. Do you recall what ethical provisions prohibit the assisting legal professional from suggesting that a client lie or deceive? Do you recall the criminal liability that can result from such behavior?

Illustration 16-c: QUESTIONS THE BANKRUPTCY TRUSTEE IS REQUIRED TO ASK THE CHAPTER 7 DEBTOR AT THE FIRST MEETING OF CREDITORS

- Debtor's awareness of the consequences of receiving a discharge in bankruptcy, including the effect on credit history
- Debtor's ability to file for relief under another chapter of the Code
- Debtor's awareness of the effect of a discharge of debt under Chapter 7
- Debtor's awareness of the effect of reaffirming debt rather than discharging it

---

Section 341(d) requires that the bankruptcy trustee examine a Chapter 7 debtor on several matters at the 341 meeting. Those required topics are set forth in Illustration 16-c.

One question that has arisen historically in 341 meetings is whether a **non-attorney employee** of a creditor can attend and ask questions of the debtor on behalf of the creditor. Some courts have allowed that and some have not on the grounds that asking questions on behalf of another at the 341 hearing is the practice of law. Under that view, an individual creditor could appear and ask questions himself at the hearing, but if he sent an agent to speak for him, that agent must be an attorney. Since corporations are not natural persons like the individual creditor and must always be represented by an agent, the practical effect of this view is to require entity creditors such as corporations to always be represented by counsel at the 341 meeting, adding to the expense of the proceeding for that creditor. BAPCPA revised §341(c) to provide that a creditor holding a consumer debt (one related to personal or household goods) may be represented at the meeting by an employee or agent of the creditor who need not be an attorney.

EC 16-d: A related question is whether a paralegal for the attorney representing a creditor can attend and ask questions of the debtor in lieu of the attorney herself. In some districts that has been prohibited, as constituting the practice of law. Research the court rulings or ethical rules of your state to determine the prevailing rule there, or check the local rules of your bankruptcy court to see if that issue is addressed there.

Within ten days following the 341 meeting, the U.S. Trustee is required by §704(b)(1) to file a report with the bankruptcy court advising whether any **presumption of abuse** should arise in the case because of the **means test** of §704(b). The clerk then provides a copy of that statement to creditors within five days. If the U.S. Trustee concludes that the presumption of abuse is still present, he is required to file a motion to dismiss the case or convert it to a Chapter 13 within 30 days of filing the §704(b)(1) report. The §704(b)(1) report filed by the U.S. Trustee in Marta Carlson's case can be seen in Document 29 in the Carlson case file.

The 341 meeting is not the only time that a debtor can be examined under oath in a case. If at any time there is a dispute about the debtor's 341 meeting testimony or if any new issue arises in the case requiring sworn testimony of the debtor or anyone else, FRBP 2004 authorizes any party in interest to file a motion with the courts asking permission to conduct a sworn examination of the debtor or any other witness. This is called a **Rule 2004 examination**.

EXAMPLE

> Assume that the bankruptcy trustee in Marta Carlson's case is considering an objection to the claim of Pine Ridge Nursing Home based on the debtor's dispute of that debt. The trustee may want to examine Marta further on this dispute and he may want to examine one or more persons from Pine Ridge as well. To accomplish those examinations, the trustee may utilize Rule 2004.

OBF B254 contains the subpoena form to compel a witness's attendance at a 2004 examination.

CONCLUSION

Much more remains to be considered in connection with the administration of a Chapter 7 case. Creditor claims must be filed and examined for validity. Property of the estate must be identified and turned over to the trustee for liquidation. The trustee may need the assistance of professionals to assist in gathering property of the estate, valuing it and liquidating it. These are the topics we will address in the next chapter.

CHAPTER SUMMARY

Upon the filing of the petition, an order for relief is entered or deemed entered. In a Chapter 7 case, a bankruptcy trustee is appointed from the panel of trustees overseen by the U.S. Trustee. The trustee's duties include locating and taking possession of the nonexempt property of the debtor to be liquidated, liquidating that property, and distributing the proceeds to creditors in the order of priority mandated by the Code. Approximately 90 percent of all Chapter 7 cases are no-asset cases.

Upon filing of the petition, a notice of commencement of case is sent by the clerk to creditors, advising of the filing and providing deadlines and other information regarding the case, including the automatic stay. Upon filing the petition, most efforts to collect debt from the debtor are automatically stayed and a creditor or its representative can be found in contempt of the court, enjoined, and fined or sanctioned for violating it. Secured creditors properly perfected in property of the debtor and in which the estate has no equity will routinely file a motion with the court asking it to lift the stay to allow the creditor to foreclose on or repossess the property unless the debtor redeems the property or reaffirms the debt with the creditor's consent. In Chapter 7 cases only, the automatic stay against personal property of an individual debtor is subject to the 45-day automatic expiration rule.

Within 20 to 40 days following the order for relief a first meeting of creditors is held where the debtor must answer case-relevant questions under oath.

REVIEW QUESTIONS

1. Explain how the panel of trustees operates. Who can serve as a bankruptcy trustee? Who appoints them? What does it mean that they are bonded and why is that required? On what basis can a bankruptcy trustee be removed from a case?

2. Summarize the duties of a bankruptcy trustee in a Chapter 7 case.

3. What is a no-asset case? What difference does that make for unsecured creditors of the debtor? What difference does that make in the fee of the bankruptcy trustee?

4. Summarize the different information provided to creditors in the notice of commencement of case.

5. Give examples of collection efforts that are subject to the automatic stay. Give examples of collection efforts that are not subject to it. How is the automatic stay enforced? What are likely penalties for violating the stay? What changes did BAPCPA make to the operation of the automatic stay for some individual debtors?

6. What do we mean by saying that there is equity in an item of property? What do we mean by asking if the estate has equity in property of the debtor pledged as security to a creditor?

7. Explain how the 45-day automatic expiration rule works in an individual debtor's Chapter 7 case.

8. Explain the difference between a debtor's surrender of property of the estate and the bankruptcy trustee's abandonment of such property.

9. List questions that the bankruptcy trustee must ask the debtor at the first meeting of creditors. List other questions the debtor is likely to be asked at the meeting.

10. What is a Rule 2004 examination and how is it different from the first meeting of creditors?

WORDS AND PHRASES TO REMEMBER

abandon (property)
adequate assurance
adequate protection (or lack of)
adversary proceedings
answer
Article 9
asset case
attorney's fees
automatic expiration of stay
automatic stay
bankruptcy trustee
bonded
contempt
continuation statement
court costs
creditors' committee
discharge in bankruptcy

enjoin
equity
financing statement (UCC-1)
fines and penalties
first meeting of creditors
   (341 meeting)
good faith
inventory of the property of the estate
involuntary petition
means test
motion
motion to lift (or extend) stay
movant
no-asset report
nonattorney employee
nonconsensual statutory lien
non-residential lease

notice of commencement of case
order (entry of)
order for relief
panel of trustees
presumption of abuse
property of the estate
punitive damages
relation back

residential lease
Rule 2004 examination
safe harbor provision
statement of intent
surrender (of property)
341 meeting
Uniform Commercial Code (UCC)

TO LEARN MORE: A number of TLM activities to accompany this chapter are accessible on the student disc accompanying the text and on the Author Updates link to the text Web site at http://www.aspenparalegaled.com/ books/parsons_abcdebt/default.asp.

Chapter Seventeen

The Chapter 7 Case: Creditor Claims and Property of the Estate

Debts are nowadays like children: conceived in pleasure but brought forth in pain.

—*Moliere*

A. Creditor Claims

1. Distinguishing Between Secured and Unsecured Claims in Bankruptcy: Bifurcation of the Undersecured Claim

In Chapters Four and Five we considered consensual security interests in a debtor's personal property and consensual mortgages in a debtor's real property in detail. In Chapter Six we considered circumstances under which a creditor may obtain a nonconsensual lien on a debtor's property, whether by statutory lien or declared constructive trust. In Chapter Eight we examined the various factors both an unsecured and secured creditor will consider in deciding whether to file suit to collect an arrearage, a collection suit. In Chapter Ten we considered the significance of property of the debtor being subject to a preexisting consensual or nonconsensual security interest when a judgment debtor seeks to execute on that property. And in Chapter Eleven we considered the priority of liens created by execution on a debtor's property.

The distinction between secured and unsecured debt is no less significant when the debtor files for bankruptcy relief under any chapter of the Code. When a creditor files a claim against a debtor in a bankruptcy case, the claim will be treated as an **unsecured claim** if the creditor is unsecured and as a **secured claim** to the extent the creditor holds a consensual or nonconsensual security interest or lien in any of the debtor's property.

To understand how the Code treats secured claims, you must keep in mind that a creditor may be **fully secured** (the dollar value of the collateral is at least as much as the dollar amount of the claim), **oversecured** (the dollar value of the collateral exceeds the dollar amount of the claim), or **undersecured** (sometimes called **partially secured**) (the dollar value of the collateral is less than the dollar amount of the claim).

EXAMPLE

Creditor #1 has a prepetition secured claim against the debtor in the amount of $100,000 and the property in which he is secured has a value of $100,000. That creditor is fully secured. Creditor #2 has a prepetition secured claim against the debtor in the amount of $100,000 and the property in which he is secured has a value of $125,000. That creditor is oversecured. Creditor #3 has a prepetition secured claim against the debtor in the amount of $100,000 and the property in which he is secured has a value of $75,000. That creditor is under-secured, or only partially secured.

Section 506(a)(1) of the Code provides that a secured claim in bankruptcy is only secured up to the value of the collateral at the time the petition is filed. For the wholly secured and oversecured creditor that presents no problem—their secured claim will be valued at the full amount of the indebtedness. But for the undersecured creditor that means his secured claim will be allowed only up to the value of the collateral. For the balance of what he is owed over the value of the collateral, his claim will be unsecured. Thus, §506(a) effectively **bifurcates** the undersecured claim into its secured and unsecured portions. Practitioners sometimes refer to this mandated bifurcation as a **strip down** or **write down** of an undersecured claim to the value of the collateral. Note that the under-secured creditor does not forfeit the unsecured portion of his claim, but he can only pursue that claim through the bankruptcy process as an unsecured claim.

EXAMPLE

As a result of the bifurcation mandated by §506(a), creditor #3 in our last example will have a secured claim of $75,000 and an unsecured claim of $25,000 in the bankruptcy proceeding.

There are numerous consequences of this bifurcation of an undersecured claim in a bankruptcy case, including how the collateral securing the claim is to be valued. We will consider each consequence and valuation issue as we come to it in our study of Chapters 7, 13, and 11 throughout the remainder of the text.

2. The Proof of Claim

Proof of claim The writing that a creditor submits as evidence of its claim against the estate.

Claims bar date The deadline set for creditors in a case to file proofs of claim.

The notice of commencement of a Chapter 7 case advises the creditors whether to file a written **proof of claim** and, if so, the deadline (called the **claims bar date**) by which such claim must be filed. If a case is a no-asset one, creditors will be advised not to file a proof of claim since no distribution (payout) to creditors is anticipated. Since the Marta Rinaldi Carlson case is an asset case, the **notice of commencement** in the case does advise creditors of a filing dead-line for proofs of claim (see Document 26 in the Carlson case file).

Section 501(a) of the Code authorizes the filing of the proof of claim. OBF 10 is the proof of claim form. In some districts, the court clerk will attach a copy of the form to the notice of commencement. In other districts, the creditor must down-load the form from the clerk's Web site or obtain one from the clerk's office. Pursuant to FRBP 3001 and 3002, the proof of claim form must be completed by the creditor, signed, and mailed or delivered to the bankruptcy court clerk or the bankruptcy trustee or both, as the form directs.

FRBP 3001 requires that if the claim is based on a writing (e.g., promissory note, written contract, security agreement, mortgage), a copy of the writing must be attached to the proof of claim.

EXAMPLE

> The proof of claim filed by Pine Ridge Nursing Home in Marta Carlson's Chapter 7 case is Document 30 in the Carlson case file. Note that the guaranty she executed, which forms the basis of the claim, is attached.

If the creditor asserts a security interest in any property of the debtor, proof of perfection of that interest must accompany the claim form.

FRBP 3001 and OBF 10 were amended in 2012 to require creditors to provide more specific information where claims are filed in cases of individual debtors, including:

- An itemized statement of interest, fees, expenses, or other charges sought in addition to the principal indebtedness
- If a security interest is asserted in debtor's property, the amount of any arrearge (amount needed to cure any default) as of the date of the petition
- If a mortgage is asserted in debtor's principal residence, an attachment (OBF 10A) must accompany the proof of claim, providing details of the outstanding loan as of the date the petition is filed
- If the claim is based on a revolving or open-end consumer credit account (like a credit card or department store account), a statement containing details of the last transaction, payment, and posting on the account

It is important that creditors in a Chapter 7 who wish to participate in any distribution from the estate file the proof of claim and file it within the time allowed. If an **unsecured creditor** fails to file a proof of claim the bankruptcy trustee will *not* include that creditor in a distribution. If the proof of claim is filed late (after the claims bar date), the trustee may object to it on that basis under §502(b)(9) or seek to have it subordinated (made inferior or junior in status) to other claims of equal rank, pursuant to the **equitable subordination** doctrine of §510 (discussed in more detail in Chapter Eighteen, Section B). FRBP 3002(c) provides that the proof of claim must be filed within 90 days following the **first meeting of creditors** (the **341 meeting**). A governmental unit, however, has 180 days from the date the case is filed to file its claim.

Pursuant to §726(a)(1), **priority claims** (discussed in Chapter Eighteen, Section B) are to be allowed if filed on or before ten days after the date the trustee mails a summary of his final report to creditors or the date on which final distribution in the case is commenced, whichever is earlier. And §726(a)(2)(C) provides that any late-filed unsecured claim will be allowed if the filing was late due to the creditor's lack of notice or actual knowledge of the case filing and the claim is filed in time to permit payment. If the initial notice to creditors did not require that a proof of claim be filed but a later notice is given to that effect, the proof of claim must be filed within 90 days of the later notice.

The failure of a secured creditor to file a timely claim does *not* impair its secured position in the property of the debtor per §506(d)(2). So, technically, if the creditor is fully secured in the pledged property (the value of the collateral equals or exceeds the amount owed), there will be no detriment to the late filing of the claim or the failure to file a claim at all. But despite that technicality, the secured creditor, as a practical matter, should always file a proof of claim and attach proof of his security interest in the debtor's property and the perfected status of that interest in order to prove that status to the trustee, who otherwise will be looking to take that property for the benefit of the estate.

Furthermore, if the secured creditor is undersecured, failing to file a claim or filing a claim late could result in the lost opportunity to participate in any distribution the creditor might otherwise have received on the unsecured portion of his claim.

EXAMPLE

Assume that Marta Carlson owes Automotive Financing, Inc. (AFI) $10,000 on the Toyota Camry that is worth only $8,500. When the automatic stay is lifted, AFI will repossess and sell the car. But even if the sale brings the maximum value of the car, AFI would still be owed $1,500. Pursuant to §506(a), AFI's claim is secured only up to the value of the collateral and is unsecured as to the balance owed in excess of that value. As we have seen, §506(a) effectively bifurcates the claim of the undersecured creditor into its secured and unsecured portions. Consequently, the $1,500 balance owed to AFI over the value of its collateral will be treated as a **general unsecured claim** in Marta's bankruptcy case. If there is a distribution from the estate to general unsecured creditors, AFI will participate *only* if it files a timely proof of claim.

3. Objections to Claims

Claims docket A list of claims filed in a bankruptcy case.

As claims are filed, they will be entered on a **claims docket** by the clerk of the court. One of the duties of the bankruptcy trustee is to examine the proofs of claim filed by creditors to determine if they are valid (see Illustration 16-a). Section 502(a) provides that unless an **objection to claim** by the trustee or other **party in interest** is filed, the claim will be **deemed allowed**.

Sections 502(b)(d)(e) and (k) set forth several grounds for objecting to a claim. The most general of these grounds is §502(b)(1), which authorizes an objection if the claim is *unenforceable against the debtor under the terms of the underlying agreement or due to controlling law.* Thus, the trustee's (or other party in interest's) examination will include a determination of whether the claim is valid at all, whether it is made in the correct amount, whether the creditor is secured in property of the estate (discussed in detail in Chapter Eighteen), or whether the debtor has any counterclaim or other offset (discussed below) to the claim. In addition, a creditor who is in possession of debtor's property or who is the transferee of a voidable transfer from the debtor (to be considered in Sections D and E) and who refuses to turn the property over or pay the amount of the voidable transfer upon proper demand by the trustee may have its claim disallowed pursuant to §502(d).

If a claim is filed as a secured one, the trustee will examine the claim not only to make sure the claim is in fact secured but to determine if the security interest is properly perfected. As we will see in Section E, below, if the security interest of the creditor is not properly perfected prior to the filing of the bankruptcy petition, the Code empowers the trustee to avoid the creditor's security interest or lien in the collateral and take the property for the benefit of the estate.

P-H 17-a: The schedules filed by the debtor will assist the trustee in the examination of the claims of creditors. Recall that Schedules D and F, on which the debtor lists secured claims and unsecured nonpriority claims, require the debtor to list whether the debtor disputes the claim. The debtor's dispute of the claim may form the basis of the trustee's challenge to that claim. The debtor's basis for disputing the claim may be a subject of inquiry at the 341 meeting. The initial task of reviewing the debtor's schedules and the creditors' proofs of claim in the bankruptcy trustee's office may be assigned to the assisting legal professional. Assume you are that legal professional. Review the schedules filed by Marta Carlson to identify claims that you might recommend to the trustee for close examination for possible dispute when the proofs of claim are filed.

EC 17-a: In addition to questioning the debtor at the 341 meeting regarding possible objections to claims, the bankruptcy trustee may also request other assistance from the debtor. Thus, there may be several unofficial meetings between personnel in the trustee's office and the debtor and the debtor's attorney. The assisting legal professional in the trustee's office may be charged with contacting the debtor or his attorney to obtain all kinds of information or further detail. Assume you are that legal professional. What ethical and professional considerations must you remember when you are given such responsibilities?

If the bankruptcy trustee concludes that any claim, secured or unsecured, is invalid in whole or in part, FRBP 3007 requires that he file a written **objection** to the claim.

EXAMPLE

> The bankruptcy trustee in Marta Carlson's Chapter 7 filed an objection to the claim of Pine Ridge Nursing Home. You can see that objection in Document 31 in the Carlson case file.

Pursuant to §502(b) and FRBP 3007, the creditor whose claim is objected to must receive a 30-day notice of the objection and of the proposed hearing date (Document 31 in the Carlson case file). Since most objections to claims are controlled by the **after notice and a hearing procedure**, the objection will be treated as a disputed matter and an evidentiary hearing conducted only if the creditor contests the objection. If the creditor does not contest the objection, it will be sustained without a hearing (see Illustrations 13-c and d). If the objection to the creditor's claim involves an attack on the validity or sufficiency of the creditor's claimed security interest in property of the debtor, however, the trustee must initiate an **adversary proceeding** to set aside that security interest as required by FRBP 7001 (see Illustration 13-f and further discussion in Section E).

Though it is most often the bankruptcy trustee who initiates an objection to a creditor's claim, note that §502(a) authorizes any party in interest to do so. If a trustee refuses to file such an objection, then another creditor who could be benefited by the disallowance of the contested claim may do so. In some situations, the Chapter 7 debtor himself may file an objection to a claim, as we will consider in Chapter Eighteen, Section C. Interestingly, the Code does not set out a time frame in which an objection to a creditor's claim must be made. Normally such objections will be made prior to **distribution of the estate** to creditors (discussed in Chapter Eighteen, Section B), but there is no time bar to a trustee who, having made a distribution to a creditor, seeks to recover it based on information learned after the distribution. Even after a case has been closed, a trustee may move to reopen it in order to object to a creditor's claim, recover the distribution to that creditor, and redistribute to others. Of course, attempts by a trustee to object to a claim after distribution may be met with defenses such as **waiver** (the voluntary relinquishment of a known right), **promissory estoppel** (the preclusion of one from acting now because he earlier made promises on which others reasonably relied, to their detriment), **equitable estoppel** (the preclusion of one from acting now because his earlier wrongful or dishonest actions or inactions worked to the detriment of others), or **laches** (the neglect of a claim or right for an inordinate period of time under the circumstances).

The validity and enforceability of most contracts as well as questions regarding attachment and perfection of security interests are controlled by state law. Thus, this topic of creditor claims and their validity is another example of how prominent a role state law plays in the administration of a bankruptcy case in a U.S. bankruptcy court.

Waiver The voluntary relinquishment of a known right.

Promissory estoppel the preclusion of one from acting now because he earlier made promises on which others reasonably relied to their detriment

Equitable estoppel The preclusion of one from acting now because his earlier wrongful or dishonest actions worked to the detriment of others.

Laches Neglect of a claim or right for a inordinate period of time.

4. Creditors' Claims and the Right to Setoff

The doctrine of **setoff** is recognized in most states by common law or by statute. The idea behind the doctrine is a simple one: If two persons are indebted to each other, the debt of either is offset by the amount of the debt of the other.

EXAMPLE

Assume that Marta Carlson borrows $1,000 from her boss, Howard Kine, at Tomorrow Today, Inc. (TTI). Later, she does $500 worth of work for him organizing his personal finances and preparing his tax return. What does she owe him now? If Kine sues her for the $1,000 she owes him, the debt will be offset by what he owes her, so he will obtain a judgment for only $500. And if the value of her services to him is $1,000, the debts mutually offset, so neither owes the other anything. If the value of her work is $1,200, the debt she owes him for the loan is completely offset and he owes her $200.

Section 553 of the Code provides that the right to setoff recognized under nonbankruptcy law (common law or statute) is alive and well in the bankruptcy context.

EXAMPLE

Assume Marta still owes Howard Kine the borrowed $1,000 when she files her Chapter 7 petition and he still owes her $500 for the work she did. Can Kine file a claim for $1,000 and will he have to pay the trustee the $500 he owes Marta since her claim for that payment is now property of the estate? If Columbiana recognizes the right to setoff, §553(a) provides that it will be recognized in the bankruptcy case. Kine can offset what Marta owes him by the amount that he owes her and file a claim in her Chapter 7 case for the $500 difference. On the other hand, if he files a claim for $1,000 the trustee can raise Marta's prepetition right to offset his claim with her claim against him and, again, Kine's claim will be no greater than $500. Of course, these examples assume that both claims involved in the setoff are otherwise valid and collectible.

5. Interest on Claims in Chapter 7 Cases

a. Interest on Unsecured and Undersecured Claims

Section 502(b)(2) disallows claims made for **unmatured interest**. That phrase refers to interest that is not yet due and owing to the creditor at the time the petition is filed and is sometimes called **postpetition interest**. Unsecured claims may include charges for **prepetition interest** that were due and owing on the date the petition was filed but are not entitled to receive postpetition interest.

EXAMPLE

> Marta owed an unsecured debt to Capitol City Bank (CCB) on her Visa credit card in the amount of $8,200 at the time her petition and Schedule F were filed (Document 12 in the Carlson case file). A portion of that $8,200 may include prepetition interest charges by CCB for a carryover balance or for late payments on the account. If the underlying card agreement permits CCB to make such interest charges, it can include them in its claim. But if CCB files a proof of claim stating a claim for not just the $8,200 balance owed at the time of the petition filing but adding a claim for interest that has accrued since the petition was filed, the trustee will object to that portion of the claim, pursuant to §502(b)(2). If Marta had not filed her petition, the interest would have continued to accrue, but once she files her petition, the unsecured creditor cannot seek to recover it on a claim made in her bankruptcy case.

Undersecured debt A debt secured by collateral of less value than the debt itself.

A secured creditor who is undersecured in the property of the debtor securing the claim is in the same situation as the unsecured creditor, like CCB in the previous example as to interest.

EXAMPLE

> Assume that Marta owes AFI $10,000 on the Toyota Camry that is worth only $8,500. Assume that the automatic stay is lifted, and AFI repossesses and sells the car for $8,500. Pursuant to §506(a)(1), AFI now has a bifurcated, general unsecured claim for the $1,500 balance but *may not* include postpetition interest in that claim per §502(b)(2). The fact that AFI was a secured creditor as to part of its claim does not change its treatment under §502(b)(2) for the unsecured portion of its claim.

In the very rare case, there may be sufficient assets in a Chapter 7 case to pay all expenses of administration and all the claims of creditors in full and still have cash left over. In that case, §726(a)(5) allows the trustee to pay postpetition interest on unsecured creditors' claims (see Illustration 18-a).

b. Interest, Fees, and Other Charges on Oversecured Claims

If a creditor is not just fully secured but oversecured in the collateral at the time the petition is filed (i.e., the value of the collateral not only equals but exceeds the amount of the claim), then §506(b) allows the creditor to include in its claim postpetition interest, as well as other fees and charges but only if those charges are authorized by the underlying agreement or by state law and only **up to the value of the collateral**.

EXAMPLE

> Capitol Savings Bank (CSB) holds the first mortgage on Marta's residence. The principal amount of its claim at the time the petition is filed is $142,500 and the residence securing the debt is valued at $255,000. CSB is fully secured in the residence because its value exceeds the principal amount of the debt. Section 506(b) allows CSB to file a claim in Marta's Chapter 7 case for the principal amount owed ($142,500) plus unpaid postpetition interest, fees, and charges up to the value of the collateral ($225,000). And CSB's right to do this would not be affected by the fact that another creditor, Dreams Come True Finance Company, is also secured in the residence. CSB has a first position in the property and its claim will take priority up to the full amount allowed by the Code.

As previously noted, the failure of a secured creditor to file a timely proof of claim does not impair its secured position in the property of the debtor per §506(d)(2). It can still seek to lift the stay on the collateral and sell it in full satisfaction of its claim or, if there is equity for the estate in the property in excess of the creditor's claim, simply wait for the trustee to sell the property, at which time its full claim plus postpetition interest, fees, and charges will be paid to it, per §506(d)(2). For this reason, many bankruptcy courts do not require fully secured creditors to file formal proofs of claim and instead require only that the creditor informally make available to the trustee the documentation demonstrating that the creditor holds a perfected security interest in the property.

EXAMPLE

> The local rules of the bankruptcy court handling Marta's Chapter 7 case might not require Capitol Savings Bank to file a formal proof of claim but to, instead, provide the trustee with a copy of the mortgage or deed of trust establishing its secured, perfected position in the residence.

Reorganization cases (cases under Chapters 13, 12, and 11) raise other issues regarding interest on secured claims that we will consider when we study those types of cases.

B. ▷ Property of the Estate

Property of the estate All property in which the debtor holds a legal or equitable interest at the commencement of a bankruptcy case.

What constitutes the **property of the estate** is one of the most important concepts in bankruptcy law. Section 541(a) of the Code provides that the commencement of a case under any chapter of the Code creates such estate and that it consists of all property in which the debtor holds a **legal or equitable interest** at the time of commencement. Section 541(b) contains some minor exceptions to this very broad definition of what constitutes property of the estate. Generally, property acquired by the debtor *after* the commencement of the Chapter 7 case does *not* belong to the estate because that will be the property available to the debtor for his **fresh start**. But read the following example to get a feel for how truly broad the concept of "property of the estate" is.

EXAMPLE

If the debtor inherits property up to 180 days *after* the petition is filed, that property belongs to the estate. The debtor is considered to have had an equitable interest in the inheritance at the time he filed. The same is true as to insurance proceeds received within 180 days of filing. If the debtor is the beneficiary of a trust, the trust property to which the debtor is entitled now belongs to the estate unless the trust was set up as a spendthrift trust (discussed in Chapter Ten, Section F). If the debtor has earned a paycheck or commission at the time he files the petition, that property belongs to the estate even though it is not paid until after the petition is filed. Stock or bonds held for the debtor by a brokerage house belong to the estate. Any debts owed to the debtor by another when the case is filed become the property of the estate. If the debtor has the right to file a lawsuit at the time the petition is file, the claim underlying the lawsuit now becomes the property of the estate and the bankruptcy trustee has standing to pursue the lawsuit in the place of the debtor. If the debtor holds a mortgage on the property of another, the mortgage and all the rights under it, including the right to foreclose in the event of default, become the property of the estate. If the debtor buys a lottery ticket before filing the petition and wins after filing the petition, the proceeds belong to the estate since the ticket became property of the estate upon filing. If stock owned by the debtor at the time the petition is filed splits after the filing, the estate gets the benefit of the stock split.

Of course, some of the property of the estate will be claimed as exempt by the debtor and retained by him. And creditors holding a perfected security interest in property of the estate may have a priority claim to it over the trustee (see the next section). Additionally, the bankruptcy trustee may consider some of the property of the estate to have no value to the estate and abandon it pursuant to §554 (see discussion in Chapter Eighteen, Section A). But otherwise the property of the estate comes under the control of the bankruptcy trustee at the time the case is commenced and will be liquidated by the trustee for the benefit of all creditors of the estate. As we have seen, however, the trustee may contest the validity of a secured creditor's claim to certain property of the debtor as collateral, hoping to defeat the allegedly perfected security interest and seize that collateral as property of the estate. With the same goal in mind, the trustee may challenge exemptions claimed by the individual debtor, as we consider in the next section.

Property in which the debtor has a legal or equitable interest may not be in the debtor's possession when the case is commenced. It may be held by another. That does not prevent it becoming property of the estate. The definition in §541(a) specifically says that qualifying property belongs to the estate, "wherever located and by whomever held."

EXAMPLE

Salary the debtor has earned as of the filing of the petition may be held by the employer. A car the debtor owns may be loaned to a family member or friend. Funds of the debtor in checking and savings accounts will be held by the financial institution.

Contingent, disputed, and unliquidated claims that the debtor has against third parties are property of the estate, and the trustee has standing, pursuant to

§704(a)(1), to pursue those claims to judgment for the benefit of the estate. Normally, that will be done by filing an **adversary proceeding** against the third party (see Chapter Thirteen, Section G, and Illustration 13-f). Whether the bankruptcy court can hear and enter a final order in an adversary proceeding brought to collect a claim of the estate will depend in the first instance on whether it is a **core** or **noncore proceeding** under 28 U.S.C. §157(b), as discussed in Chapter Thirteen, Section B (see Illustration 13-a). And regardless of whether or not it qualifies as a core proceeding, if the claim is one for wrongful death or personal injury it *cannot* be tried in the bankruptcy court. Instead, it must be tried in the district court pursuant to 28 U.S.C. §157(b)(5) or a state court having jurisdiction pursuant to 28 U.S.C. §1334(c).

Noncore proceeding Disputes governed by non-bankruptcy law, the outcome of which may affect the administration of a bankruptcy estate.

EXAMPLE

Recall that Nick and Pearl Murphy (Illustration 1-a, Case Study #1) have a professional malpractice claim for Pearl and a loss of consortium claim for Nick against the doctor who performed her botched appendectomy and the hospital where the surgery was performed. If the couple files a **joint petition** in Chapter 7 before that claim is resolved, the claims themselves are assets that they must list on their Schedule B and assign a value to them. At that point the claims are contingent on their prevailing, disputed because the doctor and hospital are not admitting liability, and unliquidated because we do not know yet the dollar amount, if any, of any settlement or verdict to be rendered on the claims. But the claims are assets that become property of the estate unless properly exempted and the lawsuit to liquidate those claims likely qualifies as a core proceeding under 28 U.S.C. §157(b)(2)(O). However, since these claims are in the nature of a personal injury action, 28 U.S.C. §157(d) mandates that the claims be tried in the U.S. district court rather than in a bankruptcy court adversary action. United States district courts have **subject matter jurisdiction** to hear such cases even without diversity of citizenship between the parties under 28 U.S.C §1334. As a practical matter, however, personal injury and wrongful death cases that arise in a bankruptcy case are normally tried in the state court having jurisdiction as authorized by 28 U.S.C. §334(c). Thus in the Murphy's bankruptcy case, the trustee is likely to ask for and receive permission from the court to pursue the Murphy's malpractice claim in state court. Since the claim is property of the estate, only the trustee now has the right to file suit on it. The Murphys will be nominal (in name only) plaintiffs in that lawsuit, and proceeds from any judgment or settlement of the claim will become property of the estate.

C. Challenging the Debtor's Claimed Exemptions in Order to Increase Property of the Estate

In Chapter Fifteen, Section B, we learned that per §522(a)(2) of the Code, the individual Chapter 7 debtor sets out his claimed exemptions on Schedule C at their fair market value as that phrase has been interpreted by the U.S. Supreme Court in *U.S. v. Cartwright*, 411 U.S. 546 (1973). We also observed there that the bankruptcy trustee will *not* automatically accept the debtor's claimed exemptions or their valuation but instead will carefully examine the exemptions on Schedule C, to see if a challenge can be made to either 1) the property claimed as exempt, or 2) the valuation of the exempt property by the debtor. You may want to review that section at this time.

EXAMPLE

> Assume a Chapter 7 debtor owns a house and lot. He owes a secured creditor $200,000 on the house, lists its fair market value on Schedule C as $220,000, and claims the $20,000 of equity in the house as exempt as a homestead under Code §522(d)(1). If the trustee in his case discovers that this is actually a rental house owned by the debtor and not a residence for the debtor or a dependent, the trustee may object to the claimed exemption on the grounds that the equity in that house and lot cannot be exempted at all under §522(d)(1). On the other hand, if the house and lot are used as a residence by the debtor, but the trustee discovers the fair market value is $250,000, the trustee may object, not to the exemption itself, but to the low valuation of the exempted property by the debtor. After all, if that house and lot are worth $250,000 that means the debtor has $50,000 of equity in it—not just $20,000. And since, under §522(d)(1), the debtor may currently exempt only $22,975 of that equity, the trustee wants to claim the balance of the equity as property of the estate.

FRBP 4003(b) authorizes not just the bankruptcy trustee but any other **party in interest** to object to a debtor's claimed exemption or its value, but most commonly it is the trustee who files the **objection**. FRBP 4003(b) requires that any objection to a debtor's claimed exemptions be made within 30 days following the **first meeting of creditors** or within 30 days following any amendment to Schedule C, although that time period can be extended by motion and for cause shown. Section 522(l) of the Code provides that if no timely objection to a claimed exemption is made, the exemption is **deemed allowed** and the U.S. Supreme Court held in *Taylor v. Freeland & Kronz*, 503 U.S. 638 (1992) that the 30-day deadline for objections (or any extensions thereof granted by the court) is to be strictly construed. In a hearing on an objection to a debtor's exemption, FRBP 4003(c) places the *burden* of showing why the debtor is not entitled to the claimed exemption on the objecting party.

As we saw in Chapter Fifteen, *Taylor v. Freeland & Kronz* effectively mandates that where the *actual value* of property the debtor claims as fully exempt is unknown or undetermined as of the first meeting of creditors, the trustee files a timely objection just in case the exempted property may turn out to have more value than the dollar limit of the exemption claimed. Otherwise, the excess value of exempted property that could have been captured as property of the estate will be lost to the estate. Conversely, *Schwab v. Reilly*, 130 S. Ct. 2652 (2010) effectively mandates that debtors seeking to exempt property up to the full dollar value of an available exemption amount for that property must make that intention expressly clear on their Schedule C, even if they suspect that the actual full value of the property may be less than that available exemption amount. Otherwise, the trustee may be able to capture for the estate the actual value of the property sought to be exempted in excess of the debtor's designated exemption amount for the property even though the trustee fails to file a timely objection to the claimed exemption amount.

P-H 17-b: Go back to Chapter Fifteen, Section B, and reread the summaries of *Taylor v. Freeland & Kronz* and *Schwab v. Reilly* or read the opinions themselves. Why did the trustee's failure in *Taylor* to file a timely objection to the debtor's exemption bar him from including the dollar amount of the debtor's settlement in excess of the allowable exemption amount in the property of that estate when the trustee's similar failure in *Schwab* did *not* bar him from including the excess dollar value of the exempted property over the amount the debtor designated as exempt in the property of that estate? What distinguishes these two cases? Do you see how the trustees in both cases were trying to increase the property of their respective estates at the expense of the debtors' claimed exemptions?

Under FRBP 4003(c), an objection to a claimed exemption is to be decided "after hearing on notice," which some, but not all, courts treat as **after notice and a hearing**. (see Illustration 13-c). Consequently, if the debtor contests the trustee's objection to the exemption, it will be treated as a **contested matter** and a hearing scheduled. If the debtor does not contest the trustee's objection, the objection will be sustained and the challenged exemption disallowed.

D. The Trustee's Powers to Compel Turnover of Property of the Estate

The Code also grants the bankruptcy trustee broad power to locate and take possession of property of the estate from the debtor and from third parties who refuse to turn it over. There are three **turnover** provisions in the Code empowering the bankruptcy trustee to compel a person or entity holding property of the estate to deliver that property to him.

Turnover The surrender of estate property to the trustee by the debtor or other person.

1. The Debtor's Duty to Turn Over Property to the Bankruptcy Trustee

Section 521(a)(4) of the Code imposes an obligation on the debtor to turn over to the trustee, "all property of the estate and any recorded information, including books, documents, records, and papers relating to property of the estate." If the debtor fails to comply with a turnover demand from the trustee, the trustee will file **a motion to compel the turnover**, which is treated as a **contested matter**, not an **adversary proceeding**. The debtor's failure to comply with this duty is also a basis for the trustee to ask the court to deny the debtor a discharge of his debts pursuant to §727 or to dismiss the case pursuant to §707 (discussed in detail in Chapter Eighteen).

2. The Duty of Third Persons to Turn Over Property of the Estate

Section 542 of the Code empowers the trustee to compel third persons (who are not *custodians* within the meaning of §101(11)) holding the property of the debtor to turn it over to him or to account for its value if the property no longer exists. Since the trustee is seeking to recover money or property from a third party in such an action, it must be brought as an adversary proceeding pursuant to FRBP 7001 rather than by motion (see Illustration 13-f).

EXAMPLE

> Prior to filing her Chapter 7 petition Marta Carlson loaned her doll collection to her sister, Evelyn Rinaldi, as disclosed in her Schedule B (see Document 8 in the Carlson case file). When the petition is filed, the trustee will contact Evelyn and demand the return of the doll collection, not to Marta, but to the trustee. Evelyn refused and the trustee filed a complaint (Document 34 in the Carlson case file) instituting an adversary action against her, pursuant to §542 and FRBP 7001, seeking the return of the doll collection or a money judgment for its value.

P-H 17-c: In the complaint filed against Evelyn Rinaldi to recover the doll collection in her possession or its value (Document 34 in the Carlson case file), note the allegations in Paragraph 3 of the complaint regarding the subject matter jurisdiction of the bankruptcy court over the adversary proceeding. Do you understand the source of the court's power to hear this case? If not, review the discussion of those issues in Chapter Thirteen, Sections B and C.

3. The Duty of Custodians to Turn Over Property of the Estate

Custodian A person authorized to have possession of a debtor's property for a specific purpose as in a trustee, receiver, or assignee for the benefit of creditors.

If the property of the estate is in the hands of a **custodian**, including an assignee for the benefit of creditors or a trustee or receiver appointed as part of a prebankruptcy effort to work out the debtor's financial problems, §543 of the Code empowers the bankruptcy trustee to compel that custodian to deliver the property held to him or to account for its proceeds.

EXAMPLE

> If Marta Carlson had attempted an assignment for benefit of creditors prior to filing her petition in bankruptcy, the trustee designated to hold her property as part of that assignment would be the target of the bankruptcy trustee's §543 turnover demand.

If the custodian fails to turn over the property, the trustee can enforce the §543 turnover demand by filing an adversary proceeding. In addition, a third person or custodian who refuses to turn over property to the trustee pursuant to a §§542 or 543 demand and who is also a creditor of the estate can have his claim setoff per §553 or disallowed per §502(d).

E. ▶ The Trustee's Avoidance Powers Regarding Property of the Estate

Avoidance powers Trustee's powers to set aside certain prepetition transfers of property of the estate.

The bankruptcy trustee not only has power to demand the turnover of property of the debtor, but to set aside certain voluntary and involuntary transfers of the debtor's property to others that occurred before the petition was filed. In Code parlance, the trustee can *avoid* these prepetition transfers. Thus, we speak of the **avoidance powers** of the trustee. There are several of them. Since all of these avoidance actions involve the trustee's effort to determine the validity, extent, or priority of a lien on the debtor's property or to recover money or property from a third party, they must be brought as adversary proceedings pursuant to FRBP 7001 and not by motion (see Illustration 13-f). As with the targeted party in a turnover action, if the party targeted by the trustee's avoidance action is also a creditor of the estate and fails to consent to the avoidance or pay the amount demanded by the trustee, that creditor may have its claim setoff per §553 or disallowed per §502(d).

Section 550(a)(1) of the Code provides that if a transfer is avoided (set aside or reversed) under one of these avoidance powers, the trustee can recover the property itself or the value of such property from either the **initial transferee** or the **entity for whose benefit the transfer was made**.

EXAMPLE

Assume that immediately before ABC Company files for Chapter 7 bankruptcy and while the company is insolvent, the officers and directors of the company authorize a transfer of $200,000 to DEF Financial Services in consideration of "financial advisory services." After the Chapter 7 petition is filed, the bankruptcy trustee investigates the prepetition transfer and concludes that it was both a fraudulent transfer under §548 and a preferential transfer under §547. The trustee also learns that the directors and officers of ABC Company each had given DEF Financial Services personal guarantees that were satisfied by the prepetition transfer. If the trustee succeeds in setting this prepetition transfer aside as either a fraudulent transfer or a preferential transfer, the amount transferred can be recovered either from DEF as the transferee or the officers and directors as persons for whose benefit the transfer was made. If property having a value of $200,000 had been transferred to DEF instead of cash and the property was not available to be returned to the trustee following avoidance of the transfer, the trustee could then recover the value of the property ($200,000) from the transferee or the benefited parties.

Section 550(a)(2) also allows the trustee to recover the property or its value from a transferee other than the initial transferee (called an immediate or mediate transferee of the initial transferee) unless that subsequent transferee gave value for the transfer in good faith and without actual or constructive knowledge of the voidability of the transfer.

EXAMPLE

Assume that after DEF Financial Services received the property transferred to it by ABC Company and before the trustee demands its return, DEF transfers the property to GHI, Inc., for a fair value. GHI has no awareness that ABC is insolvent or that it is planning to file bankruptcy or that the officers and directors of ABC are manipulating the property of the company to satisfy their personal guarantees. On those facts, the trustee should not be able to recover the property or its value from GHI. But if GHI has actual or constructive knowledge of any such circumstances, the trustee may be able to recover the property or its value against it.

1. The Power to Avoid Unperfected Security Interests in the Debtor's Property

Strong-arm clause Practitioner's phrase for the trustee's avoidance powers under §544 of the Code.

Section 544(a) of the Code, known as the **strong-arm clause**, provides that, as of the moment the case is commenced by the filing of the petition, the bankruptcy trustee has the status of a *perfected secured creditor* in *all* the property of the estate, whether as a judicial lien creditor (§544(a)(1)) or as a judgment creditor who has had a writ of execution issued in his favor (§544(a)(2)) or as the holder of a consensual mortgage or deed of trust in the real property of the debtor (§544(a)(3)). This makes the trustee a **supercreditor** of the debtor. Note that this status given the trustee is a **legalized fiction:** The trustee need not take any action to become a judicial lien creditor or judgment creditor or mortgagee, as we considered those concepts in Part A of the text. Instead, the Code simply declares him to have that legal status as of the date the petition is filed.

The most dramatic result of that supercreditor status is that the trustee can defeat

- the claim of any unsecured creditor to the property of the debtor or
- the claim of any secured creditor whose security interest in the property was not properly perfected prior to the filing of the petition.

EXAMPLE

Recall from the Assignment Memorandum in Appendix A that Marta Carlson has two mortgages on her home, one in favor of CSB with a balance of $142,500 and one in favor of DCT with a balance of $37,500. If the trustee determines that CSB failed to properly record its mortgage or deed of trust prior to the filing of the bankruptcy petition, he would initiate an adversary proceeding by filing a complaint, pursuant to §544(a) and FRBP 7001, seeking to avoid the security interest CSB claims in the home. If the trustee prevailed in avoiding CSB's lien in the home, that would mean that when the home was sold, DCT would be paid first out of the proceeds (assuming it did properly record its mortgage or deed of trust, thus perfecting its secured interest in the home). Marta would receive her homestead exemption next, and the rest of the proceeds would go to the trustee to be used for the benefit of all other creditors of the estate. CSB would still be a creditor, of course, but its claim would now be an unsecured claim, not a secured claim.

Prepetition security interests in both the personal and real property of the debtor that were not properly perfected are subject to the avoidance powers of the trustee under §544(a).

2. The Power to Avoid Statutory Liens in Property of the Estate

Recall our study of nonconsensual statutory liens in Chapter Six: the mechanic's lien, artisan's lien, attorney's lien, and so on. Section 545 of the Code grants the bankruptcy trustee a very limited power to avoid prepetition statutory liens asserted against the property of the debtor. Most statutory liens are not subject to this particular avoidance power of the trustee. The ones that are subject to avoidance are listed in Illustration 17-a.

Illustration 17-a: PREPETITION STATUTORY LIENS SUBJECT TO AVOIDANCE UNDER §545

- A statutory lien that only goes into effect upon the debtor's insolvency or financial distress, or upon the bankruptcy filing or the commencement of a non-bankruptcy insolvency proceeding against the debtor (§545(1))
- A statutory lien that would not be enforceable under applicable state law against a bona fide purchaser of the property for value as of the date the case was commenced (§545(2))
- Landlord liens (§545(3))

EXAMPLE

Assume that Columbiana had a statute providing that car repair businesses having an unpaid bill for car repair have a lien on any car repaired for the amount owed if the owner of the car filed for bankruptcy relief before paying the debt in full. If Marta owed a repairperson for work on her car when she filed the petition, the trustee could avoid that statutory lien on Marta's car under §545(1).

EXAMPLE

Assume that Columbiana had a statute providing that car repair businesses having an unpaid bill for car repair have an automatic lien on any car repaired for the amount owed if the debt was not paid within 30 days of the repair but only if the business gives notice of its lien by certified mail. If, under state law, a bona fide purchaser of the car from Marta could take the car free from that lien by purchasing it before the 30 days ran out or before the statutory notice was given, the bankruptcy trustee could likewise defeat the lien under §545(2) if Marta filed her petition before the 30 days ran out or before the statutory notice was given.

EXAMPLE

Assume Marta rented her home instead of owning it and that, pursuant to state law, her landlord was asserting a lien against her personal property in the home for the amount of the unpaid rent. The bankruptcy trustee may avoid that landlord's lien pursuant to §545(3).

Actions brought by the trustee to avoid a statutory lien in the debtor's property pursuant to §545 are adversary proceedings.

3. The Power to Avoid a Fraudulent Transfer of Property of the Estate

Section 548 of the Code authorizes the trustee to set aside any **fraudulent transfer** of the debtor's property made within two years preceding the filing of the petition. Such transactions operate as a fraud against the debtor's creditors because the debtor's estate is depleted without exchanging property of similar value from which the creditors' claims can be satisfied.

Like the **Uniform Fraudulent Transfer Act (UFTA)**, considered in Chapter Nine, Section B, §548 defines a fraudulent transfer to include not just a transfer made with actual intent to "hinder, delay or defraud" a creditor per §548(a)(1)(A) but also constructive fraud. The constructive fraud concept is governed by §548 (a)(1)(B) and requires a showing that the transfer was made for less than the **reasonably equivalent value** and one or more of the following:

Insolvent The inability to pay debts as they come due or the state of having total liabilities in excess of total assets.

- Was made at a time when the debtor was **insolvent** (see §101(32))
- Caused the debtor to become insolvent
- Left the debtor undercapitalized for current or planned business transactions
- Was made at a time the debtor had or planned to incur other debts beyond its ability to pay or
- Was to or for the benefit of an **insider** (see §101(31) and further discussion in the next section) not in the ordinary course of business.

EXAMPLE

> Assume that Marta Carlson, instead of loaning her doll collection to her sister, Evelyn Rinaldi, had made a gift of it to the sister after deciding to file for bankruptcy but before the actual petition was filed. This gift would be disclosed in Marta's Statement of Affairs (Document 19 in the Carlson case file) because it was made within one year of filing. The circumstances of this "gift" would look very suspicious to the trustee searching for property of the estate, and the purported gift might well be attacked as a fraudulent transfer both because it was made when Marta was insolvent and it was arguably made with actual intent to defraud.

The phrase "reasonably equivalent value" is not defined in the Code. It is normally determined using the **fair market value** of the property involved as of the date of the transfer. Fair market value has been defined by the Supreme Court to be the price at which the property would change hands between a willing buyer and a willing seller, neither being under any compulsion to buy or to sell and both having reasonable knowledge of relevant facts (*United States v. Cartwright*, 411 U. S. 546, 551(1973)).

Applying a strict fair market value standard to determine reasonable equivalence does not always work, however, particularly where the benefit received by the transferee is indirect or intangible. See, e.g., *Mellon Bank N.A. v. Metro Communc'ns, Inc.*, 945 F.2d 635, 644–45 (3d Cir. 1991) (value of transfer was the intangible benefit of improving debtor's ability to borrow capital) and *In re Jumer's Castle Lodge, Inc.*, 338 B.R. 344 (C.D. Ill. 2006) (debtor received more in value than it transferred, since transfer made it more attractive to investors and financiers). The most that can be said about reasonable equivalence, then, is that it "should depend on all the facts of each case an important element of which is market value. Such a rule requires case-by-case adjudication with fair market value of the property transferred as a starting point" (*In re Morris Communications, Inc.*, 914 F.2d 458, 466-67 (4th Cir. 1990)).

P-H 17-d: An excellent case in which to see how the courts analyze the reasonably equivalent value concern in a §548 fraudulent transfer case as well as how the transferee concepts of §550 work is *In re Tousa, Inc.*, 680 F.3d 1298 (11th Cir. 2012). What was the property of the debtor transferred in that case? What made the transfer fraudulent under §548? What was the reasonably equivalent value argument made by the defendants? Did it matter that defendants received value indirectly rather than directly? What was the argument of defendants that they were not entities for whose benefit the transfer was made?

Actions brought by the trustee to avoid alleged fraudulent transfers of the debtor's property pursuant to §548 are adversary proceedings.

4. The Power to Avoid Preferential Transfers of Property of the Estate

Perhaps the most breathtaking example of avoidance powers given the bankruptcy trustee is the **preferential transfer** provision of §547. This section allows the trustee to set aside any transfer of the debtor's property made within 90 days preceding the filing of the petition if the following additional elements are present:

- The transfer was "to or for the benefit of a creditor"
- The transfer was made for or on account of an antecedent (preexisting) debt
- The debtor was insolvent at the time of the transfer
- The transfer would enable the creditor to receive more than it would have received if the transfer had not been made

EXAMPLE

One of Marta's unsecured debts is to Crisis Counseling Center (CCC) for the counseling services rendered to her son, Chris (see the Assignment Memorandum in Appendix A and Document 12 in the Carlson case file). The total amount owed to CCC was $1,250 and was due last June 1. Assume that Marta did finally make a payment of $700 to CCC on October 15 before filing her Chapter 7 petition on December 1. The bankruptcy trustee will demand that CCC return that $700 payment as a preferential transfer. It was a payment made by the debtor within 90 days of the date the petition was filed, was a payment to a creditor on account of a preexisting debt at a time when Marta was insolvent, and that payment would enable CCC to receive more than it would have had the payment not been made. If CCC refuses to return the money to the trustee, he will institute an adversary proceeding, pursuant to §547 and FRBP 7001, to recover it as a preferential transfer.

Consider why allowing CCC to keep the $700 payment in the previous example would enable it to receive more than it would have had the payment not been made. If the payment had not been made, CCC would file a proof of claim in the bankruptcy case as an unsecured creditor for the full amount owed, $1,250. When the time comes for a distribution to unsecured creditors, it is very unlikely that they will all receive 100 cents on each dollar owed. Instead they will probably receive some percentage of what they are owed. But if CCC is allowed to keep the $700 payment, it is getting 100 cents on the dollar from the debtor for that portion of the debt, more than it would receive had the payment not been made.

P-H 17-e: When Marta filed her bankruptcy petition last December, she was seriously in arrears in her payments to DCT, holder of the second mortgage on her home. She had failed to make the payments due on September 1, October 1, and November 1, YR-1. However, on October 15, YR-1, she did pay DCT $954 to cover the missed payments that were due July 1 and August 1. This October 15 payment is disclosed in Section 3a of Marta's Statement of Financial Affairs (Document 19 in the Carlson case file). Will the bankruptcy trustee demand that DCT return the $954 payment it received from Marta on October 15 to the trustee as a preferential transfer? It was a payment made by the debtor within 90 days of the date of the petition, to a creditor on account of a preexisting debt, at a time with Marta was insolvent. But the last element is missing. Based on the estimated value of the real property securing the debt owed to DCT, it is going to receive the full amount Marta owes it from the proceeds of the sale of the property. Thus, her October 15 payment does not satisfy the last element of the preferential transfer definition because the payment does not enable the creditor to receive more from the estate than it would have had the payment not been made. But assume Marta made a late mortgage payment on October 15 to CSB. If the trustee succeeds in avoiding CSB's secured position in the home, will the trustee also be able to recoup the October 15 payment to this creditor as preferential?

P-H 17-f: Assume that the October 15 payment is made to DCT as described above, but assume further that the real property securing that DCT debt is not worth as much as what DCT is owed. Will the October 15 payment to DCT now be deemed preferential?

To be preferential, the payment also has to have been made on account of an **antecedent debt**. An antecedent debt is a preexisting one.

EXAMPLE

> If Marta made a car payment to AFI on October 15 but it was an installment payment that was only then due from her, that payment cannot be considered preferential. It was a payment for a current debt, not a preexisting one.

Balance sheet test A test of *insolvency* whereby a debtor's liabilities exceed his assets.

To be preferential, the payment must also have been made while the debtor was **insolvent**. Recall from Chapter Nine, Section B, that under the UFTA, there are two definitions of fraud, the **balance sheet test** (the sum of the debtor's debts is greater than all of the debtor's assets, at a fair valuation) and the **equity test** (the debtor is not paying his debts as they become due). Section 101(32) of the Code defines insolvency using *only* the balance sheet test. Thus, when insolvency is at issue in a bankruptcy case, as in a preference action, valuation of the assets of the debtor as part of the balance sheet test of insolvency is often vigorously contested.

EXAMPLE

> The party arguing that the debtor was insolvent at the time of the transfer will urge the court to value the assets of the debtor at what they would sell for in a distress situation, a fire sale if you will, rather than what they would likely sell for if the debtor was not in distress and had the time to negotiate a fair market price for its assets. One important factor in choosing between such valuation approaches is whether, at the time the transfer was made by the debtor, the

bankruptcy filing or liquidation was imminent. See, e.g., *In re Trans World Airlines*, 134 F.3d 188 (3d Cir. 1998), where the court held that since liquidation was not imminent at the time of the transfer, the debtor's assets were to be valued as if the business was a going concern rather than in distress.

Significantly, §547(f) aids the trustee or other party asserting preferential transfer by creating a rebuttable **presumption of insolvency** during the 90-day preferential transfer period. The effect of that presumption is to effectively shift the burden of coming forward with proof of solvency on the creditor being sued.

Being forced to return a payment received from a debtor within 90 days of the petition being filed may not seem fair to the creditor. After all, the creditor receiving the payment may not even have known the debtor was insolvent when the payment was made. The creditor was legitimately owed the money and did nothing illegal or unethical to collect the payment. But the policy behind the preferential transfer avoidance power given the bankruptcy trustee is that it is not fair to all creditors for one to be "preferred" by receiving a payment or other transfer of the debtor's property so close to the date of filing bankruptcy when the debtor was already insolvent. So every transfer of property by the debtor within the 90-day window is immediately suspect and will be closely examined by the trustee to see if the elements of a preference are present. The trustee's duty is to *all* the creditors of the estate, so he will aggressively pursue each preferential transfer.

When payments from the debtor must be returned to the trustee as preferential, the creditor's only remedy is to file a proof of claim for the amount of the preferential transfer returned and stand in line with other general unsecured creditors hoping that there is eventually a distribution from the estate. Of course, how much the general unsecured creditors ultimately receive will depend on the total assets located by the trustee, and they may ultimately get only pennies on each dollar owed. We will consider the distribution to creditors in Chapter Eighteen, Section B.

A preferential transfer need not involve the payment of money by the debtor. The transfer of *any* property interest of the debtor within 90 days of filing may trigger a claim of preference if the other elements of §547 are satisfied.

EXAMPLE

Assume that Marta transferred her doll collection to her sister a month before the petition was filed but did so in payment of an old debt she owed her sister. The transfer of the doll collection is a transfer of the debtor's property within 90 days of filing to a creditor in payment of an antecedent debt and made when the debtor was insolvent. It is a preferential transfer within the meaning of §547 and the doll collection will have to be returned to the estate. If Evelyn no longer has the doll collection (e.g., it was stolen, sold, or lost) she will have to return its dollar value to the trustee. Evelyn can file a claim with the estate for the debt owed her by Marta.

EXAMPLE

> Assume that to keep the CCC from suing her for the amount she owes, Marta had agreed on September 15, YR-1, to give CCC a security interest in all her personal property. And assume she signed a proper security agreement to create that security interest and that CCC filed a proper financing statement to perfect its secured position in that property. When she files her petition on December 1, YR-1, the trustee will seek to avoid the security interest Marta granted CCC on the grounds that it was preferential. What "property" did the debtor convey to CCC on September 15? The security interest in her personal property is a type of property interest and is subject to avoidance as preferential.

a. The Right of Setoff in a Preferential Transfer

Recall the discussion of the right to setoff under §553 (Section A, supra). We learned that if a bankruptcy debtor has a claim against a creditor, the amount of the claims will offset each other. But now let's examine a setoff event in the context of an apparent preferential transfer.

EXAMPLE

> Assume Marta Carlson borrowed the $1,000 from Howard Kine last year. Then, two months before filing her bankruptcy petition, she does the work for him valued at $500. Go back and look at the elements of a §547 transfer again. They are all arguably present:
>
> - There has been a transfer (Marta's services worth $500);
> - within the 90 days preceding the filing of the petition;
> - to or on behalf of a creditor (Kine);
> - in consideration of a preexisting debt (the services rendered operate to setoff a portion of the preexisting debt owed to Kine); and
> - made while the debtor (Marta) was insolvent (per the balance sheet test of §101(32) her debts exceeded her assets at the time of the transfer).

But on the facts of this Example, and without more, §553 prevents the setoff from being treated as a preferential transfer to Kine even though all the elements appear to be present. The effect of §553 is that the right to setoff can be exercised up until the time the petition is filed without penalty to the creditor.

EXAMPLE

> Do you see why §553 operates in the creditor's favor on these facts? If the trustee could assert a preference against Kine for the $500 owed to Marta, Kine would be in a position of having to pay the $500 to the trustee, then file a claim in the Chapter 7 case for the $1,000 Marta owes him. But as an unsecured creditor, he is unlikely to receive a distribution of anything close to what he is owed or even half of it. And if Marta's case was a no-asset case he would receive nothing on his claim and be out $1,500.

P-H 17-g: What would happen if the trustee does not pursue Marta's claim against Kine for the $500 prior to the final discharge being entered in the Chapter 7 case and Kine never bothers to file a proof of claim for her debt to him raising the offset issue? Marta's debt to Kine will be discharged in the Chapter 7 case. But does that leave him vulnerable to a postdischarge suit by the trustee or Marta on the $500 debt he owes her? This question raises the interesting issue of whether the discharge of an underlying debt owed by the debtor to a creditor also discharges or bars the creditor's right to later raise offset as a defense based on that discharged debt. *In re De Laurentiis Entertainment Group, Inc.*, 963 F.2d 1269 (9th Cir. 1992), held that the creditor's right to assert the setoff survives the discharge of the underlying debt. Read that case and *In re Bare*, 284 B.R. 870 (Bankr. N.D. Ill. 2002), *Durham v. SMI Industries*, 882 F.2d 881 (4th Cir. 1989), and leading setoff cases in your own federal district or circuit to note various factual contexts in which setoff issues arise in a bankruptcy case and to clarify your understanding of how it works.

Section 553 does recognize several narrow factual situations in which the creditor will not be allowed to utilize setoff as a defense to a claim made against him by the trustee based on recovery of a debt owed the estate or on avoidance of a preferential transfer. Section 553(a)(1) disallows use of setoff by a creditor whose claim has been disallowed.

EXAMPLE

If Kine's claim against Marta for the $1,000 is disallowed for any reason, Kine will not be allowed to use it as a defense when the trustee sues to recover the $500 Kine owes Marta for the benefit of the estate.

Section 553(a)(2) provides that if the claim the creditor is using to offset his own obligation to the debtor (which is now property of the estate) was acquired by transfer from another creditor during the 90-day preferential period, setoff is not available and the transfer to the creditor asserting the setoff is itself a preferential transfer that may be avoided by the trustee.

EXAMPLE

Assume Marta borrowed the $1,000 from Rosemary Chin at TTI, not Howard Kine. Marta did the work for Kine, so he owes her $500. Kine and Chin learn that Marta is about to file for Chapter 7 relief. Kine realizes that the trustee will come after him to collect the $500 he owes Marta. Chin realizes that she will see little or nothing on her claim against Marta in the Chapter 7 distribution and that the debt will be discharged. So 30 days before Marta files her petition, Chin sells and assigns her claim against Marta to Kine for $500, which she figures is more than she will realize from the Chapter 7 distribution. Kine is happy to get the claim against Marta from Chin because he can now use it to set off what he owes Marta when the trustee comes calling. And if he gets any distribution from the estate based on the $500 difference between what he owes Marta and what she now owes him as the holder of the $1,000 debt, he comes out ahead on the deal.

Section 553(a)(2) disallows the use of the setoff attempted in the previous example. The transfer of the claim from Chin to Kine will be deemed preferential to Chin as a creditor of the estate because it allows her to receive more on her claim against the estate than she would have received had she not made the transfer during the preferential period. And the estate is prejudiced because its claim against Kine, recoverable in full absent the transfer, is set off against the debt owed by Marta. So the court will avoid the transfer from Chin to Kine as preferential under §§547 and 553(a)(2). The result will be that the trustee recovers the $500 from Kine owed to the estate and Chin gets a small distribution from the estate based on her claim, likely well under 50 percent of what she is owed.

Section 553(a)(3) disallows use of setoff as a defense to a preference action if the debt due from the creditor was incurred during the preferential period, while the debtor was insolvent, and *for the purpose* of obtaining a right of setoff against a debt owed to the creditor.

EXAMPLE

> Assume that Marta owes Kine the $1,000 loaned to her last year when she decides to file her Chapter 7. Marta knows that if she just pays Kine $500 on the preexisting debt while she is insolvent and within the preferential period, the trustee will seek to recover it from Kine under §547. So instead they agree that Marta will perform the work for Kine worth $500 and that she will then assert it as an offset against his claim against her in the upcoming Chapter 7.

Section 553(a)(3) will not permit this scheme because the services were rendered to Kine by Marta *for the purpose* of creating the setoff. Effectively, what has happened is that Marta has knowingly and intentionally repaid $500 of the preexisting debt to Kine during the preference period while she was insolvent. The trustee may recover the value of Marta's services from Kine as a preferential transfer and he can file his claim for the full $1,000 she owes him. Section 553(a)(3) reminds us that the protection of setoffs provided in §553 is limited to **bona fide** mutual debts.

P-H 17-h: Go back and look at the first example in this subsection and compare it with the preceding example. What is the only difference in the factual scenarios in those two examples, one of which suggests an offset can be available notwithstanding an apparent preferential transfer and the other of which demonstrates that an offset may be disallowed as a preferential transfer? If you recognize the answer to that question, you should understand the policy behind §553's protection of genuine setoffs and the limits of that policy. What do the cases cited in P-H 17-g have to say about the *policy* behind the favorable treatment accorded genuine setoffs in §553? If you don't recognize the policy explanations there, read *In re Davidovich*, 901 F.2d 1533 (10th Cir. 1990); *In re United Sciences of America, Inc.*, 893 F.2d 279 (5th Cir. 1990); or *In re Elcona Homes Corp.*, 863 F.2d 483 (7th Cir. 1988). Then you should be able to explain how bona fide mutual debts are considered analogous to a consensual security interest and thus entitled to more favorable treatment via setoff.

Finally, §553(b) prohibits use of a debt arising during the preference period to improve the creditor's position beyond what it would have been had the debt been incurred outside the preference period.

EXAMPLE

> Assume that instead of organizing Kine's personal services and preparing his tax return, Marta paints him a picture two months before filing her Chapter 7 petition and the value of that service is deemed to be $500. If the trustee can show that the picture is worth $500 only because Marta has gained some notoriety during the preferential period and that had she painted the picture for Kine

> more than 90 days before the petition was filed (and pre-notoriety) it would have been worth only $100, the trustee may recover the $400 difference in the preference period value ($500) and the prepreference period value ($100) as a preferential transfer.

This **improvement of position exception** to the favorable treatment accorded setoffs in §553 reflects another policy-driven limitation to that treatment.

b. Transfers to Insiders

Insider A person in close relationship with a debtor such that he may be assumed to have superior access to information and be subject to special treatment.

In addition to the standard 90-day preferential transfer provision, §547 allows the bankruptcy trustee to avoid preferential transfers to **insiders** of the debtor made within one year preceding the date the petition was filed. Section 101(31) contains an extensive definition of who an insider is. Review that definition and then work through P-H 17-i.

> **P-H 17-i:**   Assume that Marta transfers her doll collection to her sister, Evelyn, six months before the bankruptcy petition is filed in payment of an old debt. The transfer occurred more than 90 days prior to the filing of the petition, but can the trustee avoid the transfer of the doll collection to Evelyn on the basis that she was an insider as to the debtor? What if the debtor is a partnership and the questioned transfer was made to a partner six months before the partnership files its bankruptcy case? To a receptionist who works for the partnership as an employee only? To the wife of a partner? What if the debtor is a corporation and the transfer was to a shareholder? An officer? A director? To an attorney who does legal work for the corporation?

Contemporaneous exchange for equivalent value A transaction supported by adequate present consideration.

c. Exceptions to the Trustee's Right to Avoid Preferential Transfers

Section 547(c) recognizes important exceptions to the trustee's right to avoid and recover preferential transfers. Transfers that would otherwise be preferential are not if the transfer

Ordinary course of business or financial affairs In general, following the typical, usual practices engaged in by a business.

- Was intended as and in fact was a contemporaneous exchange for *equivalent value* or
- Was in payment of a debt incurred in the ordinary course of business or financial affairs of the debtor and transferee and the transfer itself was either made in the *ordinary course of business or financial affairs* of the debtor and transferee or was made according to *ordinary business terms*.

The next two examples illustrate the **equivalent value exception.**

EXAMPLE

> Assume that Marta Carlson had ordered a new car on June 1, YR-1, from AAA Chevrolet. The purchase price was $15,000 and was to be paid on delivery. The car is delivered on October 1, YR-1, and Marta pays AAA cash for it. She is insolvent at the time she does so. When she files her bankruptcy petition on December 1, YR-1, the trustee will look at the October 1 payment and see a transfer of the debtor's property made within the 90-day preference window to a creditor in payment of a preexisting debt made at a time when the debtor was

insolvent, all of which enables the creditor to receive more than it would have had the payment not been made. Looks like a preferential payment alright. But if the car purchased was in fact worth $15,000, it is not preferential because the transfer of cash was in exchange for something of "equivalent value," the $15,000 car, which is now property of the estate. So this transfer would not be preferential under the Code and the trustee could not set it aside.

EXAMPLE

Assume that the car Marta purchases from AAA for $15,000 is actually worth only $12,000. That's not equivalent value. On those facts, the trustee would likely succeed in his preference claim against AAA to recover the full $15,000 for the estate. Could AAA get the car back under those circumstances? Not unless it retained a perfected security interest in it, which it would not do if it received cash in full payment. That car is property of the estate. File your proof of claim, AAA, and get in line with the other unsecured creditors.

The next three examples illustrate the **ordinary course of business exception**.

EXAMPLE

Assume that the bankruptcy debtor is in the grocery business. Sixty days before filing his bankruptcy petition the debtor orders inventory for his store, which is delivered five days later, together with an invoice stating that payment is due within ten days of receipt of the goods. The debtor pays the invoice from his supplier within the ten days even though he is insolvent at the time. But then he files bankruptcy. That payment to the supplier is immediately suspect because it was made within the 90-day preferential window. But there is nothing extraordinary about the payment because the debtor only paid what was owed and he paid it on time. The debt was created in the ordinary course of the debtor's business as well as the supplier's business and it was paid (the transfer) in the ordinary course of both the debtor's business as well as the supplier's business. This transfer is probably not preferential and the supplier can keep the money.

It has long been understood that whether a debt is created or a transfer made in the ordinary course of the debtor's and transferee's business is a subjective inquiry focusing on what is "ordinary" for those particular parties. See, e.g., *In re Fred Hawes Organization, Inc.*, 957 F.2d 239 (6th Cir 1992).

EXAMPLE

Now assume that our bankruptcy debtor who is in the grocery business pays the invoice 12 days after the goods are delivered, two days late under the terms of the invoice. That payment is now likely to be found preferential and the trustee will recover it for the estate. Do you see why? Because payments made late will not be considered "ordinary" unless the debtor and transferee have an established course of dealing whereby past payments have been made late and accepted by the transferee without complaint. If that course of dealing exists, then the late payment maybe in the ordinary course of business as between the debtor and transferee.

Even the slightest deviation from normal business behavior or practice of a debtor and transferee may render a payment extraordinary and thus unqualified for the ordinary course of dealing exception to the preferential transfer statute.

EXAMPLE

> Assume that our bankruptcy debtor who is in the grocery business pays the invoice on time, within ten days. However, the supplier has heard rumors that the debtor may be in financial trouble and so he demands payment of this invoice by cashier's check. Previously the supplier has always allowed payment by personal check. Even if the debtor makes the payment on time, if he does so by cashier's check, that's not the usual practice and the transfer will be deemed preferential and recoverable by the trustee when the debtor files his petition.

The following example illustrates the ordinary business terms exception. Unlike the ordinary course of business exception, the ordinary business terms exception is understood to involve an objective inquiry focusing not on ordinary business terms between the debtor and the transferee, but on ordinary business terms in the relevant business or industry. See, e.g., *In re Nowlen*, 452 B.R. 619, 621-22 (Bkrtcy. E.D. Mich. 2011).

EXAMPLE

> Assume that our bankruptcy debtor who is in the grocery business cannot pay the invoice within the 10 days of delivery when it is due though he has always paid this supplier on time in the past. This time debtor calls the supplier and asks for five additional days to pay even though he knows he will be late in doing so. Debtor makes the payment on the fifteenth day after delivery, paying by check as he always has, then files bankruptcy. Must the transferee supplier disgorge the payment to the trustee as preferential? This payment was not in the ordinary course of business of the debtor and supplier since they had no course of dealing allowing debtor to pay late. But supplier may be able to successfully defend against the preference action if he can show that payment by check is a standard method of payment in the industry and that there is an industry custom of allowing customer's such as debtor to occasionally make a payment slightly late. By making such argument, supplier transferee is arguing that the payment he received from debtor was according to ordinary business terms in the industry.

P-H 17-j: Prior to BAPCPA in 2005 a transferee defending against a preferential transfer allegation on the basis of the ordinary course of business defense was required to establish both the ordinary course of business and the ordinary business terms prongs of §547(c)(2). BAPCPA changed the "and" to "or," separating those concepts in §547(c)(2)(A) and (B) and thus created two different defenses, one subjective and one objective. Note that *In re Fred Hawes*, supra, was decided prior to BAPCPA while *In re Nolen*, supra, was decided afterwards. If you are not aware of the change made in this statute by BAPCPA trying to read both decisions will likely confuse you. This illustrates how essential it is that legal professionals stay abreast of changes in areas of the law in which they work. A good Website to help you keep abreast of changes in the laws regarding preferential transfers is the Bankruptcy Preference Digest at www.burbageweddell.com/blog. Look at that site and see if you recognize a discussion there of one of the preference topics we have considered in this section.

Section 547 contains a few other miscellaneous exceptions. To the extent a transfer during the preference period was for a **domestic support obligation** (e.g., child support or alimony) it is not considered preferential. In cases involving consumer debtors, transfers having an aggregate value of less than $600 are not preferential and the same is true for transfers by business debtors having an aggregate value of less than $5,000.

5. Avoidance of Postpetition Transfers

Section 549 grants the trustee the power to avoid unauthorized transfers of the debtor's property made after commencement of the case. An exception is the postpetition transfer of real property to a good faith purchaser without knowledge of the filing who pays a fair equivalent value, unless a copy of the petition or notice of the bankruptcy filing was previously filed or recorded where the deed of transfer would be recorded. The trustee's action under §549 must be commenced within two years after the date of the transfer or before the case is closed or dismissed, whichever is earlier.

6. Limitations on the Trustee's Right to Bring an Avoidance Action

Section 546(a) establishes a time limitation on the right to bring an avoidance action under any of the provisions we have just considered other than §549. Under all the other avoidance sections the suit it must be commenced within two years from the order of relief or one year from the date a trustee is first appointed, whichever is later. And, in any event, it must be filed before the case is closed which could occur earlier than either of those two events.

Section 546(b) recognizes the right of a creditor to perfect its security interest in property of the estate postpetition so long as, under applicable law (usually the law of the state where the property is located), the creditor's interest relates back to a date prior to the commencement of the case.

EXAMPLE

Under Article 9 of the Uniform Commercial Code, adopted in all 50 states, a lender who provides a debtor with a loan to purchase personal property and the loan is in fact used for that purpose has a **purchase money security interest** (**PMSI**) in the property purchased by the debtor. That PMSI can be perfected by the creditor's filing a **financing statement** (see Illustration 5-e) with the appropriate state agency. In most states, the creditor has ten days from the date the debtor takes possession of the property to file the financing statement and the creditor will then be deemed to have been perfected in the property, not on the date the financing statement is filed, but on the date the money was loaned. In other words, the interest of the creditor in the property relates back to the date of the transaction and if perfected within the time allowed will be deemed under state law to be superior to any intervening creditor's interest in the property. Section 546(b) grants that priority to the creditor even against a bankruptcy trustee acting under the authority of a bankruptcy case filed by the debtor between the time the money was loaned and the time the creditor perfected its PMSI.

Section 546(c) recognizes the superiority of the rights of a seller of goods to **reclaim** such goods from possession of a debtor/buyer who has taken possession of the goods within 45 days of the commencement of the case and at a time when the debtor was insolvent (compare the right of reclamation outside of bankruptcy given a seller for buyer's insolvency under UCC §2-702). To exercise this reclamation right in the goods, the seller must give the trustee a written demand for reclamation of the goods within 20 days following commencement of the case.

F. ▶ Hiring Professional Persons to Assist the Trustee

Section 327 of the Code and FRBP 2014 authorize the bankruptcy trustee to hire **professional persons** such as attorneys, accountants, appraisers, auctioneers, real estate agents, or other professionals to assist the trustee with administering the estate.

EXAMPLE

> If the trustee is going to initiate an adversary proceeding, he will hire an attorney to represent him in that litigation. When the time comes to liquidate property of the estate the trustee may conduct a public auction and need to retain the services of an auctioneer for that purpose. If the trustee encounters complicated financial dealings by the debtor or other party that he lacks the sophistication to understand, he may need an accountant or other financial professional to assist him. If he has a question regarding the value of realty, he may need an appraiser to tell him the likely value and, later, a real estate agent to help sell it.

Professionals can only be hired with the approval of the bankruptcy court. So the trustee will file a motion with the court for permission to do so and obtain a court order approving the hiring.

EXAMPLE

> In the Marta Carlson case, the bankruptcy trustee has decided that her home needs to be appraised to determine its potential value to the estate. He has filed a motion for permission to hire a real estate appraiser, which is shown in Document 32 in the Carlson case file. The order granting that permission is shown in Document 33.

FRBP 6003 provides that, absent a showing of **immediate and irreparable harm**, the court cannot grant an application for permission to hire a professional person during the first 21 days following the filing of the petition.

CONCLUSION

Once the trustee has reviewed creditor claims in an asset case and gathered property of the estate, it is time to liquidate that property and complete the administration of the Chapter 7 case. Priority of distribution of the proceeds of estate property must be determined. There may be challenges to the debtor's right to discharge certain debts or to receive any discharge at all. In Chapter Eighteen we will consider all this as we conclude our study of Chapter 7.

CHAPTER SUMMARY

In an asset case, creditors generally must file a proof of claim by the claims bar date in order to participate in any distribution from the estate. The bankruptcy trustee reviews submitted claims and may object to their allowance, raising a contested matter. Generally, unsecured and undersecured creditors do not receive postpetition interest on their claims. Fully secured creditors do receive postpetition interest on their claims, up to the value of the collateral. Property of the bankruptcy estate includes all property in which the debtor has a legal or equitable interest at the time the case is commenced.

The bankruptcy trustee is empowered to compel the turnover of property of the estate by the debtor or third persons, including legal custodians of that property. The trustee is also empowered to set aside certain prepetition transfers of the debtor's property. Using the strong-arm clause of the Code, the trustee, as a supercreditor, can defeat the claim of any unsecured creditor to the property of the debtor or the claim of any secured creditor whose claim to the debtor's property was not perfected prior to the filing of the petition. The trustee may avoid some prepetition statutory and equitable liens in the debtor's property. He can avoid fraudulent transfers of the debtors property made two years prior to the petition's filing. And he can avoid preferential transfers of the debtor's property made within 90 days preceding the filing of the petition to noninsiders and within one year to insiders. Exceptions to preferential transfer claims are recognized for transfers for equivalent value and transfers in the ordinary course of business or financial affairs of the debtor and the recipient. The right to setoff is recognized in bankruptcy and a setoff claim on behalf of the debtor arising within 90 days preceding the filing of the petition will generally not be treated as a preferential transfer to the creditor. Professionals may be hired to assist the bankruptcy trustee in the administration of the case but only with prior court approval.

REVIEW QUESTIONS

1. Why does a creditor in a no-asset case not need to file a proof of claim? What is the risk to an unsecured creditor of not filing a proof of claim in an asset case? What is the risk to an undersecured creditor? What is the risk to a fully secured creditor?
2. Explain the procedure the trustee must follow in objecting to a creditor's claim, including the time frame for making the objection.
3. Under what circumstances might a creditor be entitled to recover postpetition interest on its claim?
4. What do we mean by property in which the debtor holds a legal or equitable interest for purposes of determining what is or is not property of the estate? Give examples.
5. Describe the turnover powers of the bankruptcy trustee. Who might be a custodian of the debtor's property?

6. What is the strong-arm clause of the Code? What do we mean when we say that the bankruptcy trustee is a supercreditor of the debtor? What does that mean for unsecured claims to the debtor's property? Secured claims not properly perfected prepetition?

7. What are the four elements of a preferential transfer? How is insolvency determined for purposes of a preferential transfer? Who will be considered an insider for purposes of a preferential transfer claim and what difference does it make?

8. Explain the exchange for reasonably equivalent value in connection with fraudulent transfers. What is fair market value?

9. Explain the right to setoff. Why does having a right of setoff matter to a creditor targeted in a preferential transfer action?

10. Give examples of various kinds of professional persons that a trustee might request permission to hire to assist in the administration of a case, and explain why the trustee might need the assistance of each professional mentioned.

WORDS AND PHRASES TO REMEMBER

avoidance powers
balance sheet test
bifurcated claim
claims bar date
contemporaneous exchange
   for equivalent value
core or noncore proceeding
custodian
deemed allowed
distribution of the estate
domestic support obligation
entity for whose benefit the transfer
   was made
equitable estoppel
equity test of insolvency
equivalent value exception
fair market value
financing statement
fully secured claim
improvement of position exception
   to setoff
immediate and irreparable harm
initial transferee
insider
insolvent
laches

legal or equitable interest
legalized fiction
motion
objection to claim
on account of an antecedent debt
ordinary business terms exception
ordinary course of business exception
oversecured
partially secured claim
postpetition interest
preferential transfer
presumption of insolvency
professional persons
proof of claim
promissory estoppel
property of the estate
purchase money security interest
   (PMSI)
reasonably equivalent value
reclaim
stripped down claim
strong-arm clause
undersecured claim
waiver
written down claim

TO LEARN MORE: A number of TLM activities to accompany this chapter are accessible on the student disc accompanying the text and at the Author Updates link to the text Web site at http://www.aspenparalegaled.com/books/parsons_abcdebt/default.asp.

Chapter Eighteen

The Chapter 7 Case: Liquidation, Distribution, Reaffirmation or Redemption, and Final Discharge

If the Devil danced in empty pockets, he'd have a ball in mine.

—Joe Diffie

A. Liquidating Property of the Estate

In a Chapter 7 asset case, the trustee will **liquidate** nonexempt property of the estate and distribute the proceeds in an order of priority we consider in Section B, below. First, we consider how the trustee liquidates the property of the estate. Of course, if the trustee determines the filing to be a **no-asset case** and files a **no-asset report**, that means there is no nonexempt property to liquidate and the case will be closed quickly.

1. Abandonment of Property of the Estate

If a timely objection to the debtor's claimed Schedule C exemptions is not made (see Chapter Seventeen, Section B), that property is **deemed abandoned** by the trustee and the estate has no further interest in it.

Pursuant to §554 and FRBP 6007, the trustee can abandon any other property of the estate that is

- Of inconsequential value to the estate or
- Burdensome to the estate.

a. Abandonment of Secured Property

The most common example of abandonment arises in connection with property pledged as security for debt. If the security interest is **perfected** and the trustee cannot **avoid** it as considered in the last chapter, the **secured claim** will be **allowed** under §502. And if there is no **equity** for the estate in the pledged

441

property (i.e., the amount of the allowed claim equals or exceeds the value of the collateral), that property is of no value to the estate and will be abandoned to the creditor. If the value of the collateral abandoned to the creditor is equal to the full amount of the allowed claim, the claim of the creditor is fully satisfied by that abandonment. On the other hand, if the value of the abandoned collateral is insufficient to satisfy the full amount of the allowed claim (i.e., the creditor is **undersecured** or **partially secured**), the creditor's claim is **bifurcated** pursuant to §506(a)(1), as was discussed in Chapter Seventeen, Section A. The trustee will abandon the collateral to the undersecured creditor in full satisfaction of the secured portion of the creditor's bifurcated claim. But the creditor still has a **general unsecured claim** for the balance owed in excess of the value of the collateral.

If there is equity for the estate in the pledged property (i.e., the creditor is **oversecured**; the value of the property exceeds the amount owed), the trustee will usually *not* abandon the property to the creditor. Instead, the trustee will sell the property himself, pay the creditor the full amount of his allowed secured claim from the proceeds (which may include postpetition interest and fees per §506(b) as we saw in Chapter Seventeen, Section A), and will then include the excess proceeds of the sale in the property of the estate available to other creditors.

b. Abandonment of Other Property of the Estate

Any property of the estate may be abandoned by the trustee whether it is pledged as collateral for a security interest or not, if the trustee concludes that it is burdensome to the estate.

EXAMPLE

Assume the property of the estate includes a claim the debtor has made against a local clothes cleaning business alleging that the cleaner lost a shirt worth $20. The cleaner denies liability on the claim and refuses to settle. The trustee may conclude that it will cost the estate more to litigate that small claim than it is worth and abandon the claim as burdensome to the estate.

c. Procedure for Abandonment

Abandonment The trustee's releasing of any claim by the estate to property deemed burdensome or of inconsequential value to the estate per §544 of the Code.

Section 554 **abandonment** is governed by the Code's "after notice and a hearing" procedure (discussed in Chapter Thirteen, Section G, and see Illustration 13-c), which means the trustee must give notice to all parties in interest of his intent to abandon and a hearing is conducted only if an objection is made within 14 days following notice. A notice of intent to abandon property filed by the trustee in Marta Carlson's case is seen in Document 36 in the Carlson case file.

Recall that in Chapter Fifteen, Section B, we learned that an individual Chapter 7 debtor must file a **statement of intent** with regard to property pledged as collateral, indicating whether he will **surrender** that property to the secured creditor or seek to retain it. If the debtor does indicate an intent to surrender pledged property, the secured creditor must still await the trustee's decision as to whether to abandon that property as having no benefit to the estate or to assert an interest in it for the benefit of the estate as by avoiding the creditor's security interest or lien as we considered in Chapter Seventeen, Section E, or by contending that there is **equity** in the property for the estate (i.e., it is worth more than the amount owed the creditor). And even if the trustee does decide to abandon, the secured creditor must take appropriate action to have the automatic stay of §362 lifted per the procedures discussed in Chapter Sixteen, Section E.

As a practical matter, the trustee will make the decision as to whether to abandon pledged property or challenge the lien at or shortly after the **first meeting of creditors**. By then the individual Chapter 7 debtor will have filed his statement of intent with regard to the property so his intent to surrender the property or not will be known to all parties. Some secured creditors will await the decision of the debtor and trustee regarding surrender and abandonment before filing a motion to lift stay while others will file a motion to lift stay as soon as the petition is filed and they receive notice of the case.

2. The Sale of Property Free and Clear of Liens

When a creditor has a perfected security interest in some property of the estate but there is still **equity** (dollar value of the property in excess of the claim that it secures) for the estate in that property (i.e., the creditor is oversecured), the trustee may seek permission from the court to sell the property **free and clear of liens**, pursuant to §363(f) and FRBP 6004(c). The property is sold and the security interest then attaches to the proceeds of sale up to the amount of the secured claim. Permission for a sale free and clear of liens is obtained by filing a motion subject to the "after notice and a hearing" procedure.

EXAMPLE

> Recall from the Assignment Memorandum in Appendix A that Marta Carlson has two mortgages on her home, one in favor of Capitol Savings Bank (CSB) with a balance of $142,500 and one in favor of Dreams Come True Finance Company (DCT) with a balance of $37,500. In her Schedule C (Document 9 in the Carlson case file) Marta has claimed her full §522(d)(1) homestead exemption of $22,975 in the home. No objection has been filed to these secured claims or to Marta's claimed exemption amount. The home has appraised for $255,000 and the trustee has filed a motion for permission to sell the home free and clear of liens (Document 37 in the Carlson case file). If permission is granted by the court and the sale brings the full $255,000, the proceeds will be distributed as follows: the realtor's 6 percent fee ($15,300) as an administrative expense; $142,500 to pay off CSB; $37,500 to pay off DCT; $22,975 to Marta for her exemption; and the balance of $36,725 will go to the estate. But by order of the court, that sale will terminate the liens of CSB and DCT in the property, as well as Marta's exemption in it. It is a sale free and clear of liens.

Credit-bidding (or **bidding-in**) The practice of a creditor secured in property foreclosed on or repossessed bidding the amount owed at the foreclosure/repossession sale and receiving credit for the amount owed against the sales price.

Section 363(k) preserves the right of a creditor secured in the property to be sold to bid on the property at the sale and in doing so to receive credit against the purchase price for the amount of its unpaid claim, a practice known as **credit-bidding** (or **bidding in**).

EXAMPLE

> If Marta's trustee receives permission to sell her home free and clear of liens, either or both of the secured creditors have the right under §363(k) to bid at the sale. If CSB chose to credit-bid at the sale and the amount of its winning bid was $151,050 (an amount equal to the $142,500 balance owed to it, plus $8,550 representing the 6% realtor's fee), CSB would only have to pay cash in the amount of $8,550 because the amount CSB is owed is credited against the bid amount.

The Code gives a secured creditor this right as a means of assuring that the property is not sold at a price less than what is owed to the creditor. After all, the sale is going to extinguish the creditor's security interest in the property.

EXAMPLE

If a third party appears at the sale and bids in at the $255,000 appraised value, then neither CSB nor DCT are likely to bid—the sale will bring enough to satisfy both their claims. But what if the high bid by a third party at the sale is only $125,000? If that bid is accepted, CSB is going to receive only a portion of what it is owed and DCT, whose lien on the property is junior to CSB's, will get nothing. So both CSB and DCT will likely be ready to credit-bid as necessary to protect their respective interests.

P-H 18-a: What would DCT have to do to protect itself if this scenario played out? A third party bids $125,000 for the property. CSB then enters a credit-bid in the amount of $151,050 to protect its interest in the property. But that bid by CSB will not result in DCT's receiving anything and its second mortgage will be wiped out by the sale. If it wants to protect itself, then it will need to bid an amount in excess of CSB's bid, and it will only receive credit against the amount owed for the balance owed to it (i.e., it will actually have to pay enough to satisfy CSB's senior claim plus the realtor's fee). What practical considerations would go into DCT's decision to do this in order to acquire the property?

P-H 18-a and the two Examples preceding it are offered to show how credit-bidding works but present unlikely scenarios in the real world. A trustee will not seek to sell property unless the trustee is confident that there is equity in the property for the estate over and above all administrative expenses of sale, all perfected liens on the property, and any exemption amount due the debtor. To assure that result, the trustee's auction sale will likely not be an **absolute sale** (high bid takes title regardless of amount) but will instead be conducted as a **reserve sale** (high bid will not be accepted unless it meets a minimum amount decided by the trustee).

P-H 18-b: When a creditor purchases property of the estate using a credit bid as authorized under §363(k), that bid extinguishes the creditor's claim in the bankruptcy case. But does it also extinguish the underlying debt that the creditor might pursue against persons other than the debtor in bankruptcy, for example, guarantors of the debt? Compare *In re Five Boroughs Mortg. Co., Inc.*, 176 B.R. 708, 712 (Bankr. E.D. N.Y. 1995) (a bankruptcy court can determine a claim in the case but not the underlying debt) with *In re Spillman Development Group, Ltd.*, 710F.3d 299, (5th Cir. 2013) (credit bid in bankruptcy case extinguished both the creditor's claim and the underlying debt, freeing guarantors).

3. The Sale of Other Property of the Estate

Section 363(b)(1) and FRBP 6004(a) permit the trustee to notice his intent to sell other property of the estate "after notice and a hearing." No hearing will be conducted unless an objection is filed not less than five days before the date of the proposed sale per FRBP 6004(b). If an objection is filed, it becomes a contested matter and a hearing will be conducted.

The sale of property of the estate can be accomplished by **public** or **private sale**. FRBP 2002(c) requires that the notice of a proposed sale, use, or lease of property include:

- The time and place of a public sale;
- The terms and conditions of a private sale; and
- The time fixed for filing objections.

A public sale is by **auction**, properly advertised and usually conducted by an auctioneer retained as a professional, pursuant to §327 and FRBP 2014. If the order authorizing the hiring of the professional person did not specifically approve the manner of his compensation, the trustee must obtain court approval for that compensation before paying the professional from the assets of the estate.

P-H 18-c: Look at the motion for permission to hire real estate appraiser filed by the trustee in Marta Carlson's case (Document 32 in the Carlson case file) and the order approving that hiring (Document 33 in the Carlson case file). Did the trustee properly obtain permission in that motion and order to compensate the appraiser from estate funds?

Section 363 and other sections of the Code deal with other ways the bankruptcy trustee may need to utilize property of the estate, some of which include:

- Operating an ongoing business of the debtor;
- Leasing estate property; or
- Pledging property of the estate as collateral to raise cash or obtain credit.

Though these issues can arise in a Chapter 7 case, they rarely do, and we will examine them later in connection with our study of the Chapter 11 case where they arise routinely.

P-H 18-d: Bankruptcy trustees are increasingly using the Internet to liquidate property of the estate. Go to www.bankruptcysales.com/index.cfm and note the kinds of property being offered for sale by trustees around the country. See if you can find a property listing for a case pending in your federal district.

---

4. Continuing Operation of a Business Debtor as Part of the Liquidation

When an ongoing business files for Chapter 7 liquidation, the bankruptcy trustee may determine that it is in the best interest of the creditors to continue operating the business for a certain period of time postpetition in order to maximize the value of the property of the estate and the ultimate payout to creditors. This is unusual but §721 of the Code authorizes the trustee to seek court permission to operate the business postpetition for this purpose.

When a liquidating business debtor does continue to operate postpetition under Chapter 7, there are a number of operational motions that will need to be made to deal with matters such as using property of the estate postpetition, which could put that property at risk of deterioration or loss; using property—such as cash—postpetition that has been pledged as collateral to one or more creditors who thus have rights in it; obtaining postpetition financing, thus increasing the total indebtedness of the business; and so on. These operational concerns are similar to those that routinely arise in a Chapter 11 reorganization in which the business debtor is not liquidating but continuing to operate under the postpetition protection of the Code. We will not consider these operational concerns until we look at Chapter 11 in detail, but for an idea of the types of operational motions routinely filed in a Chapter 11 and in connection with the postpetition operation of a business debtor liquidating under Chapter 7, see the discussion of first day orders in Chapter Twenty-Three, Section D, and of operational motions in Chapter Twenty-Four, Section D.

B. Distribution of the Estate to Creditors and the Order of Priority

Once the bankruptcy trustee has liquidated the other property of the estate, including the settlement of allowed secured claims as discussed in the last section, the proceeds will be distributed to pay **administrative expenses** and **claims of creditors** in a certain order of priority. Administrative expenses are defined in §503(b) and include:

Administrative expenses Postpetition expenses incurred in preserving the property of the estate and in administering the estate by the trustee or debtor in possession.

- The trustee's fee;
- Fees of professionals hired by the trustee;
- Certain taxes incurred by the estate;
- "Actual and necessary" costs and expenses of preserving the estate, which can include wages, salaries, and commissions incurred after the commencement of the case; and
- "Actual and necessary" expenses incurred by creditors who file an involuntary petition in the case or who, with court permission, recover property for the estate transferred or concealed by the debtor.

Section 507 establishes an order of priority for various administrative expenses and other claims. Section 726 then mandates the particular order in which distributions on claims *not* secured by property of the estate are to be made by the Chapter 7 trustee. Section 507 **priority claims** must be paid first, then the claims of general unsecured creditors, and then certain miscellaneous claims. Illustration 18-a summarizes the order of distribution mandated by the Code.

Priority claim An unsecured claim entitled to a certain order of preferment and payment under §507.

Each class of claims listed in Illustration 18-a is entitled to be paid in full before the next class in priority receives anything.

EXAMPLE

If all the available assets are exhausted in paying §507 priority claims, general unsecured creditors will receive nothing. If all available assets are exhausted paying priority and general unsecured claims that were timely filed, general unsecured claims not timely filed will receive nothing.

Illustration 18-a: ORDER OF DISTRIBUTION FOR ADMINISTRATIVE EXPENSES AND CREDITOR CLAIMS

A.   Secured claims

   1)   Allowed fully secured or oversecured claims are satisfied entirely out of the secured property up to its value, per §§506(a) and (b)
   2)   Allowed partially secured (undersecured) claims are satisfied out of the secured property up to the value of the secured property and the deficiency is treated as a general unsecured claim, per §506(a)(1)

B.   Section 507 priority claims

   1)   The bankruptcy trustee's fee and expenses attributable to payment of domestic support obligations of the debtor, per §507(a)(1)(C)
   2)   Domestic support obligations of the debtor, per §507(a)(1)(A)
   3)   Administrative expenses authorized by §503(b), per §507(a)(2)
   4)   Allowed §502(f) unsecured claims arising in an involuntary case between the time the petition is filed and the time the trustee is appointed (called the **gap period**), per §507(a)(3)
   5)   Claims for employee's wages, salaries, or commissions and some benefits earned within 180 days prior to the filing of the petition not to exceed $10,000 per claim, per §507(a)(4)
   6)   Claims for unpaid contributions to any employee benefit plan arising from services rendered within 180 days prior to filing of the petition not to exceed $10,000 per claim, per §507(a)(5)
   7)   Certain farmer and fishermen claims up to $10,000 each, per §507(a)(6)
   8)   Prepetition deposits of money for the lease or purchase of real property or consumer services up to $2,225 per claimant, per §507(a)(7)
   9)   Various tax claims including income and property taxes assessed at varying times before the petition was filed, per §507(a)(8)
   10) Certain claims arising out of federal depository insurance, per §507(a)(9)
   11) Personal injury or wrongful death claims arising out of DUI, per §507(a)(10)

C.   General (i.e., nonpriority) unsecured claims, per §726, including deficiency claims of partially secured creditors whose collateral was insufficient to cover the entire debt per §506(a)(1)

   1)   General unsecured claims timely filed, per §726(a)(2)
   2)   General unsecured claims untimely filed, per §726(a)(3)

D.   Claims for fines, penalties, forfeiture, or punitive damages other than compensation for actual pecuniary loss, per §726(a)(4)
E.   Interest at the legal rate on priority and general unsecured claims, per §726(a)(5)
F.   Remaining surplus, if any, returned to debtor, per §726(a)(6)

Within a particular priority classification, the distribution will be *pro rata*.

EXAMPLE

> Assume the trustee has $10,000 available to distribute to general unsecured claimants. But there is a total of $100,000 owed to all the creditors in that classification. The distribution will be *pro rata*, with each unsecured creditor receiving ten cents on the dollar for its claim regardless of whether their claim was larger or smaller than others in the same class.

P-H 18-e: Assume the following expenses and claims are present in an estate and that the trustee has funds to pay most but not all of them: unpaid federal income taxes for the past two tax years; unpaid unsecured bills from the debtor's suppliers; unpaid child support; unpaid Social Security withholdings on the debtor's employees; an unpaid student loan; and travel expenses of the bankruptcy trustee. Arrange the list in the order of priority mandated by §726.

A general unsecured debt that is not dischargeable (see discussion in Section C) still participates in the distribution under §726.

EXAMPLE

> The educational loans that Marta Carlson owes to Columbiana Federal Savings & Loan, in the amount of $5,000, and Capitol City Bank (CCB), in the amount of $10,000, are unsecured nonpriority but non-dischargeable debts. Even though Marta cannot discharge those debts and will remain liable for them, they will participate with other general unsecured creditors in any distribution to that class of creditors.

P-H 18-f: Assume the total administrative expenses for Marta Carlson's estate, excluding the realtor's fee associated with selling the residence on Spruce Street, and other §507 priority claims total $3,000. All of Marta's claimed exemptions are allowed. The residence is sold free and clear of liens, netting the estate $38,075. The doll collection is purchased from the estate for $4,000 after expenses of sale. The Toyota Camry is sold, netting the estate $2,150 after the claim of AFI in the amount of $1,750 secured by the vehicle is satisfied and Marta's $4,600 exemption in the car is paid. The Shears washer and dryer are not sold but instead are retained by Marta after she agrees to remain liable for that debt postdischarge (discussed in Section F). Finally, assume that the trustee's objection to the claim of Pine Ridge Nursing Home is upheld so that creditor receives nothing. All other unsecured claims are allowed. How much cash will the estate have available to distribute to general unsecured creditors? Based on the total amount of general unsecured debt owed on the allowed unsecured claims, what percentage of the total unsecured debt will be paid?

Subordination The treatment of a claim in a less favored way than others either by consent of the creditor or by court order where the creditor has either filed a claim after the **claims bar date** or has acted dishonestly.

Section 510 provides for the **subordination** of a claim to others of equal rank under certain circumstances. Section 510(a) provides that a pre-petition **subordination agreement** will be enforced in bankruptcy if it is otherwise valid under non-bankruptcy law. A subordination agreement is most commonly used where the owner of property needs to refinance property on which there is an existing mortgage. The new lender will not agree to loan funds unless the existing mortgagee agrees to take a second or junior position to the new lender who will take a first mortgage position in the property after it makes the loan.

P-H 18-g: Can you think of reasons *why* the original mortgagee would voluntarily agree to subordinate its mortgage position to the new lender? If the owner is in arrears on its payments to the original mortgagee, might the original mortgagee benefit from the refinancing?

The court may order involuntary **equitable subordination** of all or part of a creditor's claim pursuant to §510(c). Equitable subordination is most typically exercised where the creditor has engaged in inequitable or dishonest conduct that resulted in unfair advantage to him or prejudice to other creditors.

EXAMPLE

> Assume a creditor holding a senior security interest in property of the estate misrepresents the value of its secured claim to a creditor holding a junior secured position in the same property. If that misrepresentation causes the junior creditor to be prejudiced in some way, the court may order the senior claim equitably subordinated to the junior claim.

C. The Debtor's Right to Retain Property in a Chapter 7: Reaffirmation, Redemption, Exemption, Ride Through, and Lien Stripping

1. The Reaffirmation Agreement

Recall from Chapter Fifteen, Section B, that the individual Chapter 7 debtor must file OBF 88, **Statement of Intent by Individual Debtor**, indicating his intent with regard to his secured property. One option is to **surrender** the collateral to the secured creditor and discharge the balance of the debt.

Another option, provided by §524(c) of the Code, permits a Chapter 7 debtor to agree with the creditor to retain the collateral and **reaffirm** the secured debt. The typical example of a debt that the debtor is eager to reaffirm rather than to discharge is one that is secured by property that the debtor needs to keep, such as a home or car.

EXAMPLE

> Assume that a Chapter 7 debtor owns a car that is worth $6,000 and on which he owes $6,500 to the creditor who holds a security interest in it. There is no equity in the car for the debtor to exempt and no equity for the estate either since the creditor's secured claim against the car exceeds its value. The trustee will abandon this property for the estate. The debtor could allow the creditor to repossess the car and discharge the $6,000 debt he owes the creditor. But the debtor needs a car, and he would like to keep this one. The debtor may therefore enter into a reaffirmation agreement with the creditor in which he agrees to remain legally liable for the debt following his discharge in bankruptcy.

P-H 18-h: Do you see the risk to the debtor in reaffirming a debt that he could discharge in the Chapter 7? If he reaffirms this debt and then receives his discharge in bankruptcy, how long will it be before he can file another Chapter 7 proceeding? If, following the reaffirmation and the discharge, the debtor defaults on payments to the still-secured creditor, what rights does the creditor have against the debtor?

Debtors may choose to reaffirm a dischargeable debt in the full amount owed and according to the original terms of the obligation. Or they may negotiate with the creditor to reaffirm only a portion of the balance owed or on more favorable terms (e.g., lower monthly payments, longer amortization, or lower interest rate). You can understand why unsecured creditors facing the possibility of a full discharge of the obligation owed to them would be amenable to such compromise in order to obtain a reaffirmation.

It is important that the individual debtor seeking to reaffirm a secured debt indicate his intention to retain the property by reaffirming on the statement of intent. If the debtor's original statement of intent indicated the intent to surrender the pledged property and the debtor later decides to reaffirm the debt and keep the property, the statement of intent must be amended.

Reaffirmation agreement The bankruptcy debtor's agreement with a creditor to pay the creditor a debt that could have been discharged in bankruptcy.

Section 524(c) requires that in order to reaffirm a debt the debtor and creditor must enter into a written **reaffirmation agreement**. The bankruptcy court must review the agreement and has the power to disapprove it. The reaffirmation agreement will provide that the debtor will remain liable and pay all or a portion of the money owed, even though the debt would otherwise be discharged in the bankruptcy. In return, the creditor promises that it will not repossess or take back the automobile or other property so long as the debtor continues to pay the debt.

EXAMPLE

> Recall that Marta Carlson owes Shears Department Store $900 and the debt is secured by her washer and dryer, worth only $600 together. Marta would like to reaffirm her debt to Shears in order to keep her washer and dryer. Although Marta claimed an exemption in the washer and dryer in her Schedule C (Document 9 in the Carlson case file) under §522(d)(3), that alone will not entitle her to keep possession of that property since she has given Shears a security interest in the washer and dryer. So Marta decides to enter a reaffirmation agreement with Shears, promising to pay the entire indebtedness in exchange for Shears allowing her to keep the washer and dryer. That reaffirmation agreement is set out in Illustration 18-b (and Document 38 in the Carlson case file). The court still has to approve the agreement.

The procedure for obtaining the approval of a reaffirmation agreement set out in §524 is quite complex. The reaffirmation agreement must be entered into before the discharge is entered by the court in order to be valid. The agreement must be signed by the parties and filed with the court. The Code requires that reaffirmation agreements contain an extensive set of disclosures described in §524(k). Among other things, the disclosures must advise the debtor of the amount of the debt being reaffirmed and how it is calculated, and that reaffirmation means that the debtor's personal liability for that debt will not be discharged in the bankruptcy. The disclosures also require the debtor to sign and file a statement of his or her current income and expenses that shows that the balance of income paying expenses is sufficient to pay the reaffirmed debt. If the balance is not enough to pay the debt to be reaffirmed, there is a **presumption of undue hardship**, and the court may decide not to approve the reaffirmation agreement. If the court is inclined to disapprove the reaffirmation agreement because the presumption of hardship is present or for any other reason, the court must conduct a hearing and give the debtor and creditor an opportunity to overcome the presumption of undue hardship or to otherwise convince the court that the agreement is in the debtor's best interest.

Illustration 18-b: REAFFIRMATION AGREEMENT BETWEEN MARTA CARLSON AND SHEARS DEPARTMENT STORE

B240A (Form B240A) (04/10)

> Check one.
>
> ☐ **Presumption of Undue Hardship**
>
> ☒ **No Presumption of Undue Hardship**
> *See Debtor's Statement in Support of Reaffirmation, Part II below, to determine which box to check*

United States Bankruptcy Court
Middle District of Columbiana

In re   **Marta Rinaldi Carlson** _____   Case No.   **081441-CP** _____
　　　　　　　　　　　　　　　　　Debtor(s)　　　　　　　　　Chapter   **7** _____

REAFFIRMATION DOCUMENTS

Name of Creditor: **Shears Department Store** _____

☐ Check this box if Creditor is a Credit Union

PART I. REAFFIRMATION AGREEMENT

Reaffirming a debt is a serious financial decision. Before entering into this Reaffirmation Agreement, you must review the important disclosures, instructions, and definitions found in Part V of this form.

A. Brief description of the original agreement being reaffirmed:　　　 Purchase agreement for Shears washer & dryer
　　　　　　　　　　　　　　　　　　　　　　　　　　　　　　　For example, auto loan

B. ***AMOUNT REAFFIRMED:***　　　　　$ _____ 900 _____

>   The Amount Reaffirmed is the entire amount that you are agreeing to pay. This may include unpaid principal, interest, and fees and costs (if any) arising on or before   **April 30, YR-1** , which is the date of the Disclosure Statement portion of this form (Part V).
>
>   *See the definition of "Amount Reaffirmed" in Part V, Section C below.*

C. The ***ANNUAL PERCENTAGE RATE*** applicable to the Amount Reaffirmed is   **6.5** _____ %.

>   *See definition of "Annual Percentage Rate" in Part V, Section C below.*
>
>   This is a *(check one)*   ☒ Fixed rate　　　　　☐ Variable rate

If the loan has a variable rate, the future interest rate may increase or decrease from the Annual Percentage Rate disclosed here.

D. Reaffirmation Agreement Repayment Terms *(check and complete one)*:

>   ☐ $ **45** per month for **20** __ months starting on **June 1, YR-1** .
>
>   ☐ Describe repayment terms, including whether future payment amount(s) may be different from the initial payment amount. ____ .

E. Describe the collateral, if any, securing the debt:

B240A, Reaffirmation Documents

Description: **Shears washer and dryer**

Current Market Value $ **600**

F. Did the debt that is being reaffirming arise from the purchase of the collateral described above?

☒ Yes. What was the purchase price for the collateral? $ **1,200**

☐ No. What was the amount of the original loan? $ _____

G. Specify the changes made by this Reaffirmation Agreement to the most recent credit terms on the reaffirmed debt and any related agreement:

	Terms as of the Date of Bankruptcy	Terms After Reaffirmation
Balance due (including fees and costs)	$ 900	$ 900
Annual Percentage Rate	6.5 %	6.5 %
Monthly Payment	$ 45	$ 45

H. ☐ Check this box if the creditor is agreeing to provide you with additional future credit in connection with this Reaffirmation Agreement. Describe the credit limit, the Annual Percentage Rate that applies to future credit and any other terms on future purchases and advances using such credit:

_____

PART II. DEBTOR'S STATEMENT IN SUPPORT OF REAFFIRMATION AGREEMENT

A. Were you represented by an attorney during the course of negotiating this agreement?

Check one. ☐ Yes   ☒ No

B. Is the creditor a credit union?

Check one. ☐ Yes   ☒ No

C. If your answer to EITHER question A, or B, above is "No" complete 1. and 2. below.

   1. Your present monthly income and expenses are:

     a. Monthly income from all sources after payroll deductions (take-home pay plus any other income) $ **2,267**

     b. Monthly expenses (including all reaffirmed debts except this one) $ **2,000**

     c. Amount available to pay this reaffirmed debt (subtract b. from a.) $ **267**

     d. Amount of monthly payment required for this reaffirmed debt $ **45**

*If the monthly payment on this reaffirmed debt (line d.) **is greater than** the amount you have available to pay this reaffirmed debt (line c.), you must check the box at the top of page one that says "Presumption of Undue Hardship." Otherwise, you must check the box at the top of page one that says "No Presumption of Undue Hardship."*

   2.   You believe this reaffirmation agreement will not impose an undue hardship on you or your dependents because:

      Check one of the two statements below, if applicable:

      ☒ You can afford to make the payments on the reaffirmed debt because your monthly income is greater than your monthly expenses even after you include in your expenses the monthly payments on all debts you are reaffirming, including this one.

      ☐ You can afford to make the payments on the reaffirmed debt even though your monthly income is less than your monthly expenses after you include in my expenses the monthly payments on all debts you are reaffirming, including this one, because:

      _____

      Use an additional page if needed for a full explanation.

D. If your answers to BOTH question A or B above were "Yes," check the following statement, if applicable:

      ☐ You believe this Reaffirmation Agreement is in your financial interest and you can afford to make the payments on the reaffirmed debt.

Also, check the box at the top of page one that says "No Presumption of Undue Hardship."

B240A, Reaffirmation Documents   Page 4

PART III. CERTIFICATION BY DEBTOR(S) AND SIGNATURES OF PARTIES

I hereby certify that:

(1)   I agree to reaffirm the debt described above.

(2)   Before signing this Reaffirmation Agreement, I (we) read the terms disclosed in this Reaffirmation Agreement (Part I) and the Disclosure Statement, Instructions and Definitions included in Part V below;

(3)   The Debtor's Statement in Support of Reaffirmation Agreement (Part II above) is true and complete;

(4)   I am entering into this agreement voluntarily and fully informed of my rights and responsibilities; and

(5)   I have received a copy of this completed and signed Reaffirmation Documents form.

SIGNATURE(S) If this is a joint Reaffirmation Agreement, both debtors must sign.):

Date   **April 30, YR-1**   Signature **/s/ Marta Rinaldi Carlson**
                                                         Marta Rinaldi Carlson
                                                                    Debtor

Date   _____   Signature _____

                                                         Joint Debtor, if any

Reaffirmation Agreement Terms Accepted by Creditor:

Creditor   Shears Department Store   1129 Loveland Mall Rd., Capitol City, CL.
                    Print Name   Address

        Martha Adkins, Regional Mgr   **/s/ Martha Adkins**   **April 30, YR-1**
        Print Name of Representative   Signature   Date

PART IV. CERTIFICATION BY DEBTOR'S ATTORNEY (IF ANY)

To be filed only if the attorney represented the debtor during the course of negotiating this agreement.

I hereby certify that: (1) this agreement represents a fully informed and voluntary agreement by the debtor; (2) this agreement does not impose an undue hardship on the debtor or any dependent of the debtor; and (3) I have fully advised the debtor of the legal effect and consequences of this agreement and any default under this agreement.

☐ A presumption of undue hardship has been established with respect to this agreement. In my opinion, however, the debtor is able to make the required payment.

Check box, if the presumption of undue hardship box is checked on page 1 and the creditor is not a Credit Union.

Date   _____   Signature of Debtor's Attorney   _____

                                     Print Name of Debtor's Attorney   _____

As curious as it may sound, it is not unusual for the debtor's attorney to abstain from representing the debtor in connection with a reaffirmation agreement. This is so because if the attorney chooses to represent her client in connection with the agreement, the attorney must certify in writing that she advised the debtor of the legal effect and consequences of the agreement, including a default under the agreement. The attorney must also certify that the debtor was fully informed and voluntarily entered into the agreement and that reaffirmation of the debt will not create an undue hardship for the debtor or the debtor's dependants. It is no small thing for a debtor with a history of severe financial problems to reaffirm a debt that he could discharge in bankruptcy. There may be disagreements between the debtor and the attorney regarding whether it is in the best interests of the debtor to reaffirm. Even if it appears to be at the time, it may not turn out well if the debtor reaffirms, then defaults later and can no longer discharge the debt. The attorney who has certified that reaffirmation will not create an undue hardship for the debtor could face malpractice charges when it does.

P-H 18-i: Look at Part IV of Marta Carlson's reaffirmation agreement with Shears in Illustration 18-b. Did her attorney represent her in connection with that agreement? Discuss with a debtor's lawyer in your area or a member of the panel of trustees or the U.S. trustee in your federal district whether debtors' lawyers in your area routinely represent their clients on reaffirmation agreements and sign off on them.

If the debtor who enters the reaffirmation agreement and files it with the court is not represented by counsel in connection with the agreement, a hearing on the proposed reaffirmation agreement will be held, and the bankruptcy judge will decide whether to approve the agreement. However, in many districts, if the debtor is represented by an attorney in connection with the reaffirmation agreement, and the presumption of undue hardship is not present, the reaffirmation agreement may become effective without court approval. Even if the debtor is represented by counsel, if the presumption of hardship arises in connection with the proposed reaffirmation agreement, a hearing will be held and the judge will decide whether the reaffirmation is in the best interests of the debtor.

P-H 18-j: Look at Marta Carlson's reaffirmation agreement with Shears again. Did the presumption of hardship arise in connection with that agreement? Check the local rules of the bankruptcy court nearest you. If Marta was a debtor in that court, would a hearing be needed on her reaffirmation agreement? Interview local debtors' attorneys or a member of the trustee panel or the U.S. trustee for your district. How strict are the bankruptcy judges in your district on allowing or disallowing reaffirmation agreements proposed by Chapter 7 debtors? For example, if a debtor wanted to reaffirm debts on three different vehicles when he needed only one or two for personal and business purposes, or on his recreational boat, would the judge have a problem approving that?

Sometimes debtors see reaffirmation as a way to salvage their credit history or their relationship with a particular creditor, even though it is not essential to do so and the obligation is unsecured by any property of the debtor.

EXAMPLE

> A debtor may have a long-standing credit account with a local or national department store where the debtor likes to shop. Even though the balance owed the department store is unsecured and the debtor could discharge it, the debtor chooses to reaffirm the debt just to keep the credit account with the department store in good standing.

Of course, a debtor who has received a discharge may repay any debt voluntarily whether or not a reaffirmation agreement exists and this does sometimes occur.

EXAMPLE

> A debtor may formally discharge a debt arising from a family loan but still feel a moral obligation to pay the debt. The creditor whose debt has been discharged will not be able to sue or otherwise take action to collect that debt; it has been discharged.

2. The Right to Redeem Personal Property

Another option available to the Chapter 7 debtor to retain secured property arises from §722, which allows an individual consumer debtor in Chapter 7 the right to **redeem** tangible personal property (not realty) intended primarily for personal, family, or household use (consumer property) from a lien securing such property where the property has been claimed as exempt by the debtor under §522 or has been abandoned by the trustee under §554.

This **right of redemption** is exercised by the debtor paying the amount of the **allowed secured claim** to the creditor. Recall that §506(a)(1) provides that a secured creditor's claim is only a secured claim up to the value of the collateral. The creditor's claim is unsecured as to all amounts owed over that value. The value of personal property securing a claim for purposes of determining the secured portion of the claim is defined in §506(a)(2), added by BAPCPA, as the **replacement value** of the goods on the date the petition is filed without deduction for sale or marketing costs. For goods acquired for personal, family, or household purposes (consumer goods), such as those subject to §722 redemption, replacement value means *the price a retail merchant would charge for property of that kind, given its age and condition.*

Present value Calculation of the current value of property for purposes of determining the value of a secured claim in bankruptcy.

EXAMPLE

> Marta Carlson owes Shears Department Store $900 and the debt is secured by her washer and dryer, which she values at only $600 together. In her Schedule C (Document 9 in the Carlson file), she has exempted the total $600 value of the washer and dryer from any claim of the trustee. The trustee has abandoned this property for the estate because there is no equity in it since both Shears' lien and Marta's claimed exemption in the property are superior to his claim (see Document 36 in the Carlson case file). It is tangible consumer property within the meaning of §722 since it is property used for personal, family, or household purposes. As an alternative to reaffirming her debt to

Shears, Marta could seek to redeem this property from the lien by paying the debtor "the full amount of the allowed secured claim." But Shears may not agree that Marta's valuation of the washer and dryer at $600 is accurate. Shears may contend that the value she has placed on the washer and dryer is the liquidation value of the property but not the replacement value, which is the required valuation under §506(a)(2). The court may have to decide the valuation dispute. But if the court does find the replacement value of the washer and dryer to be less than the full amount of the debt ($900) and Marta can exempt that value in her Schedule C, then Marta can redeem the property by paying Shears that replacement value. The balance owed to Shears becomes an unsecured claim that can be discharged if there are insufficient nonexempt assets in the estate available to pay it. Of course, Marta will have to come up with the $600 or other dollar amount determined to be the replacement value of the collateral to pay Shears and that may be difficult for someone already in bankruptcy. Perhaps Howard Kine, her boss at TTI, will loan it to her.

P-H 18-k: Prior to BAPCPA's addition of the new §506(a)(2), the Supreme Court had adopted the replacement value rule in the important case of *Associates Commercial Corp. v. Rash*, 520 U.S. 953 (1997). *Rash* rejected the debtor's argument that the present value of the collateral under §506(a)(1) should be the **liquidation** or **foreclosure value** of the property, which is essentially what the property would sell for in a rushed, even emergency, situation, likely to produce far less than its retail value. So the replacement value of the washer and dryer that Marta Carlson might like to redeem from the lien of Shears would be not what a consumer would sell it for in a garage sale, and not what a consumer who needed quick cash would sell it for to a neighbor or friend, and not what it would be sold for wholesale, but instead what a retail merchant would ask for it given its present age and condition. Do you see how the latter value is likely to be higher than the others? Those interested in the history of bankruptcy practice might want to read *Rash* to understand why BAPCPA did what it did on this issue and to understand that the debtor's argument in *Rash* was by no means unreasonable.

In actual practice, the codification of the *Rash* replacement value rule in §506(a)(2) is highly beneficial to the secured creditor and has made it exceedingly difficult for Chapter 7 consumer debtors to utilize the §722 right of redemption in consumer property. It is now the rare case in which a right to redeem is exercised by the debtor. Instead, debtors will opt for a reaffirmation for property they would like to keep.

As with the intent to reaffirm a debt, the individual debtor's intent to redeem property pledged as collateral must be noted on his statement of intent.

3. Debtor's Right to Avoid Liens Impairing an Exemption

In Chapter Fifteen, Section B, we learned that an individual debtor can exempt certain real and personal property from the bankruptcy trustee. In most situations, however, an exemption cannot prevail over a perfected security interest of a creditor in the property sought to be exempted. Thus exemptions are mostly claimed in unsecured property. However, §522(f)(1)(A) of the Code empowers the individual debtor to avoid a **judicial lien** on his property to the extent that the lien impairs an exemption the debtor would otherwise have in the property. Judicial liens are defined by §101(36) as liens obtained by judgment, levy sequestration, or other legal or equitable process and include those prejudgment remedies we considered in Chapter Nine and the postjudgment execution remedies we considered in Chapter Eleven.

EXAMPLE

> Assume that an individual Chapter 7 debtor owns a residence worth $200,000 that is encumbered by a mortgage in favor of the bank in the amount of $150,000. If the jurisdiction allows the debtor a $30,000 homestead exemption, then there would be only $20,000 in nonexempt equity in the residence. If another creditor of the debtor had taken a prepetition final judgment against the debtor in the amount of $40,000 and filed a judgment lien against the debtor's residence in that amount, once the debtor files in Chapter 7 he can avoid $20,000 of that judgment lien on the residence, the amount by which the judgment lien impairs his exemption based on the value of the property.

Section 522(f)(1)(A) prohibits a judicial lien resulting from a **domestic support obligation** (child support, alimony, or maintenance recoverable by a spouse, former spouse, or child of the debtor) from being avoided by the debtor.

Section 522(f)(1)(B) also authorizes the debtor to avoid a **nonpossessory, nonpurchase money security interest** (PMSI is defined in Chapter Five, Section D) in certain household items and tools of the trade to the extent the lien impairs an exemption (illustrated in connection with a Chapter 13 case in Chapter Twenty-One, Section B). Moreover, §§522(g)(h)(i) authorize the Chapter 7 debtor to initiate turnover, avoidance, or setoff actions (discussed in Chapter Seventeen, Sections A, D, and E) if the trustee refuses to do so in order to assert an exemption in property recovered.

As with the intent to reaffirm a debt and the right to redeem, the individual debtor's intent to avoid one of these liens in order to claim an exemption must be noted on his statement of intent. Per FRBP 4003(d), the proceeding to avoid judicial lien impairing an exemption is brought by motion, not adversarial proceeding. FRBP 4003(d) also recognizes the creditor's right to object to such a motion by challenging the exemption claimed by the debtor.

4. The Ride Through Option

Before BAPCPA, many federal circuits recognized an additional option for a Chapter 7 debtor to retain secured property following closure of the case. A typical scenario was this: The debtor owns a car worth $10,000 and owes $10,500 on it to the creditor holding a security interest in the car to secure payment of the debt. The bankruptcy trustee has abandoned the car since there is no equity in it for the estate. The debtor is not in default on the payments to the creditor and the creditor has not and does not want to repossess. The debtor needs the car but is unable to redeem it. So the debtor asks the court for permission to reaffirm the debt. The court refuses the application to reaffirm, finding that it is not in the best interests of the debtor (perhaps he has another car and the judge concludes that all he needs is one car, or perhaps he is reaffirming other debts that the court believes will put him at high risk of default on the car note if it is reaffirmed as well so the presumption of hardship is not overcome). What happens now? Must the debtor surrender the car he would like to keep, is paying for, and that the creditor would like him to keep and continue paying for?

Prior to 2005, five federal circuits recognized that a debtor had an additional option. With the acquiescence (rather than formal agreement, as in a reaffirmation) of the creditor, he could allow the debt to the secured creditor to be formally discharged but keep the car and continue making the payments. This option was called a **ride through** (or a **pay through** or, if the collateral was a vehicle, a **pay and ride**) by practitioners because the debtor's possession of the collateral was riding through and beyond the bankruptcy case. This arrangement was quite favorable to the debtor because the underlying debt to the creditor was discharged. If at any time before the debtor completed the payments due the creditor he no longer wanted the car (or if it were wrecked), he could simply surrender it back to the creditor and have no further liability on the debt—it had been discharged. Of course, the lien on the property survived the bankruptcy case even if the underlying debt did not; if there were a postdischarge default by the debtor, the creditor could repossess. However, with ride through that was the creditor's sole remedy upon default.

P-H 18-l: The rationale for the ride through option was that §521(a)(2), the Code provision requiring the individual debtor to file his statement of intent regarding property (see Chapter Fifteen, Section B), was not limited by that section to the options of surrender, exemption, redemption, or reaffirmation. Though the ride through option was not expressly granted in the Code, it was a long-recognized practice and, because it was not prohibited by §521(a)(2), was allowed in these circuits for debts secured by both personal property (e.g., vehicles) and real property (e.g., home mortgages). Although debtors often sought reaffirmation before choosing the ride through option, doing so was not a necessary prerequisite to ride through. Read *In re Waller*, 394 B.R. 111 (S.D.C. 2008) for a discussion of the pre-BAPCPA ride through practice and a list of the federal circuits that recognized it. Determine if your federal circuit authorized this practice or rejected it.

In 2005 BAPCPA added new §362(h)(1), stating that the automatic stay terminates with respect to personal property pledged as collateral and such property is no longer deemed property of the estate if the debtor does not file a statement of intention in a timely manner or does not perform the stated intention (surrender, redemption or reaffirmation) by the statutory deadline—30 days after the petition is filed or before the first meeting of creditors, whichever is earliest per §521(a)(2). This new provision has been interpreted as eliminating the ride through option concerning personal property pledged as collateral. See, e.g., *In re Jones*, 591 F.3d 308, 311-12 (4th Cir. 2010). But what about debts secured by the debtor's real property? Courts that recognized the pre-BAPCPA ride through option are holding that new §362(h)(1) is limited in its effect to debts secured by personal property and that the ride through is still available in connection with debts secured by mortgages on the debtor's property. See, e.g., *In re Waller*,

394 B.R. 111 (Bankr. S.C. 2008); *In re Caraballo*, 386 B.R. 398 (Bankr. Conn. 2008); and *In re Wilson*, 372 B.R. 816 (Bankr. S. C. 2007).

P-H 18-m: See if the courts of your federal district or circuit are allowing post-BAPCPA ride throughs for debts secured by mortgages on the debtor's property.

But has BAPCPA totally eliminated the ride through option for debts secured by personal property? Maybe not. Some courts are construing §§521(a)(2) and new 362(h) together to mean that what the debtor must do is ask the court to reaffirm the debt secured by personal property. If a timely notice of intent to reaffirm is filed and a timely application to reaffirm the debt is sought but not approved, those courts are saying the requirements of §362(h) are complied with and the debtor may still choose ride through with the acquiescence of the creditor. Called a **back door ride through** by practitioners, the procedure is being recognized in those federal districts where pre-BAPCPA ride through was recognized. See, e.g., *In re Chim*, 381 B.R. 191 (Bkrtcy. D. Md. 2008), and *In re Moustafi*, 371 B.R. 434 (Bkrtcy. D. Ariz. 2007).

Once the bankruptcy case is closed, the postdischarge legal rights as between the ride through debtor and the secured creditor will be governed by state law. The lien on the personal property (or the mortgage in the case of real property) survives the end of the bankruptcy case and the creditor will have the right to repossess (or foreclose) upon default. But regarding what constitutes default state law, not bankruptcy law, will control (e.g., some state consumer protection laws prohibiting repossession of a vehicle or other personalty when there is no default on payments). See, e.g., *In re Dumont*, 383 B.R. 481 (9th Cir. BAP 2008), and *In re Steinhaus*, 349 B.R. 694 (Bkrtcy. D. Idaho 2006).

In bankruptcy courts where ride through is deemed an option, debtors will often state their intent to pursue that option on their statement of intent even though the official form (OBF B8) does not contain that option. And in many bankruptcy courts where the controlling law says ride through is not a viable option, it has been and still is done informally between debtor and acquiescing creditor. After all, who is to complain? The trustee has abandoned the property as having no value to the estate. For the same reason no other creditor will care, having no interest in the collateral. The debtor is delighted to keep the property and the creditor is delighted to keep receiving payments. All's well that ends well?

P-H 18-n: See if the courts of your federal district or circuit recognize post-BAPCPA back door ride through for personalty. If not, ask a practitioner if it is done informally. For a good discussion of this interesting post-BAPCPA development, read Christopher M. Hogan, "Will the Ride Through Ride Again?" 108 Colum. L. Rev. (2008).

Section 362(h)(1)(B) provides an alternative method of achieving back door ride through. Per the new statute, the automatic stay is lifted on liens secured by personal property and the property is no longer considered property of the estate if the debtor fails to file a timely statement of intent or, having stated an intent to reaffirm, fails to do so in a timely manner. But subsection (B) says that if the creditor refuses reaffirmation (and why would a creditor do that?), then the lien lifting does not occur. See an interesting application of this exception in *In re Perkins*, 418 B.R. 680 (M.D.N.C. 2009). (In *Perkins,* the creditor did not file a timely reaffirmation agreement signed by debtor, so approval could not be granted by court. In that case, stay was not lifted as to lien on personalty and the creditor could not declare the debtor in default and repossess unless the debtor defaulted on payments. The creditor was deemed to have waived its right to declare default based on *ipso facto* **clause** [filing for bankruptcy relief is an act of default] in contract.)

P-H 18-o: An *ipso facto* (Latin for "by the act itself") clause in a contract is one that makes the act of one party becoming insolvent, acknowledging insolvency, filing (or having filed involuntarily for them) a bankruptcy case or state law receivership proceeding, or making an assignment for the benefit of creditors an act of default by that party. Section 365(e) of the Code together with §541(c) effectively make *ipso facto* clauses ineffective in a bankruptcy case concerning executory (ongoing) contracts. However, BAPCPA added §521(d), which together with new §362(h)(1)(A) make such clauses operative in the bankruptcy case upon the failure of the debtor to file in a timely manner the required statement of intent and seek in a timely manner redemption or reaffirmation of a debt secured by personal property. The continuing postconfirmation effect of an *ipso facto* clause in a contract where the debtor rides through on a debt secured by personal property is one of those to be decided by state law. Determine if your state enforces *ipso facto* clauses in consumer contracts.

---

5. The Lien Stripping Option

Recall the bifurcation of an undersecured claim mandated by §506(a) pursuant to which the value of a secured claim is stripped down to the value of the collateral and bifurcated between its secured and unsecured portion (see Chapter Seventeen, Section A). Section 506(d) provides that a lien is void "[t]o the extent that [it] secures a claim against the debtor that is not an allowed secured claim." How do those two provisions work in the following scenario? The creditor is owed $250,000 and the debt is secured by a perfected mortgage on the debtor's residence. The residence is valued at only $200,000, so the creditor is undersecured. The Chapter 7 trustee decides there is no equity in the residence for the estate and abandons it to the debtor.

Can debtor use §§506(a) and (d) to ask the court to reduce the lien of the creditor on the residence to the $200,000 value? Note that the creditor is not simply asking for what §506(a) already does—bifurcate the bankruptcy claim of this undersecured creditor into a secured claim for $200,000 and an unsecured claim for $50,000. The debtor is asking that for all purposes the secured position of creditor in the residence be limited to the $200,000 present value and the mortgage declared void for all amounts above $200,000. This is an effort to **strip down** or **write down** the lien not just for purposes of treating the creditor's claim in a distribution but to actually void the balance of the lien on the collateral for all purposes.

EXAMPLE

> Assume a Chapter 7 debtor owns a home secured by a mortgage having a balance of $200,000 but the home is only valued at $180,000 when the petition is filed. We know that this creditor is undersecured and that pursuant to §506(a) its claim is bifurcated: Its claim is secured in the amount of $180,000 and unsecured in the amount of $20,000. Can the debtor succeed in having the court void the mortgage on the $20,000? If so, consider the consequences. The trustee may abandon the residence as having no equity for the estate. The debtor may be current on the payments to the creditor. The debtor may ride through this secured obligation by continuing to make the payments as they come due. If so, the debtor will only have to pay the creditor $180,000 to satisfy the mortgage on the house, not the $200,000 note balance—the lien has been voided as to all amounts over $20,000. Or, if the creditor waits until property values go back up and then sells the residence for $220,000, the creditor can pay off the balance of the $180,000 debt secured by the mortgage and keep the balance of the sales price. In other words, any increase in equity after the mortgage is stripped down accrues to the debtor.

Sections 506(a) and (d) could certainly be read as allowing if not intending the kind of strip down illustrated in the last example. But in *Dewsnup v. Timm*, 502 U.S. 410 (1997), the Supreme Court said it was not allowable. The reasoning is that Congress intended the two sections to be read independently of each other and that the claim bifurcation feature of §506(a) does not mandate or authorize an otherwise legitimate security interest to be otherwise stripped down or voided under §506(d), regardless of the value of the collateral. The court was bothered by the idea that the debtor would benefit by any post–strip down increase in the value of the collateral and decided to preserve the pre-Code rule that liens on real property should pass through bankruptcy unaffected unless a Code provision expressly said otherwise.

Should the result in *Dewsnup* control in the following scenario? Creditor #1 is owed $250,000 and the debt is secured by a mortgage on debtor's residence. The residence is valued at only $240,000, meaning that creditor #1 is undersecured. Creditor #2 is owed $30,000 and that debt is secured by a junior mortgage on the debtor's residence; the mortgage held by creditor #1 is senior to the mortgage held by creditor #2. Both mortgages are properly perfected but if the residence is sold, all the proceeds of sale will go to creditor #1 and none to creditor #2. Is the debtor in a position to use §§506(a) and (d) to ask the court to void the mortgage securing the claim of creditor #2 on the grounds that he is effectively in the position of an unsecured creditor?

Most courts that have considered this question so far say no. See, e.g., *Talbert v. City Mortg. Serv.*, 344 F.3d 555 (6th Cir. 2003); *Ryan v. Homecomings Fin. Network*, 253 F.3d 778 (4th Cir. 2001); *Laskin v. First Nat'l Bank of Keystone*, 222 B.R. 872 (B.A.P. 9th Cir. 1998); all construe *Dewsnup* to say that §506(d) does not authorize the complete **strip off** and voiding of a junior lien on realty notwithstanding the absence of any equity for the junior lien holder in the property and regardless of the effect of the bifurcation of claim feature of 506(a). There is a minority view, however, that interprets *Dewsnup* to prohibit only strip downs, not strip offs, of wholly unsecured second mortgages. See, e.g., *In re McNeal*, 477 Fed.Appx. 562, 564 (11th Cir. 2012, unpublished), and *In re Lavelle*, 2009 WL 4043089, at *4-5 (Bankr. E.D.N.Y. 2009).

> **P-H 18-p:**   See if courts in your federal district or circuit have ruled on this interesting strip off theory for wholly unsecured second mortgages and, if so, which way they go. For a thoughtful analysis of both views, see Michael Myers, *Dewsnup Strikes Again,* Ariz. L. Rev. 1333 (2011).

 D. **Non-dischargeable Debts**

Discharge Permanent relief from debt pursuant to order of the bankruptcy court.

The primary purpose of filing a Chapter 7 petition from the individual debtor's standpoint is to receive a **discharge** of his debts. Once discharged, the debtor can never again be held legally responsible for the discharged debts. This is part of the **fresh start** public policy behind Chapter 7. The concept of a discharge is irrelevant to an entity debtor like a corporation or partnership since the effect of liquidation for such a debtor is that it will simply cease doing business. However, not all debts can be discharged in bankruptcy by the individual debtor. Section 523(a) identifies debts that cannot be discharged in bankruptcy and the primary ones are summarized in Illustration 18-c.

FRBP 4007 provides that any creditor can file a **complaint objecting to the discharge of a particular debt** or the debtor himself can file a **complaint to determine the dischargeability of a particular debt**. Any such action is an **adversary proceeding**, not just a **contested matter** (see Illustration 13-f). Rule 4007 also provides that any complaint contesting the dischargeability of a debt must be filed within 60 days following the first meeting of creditors though the time can be extended by motion. Rule 2002(f) requires the bankruptcy court clerk, or some other person as the court may direct, to provide notice by mail of the time fixed for filing a complaint objecting to discharge of a particular debt.

Illustration 18-c: DEBTS THAT CANNOT BE DISCHARGED IN A CHAPTER 7 BANKRUPTCY

- Taxes entitled to priority payment and tax obligations related to a fraudulent return, failure to file a return or a late return filed within two years preceding the petition and withholding taxes that should have been collected from third parties
- Debts for money, property, services or an extension of credit obtained by fraudulent pretenses or by the use of a false financial statement
- Last-minute consumer cash advances or spending for luxury goods or services
- Debts that were not listed on the debtor's schedules so that the creditor could not file a timely proof of claim
- Debts arising from the debtor's fraud or defalcation while acting in a fiduciary capacity
- Debts arising from embezzlement or larceny
- Domestic support obligations such as alimony and child support
- Debts or claims arising out of the willful or malicious injury to another or the property of another
- Student loans, unless the debtor can convince the court that not discharging this obligation will work an undue hardship on the debtor or his dependents
- Certain fines and penalties imposed by the government
- Claims arising from the wrongful death or personal injury caused by the debtor's driving under the influence of drugs or alcohol

1. Taxes [§523(a)(1)]

Generally speaking, income taxes (whether federal, state or local) due for the three tax years preceding the filing of the petition cannot be discharged nor can property taxes due for the year preceding the petition. Regardless of the tax year in question, a debtor filing a false tax return, no return or a late return within two years preceding the petition cannot discharge those obligations. Employer debtors who failed to withhold income tax, Social Security, or Medicare premiums from employee paychecks as required by law cannot discharge those obligations.

2. Debts Created by Fraudulent Pretenses or False Financial Statement [§523(a)(2)(A)(B)]

Debts created by means of **fraudulent pretenses** or by use of a **fraudulent financial statement** may be found to be non-dischargeable.

EXAMPLE

Assume that a person obtains a loan from a bank to buy a car. He borrows $10,000 from the bank but has a kick-back deal with the seller of the car to get $2,000 of the purchase price back after the deal is done. When the buyer of the car files for bankruptcy the bank can argue that the debt to it should be declared non-dischargeable under §523(a) due to the fraudulent pretenses used to obtain the loan. Or assume that a real estate developer obtains a million dollar loan from a bank to develop a subdivision. He presents a personal financial statement to the bank as part of the loan application but exaggerates the value of his assets in order to qualify for the loan. If he files bankruptcy the entire debt may be declared non-dischargeable due to the fraudulent financial statement.

3. Presumption of Fraud in "Last-Minute" Consumer Purchases of Luxury Goods or Services [§523(a)(2)(C)]

Luxury goods or services Goods or services not reasonably necessary for the maintenance or support of the debtor or a dependent.

Section 523(a)(2)(C) creates a **rebuttable presumption** that consumer debts aggregating more than $500 owed to a single creditor for **luxury goods or services** purchased within 90 days preceding the petition are fraudulent and non-dischargeable. The phrase "luxury goods or services" is not defined but expressly does *not* include goods or services reasonably necessary for the maintenance or support of the debtor or a dependent.

The same section also makes **cash advances** aggregating more than $750 obtained within 70 days preceding the petition on an open end credit plan non-dischargeable. The policy behind these consumer provisions is to punish last-minute spending sprees by unethical debtors. But the presumption of fraud is rebuttable by the debtor.

EXAMPLE

Assume that in the 90 days preceding the filing of her bankruptcy petition Marta Carlson charged almost $1,000 on her Capitol City Bank Visa card for an iPod, several video games, and tuition to a 3-week science camp for her son, Chris. In her bankruptcy case, CCB may seek to have these charges declared non-dischargeable under 523(a)(2)(C) as luxury goods and services. At the trial, Marta testifies that each of those purchases was necessitated by the emotional problems suffered by her son and all represented efforts on her part to provide him with healthy diversions and positive experiences to improve his emotional state. If the court concludes that these charges were reasonably necessary for the maintenance or support of Chris, she may be allowed to discharge them. How do you think the court will rule on that?

4. Debts Arising from Fraud or Defalcation in a Fiduciary Capacity [§523(a)(4)]

A **fiduciary capacity** arises when the debtor occupies a position of trust and confidence as to another person who relies on the debtor to exercise competence, honesty and loyalty. Generally speaking, some courts construe this "fraud or defalcation in a fiduciary capacity" language narrowly and hold it only applies to express or implied trusts (discussed in Chapters Six and Ten) (see, e.g., *In re Burress*, 245 B.R. 871 (Bankr. D. Colo. 2000)). Other courts construe the language more broadly to apply to any person entrusted with the property or confidential affairs of others raising an expectation of loyalty and care (e.g., attorneys, trustees, brokers, bankers) (see, e.g., *In re McDade*, 282 B.R. 650 (N.D. Ill. 2002)). If an obligation arises out of fraud or defalcation (dishonesty) by the debtor acting in such capacity, that obligation may not be dischargeable in bankruptcy.

EXAMPLE

Assume an accountant (or lawyer or trustee) is sued for lying to his client regarding the investment of the client's money entrusted to him for safe investment, and a pre-petition judgment is entered against him for fraud. If the accountant files in Chapter 7 to discharge that judgment, it may be deemed non-dischargeable since it arose out of the accountant's fraud in a fiduciary capacity depending on whether the bankruptcy court follows *Burress* or *McDade* in interpreting the scope of §523(a)(4).

There has also been a question regarding the degree of culpability that should be required to bar the fiduciary from discharging an obligation arising from defalcation of his obligation. Should a knowing, intentional violation of the fiduciary duty be required in order to block discharge, or is a negligent or technical but innocent violation of duty that results in loss to the beneficiary enough? The lower courts were split on this issue until the recent Supreme Court decision in *Bullock v. BankChampaign N.A.*, 133 S. Ct. 1754 (2013) holding that defalcation does require a culpable state of mind beyond mere negligence, which can consist of knowledge of, or gross recklessness in respect to, the improper nature of the relevant fiduciary behavior.

If the accountant in the last example files for bankruptcy relief before the claim is reduced to judgment the bankruptcy court can do either of two things: it can conduct a trial itself on the issue of the accountant's misfeasance or it can lift the stay on the lawsuit that was pending when the petition was filed, allow that court (probably a state court) to enter a final judgment on the issues and then apply **collateral estoppel** (a doctrine prohibiting the relitigation of an issue already decided) to the state court judgment.

EXAMPLE

Assume that the beneficiaries of a trust have sued the trustee in state court alleging misappropriation of trust funds. The case is still pending when the trustee files a Chapter 7 petition and seeks to discharge this contingent unliquidated claim of the beneficiaries. The beneficiaries file a complaint to have the debt liquidated and declared non-dischargeable under §523. Factors the bankruptcy judge may consider in making the decision of whether to try the case herself or lift the stay and allow the case to proceed to judgment in state court include:

- How far along the state court proceeding was at the time the petition was filed;
- How long it will take the case to move through the state court trial and appellate system;
- Whether a jury has been demanded in the state court action (see the discussion of jury trials in bankruptcy court in Chapter Thirteen, Section B);
- The complexity of the state law issues raised in the case; and
- Wishes of the parties.

P-H 18-q: Using the hypothetical in the last example and the factors enumerated there, which factors argue for the bankruptcy judge hearing the case and which for lifting the stay and allowing the case to proceed in state court? If your supervising lawyer represented the debtor can you think of reasons she might favor or disfavor the bankruptcy judge keeping the case in bankruptcy court?

5. Debts Arising from Embezzlement or Larceny [§523(a)(4)]

Regardless of whether a fiduciary capacity is involved, any obligation arising out of embezzlement or larceny cannot be discharged in bankruptcy.

EXAMPLE

Assume a bookkeeper employee steals from her employer. The obligation arising from that embezzlement will be non-dischargeable if the employee files for Chapter 7 relief.

6. Domestic Support Obligations [§523(a)(5)]

Section 101(14A) of the Code defines **domestic support obligations** generally as debts for "alimony, maintenance or support" of a spouse, former spouse or child of the debtor. Generally these obligations must arise from a court decree of divorce of separation or from a property settlement agreement. Both domestic support obligations and other debts to a former spouse or child of the debtor arising in the course of a divorce or separation are exempted from discharge by §523(a)(5)(15).

7. Debts Arising from Willful or Malicious Injury to the Person or Property of Another [§523(a)(6)]

Assume a person is sued for the intentional infliction of emotional distress (discussed in Chapter Seven, Section B) or any other intentional tort. The judgment arising out of that claim may be non-dischargeable when the defendant files for bankruptcy relief.

8. Student Loans [§523(a)(8)]

At one time, student loan debt could be discharged in bankruptcy as easily as an auto loan or credit card debt. Congress implemented the prohibition on discharge of student loans in 1976 after widespread reports of some newly graduated doctors and lawyers filing Chapter 7 cases to discharge their considerable (and taxpayer guaranteed) student loan debt before undertaking lucrative careers.

P-H 18-r: The problem still exists apparently. A 2013 investigation by Scripps Howard News Service reported that nearly 1,000 medical professionals in the country are in default on government-backed student loans totaling more than $116 million, with some of the loans nearly 20 years old. See www.naplesnews. com/news/2013/feb/18/scripps-special-report-900-doctors-owe-116-in/.   What does the report suggest is the problem with collecting these overdue loans?

Until BAPCPA in 2005, the prohibition on discharge only applied to a **federal student loan** meaning an educational loan made, subsidized, or guaranteed by the government or made under a program funded by either a governmental unit or a nonprofit institution. In one of its more controversial provisions, BAPCPA expanded the non-dischargeability provision to include **private student loans** (meaning loans made by for-profit lenders, not subsidized or guaranteed by the government and thus not subject to government regulation on amount, interest rate, or fees) as well. Thus today, neither a public nor a private student loan can be discharged absent a showing of undue hardship.

The only exception to the prohibition on discharge of student loans is a showing by debtor that disallowing discharge of the student loan obligation will cause **undue hardship** to the debtor and his dependents. Undue hardship is an undefined term in the Code but has always been construed by the courts as a demanding standard. In the oft-cited case of *In re Briscoe*, 16 B.R. 128, 131 (Bkrtcy. S.D.N.Y. 1981), the court said, "Dischargeability of student loans should be based upon the certainty of hopelessness, not simply present inability to fulfill financial commitment." That **certainty of hopelessness test** was cited with approval in the leading case of *Brunner v. New York State Higher Edu. Serv. Corp.*, 831 F.2d 395, 396 (2d Cir. 1987), which held that in order to establish undue hardship the debtor must show:

- That the debtor cannot maintain, based on current income and expenses, a "minimal" standard of living for herself and her dependants if forced to repay the loan;
- That additional circumstances exist indicating that this state of affairs is likely to persist for a significant portion of the repayment period of the student loan; and

• That the debtor has made good faith efforts to repay the loan.

In *Brunner* the Second Circuit said of Congress's decision to exempt student loan debt from discharge in bankruptcy: "In return for giving aid to individuals who represent poor credit risks, it strips these individuals of the refuge of bankruptcy in all but extreme circumstances." It was, "a conscious Congressional choice to override the normal 'fresh start' goal of bankruptcy."

P-H 18-s: See if the courts of your federal circuit follow *Brunner* and the certainty of hopelessness test in applying the undue hardship standard for discharge of student loan debt. If not, what standard do they apply? Marta Carlson has two educational loans (see the Assignment Memorandum in Appendix A and her Schedule F, Document 12 in the Carlson case file), one to Columbiana Federal Savings & Loan in the amount of $5,000 and one to Capitol City Bank in the amount of $10,000, both insured by the U.S. government. Looking at Marta's overall financial situation and that of her two children, can you construct a plausible argument under the standard used in your federal circuit that excepting these two loans from discharge would work an undue hardship on her or her dependents?

The second prong of the *Brunner* formula, requiring the debtor seeking to discharge student debt to show "additional circumstances" indicating that the debtor's inability to maintain a minimal standard of living will continue for all or a significant portion of the loan payback period, has proved to be the most difficult for debtors to meet. As summarized in *In re Nys*, 308 B.R. 436 (9th Cir. BAP 2004), such circumstances may include:

• Serious mental or physical disability of the debtor or the debtor's dependents that prevents employment or advancement
• The debtor's obligations to care for dependents
• Lack of, or severely limited, education
• Poor quality of education
• Lack of usable or marketable job skills
• Underemployment, maximized income potential in the chosen educational field, and no other, more lucrative job skills
• Limited number of years remaining in the debtor's work life to allow payment of the loan
• Age or other factors that prevent retraining or relocation as a means for payment of the loan
• Lack of assets, whether or not exempt, which could be used to pay the loan
• Potentially increasing expenses that outweigh any potential appreciation in the value of the debtor's assets and/or likely increases in the debtor's income
• Lack of better financial options elsewhere

P-H 18-t: What about a prolonged depression of the job market as we have experienced as a result of the Great Recession? See *In re Gibson*, 428 B.R. 385 (Bkrtcy. W.D. Mich. 2010), where that argument was rejected. Have the courts of your federal district or circuit accepted or rejected such an argument in a student loan case?

P-H 18-u: Congress removed commercial banks from the federal student loan business by provisions of the **Health Care and Education Reconciliation Act of 2010**. Through the law's new **Direct Loan Program** administered by the U.S. Department of Education, federal student loans are made directly by the federal government with no bank middleman, saving the government billions of dollars that had been paid to those banks in subsidies to make the loans while the government guaranteed payment to the lender upon default by the borrower. (Private educational bank loans can still be made but will not be government backed.) The savings, projected at $68 billion over 11 years, will go primarily to expand the Pell Grant program. Is this a brilliant idea or a socialist takeover of the college loan market?

P-H 18-v: Maybe the undue hardship test is not as intimidating in the application as it sounds in theory. A 2012 study found that 4 out of 10 debtors who sought partial or total discharge of student debt in bankruptcy were successful notwithstanding the undue hardship test. Remarkably, the study found that only one-tenth of 1 percent of bankruptcy debtors with student loan debt even attempted to discharge it. See Jason Iuliano, *An Empirical Assessment of Student Loan Discharges and the Undue Hardship Standard*, 86 Am. Bankr. L. J., 495 (Sep. 25, 2012). Read the study and determine what were the common characteristics of the debtors whose student debt was discharged in whole or part.

The U.S. Department of Education has instituted a new **Income Based Repayment (IBR) Plan** that caps the required monthly payment on a federal student loan obligation at an amount calculated based on the former student's income and family size. The qualifying former student is given 25 years to repay the loan rather than the standard 10 years and any amounts still owing after 25 years will be forgiven under the plan. The DOE also offers a **Public Service Loan Forgiveness (PSLF) Plan**, pursuant to which graduates who choose to work as public school teachers or in other government positions or for nonprofit organizations can repay their student loans at reduced amounts and receive forgiveness of the balance after only 10 years. You can read up on these DOE repayment options at http://studentaid.ed.gov/.

P-H 18-w: The decision of a debtor in bankruptcy to participate or not in one of these DOE programs could have a bearing on whether the debtor can satisfy the third prong of the *Brunner* formula for determining undue hardship— whether the debtor has made a good faith effort to repay the loan. Generally, whether the debtor chose to participate or not is a relevant factor on good faith but not per se decisive (see, e.g., *In re Barrett*, 487 F.3d 353, 364 (6th Cir. 2007) and the weight it is given by different courts therefore varies. Compare *In re Gibson*, 428 B.R. 385, 391-92 (Bkrtcy. W.D. Mich. 2010) (debtor who declined to participate in DOE IBR plan did not use good faith efforts to repay her loans) with *In re Bene*, 474 B.R. 56, 71-72 (Bkrtcy. W.D.N.Y. 2012) (debtor's decision not to participate outweighed by other circumstances and no bar to finding of good faith).

P-H 18-x: Another issue raised by these DOE programs for student loan repayment is the potential tax liability for debtors who are ultimately able to write off all or a portion of the student loan debt as a result of participating in such a program (cancellation of debt income or COD). Should a debtor who chooses not to participate because of the potential for tax liability years down the road when the balance of a loan is written off nonetheless be held to have failed the good faith prong of the *Brunner* test? The courts are split. Compare *In re Gibson*, 428 B.R. 385 (Bkrtcy. W.D. Mich. 2010) ("the court is not persuaded that a debtor's long-term tax strategy or concerns should foreclose the possibility of at least some debt repayment over the next twenty-five years, particularly in the case of a bright, well-educated, healthy debtor") and *In re Nixon*, 453 B.R. 311, 335, 392-93 (Bankr. S.D. Ohio 2007) ("At the end of the 25-year repayment period, if the debt is cancelled, there are tax consequences for the Debtor. The Debtor would be 81 years old at the end of the 25-year repayment period, and likely still on a fixed income. The tax consequences for someone in that position could be devastating."). See if your district or circuit has a case dealing with this aspect of the dischargeable student loan issue.

P-H 18-y: In the last generation the cost of a college education has accelerated far faster than inflation. At the same time, most states have reduced aid to public institutions placing more of the increasing cost on the student and her family. In 2012 the total student loan debt in the United States ($914 billion) actually exceeded total consumer credit card debt ($858 billion) and is second only to total indebtedness for home loans ($8.15 trillion). Is it time to revisit the undue hardship standard for discharge of student loan debt and give bankruptcy judges more flexibility to modify such obligations in particular cases? Should BAPCPA's expansion of the discharge restriction to private student loans made by for-profit lenders be reconsidered? Can you think of other approaches to this vexing problem that ought to be considered?

9. Fines, Penalties, and Forfeitures Owed to the Government [§523(a)(7)]

Governmental fines and penalties imposed to punish the debtor for wrongdoing are non-dischargeable if not more than three years old when the petition is filed. Examples might include speeding tickets, penalties on unpaid taxes, and liability for bail bond forfeiture.

10. Personal Injury and Wrongful Death Claims Arising from DUI [§523(a)(9)]

Judgments arising out of simple or even gross negligence are generally dischargeable in bankruptcy, but if the wrongful death, personal injury, or property damage claim against the debtor arises out of the debtor's driving while intoxicated by alcohol or drugs, it will not be a dischargeable debt.

11. Unlisted Debts [§523(a)(3)]

When preparing their schedules and lists to accompany the bankruptcy petition, debtors must be very careful to list every single debt they owe whether contingent or fixed, disputed or undisputed. Any debt not listed may not be discharged whether the error was intentional or accidental. Legal professionals assisting debtors complete their schedules must help them be thorough. When a debt has been omitted by mistake, it may be possible to amend the schedules to include the debt and discharge it.

FRBP 1009 provides that a voluntary petition, list, statement or schedule can be amended by the debtor at any time before the case is closed. If the case has been closed when the omission of a creditor from the schedules is discovered, the case may be **reopened** by motion pursuant to §350(b) and FRBP 5010, and the schedules then amended. However, the debtor will be required to pay a new filing fee for reopening the case as well as the additional attorney fee involved.

E. Objections to Discharge

An individual Chapter 7 debtor can be denied any discharge at all (i.e., no relief from any debts) if one of the grounds set forth in §727(a) of the Code and summarized in Illustration 18-d is established.

The bankruptcy trustee, U.S. Trustee or any creditor is given standing to object to the debtor's discharge by filing a complaint and instituting an adversary proceeding (see Illustration 13-f). FRBP 4004 requires that a complaint to deny discharge be initiated within 60 days following the first meeting of creditors subject to extension by motion and as with complaints objecting to discharge of a particular debt, FRBP 2002(f) requires the bankruptcy court clerk, or some other person as the court may direct, to provide notice by mail of the time fixed for filing a complaint objecting to discharge.

1. Dealing with Property for the Purpose of Hindering, Delaying, or Defrauding a Creditor [§727(a)(2)]

Debtors must be very careful not to play games with the bankruptcy process by hiding assets, putting them into the name of a third person prior to filing, or similar gambits. The trustee will aggressively look for that type of thing and most bankruptcy judges will have little sympathy for debtors engaged in them when a denial of discharge is requested.

2. Concealing, Destroying, Falsifying, or Not Keeping Books and Records [§727(a)(3) & (4)(D)]

Debtors must be very careful not to destroy, alter, or hide their financial records as part of an attempt to hide assets or deceive as to their value. Bankruptcy trustees know the kinds of records consumer and business debtors should have and will aggressively pursue any situation that looks suspicious. Note that it is not just concealing, destroying, or falsifying books and records that is punishable, but the failure to keep adequate records.

Illustration 18-d: GROUNDS FOR DENYING A DISCHARGE TO AN INDIVIDUAL CHAPTER 7 DEBTOR

- The debtor has transferred, removed, destroyed or concealed property with the intent to hinder, delay or defraud a creditor or the trustee within either a year preceding the filing of the petition or after the petition was filed
- The debtor has concealed, destroyed, falsified or failed to keep books and records from which his financial condition or business transactions may be ascertained unless there is justification
- The debtor has knowingly made a false oath or account, or presented or used a false claim or in connection with the bankruptcy case
- The debtor has failed to satisfactorily explain any loss of assets or deficiency of assets to meet his liabilities
- The debtor has failed to obey a lawful order of the bankruptcy court
- The debtor has been previously granted a discharge in a Chapter 7 or 11 within eight years prior to the filing the petition in the current case or a discharge in a Chapter 13 within six years prior to the filing the petition in the current case
- The debtor has failed to complete an instructional course concerning financial management

---

3. Making a False Oath or Account or Using a False Claim [§727(a)(4)]

The petition and supporting schedules and lists filed by the debtor are signed under penalty of perjury and the debtor must be sure before signing that they are accurate and complete. The failure to do so can be construed as a false oath and a discharge denied. In addition, the debtor is examined under oath at the first meeting of creditors (the 341 meeting) and must be careful to give truthful answers there.

4. Lack of Satisfactory Explanation of Loss of or Inadequate Assets [§727(a)(5)]

At the 341 meeting and at informal meetings with the bankruptcy trustee the debtor may be questioned closely regarding assets he once had but now does not. Where did those assets go? If the debtor seemed to have adequate income flow to pay his obligations but did not, where did that income go? If the debtor cannot give a plausible explanation, deception may be suspected and the unsatisfactory explanation will form the basis of this objection to discharge.

5. Failure to Obey a Lawful Court Order or to Answer When Asked [§727(a)(6)]

Assume a debtor fails to come to his 341 meeting as required by §521 and the court orders him to be present for the rescheduled date. Assume a debtor refuses to turn over property to the trustee as required by §521 and the court orders the turnover. Assume the trustee requests a Rule 2004 examination of a debtor, the debtor fails to attend and the court orders his attendance. The debtor must obey the court's orders. Failure to obey even one lawful order forms the basis for this objection to discharge. A pattern of refusal to obey practically guarantees the motion being granted.

The debtor must also respond to material questions put to him by the court and to testify when asked to do so whether at his 341 meeting or at a Rule 2004 examination (discussed in Chapter Sixteen, Section F), at any other evidentiary hearing, or in connection with discovery undertaken in an adversary proceeding (see Chapter Thirteen, Section G). A claim by the debtor of the Fifth Amendment privilege against self-incrimination will not prevent denial of discharge on this basis if the judge has granted the debtor immunity in connection with the testimony.

6. A Prior Discharge [§727(a)(8)(9)]

Section 727(a)(8) stipulates that a bankruptcy court is to deny a Chapter 7 discharge if the debtor previously received a discharge in a Chapter 7 or 11 case within eight years preceding the filing of the petition.

P-H 18-z: BAPCPA increased the mandatory waiting period between Chapter 7 discharges from six years to eight. Although the purported reason for the extension was to prevent unscrupulous utilization of the discharge privilege by debtors, the change also means that honest debtors will remain vulnerable for a longer period to unscrupulous lenders able to charge such individuals higher rates of interest knowing that, regardless of their circumstances, they cannot discharge that obligation during the eight-year term. Do you agree with the eight-year waiting period? If so, what waiting period do you think would be fair? Should Congress have offset the extension of the prior discharge term with other legislation protecting former debtors from predatory lenders?

The court will also deny a Chapter 7 discharge if the debtor previously received a discharge in a Chapter 13 or 12 case within six years preceding the petition under §727(a)(9) unless:

- The debtor paid all allowed unsecured claims in the earlier case in full, or
- The debtor made payments under the plan in the earlier case totaling at least 70 percent of the allowed unsecured claims and the debtor's plan was proposed in good faith and the payments represented the debtor's best effort.

P-H 18-aa: Is the conditional six-year waiting period after a Chapter 13 or 12 reasonable? Why did Congress recognize exceptions for the six-year waiting period but none for the eight-year waiting period between Chapter 7 cases? Would a "good-faith filing" exception to the eight-year waiting period be reasonable? Workable?

7. Failure to Complete the Postpetition Financial Management Course [§727(a)(11)]

In addition to the prepetition credit counseling requirement imposed on individual debtors considered in Chapter Fourteen, Section D, §727(a)(11), added by BAPCPA, requires those debtors to complete a postpetition **financial management instructional course** before the discharge will be granted.

Credit counseling agencies A nonprofit entity approved by the U.S. Trustee to provide prepetition credit counseling or predischarge financial management services to individual debtors.

The individual debtor must also file a **Certificate of Completion of Instructional Course Concerning Personal Financial Management** (OBF 23) along with a copy of any **debt management plan** that was developed in counseling as required by Exhibit D to the bankruptcy petition. (FRBP 1007 as amended effective December 1, 2013 eliminates the debtor's obligation to file OBF 23 if the provider of the course notifies the court that the debtor has completed the course.) The certification of completion prepared on behalf of Marta Carlson can be seen in Document 35 in the Carlson case file. As with the prepetition credit counseling, the postpetition and predischarge financial management instructional course will be conducted by nonprofit **budget and credit counseling agencies** that are approved by the U.S. Trustee per §111 of the Code.

F. Dismissal or Conversion of a Chapter 7 Case

Related to the topic of the §727 objection to discharge is the possibility that a Chapter 7 case may be dismissed by the bankruptcy judge for other reasons or converted to a Chapter 13 case. This can happen for a number of different reasons.

1. For Delay, Nonpayment of Fees, or Failure to File Schedules

Section §707(a) provides that the court may dismiss a Chapter 7 case for:

- Unreasonable delay by the debtor that is prejudicial to creditors;
- Nonpayment of any required fees or charges; or
- Failure to timely file the required schedules supporting the of the debtor's petition.

2. For Bad Faith or Abuse Demonstrated by the Totality of Circumstances

Section 707(b)(1) authorizes the court to dismiss a Chapter 7 case filed by a consumer debtor if it finds that the granting of relief would be an "abuse of the provisions of this chapter." We learned in Section C of Chapter Thirteen that §707(b)(2) raises a **presumption of abuse** if the debtor fails the means test that can only be overcome by the debtor showing **special circumstances** involving extraordinary expenses or adjustments to income. But "abuse" under §707(b) is a much broader concept than the means test and presumption of abuse that apply only to consumer debtors.

Section 707(b)(3) allows the court in all Chapter 7 cases to consider whether a) the debtor filed the petition in **bad faith** or b) the **totality of the circumstances** of the debtor's financial situation demonstrates that it would be an **abuse of the system** to allow the debtor a Chapter 7 discharge. The court can look at any relevant factors in making the decision except that §707(b)(1) specifically says the court may *not* consider charitable contributions by the debtor.

EXAMPLE

> Assume a debtor files a Chapter 7 to stop foreclosure on his home. He fights the lifting of the stay on the creditor's foreclosure on his home then dismisses that case without receiving a discharge. A year and a day later (to avoid the application of the 30-day automatic stay of §362(c) discussed in Chapter Sixteen, Section E) he files another Chapter 7 case to prevent foreclosure and again fights the lifting of the stay for a while and dismisses this case too. Now, another year and a day later (again to avoid the application of §362(c)), he files yet another Chapter 7 to delay the latest foreclosure actions against him. Regardless of other circumstances, the bankruptcy court could conclude that this third filing is in bad faith and that the debtor is abusing the system by manipulating it only to stop foreclosures using the automatic stay while never intending to allow the case to proceed against his nonexempt assets for the benefit of his creditors. A case like that might well be dismissed under §707(b)(3).

EXAMPLE

> Assume a physician just finishing his residency and carrying a substantial amount of debt from his medical education and training signs a personal services contract agreeing to provide medical services for a physician's group for three years. The physician begins performance on the agreement but is immediately sorry he entered into it. Unhappy with where he is living and working, he breaches the agreement after six months and moves to another location to practice. When the physician's group with which he contracted files suit, the physician files a Chapter 7 case to discharge the claims arising from the agreement. In examining the totality of the physician's financial circumstances the court may conclude that although the debtor can overcome the presumption of abuse based on the educational loan debt he is still carrying, that his projected income in the near future will quickly enable him to pay off that debt at which point he will not be able to rebut the presumption of abuse from the means test. Based on the totality of circumstances the court may dismiss this case.

EXAMPLE

> Assume a debtor files for Chapter 7 relief and it is learned that the debtor is unable to pay his debtors because he gave almost everything he owned away to charities. Per §707(b)(1) this arguably cannot be a ground for dismissal based on either bad faith or abuse from the totality of the circumstances.

It is important not to confuse the bad faith and abuse from totality of the circumstances tests with the means test and presumption of abuse that involves only individual consumer debtors and is normally resolved at the beginning of a case in connection with that debtor's Form 22A discussed in Chapter Fourteen, Section C. The bad faith and abuse from totality of the circumstances tests apply to *all* Chapter 7 debtors whether individuals or entities and whether involving consumer or business debts. And a motion based on these grounds can be raised at any point in a Chapter 7 case to seek dismissal of the case or conversion to a Chapter 13 case with the individual debtor's consent.

3. The Debtor's Right to Convert

So long as the case was originally filed as a Chapter 7 (and not converted to a Chapter 7 from another chapter of the Code), §§706(a) and (d) permit the debtor to **convert** the case to a case under Chapters 11, 12, or 13 so long as the debtor qualifies as a debtor under the chapter of the Code to which he converts the case.

On motion, a party in interest may request the conversion of a Chapter 7 case to one under Chapter 11 and such motion is decided using the "after notice and a hearing" procedure per §706(b). But a Chapter 7 case cannot be converted to one under Chapter 12 or 13 without the debtor's request or consent per §706(c).

A case that has been or is likely to be converted from one chapter of the Code to another is commonly referred to by practitioners as one that has or is likely to go **downstream**. For example, if a debtor files a shaky Chapter 13 case that is likely to be converted later to a Chapter 7 liquidation, a practitioner might say, "That is a downstream liquidation if I ever saw one."

G. ▶ The Final Discharge, Closing the Case, and Prohibition on Discrimination

The individual Chapter 7 debtor receives a final **discharge in bankruptcy** from the court under §727 of the Code (see OBF 18). The final discharge entered in Marta Carlson's case is Document 39 in the Carlson case file. In a no-asset case the discharge may be entered in as little as 30–60 days following filing of the petition. In asset cases it takes approximately four months. Some cases get bogged down with disputes and go on significantly longer.

The procedure for handling the final discharge varies among federal districts. In most districts the entry of the discharge is done automatically without any hearing being held. In the past bankruptcy judges routinely conducted a discharge hearing where they would endeavor to make sure the debtor understood the significance of the discharge but most judges now do not. In some districts the court requires the debtor's attorney to file a certification or affidavit stating that the attorney has reviewed the significance of the discharge with the debtor before the discharge will be granted. The local rules of the bankruptcy court will typically address how the judge handles the discharge.

P-H 18-bb: Determine the discharge procedure used in the bankruptcy court in your federal district. Does the judge conduct a formal discharge hearing? Is the debtor's attorney required to make any certifications or to file an affidavit concerning discussions with his client? Check the local rules of your court or discuss this issue with the U.S. Trustee, a trustee panel member or bankruptcy practitioner.

The discharge releases the debtor from any further personal liability for dischargeable debts. The debtor is no longer legally required to pay those debts and the discharge operates as a permanent **injunction** prohibiting creditors from ever undertaking any form of collection action on the discharged debts.

EXAMPLE

> Look at the second page of OBF 18, Discharge of Debtor and note the various warnings and other information set out there concerning the effect of the discharge.

If a creditor does violate the permanent injunction against attempting to collect a discharged debt the debtor can file a motion with the bankruptcy court asking that the offending creditor be enjoined for continuing to violate the discharge order and found in contempt of the court's discharge order. An injunction and a monetary fine for civil contempt is the usual result. If the case has been closed when the creditor violates the order of discharge, the debtor must move to reopen the case pursuant to §350(b) and FRBP 5010 in order to seek relief from the court. The filing fee is waived when a case is reopened for this purpose.

As has been mentioned, only an individual debtor actually receives a discharge. An entity debtor simply goes out of business.

A discharge, once granted, can be revoked. Section 727(d) sets forth the reasons why a **revocation of discharge** can be entered by the bankruptcy court upon request of the bankruptcy trustee, U.S. Trustee, or a creditor and those are summarized in Illustration 18-e.

A request to revoke the debtor's discharge on the first ground listed in Illustration 18-e must be filed within one year of the date the discharge was granted. For the other grounds the request must be filed within a year of the date the discharge was granted or the date that the case is closed whichever is later. If the case has been closed when the creditor seeks to revoke the discharge it must move pursuant to §350(b) and FRBP 5010 to reopen the case.

The granting of the discharge does not mean that the case itself is closed. Following discharge, the bankruptcy trustee may still have property of the estate to seize or liquidate and proceeds to distribute. When that process is completed and if there are no other matters pending, the trustee will file the **final report and accounting** required by §704(a)(9) and the case will be **closed** pursuant to §350(a).

P-H 18-cc: Let's look at Marta Carlson's fresh start following her discharge in Chapter 7. What property was she able to exempt and keep for use in her fresh start? What debts does she remain liable for post-discharge? She lost her house in the liquidation so will now need a new place to live with her children. Note the new address for her in the heading of the order of discharge (Document 39 in the Carlson case file). She lost her car in the liquidation so will need a new one. She needs to make wise financial decisions now. How long will it be before she can file another Chapter 7 case?

Section 525 of the Code contains a broad prohibition on discrimination against a debtor because he has been through bankruptcy. Though §525 applies to any debtor invoking any chapter of bankruptcy relief, it is the Chapter 7 debtor who is most likely to suffer discrimination as a result of the stigma of having filed. Section 525(a) prohibits any governmental entity from denying, revoking, conditioning or refusing to renew any license, permit, charter, or employment

Illustration 18-e: GROUNDS SUPPORTING A REVOCATION OF DISCHARGE

- The debtor obtained the discharge fraudulently
- The debtor failed to disclose the fact that he or she acquired or became entitled to acquire property that would constitute property of the bankruptcy estate
- The debtor has refused to obey any lawful order of the court
- The debtor has failed to explain misstatements discovered in an audit of the case
- The debtor has failed to provide documents or information requested in an audit of the case

solely because the person or entity has been a bankruptcy debtor. Section 525(b) prohibits private employers from discriminating in employment solely because the person or someone associated with the person has been a bankruptcy debtor. And §525(c) prohibits both public and private makers of student loans from discriminating in making such a loan on that basis.

CONCLUSION

We have now examined a Chapter 7 liquidation case from filing through discharge. Many individual debtors are able to repay some or all of their debts if given sufficient time and relief from creditor collection efforts. For those debtors, a Chapter 13 reorganization case is often the perfect solution. We will examine the Chapter 13 case next.

CHAPTER SUMMARY

The bankruptcy trustee can abandon property of the estate that is of inconsequential value or burdensome to the estate on notice and a hearing. Property which is burdened by a perfected security interest but in which there is equity for the estate may be sold by the trustee free and clear of all liens with prior permission of the court. The trustee will liquidate other property of the estate by selling it on notice and a hearing. Assets of the estate are distributed by the trustee to satisfy administrative expenses of the case and creditor claims in a mandated order of priority. Within a particular priority classification, distribution is *pro rata* among creditors in the class. A Chapter 7 debtor may attempt to retain property pledged as collateral that the trustee has abandoned on behalf of the estate either by reaffirmation of the debt, redemption, avoiding certain liens in order to claim an exemption, ride through, or, in a few courts, by stripping off a junior lien on the property. Some debts cannot be discharged in a Chapter 7 case and a complaint to determine the dischargeability of a debt is an adversary proceeding. A number of grounds exist for the denial of any discharge to an individual Chapter 7 debtor. A complaint objecting to discharge is an adversary proceeding. Entity debtors such as corporations and partnerships do not receive a technical discharge in a Chapter 7 case, they merely cease legal existence. A Chapter 7 case can be dismissed for various reasons or, in the case of an individual debtor, converted to a case under Chapter 13, 12, or 11 with the debtor's consent and assuming the debtor qualifies for relief under the Chapter converted to. Among the reasons for dismissal or conversion is a finding that the Chapter 7 case was filed in bad faith or that, under the totality of circumstances, it would be an abuse of the system to permit a discharge. A debtor may reaffirm a debt that could have been discharged in bankruptcy but the reaffirmation agreement must be in writing and be approved by the court. An individual Chapter 7 debtor has the right to redeem consumer property pledged as security to a creditor and which the debtor wishes to exempt from the trustee or which the trustee has abandoned by paying the present value of the property to the creditor. The individual Chapter 7 debtor receives a discharge from the bankruptcy court which operates as a permanent injunction prohibiting creditors from ever undertaking any form of collection action on the discharged debts. For a year following the discharge it can be revoked upon the showing that it was obtained by fraud and other limited grounds for revoking a discharge also exist.

REVIEW QUESTIONS

1. List as many types of debts that cannot be discharged in a Chapter 7 bankruptcy as you can recall.
2. Explain how the presumption of fraud in "last-minute" consumer purchases of luxury goods and services arises. And the presumption in "last-minute" cash advances. What is the undue hardship exception to the non-dischargeability of educational loans?
3. List as many of the grounds as you can recall for denying a discharge to an individual debtor in a Chapter 7 case.
4. Explain the difference between the presumption of abuse that prevents a Chapter 7 case from going forward and the concepts of bad faith and abuse from totality of the circumstances that may justify dismissing or converting a Chapter 7 case.
5. Describe the process the bankruptcy trustee will go through in deciding whether to abandon property of the estate and in obtaining court authorization to do so.
6. What do we mean by selling property of the estate free and clear of liens and what is the procedure for doing so?
7. What are administrative expenses? What priority do they receive in the distribution of an estate?
8. List as many Section 507 priority claims as you can recall. Explain how the claims of under-secured creditors are treated in the distribution. Explain how the claims of fully secured creditors are treated.
9. Describe generally the procedure for reaffirming a debt. What is the risk to the debtor in reaffirming a debt he could have discharged? Why would a debtor reaffirm a dischargeable debt? What is the scope of the Chapter 7 debtor's right to redeem property? What must he pay in order to do so?
10. What are the grounds upon which a discharge may be revoked? What are the time frames for moving to revoke a discharge?

WORDS AND PHRASES TO REMEMBER

abandonment of property
absolute sale
abuse of the system
administrative expenses
allowed (claim)
auction
back door ride through
bad faith
bidding in
bifurcated (claim)
cash advances
certainty of hopelessness test
closed case
collateral estoppel
convert (case)
credit-bidding
Direct Loan Program
discharge in bankruptcy (final
    discharge)
downstream
final report and accounting
financial management instructional
    course
foreclosure value
fraudulent financial statement
fraudulent pretenses
free and clear of liens
fresh start
fully secured
gap expenses
Health Care and Education
    Reconciliation Act of 2010
Income Based Repayment (IBR) Plan
ipso facto clause
judicial lien
liquidation value
luxury goods or services

no-asset report
nonpossessory, nonpurchase money
    security interest
nonprofit budget and credit
    counseling service
oversecured
partially secured
pay and ride
pay through
permanent injunction
present value
presumption of abuse
presumption of undue hardship
priority claims
private sale
public sale
Public Service Loan Forgiveness
    (PSLF) Plan
reaffirmation agreement
rebuttable presumption
reopen case
replacement value
reserve sale
revocation of discharge
ride through
right of redemption
sale free and clear of liens
special circumstances
Statement of Intent by Individual
    Debtor
strip down
surrender
totality of circumstances
undersecured
undue hardship
write down

TO LEARN MORE: A number of TLM activities to accompany this chapter are accessible on the student disc accompanying the text and at the Author Updates link to the text Web site at http://www.aspenparalegaled.com/ books/parsons_ abcdebt/default.asp.

Chapter Nineteen:

The Chapter 13 Case: Reorganization for an Individual with Regular Income—Filing the Case

By no means run in debt; take thine own measure.
Who cannot live on twenty pounds a year cannot on forty.

—*George Herbert*

A. Introduction to the Chapter 13 Case

1. The Purpose of Chapter 13

A Chapter 13 bankruptcy case is not a liquidation proceeding like Chapter 7. It is a **reorganization proceeding** designed for an **individual with regular income** (see §109(e)). In a Chapter 13 case the debtor proposes a plan which requires the debtor to use **future income** to pay all or some of his debts in exchange for which the debtor will be able to keep all or most of his nonexempt assets.

The plan may call for the **modification of debt obligations** to enable the debtor to repay what is owed on more favorable terms.

EXAMPLE

> Assume a debtor borrows money and signs a promissory note calling for repayment to the creditor over five years at $100 per month. The debtor files for Chapter 13 relief when he still owes 24 more payments at $100 per month, or $2,400. The debtor's Chapter 13 plan may call for the balance of the debt to be paid over 60 additional months at $40 per month. If approved by the court, the creditor must accept the extended plan payments.

The plan may also call for all or a portion of some debts to be discharged.

EXAMPLE

> For the debt described in the preceding Example, the plan may call for 60 payments of $20 each to the creditor, for a total of $1,200, and for the remaining $1,200 balance to then be discharged. If the plan is approved, the 60 monthly payments of $20 each will be the only payments to which the creditor is entitled and the balance will be discharged.

Of course, the debtor cannot arbitrarily alter the repayment schedule or reduce the payments due a creditor. In Chapter Twenty-One we will learn what kinds of debt modification Chapter 13 allows. And in Chapter Twenty-Two we will consider the requirements for approval of a Chapter 13 plan by the bankruptcy court.

Chapter 13 plans run three to five years under the close supervision of a named trustee. Because the Chapter 13 debtor is using **future income** to fund the plan, the plan itself is sometimes referred to informally as a **wage earner plan**, though, as we will see, the Chapter 13 debtor need not necessarily be a wage earner.

Wage earner plan Informal and inaccurate name for a Chapter 13 plan.

After BAPCPA and the new **means test** that we considered in Chapter Fourteen, Section C, the Code now contains a clear bias in favor of an individual debtor filing a Chapter 13 rather than a Chapter 7. The idea is that if the debtor is in a position to pay off even some of his debt, he should do that rather than liquidating under a Chapter 7. Thus, if the debtor filing for Chapter 7 relief triggers the presumption of abuse under that chapter and cannot rebut it, his case will be dismissed unless he voluntarily converts it to a Chapter 13. The means test and the presumption of abuse are the Code's way of not so gently pushing individual debtors toward a Chapter 13 and away from a Chapter 7.

2. Eligibility to File a Chapter 13 Case

Chapter 13 is limited to debtors with relatively small amounts of debt. Section 109(e) places strict dollar limits on how much debt a prospective Chapter 13 debtor can have. The dollar limits are subject to adjustment every third year, as mandated by §104. As of April 1, 2013, an individual filing for Chapter 13 relief can have no more than $383,175 in unsecured debt and $1,149,525 in secured debt. These amounts will be adjusted next in April 2016. Individuals with debt in excess of either the secured or unsecured debt limits can reorganize under Chapter 11, though, as we will learn, a Chapter 11 case contains many more technicalities and is much more expensive. In order to file for Chapter 13 relief, the individual must have "**regular income**," which will be used to fund the reorganization plan. Section 101(30) defines the phrase, "an individual with regular income" to mean an "individual whose income is sufficiently stable and regular to enable such individual to make payments under a plan under Chapter 13. . . ."

What is or is not "regular income" has been left largely to the courts to determine, and the courts have identified a congressional intent that the phrase be interpreted broadly. As stated in *In re Baird*, 228 B.R. 324, 327-328 (Bankr. M.D. Fla. 1999):

> The legislative history of §101(30) is unusually clear and indicates that Congress intended to expand and broadly define "individual with regular income" to include funding from diverse and nontraditional sources.

Where the debtor is employed and has a regular wage or salary, there is rarely a problem, even if that wage or salary varies from period to period.

EXAMPLE

Assume the debtor is a used car salesperson whose monthly income depends on commissions from sales. Though his income may vary depending on how well he does from month to month, he will qualify as an individual with regular income. The same is true for a debtor who works construction and whose income may be both seasonal and weather-dependent.

If a debtor is retired or disabled and living on a fixed income (e.g., pension, disability, or Social Security benefits), he will qualify for a Chapter 13 so long as those payments are regular and stable. A debtor who is unemployed at the time the petition is filed but who has good prospects for employment in the immediate future, will also qualify. A debtor who receives regular voluntary support from a nondebtor spouse or other family member qualifies, despite the argument that such voluntary funding could be cut off at any time. How about the promise of a live-in boyfriend to support his debtor girlfriend? See *In re Murphy*, 226 B.R. 601 (Bankr. M.D. Tenn. 1998).

Married couples can be **joint debtors** in a Chapter 13 case, under §§109(e) and 302(a), and commonly are because they share joint liability for debts and joint ownership of property. However, the combined debts of the joint debtors cannot exceed the monetary debt limits set by §109(e), discussed above. Only one of the spouses need have regular income to fund the plan in a joint case.

The most obvious requirement for Chapter 13 eligibility is that the debtor must be an individual. Thus, Chapter 13 is not available to an entity. (Entities can reorganize under Chapter 11, as can individuals.) Pursuant to §1304, an individual who owns a business as a **sole proprietor** can file Chapter 13 since the law does not consider the owner to be a separate legal person from his business. Such a debtor is permitted by §1304 to maintain control of his business and to operate it postpetition. The trustee in the case (discussed below) is required by §1302(c) to monitor the business and to provide reports on its operation to the court and creditors.

Pursuant to §109(g), an individual cannot file under Chapter 13 or any other chapter if, during the preceding 180 days, a prior bankruptcy petition was either a) involuntarily dismissed due to the debtor's willful failure to appear before the court or comply with orders of the court, or b) voluntarily dismissed by the debtor after creditors sought relief from the automatic stay to recover property of the debtor upon which they hold liens.

P-H 19-a: Decide which of the following debtors qualifies to file a petition for Chapter 13 relief:

- A corporation, owned by husband and wife, that operates a small deli and has only $100,00 in unsecured debt and $225,000 in secured debt
- An unemployed, single woman who has a job set to begin the first of next month
- A man who is sole owner of an unincorporated real estate brokerage and has $300,000 in unsecured debt and $750,000 in secured debt
- A retired couple living on a small pension and Social Security benefits
- A woman who owns stock in the company she works for
- A man who filed a Chapter 7 case six months ago and dismissed it voluntarily three months ago when the company holding the mortgage on his home sought to lift the automatic stay

- A man, who owns an unincorporated car repair shop, and his wife, who is a homemaker
- A lawyer who has her own unincorporated solo law practice and who has $400,000 in unsecured debt and $500,000 in secured debt

Ever heard of a **Chapter 20 case?** There is no Chapter 20 in the Code, of course, but that phrase is used by practitioners to describe the not uncommon practice of a debtor obtaining a discharge in a Chapter 7 case and then filing a Chapter 13 case shortly thereafter (7 + 13 = 20). Section 1328(f) provides that a Chapter 13 debtor cannot receive a discharge in his Chapter 13 case if he has received a discharge under Chapter 7, 11, or 12 during the four years preceding his filing of the Chapter 13 petition (we will consider discharge in a Chapter 13 case in detail in Chapter Twenty-Two). But a Chapter 13 case can be filed and a plan approved even though no discharge is granted in the case.

P-H 19-b: Why would a debtor who has received a discharge in Chapter 7 file a Chapter 13 less than four years later? Sometimes it is planned, a calculated strategy. A debtor goes through a Chapter 7 to discharge all the debt he can and then immediately files a Chapter 13 and proposes a plan that will enable him to make payments on his remaining debt on a more flexible schedule than his creditors would allow otherwise. Or he proposes a plan to take advantage of the more generous lien stripping options that Chapter 13 allows, as we will learn in Chapter Twenty-One of the text. Often the Chapter 13 filing so soon after the Chapter 7 discharge is unplanned but necessary because the debtor has fallen behind on payment schedules and needs a Chapter 13 plan to cure arrearages and perhaps even to obtain court assistance to control his own spending. See if you can determine from a practitioner in your area how common Chapter 20 filings are there.

Prepetition credit counseling Counseling that an individual debtor must receive from an approved **credit counseling agency** as a qualification for filing for bankruptcy relief.

Since the Chapter 13 filer is by definition an individual, he must comply with the **prepetition credit counseling** requirement of §109(h)(1), imposed on all individuals filing under any chapter of the Code. (See discussion of this requirement in Chapter Fourteen, Section D.)

For our detailed study of how a Chapter 13 proceeding works, we will focus on a married couple that in many ways fits the profile of typical Chapter 13 debtors. Let's meet Roger and Susan Matthews. Go to Appendix B at this time and read the Assignment Memorandum.

P-H 19-c: Based on the budget for Roger and Susan Matthews shown in the Assignment Memorandum in Appendix B, how much money do the Matthews have available each month to apply to the bills not being paid? How financially vulnerable are they to unexpected expenses in excess of those budgeted or to job loss? Does it appear likely at this point that the Matthews will be able to propose a plan that will pay 100 percent of their secured and unsecured debts over a three- to five-year period?

B. Filing a Chapter 13 Case

1. The Petition, Schedules, and Other Documents

Petition Document filed to initiate a bankruptcy case under the Code.

A Chapter 13 case is commenced in the same way as a Chapter 7, by filing a **petition** with a bankruptcy court (see the Matthews' Chapter 13 petition, Document 1 in the Matthews case file on the disc accompanying this text) that has proper venue (see discussion of venue in Chapter Fifteen, Section A). Like the Chapter 7 debtor, the Chapter 13 debtor must also file a list of creditors (see Document 2 in the Matthews case file), along with the various schedules of assets and liabilities, a statement of financial affairs, and the other statements and documents discussed in Chapter Fourteen, Section B (see Documents 2 through 15 and 17-20 in the Matthews case file, except for the Statement of Intent (OBF B8)). Section 521(a)(2) requires the filing of a Statement of Intent only of an individual Chapter 7 debtor. The Chapter 13 debtor's (and the Chapter 11 debtor's) proposed plan will indicate how he intends to deal with property that is subject to a security interest.

P-H 19-d: Review the exemptions claimed by the Matthews on their Schedule C (Document 5 in the Matthews case file). Do all of those claimed exemptions appear to comply with §522? Note that Roger Matthews is reporting a priority claim on Schedule E in favor of the IRS for $1,000 in back taxes he has not paid. You may want to review the discussion of priority claims in Chapter Eighteen, Section B, and the treatment such claims receive in a Chapter 7 liquidation. In Chapter Twenty-One, Section A we will see how they are treated in a Chapter 13. Go ahead and look at the Matthews' Chapter 13 plan (Illustration 21-b). The plan indicates that they are going to surrender one of their vehicles to the secured creditor. Since the Chapter 13 plan states the debtor's intent with regard to secured property, no statement of intent is required.

Disposable income Income a bankruptcy debtor has available to pay creditors after deducting income necessary for the support or maintenance of the debtor and his dependents.

Significantly, the Chapter 13 debtor must also file OBF 22C, **Chapter 13 Statement of Current Monthly Income and Calculation of Commitment Period and Disposable Income** (see Document 16 in the Matthews case file; to be discussed in detail in Chapter Twenty), for the purpose of determining the **applicable commitment period** (i.e., required duration) of the debtor's plan and the amount of **disposable income** the debtor is expected to have available during the plan term to pay to creditors. Recall that the Chapter 7 debtor files OBF 22A (see Document 21-A in the Carlson case file).

The signatures on a Chapter 13 petition involve the same considerations as those on a Chapter 7 petition. This might be a good time to review that discussion in Chapter Fifteen, Section A.

A Chapter 13 case can only be commenced voluntarily. The Code does *not* authorize an involuntary Chapter 13 filing.

2. Attorney's Fees in a Chapter 13 Case

As previously noted, in all bankruptcy cases the attorney fee agreement between the debtor and his attorney must be in writing, per §528(a)(1). As in a

Chapter 7 case, FRBP 2016 requires the **Statement Disclosing Compensation Paid or to Be Paid to the Attorney for the Debtor** to be filed in a Chapter 13 case. (See Document 19 in the Matthews case file.) However, attorney's fees work differently in a reorganization case than in a Chapter 7 liquidation (see Chapter Fifteen, Section B). In a Chapter 13 case, the fees charged by the debtor's attorney must not only be *disclosed*, they must also be *approved* by the court. And they can be paid by the debtor through the plan. If the fees are disclosed and payment is provided in the plan, the **order confirming the plan** (see Chapter Twenty-Two, Section B) is a sufficient court approval of the fees. Some federal districts may require a formal application for payment of attorney's fees separate from the plan.

EXAMPLE

As the Matthews' disclosure on attorney's fees indicates (Document 19 in the Matthews case file), part of the payment is to be made through the plan (Document 21 in the Matthews case file) and the order confirming the plan (Document 24 in the Matthews case file) is sufficient court approval.

Sometimes attorneys for the Chapter 13 debtor are called upon to provide legal assistance not contemplated by the initial fee paid prepetition or through the plan. In that event, the attorney will be required to file an **application for additional compensation** and obtain court approval of the proposed fee.

EXAMPLE

Assume that the attorney for the Matthews discloses his initial fee agreement with the clients and a plan is confirmed that calls for that fee to be paid through the plan. A year later, the Matthews need to modify the plan due to changed circumstances (see Chapter Twenty-Two, Section D) and call on the attorney again. The original fee did not contemplate this additional work, and so the attorney will file an application for additional compensation and obtain court approval for the additional fee. FRBP 2016 will apply, requiring the attorney to submit a detailed, itemized statement of services rendered and expenses incurred.

Fees allowed to debtor's attorneys for Chapter 13 work vary considerably among bankruptcy courts across the country.

3. The Standing Chapter 13 Trustee

In most federal districts, the trustee in a Chapter 13 case is not appointed from the **trustee panel**, as are trustees in Chapter 7 cases (see discussion in Chapter Sixteen, Section B). Instead, there is one individual designated by the U.S. Trustee to serve as the Chapter 13 **standing trustee**, who will automatically serve as trustee in all Chapter 13 cases filed in that district. In districts with heavier Chapter 13 filings, there may be more than one standing trustee.

Standing trustee A person appointed by the U.S. Trustee to serve as trustee in all Chapter 12 and 13 cases filed in the district. Cf. trustee panel.

Section 1302(b) assigns the Chapter 13 standing trustee many of the same duties as those of the Chapter 7 trustee (see Illustration 16-a), except that in a Chapter 13 the trustee will not seize nonexempt assets, liquidate them, and distribute the proceeds to creditors. Remember, Chapter 13 is a reorganization, not a

Illustration 19-a: UNIQUE DUTIES OF THE CHAPTER 13 STANDING TRUSTEE

- To evaluate the case to make sure it is filed in good faith and in compliance with all Code requirements
- To ensure that the debtor begins making payments under the plan as required by the Code (which often occurs before plan confirmation, as discussed later)
- To review the debtor's proposed plan for feasibility and good faith and to be heard in support or opposition to its confirmation
- To review any proposed modifications of the debtor's plan after confirmation or to propose such modification and to be heard in support or opposition to any proposed modification
- Upon approval of the plan, to collect the payments made by the debtor under the plan and to distribute those payments to pursuant to the plan
- To assist the debtor in complying with a confirmed plan, other than by giving legal advice
- If any claim for a domestic support obligation is made in the case, to advise the holder of the claim of their rights including the right to utilize the state child support enforcement agency to collect the amount owed

liquidation. But §1302(b) imposes unique duties on the Chapter 13 standing trustee, and those duties are summarized in Illustration 19-a.

We will have more to say about the duties of the Chapter 13 standing trustee as we consider other aspects of administering a Chapter 13 case.

C. The Order for Relief, Notice to Creditors, and Automatic Stay Under Chapter 13

As was discussed in Chapter Sixteen, Section A, most bankruptcy courts treat the filing of the petition as the entry of an **order for relief** in the case, while some enter a formal order to that effect. Pursuant to §342, the clerk of the bankruptcy court will give immediate notice to all creditors and other parties in interest of the commencement of the case using OBF B9I. (See Document 22 in the Matthews case file.)

Automatic stay The prohibition on creditors continuing collection efforts against a debtor that arises automatically upon the debtor's filing of a bankruptcy petition.

Filing the petition under Chapter 13 triggers the **automatic stay** provision of §362. As we have learned, the stay arises by operation of law, with the exception of the BAPCPA limitations imposed on debtors who have filed once (stay limited to 30 days unless debtor moves for extension) or twice (no stay at all) in the year preceding the current filing. (See discussion in Chapter Sixteen, Section E.) As long as the stay is in effect, creditors may not initiate or continue collection demands, lawsuits, or execution on judgments. The notice of commencement to creditors advises creditors of the stay and the danger of penalties if they continue collection efforts.

Co-debtor stay A Chapter 13 provision extending the automatic stay to co-debtors of the Chapter 13 debtor.

Section 1301(a) of the Code provides that unless the bankruptcy court authorizes otherwise, a creditor may *not* seek to collect a **consumer debt** from any individual who is liable along with the debtor. This is the unique **co-debtor stay** of Chapter 13. It does not apply in Chapter 7, 11, or 12 cases at all or to co-debtors on nonconsumer debts in Chapter 13. As we have learned, consumer debts are those incurred by an individual primarily for a personal, family, or household purposes (see §101(8)).

EXAMPLE

> A married person may file a Chapter 13 and the debtor's spouse, who does not file, will be protected by the stay from being pursued on any consumer debts she owes with her debtor/husband. Of course, if the spouse files as a joint debtor, they both have the benefit of the automatic stay.

The rationale behind the co-debtor stay of Chapter 13 is that persons who do not themselves receive the actual consideration for a consumer debt often volunteer to become liable for such a debt and it would be unfair to stay collection against the person who did receive the actual consideration while collection proceeded against the person who didn't.

EXAMPLE

> Assume Susan Matthews' parents co-signed the promissory note when Roger and Susan borrowed money to purchase furniture for their house. When Roger and Susan file for Chapter 13 relief, the automatic stay goes into effect on their behalf. But what about the parents? They are not in a bankruptcy proceeding. Without the co-debtor stay, the creditor could proceed with collection efforts against the parents even though they received no actual consideration (furniture) for the debt.

Sections 1301(a)(1) and (2) provide that the co-debtor stay is automatically lifted when the Chapter 13 debtor receives a discharge and the case is closed or when the case is dismissed or converted to a Chapter 7. Per §§1301(c)(2) and (d), the co-debtor stay is to be lifted on motion of the creditor and **after notice and a hearing** (considered in Chapter Thirteen, Section G) *to the extent that* the plan does not provide for paying the creditor. Twenty days after the filing of a motion to lift stay under §1301(c)(2), the stay is **automatically terminated** per the mandate of §1301(d) unless the debtor or co-debtor files a written objection in which a hearing will be conducted.

EXAMPLE

> Assume a married person files a Chapter 13 case but the spouse does not. The spouse initially gets the benefit of the co-debtor stay as to consumer debts. But if the debtor files a plan that calls for paying only half of that debt and the plan is confirmed, the creditor may file a motion to have the co-debtor stay lifted as to the half of the debt not to be paid under the plan. The co-debtor stay will automatically terminate 20 days after the motion is filed unless the debtor or co-debtor files a written objection. If an objection is filed a hearing will be conducted at which the burden will be on the party filing the objection to show cause why the stay should be continued as to the co-debtor.

Per §1301(c), the co-debtor stay can also be lifted by motion of the creditor and after notice and a hearing if the creditor can show that either

- The creditor will be irreparably harmed if the stay is not lifted or
- That between the debtor and the co-debtor, the co-debtor received the actual consideration for the claim.

EXAMPLE

> Assume a married person files a Chapter 13 but the spouse does not. The spouse gets the benefit of the co-debtor stay as to consumer debts, but if the creditor can show that the consumer item purchased was for the exclusive benefit of the spouse and not the debtor, the stay may be lifted. Or, if the creditor can show that the co-debtor is disposing of assets and will be judgment proof when the case is over, that may constitute irreparable harm to the creditor.

D. Property of the Estate in a Chapter 13

Property of the estate All property in which the debtor holds a legal or equitable interest at the commencement of a bankruptcy case.

Just as in a Chapter 7, all of the Chapter 13 debtor's nonexempt property becomes **property of the estate** upon filing of the petition and, as such, is subject to the control of the court, per §§1306(a) and 541(a). However, the standing trustee will not take possession of and sell the property of the estate unless the debtor's plan contemplates an abandonment and sale of property. Instead the debtor will retain possession of the property, subject to the terms of his plan per §1306(b).

The standing trustee in a Chapter 13 case has the same powers as a Chapter 7 trustee to challenge a debtor's claimed exemptions (Chapter Seventeen, Section C) and to pursue disputed, contingent, or unliquidated claims of the creditor against third parties (see Chapter Seventeen, Section B). If the debtor has already filed suit to collect on those claims when the petition is filed, the standing trustee may simply authorize the debtor to continue that suit.

The standing trustee has the same power to compel turnover of the debtor's property from third persons and custodians holding it (see Chapter Seventeen, Section D) and to avoid other prepetition transfers of the debtor's property (see Chapter Seventeen, Section E) as a Chapter 7 trustee. However, Chapter 13 standing trustees rarely exercise their turnover and avoidance powers, leaving it to the debtor to either regain possession of his property on his own or to live with the consequences of his (usually voluntary) prepetition transfers. The debtor may be handicapped in accomplishing that task since, other than the power to avoid a lien to protect an exemption (discussed in Chapter Fifteen, Section B), the Code does not grant the Chapter 13 debtor the power to compel turnover or to avoid prepetition transfers. Those powers only belong to "the trustee" (see *Hartford Underwriters Ins. Co. v. Union Planters Bank*, 530 U.S. 1 (2000)). The Chapter 13 debtor who is unable to convince a third person to return his property must therefore file suit under state law to compel the return of such property, but few Chapter 13 debtors have the resources to do so. Ironically, that debtor's failure to bring property transferred prepetition back into the estate to be made available to creditors through the plan may cause the standing trustee to object to the plan on the basis that it doesn't provide creditors as much as they would receive in a Chapter 7 liquidation (a requirement for plan confirmation discussed in Chapter Twenty-Two, Section B). This can be a real catch-22 for Chapter 13 debtors.

P-H 19-e: In contrast to the Chapter 13 debtor not being given the turnover and avoidance powers of the trustee, §1203 *does* grant those powers to a Chapter 12 debtor (as discussed in Chapter Twenty-Two, Section G), and §1107(a) grants those powers to a Chapter 11 debtor (as discussed in Chapter Twenty-Four,

Section E). Technically, the reason for that distinction is that a bankruptcy trustee is not initially appointed in a Chapter 11 case and the debtor continues to operate his business as a debtor in possession. Although there is a standing trustee in a Chapter 12 case, that debtor, too, is considered a debtor in possession and given some of the powers of a trustee. Is this an oversight in the Code's treatment of a Chapter 13 debtor? Should the standing trustee in a Chapter 13 be required to pursue turnover and avoidance actions that appear to have merit? Is the fact that most such prepetition transfers by the Chapter 13 debtor were voluntary a sufficient reason to deny him the right to exercise such powers if the standing trustee declines?

The definition of property of the estate is actually broader in a Chapter 13 than in a Chapter 7. Per §1306(a), what becomes property of the estate in a Chapter 13 includes **postpetition property**: all nonexempt property acquired by the debtor *after* the petition is filed and while the plan is in effect, including postpetition earnings and other income received by the debtor. The reason for including postpetition property, including income and earnings in the Chapter 13 estate, is that the plan is going to be funded from the postpetition income of the debtor, and that income and any other property the debtor acquires during the term of the plan must be subject to court supervision.

EXAMPLE

> Assume a Chapter 13 debtor's petition was filed 1 month ago and the proposed plan was confirmed today and will last for 48 months. The property of the estate will include: all nonexempt property owned by the debtor as of the date the petition was filed; all income received by the debtor between the date the petition was filed and the date of confirmation; all income received by the debtor during the 48 months that the plan will run; and all nonexempt property acquired by the debtor by purchase, gift, inheritance, or otherwise during the 48 months of the plan's duration.

The rights of creditors secured in the property of the debtor when a Chapter 13 petition is filed are governed in the first instance by §506, which provides that such claim is secured up to the value of the property securing the claim. We will consider the options of a Chapter 13 debtor in dealing with secured claims in Chapter Twenty-One, Section B.

E. ▶ The First Meeting of Creditors and Filing Proofs of Claim

Pursuant to §341 and FRBP 2007(a), between 21 and 50 days after the debtor files the Chapter 13 petition the **first meeting of creditors** (the **341 meeting**) is held. The notice of commencement will advise the creditors of the time and place of the meeting. (See Document 22 in the Matthews case file.) As in a Chapter 7 case, the Chapter 13 debtor is placed under oath at the meeting and will answer questions asked by the standing trustee and creditors. Significantly, the reorganization plan proposed by the debtor will be available to the trustee and creditors at the meeting because per FRBP 3015(b) it must be filed by the debtor with the petition or within 14 days thereafter. Most of the questions at the 341 meeting will typically relate to the plan.

In order to participate in distributions under the plan in a Chapter 13 case, both secured and unsecured creditors must file their claims with the court within 90 days after the first date set for the meeting of creditors pursuant to FRBP 3002(c). A governmental unit, however, has 180 days from the date the petition is filed to file its proof of claim.

> **EC 19-a:**   The timing rule for filing proofs of claim in a Chapter 13, set forth in FRBP 3002(c), illustrates how tricky such deadlines can become and the importance of the legal professional knowing the deadlines that apply and of having a system in place to make sure those deadlines are met. Assume a Chapter 13 case is filed and the 341 meeting is scheduled for September 1. Then, the meeting is rescheduled for September 15. The proofs of claim are due in that case 90 days from September 1, not 90 days from September 15. If you are responsible for preparing the proof of claim for a client or if you are a legal professional assisting the standing trustee, the debtor's attorney, or the attorney for another creditor, it is imperative that you know the applicable deadline and meet it, if that is your responsibility. If you work for another party, your responsibility might be to point out the failure of a creditor to meet the applicable deadline. Failure to do so is both professional malpractice and an ethical violation for failure to act with competence.

Any **party in interest** may object to a claim filed by a creditor in a Chapter 13 case pursuant to §502, just as can be done in a Chapter 7 (see Chapter Seventeen, Section A). That objecting party is most likely to be the debtor himself or the standing trustee.

> **P-H 19-f:**   The leading treatise regarding all things Chapter 13 is *Chapter 13 Bankruptcy*, by Keith M. Lundin and William H. Brown (4th ed., 2011, Bankruptcy Press, Nashville, TN, available by online subscription only at www.ch13online.-com). If you have access to this work, consult it regarding questions you may have as we continue our study of Chapter 13.

CONCLUSION

Thus begins a Chapter 13 case. But the heart of a Chapter 13 case is the debtor's plan of reorganization that, as noted, must be filed with the petition or within 14 days thereafter. In Chapter Twenty we will see how the required term of a Chapter 13 plan is determined (called the applicable commitment period) as well as the minimum amount the debtor must pay into it (called the debtor's projected disposable income).

CHAPTER SUMMARY

A Chapter 13 bankruptcy case is a reorganization proceeding for an individual with regular income in which the debtor formulates a plan to use future income to pay some or all of his debts over the following three to five years. Only individuals with secured and unsecured debts below stipulated ceilings can file for Chapter 13 relief, though husbands and wives may be joint debtors in Chapter 13. Fees of the debtor's attorney in a Chapter 13 must be approved by the court and can be paid through the plan.

A Chapter 13 is commenced by filing a petition, and the debtor must complete a form calculating monthly disposable income and the applicable plan commitment period. The proposed plan of reorganization must be filed with the petition or within 15 days thereafter. An order for relief is entered or deemed entered with the filing of the petition, and the automatic stay goes into effect. In a Chapter 13, the automatic stay includes a stay against proceeding against co-debtors on consumer debts. A Chapter 13 standing trustee will administer the case under the supervision of the U.S. Trustee. The standing trustee will ensure that the plan of reorganization is proposed in good faith and is feasible and will then collect debtor's plan payments and distribute funds to creditors pursuant to the plan.

Property of the estate in a Chapter 13 includes both prepetition and postpetition property of the debtor for the duration of the plan. However, in a Chapter 13, the standing trustee does not take possession of, abandon, or sell property of the estate unless the plan calls for it; the debtor retains possession of his property. The Chapter 13 standing trustee may, but rarely does, pursue contested claims on behalf of the estate or exercise his turnover or avoidance powers, leaving it to the debtor to pursue such matters as state law allows.

A first meeting of creditors is conducted at which questions about the plan or objections to it are often resolved. In order to participate in distributions under the plan, both secured and unsecured creditors must file proofs of claim within 90 days following the meeting of creditors. A governmental creditor, however, has 180 days from the date the petition is filed to file its proof of claim.

REVIEW QUESTIONS

1. Why are Chapter 13 plans sometimes called "wage earner" plans? Must the Chapter 13 debtor be a wage earner? What is the "regular income" requirement for Chapter 13 relief?
2. What are the secured and unsecured debt limitations on filing for Chapter 13 relief? If a debtor does not qualify for Chapter 13 relief due to exceeding those limits, what other reorganization proceeding might the debtor choose?
3. Can a Chapter 13 be commenced involuntarily? Must a Chapter 13 debtor comply with the prepetition credit counseling requirement?
4. How are debtor's attorney's fees handled differently in a Chapter 13 than in a Chapter 7 case? If a debtor's attorney is required to do unexpected work for the debtor after the plan has been approved, what is the procedure for receiving compensation?
5. How does a Chapter 13 debtor determine the required duration of his plan of reorganization?
6. What do we mean by a "standing trustee" and how is that different from a "trustee panel"?

7. List all the duties of a Chapter 13 standing trustee that you can recall. How are the duties of a Chapter 13 standing trustee different from those of a Chapter 7 trustee?

8. What is the co-debtor stay of Chapter 13? What is the policy behind the co-debtor stay? How can the co-debtor stay be lifted?

9. How is the property of the estate defined differently in a Chapter 13 than in a Chapter 7 and why?

10. Why might a Chapter 13 debtor have difficulty setting aside prepetition transfers of his property or liquidating contingent claims he has against others?

WORDS AND PHRASES TO REMEMBER

after notice and a hearing
automatic stay
Chapter 13 plan
Chapter 13 standing trustee
co-debtor stay
consumer debts
disposable income
first meeting of creditors
future income
individual with regular income
joint debtors

order for relief
petition
postpetition property
prepetition credit counseling
property of the estate
reorganization
sole proprietor
Statement of Current Monthly
    Income
wage earner plan

TO LEARN MORE: A number of TLM activities to accompany this chapter are accessible on the student disc accompanying the text and at the Author Updates link to the text Web site at http://www.aspenparalegaled.com/books/parsons_abcdebt/default.asp.

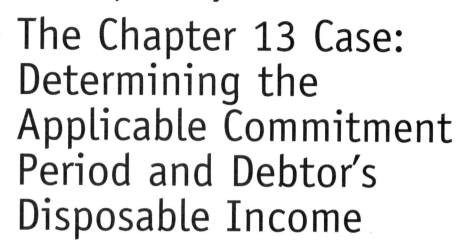

Chapter Twenty:

The Chapter 13 Case: Determining the Applicable Commitment Period and Debtor's Disposable Income

And I won't tell 'em at the bank
What I'm gonna do with all my dough
I'll just smile and tell 'em thanks
For it's better they shouldn't know

—*Dan Hicks, Payday Blues*

 A. **Determining the Applicable Commitment Period of a Chapter 13 Plan**

1. The Applicable Commitment Period for the Below Median Debtor

Applicable commitment period The required duration of a Chapter 13 plan, between three and five years.

Projected disposable income Income that a bankruptcy debtor is projected to have available during the term of his plan to pay unsecured creditors after deducting income necessary for the support or maintenance of the debtor and his dependents and to pay secured creditors.

The idea behind a Chapter 13 plan is that for the term of the plan, three to five years (the **commitment period**), the debtor retains enough monthly income to pay his basic living expenses, either surrenders secured property to the secured creditors or makes arrangements to pay the full value of secured debt on some allowed terms (to be considered in the next chapter), and then turns over the excess income, called his **disposable income**, to the trustee, who will disperse that amount to unsecured creditors as called for in the plan. Thus, the first step in calculating a Chapter 13 plan is to determine the **applicable commitment period** for the debtor's plan. The second step is to determine the debtor's **projected disposable income** during the plan period. We will consider these two important steps in this chapter. In the next chapter we will look at the various ways that a Chapter 13 debtor can propose to deal with secured and unsecured debts in his plan.

Looming over the questions of applicable commitment period and projected disposable income is §1325(b)(1), which provides that if the trustee or an unsecured creditor objects to a proposed plan, the court *may not* confirm it unless the

495

plan *either* 1) provides for the payment in full of all unsecured claims (called a **100% plan**), or 2) provides that all of the debtor's projected disposable income to be received in the applicable commitment period is paid to unsecured creditors.

The form used to calculate the debtor's applicable commitment period and his disposable income is Official Bankruptcy Form (OBF) 22C, **Chapter 13 Statement of Current Monthly Income and Calculation of Commitment Period and Disposable Income**. In this section we will use Parts I and II of the Matthews' Form 22C set out in Illustration 20-a (and in Document 16-A in the Matthews case file) to learn how the applicable commitment period is determined. In the next section we will use it to learn how the debtor's projected disposable income is calculated.

Disposable income is defined by §§1325(b)(2)(A) and (B) as **current monthly income** (other than child support payments received by the debtor) less amounts "reasonably necessary" for the maintenance or support of the debtor or dependents and less charitable contributions up to 15 percent of the debtor's gross income. If the debtor operates a business, the definition of disposable income excludes those amounts that are necessary for ordinary operating expenses.

The phrase *current monthly income* (CMI) is defined in §101(10A) to include the **average monthly income from all sources** that the debtor has received during the six months preceding the filing of the petition (known as the **look back period**) regardless of whether such income is taxable, as well as any amounts paid by a third party for the household expenses of the debtor. The sixth month to be included in the look back period is the month immediately preceding the date the case is filed.

EXAMPLE

> If a Chapter 13 petition is filed on September 15, the applicable look back period for calculating the debtor's CMI will be income from all sources received from March through August of that year. Income from those six months will be averaged to arrive at the current monthly income figure. So if the debtor had income totaling $26,400 during the look back period, the applicable CMI will be $4,400 ($26,400 divided by 6).

You can see the §101(10A)(A) definition of CMI reflected on Line 1 in Part I of the form. The remainder of Part I of the form then requires the debtor to report his average monthly income, so defined, from a number of different categories. Joint debtors must report the average income figures separately in Columns A and B. On Line 2 the debtor lists his gross wages, salary, and tips. That gross wages, etc., figure is to be entered *without* deductions or withholdings for tax, insurance, etc.; it is a **gross income** figure. On Line 3 the debtor who operates a business reports his **net income** from that business (gross income minus ordinary and necessary business expenses). Similarly, on Line 4, the debtor who leases a house or apartment and had rental income for the preceding six months will report that net rental income. Line 5 requires the inclusion of **passive income** from various kinds of investments, Line 6 retirement income, Line 7 child support or alimony payments, Line 8 unemployment income, and Line 9 income from any other source excluding Social Security benefits. Remember, the amounts entered in each of the lines in Part I of the form are an average of the monthly amounts received during the applicable look back period.

Illustration 20-a: PARTS I AND II OF THE MATTHEWS' OBF 22C

B 22C (Official Form 22C) (Chapter 13) (04/13)

In re **Roger H Matthews**
_____ **Susan J Matthews** _____
                        Debtor(s)
Case Number: _____
                        (If known)

According to the calculations required by this statement:
☒ The applicable commitment period is 3 years.
☐ The applicable commitment period is 5 years.
☐ Disposable income is determined under § 1325(b)(3).
☒ Disposable income is not determined under § 1325(b)(3).
(Check the boxes as directed in Lines 17 and 23 of this statement.)

CHAPTER 13 STATEMENT OF CURRENT MONTHLY INCOME
AND CALCULATION OF COMMITMENT PERIOD AND DISPOSABLE INCOME

In addition to Schedules I and J, this statement must be completed by every individual chapter 13 debtor, whether or not filing jointly. Joint debtors may complete one statement only.

	Part I. REPORT OF INCOME		
1	**Marital/filing status.** Check the box that applies and complete the balance of this part of this statement as directed. a. ☐ Unmarried. **Complete only Column A ("Debtor's Income") for Lines 2-10.** b. ☐ Married. **Complete both Column A ("Debtor's Income") and Column B ("Spouse's Income") for Lines 2-10.**		
	All figures must reflect average monthly income received from all sources, derived during the six calendar months prior to filing the bankruptcy case, ending on the last day of the month before the filing. If the amount of monthly income varied during the six months, you must divide the six-month total by six, and enter the result on the appropriate line.	Column A Debtor's Income	Column B Spouse's Income
2	**Gross wages, salary, tips, bonuses, overtime, commissions.**	$ 3,000.00	$ 2,167.00
3	**Income from the operation of a business, profession, or farm.** Subtract Line b from Line a and enter the difference in the appropriate column(s) of Line 3. If you operate more than one business, profession or farm, enter aggregate numbers and provide details on an attachment. Do not enter a number less than zero. **Do not include any part of the business expenses entered on Line b as a deduction in Part IV.** a. Gross receipts $ 0.00 (Debtor) $ (Spouse) b. Ordinary and necessary business expenses $ 0.00 c. Business income — Subtract Line b from Line a	$ 0.00	$ 0.00
4	**Rents and other real property income.** Subtract Line b from Line a and enter the difference in the appropriate column(s) of Line 4. Do not enter a number less than zero. **Do not include any part of the operating expenses entered on Line b as a deduction in Part IV.** a. Gross receipts $ 0.00 (Debtor) $ (Spouse) b. Ordinary and necessary operating expenses $ 0.00 c. Rent and other real property income — Subtract Line b from Line a	$ 0.00	$ 0.00
5	**Interest, dividends, and royalties.**	$ 0.00	$ 0.00
6	**Pension and retirement income.**	$ 0.00	$ 0.00
7	**Any amounts paid by another person or entity, on a regular basis, for the household expenses of the debtor or the debtor's dependents, including child support paid for that purpose.** Do not include alimony or separate maintenance payments or amounts paid by the debtor's spouse. Each regular payment should be reported in only one column; if a payment is listed in Column A, do not report that payment in Column B.	$ 0.00	$ 0.00
8	**Unemployment compensation.** Enter the amount in the appropriate column(s) of Line 8. However, if you contend that unemployment compensation received by you or your spouse was a benefit under the Social Security Act, do not list the amount of such compensation in Column A or B, but instead state the amount in the space below: Unemployment compensation claimed to be a benefit under the Social Security Act Debtor $ 0.00 Spouse $	$ 0.00	$ 0.00

B 22C (Official Form 22C) (Chapter 13) (04/13)   2

			Debtor	Spouse		
9	**Income from all other sources.** Specify source and amount. If necessary, list additional sources on a separate page. Total and enter on Line 9. **Do not include alimony or separate maintenance payments paid by your spouse, but include all other payments of alimony or separate maintenance. Do not include** any benefits received under the Social Security Act or payments received as a victim of a war crime, crime against humanity, or as a victim of international or domestic terrorism.					
		a.	$	$		
		b.	$	$	$ 0.00	$ 0.00
10	**Subtotal.** Add Lines 2 thru 9 in Column A, and, if Column B is completed, add Lines 2 through 9 in Column B. Enter the total(s).				$ 3,000.00	$ 2,167.00
11	**Total.** If Column B has been completed, add Line 10, Column A to Line 10, Column B, and enter the total. If Column B has not been completed, enter the amount from Line 10, Column A.				$	5,167.00

Part II. CALCULATION OF § 1325(b)(4) COMMITMENT PERIOD

12	Enter the amount from Line 11			$	5,167.00
13	**Marital Adjustment.** If you are married, but are not filing jointly with your spouse, AND if you contend that calculation of the commitment period under § 1325(b)(4) does not require inclusion of the income of your spouse, enter on Line 13 the amount of the income listed in Line 10, Column B that was NOT paid on a regular basis for the household expenses of you or your dependents and specify, in the lines below, the basis for excluding this income (such as payment of the spouse's tax liability or the spouse's support of persons other than the debtor or the debtor's dependents) and the amount of income devoted to each purpose. If necessary, list additional adjustments on a separate page. If the conditions for entering this adjustment do not apply, enter zero.				
	a.		$		
	b.		$		
	c.		$		
	Total and enter on Line 13			$	0.00
14	**Subtract Line 13 from Line 12 and enter the result.**			$	5,167.00
15	**Annualized current monthly income for § 1325(b)(4).** Multiply the amount from Line 14 by the number 12 and enter the result.			$	62,004.00
16	**Applicable median family income.** Enter the median family income for applicable state and household size. (This information is available by family size at www.usdoj.gov/ust/ or from the clerk of the bankruptcy court.)				
	a. Enter debtor's state of residence: **CL (MO)** b. Enter debtor's household size: **4**			$	70,687.00
17	**Application of § 1325(b)(4).** Check the applicable box and proceed as directed. ☒ **The amount on Line 15 is less than the amount on Line 16.** Check the box for "The applicable commitment period is 3 years" at the top of page 1 of this statement and continue with this statement. ☐ **The amount on Line 15 is not less than the amount on Line 16.** Check the box for "The applicable commitment period is 5 years" at the top of page 1 of this statement and continue with this statement.				

E X A M P L E

Mr. and Mrs. Matthews are joint debtors, so they list their income separately in Columns A and B of Part I. The only source of income for either of them is the salaries they are paid by their respective employers, so they enter the six-month average of their respective salaries in Columns A and B of Line 2. In Lines 3-9 they enter zero, then show the subtotals and total in Lines 10 and 11.

P-H 20-a: The definition of CMI used in connection with OBF 22C in a Chapter 13 case is the same as that used in connection with OBF 22A utilized for the means test in a Chapter 7 case filed by an individual debtor with primarily consumer debts (see discussion in Chapter Fourteen, Section C). And Part I of

OBF 22C is essentially identical to Part II of OBF 22A. In both forms, CMI is calculated using the same definition of that term. But the two forms are used for different purposes. This is a good time to review the reason why OBF 22A is used in Chapter 7 cases for individual consumer debtors. There is no means test for a Chapter 13 debtor, however. If you are ready to do so, verbalize the reasons for using the OBF 22A form in a Chapter 7 bankruptcy case involving a consumer debtor and the different reasons for using the OBF 22C form in a Chapter 13 case. What is the purpose for calculating CMI in each form? If you can't verbalize that distinction yet, you certainly should be able to do so once you've finished this chapter.

Note that the Code's formula for calculating projected disposable income the Chapter 13 debtor will have during the term of his plan is derived from considering his *prepetition income* during the six-month look back period. In the vast majority of cases this makes perfect sense, because the debtor expects his income during the upcoming plan period to be identical or very similar to what it has been during the look back period. But occasionally that is not the case because the debtor's income during the look back period was higher or lower than what it will be during the plan period.

EXAMPLE

Debtor receives a one-time buyout from an employer during the look back period, causing her CMI figure calculated per §101(10A)(A) to be substantially higher than what her actual monthly income will be during the period of her plan. In this situation the CMI calculated per §101(10A)(A) seems to conflict with the idea of a debtor making available all of her *projected* disposable income (PDI) as contemplated by §1325(b)(1)(B) because her projected income is clearly lower than her CMI calculated based on the look back period. Or a debtor could have just gotten a new job that will significantly increase her real income during the plan period over what the CMI calculated using income from the look back period would suggest, raising the same dilemma. The same dilemma could be created by a significant increase or decrease in debtor's expenses between the look back period and the plan period, which will leave the debtor with more or less disposable income during the plan period.

In dealing with debtors like the ones in the example, some bankruptcy courts utilized a strict **mechanical approach** to CMI calculation that focused exclusively on income/expenses in the look back period without regard to the upcoming changes. In these districts, debtors either had to delay filing until the applicable look back period encompassed the change in income or expenses (which was not always possible due to repossessions, foreclosures, or other financial emergencies) or go ahead and propose a plan based exclusively on numbers from the look back period, have it confirmed, and then file a proposed modification to the plan based on changed circumstances (to be considered in Chapter Twenty-Two, Section D), which would add to the expense of the case. Other courts developed a **forward-looking approach** that allowed/required debtors when doing their initial CMI calculation to consider the upcoming changes, notwithstanding the unequivocal language of §101(10A)(A).

In *Hamilton v. Lanning*, 130 S. Ct. 2464 (2010), the U.S. Supreme Court (SCOTUS) finally clarified the matter by holding that the forward-looking approach was the proper one. Specifically SCOTUS held that bankruptcy courts may confirm plans in which the debtor's disposable income has been calculated taking into account changes in the debtor's income or expenses that are *known or virtually certain* at the time of confirmation of the debtor's plan.

P-H 20-b: Read the SCOTUS decision in *Hamilton v. Lanning*. What were the statutory construction arguments favored by lower courts utilizing the mechanical approach to the calculation of CMI and disposable income? What were the statutory construction arguments of those favoring the forward looking approach? Why did SCOTUS choose the latter over the former? Do you think SCOTUS got this one right in terms of statutory construction? In terms of policy?

Once the CMI itemized in Part I of OBF 22C has been totaled on Line 11, we then take that total to Part II of the form and enter it on Line 12. Chapter 13 debtors who are married but who did *not* file jointly and who entered the non-filing spouse's average income in Column B of Part I may subtract that portion of the nonfiling spouse's income on Line 13 that was not paid on a regular basis to defer household expenses of the debtor or dependents of the debtor and enter the balance on Line 14. This is the **marital adjustment** of OBF 22C. The income of a nonfiling spouse must be reported in Column B. And if the income of the nonfiling spouse is regularly available for household expenses of the debtor or his dependents, it must be listed and included in the debtor's total CMI entered on Line 11. It is only where the nonfiling spouse's income is not regularly available for household expenses that it can be deducted from the debtor's CMI. And the reason that the nonfiling spouse's income is not available for household expenses must be stated. The most common reason is that the nonfiling spouse is required to pay spousal or child support from an earlier marriage.

EXAMPLE

The Matthews enter the total of their joint CMI on Line 12 of their form 22C. No reduction is made for the marital adjustment since they are both debtors. Instead, a zero is entered on Line 13, and the total from Line 13 is carried forward to Line 14.

P-H 20-c: Be sure you understand why the Matthews cannot use the marital adjustment. Or why a single Chapter 13 debtor could not use it. Or why a married debtor must include his nonfiling spouse's average income in his own CMI if the spouse's income is available to defer household expenses. The marital adjustment seen on Line 13 of OBF 22C is similar to that seen on Line 14, Part III of OBF 22A as part of the Chapter 7 individual consumer debtor's means test (see discussion in Chapter Thirteen, Section C). Both the qualifying Chapter 13 debtor and the qualifying Chapter 7 consumer debtor can make this adjustment to CMI. But don't forget, we're calculating the debtor's CMI in each case for different reasons.

On Line 15 of the form, the CMI total from Line 14 is **annualized** by being multiplied by 12 on Line 13 (current monthly income × 12). Then on Line 16 we

Median income figure State by state statistics compiled by the U.S. Census Bureau every ten years when a constitutionally mandated census is taken and set out by family size.

enter the **median family income** figure for a family the size of the debtor's family living in the debtor's state of residence. The median family income figures are drawn from the **Census Bureau**'s tables and posted on the U.S. Trustee Program's website at www.usdoj.gov/ust/eo/bapcpa/meanstesting.htm.

P-H 20-d: Assume that the fictional state of Columbiana, the Matthews' state of residence, has the same median family numbers as the actual state of Missouri. There are four persons in the Matthews' family. Go to the U.S. Trustee website and locate the Census Bureau's current tables for median family income for a family of four in the state of Missouri. This is the median family income figure the Matthews use on Line 16 of their Form 22C. (Remember that the median income figures from the Census Bureau are adjusted annually. The Matthews' form uses the correct median income figure for Missouri as of January 2013 but that figure may be different when you read this.) Determine the median income for a family of four in your state of residence.

Next we compare the debtor's annualized CMI on Line 15 with the state's median family income number on Line 16. This comparison will determine the applicable commitment period for the debtor's Chapter 13 plan. If the Chapter 13 debtor's annualized CMI is *less than* the applicable median family income figure, he is what practitioners call a **below median debtor** and §1325(b)(4)(A) provides that his plan may run anywhere from 36 months (3 years) to 60 months (5 years). It *must* run at least 3 years. However, if the debtor's annualized CMI is *equal to or more than* the applicable median family income figure, he is an **above median debtor** and §1325(b)(4)(A) requires that his plan run for a full 5 years, *unless* the plan calls for unsecured creditors to be paid 100 percent of what they are owed. So long as the plan of the above median debtor proposes to pay unsecured creditors 100 percent of what is owed, it can run for as little as 3 years or up to 5 years. After all, those unsecured creditors are going to be pleased to receive 100 percent of what they are owed and would much rather receive it in fewer than 5 years. They will be delighted to see that the plan is approved to run fewer than 5 years; they're going to get their money sooner.

EXAMPLE

The Matthews' annualized CMI falls below their state's median family income figure, making them below median debtors. They can propose a plan that will call for them to pay out their disposable income to unsecured creditors for as little as three years and no more than five. Their plan must run for at least three years.

P-H 20-e: The applicable commitment period of the Matthews is only three years (see Illustration 20-a and Document 16-A in the Matthews case file) but they have proposed a five-year plan (see Illustration 21-b). Can you think of reasons why a debtor might choose to do this? Might moral attitudes regarding a perceived duty to pay as much debt as possible be involved in this decision? Might practical concerns regarding the impact on the debtor's credit rating, as discussed in Chapter Three, Section G, be involved? Or the debtor's desire to do business in the future with certain creditors?

Illustration 20-b: PARTS I AND II OF THE MATTHEWS' OBF 22C ASSUMING ABOVE MEDIAN INCOME

B 22C (Official Form 22C) (Chapter 13) (04/13)

In re   **Roger H Matthews**
____**Susan J Matthews**_____
                Debtor(s)

Case Number: _____
                    (If known)

According to the calculations required by this statement:
☐ **The applicable commitment period is 3 years.**
☒ **The applicable commitment period is 5 years.**
☒ **Disposable income is determined under § 1325(b)(3).**
☐ **Disposable income is not determined under § 1325(b)(3).**
(Check the boxes as directed in Lines 17 and 23 of this statement.)

CHAPTER 13 STATEMENT OF CURRENT MONTHLY INCOME
AND CALCULATION OF COMMITMENT PERIOD AND DISPOSABLE INCOME

In addition to Schedules I and J, this statement must be completed by every individual chapter 13 debtor, whether or not filing jointly. Joint debtors may complete one statement only.

		Part I. REPORT OF INCOME		
1	**Marital/filing status.** Check the box that applies and complete the balance of this part of this statement as directed. a. ☐ Unmarried. **Complete only Column A ("Debtor's Income") for Lines 2-10.** b. ☐ Married. **Complete both Column A ("Debtor's Income") and Column B ("Spouse's Income") for Lines 2-10.**			
	All figures must reflect average monthly income received from all sources, derived during the six calendar months prior to filing the bankruptcy case, ending on the last day of the month before the filing. If the amount of monthly income varied during the six months, you must divide the six-month total by six, and enter the result on the appropriate line.		**Column A** Debtor's Income	**Column B** Spouse's Income
2	**Gross wages, salary, tips, bonuses, overtime, commissions.**		$ 4,000.00	$ 3,000.00
3	**Income from the operation of a business, profession, or farm.** Subtract Line b from Line a and enter the difference in the appropriate column(s) of Line 3. If you operate more than one business, profession or farm, enter aggregate numbers and provide details on an attachment. Do not enter a number less than zero. **Do not include any part of the business expenses entered on Line b as a deduction in Part IV.** a. Gross receipts — Debtor $ 0.00 Spouse $ b. Ordinary and necessary business expenses — Debtor $ 0.00 Spouse $ c. Business income — Subtract Line b from Line a		$ 0.00	$ 0.00
4	**Rents and other real property income.** Subtract Line b from Line a and enter the difference in the appropriate column(s) of Line 4. Do not enter a number less than zero. **Do not include any part of the operating expenses entered on Line b as a deduction in Part IV.** a. Gross receipts — Debtor $ 0.00 Spouse $ b. Ordinary and necessary operating expenses — Debtor $ 0.00 Spouse $ c. Rent and other real property income — Subtract Line b from Line a		$ 0.00	$ 0.00
5	**Interest, dividends, and royalties.**		$ 0.00	$ 0.00
6	**Pension and retirement income.**		$ 0.00	$ 0.00
7	**Any amounts paid by another person or entity, on a regular basis, for the household expenses of the debtor or the debtor's dependents, including child support paid for that purpose.** Do not include alimony or separate maintenance payments or amounts paid by the debtor's spouse. Each regular payment should be reported in only one column; if a payment is listed in Column A, do not report that payment in Column B.		$ 0.00	$ 0.00
8	**Unemployment compensation.** Enter the amount in the appropriate column(s) of Line 8. However, if you contend that unemployment compensation received by you or your spouse was a benefit under the Social Security Act, do not list the amount of such compensation in Column A or B, but instead state the amount in the space below: Unemployment compensation claimed to be a benefit under the Social Security Act Debtor $ 0.00 Spouse $		$ 0.00	$ 0.00

B 22C (Official Form 22C) (Chapter 13) (04/13)   2

			Debtor	Spouse		
9	**Income from all other sources.** Specify source and amount. If necessary, list additional sources on a separate page. Total and enter on Line 9. **Do not include alimony or separate maintenance payments paid by your spouse, but include all other payments of alimony or separate maintenance. Do not include** any benefits received under the Social Security Act or payments received as a victim of a war crime, crime against humanity, or as a victim of international or domestic terrorism.					
		a.		$	$		
		b.		$	$	$ 0.00	$ 0.00
10	**Subtotal.** Add Lines 2 thru 9 in Column A, and, if Column B is completed, add Lines 2 through 9 in Column B. Enter the total(s).					$ 4,000.00	$ 3,000.00
11	**Total.** If Column B has been completed, add Line 10, Column A to Line 10, Column B, and enter the total. If Column B has not been completed, enter the amount from Line 10, Column A.					$	7,000.00

Part II. CALCULATION OF § 1325(b)(4) COMMITMENT PERIOD

12	Enter the amount from Line 11			$	7,000.00
13	**Marital Adjustment.** If you are married, but are not filing jointly with your spouse, AND if you contend that calculation of the commitment period under § 1325(b)(4) does not require inclusion of the income of your spouse, enter on Line 13 the amount of the income listed in Line 10, Column B that was NOT paid on a regular basis for the household expenses of you or your dependents and specify, in the lines below, the basis for excluding this income (such as payment of the spouse's tax liability or the spouse's support of persons other than the debtor or the debtor's dependents) and the amount of income devoted to each purpose. If necessary, list additional adjustments on a separate page. If the conditions for entering this adjustment do not apply, enter zero.				
	a.		$		
	b.		$		
	c.		$		
	Total and enter on Line 13			$	0.00
14	Subtract Line 13 from Line 12 and enter the result.			$	7,000.00
15	**Annualized current monthly income for § 1325(b)(4).** Multiply the amount from Line 14 by the number 12 and enter the result.			$	84,000.00
16	**Applicable median family income.** Enter the median family income for applicable state and household size. (This information is available by family size at www.usdoj.gov/ust/ or from the clerk of the bankruptcy court.)				
	a. Enter debtor's state of residence: **CL (MO)** b. Enter debtor's household size: **4**			$	70,687.00
17	**Application of § 1325(b)(4).** Check the applicable box and proceed as directed. ☐ **The amount on Line 15 is less than the amount on Line 16.** Check the box for "The applicable commitment period is 3 years" at the top of page 1 of this statement and continue with this statement. ☒ **The amount on Line 15 is not less than the amount on Line 16.** Check the box for "The applicable commitment period is 5 years" at the top of page 1 of this statement and continue with this statement.				

P-H 20-f: Notwithstanding the preceding examples and the literal language of §1325(b)(4), some bankruptcy courts are interpreting that section to *not* require a full five-year plan, even where the above median debtor does not propose to pay unsecured creditors 100 percent. Instead, those courts are focusing on the final monthly disposable income figure entered by such debtors in Line 59 in Part V of OBF 22C (discussed in the next section) and using it as a multiplier to determine how much the debtor must pay to unsecured creditors over the duration of the plan, regardless of its length. If the debtor is going to pay an amount equal to 60 times the number in Line 59 over the course of the plan, those courts do not care if he pays it over five years or four years or three years. They reason that the same amount is going to be paid regardless of the duration of the plan, and so the debtor need not be compelled to stay in a plan the full five years. They also reason that creditors come out ahead with plans lasting fewer than five years because creditors receive their payout sooner. See a good discussion of both views in *In re Frederickson*, 375 B.R. 829 (BAP 8th Cir. 2007).

2. The Applicable Commitment Period for the Above Median Debtor

Let's assume for the moment that Roger Matthews has a gross salary of $48,000 per year ($4,000 per month) at City Plumbing Company and Susan Matthews has a gross salary of $36,000 ($3,000 per month) at Heart and Soul Academy. Based on those assumptions, their CMI is $7,000 and their annualized CMI is $84,000, which puts them above their applicable median income level. They are now **above median debtors** and will be required to propose either a five-year plan or a shorter 100 percent plan. Illustration 20-b and the alternative OBF 22C in Document 16-B in the Matthews file show what Parts I & II of the Matthews OBF 22C would look like if they had the higher incomes. (Since the median income figures are adjusted annually, if the applicable median income figure for a family of four in Missouri exceeds the $84,000 used in Document 16-B and Illustration 20-b at the time you are reading this, then raise the Matthews' combined hypothetical income to $5,000 in excess of that number.)

Whether a Chapter 13 debtor's applicable commitment period is three or five years, the debtor is required to note the applicable period in the box at the top of page 1 of his Form 22C and on Line 17, then continue by completing the remaining parts of the form dealing with his projected disposable income for the applicable commitment period.

B. ▶ Calculating the Chapter 13 Debtor's Projected Disposable Income

1. Calculating Disposable Income for the Below Median Debtor

Part III and, if necessary, Parts IV-VI of OBF 22C are used to calculate the debtor's projected disposable income for the term of the plan. Illustration 20-c and Document 16-A in the Matthews case file show Part III of the Matthews Form 22C. What constitutes disposable income for purposes of a Chapter 13 plan is controlled by §1325(b)(2) and (3). Essentially it is a determination of how much money the debtor will have available on a monthly basis to pay his unsecured creditors during the term of the plan. We are concerned at this point with money available for unsecured creditors because the debtor is going to retain sufficient funds to support himself and his dependents during the plan and he will propose separate treatment of his various secured debts as we will consider in the next chapter. But remember the dictate of §1325(b)(1): The Chapter 13 plan cannot be confirmed over an objection unless it proposes to pay unsecured creditors 100 percent of what they are owed or to utilize *all* of the debtor's projected disposable income to be received in the applicable commitment period to pay those unsecured creditors.

Illustration 20-c: PART III OF THE MATTHEWS OBF 22C

	Part III. APPLICATION OF § 1325(b)(3) FOR DETERMINING DISPOSABLE INCOME		
18	Enter the amount from Line 11.	$	5,167.00
19	**Marital Adjustment.** If you are married, but are not filing jointly with your spouse, enter on Line 19 the total of any income listed in Line 10, Column B that was NOT paid on a regular basis for the household expenses of the debtor or the debtor's dependents. Specify in the lines below the basis for excluding the Column B income(such as payment of the spouse's tax liability or the spouse's support of persons other than the debtor or the debtor's dependents) and the amount of income devoted to each purpose. If necessary, list additional adjustments on a separate page. If the conditions for entering this adjustment do not apply, enter zero. a. $ b. $ c. $ Total and enter on Line 19.	$	0.00
20	**Current monthly income for § 1325(b)(3).** Subtract Line 19 from Line 18 and enter the result.	$	5,167.00
21	**Annualized current monthly income for § 1325(b)(3).** Multiply the amount from Line 20 by the number 12 and enter the result.	$	62,004.00
22	**Applicable median family income.** Enter the amount from Line 16.	$	70,687.00
23	**Application of § 1325(b)(3).** Check the applicable box and proceed as directed. ☐ **The amount on Line 21 is more than the amount on Line 22.** Check the box for "Disposable income is determined under § 1325(b)(3)" at the top of page 1 of this statement and complete the remaining parts of this statement. ☒ **The amount on Line 21 is not more than the amount on Line 22.** Check the box for "Disposable income is not determined under § 1325(b)(3)" at the top of page 1 of this statement and complete Part VII of this statement. **Do not complete Parts IV, V, or VI.**		

Calculation of the debtor's projected disposable income begins by entering his CMI from Line 11 at the end of Part I of the form on Line 18 in Part III. On Line 19, the married debtor who has included the average monthly income of his nonfiling spouse in Column B of Part I may deduct whatever portion of the spouse's income is not available for household expenses of the debtor or a dependent of the debtor. The factors determining the availability of the marital adjustment here in Part III of the form are the same as for that adjustment on Line 13 in Part II of the form where we were determining the applicable commitment period (see discussion of the Line 13 marital adjustment above). After subtracting the marital adjustment on Line 19 and entering the balance of CMI on Line 20, the CMI is then annualized again on Line 21 using the multiple of 12 (CMI × 12). The applicable state median income figure for a similar size family is entered on Line 22.

EXAMPLE

The Matthews enter their CMI of $5,167 from Line 11 on Line 18. Since they are joint debtors, the marital adjustment is not available, so zero is entered on Line 14 and the CMI balance of $5,167 is again entered on Line 20 before being annualized on Line 21 to $62,004. The state median income figure for a family of four in Columbiana (Missouri) is entered on Line 22.

> **P-H 20-g:**   Do the calculations involving CMI in Part III of the form look familiar? They should since they are identical to those in Part II. But they are done for different purposes: in Part II to determine the applicable commitment period and in Part III to determine projected disposable income.

On Line 23 of Form 22C the debtor compares his annualized CMI on Line 21 with the applicable state median income figure on Line 22. If his annualized CMI is *less than* the median income figure we now know to call him a *below median debtor*. That debtor must check the second box on Line 23 and the box at the top of page 1 of the form reading, "Disposable income is not determined under §1325(b)(3)," complete the verification in Part VII of the form, and he is done with the form.

If the debtor's annualized CMI is *equal to* or *greater than* the applicable median income we now know to call him an *above median debtor*. That debtor must check the second box on Line 23 to that effect and the box at the top of page 1 of the form reading, "Disposable income is determined under §1325(b)(3)" then complete Parts IV-VI of the form to determine his projected disposable income. Section 1325(b)(3) controls the calculation of the disposable income of the above median debtor and involves the same listing of deductions from the debtor's CMI that we saw in Parts IV-VI of OBF 22A in connection with the means test of the above median debtor in a Chapter 7 consumer bankruptcy case (see Chapter Fourteen, Section C). More specifically, §1325(b)(3) dictates that the above median debtor's reasonably necessary living expenses be determined under §707(b)(2), the same section that Chapter 7 debtors use to determine whether they meet the means test.

EXAMPLE

The Matthews' annualized CMI entered on Line 21 is less than the applicable median income figure entered on Line 22 so they check the second box in Line 23 and the box on top of page 1 of the form indicating that their calculation of disposable income is not controlled by §1325(b)(3). They need only sign the verification in Part VII and they are done with Form 22C. They do not need to complete Parts IV–VI of the form.

But all we know when the below median debtor has completed his Form 22C is 1) his applicable commitment period and 2) that he is in fact a below median debtor because his CMI is less than the state median income figure. We still don't know what his disposable income is for purposes of determining how much he actually has to pay to unsecured creditors in order to have his Chapter 13 plan confirmed: remember that the debtor's plan must pay his unsecured creditors 100 percent over the term of the plan or pay all his disposable income to them. But for all its charms and horrors, Form 22C does not give us the below median debtor's disposable income number.

It is §1325(b)(2) that controls the disposable income calculation for the below median debtor. It provides that the debtor will deduct amounts **reasonably necessary** for the maintenance or support of himself and his dependents and his **actual expenses** will be used for that purpose so long as they are reasonable. The actual expenses of the debtor and his anticipated disposable income will then be derived, at least initially, from his Schedule J, Current Expenditures of Individual Debtors.

The Matthews' Schedule J is Document 12 in the Matthews case file. Notice how much like a budget it is. Compare the Schedule J with the informal budget drawn up by their lawyer in the Assignment Memorandum in Appendix B of the text. From the budget document, can you determine where much of the Schedule J information came from?

P-H 20-h: Where did the *net* average monthly income for Roger and Susan that you see on Line 20a on Schedule J come from? Look at the Matthews' Schedule I, Current Income of Individual Debtor, Document 11 in their case file. That form instructs the debtor to enter an estimate of average or projected gross income at the time the case is filed rather than the CMI formula used in Part I of OBF 22C. The deductions from that gross income and inclusion of income from other sources is similar to but not identical with Part I of OBC 22C (e.g., royalty income is included on Line 5 of OBF 22C but not mentioned on Schedule I). Since the below median debtor has calculated his CMI in Part I of OBF 22C, should that figure be used on Line 20a of Schedule J? Or should the OBF calculation of CMI on OBF 22C be ignored for the below median debtor and the average monthly income calculated on his Schedule I used instead? Almost a decade after BAPCPA became law, these questions have no clear answer. OBF 22C was created to comply with BAPCPA mandates, but pre-BAPCPA Schedules I and J have not yet been amended to conform. Of course, that could have changed after this was written. Check the current forms to see if this anomaly has been dealt with.

Although the Schedule J now in use is a starting point to determine the below median debtor's disposable income, the monthly net income figure calculated on Line 20c of Schedule J is not that debtor's actual disposable income that must be paid to unsecured creditors. It is only the *starting point* to determine it. Why do we say that? In part because the monthly net income figure from Line 20c on Schedule J does not take into consideration installment payments on nonmortgage secured debt that the debtor may need to make during the plan.

EXAMPLE

> Look at Line 13 of Schedule J where the Matthews would normally list the monthly payment due on all three auto loans they are carrying, totaling $720 (see the budget set out in the Assignment Memorandum in Appendix B and the Matthews' Schedule D, Document 6 in their case file). But the form instructs the Chapter 13 debtor (or Chapter 11 or 12 debtor) to *not* list payments to be included in the plan there. That's because auto loan payments are commonly modified in the actual Chapter 13 plan either because the auto securing the loan is surrendered to the creditor or because the secured value of the loan is crammed down to current value of the auto and payments adjusted accordingly as we will see in the next chapter.

Decisions the debtor makes regarding the treatment of secured debt in his actual plan will have an impact on the total amount of disposable income available for unsecured creditors that Schedule J does not reflect.

EXAMPLE

The Matthews currently make monthly payments totaling $720 on three vehicles. If their plan proposes to reaffirm those three debts, retain possession of all three vehicles, and continue paying the monthly obligations as they come due, that will be $720 per month that will not be available to unsecured creditors during the term of the plan. However, if the Matthews' plan proposes to surrender one or more of the vehicles or other secured property and stop paying the affected secured creditors, that decision will free up additional "disposable" dollars to go to unsecured creditors each month. That decision is not reflected on Schedule J. Thus, for this reason too, the amount of monthly net income entered on Line 20c of Schedule J is only a suggestion or a starting point for the trustee to determine if the debtor is making all of his projected disposable income available to unsecured creditors as required by §1325(b).

Another reason that current Schedule J does not calculate the debtor's disposable income for plan purposes is that it does not calculate certain anticipated expenses that may arise during the term of the plan.

EXAMPLE

Line 19 of the Matthews' Schedule J indicates that they expect to begin incurring child care expenses of $250 per month in the next year. That expense will obviously have an impact on their disposable income. But note that Schedule J does not allow that anticipated future expense to be added to the average monthly expense total showing on Line 18. In *Hamilton v. Lanning*, the Supreme Court held that upcoming changes in debtor's income or expenses, "virtually known or certain," can be considered in determining the debtor's disposable income. But Schedule J does not include that calculation.

For these reasons, Schedule J does not calculate the Chapter 13 debtor's disposable income. It is nothing more than a starting point to figure it out. Thus, though Line 20c on the Matthews' Schedule J shows a *monthly net income* available to the Matthews of $823 after deducting the various expenses listed on the form, that is not their disposable income for purposes of determining debtors' projected disposable income under §1325(b)(2).

In actuality, the debtor must decide on the specific terms of his plan, including how secured claims will be treated and what likely changes there will be to his income and expenses during the term of the plan before his disposable income can be determined. In Chapter Twenty-One, we will look at the decisions the Matthews' have made regarding those things and the actual terms of the Chapter 13 plan they put together. Only then can we determine if the plan actually proposes paying all their disposable income to unsecured creditors over the term of the plan as required by §1325(b).

2. Calculating Disposable Income for the Above Median Debtor

To learn how the calculation of projected disposable income works for the above median Chapter 13 debtor, let's again assume that Roger Matthews has a gross salary of $48,000 per year ($4,000 per month) at City Plumbing Company and Susan Matthews has a gross salary of $36,000 ($3,000 per month) at Heart and Soul Academy. Based on those assumptions, their CMI is $7,000 and their annualized CMI is $84,000, which puts them above their applicable median income level. As above median debtors they will need to complete Parts IV–VI of Form 22C. Let's also assume that the fictional county of Capitol County, Columbiana, where the Matthews reside, has the same local standards data as Boone County, Missouri. The Matthews' alternative Form 22C is Document 16-B in their case file. Illustration 20-d displays parts III through VI of that form, assuming the higher income numbers for the Matthews.

Before we go through Parts IV–VI of the Matthews' alternative OBF 22C using the higher income assumptions for the Matthews, it may be helpful for you to review the step-by-step discussion of preparing Parts IV-VI of Marta Carlson's alternative OBF 22A in Chapter Fourteen, Section C, Illustration 14-c and Document 21-B in the Carlson case file, since the deductions allowed on the two forms are substantially similar and calculated in the same way. As we have noted, this is the case because §1325(b)(3) dictates that the reasonably necessary expenses of the above median Chapter 13 debtor allowed in order to determine his disposable income are to be calculated according to §707(b)(2), the same section that controls the determination of the means test for the Chapter 7 consumer debtor.

In Part IV, Lines 24A through 29 of their alternative Form 22C, the Matthews enter standardized expense amounts for food and clothing (Line 24A), health care (Line 24B), nonmortgage housing and utility expenses (Lines 25A and 26),

Illustration 20-d: PARTS III Through VI OF THE MATTHEWS' OBF 22C ASSUMING ABOVE MEDIAN INCOME

Part III. APPLICATION OF § 1325(b)(3) FOR DETERMINING DISPOSABLE INCOME		
18	**Enter the amount from Line 11.**	$ 7,000.00
19	**Marital Adjustment.** If you are married, but are not filing jointly with your spouse, enter on Line 19 the total of any income listed in Line 10, Column B that was NOT paid on a regular basis for the household expenses of the debtor or the debtor's dependents. Specify in the lines below the basis for excluding the Column B income(such as payment of the spouse's tax liability or the spouse's support of persons other than the debtor or the debtor's dependents) and the amount of income devoted to each purpose. If necessary, list additional adjustments on a separate page. If the conditions for entering this adjustment do not apply, enter zero. a. ___ $ b. ___ $ c. ___ $ Total and enter on Line 19.	$ 0.00
20	**Current monthly income for § 1325(b)(3).** Subtract Line 19 from Line 18 and enter the result.	$ 7,000.00
21	**Annualized current monthly income for § 1325(b)(3).** Multiply the amount from Line 20 by the number 12 and enter the result.	$ 84,000.00
22	**Applicable median family income.** Enter the amount from Line 16.	$ 70,687.00
23	**Application of § 1325(b)(3).** Check the applicable box and proceed as directed. ☒ **The amount on Line 21 is more than the amount on Line 22.** Check the box for "Disposable income is determined under § 1325(b)(3)" at the top of page 1 of this statement and complete the remaining parts of this statement. ☐ **The amount on Line 21 is not more than the amount on Line 22.** Check the box for "Disposable income is not determined under § 1325(b)(3)" at the top of page 1 of this statement and complete Part VII of this statement. **Do not complete Parts IV, V, or VI.**	

 Best Case Bankruptcy

Part IV. CALCULATION OF DEDUCTIONS FROM INCOME

Subpart A: Deductions under Standards of the Internal Revenue Service (IRS)

24A	**National Standards: food, apparel and services, housekeeping supplies, personal care, and miscellaneous.** Enter in Line 24A the "Total" amount from IRS National Standards for Allowable Living Expenses for the applicable number of persons. (This information is available at www.usdoj.gov/ust/ or from the clerk of the bankruptcy court.) The applicable number of persons is the number that would currently be allowed as exemptions on your federal income tax return, plus the number of any additional dependents whom you support.		$ 1,450.00

National Standards: health care. Enter in Line a1 below the amount from IRS National Standards for Out-of-Pocket Health Care for persons under 65 years of age, and in Line a2 the IRS National Standards for Out-of-Pocket Health Care for persons 65 years of age or older. (This information is available at www.usdoj.gov/ust/ or from the clerk of the bankruptcy court.) Enter in Line b1 the applicable number of persons who are under 65 years of age, and enter in Line b2 the applicable number of persons who are 65 years of age or older. (The applicable number of persons in each age category is the number in that category that would currently be allowed as exemptions on your federal income tax return, plus the number of any additional dependents whom you support.) Multiply Line a1 by Line b1 to obtain a total amount for persons under 65, and enter the result in Line c1. Multiply Line a2 by Line b2 to obtain a total amount for persons 65 and older, and enter the result in Line c2. Add Lines c1 and c2 to obtain a total health care amount, and enter the result in Line 24B.

24B:

Persons under 65 years of age			Persons 65 years of age or older		
a1.	Allowance per person	60	a2.	Allowance per person	
b1.	Number of persons	4	b2.	Number of persons	
c1.	Subtotal	240	c2.	Subtotal	

24B total: $ 240.00

25A	**Local Standards: housing and utilities; non-mortgage expenses.** Enter the amount of the IRS Housing and Utilities Standards; non-mortgage expenses for the applicable county and family size. (This information is available at www.usdoj.gov/ust/ or from the clerk of the bankruptcy court). The applicable family size consists of the number that would currently be allowed as exemptions on your federal income tax return, plus the number of any additional dependents whom you support.		$ 544.00

Local Standards: housing and utilities; mortgage/rent expense. Enter, in Line a below, the amount of the IRS Housing and Utilities Standards; mortgage/rent expense for your county and family size (this information is available at www.usdoj.gov/ust/ or from the clerk of the bankruptcy court) (the applicable family size consists of the number that would currently be allowed as exemptions on your federal income tax return, plus the number of any additional dependents whom you support); enter on Line b the total of the Average Monthly Payments for any debts secured by your home, as stated in Line 47; subtract Line b from Line a and enter the result in Line 25B. **Do not enter an amount less than zero.**

25B:

a.	IRS Housing and Utilities Standards; mortgage/rent expense	$ 1,146.00	
b.	Average Monthly Payment for any debts secured by your home, if any, as stated in Line 47	$ 1,550.00	
c.	Net mortgage/rental expense	Subtract Line b from Line a.	$ 0.00

26	**Local Standards: housing and utilities; adjustment.** If you contend that the process set out in Lines 25A and 25B does not accurately compute the allowance to which you are entitled under the IRS Housing and Utilities Standards, enter any additional amount to which you contend you are entitled, and state the basis for your contention in the space below:		$ 0.00

B 22C (Official Form 22C) (Chapter 13) (04/13)   4

27A	**Local Standards: transportation; vehicle operation/public transportation expense.** You are entitled to an expense allowance in this category regardless of whether you pay the expenses of operating a vehicle and regardless of whether you use public transportation. Check the number of vehicles for which you pay the operating expenses or for which the operating expenses are included as a contribution to your household expenses in Line 7. ☐ 0 ☐ 1 ☒ 2 or more. If you checked 0, enter on Line 27A the "Public Transportation" amount from IRS Local Standards: Transportation. If you checked 1 or 2 or more, enter on Line 27A the "Operating Costs" amount from IRS Local Standards: Transportation for the applicable number of vehicles in the applicable Metropolitan Statistical Area or Census Region. (These amounts are available at www.usdoj.gov/ust/ or from the clerk of the bankruptcy court.)	$	424.00
27B	**Local Standards: transportation; additional public transportation expense.** If you pay the operating expenses for a vehicle and also use public transportation, and you contend that you are entitled to an additional deduction for your public transportation expenses, enter on Line 27B the "Public Transportation" amount from the IRS Local Standards: Transportation. (This amount is available at www.usdoj.gov/ust/ or from the clerk of the bankruptcy court.)	$	0.00

28	**Local Standards: transportation ownership/lease expense; Vehicle 1.** Check the number of vehicles for which you claim an ownership/lease expense. (You may not claim an ownership/lease expense for more than two vehicles.) ☐ 1 ☒ 2 or more. Enter, in Line a below, the "Ownership Costs" for "One Car" from the IRS Local Standards: Transportation (available at www.usdoj.gov/ust/ or from the clerk of the bankruptcy court); enter in Line b the total of the Average Monthly Payments for any debts secured by Vehicle 1, as stated in Line 47; subtract Line b from Line a and enter the result in Line 28. **Do not enter an amount less than zero.**			
	a.	IRS Transportation Standards, Ownership Costs	$ 517.00	
	b.	Average Monthly Payment for any debts secured by Vehicle 1, as stated in Line 47	$ 360.00	
	c.	Net ownership/lease expense for Vehicle 1	Subtract Line b from Line a.	$ 157.00

29	**Local Standards: transportation ownership/lease expense; Vehicle 2.** Complete this Line only if you checked the "2 or more" Box in Line 28. Enter, in Line a below, the "Ownership Costs" for "One Car" from the IRS Local Standards: Transportation (available at www.usdoj.gov/ust/ or from the clerk of the bankruptcy court); enter in Line b the total of the Average Monthly Payments for any debts secured by Vehicle 2, as stated in Line 47; subtract Line b from Line a and enter the result in Line 29. **Do not enter an amount less than zero.**			
	a.	IRS Transportation Standards, Ownership Costs	$ 517.00	
	b.	Average Monthly Payment for any debts secured by Vehicle 2, as stated in Line 47	$ 240.00	
	c.	Net ownership/lease expense for Vehicle 2	Subtract Line b from Line a.	$ 277.00

30	**Other Necessary Expenses: taxes.** Enter the total average monthly expense that you actually incur for all federal, state, and local taxes, other than real estate and sales taxes, such as income taxes, self employment taxes, social security taxes, and Medicare taxes. **Do not include real estate or sales taxes.**	$	960.00
31	**Other Necessary Expenses: involuntary deductions for employment.** Enter the total average monthly deductions that are required for your employment, such as mandatory retirement contributions, union dues, and uniform costs. **Do not include discretionary amounts, such as voluntary 401(k) contributions.**	$	0.00
32	**Other Necessary Expenses: life insurance.** Enter total average monthly premiums that you actually pay for term life insurance for yourself. **Do not include premiums for insurance on your dependents, for whole life or for any other form of insurance.**	$	0.00
33	**Other Necessary Expenses: court-ordered payments.** Enter the total monthly amount that you are required to pay pursuant to the order of a court or administrative agency, such as spousal or child support payments. **Do not include payments on past due obligations included in line 49.**	$	0.00
34	**Other Necessary Expenses: education for employment or for a physically or mentally challenged child.** Enter the total average monthly amount that you actually expend for education that is a condition of employment and for education that is required for a physically or mentally challenged dependent child for whom no public education providing similar services is available.	$	0.00
35	**Other Necessary Expenses: childcare.** Enter the total average monthly amount that you actually expend on childcare - such as baby-sitting, day care, nursery and preschool. **Do not include other educational payments.**	$	0.00
36	**Other Necessary Expenses: health care.** Enter the total average monthly amount that you actually expend on health care that is required for the health and welfare of yourself or your dependents, that is not reimbursed by insurance or paid by a health savings account, and that is in excess of the amount entered in Line 24B. **Do not include payments for health insurance or health savings accounts listed in Line 39.**	$	50.00

B 22C (Official Form 22C) (Chapter 13) (04/13)   5

37	**Other Necessary Expenses: telecommunication services.** Enter the total average monthly amount that you actually pay for telecommunication services other than your basic home telephone and cell phone service - such as pagers, call waiting, caller id, special long distance, or internet service-to the extent necessary for your health and welfare or that of your dependents. **Do not include any amount previously deducted.**	$	0.00
38	**Total Expenses Allowed under IRS Standards.** Enter the total of Lines 24 through 37.	$	4,102.00

Subpart B: Additional Living Expense Deductions
Note: Do not include any expenses that you have listed in Lines 24-37

39	**Health Insurance, Disability Insurance, and Health Savings Account Expenses.** List the monthly expenses in the categories set out in lines a-c below that are reasonably necessary for yourself, your spouse, or your dependents.		
	a. Health Insurance $ 74.00		
	b. Disability Insurance $		
	c. Health Savings Account $		
	Total and enter on Line 39	$	74.00
	If you do not actually expend this total amount, state your actual total average monthly expenditures in the space below: $		
40	**Continued contributions to the care of household or family members.** Enter the total average actual monthly expenses that you will continue to pay for the reasonable and necessary care and support of an elderly, chronically ill, or disabled member of your household or member of your immediate family who is unable to pay for such expenses. **Do not include payments listed in Line 34.**	$	0.00
41	**Protection against family violence.** Enter the total average reasonably necessary monthly expenses that you actually incur to maintain the safety of your family under the Family Violence Prevention and Services Act or other applicable federal law. The nature of these expenses is required to be kept confidential by the court.	$	0.00
42	**Home energy costs.** Enter the total average monthly amount, in excess of the allowance specified by IRS Local Standards for Housing and Utilities that you actually expend for home energy costs. **You must provide your case trustee with documentation of your actual expenses, and you must demonstrate that the additional amount claimed is reasonable and necessary.**	$	0.00
43	**Education expenses for dependent children under 18.** Enter the total average monthly expenses that you actually incur, not to exceed $156.25 per child, for attendance at a private or public elementary or secondary school by your dependent children less than 18 years of age. **You must provide your case trustee with documentation of your actual expenses, and you must explain why the amount claimed is reasonable and necessary and not already accounted for in the IRS Standards.**	$	0.00
44	**Additional food and clothing expense.** Enter the total average monthly amount by which your food and clothing expenses exceed the combined allowances for food and clothing (apparel and services) in the IRS National Standards, not to exceed 5% of those combined allowances. (This information is available at www.usdoj.gov/ust/ or from the clerk of the bankruptcy court.) **You must demonstrate that the additional amount claimed is reasonable and necessary.**	$	0.00
45	**Charitable contributions.** Enter the amount reasonably necessary for you to expend each month on charitable contributions in the form of cash or financial instruments to a charitable organization as defined in 26 U.S.C. § 170(c)(1)-(2). **Do not include any amount in excess of 15% of your gross monthly income.**	$	50.00
46	**Total Additional Expense Deductions under § 707(b).** Enter the total of Lines 39 through 45.	$	124.00

B 22C (Official Form 22C) (Chapter 13) (04/13)   6

	Subpart C: Deductions for Debt Payment			
47	**Future payments on secured claims.** For each of your debts that is secured by an interest in property that you own, list the name of creditor, identify the property securing the debt, state the Average Monthly Payment, and check whether the payment includes taxes or insurance. The Average Monthly Payment is the total of all amounts scheduled as contractually due to each Secured Creditor in the 60 months following the filing of the bankruptcy case, divided by 60. If necessary, list additional entries on a separate page. Enter the total of the Average Monthly Payments on Line 47.			

	Name of Creditor	Property Securing the Debt	Average Monthly Payment	Does payment include taxes or insurance	
a.	**First Bank of Capitol City**	**Residence at 419 W. Rockwood Ave**	$ 850	☒yes ☐no	
b.	**Capitol Savings Bank**	**Residence at 419 W. Rockwood Ave**	700	no	
c.	**Automotive Financing, Inc.**	**YR-3 Ford truck F150**	360	no	
d.	**Columbiana Federal Savings & Loan**	**YR-4 Honda Civic**	240	no	
			Total: Add Lines	$	2,150.00

48	**Other payments on secured claims.** If any of debts listed in Line 47 are secured by your primary residence, a motor vehicle, or other property necessary for your support or the support of your dependents, you may include in your deduction 1/60th of any amount (the "cure amount") that you must pay the creditor in addition to the payments listed in Line 47, in order to maintain possession of the property. The cure amount would include any sums in default that must be paid in order to avoid repossession or foreclosure. List and total any such amounts in the following chart. If necessary, list additional entries on a separate page.			

	Name of Creditor	Property Securing the Debt	1/60th of the Cure Amount	
a.	**First Bank of Capitol City**	**Residence at 419 W. Rockwood Ave.**	$ 14.17	
			Total: Add Lines	$ 14.17

49	**Payments on prepetition priority claims.** Enter the total amount, divided by 60, of all priority claims, such as priority tax, child support and alimony claims, for which you were liable at the time of your bankruptcy filing. **Do not include current obligations, such as those set out in Line 33.**	$ 16.67

50	**Chapter 13 administrative expenses.** Multiply the amount in Line a by the amount in Line b, and enter the resulting administrative expense.		
	a.	Projected average monthly Chapter 13 plan payment.	$ 1,998.00
	b.	Current multiplier for your district as determined under schedules issued by the Executive Office for United States Trustees. (This information is available at www.usdoj.gov/ust/ or from the clerk of the bankruptcy court.)	x 4.2%
	c.	Average monthly administrative expense of chapter 13 case	Total: Multiply Lines a and b	$ 83.92

51	**Total Deductions for Debt Payment.** Enter the total of Lines 47 through 50.	$ 2,264.76

	Subpart D: Total Deductions from Income	
52	**Total of all deductions from income.** Enter the total of Lines 38, 46, and 51.	$ 6,490.76

	Part V. DETERMINATION OF DISPOSABLE INCOME UNDER § 1325(b)(2)	
53	**Total current monthly income.** Enter the amount from Line 20.	$ 7,000.00
54	**Support income.** Enter the monthly average of any child support payments, foster care payments, or disability payments for a dependent child, reported in Part I, that you received in accordance with applicable nonbankruptcy law, to the extent reasonably necessary to be expended for such child.	$ 0.00
55	**Qualified retirement deductions.** Enter the monthly total of (a) all amounts withheld by your employer from wages as contributions for qualified retirement plans, as specified in § 541(b)(7) and (b) all required repayments of loans from retirement plans, as specified in § 362(b)(19).	$ 0.00
56	**Total of all deductions allowed under § 707(b)(2).** Enter the amount from Line 52.	$ 6,490.76

B 22C (Official Form 22C) (Chapter 13) (04/13)   7

	Deduction for special circumstances. If there are special circumstances that justify additional expenses for which there is no reasonable alternative, describe the special circumstances and the resulting expenses in lines a-c below. If necessary, list additional entries on a separate page. Total the expenses and enter the total in Line 57. **You must provide your case trustee with documentation of these expenses and you must provide a detailed explanation of the special circumstances that make such expense necessary and reasonable.**		
57	Nature of special circumstances	Amount of Expense	
	a.	$	
	b.	$	
	c.	$	
		Total: Add Lines	$ 0.00
58	**Total adjustments to determine disposable income.** Add the amounts on Lines 54, 55, 56, and 57 and enter the result.		$ 6,490.76
59	**Monthly Disposable Income Under § 1325(b)(2).** Subtract Line 58 from Line 53 and enter the result.		$ 509.24

Part VI. ADDITIONAL EXPENSE CLAIMS

	Other Expenses. List and describe any monthly expenses, not otherwise stated in this form, that are required for the health and welfare of you and your family and that you contend should be an additional deduction from your current monthly income under § 707(b)(2)(A)(ii)(I). If necessary, list additional sources on a separate page. All figures should reflect your average monthly expense for each item. Total the expenses.	
60	Expense Description	Monthly Amount
	a.	$
	b.	$
	c.	$
	d.	$
	Total: Add Lines a, b, c and d	$

mortgage/rent expense (Lines 25B and 26), vehicle operation expense (Lines 27A and 27B), vehicle ownership expense (Lines 28 and 29), based on the **National Standards for Allowable Living Expenses** and **Local Standards for Transportation and Housing and Utilities Expenses** published by the **Internal Revenue Service** and posted on the U.S. Trustee Program website at www.usdoj.gov/ust/eo/bapcpa/meanstesting.htm for a family of their size living in Capitol County, Columbiana (Boone County, Missouri). Go to that site and see for yourself how the numbers entered on the form were determined. (Remember when comparing the current IRS national and local standard amounts that they are adjusted annually. Document 16-B in the Matthews case file reflects the applicable amounts as of January 2013.)

P-H 20-i: With regard to the deduction for vehicle ownership expense on Lines 28-29 of OBF 22C, recall that there was an issue of whether that deduction is allowable where the Chapter 13 debtor owns the vehicle outright so there is no lease or debt secured by the vehicle. The Supreme Court resolved the issue in *Ransom v. FIA Card Services, N.A.,* 131 S. Ct. 716 (2011), holding that the deduction is not allowable for a car that is owned free of debt or lease obligations. All three vehicles owned by the Matthews are security for debt, so *Ransom* is no bar to their taking the deduction for all three vehicles. However, the Matthews plan to surrender the YR-10 Oldsmobile Intrigue to Car World, the creditor secured in it, and some courts are construing *Ransom* to mean that the vehicle ownership expense is also unavailable for even pledged vehicles to be surrendered by the debtor (see P-H 14-j). Counsel for the Matthews has elected to follow that construction of *Ransom* and not to deduct the expense for the Intrigue.

P-H 20-j: Ironically, it appears that allowing above median Chapter 13 debtors to determine projected disposable income using the IRS standards for their expenses is resulting in 80 percent of those debtors paying *less* to unsecured creditors than they would have under pre-BAPCPA procedure that used the debtor's actual expenses to calculate deductions. (See the 2007 Report of the U.S. Trustee Program to Congress available online at www.usdoj.gov/ust/eo/public_affairs/reports_studies/docs/Rpt_to_ Congress_on_IRS_Standards.pdf.) Since approximately a quarter of Chapter 13 debtors are above median, this is no small thing. The irony arises because a fundamental premise of BAPCPA was that debtor abuse was occurring in bankruptcy cases resulting in debtors paying less to unsecured creditors than they could and should. Not only was the premise of abuse highly questionable as discussed in Chapter Fourteen (see P-H 14-m and 14-n), but it would appear that BAPCPA has, if anything, created an abuse in this instance.

In Part IV, Lines 30-37 of the form, the Matthews enter average monthly amounts (based on an average of payments made during the six months preceding filing of the petition) actually expended on expenses related to the IRS standards but not expressly covered by them including taxes (other than real estate and sales taxes) (Line 30), involuntary deductions from pay checks for things such as union dues, uniforms, etc. (Line 31), life insurance premiums on the debtor's life (Line 32), court-ordered payments such as spousal or child support (in their full amount, not averaged) (Line 33), expenses necessary for continued employment or for a physically or mentally challenged dependent child for whom no similar public service is available (Line 34), child care expenses (Line 35) (zero entered here by the Matthews because they are not incurring those expenses yet), unreimbursed health care expenses in excess of the national standard deduction allowed on Line 24B and not including insurance premiums (Line 36), and necessary additional telecommunication expenses (Line 37).

In Part IV, Lines 39-45, the Matthews can enter deductions they have for other monthly living expenses, such as health/disability insurance premiums (Line 39); reasonable and necessary costs of supporting an elderly, chronically ill, or disabled member of the household or a member of the debtor's immediate family (Line 40); expenses related to keeping the debtor's family safe where a member of the family has been the victim of domestic violence or stalking and qualifies for protection under the Family Violence Prevention and Services Act (Line 41); home energy costs in excess of the IRS standards for nonmortgage utility costs; school costs incurred in connection with a dependent child's attendance at a public or private elementary or secondary school up to a current maximum of $156.25 per child (that amount will be next adjusted in April, 2016) (Line 43); food and clothing expenses in excess of the IRS standards up to a maximum of 5 percent of the combined IRS allowances (Line 44), and *continuing* charitable contributions not to exceed 15 percent of the debtor's gross monthly income (compare the treatment of this item on Line 40 of OBF 22A for purposes of the Chapter 7 means test and see P-H 14-i) (Line 45).

In Part IV, Lines 47-50 of the form, the Matthews can enter deductions they have for debt payments, including the average monthly scheduled payment on secured debts (Line 47) (excluding the payment on the YR-10 Oldsmobile Intrigue that they plan to surrender to Car World, as discussed in P-H 20-i); monthly amounts needed over the term of the 60-month plan to cure arrearages on secured debt where the debtor intends to retain the property (Line 48); monthly amounts needed over the term of the 60-month plan to pay prepetition priority debts (such as Mr. Matthews' $1,000 obligation to the IRS for back taxes) (Line 49); and the projected monthly administrative expense of the plan, calculated by multiplying the current multiplier for administrative expense established by the U.S. Trustee Program (4.20% or .042 as of January 2013) by the monthly amount the debtors estimates paying into their Chapter 13 plan ($1,998 for the Matthews; thus $1,998 × .042 = $83.92) (Line 50).

In Part V, Line 54 of the form, the Matthews are allowed to deduct any amounts of income received and included in Part I of the form that were for child support, foster care payments, or disability payments for a dependent child. Section 1325(b)(2) expressly excludes these items from the definition of disposable income. On Line 55 the Matthews can deduct amounts withheld by the employer from the debtor's paycheck for qualified retirement plan contributions or to repay loans from such retirement plans. Section 1322(f) expressly excludes these items from disposable income. A **qualified retirement plan** is one approved by the IRS allowing the withholding of pre-tax contributions and deferring tax on the amounts withheld until withdrawal from the plan, usually at retirement.

On Line 57 the Matthews can enter deductions for expenses related to special circumstances for which there is no reasonable alternative. This **special circumstances expense** deduction derives from §707(b)(2)(B) and is the same as that allowed a Chapter 7 consumer debtor who can use it to rebut the presumption of abuse arising from the means test (see discussion in Chapter Fourteen, Section C and P-H 14-k). Special circumstance expenses may be unusual expenses arising from a serious medical condition or a decrease in income or increase in expenses due to a call to active duty in the military. Special circumstances expenses must be itemized, explained, and well documented.

The total adjustments (deductions) claimed by the debtor are entered on Line 58 of the form, subtracted from the current monthly income figure, and the result entered on Line 59. Though the form identifies the figure on Line 59 as the above median debtor's monthly disposable income under §1325(b)(2) (the amount that must be distributed to unsecured creditors in the plan if they are not paid 100%), that's not exactly right. As established by SCOTUS in *Hamilton v. Lanning*, known or virtually certain changes in the debtor's income or expenses must be taken into account even if the forms, using prepetition numbers, do not. And as we mentioned in connection with the below median debtor's Schedule J, the terms of the plan itself may alter the disposable income figure (e.g., by surrendering secured property, freeing up more disposable dollars for unsecured creditors).

P-H 20-k: The variableness of the debtor's disposable income as calculated using OBF 22C is highlighted by Line 60 of the form, where the Chapter 13 debtor can list any additional average monthly expenses related to the health and welfare of the family that are not covered elsewhere in the form. But there is no place on the form to deduct such claimed expenses from current income. Presumably, the debtor claiming such expenses will draft a plan in which such expenses are retained by the debtor and then fight it out when the trustee or a creditor objects to plan confirmation.

Consequently, the monthly disposable income figure listed on Line 59 is only another starting point to determine the real disposable income figure for purposes of §1325. See *In re Risher*, 344 B.R. 833, 836-837 (Bankr. W.D. Ky. 2006) (OBF 22C calculation provides a "starting point . . . a floor not a ceiling" for determination of debtor's disposable income). Having stated those caveats, if none of the deductions taken by the Chapter 13 debtor on OBF 22C are challenged by the trustee, the number entered on Line 59 ($509.24 for the Matthews) will certainly be the *starting point* for the trustee to determine if the debtor is in fact making all of his projected disposable income available to unsecured creditors in a non–100 percent plan and to decide whether to object to plan confirmation.

EXAMPLE

Assuming the Matthews had the higher income we have theorized on their alternative Form 22C and assuming their trustee did not challenge their calculations on that form, that trustee would likely begin her inquiry into whether the Matthews' plan meets the disposable income requirement with the $509.24 figure on Line 59. But that would only be the starting point for the inquiry.

Recall that for the below median debtor, we said earlier that the monthly net income entered on Line 20c of the debtor's Schedule J is no more than a starting point determination of the debtor's disposable income. The same is true of Line 59 in the above median debtor's Form 22C and for the same reasons. In both circumstances, we have to look at the debtor's final determination of how secured debt will be treated in the plan and whether there are likely to be changes to income or expenses during the term of the plan not dealt with in Schedule J or Form 22C. Those types of issues will ultimately determine the actual disposable income amount. In the next chapter we will see that done in the Matthews' case.

P-H 20-l: This discussion of calculating the disposable income of the Chapter 13 debtor, whether under or above median, demonstrates that the BAPCPA-inspired procedures and forms now utilized to determine this critical concept are not just complex and confusing, but inconsistent, relative, and even arbitrary. A leading commentary on Chapter 13 matters has referred to BAPCPA's decision to import the means test of §707(b) into the calculation of disposable income for an above median Chapter 13 debtor as "a fundamentally flawed enterprise" (Keith M. Lundin & William H. Brown, *Chapter 13 Bankruptcy*, 4th ed., 2011). Certainly, the forms used in the disposable income calculation, particularly Schedules I and J and OBF 22C, should be amended by the **Administrative Office of**

the U.S. Courts to reflect the decision in *Hamilton v. Lanning* and the other variables we have considered. Check to see if recent changes have been made to those forms as you see them in the illustrations and case file documents used here. As changes are made, the author will update the illustrations and case file documents on the text website at www.aspenparalegaled.com/books/parsons_abc-debt/default.asp. But the task of the legal professional is always to learn how to competently use what we are given.

CONCLUSION

The Chapter 13 plan of a below median debtor must run at least three and no more than five years. The plan of an above median debtor must run five years unless it is a 100 percent plan. A Chapter 13 plan cannot be confirmed unless it is a 100 percent plan or all projected disposable income of the debtor over the term of the plan is made available to pay unsecured creditors. In the next chapter we will see what a Chapter 13 plan actually looks like, how it provides for treatment of both secured and unsecured claims, and how the ultimate disposable income figure is arrived at.

CHAPTER SUMMARY

A Chapter 13 plan runs three to five years. The debtor must complete and file OBF 22C to determine the applicable commitment period. For the debtor whose annualized CMI is below the applicable state median the commitment period will be three years, although that debtor may propose a plan of up to five years. The plan of an above median debtor must run for five years, unless it proposes to pay unsecured creditors 100 percent over a shorter term.

A Chapter 13 plan must propose to pay unsecured creditors 100 percent of what is owed to them or all of the debtor's projected disposable income over the term of the plan. The disposable income of an above median debtor is calculated in the first instance using OBF 22C, while the disposable income of a below median debtor is calculated starting with his Schedule J. Disposable income calculated using either OBF 22C or Schedule J may be subject to modification by changes in the debtor's income or expenses and by proposals affecting secured claims.

REVIEW QUESTIONS

1. Explain the difference between an above median debtor and a below median debtor.
2. What do we mean by the applicable commitment period and how is it affected by whether the debtor is above or below median income?
3. How is the current monthly income of a Chapter 13 debtor determined for use on OBF 22C? What do we mean by annualized CMI?
4. What do we mean by the Chapter 13 debtor's projected disposable income?

5. What is the role of the debtor's projected disposable income in determining if his proposed plan can be confirmed by the court?

6. What is the significance of the Supreme Court's holding in *Hamilton v. Lanning*?

7. Why isn't projected disposable income as calculated on OBF 22C or Schedule J conclusive?

8. What limits does OBF 22C place on the debtor's charitable contribution deduction and do those limitations arguably conflict with the Code itself?

9. List five different deductions other than charitable contributions that a debtor can make to his gross income in determining his disposable income.

10. What is a 100 percent plan?

WORDS AND PHRASES TO REMEMBER

Administrative Office of the U.S.
    Courts
applicable commitment period
Chapter 13 plan
cure (default)
disposable income
gross income
marital adjustment

median income figure
objection to confirmation
projected disposable income
qualified retirement plan
special circumstances expense
surrender of property
100 percent plan

TO LEARN MORE: A number of TLM activities to accompany this chapter are accessible on the student disc accompanying the text and at the Author Updates link to the text Web site at http://www.aspenparalegaled.com/ books/parsons_abcdebt/default.asp.

Chapter Twenty-One

The Chapter 13 Case: The Plan: Treatment of Expenses and Claims and the Disposable Income Determination

The young folks roll on the little cabin floor,
All merry, all happy and bright;
By 'n' by Hard Times comes a-knocking at the door,
Then my old Kentucky home, goodnight.

—*Stephen C. Foster*

In this chapter we will look at the actual terms of a Chapter 13 plan, that is, how it treats the various claims of creditors, secured and unsecured, priority and nonpriority. It may be helpful to you to first review Chapter Eighteen, Section B, regarding how such claims are paid out in a Chapter 7 liquidation. Of course, a Chapter 13 is not a liquidation, it is a type of reorganization for the individual debtor. So we will see some similarities to Chapter 7 treatment of claims and some dramatic differences.

A. Treatment of Priority Claims in the Chapter 13 Plan

Priority claims An unsecured claim entitled to a certain order of preferment and payment under §507.

In Chapter Eighteen, Section B, we saw that §507 designates some claims as **priority claims** for purposes of payment. Section 1322(a)(2) requires that a Chapter 13 plan provide for the payment of all §507 priority claims in full (100%) although the payment may be made in deferred installments over the term of the plan.

EXAMPLE

> The Matthews' Chapter 13 plan (Illustration 21-b) calls for the payment in full of a tax obligation resulting from federal income taxes assessed for tax year YR-2. That tax obligation is given a priority status by §507(a)(8) (see Illustration 18-a).

One exception to the requirement of full payment of priority claims is where the priority creditor agrees to a different treatment under the plan, which would be unusual. Another exception applies to the priority granted by §507(a)(1)(B) to domestic support obligations that have been assigned for collection to a governmental agency. Section 1322(a)(4), added by BAPCPA, provides that the plan can call for less than full payment of that priority claim if the plan runs a full five years and calls for the distribution of all the debtor's projected disposable income during that term.

B. Treatment of Secured Claims in the Chapter 13 Plan

The debtor has a number of options in deciding how to deal with secured debts in his proposed Chapter 13 plan, a number of which involve the right to **modify** the terms of a secured claim.

1. Payment of the Secured Claim in Full and Retention of the Lien: The Pay Through Proposal

Per §1322(b)(2), the plan may propose to pay a secured claim in full as called for in the underlying contract and for the creditor to retain its lien on the secured property. The secured creditor is not likely to object to such a plan because its interest is not **impaired** in any way, and the debtor is able to keep the property.

EXAMPLE

> The Matthews' plan (Illustration 21-b) calls for First Bank of Capitol City (FBCC) to retain its first mortgage position in their home and for the monthly payments of $850 to continue unimpaired by the plan. FBCC should have no objection to this arrangement. So long as the Matthews make the mortgage payments, they will be able to retain the home.

Practitioners sometimes call this proposal a **pay through** (or sometimes a **ride through**) provision since the debtor is proposing to pay installments as they come due throughout the duration of the plan and beyond.

2. Avoiding a Lien That Impairs an Exemption in Property of the Debtor

In Chapter Fifteen, Section B, we considered the exemptions that an individual Chapter 7 debtor may claim. The Chapter 13 debtor, like the individual Chapter 7 debtor, may claim these exemptions and must file a Schedule C in order to do so. We saw there that a debtor cannot normally claim an exemption in property in which the debtor has granted a consensual security interest or in property subject to a statutory lien. However, we also saw that §522(f)(1)(A) permits a debtor to avoid a **judicial lien** on his property that impairs an exemption unless the judicial lien arises out of a domestic support obligation. Section §522(f)(1)(A) is available to the Chapter 13 debtor as well, as is §522(f)(1)(B), which permits the debtor to avoid even a **consensual lien** in household goods and furnishings, wearing apparel, appliances, tools of the

Consensual lien A security interest (lien) in property voluntarily granted by a debtor to a creditor in a contract such as a mortgage instrument or security agreement.

Purchase money security interest A security interest in personal property created by loaning or extending credit to a debtor for the express purpose of purchasing the property.

trade, and other such items to the extent the lien is not a **purchase money security interest** (discussed in Chapter Five, Section D) and it impairs the debtor's right to exempt such property. Per FRBP 4003(d), the proceeding to avoid a lien impairing an exemption is brought by motion.

EXAMPLE

> The Matthews' Chapter 13 plan (Illustration 21-b) seeks to avoid the lien of Capitol City Finance Company (CCFC) in Roger's plumbing tools and the couple's furniture under §522(f)(1)(b). The debt of CCFC is not a purchase money one because Roger and Susan already owned these items before he and Susan incurred the debt to CCFC and CCFC does not have possession of the items in which it claims the security interest. Consequently, the debtors should be able to avoid the CCFC lien in those goods entirely, have the $2,000 balance of the debt to CCFC treated as a general unsecured claim, and keep the items because they claim them as exempt, pursuant to §522(d)(3) (see the Matthews' Schedule C, Document 5 in their case file). If Roger had pledged a gun collection as security for the CCFC loan, there might be a question as to whether the guns constitute "household goods" within the meaning of that section. If Roger was a traveling salesman and had pledged his car as security for this loan, there might be a question as to whether the car was a "tool of the trade" for purposes of §522(f)(1)(B).

3. Curing of Arrearages Created by Default

At the time the Chapter 13 petition is filed, a debtor frequently has defaulted on some payments due to secured creditors and owes the arrearages, as well as future payments. Simply promising to make all future payments is not going to appease the creditor in that situation. Pursuant to §§1322(b)(3) and (5), the debtor's plan may propose to **cure the arrearage** by making up the past-due payments. However, the plan *must* call for the arrearages to be paid

Cure Payment of an arrearage to bring the defaulting party into compliance with its obligations under a contract.

- Over a reasonable time, and
- Within the term of the plan

Section 1322(b)(5) allows the curing of arrearage on debt secured by either real or personal property. This includes the debtor's principal residence, the mortgage on which is often in default due to missed payments when a debtor files for Chapter 13 relief. Foreclosure looms. Saving the residence becomes the highest priority for such a debtor and the right to cure the arrearage on the mortgage arising from the defaults is critical to the debtor's hopes. If the debtor can cure the arrearage as part of the plan *and* make the future payments as they come due, he can keep the secured property.

In the case of a debt secured by a mortgage in the debtor's principal residence, however, there is an important exception. Section 1322(c)(1) provides that curing the arrearage is only possible *until such residence is sold at a foreclosure sale conducted in accordance with applicable nonbankruptcy law*. Most foreclosures are conducted under state law. So what this provision means is that if the debtor does not file his Chapter 13 petition triggering the automatic stay of a foreclosure proceeding prior to the time the residence has been sold in foreclosure, it is too late to cure the arrearage and the debtor loses the house.

EXAMPLE

> When the Chapter 13 petition was filed, the Matthews had failed to make their last monthly mortgage payment of $850 to FBCC (see the Assignment Memorandum in Appendix B). Their plan (Illustration 21-b) calls for curing that arrearage over the first 12 months of the plan, along with payment of the remaining installments as they come due. So long as a foreclosure action has not been completed by the sale of the property in foreclosure when the Matthews' Chapter 13 petition is filed, this is permissible. If the court concludes that the 12 months is a reasonable time over which to cure the arrearage, the plan may be approved and the Matthews will be able to keep their house.

Note in the last example that the plan calls for curing the arrearage during the term of the plan, over the first 12 months of it. If the plan called for the arrearage to be cured over 6 years when the plan itself is only 5 years in duration, the proposal could not be approved. Under §1322(b)(5), it doesn't matter if the payment schedule on the underlying secured debt runs longer than the plan (e.g., the plan runs for 5 years and the FBCC mortgage has another 23 years to run) so long as the *arrearage* is cured during the term of the plan.

EXAMPLE

> The mortgage payments owed by the Matthews to FBCC run for longer than the term of their plan (five years). That is no bar to their plan calling for the curing of the arrearage within a reasonable time and for continuing the payments in order to retain the secured property.

P-H 21-a: Since it is too late to cure an arrearage on a mortgage in Chapter 13 once the residence has been sold in foreclosure, questions can and do arise over exactly when a foreclosed-on residence has been "sold." And that question will be determined by the controlling state law. Is the sale final when the gavel falls at the foreclosure sale? When the trustee's deed of conveyance is actually signed satisfying the statute of frauds? When that deed is delivered to the buyer? When that deed is properly recorded? When the debtor's right of redemption expires? When a court enters an order approving the sale where that is required by law? The cases are all over the board. Compare *In re Medaglia*, 402 B.R. 530 (Bkrtcy. D.R.I. 2009); *In re Spencer*, 263 B.R. 227 (Bkrtcy. N.D. Ill. 2001); and *In re Connors*, 497 F.3d 314 (3d Cir. 2007) (applying New Jersey law) then determine the rule on this point in your state.

E-C 21-a: Commonly, debtors do not approach a lawyer for assistance until the mortgage on their residence has been declared in default and foreclosure proceedings begun. If the foreclosure sale is imminent, the need to get the Chapter 13 petition filed and stop the foreclosure sale using the automatic stay is paramount. Debtors' lawyers and the legal professionals assisting them must understand the legal implications of delay in handling such a matter. What are the specific ethical and professional obligations of legal professionals in your state regarding competence, zealous representation, and the timely performance of agreed legal services that come into play in this situation?

Although the curing of an arrearage in secured debt does not normally require the payment of **postpetition interest** to the creditor, §1322(e) requires the payment of such interest *if* the terms of the underlying agreement itself or state law do so.

> **EXAMPLE**
>
> The Matthews' plan calls for interest to be paid to FBCC on the arrearage payments. This is necessary because the promissory note between the Matthews and FBCC requires the payment of interest on arrearages.

When a Chapter 13 debtor's plan proposes to cure an arrearage on a debt secured by a mortgage on his principal residence under §1322(b)(5), FRBP 3002.1, effective in December 2011, imposes significant notice requirements and filing deadlines on the creditor secured by such mortgage.

> **EXAMPLE**
>
> The holder of the mortgage must give written notice to the debtor, debtor's attorney, and the trustee of changes in the payment amount caused by changes in the applicable interest rate or by adjustments in the escrow account balance at least 21 days before the change become effective. And the mortgage holder must give written itemization of any postpetition fees, expenses, or charges it alleges are due under the mortgage within 180 days after such costs were incurred. Significant penalties are imposed on the mortgage holder for noncompliance with these requirements.

4. Reducing an Undersecured Claim to Present Value: Cramdown

a. How Cramdown Works in General

Recall that §506(a) provides that a secured claim in bankruptcy is only secured up to the value of the collateral and is unsecured to the extent the claim exceeds that value. Consequently, the claim secured by collateral having a value equal to or greater than the amount of the claim has is a **fully secured claim** (or even **oversecured**). But a claim secured by collateral having a value less than the amount of the claim is an **undersecured claim** (sometimes called **partially secured**) and it is this claim that §506(a) effectively **bifurcates** into its secured and unsecured portions. We have already considered the implications of a secured claim's status as fully or oversecured or undersecured for purposes of deciding how such claims are calculated and satisfied in a Chapter 7 case (see Chapters Seventeen, Section A, and Eighteen, Sections A and C, and Illustration 18-a).

Sections 1322(b)(2) and 1325(a)(5) authorize a Chapter 13 debtor to utilize the bifurcation feature of §506 (sometimes called **strip down** or **write down**) to propose a plan in which the debtor will retain possession of secured property while paying the undersecured creditor only the value of the collateral (referred to by practitioners as its **present value**) as a secured claim over the term of the plan rather than the entire amount of the debt. The unsecured portion of the debt is then treated as an unsecured claim under the plan. This right of the Chapter 13 debtor to reduce the amount of a secured claim to the present value of the property securing the claim while retaining that property is known as the **cramdown** since it can be approved by the bankruptcy court without creditor approval and

Present value Calculation of the current value of property for purposes of determining the value of a secured claim in bankruptcy.

Cramdown The right of a Chapter 13 debtor to reduce the amount of an undersecured claim to the present value of the collateral and to retain that collateral by paying that value over the term of the plan.

over creditor objection. The arrangement is effectively crammed down on the secured creditor. Technically, the secured claim is stripped down or written down to its present value per §506(a) and then crammed down per §§1322(b)(2) and 1325(a)(5).

EXAMPLE

The YR-3 Ford Truck F-150 that Roger drives is worth $7,500 but the Matthews still owe $9,000 for it. Thus the claim of the creditor holding a security interest in the truck, Automotive Financing, Inc. (AFI) is undersecured on its claim. The Matthews' Chapter 13 plan (Illustration 21-b) proposes to pay AFI the $7,500 present value of the truck over the 60-month term of the plan and for debtors to retain possession of the truck. This is a cramdown proposal. The balance of $1,500 owed to AFI is treated and paid as a general unsecured claim in the Matthews' plan. If AFI was fully secured or oversecured (i.e., the truck had a present value equal to or in excess of the $9,000 balance owed) the Matthews could not propose this cramdown. They would have to propose paying the full $9,000 in order to keep the truck.

Note in the last example that the cramdown proposal on the truck calls for the Matthews to pay the full present value of AFI's secured claim during the term of the plan. This is a strict requirement of the cramdown option. The present value to which the secured claim is crammed down must be paid in full during the term of the plan.

EXAMPLE

If the Matthews plan called for the truck value to be crammed down to its present value of $7,500 and paid over six years, it would not be approved since the plan can only run for five years.

In Chapter Eighteen, Section C, we considered whether a Chapter 7 individual debtor could use lien stripping together with a ride through option to retain possession of pledged property while paying only the secured value of a claim. And we learned that the answer is no owing to the decision in *Dewsnup v. Timm*, 502 U.S. 410 (1997), with one possible exception recognized in a minority of courts as discussed in P-H 18-o. Do not confuse that rule in Chapter 7 cases with the cramdown option available in Chapter 13 cases using §§1322(b)(2) and 1325(a)(5). There are no equivalent provisions in Chapter 7.

b. Exclusion of the Debtor's Principal Residence from the Cramdown Option—and Some Exceptions

Pursuant to §1322(b)(2) as interpreted by the Supreme Court in *Nobleman v. American Savings Bank*, 508 U.S. 324 (1993), the right to cramdown a secured claim to the present value of the collateral does not apply to a debt secured *only by a security interest in real property that is the debtor's principal residence.* Thus, in most Chapter 13 cases, the debtor is unable to modify the mortgage on his home even if the value of the home has fallen below the balance of the mortgage (i.e., the creditor is undersecured).

There are, however, a number of exceptions to the §1322(b)(2) prohibition on cramdown of a claim secured by a mortgage in the debtor's primary residence. First, note that the restriction just quoted applies only to real property used as the debtor's **principal residence**. If the Chapter 13 debtor owns a second home that is *not* his principal residence, he can cramdown the mortgage on that second home if its value has fallen below the balance of the mortgage. This disparity in the Code gives a curious advantage to debtors who are better off (i.e., those who own two or more homes rather than one), one that is troubling during this time of economic distress (see discussion of the Great Recession and the mortgage foreclosure crisis in Chapter Four, Section E). To date, efforts to extend the cramdown option to the principal residence of Chapter 13 debtors even temporarily have failed in Congress.

Second, note also that the restriction of §1322(b)(2) applies only to a security interest in **real property** used as the debtor's principal residence. What if the debt is secured by a **mobile home** used as the debtor's principal residence? Can the mobile home ever be considered **personal property** and thus subject to §1322(b)(2) modification? Some courts say yes if, under state law, the mobile home is not so permanently attached to the real property on which it sits to be considered real property itself. See, for example, *In re Reinhardt*, 563 F.3d 558 (6th Cir. 2009) (mobile home used as principal residence but not considered real property under Ohio law so debt secured by it subject to modification) and *In re Ennis*, 558 F.3d 343 (4th Cir. 2009) (same result under Virginia law).

Third, what if there is a second mortgage on the debtor's primary residence that is wholly undersecured?

EXAMPLE

> Assume the Chapter 13 debtor's primary residence is valued at $200,000. Bank #1 holds a first mortgage on the residence, the balance on which is $225,000. Bank #1 is undersecured in the amount of $25,000 per §506(a) so that the value of its secured claim in the residence is only $200,000. But bank #1 is not wholly undersecured because the secured portion of its claim does have that $200,000 value. However, assume that bank #2 holds a second mortgage on the residence the balance on which is $30,000. Bank #2 is wholly undersecured—all the secured value of the residence ($200,000) will go to satisfy the mortgage of bank #1. Can the Chapter 13 debtor cramdown that second mortgage?

Most courts have construed *Nobleman* to not prohibit the cramdown of a wholly undersecured second mortgage such as that held by bank #2 in the last example. See, e.g., *In re Zimmer*, 313 F.3d 1220 (9th Cir. 2002); *In re Lane*, 280 F.3d 663 (6th Cir. 2002); *In re Pond*, 252 F.3d 122 (2d Cir. 2001); *In re Tanner*, 217 F.3d 1357 (11th Cir. 2000); *In re Bartee*, 212 F.3d 277 (5th Cir. 2000); and *In re McDonald*, 205 F.3d 606 (3d Cir. 2000). The reasoning is that since the second mortgage is wholly undersecured by the operation of §506(a), it is effectively unsecured and thus does not have the protection from cramdown afforded by §1322(b)(2). In this situation, the mortgage is not stripped down, it is stripped off.

P-H 21-b: See if the courts of your federal circuit have adopted the majority view of *In re Zimmer*, et al., in connection with the cramdown of a wholly undersecured second mortgage in a Chapter 13 case. Does it matter if the case in which the wholly undersecured second mortgage to be stripped off is a "Chapter 20" (a Chapter 13 case that closely follows a Chapter 7 case for the same debtor; see P-H 19-b). Here there is a split among bankruptcy courts. Compare *In re Dang*, 467 B.R. 227 (Bankr. M.D. Fla. 2012) and *In re Okosisi*, 451 B.R. 90 (Bankr. D. Nev. 2011) with *In re Gerardin*, 447 B.R. 342 (Bankr. S.D. Fla 2011) and *In re Victorio*, 454 B.R. 759 (Bankr. S.D. Cal. 2011). The only circuit court to decide the issue is the Fourth Circuit which allowed the Chapter 20 strip off. See *In re Davis*, No. 12-1184 (4th Cir. May 10, 2013). What are the competing arguments on this issue? Who gets it right, do you think?

Fourth, the §1322(b)(2) prohibition applies to debts secured *only* by the debtor's principal residence. So if the debt on a debtor's principal residence is secured not only by the real property itself but by some other property (e.g., another parcel of real property or any personal property), that debt is subject to cramdown. Of course, the fact that the debt is secured by other property makes it less likely that the debt will be undersecured.

Fifth, §1322(c)(2) provides that if the original payment schedule for a loan secured only by the debtor's primary residence calls for the last payment to be made *before* the Chapter 13 plan expires, the plan can provide for "payment of the claim as modified pursuant to §1325(a)(5)." A number of courts have construed §1322(c)(2) to mean that the amount of the secured claim to be paid in full during the term of the plan can be reduced to the extent that it *exceeds* the available equity in the residence. In other words the secured claim can be crammed down to the present equity so long as it is paid in full during the term of the plan. The balance of the debt will be bifurcated pursuant to §506(a) and treated as a general unsecured claim.

EXAMPLE

Capitol Savings Bank (CSB) holds a second mortgage in the residence of Roger and Susan Matthews, and the balance on that debt is $30,000. The CSB debt is scheduled to be paid off in 48 more months. However, the value of the house is only $120,000 and the balance owed on the first mortgage to FBCC is $100,000. That means there is only $20,000 of equity in the home available to CSB. Because the Matthews have proposed a 60-month (5-year) plan, they have proposed to reduce the claim of CSB to that $20,000 equity amount, pursuant to §1322(c)(2), and to pay it off entirely during the plan. Note that if there was $30,000 or more equity in the residence available for CSB or if the original term of the CSB loan extended beyond the term of the Matthews' plan, they could not take advantage of this cramdown provision. Because the principal amount owed to CSB has been crammed down from $30,000 to $20,000, the $10,000 difference will be treated as an unsecured claim under the plan.

The §1322(c)(2) cramdown exception is usually directed at shorter term home equity loans wherein the lender has loaned an amount in excess of the true equity in the residence. For a good discussion of this interpretation of §1322(c)(2), see *In re Young*, 199 B.R. 643 (Bankr. E.D. Tenn. 1996), followed in *In re Eubanks*, 219 B.R. 468 (B.A.P. 6th Cir. 1998), and *In re Paschen*, 296 F. 3d 1203 (11th Cir. 2002). Not all courts agree with this construction of §1322(c)(2). See, e.g., *In re Witt*, 113 F.3d 508 (4th Cir. 1997), (§1322(c)(2) was only intended to permit payment of the full amount of the claim during the term of the plan including arrearages, not to cramdown such a claim even though it is undersecured under §506(a)).

P-H 21-c: See if the courts of your federal circuit follow *In re Young* or *In re Witt* in their construction of §1322(c)(2) or if they have yet to rule on this interesting question.

---

c. *Cramdown of Purchase Money Claim Secured by a Motor Vehicle: The 910-Day Rule of the §1325(a) "Hanging Paragraph"*

By far the most common use of this cramdown power is in connection with automobiles. It is very common for debtors to owe more on their vehicles than they are worth, as the Matthews do on the YR-3 Ford Truck F-150 mentioned in earlier examples, and to propose Chapter 13 plans seeking to cramdown on that value. However, BAPCPA has imposed some severe limitations on the right of a Chapter 13 debtor to cram down the amount owed on a vehicle to its value. The last paragraph of §1325(a), added by BAPCPA and known to practitioners as the infamous **hanging paragraph** (so-called because it "hangs" to the end of §1325(a) like an afterthought), provides that the cramdown to value provision *cannot* be used for automobiles if

- The debt secured by the automobile is a **purchase money security interest** (the debt was incurred to enable the debtor to purchase the vehicle);
- The debt was incurred within 910 days (two-and-a-half years) preceding the filing of the petition; *and*
- The vehicle was acquired for the "personal use of the debtor."

EXAMPLE

> The Matthews purchased the Ford Truck F-150 new almost three years ago and borrowed money from Automotive Financing, Inc. (AFI) in order to do so. Although the debt owed on the truck is therefore a purchase money security interest, and although the truck was purchased for Roger's personal use, the Matthews' plan can cram down the debt owed to AFI to the truck's value because it was purchased more than 910 days (two-and-a-half years) prior to the filing of the petition, triggering the **910-day rule** of §1325(a). On the other hand, the Honda Civic was purchased only two years ago, making it a **910 vehicle**, so this option is not available to the Matthews as to it even if the debt secured by it is undersecured.

Technically what the hanging paragraph of §1325(a) says is that §506 is *not to apply* to 910 vehicles for purposes of the cramdown provisions of Chapter 13. This is being construed by the courts to mean that claims secured by 910 vehicles cannot be bifurcated under §506(a). Thus the creditor is entitled to receive the full value of its claim rather than the present value of the collateral if the debtor wishes to retain possession of the vehicle. (See, e.g., *In re Dean*, 537 F.3d 1315 (11th Cir. 2008).) In order to retain 910 vehicles, Chapter 13 debtors will either have to propose a pay through on such claims or a payoff of the entire value of the unmodified claim during the term of the plan.

d. Cramdown of Purchase Money Claim Secured by Property Other Than a Motor Vehicle: The Hanging Paragraph Strikes Again

The hanging paragraph of §1325(a) also provides that any debt secured by property *other than* vehicles is not subject to bifurcation under §506 and thus cannot be crammed down to value if

- It is a purchase money security interest and
- The debt was incurred during the one-year period preceding the filing of the petition.

EXAMPLE

> Assume a debtor purchases $5,000 of household appliances on credit and pledges those appliances to the seller as collateral to secure payment. Since the credit was extended for the purchase of consumer goods, this is a purchase money security interest. Nine months later, the debtor files for Chapter 13 relief and still owes $4,000 on the debt. He would like to cram down this obligation because his household appliances that secure the debt only have a total value of $2,500. But he will be unable to do so because of the **one-year rule** of §1325(a). This debtor might be well advised to, if feasible, delay his Chapter 13 filing until the one-year period has run.

As with 910 vehicles, if the Chapter 13 debtor wants to retain possession of secured property falling within the one-year rule, he will have to propose a pay through or a payoff of the entire value of the unmodified claim during the plan period.

e. How the Cramdown Value of Collateral Is Determined

Liquidation or foreclosure value The dollar value of property resulting from a forced sale.

The value of personal property securing a claim for purposes of determining the secured portion of the claim and exercising the cramdown right where it is available is defined in §506(a)(2), added by BAPCPA, as the **replacement value** of the goods on the date the petition is filed without deduction for sale or marketing costs. For goods acquired for personal, family, or household purposes (consumer goods), replacement value means *the price a retail merchant would charge for property of that kind, given its age and condition*, on the date the petition is filed.

EXAMPLE

> In determining the value of the Ford Truck F-150 that the Matthews are cramming down, we would determine the replacement value of that vehicle as of the date the petition is filed. Common sources for determining automobile values are the **Kelly Blue Book** or the **National Automobile Dealers Association (NADA)**. Debtor's lawyers are more likely to use the former since its values are usually lower than those in NADA.

P-H 21-d: Go back and read P-H 18-j in Chapter Eighteen, Section C, dealing with the right of an individual consumer debtor in Chapter 7 to redeem property under §722. That P-H discusses *Associates Commercial Corp. v. Rash*, 520 U.S. 953 (1997) and the codification by BAPCPA of the *Rash* replacement value standard in §506(a)(2). Do you see why the replacement value will almost always be greater than the liquidation or foreclosure value of the property, or the casual garage sale value of the property, or even the wholesale value whether you're dealing with a Chapter 7 redemption or a Chapter 13 cramdown?

Defining value in §506(a)(2) as replacement value has by no means ended disputes over what replacement value is with regard to many kinds of property. If the creditor or trustee will not accept the debtor's proposed cramdown value, he or she can object to the confirmation of the plan and an evidentiary hearing may be conducted by the court on the issue of value. Experts may be called by either or both sides to testify on the value dispute. That can be time-consuming and expensive, of course. As a practical matter, determination of the value of property in a cramdown is often arrived at by negotiations between the debtor and the affected creditor, usually at the first meeting of creditors. And though the replacement value standard obviously favors the creditor, the debtor often has *leverage* to negotiate a more favorable value since he has the option to simply surrender the property to the creditor as discussed later in this section and perhaps to even discharge the balance of the debt.

f. Determining the "Present Value" of the Collateral for Purposes of Plan Payments

Determining the payments to be made to a secured creditor to give it the value of its collateral as calculated under §506(a) is not simply a matter of dividing the replacement value by the number of plan payments to be made. That is because the debtor is not going to pay the creditor that replacement cost as a lump sum at the beginning of the plan. Instead, the debtor is proposing to pay that amount to the creditor in installments over the time of the plan (three to five years). The secured creditor is entitled to receive the value of its collateral, but since that value is going to be paid to him over time rather than immediately, the creditor must be

Interest The cost of using another person's money or property.

compensated for the delay with some amount of **interest**, just as a lender of money is entitled to interest until the loan is repaid in full. By adding an interest component to the installment payments of the replacement value of the collateral, we are seeking to quantify the **time-price differential** involved in the delayed payment to the creditor of the full replacement value of the collateral. Since the full value is being paid over time, the total amount of the debtor's plan payments to the creditor must equal the **present value** of the collateral. In essence, the plan payments must be **discounted** by a rate of interest that will ultimately provide the creditor with that present value.

When a Chapter 13 plan calls for a secured claim to be crammed down to present value and for the payments of that value to be made in installments during the term of the plan, as the Matthews are doing on their truck, §1325(a)(5)(B)(ii) and (iii) require that

- The present value be paid in full during the term of the plan
- The payments be made in equal installments and
- The payments be increased to compensate the creditor for the delay in receiving the present value of the collateral in order to give the creditor **adequate protection**.

EXAMPLE

When the Matthews cram down on the Ford Truck F-150, they are declaring that AFI will get only the replacement value of the collateral in payment of its claim. If they simply surrendered the truck to AFI, it would be getting that replacement value immediately. But the Matthews' plan contemplates the

> debtors keeping the truck and paying AFI the value of its claim in installments over the term of the plan. The plan is therefore delaying AFI's receipt of the value of its claim. The Matthews plan must increase the payments by an appropriate rate of interest to account for that delay and to adequately protect AFI by providing it with the present value of its claim.

Though the Code recognizes that the secured creditor receiving the value of its collateral in delayed payments is entitled to interest to compensate for that delay, it does not specify the appropriate interest rate to be applied to those payments. In *Till v. SCS Credit Corp.*, 541 U.S. 465 (2004), the Supreme Court rejected a creditor's argument that the appropriate rate of interest in such situations is the rate set forth in the contract between the debtor and creditor. The court held instead that the appropriate interest rate to be used is the national **prime rate** plus an **upward adjustment** to reflect the *risk of nonpayment* by the bankrupt debtors. The court left the question of the appropriate upward **risk adjustment** to be decided by the court, based on the circumstances of each case. In most cases the risk adjustment will run one to three percentage points.

Prime rate The interest rate that commercial banks charge their best customers.

EXAMPLE

Assume that the **contract rate** of interest that the Matthews agreed to pay AFI when they purchased the Ford Truck F-150 was 10 percent per annum. At the time the petition is filed, the prevailing national prime rate is 6 percent. In the Matthews' plan they cram down the debt owed to AFI to its replacement value and propose to pay that value in installments through the term of the plan. Since AFI is being delayed in receiving the replacement value of the collateral to which it is entitled, the plan adds a *Till* rate of interest based on the 6 percent prime plus an upward risk adjustment factor of a half point, for a total rate of interest of 6.5 percent. This is the Matthews' proposal to give AFI the *present value* of its collateral. AFI may object to the half-point risk adjustment and argue for more, perhaps one to two points higher. But the plan rate will still be lower than the contract rate. Do you see why *Till* is, in most situations, a pro-debtor decision?

P-H 21-e: Under the hanging paragraph of §1325(a), claims secured by 910 vehicles or property subject to the one-year rule cannot be crammed down; they are not controlled by the bifurcation concept of §506(a). We noted that as to such claims, the debtor, in order to keep the property, will either have to propose a pay through, in which case the contract rate of interest will continue to apply, or a payoff of the full value of the unmodified claim during the term of the plan. If the debtor chooses the latter, however, the creditor is being denied immediate payment of that value, again raising the question of what interest the creditor should receive on those payments in order to compensate it for the delayed receipt of value and the risk of debtor's nonpayment. Should we use the *Till* rate of interest in such cases? Or, since the whole basis for excepting such property from cramdown is that the bifurcation of §506(a) is inapplicable to such property, is use of the *Till* rate inappropriate and the contract rate the one to use? Read *In re Dean*, 537 F.3d 1315 (11th Cir. 2008) and see what interest rate the creditor secured by the 910 vehicle asked for if the debtor chose to pay off the entire amount of its unmodified claim over the term of the plan. See what the court said about the creditor's choice. Then see if any later cases have addressed this issue.

5. Modifying a Secured Claim by Adjusting Payments

As we have seen, when a secured claim is crammed down to the value of its collateral, that will result in a modification downward of the contractual payments to be made by the debtor to the creditor under the terms of the plan simply because less principal is being paid to that creditor on the debt. But can a Chapter 13 debtor who does not or cannot cram down a secured claim to its value propose to modify installment payments to a secured creditor by lowering those payments during the term of the plan? Sections 1322(b)(2) and 1325(a)(5) do allow such a modification with one important caveat: Per §1325(a)(5)(B)(ii), the full value of the claim must be paid during the term of the plan.

EXAMPLE

> The Matthews owe Columbiana Federal Savings & Loan (CFSL) a total of $7,500 on an original loan of $12,000 made two years ago for which they obligated themselves to pay $240 per month for five years. There are currently 36 monthly payments remaining on the contract. The debt is secured by the Honda Civic automobile that Susan drives. The vehicle is a 910 vehicle since they have owned it only two years, which means they cannot cram down CFSL's secured claim to the present value of the vehicle. However, their Chapter 13 plan (Illustration 21-b) proposes to pay CFSL the full amount of the unmodified claim at the *contract rate* of 7.5 percent but over the full 60 months of the plan, rather than over the remaining 36 months of the contract. This will require them to pay CFSL only $150 per month over the term of the plan. CFSL will retain its lien on the automobile. The court can approve this plan even over CFSL's objection pursuant to §1325(a)(5)(B)(ii) because the creditor is receiving the full amount of its allowed claim during the term of the plan. Note that this saves the Matthews $90 per month over what they were paying CFSL (see the budget in the Assignment Memorandum in Appendix B).

P-H 21-f: Even though this plan provision saves the Matthews $90 a month over what they were paying CFSL, it may not mean that they come out better in the long run. How much total principal and interest would the Matthews have paid CFSL if they paid off the car over the remaining 36 months of the contract? How much will they pay CFSL in principal and interest over the 60 months of the plan?

In the last example, if the Matthews' plan proposed to not only extend the number of installment payments to CFSL but to also use a *Till* rate of interest for such payments rather than the contract rate, that would raise the unanswered question we raised in P-H 21-e. And if the contract rate on that debt was 15 percent per annum rather than 7.5 percent, it would be very tempting for their attorney to propose a *Till* rate. But often Chapter 13 debtors will choose *not* to propose a lower *Till* rate for modified plan payments when they could do so because they do not wish to offend a creditor with whom they hope to do business in the future.

6. Surrender of Secured Property

Surrender (of property) The debtor's act of voluntarily relinquishing possession of pledged property to the secured creditor.

Pursuant to §1325(a)(5)(C), a Chapter 13 debtor may propose to **surrender** property subject to a security interest to the secured creditor. The creditor must then move to have the **automatic stay** lifted in order to take possession of the property. If there is no **equity** in the property for the estate (the debt exceeds the value of the property) and no basis to avoid the lien securing the property, the trustee will **abandon** the property to the creditor pursuant to §554 of the Code on the grounds that it is not needed for the reorganization. (See discussion of **abandonment** in Chapter Eighteen, Section A.)

As we know, §506(a) bifurcates most secured claims by providing that a secured creditor's claim is secured only up to the value of the collateral and is an unsecured claim to the extent the debt exceeds the value of the collateral. Thus if the debtor surrenders the property securing the debt but its value is less than the amount owed (i.e., the creditor is undersecured or partially secured), the balance still owing on the debt after the property is repossessed and sold will be treated as a general unsecured claim.

EXAMPLE

The Matthews have decided to surrender the YR-10 Oldsmobile. This surrender is referenced in their plan. Note that this relieves them of the $120 per month payment they were making to Car World (see the budget in the Assignment Memorandum in Appendix B). They owed Car World $5,000 on that debt. Upon surrender, Car World will move the court, pursuant to §362, to lift the automatic stay. Since there is no equity in the car (it is worth only $2,000 and the amount owed is $5,000), the trustee will not object to the motion to lift stay and will abandon pursuant to §554. Assuming the car is in fact worth $2,000, the $3,000 balance of the debt ($5,000 minus the $2,000 value of the car surrendered) will be treated as a general unsecured debt under the plan.

P-H 21-g: What happens when a debtor surrenders a 910 vehicle or other collateral subject to the one-year rule of the §1325(a) hanging paragraph? Since that paragraph says that such claims are not governed by the bifurcation concept of §506(a) and the debtor therefore cannot cramdown the value of the secured claim to the value of the collateral, it might follow that when the debtor chooses to surrender such property, the creditor must accept that surrender as a full satisfaction of its claim rather than bifurcating its secured claim into an unsecured claim for the deficiency owing after disposition of the surrendered collateral. Isn't what's good for the goose, good for the gander? Apparently not. Read *In re Barrett*, 543 F.3d 1239 (11th Cir. 2008). What was the reasoning of the Eleventh Circuit on this issue? See if you can locate cases decided in your federal circuit dealing with the issue.

P-H 21-h: Before you leave this section, take a look at the Matthews' Schedule C (Document 5 in their case file). Be sure you understand why they claimed Roger's plumbing tools and their furniture as exempt notwithstanding the judicial lien of CCFC in those items. Why didn't they claim an exemption in their residence? In the YR-3 Ford truck? In the YR-10 Oldsmobile? Why was it necessary to claim an exemption in the YR-4 Honda Civic?

7. Sale of Property Free and Clear of Liens

Section 1303 of the Code authorizes a Chapter 13 debtor to ask that secured property be sold **free and clear of liens** pursuant to §363(f). As in a Chapter 7 liquidation, such sale will be subject to the secured creditor's §363(k) right to **credit-bid** for the property at the sale (see the discussion in Chapter Eighteen, Section A).

C. ▶ Treatment of Nonpriority Unsecured Claims Under the Chapter 13 Plan

1. Curing Defaults and Modifying the Obligation of Unsecured Debt

Sections 1322(b)(3) and (5) allow a Chapter 13 debtor to propose curing arrearages arising from default on unsecured debt just as he can on secured debt. If a debtor plans to propose a 100 percent plan in which all his unsecured debt will be paid, the plan *must* cure any arrearages.

Section 1322(b)(2) allows the Chapter 13 debtor to modify the rights of unsecured creditors just as he can for secured creditors by modifying the amount of payments due or the time over which they will be paid again.

EXAMPLE

> The Matthews owe $25,000 in unsecured debt for hospital and doctor bills at the time their petition is filed. This amount is due and payable immediately to the various creditors. But their plan calls for paying these creditors some amounts in monthly installments over the term of the plan. Section 1322(b)(2) permits this modification of these unsecured obligations.

Interest is not normally an issue when unsecured debt is modified in a Chapter 13 plan since the creditor's claim is not being valued by any collateral and the creditor is not being deprived of the right to possess any such collateral. Moreover, as we consider in the next section, a Chapter 13 plan may propose to pay unsecured creditors less than the full amount of their claim anyway subject to the various requirements for plan confirmation.

Classes Designated groupings of creditor claims or equity interests with members of each class receiving equal treatment.

2. Classes of Unsecured Creditors in a Chapter 13 Plan

Section 1322(b)(1) permits a Chapter 13 plan to create separate **classes** of unsecured creditors and to treat each class of creditors differently from one another.

EXAMPLE

> A debtor engaged in business may put unsecured consumer debt in one class and unsecured business debt in another. A consumer who is jointly liable with a nondebtor on a debt may choose to place that debt in a separate class for favorable treatment in order to protect the nondebtor.

The debtor is not free to create any classes of unsecured debt he wishes or to propose favorable treatment for some over others. If that were so, debtors would routinely put **nondischargeable debts** (discussed in Chapter Twenty-Two, Section E) in one class for favorable treatment over dischargeable debts in another class, a practice that has been ruled impermissible in many cases (see, e.g., *In re Simmonds*, 288 B.R. 737 (Bankr. N.D. Tex. 2003)). Instead, there are three requirements imposed on classifications of unsecured debt:

- §1322(b)(1) requires that only claims that are *substantially similar* can be grouped in the same class;
- §1322(b)(1) provides that a plan cannot *discriminate unfairly* against any class; and
- §1322(a)(3) requires that claims within the same class be treated the same for purposes of payment.

The second requirement, that the plan not discriminate unfairly against any class, is the one most likely to draw objection. If a debtor's proposed plan with classes of debt draws an objection, the burden is on the debtor to show why the differing treatment of the classes is fair.

P-H 21-j: Section 1322(b)(1) expressly recognizes the right to treat a consumer debt on which a nondebtor is jointly liable with the debtor differently. And the unfairness of attempting to treat non-dischargeable debt more favorably than dischargeable debt can be readily seen. But what about the individual business debtor seeking more favorable treatment for his business debts over his consumer debts in order to keep his business? What about disputed debt being treated differently than undisputed debt? If Marta Carlson, our Chapter 7 debtor, was in a Chapter 13 plan, could she place the debt her former husband was responsible for paying but didn't in one class for less favorable treatment? Could the Matthews put their credit card debt attributable to fees and penalties in one class for less favorable treatment? Or could they put some or all of their credit card debt in one class for more favorable treatment because of their desire to keep those particular credit cards? Could they classify their medical or hospital debt separately and provide for more favorable treatment in order to maintain the relationship with a particular doctor or hospital? What other classifications can you think of that might arguably be fair?

Section 502(b)(2) disallows claims for unmatured (postpetition) interest, and so postpetition interest need not be paid to unsecured creditors in a Chapter 13 plan.

You can see from this discussion that a great deal of flexibility is possible in a Chapter 13 plan. And fashioning a plan for a debtor involves understanding the provisions of the Code, budgets, and how various financial arrangements work. If you are an assisting legal professional in this field, whether for the debtor's attorney, a creditor's attorney, the U.S. Trustee, or the standing trustee, this is the type of calculating, projecting, and testing you will be doing constantly. For the debtor's attorney, you will do this in order to draft the proposed plan. For the creditor's attorney or one of the trustees, you will do this to determine why the debtor proposed what he did and to decide whether the plan should be accepted or objected to during the confirmation process.

D. ▶ Nonpayment of Unsecured Debt: The Less Than 100 Percent Plan and Disposable Income Requirement

100 percent plan A Chapter 13 plan in which unsecured claims are paid in full.

A Chapter 13 plan may propose to pay unsecured claims in full over the term of the plan. We call that a **100 percent plan**. Such a plan may modify the original terms of payment to unsecured creditors, as discussed in the preceding section, and if the court approves the debtor's proposed plan, the creditors must accept the modified payments. Most unsecured creditors will not complain about proposed modifications if the plan does in fact pay them all they are owed.

A Chapter 13 plan need not pay unsecured claims in full but a less than 100 percent plan must meet two requirements. First, pursuant to §1325(b)(1)(B), the plan must propose to pay unsecured creditors all **projected disposable income** over the **applicable commitment period** (the term of the plan). Second, pursuant to §1325(a)(4), the plan must provide that the unsecured creditors will receive at least as much under the plan as they would receive if the debtor's assets were liquidated under Chapter 7. This is the best interests test. Let's consider both of these requirements in order.

1. The Disposable Income Requirement

The disposable income requirement for a non–100 percent plan is illustrated in the following example.

EXAMPLE

> Assume a debtor calculates that he will have $150 per month, or $9,000, in disposable income using during the term of his five-year plan. He has $45,000 in unsecured debt. He cannot propose a plan that will pay his unsecured creditors less than 100 percent of what they are owed unless his plan calls for paying all of that projected disposable income to those unsecured creditors. If his plan does call for paying the full $150 a month to unsecured creditors for the full term of the plan, it can be confirmed. But if his plan only calls for paying $125 a month to the unsecured creditors for the term of the plan, it will not be confirmed.

But still, we are left with the question of what exactly the debtor's disposable income is that must be paid in full to on unsecured claims for the term of the plan. In Section C of Chapter Twenty, we discovered that neither the debtor's Schedule J nor his Form 22C calculates the actual disposable income number to determine if the debtor's plan meets this test. Both, we said, are merely starting points because the final calculation must await the debtor's decisions about how to treat secured claims and about likely future changes in income and expenses. So how do we, finally, determine the debtor's disposable income when he proposes a less than 100 percent plan? Remember, §1325(b)(1) provides that a non–100 percent plan must propose to pay use *all* of the debtor's projected disposable income over the term of the plan to unsecured creditors.

The Matthews have finally made those decisions in consultation with their lawyer. They know what their income is and is likely to be over the term of the plan. They have calculated their likely living expenses over the term of the plan. As we've seen in this chapter, they've made decisions about what to do with their various secured debts. In Illustration 21-a you will find the final budget that the attorney for the Matthews has put together reflecting these decisions and what

Illustration 21-a: MONTHLY BUDGET FOR ROGER AND SUSAN MATTHEWS UNDER PROPOSED PLAN

<u>Net monthly income:</u>

Roger:	$ 2,400
Susan:	$ 1,733
Total monthly income	$ 4,133

<u>Living expenses:</u>

Food	$ 500
Home maintenance	100
Clothing	175
Dry cleaning/laundry	25
Gas	150
Utilities & phone	500
Insurance (auto)	60
Medical/dental	100
Charitable contributions	50
Entertainment/recreation	50
Child care	250
Miscellaneous	175
Total monthly living expenses	$ 2,135

<u>Payments on secured debt:</u>

House payments	$ 1,241
(FBCC $850)	
(CSB $391)	
Car payments	297
(AFI for Ford Truck F-150 $147)	
(CFSL for Honda Civic $150)	
Total monthly secured debt payments	$ 1,538
Available to apply to unsecured debt	$ 460
Total monthly plan payments	$ 1,998

<u>Unsecured debt with priority:</u>

IRS (U.S.) Tax bill from YR-2	$ 1,000
Attorney's fee	1,000

<u>Unsecured debts with no priority:</u>

Credit cards	$35,000
Doctor & hospital	25,000
CCFC vacation debt	2,000
CSB	10,000
AFI	1,500
Car World	3,000
Total nonpriority unsecured debt	$76,500

the Matthews will be able to pay out of their projected income on the secured debt they plan to reaffirm and retain through the plan, on the priority unsecured debt that they must pay in full, and on their remaining unsecured debt.

Out of a total combined net monthly income of $4,133 (after employer deductions for taxes, health insurance, etc.), the Matthews expect to have monthly living expenses of $2,135 and will keep that amount from their monthly paychecks to pay themselves. That leaves $1,998, and $1,538 of that will go each month to pay the secured debt that they plan to retain in the plan. That leaves $460 available each month to be applied to administrative expenses, priority unsecured debt, the curing of arrearages proposed in the plan, and, finally, to nonpriority unsecured debt. Of that $460, only $311.86 per month will wind up being paid to nonpriority unsecured creditors and that $311.86 is the Matthews' monthly projected disposable income number. (See the detailed analysis of the Matthews' plan in Section F.)

2. The Liquidation Comparison Requirement

Best interests test A test for confirmation of a plan of reorganization under Chapter 11 or 13 of the Code which requires a showing that unsecured creditors will receive at least as much under the plan as they would have received in a Chapter 7 liquidation.

Pursuant to §1325(a)(4), a non–100 percent plan must result in the unsecured creditors receiving at least as much under the plan as they would receive if the debtor's assets were liquidated under Chapter 7. This is sometimes called the **best interests test** and requires a comparison of the proposed payout to what unsecured creditors would have received if the debtor had filed a Chapter 7 liquidation proceeding. If creditors receive more under the Chapter 13 plan than they would have received in the liquidation, this test is met. If creditors would have received more in the Chapter 7, then this test is not met and the plan will not be confirmed.

P-H 21-i: Assume the debtor in the last Example has assets that, in a Chapter 7, would have been liquidated by the trustee and would have produced sufficient proceeds to pay all the priority claims of §507(a) in full, with $5,000 left over available to be paid to his unsecured creditors. If he proposes a Chapter 13 plan paying $150 a month to his unsecured creditors over five years, can it be confirmed? If he proposes a plan paying $75 a month to his unsecured creditors over five years, can it be confirmed?

Look at the Matthews' final budget in Illustration 21-a and the detailed analysis of the plan in Section F below. The Matthews are proposing to pay $311.86 per month on nonpriority unsecured claims over the 60 months of the plan or a total of $18,711.60. They have nonpriority unsecured claims totaling $76,500. So in their Chapter 13 plan they will pay 24 to 25 percent of their unsecured debt. Now look at the Matthews' bankruptcy schedules setting out their assets and their value. If the Matthews simply liquidated in Chapter 7 bankruptcy, would the unsecured creditors get anything close to 24 or 25 percent of their claims?

Discharged Permanent relief from debt pursuant to order of the Bankruptcy Court.

Unsecured debt that is not paid in an approved Chapter 13 plan will be **discharged**, just as in a Chapter 7 case (unless the obligation is of a type treated by the Code as nondischargeable, a topic discussed in Chapter Twenty-Two, Section E).

A Chapter 13 plan that is not a 100 percent plan is often referred to by the percentage of unsecured debt that it does pay.

EXAMPLE

The debtor who proposes to pay $150 a month, or $9,000 over 60 months in his plan on $45,000 of unsecured debt, has proposed a 25 percent plan. If it is approved, the $36,000 of unsecured debt not paid will be discharged. The Matthews' plan will be referred to as a 24 to 25 percent plan because it proposes to pay nonpriority unsecured claims at 24 to 25 percent of the amount owed.

Illustration 21-b: CHAPTER 13 PLAN OF ROGER AND SUSAN MATTHEWS

CHAPTER 13 PLAN

UNITED STATES BANKRUPTCY COURT
MIDDLE DISTRICT OF COLUMBIANA

In re Roger H. Matthews and wife,	)	Case no. 081661-CP
Susan J. Matthews	)	
	)	Chapter 13
Debtors	)	
	)	

CHAPTER 13 PLAN

---

1. **PLAN TERM AND PAYMENT**: The term of this plan is 60 months, during which period the Debtors will pay the Chapter 13 Trustee the total sum of $1,998 per month by wage order of both debtors.

2. **TAX REFUNDS** to be paid into the plan as follows: All refunds in excess of $500 annually during plan.

3. **PROPERTY OF THE ESTATE/INSURANCE**: Debtors' income and nonexempt assets remain property of the estate and do not vest in debtors until completion of the plan. The Chapter 13 Trustee has no obligation to insure property of the estate, which is the responsibility of the debtors.

4. **ADMINISTRATIVE EXPENSES** under 11 U.S.C. §§503 and 1326 are to be paid in full. Balance of attorney's fee to debtor's attorney in the amount of $1,000 to be paid in first 5 months at $200 per month.

5. **PRIORITY CLAIMS**: Claims entitled to priority under 11 U.S.C. §507 are to be paid in full in deferred cash payments, including the claim of the United States of America in the amount of $1,000 for Tax YR-2 to be paid in full in installments of $16.67 per month.

6. **POSTPETITION DEBT** cannot be incurred by the Debtors without the prior written approval of the Chapter 13 Trustee unless debt is incurred for medical expenses for the Debtors or Debtors' dependents, utilities for the Debtors' household, and/or for repairs to Debtors' vehicles that are used for transportation necessary for the Debtors' performance under the plan. If postpetition debt is incurred, it will be paid under the plan as allowed under 11 U.S.C. §1305.

7. **LIEN RETENTION**: Secured claims remain subject to objection by the Trustee if not properly documented or perfected regardless of confirmed plan treatment. Secured creditors retain their liens, which shall be released upon satisfaction of the secured amount except as modified in Paragraphs 10 or 11 below. If the title with lien released is not received by counsel for Debtors within thirty (30) days of satisfaction of the secured amount, then the creditor will be responsible for any court costs and/or legal fees incurred by the Debtors in obtaining release of the lien.

8. **TAX LIABILITY** claims for secured, priority, and unsecured debts paid per claim unless objected to.

9. **UNSECURED CREDITORS**: If no secured plan treatment is provided herein, the claim will be treated as unsecured and, depending on the allowed claims, will be paid the resulting dividend within the designated range below; provided, however, that if the funds available exceed the specified dividend range allowed, unsecured claims will be entitled to the greater dividend.

24-25%

10. **SECURED DEBT:**

a. Arrearage on mortgage payment to First Bank of Capitol City in the amount of $850 to be cured over first 12 months of plan together with interest at 8% per annum in 12 monthly installments of $74 each per 11 U.S.C. §1322(b)(5). Future mortgage payments to be paid as per Paragraph 11.

b. YR-8 Oldsmobile pledged as security for indebtedness to Car World to be surrendered to Car World and balance of debt owed to Car World to be treated as nonpriority unsecured debt.

c. Lien of Capitol City Financing Company in debtor's plumbing tools and furniture to be avoided per 11 U.S.C. §522(f)(1)(B) and exempted per 11 U.S.C. §522(d)(3). Balance owed Capitol City Financing Company to be treated as nonpriority unsecured debt.

d. Prepetition debt owed to Automotive Financing, Inc. secured by YR-3 Ford Truck F-150 to be modified to current value of $7,500 and paid in full over 60 months of plan together with interest at 6.5% per annum in monthly installments of $147 per 11 U.S.C. §§1322(b)(2) and 1325(a). Balance owed Automotive Financing, Inc. to be treated as nonpriority unsecured debt.

e. Claim of Columbiana Federal Savings & Loan secured by YR-4 Honda Civic to be modified and paid in full over 60 months of plan together with interest at 7.5% per annum in monthly installments of $150 per month per 11 U.S.C. §§1322(b)(2) and 1325(a)(5).

11. **MORTGAGES:**

a. The Debtors own a house and 1/2 acre located at 419 West Rockwood Avenue, Capitol City, Columbiana, with a first mortgage held by First Bank of Capitol City, which is to be paid through the plan in monthly installments of $850. Debtors to pay any future mortgage increases due to escrow changes. Mortgage balance and lien survive beyond the plan.

b. A second mortgage on the house and 1/2 acre is held by Capitol Savings Bank. Prepetition mortgage balance of $30,000 to be modified to $20,000 per 11 U.S.C. §1322(c)(2) and paid in full through the plan together with interest at 6.5% per annum in 60 monthly installments of $391. Unpaid balance to be treated as nonpriority unsecured claim.

Date: 12/1/YR-1   /s/ Roger H. Matthews___   /s/ Susan J. Matthews____
                  Roger H. Matthews, Debtor   Susan J. Matthews, Debtor

                                                     /s/ Carolyn A. Thomas
                                                     Carolyn A. Thomas
                                                     Attorney for Debtors
                                                     912 Court Street
                                                     Capitol City, Columbiana
                                                     (555) 555-1234
                                                     Bar # CL-7735

P-H 21-k   Do you see why the child care expense is included in this budget when it was not in the prepetition budget in the Assignment Memorandum in Appendix B? Why do you think the attorney increased the "Miscellaneous" category from $100 in the prepetition budget to $175 in this budget and the food budget from $475 to $500? Do you understand why the total of unsecured debt in Illustration 21-a is higher than the total of debt not being paid shown in the budget in the Assignment Memorandum? Do you see why the debt owed to CCFC on the vacation debt is now treated as unsecured debt, even though it was originally a secured debt? Do you see why a portion of the secured debt owed to CSB, AFI, Car World, and CCFC is now regarded as unsecured debt? Based on the revised budget you see in Illustration 21-a, how much disposable income should be available to pay a portion of the Matthews' unsecured debts over the term of the plan? Compare the revised budget you see in Illustration 21-a with the terms of the actual plan.

The Matthews' proposed Chapter 13 plan, based on the foregoing budget, is shown in Illustration 21-b.

E. ▶ Payments Outside the Chapter 13 Plan and the Wage Order

In general, the payments that a Chapter 13 debtor is going to make to creditors under his plan will not be made by the debtor directly. Instead, the Code envisions that the portion of the debtor's income that is to be paid to creditors go to the standing trustee, who then distributes the funds to the creditors under the terms of the plan. That portion of the debtor's income that he needs for his regular recurring living expenses will be retained by the debtor and he will be expected to pay those living expenses as they come due. These living expense payments are considered **payments outside the plan** since the debtor pays those debts directly as they come due.

If the source of the debtor's income to fund the plan is wages or salary, the employer will be served with a **wage order** from the bankruptcy court, directing the employer to make a **payroll deduction** from the debtor's paycheck each pay period and to pay that amount directly to the trustee rather than to the debtor. The debtor is to receive only that portion of his paycheck that goes toward his living expenses. The trustee receives the rest and pays it to the creditors as called for by the plan. The wage order served on the employer of Roger Matthews is shown in Illustration 21-c. (Both wage orders are shown in Document 25 of the Matthews case file.)

This system means the standing trustee's office in any give federal district is handling a tremendous amount of money coming in from Chapter 13 debtors or their employers. Nationwide, Chapter 13 standing trustees collect and disburse hundreds of millions of dollars to creditors every year.

Chapter 13 plans sometimes propose that certain debts, other than regular living expenses, be paid *outside the plan*. This is most commonly proposed when a third person (someone other than the debtor) is making part or all of the payment.

Illustration 21-c: ITL WAGE ORDER TO EMPLOYER OF ROGER MATTHEWS

<u>UNITED STATES BANKRUPTCY COURT MIDDLE DISTRICT OF COLUMBIANA</u>

In re: Roger H. Matthews and wife, Susan J. Matthews   )   Case No. 081661-CP
Debtors   )   Chapter 13

To Employer: City Plumbing Company
Attn. Payroll Department
[Address]
Re employee Roger H. Matthews
Deduction: $1,119 monthly

<u>ORDER TO EMPLOYER TO DEDUCT AND REMIT A PORTION OF DEBTOR'S EARNINGS</u>
<u>FOR THE VOLUNTARY PAYMENT OF DEBTS</u>

This is an ORDER of the United States Bankruptcy Court, NOT a garnishment. **It supersedes any previous order of this Court issued with respect to the Debtor/Employee's wages.** The above-named Debtor/Employee has voluntarily filed a petition and plan under Chapter 13 of the United States Bankruptcy Code seeking to pay certain debts under the protection of this Court. These debts are to be paid by the Chapter 13 Trustee from the Debtor/Employee's future earnings. Debtor/Employee has requested an Order to have his future earnings withheld and paid to the Chapter 13 Trustee. This Court is empowered under Title 11 Section 1325(c) of the United States Code to direct any entity from which the Debtor/Employee receives income to pay all or any part of such income to the Trustee. Accordingly, it is hereby ORDERED that:

Until further order of the Court, you are directed to immediately begin withholding the above stated amount from the wages, salary, commission, and all other earnings or income of Debtor/Employee and remit same promptly to the Chapter 13 Trustee no less frequently than once each month. (Make check payable to "Carmen W. Evans, Chapter 13 Trustee" at the address shown below).

MAIL ALL REMITTANCES WITH CASE NAME AND NUMBER TO:

Carmen W. Evans
Chapter 13 Trustee
Metro Building, Suite 625
Capitol City, Columbiana

ENTER: January 7, YR00

<u>/s/ Cynthia H. Parks</u>
Cynthia H. Parks
United States Bankruptcy Judge

EXAMPLE

> There may be a nondebtor who is also liable on the debt and who will be making all or part of the payments to avoid his own default. Or a relative or friend of the debtor may volunteer to pay all or part of the debt for the debtor.

In some federal districts it is customary for secured debt subject to a *pay through* proposal to be paid outside the plan since the obligation is not modified (scheduled payments will be made per the contract throughout the plan and beyond). However, if an obligation is impaired by the plan either because it is not being paid 100 percent or because it is not being paid on the terms of the original contract, that obligation normally must be made through the plan.

EXAMPLE

> In some districts the Matthews plan might call for the monthly payments to FBCC, holder of the first mortgage, to be paid outside the plan since that obligation is not impaired and will be paid as called for in the contract during and beyond the plan. In districts where that is not customary, the plan might still propose to pay that obligation outside the plan if a nondebtor was also liable on the debt along with the Matthews or if a third party (e.g., Roger or Susan's parents) had agreed to help the couple make the payments to FBCC. On the other hand, the plan could not call for the payments to CSB, holder of the second mortgage, to be made outside the plan because that obligation is impaired by the plan with the cramdown to equity value.

A desire to avoid the trustee's administrative costs for handling plan payments may also explain a proposal to make certain payments outside the plan, but many Chapter 13 trustees would object to a proposal based solely on such a rationale and some bankruptcy judges would not confirm a plan on that basis. This is the kind of thing on which there is wide variation of practice among the federal districts.

F. ▶ Analysis of the Matthews' Chapter 13 Plan

The Matthews have a combined net monthly income of $4,133. Under the terms of their plan, each month they will retain a total of $2,135 to pay their monthly living expenses as itemized in the budget in Illustration 21-a.

The balance of the Matthews net monthly income, $1,998 ($4,133 minus $2,135) will be paid by wage order to the Chapter 13 trustee each month; the trustee will distribute those funds as follows:

$16.67	to the United States on the YR-2 tax obligation
$200	to attorney Carolyn A. Thomas for five months on the balance of the fee owed
$850	to FBCC on the first mortgage
$391	to CSB on the second mortgage
$74	to FBCC for 12 months to cure the arrearage
$147	to AFI on the Ford Truck F-150

$150 .... to CFSL on the Honda Civic
$100 .... to Chapter 13 Trustee for administrative expenses
$69.33 .... to unsecured creditors pro rata

Obviously, the Matthews are not proposing a 100 percent plan. And initially only $69.33 per month will be available for distribution to unsecured creditors. But remember that the $200 per month payment to attorney Carolyn A. Thomas will only be made for five months and the $74 per month payment to FBCC only for 12 months. As those obligations are satisfied, the monthly *pro rata* payment to unsecured creditors will increase for the duration of the plan.

EXAMPLE

Excluding the $100 administrative expense to the Chapter 13 trustee that will be paid each of the 60 months of the plan, the $200 administrative expense for attorney's fees that will be paid for the first 12 months of the plan, the $16.67 paid each month on the priority claim of the United States for Roger's tax obligation (all of which must be paid in full), and recognizing that the $74 paid for 12 months to secured creditor FBCC to cure that arrearage will thereafter be available to distribute to unsecured creditors, this plan calls for a total of $18,711.80 to be paid to nonpriority, nonadministrative, unsecured creditors over the 60 months of the plan or an average of $311.86 per month. Note in Illustration 21-a that the Matthews have a total of $76,500 in nonpriority, unsecured debt. Thus they are proposing a 24 to 25 percent plan ($18,711.80 divided by $76,500).

P-H 21-l: Recall that per §1325(b)(1), the Matthews' plan cannot be confirmed unless it is either a 100 percent plan (which it is not) or it makes all the debtors' projected disposable income available to unsecured creditors over the term of the plan. Review the discussion of that requirement for the below median debtor in Chapter Twenty, Section B. Does the Matthews plan that you see in Illustration 21-b appear to satisfy that requirement?

P-H 21-m: If the Matthews had the higher joint monthly income of $7,000 ($84,000 annually) that we assumed for purposes of completing their alternative OBF 22C in Chapter Twenty (see Illustration 20-b), would they be able to propose a 100 percent plan based on the analysis in the last example?

Questions regarding the amount of living expenses claimed in Schedule J and/ or Form 22C and used to calculate the amount retained by the debtors in the plan are typically raised and resolved at the first meeting of creditors.

EXAMPLE

At the Matthews' 341 meeting, the Chapter 13 trustee may question the inclusion of $175 in "miscellaneous" expenses in the Matthews calculation of living expenses in their plan since only $100 was included for such expenses on their Schedule J (Document 12 in the Matthews case file). Or, the trustee might question the inclusion of the $250 for childcare expenses in their projected living expenses if the couple is not yet actually incurring that expense. What modifications in the plan as proposed might the trustee make on these issues? Since

> the Matthews have included an amount in their living expenses for charitable contributions, the trustee may ask for documentation that the debtor has historically made such contributions in that amount to insure the debtor isn't just looking for a way to keep more cash from creditors. Of course, if the plan is a 100 percent plan, the trustee will have less reason for concern.

Questions regarding other aspects of the proposed plan are also raised at the 341 meeting and are often resolved there.

EXAMPLE

> The Chapter 13 trustee for the Matthews may question the plan proposing to pay the full contract rate of interest on the cramdown of the claim of CFSL when it is not doing so on the crammed down claims of either AFI or CSB. If the plan proposed to pay the first mortgage payments owed to FBCC outside the plan, the trustee might object either because the parents' promise to help is not a sufficiently valid reason or because the trustee considers that claim impaired due to the arrearage that has to be cured. Again, attitudes and practice on such matters vary widely across the country.

Disputes raised at the 341 meeting regarding the plan that cannot be resolved there often lead to an **objection to confirmation** being made by the trustee or a creditor, and that objection can threaten the confirmation of the plan.

CONCLUSION

The Code provides the Chapter 13 debtor a number of options in dealing with secured and unsecured claims while protecting the rights of a secured claim in its collateral. The plan must be confirmed by the bankruptcy court and the debtors must then live under the terms of the plan for its duration. In Chapter Twenty-Two, we consider the Chapter 13 plan confirmation process and the challenges that may arise for debtors trying to successfully complete the Chapter 13 plan. We will also take a cursory look at the rarely filed Chapter 12 bankruptcy proceeding, which is much like a Chapter 13.

CHAPTER SUMMARY

Priority claims must be paid in full in a Chapter 13 plan, though payment may be made in deferred installments over the term of the plan. A debtor may surrender pledged property to a secured creditor as part of a plan and the trustee will abandon the property for the estate. The plan may propose to pay a secured claim in full during the term of the plan and beyond and for the creditor to retain its lien on the secured property. Arrearages on secured debt may be cured by installment payments over a reasonable time under the plan. As in a Chapter 7, the Chapter 13 debtor can avoid a judicial lien in property that impairs an exemption, unless the lien arises out of a domestic support obligation. But in Chapter 13 the debtor may also avoid a consensual security interest in household goods and furnishings, wearing apparel, appliances, tools of the trade, and other such items to the extent the lien impairs an exemption in such property, so long as it is not a purchase money security interest.

A plan can modify the rights of a secured creditor by adjusting downward the amount of the periodic payments the secured creditor is to receive and/or extending the payment period accordingly so long as the full value of the secured creditor's claim is paid during the term of the plan. Or it may propose to cram down the amount of the secured claim to the present value of the collateral, pay the full amount of the reduced secured claim over the term of the plan, treat the balance of the debt as unsecured, and retain the collateral. Present value is the replacement value of the property involved as of the date the petition is filed. In a cramdown to value, if the value will be paid to the creditor in installments, interest must be added to the payments based, not on the contract rate, but on the national prime together with an appropriate risk adjustment. The debtor's mortgage in his principal residence cannot be crammed down to value unless the original payment schedule calls for the last payment to be made before the plan expires, in which event the amount of the claim can be reduced to the extent it exceeds the available equity in the residence. Liens on vehicles subject to the 910-day rule cannot be crammed down. A Chapter 13 plan can cure arrearages in unsecured debt and pay or modify unsecured obligations, including proposing to discharge some or all of them subject to the requirement that a plan pay all projected disposable income over the term of the plan and subject to the best interests tests that requires that unsecured creditors receive more in the Chapter 13 plan than they would have received in a Chapter 7 liquidation.

A Chapter 13 plan may create classes of creditors if creditors in each class have substantially similar claims and are treated alike and so long as no class is discriminated against unfairly. Plan payments are channeled through the standing trustee to creditors unless the plan provides that they are to be paid outside the plan. If the debtor is employed, a wage order will issue to the employer directing the employer to make payroll deductions and remit the designated amount to the trustee.

REVIEW QUESTIONS

1. What is a priority claim? What percentage of a priority claim must be paid in the Chapter 13 plan?
2. What is a pay through proposal in a Chapter 13 plan and how does it work?
3. What two liens can a Chapter 13 plan avoid in order to claim an exemption in the collateral subject to the liens?
4. Explain the bifurcation feature of a secured claim under §506(a) and how that impacts on the Chapter 13 debtor's right to cram down a secured claim in his plan.
5. How is the value of the secured portion of a bifurcated secured claim determined?
6. What do we mean by paying the present value of a secured claim in a Chapter 13 plan and how is that present value calculated?
7. When can the debtor's principal residence be subject to cramdown treatment in a Chapter 13 plan?
8. What is a 910 vehicle?

9. What happens to a secured creditor's claim when the Chapter 13 debtor surrenders the collateral to him?

10. Over what period of time can a prepetition arrearage in secured or unsecured debt be cured in a Chapter 13 plan?

11. Explain what we mean by payments outside the plan.

12. Explain what a wage order is and what the employer must do to comply with it.

WORDS AND PHRASES TO REMEMBER

Abandonment
Administrative Office of the U.S. Courts
applicable commitment period
best interests test
Chapter 13 plan
classes (of creditors)
confirmation (hearing)
consensual lien
cramdown
credit-bid
cure (default)
discriminate unfairly
disposable income
exempt property
feasibility (of plan)
free and clear of liens
gross income
hanging paragraph
impaired interest
interest
Kelly Blue Book
marital adjustment
median income figure
mobile home
modification of rights
National Automotive Dealers Association (NADA)

nondischargeable debts
objection to confirmation
one-year rule
payment outside the plan
payroll deduction
pay through
projected disposable income
postpetition interest
present value (of collateral)
prime rate
principal residence
priority claims
purchase money security interest
qualified retirement plan
replacement value
ride through
risk adjustment
special circumstances expense
substantially similar
surrender of property
Till rate
unmatured interest
value of collateral
wage order
100 percent plan
910-day rule
910 vehicle

TO LEARN MORE: A number of TLM activities to accompany this chapter are accessible on the student disc accompanying the text and at the Author Updates link to the text Web site at http://www.aspenparalegaled.com/ books/parsons_abcdebt/default.asp.

Chapter Twenty-Two

The Chapter 13 Case: Plan Confirmation, Modification, Discharge, and Comparisons with Chapter 12

I wake up every morning
Keep an eye on what I spent
Gotta think about eating
Gotta think about paying the rent

—Mark Knopfler, Get Lucky

A. Timing of the Chapter 13 Plan and Initial Payments

Federal Rules of Bankruptcy Procedure (FRBP) 3015(b) requires that the debtor's proposed Chapter 13 plan be filed at the time the petition is filed or within 14 days thereafter. Section 1322(a) permits the debtor to modify the plan at any time before confirmation. This allows the plan to be proposed prior to the 341 meeting, discussed there with creditors and the trustee, and then modified if necessary prior to the court's confirmation of the plan.

Section 1326(a)(1) of the Code requires the debtor to begin making payments on the plan within 30 days following the entry for the order of relief or the filing of the proposed plan, whichever is earlier. This means the debtor is making payments to the trustee on his plan even *before* it is confirmed. One of the duties imposed on the standing trustee is to ensure that the debtor begins making these payments (see Illustration 19-a). Per §1326(a)(2), the trustee retains these preconfirmation payments until the plan is confirmed and only then distributes them to creditors.

EXAMPLE

Under their plan (Illustration 21-b or Document 21 in the Matthews case file), the Matthews propose to pay a total of $1,998 per month into their plan. Since they filed their plan with the petition, they must begin making payments within 30 days after the filing, even though their plan is not yet confirmed. (Compare the

> date the plan was filed with the date the plan was confirmed in Document 24 in the Matthews case file.) The standing trustee retains these payments until the plan is confirmed and then distributes them to creditors, per the now-confirmed plan.

B. ▶ Confirmation of the Chapter 13 Plan

Section 1324 provides that the court "shall hold" a **confirmation hearing** on the plan no earlier than 20 days and no later than 45 days after the first meeting of creditors. Creditors must be given 28 days' notice of the confirmation hearing, pursuant to Federal Rules of Bankruptcy Procedure (FRBP) 2002(b). Creditors or the standing trustee may object to confirmation. Notwithstanding the mandatory language of §1324, many bankruptcy judges only conduct a confirmation hearing if an objection to confirmation is filed. In those districts, absent an objection, confirmation will be automatic when the deadline for making objections passes.

In addition, §1324 allows the confirmation hearing to be held earlier than 20 days following the first meeting of creditors if the court determines it would be in the **best interests** of the estate and creditors to do so and there is no objection. As a result, many bankruptcy judges conduct the confirmation hearing shortly after the first meeting of creditors if no objection is filed at that time. Others wait until the time for filing claims (the **claims bar date**) has expired.

P-H 22-a: Look at the Notice of Commencement of Case that was sent to creditors in the Matthews' Chapter 13 case (Document 22 in the Matthews case file). What is the deadline established there for filing proofs of claim in the Matthews' case? Now look at the Order Confirming Chapter 13 Plan (Document 24 in the Matthews case file) to see when it was entered. Does it appear that any objection to the plan was made at or following the 341 meeting? How does the judge in the Matthews' case interpret §1324?

The debtor may **modify the plan** any time prior to confirmation, per §1323. Section §1325 sets out the criteria that the court must consider in deciding whether to confirm a plan; those criteria are summarized in Illustration 22-a.

Any party in interest may **object to the confirmation** of a proposed Chapter 13 plan. In most Chapter 13 cases, any objections to the plan by creditors or the trustee are worked out at the 341 meeting prior to the confirmation hearing so that the confirmation hearing is perfunctory and brief. If they cannot be worked out, the creditor or the trustee will file a formal objection to confirmation of the plan and the matter will be resolved at the confirmation hearing. Upon confirmation of the plan, the court will enter an order complying with Official Bankruptcy Form (OBF) 230B, **Order Confirming Chapter 13 Plan**. (See Document 24 in the Matthews case file.)

Most of the requirements for confirmation in §1325 are self-explanatory and some we have already considered. But note the first two requirements in Illustration 22-a, one relating to the good faith of the debtor in filing the petition, and the other relating to the plan being proposed in good faith. **Good faith** is not

Good faith Generally, honesty in fact and compliance with the letter and spirit of the Code.

Illustration 22-a: CRITERIA FOR CONFIRMING A CHAPTER 13 PLAN

- The Chapter 13 petition was filed in *good faith*
- The Chapter 13 plan "has been proposed in *good faith* and not by any means forbidden by law"
- The plan is *feasible*, in the sense that the debtor will be able to make all payments called for in the plan and will be able to comply with the plan
- The debtor has filed all federal, state, and local tax returns due
- The debtor is current on all domestic support obligations
- The value to be distributed to all unsecured creditors under the plan is not less than they would have received in a Chapter 7 liquidation
- Each secured creditor has either a) accepted the plan or b) will receive at least the value of the collateral and have the security interest in the property continued or c) has had the secured property surrendered to it
- All administrative and priority claims, as well as fees associated with the filing, have been paid or will be paid through the plan
- The case filing and the plan otherwise comply with all provisions of the Code

a defined term under the Code and the concept has been left to court interpretation. The various issues that we indicated in the previous section might be raised for discussion at the 341 meeting may, if they cannot be resolved there, give rise to an objection to confirmation on the basis of lack of good faith.

Good faith also emerges as a consideration in other contexts in Chapter 13 cases when the debtor seeks to modify a confirmed plan and as an implicit (not explicit) factor in a court's decision to dismiss a Chapter 13 case or convert it to a Chapter 7 liquidation under §1307, as discussed in Section F, where the good faith concept is discussed further.

Recall that the Chapter 13 debtor is required to make the first payments on his proposed plan to the trustee within 30 days following the filing of the petition or the proposal of the plan, whichever is earlier, per §1326(a)(1), and that the trustee retains these preconfirmation payments until the plan is confirmed, per §1326(a)(2). Once the plan is confirmed, §1326(a)(2) requires the trustee to distribute funds received under the plan "as soon as is practicable."

If the court declines to confirm the plan, the debtor may file a modified plan or, pursuant to §1307(a), he may convert the case to a liquidation case under Chapter 7 without the need for court permission.

C. Living with the Confirmed Chapter 13 Plan

Pursuant to §1327(a), the provisions of a confirmed plan bind the debtor and each creditor. Sections 1327(b) and (c) provide that, upon confirmation, the property of the estate **vests** in the debtor free and clear of any claim or interest of any creditor provided for in the plan, unless the plan or the order of confirmation state otherwise. The idea is that, upon filing the petition, the bankruptcy estate is created and is subject to the control of the court per §§1306 and 541. However, upon confirmation, all the property not abandoned passes back to the debtor except for the income or other property needed to perform the plan. And, of course, **postpetition property** continues to enter the estate, per §1306, either to be used for performance of the plan (the income) or to pass through the estate back to the debtor.

After confirmation, it is up to the debtor to make the plan succeed. The debtor must make the payments to the trustee either directly or through payroll deduction and must make sure that any payments to be made to creditors outside the plan are made as well, either by himself or a third party. And the debtor must accept living under the strictures of what is essentially a fixed budget for the term of the plan.

Furthermore, while confirmation of the plan entitles the debtor to retain property as long as payments are made, §1305(c) has been interpreted by the courts to mean that the Chapter 13 debtor may not incur **new debt** after the Chapter 13 petition has been filed without consulting with and obtaining the permission of the trustee. The reason for that limitation is that new debt may compromise the debtor's ability to complete the plan. The only exceptions to this requirement are recurring living expenses that were anticipated when the plan was confirmed and emergency expenses the debtor incurs without time to seek prior permission from the trustee.

EXAMPLE

If the debtor, or his dependent, living under a confirmed plan has a medical emergency, or if a vehicle breaks down and needs immediate repair, the debt incurred is allowable and the creditor can file a postpetition claim to be paid.

A debtor incurring unapproved new debt due to an emergency situation must seek the trustee's ratification of the expense promptly after it has been incurred or risk a motion by the trustee of dismissal of the case (see Section E). The limitations on incurring postpetition debt are normally set out in the plan itself. (See Paragraph 6 of the Matthews plan, Illustration 21-b and Document 21 in the Matthews case file.)

If the debtor fails to make the payments due under the confirmed plan, the court may dismiss the case or convert it to a liquidation case under Chapter 7, pursuant to §1307(c), on the motion of the trustee or an unpaid creditor. If the payments that are to be made to the standing trustee are not received as called for by the plan, the trustee's office will typically contact the debtor's lawyer or the debtor to find out what the problem is. The trustee has some discretion to work with a debtor who has gotten behind to allow the debtor time to catch up on his payments. When a motion to dismiss or convert the case is made due to delinquencies in payments under the plan bankruptcy judges may also exercise discretion to allow the debtor some time to make up the missed payments before granting the relief requested if they are convinced the debtor has good intentions and a reasonable chance of making up the delinquencies.

EXAMPLE

Assume that a year after confirmation of the Matthews' Chapter 13 plan Roger is laid off and their plan payments become delinquent. The trustee or creditors may move the court to dismiss or convert the case. If Roger appears before the court and explains that the layoff was due to no fault of his own, that he is desperately seeking new employment, and is confident of finding a job within 30 to 45 days, the court may stay a ruling on the motion to give him time to find a new job, make up the deficiencies, and begin making regular contributions to the plan again. The hearing on the motion will likely be continued for some number of days until Roger can return and report back to the court.

D. ▶ Modifying a Confirmed Chapter 13 Plan

Sometimes events occur that call for a plan to be **modified** after it has been confirmed. The debtor may lose his job, have to change jobs, or take time off from a job due to illness or the debtor may incur new unexpected expenses (e.g., medical expenses due to health problems, a new child). Or the debtor may have a significant increase in income, enabling him to pay more than at the time of confirmation.

Section 1329(a) authorizes the debtor, the trustee, or a creditor to file a **motion to modify plan** with the court. The matter is determined after notice and a hearing, which, as we know, means the proposed modification will be approved without a hearing unless an **objection to modification** is filed. Notice is provided using OBF 231B, **Order Fixing Time to Object to Proposed Modification of Confirmed Chapter 13 Plan**.

Section 1329(c) requires that, to be approved, the modified plan must comply with all the requirements of §§1322 and 1325 that we considered in connection with the original plan, including the good faith requirement. Assuming that the proposed modification does comply with those requirements, §1329(a) provides that the plan as modified can extend or reduce the time for payments, increase or reduce the amount to be paid on a particular class of claims, and even extend the length of the plan, but §1329(c) provides that the plan, as modified, cannot, in any event, extend more than five years beyond the time that the first payment was due under the original plan.

The typical motion to modify plan is made by the debtor seeking some relief from the commitments made in the confirmed plan based on changed circumstances or on a tardy realization that the commitments taken on were too onerous. Courts take varying approaches to such requests, some requiring a showing of a **substantial change in circumstances** to merit modification and rejecting mere difficulty in compliance as a legitimate ground if such difficulty was reasonably foreseeable at the time the plan was confirmed. Other courts are more lenient, noting that the Code itself does not impose any such requirements on the approval of a modification request and concluding that Congress intended to leave the determination of sufficient grounds for modification to the discretion of the bankruptcy judge.

P-H 22-b: The two approaches to ease of plan modification are reflected in *In re Meeks*, 237 B.R. 856, 859 (Bankr. M.D. Fla. 1999) (Congress did not include any language indicating an intent to make any substantial change a threshold requirement for modification of a plan) and *In re Mellors*, 372 B.R. 763, 769-770 (Bankr. W.D. Pa. 2007) (declining to follow *Meeks* because §1327 demonstrates a congressional intent that confirmed plans be accorded a great deal of finality). Read both. Which approach do you think better reflects true congressional intent re modification?

P-H 22-c: Which of the following do you think would form a legitimate good faith basis for the Matthews to seek a modification of their confirmed plan?

- A request to abandon the Ford Truck F-150 to the creditor since it has just been wrecked and to treat the balance owed to the creditor as an unsecured claim under the plan

- A request to convert the plan to a 10 percent plan, from a 24 percent case, so that Susan can go back to school full time and earn her masters degree
- A request to convert the case to a 2 percent plan, from a 24 percent case, so that both Roger and Susan can pursue a recent religious calling to donate all their time to missionary work for their religion

Which of the following do you think would form a legitimate good faith basis for the trustee or a creditor to seek a modification in the confirmed plan?
- A request to increase the plan to 100 percent because Susan just won $1 million in the lottery
- A request to extend the plan to five-and-a-half years so another 10 percent could be paid to unsecured creditors
- A request to increase the plan from a 24 percent plan to a 50 percent plan because Roger got the promotion and raise he mentioned at their 341 meeting that he might be in line for

---

E. The Chapter 13 Discharge

1. Timing of the Discharge

Discharge Permanent relief from debt pursuant to order of the bankruptcy court.

Confirmation of a Chapter 13 plan does *not* result in an immediate discharge of the debts not to be paid under the plan. Section 1328(a) of the Code provides that the **discharge** in a Chapter 13 is granted only upon *completion* of the plan. One exception to that rule is that an **early discharge** can be granted under §1328(b) for hardship (thus, sometimes called a **hardship discharge**), if the debtor can establish the three requirements shown in Illustration 22-b.

A hardship discharge is reserved for extreme cases, as where a debtor becomes permanently disabled and is unable to further fund any feasible plan.

2. Requirements for Receiving a Chapter 13 Discharge

In addition to completing the plan, receiving a discharge under Chapter 13 is contingent upon meeting other requirements, shown in Illustration 22-c.

Unlike Chapter 7, creditors have no standing to object to a debtor's discharge under Chapter 13. Of course, they can object to the plan's confirmation or modification and move to dismiss or convert the case if plan payments are not being made (see discussion in Section F), but only the trustee can object to a discharge under Chapter 13.

3. Scope of the Chapter 13 Discharge: Non-dischargeable Debts

Nondischargeable debt A debt that may not be discharged in bankruptcy

The discharge releases the debtor from all unpaid claims designated for non-payment in the plan or disallowed under §502, with limited exceptions. Sections 1328(a) and (d) set forth the debts that cannot be discharged in a Chapter 13, and those are summarized in Illustration 22-d.

Illustration 22-b: REQUIREMENTS TO RECEIVE AN EARLY DISCHARGE (HARDSHIP DISCHARGE) IN CHAPTER 13

- The failure to complete payments under the plan is beyond the control of the debtor
- The payments made to unsecured creditors up to the time of discharge are at least as much as they would have received in a Chapter 7 liquidation (this is sometimes called the "good faith test" of §1328(b))
- Modification of the plan is not feasible

Illustration 22-c: REQUIREMENTS FOR RECEIVING A CHAPTER 13 DISCHARGE, IN ADDITION TO COMPLETING PLAN PAYMENTS

- Certification by the debtor (if appropriate) that all domestic support obligations that came due prior to making such certification have been paid (§1328(a) using OBF 283)
- The debtor has not received a discharge in a prior Chapter 13 case (within two years preceding the order for relief in the instant case or within four years in a prior Chapter 7, 11, or 12 case; §1328(f))
- The debtor has completed the postpetition course in financial management (§1328(g); see Document 23 in the Matthews case file)

Illustration 22-d: DEBTS THAT CANNOT BE DISCHARGED IN A CHAPTER 13 BANKRUPTCY

- Long-term obligations, such as the home mortgage extending beyond the term of the plan and that, the plan contemplated, would continue to be paid (§1322(b)(5))
- Unpaid taxes on returns filed two years preceding the petition or on returns not filed or for fraudulent returns
- Debts for money, property, services, or an extension of credit obtained by fraudulent pretenses or by the use of fraudulent financial statements
- Last-minute consumer cash advances or spending for luxury goods or services
- Debts that were not listed on the debtor's schedules so that the creditor could not file a timely proof of claim
- Debts arising from the debtor's fraud or defalcation while acting in a fiduciary capacity
- Domestic support obligations, such as alimony and child support
- Student loans, unless the debtor can convince the court that not discharging this obligation will work an undue hardship on the debtor or his dependents
- Claims arising from the wrongful death or personal injury caused by the debtor's driving under the influence of drugs or alcohol
- Restitution or fine included on the sentence of the debtor for a crime
- Restitution or damages awarded in a civil action against the debtor based on willful or malicious injury that caused personal injury or death
- Postpetition debts for consumer necessities allowable under §1305(a)(2), for which trustee approval could have been sought but was not

---

P-H 22-d: How much debt are the Matthews discharging upon completion of their plan? Do you recognize one debt the Matthews had that would probably be considered non-dischargeable had they not agreed to pay it in full?

Most of the non-dischargeable debts you see in Illustration 22-d are identical to the debts declared non-dischargeable in a Chapter 7, pursuant to §523(a). You may want to go back and read the discussion of these various non-dischargeable obligations (see Chapter Eighteen, Section D, and review Illustration 18-c).

However, a slightly more generous discharge is available under a Chapter 13 than under a Chapter 7. In a Chapter 13, debts or claims arising out of the willful or malicious injury to the property (but not the person) of another, referenced in §523(a)(6), and certain fines and penalties imposed by the government, referenced in §523(a)(7), *can* be discharged. Curiously, §1328(c) provides that a Chapter 13 debtor receiving an early hardship discharge under §1328(b) does not discharge that debtor from any of the debts listed in §523(a).

EXAMPLE

> Assume an individual is sued for civil damages by another who alleges that the individual committed an intentional and malicious physical assault with a baseball bat on his automobile, totally destroying it. The case goes to trial and a verdict for the plaintiff in the amount of $20,000 is returned for the plaintiff. A final judgment is entered on the jury's verdict. The final judgment is now enforceable. If the individual against whom the verdict has been returned consults a debtor's attorney as to whether the judgment can be discharged in bankruptcy, he will likely be told that cannot be accomplished in a Chapter 7 case but might be accomplished in a Chapter 13 case subject to the Code requirements for confirmation and discharge already discussed.

P-H 22-e: Look again at Illustration 22-a. Assume the individual described in the last example files for Chapter 13 relief and proposes a plan to pay all his creditors 100 percent over five years, except for the judgment creditor in the lawsuit described. The plan proposes to pay nothing on that claim and to discharge it. Which criteria for confirmation of a Chapter 13 plan is the judgment creditor most likely to say is not satisfied by this plan? How would you rule on that issue if you were the bankruptcy judge? Would it matter that the debtor can show that in fact *all* of his projected disposable income for the five years of the plan will be needed to pay the other creditors 100 percent?

The **order granting discharge** will follow OBF 18W, Discharge of Debtor after Completion of Chapter 13 Plan.

Note that Chapter 13 does *not* contain a provision similar to §727, which sets out various grounds for denying any discharge at all to a Chapter 7 debtor (see Chapter Eighteen, Section E, and Illustration 18-d). The types of conduct that might serve as a basis for denying a discharge in a Chapter 7 (fraud, dishonesty, lack of cooperation, etc.) will be relevant in the decision to confirm the Chapter 13 debtor's plan or in deciding to dismiss or convert the Chapter 13 case, as discussed in the next section.

F. ▶ Conversion or Dismissal of a Chapter 13 Case

Section 1307(a) provides that the debtor can convert his case to a Chapter 7 liquidation at any time. Of course, the debtor wishing to convert his case will have to meet the requirements for being a Chapter 7 debtor, as stipulated in §1307(g). Conversion is accomplished by the debtor filing a **notice of conversion**.

Illustration 22-e: BASES FOR DISMISSAL OR CONVERSION OF A CHAPTER 13 CASE

- Unreasonable delay by the debtor that is prejudicial to creditors
- Nonpayment of any required fees and charges
- Failure to timely file a plan
- Failure to commence making timely payments under the plan, as required by §1326(a)(1)
- The denial of confirmation of a plan and the denial of a request made for additional time for filing another plan or a modification of a plan
- A material default by the debtor with respect to a term of a confirmed plan
- The revocation of the order of confirmation
- The termination of a confirmed plan by reason of the occurrence of a condition specified in the plan, other than completion of payments under the plan
- Only on request of the U.S. Trustee, failure of the debtor to timely file the various schedules of assets and liabilities and statement of affairs, as required by §521
- Failure of the debtor to pay any domestic support obligation that first becomes payable after the date of the filing of the petition
- Failure of the debtor to file all tax returns due for the preceding four years by the day before the first meeting of creditors is first scheduled, as required by §1308(a)

Illustration 22-f: RELEVANT AREAS OF INQUIRY TO DECIDE A GOOD FAITH ISSUE IN A CHAPTER 13 CASE

1. The prepetition activities of the debtor that gave rise to her debts
2. The motives of the debtor in deciding to file the Chapter 13 case
3. The accuracy of the disclosures made in the debtor's petition and supporting schedules
4. The terms of the plan that the debtor proposes in the Chapter 13
5. The debtor's compliance with the terms of a confirmed plan

Pursuant to §1307(b), the debtor may request the court to *dismiss* his Chapter 13 case at any time, and the court will grant that request unless the Chapter 13 case was itself converted from an earlier Chapter 7 or Chapter 11 case. Request for dismissal is accomplished by filing a motion for permission to dismiss Chapter 13 case.

Sections 1307(c) and (e) provide a number of circumstances under which a party in interest (the trustee, U.S. Trustee, or a creditor) can move the bankruptcy court to either dismiss the Chapter 13 case or convert it to a Chapter 7, "whichever is in the best interest of creditors and the estate." Those circumstances are summarized in Illustration 22-e.

An important concept that often comes into play when the court considers a motion to dismiss or convert a Chapter 13 case, even though it is not expressly mentioned in §1307, is **good faith**. As we mentioned above in connection with the confirmation of a proposed plan, (see Illustration 22-a), the courts construe good faith the same in any context in which it may arise in a Chapter 13: confirming a plan, modifying a plan, or deciding whether to dismiss or convert the case.

The focus of the good faith inquiry is, generally speaking, the honesty of the debtor and whether he has acted with integrity and fairness in connection with five different stages of the Chapter 13 process as listed in Illustration 22-f.

Generally speaking, all five of the areas listed in Illustration 22-f are relevant areas of inquiry in both an objection to confirmation of a plan under §1325, an objection to modification of a plan under §1329, and a motion to dismiss or convert the case under §1307. Let's summarize the kinds of specific issues that may be raised under each of the areas identified in Illustration 22-f.

1. Prepetition Activities of the Debtor That Gave Rise to Her Debts

Did any of the debts arise from dishonest or intentional conduct by the debtor? Did the debtor make bona fide efforts to pay his legitimate debts? Did the debtor wrongfully deny liability or inappropriately delay collection by his creditors? Did the debtor attempt to hide or wrongfully transfer his property to defeat legitimate creditor claims?

2. Motives of the Debtor in Filing the Chapter 13 Case

Is the Chapter 13 filing just another step in a continuing scheme to wrongfully delay the payment of legitimate debts? Does it appear the debtor is using Chapter 13 primarily to discharge a debt that would not be dischargeable under Chapter 7? Has the debtor made prior filings under Chapters 7, 11, or 13?

3. Accuracy of the Disclosures in the Debtor's Petition and Schedules

Has the debtor disclosed all his property? Has the debtor disclosed all his debts? Has the debtor wrongfully disputed legitimate claims? Do the schedules disclose that the debtor has transferred property in an attempt to defeat legitimate creditor claims?

4. Terms of the Proposed Chapter 13 Plan

Is the plan designed to benefit the debtor by directing a disproportionate share of disposable income to non-dischargeable debts or to the detriment of unsecured creditors holding dischargeable debt? Has the debtor used classes of debt to unfairly advantage friends, relatives, or business associates over other creditors?

5. Debtor's Compliance with the Terms of a Confirmed Plan

Is the debtor making the payments called for under the plan? Does the debtor habitually make late payments for no good reason? Has the debtor delayed surrendering property or otherwise doing what he promised in the plan?

G. ▶ The Chapter 12 Reorganization for a Family Farmer or Family Fisherman with Regular Income

Family farmers A debtor engaged in farming operations and who otherwise meets the requirements to be a debtor under Chapter 12.

1. History and Purpose of Chapter 12

The Chapter 12 bankruptcy was created by Congress in 1986 exclusively for **family farmers** *with a regular income* in response to a time of economic hardship for the nation's farmers. The chapter was enacted with a *sunset clause*, pursuant to which, it would expire at a specific time if not renewed. However, it was renewed several times and finally made a permanent part of the Code by BAPCPA, which expanded it to also cover **family fishermen** *with a regular income.*

Family fishermen A debtor engaged in a commercial fishing operation and who otherwise meets the requirements to be a debtor under Chapter 12.

A "family farmer" who qualifies for relief under Chapter 12 is defined in §§101(18) and (19) as an individual or an individual and spouse engaged in a **farming operation** (see §§101(20) and (21)) either as individuals, a partnership, or a closely held corporation. Like Chapter 13, Chapter 12 imposes debt limitations on those seeking to qualify for relief, and the dollar amount of those limitations are subject to adjustment every third year as mandated by §104 (see discussion in Chapter Nineteen, Section A). As of April 1, 2013, those filing for Chapter 12 relief can have no more than $4,031,575 in total debt, at least 50 percent of which must be related to the farming operation. The qualifying individual or individual and spouse must derive more than 50 percent of their annual income from the farming operation.

A "family fisherman" who qualifies for relief under Chapter 12 is defined in §§101(19A) and (19B) as an individual or an individual and spouse engaged in a **commercial fishing operation** either as individuals, a partnership, or a closely held corporation. Currently, those filing for Chapter 12 relief as family fishermen can have no more than $1,868,200 in total debt, at least 50 percent of which must be related to the fishing operation and, like the family farmer, the qualifying individual or individual and spouse must derive more than 50 percent of their annual income from the fishing operation.

2. Similarities to Chapter 13 and Chapter 11 Reorganizations

Chapter 12 is a reorganization proceeding, *not* a liquidation. As in a Chapter 13, only the debtor can propose a plan. The definition of what constitutes property of the estate in a Chapter 12 is substantially identical to that in a Chapter 13. And the Chapter 12 debtor must commit all disposable income to pay creditors during the plan, as must a Chapter 13 debtor. The procedures for filing the case, the role of the standing trustee, and the procedures for confirmation are similar. However, as noted, Chapter 12's debt limits are much more generous than the analogous Chapter 13 provisions and, unlike Chapter 13, both individuals and entities may qualify as debtors under Chapter 12.

Chapter 12 offers debtors more powerful debt restructuring tools than Chapter 13. Section 1222(b)(9) allows a Chapter 12 debtor to restructure secured debt over a term in excess of the plan. Chapter 12 contains no prohibition on the cramdown of an undersecured mortgage on real property used as the debtor's principal residence, unlike the prohibitions on such cramdown for Chapter 13 debtors and individual Chapter 11 debtors (compare §1222(b)(2) with §§1322(b)(2) and 1123(b)(5)). Chapter 12 contains no limitation like the 910 day rule on the cramdown of an undersecured claim involving a motor vehicle as collateral or the one year rule on the cramdown of an undersecured claim involving collateral other than a motor vehicle (compare §1325 with §1225). Moreover, the Code's general adequate protection standard of §361, which comes into play in motions to lift the automatic stay under §362, is declared inapplicable in a Chapter 12 by §1205(a) and the Chapter 12 debtor has other options to satisfy that standard, including paying only "reasonable rent customary in the community" as adequate protection payments for farmland.

Another significant difference between the Chapter 12 and 13 cases is that in the former the debtor is declared a **debtor in possession**, pursuant to §1203. The debtor in possession concept is one that we will consider in depth in connection with the Chapter 11 case but, briefly, it means that the debtor retains possession and control of the business assets and continues to operate the business with the right to exercise many of the powers of a bankruptcy trustee, including, in contrast to a Chapter 13 debtor, the turnover and avoidance powers of the trustee, which we considered in Chapter Seventeen, Sections D and E. (See Chapter Nineteen, Section D, for discussion of the Chapter 13 debtor's limited rights in this regard, and see Chapter Twenty-Four, Section E, for a full discussion of the rights of a Chapter 11 debtor in possession under the Code.)

Debtor in possession The legal status given a debtor filing a Chapter 11 or 12 case.

P-H 22-f: The treatment of the Chapter 12 debtor as a debtor in possession explains the differences seen in the duties of the standing trustee in a Chapter 13 case, as set forth in §1302, and those of the standing trustee in a Chapter 12 case, as set forth in §1202. Compare those two Code sections and make a list of the duties that the standing trustee has initially in a Chapter 13 that he does not have initially in a Chapter 12 case.

Today, few Chapter 12 cases are filed in most federal districts. That is true in part because the number of family farmers continues to decline, the median age of farmers continues to rise and consolidation of farming businesses continues apace. But it is also true because debtors qualifying for relief under Chapter 12 may also qualify for relief under either Chapter 13 or 11 or both and frequently choose to file for reorganization under one of those alternative chapters.

CONCLUSION

We have now examined a Chapter 13 case from filing to plan confirmation to discharge. Many businesses seek to reorganize rather than liquidate. The chapter of the Code designed for the business reorganization is Chapter 11. We consider it next.

CHAPTER SUMMARY

The Chapter 13 plan must be filed with the petition or within 14 days thereafter. The debtor must begin making payments to the trustee under the plan within 30 days of the entry of the order for relief or filing the proposed plan even if the plan has not yet been confirmed. A Chapter 13 plan must be confirmed by the court. There are a number of criteria for confirmation of a Chapter 13 plan, and creditors or the trustee may object to confirmation, in which event a confirmation hearing will be conducted by the court. Once a plan is confirmed, the debtor cannot incur new debt without permission of the standing trustee except for recurring living expenses or emergencies. If a debtor fails to make the payments promised under the confirmed plan, the Chapter 13 case can be dismissed or converted to a Chapter 7 liquidation. A confirmed plan can be modified on motion of the debtor, trustee, or creditors, based on changed circumstances. A discharge of debts not paid through the plan is granted upon completion of the plan unless the court grants an earlier hardship discharge based on certain criteria. As in a Chapter 7, some debts cannot be discharged in a Chapter 13.

A Chapter 12 bankruptcy is designed for a family farmer, or family fisherman, with regular income and operates very similarly to a Chapter 13. Chapter 12 uses a nontrustee debtor in possession approach to case administration and allows a debtor more powerful tools for restructuring secured debt than does Chapter 13.

REVIEW QUESTIONS

1. List as many requirements as you can recall for confirming a Chapter 13 plan.
2. What do we mean by the feasibility and good faith tests for plan confirmation?
3. Under what circumstances may a Chapter 13 debtor living under a confirmed plan incur new debt obligations?
4. What happens if a debtor fails to make payments promised under the plan? Is a trustee likely to work with a struggling Chapter 13 debtor and allow him to make up missed plan payments?
5. List as many of the grounds as you can recall for dismissing or converting a Chapter 13 case.
6. What are the requirements for receiving a discharge of unpaid debt in a Chapter 13?
7. What is a hardship discharge and what are the grounds for receiving one?
8. List as many debts as you can recall that cannot be discharged in a Chapter 13.
9. Under what circumstances can a Chapter 13 debtor have his case converted to one under Chapter 7? Under what circumstances can he have his case dismissed?
10. What are the differences and similarities between a Chapter 12 case and a Chapter 13 case? Which is more frequently filed?

WORDS AND PHRASES TO REMEMBER

claims bar date	family fisherman with regular income
commercial fishing operation	feasibility (of plan)
confirmation hearing	good faith
debtor in possession	hardship discharge
early discharge	modification of plan
family farmer with regular income	new debts

notice of conversion
objection to confirmation
objection to modification
Order Confirming Chapter 13 Plan

Order Granting Discharge
sunset clause
vesting (of property)

TO LEARN MORE: A number of TLM activities to accompany this chapter are accessible on the student disc accompanying the text and at the Author Updates link to the text Web site at http://www.aspenparalegaled.com/ books/parsons_abcdebt/default.asp.

Chapter Twenty-Three:

The Chapter 11 Business Reorganization: Filing the Case

When a man is in love or debt,
someone else has the advantage.

—*Bill Balance*

A. Introduction to Chapter 11

1. The Purpose of Chapter 11

A Chapter 11 bankruptcy is known as a **business reorganization** proceeding. Although qualifying individuals may file for Chapter 11 relief, it is used mostly by **entity debtors** that need to reorganize their finances under bankruptcy court supervision as an alternative to liquidation. Chapter 11 shares the same underlying purpose of Chapter 13—to enable a debtor to reorganize—but it is much more complex. It is the difference between reorganizing the finances of an individual consumer or couple and the finances of an ongoing business that may have millions of dollars in both assets and debt; dozens or even hundreds of creditors; dozens, hundreds, or even thousands of employees; and owners eager to protect their investment in the business (their **equity interest**).

The financial affairs of a typical Chapter 11 debtor involve not only more transactions *quantity-wise* than a typical Chapter 13 debtor, but also more *quality-wise*, in the sense of legal sophistication and complexity.

EXAMPLE

Think of the shopping mall nearest to where you live. Imagine if the owner of the mall filed for Chapter 11 relief. We might discover that the "owner" of the mall is a limited partnership with a single corporate general partner and several limited partners. The corporate general partner is in turn owned by three individuals who have signed personal guaranties and mortgaged their homes to guaranty the corporate debt but not specifically the limited partnership debt. The limited partners in the limited partnership are a variety of wealthy individuals from around the state, who have not only made a capital investment in the limited partnership but who have also loaned it money and hold promissory notes issued by the limited partnership. Those notes, however, are subordinated to the master promissory note issued to the primary creditor of the company that holds a first mortgage on the mall property and a second secured

> position as to all personal property of the limited partnership. The corporate general partner has also issued corporate bonds to raise capital, some of which are convertible to stock in the corporation and all of which were purchased by another limited partnership. Sound like this could get complicated? How does the complexity of your personal financial situation compare with that?

As this example may suggest, those who are planning to work in the Chapter 11 area will benefit from studying accounting, business associations, and business financing.

2. Eligibility to File a Chapter 11 Case

Section 109(d) provides generally that any "person" (see Chapter Fourteen, Section A) qualifying to file for Chapter 7 liquidation qualifies to file for Chapter 11 as well. Thus, technically, qualified individuals, as well as entity debtors, can file for Chapter 11 reorganization. But most individuals seeking to reorganize their financial affairs will choose Chapter 13, which we know is designed for individuals with relatively small amounts of debt. Individuals filing for Chapter 11 relief will be those with debt in excess of the Chapter 13 limits (see Chapter Nineteen, Section A) or those whose debt is primarily business debt rather than consumer debt.

EXAMPLE

> In the previous example, the three individual shareholders in the corporation serving as general partner in the limited partnership that owns the mall may find it necessary to file for individual bankruptcy relief. Not only will the debt they have guaranteed likely exceed the limits imposed for filing under Chapter 13, it sounds like most of their debt is likely to be business related. For either reason, Chapter 11 would probably be the appropriate reorganization chapter for them to file under. Of course, if the limited partnership, the corporate general partner, or the individual shareholders of the corporation decide that a liquidation bankruptcy is necessary, they will file under Chapter 7.

a. The Small Business Debtor

One type of Chapter 11 debtor that receives special treatment under the Code is the debtor engaged in commercial or business activities who has aggregate, noncontingent, liquidated debts not exceeding $2,490,525 million (this amount is adjusted every three years, with the next adjustment due April 1, 2016). Such a debtor is designated a **small business debtor**, pursuant to §101(51D), and its Chapter 11 filing will be designated a **small business case**, as defined in §101(51C), if

Small business debtor A Chapter 11 debtor engaged in commercial or business activities which has aggregate non-contingent liquidated debts not exceeding $2,490,525 million and who elects to have its case treated as a small business case for expedited administration.

- The U.S. Trustee does not appoint a creditors' committee in the case (see Section C, below) or
- Such a committee is appointed but the court concludes it is not sufficiently active to provide adequate oversight to the debtor.

The designation of a proceeding as a small business case under Chapter 11 has consequences we will refer to periodically in our study but, in general, it means that

- The period for plan formulation (see Chapter Twenty-Five, Section A) is reduced;
- The procedures for plan approval (see Chapter Twenty-Five, Section E) are somewhat simplified;
- The debtor is subject to closer supervision by the U.S. Trustee; and
- Some specialized reporting requirements are required.

b. The Single Asset Real Estate Debtor

Single asset real estate debtor A Chapter 11 debtor whose primary business is the operation of a single piece of income-producing property and which derives substantially all of its income from that property.

A second type of Chapter 11 debtor that receives special treatment under the Code is the **single asset real estate debtor.** Per §§1121 and 362(d), a debtor whose primary business is the operation of a single piece of income-producing property and who derives substantially all of its income from that property is treated as a single asset real estate debtor (see definition in §101(51B)). Owners of an apartment complex whose income derives from apartment rentals are the best example. Such debtors are treated specially by the Code due to historical problems with their filing a Chapter 11 petition in order to trigger the automatic stay against creditors secured in the real property when there are no realistic prospects of successfully reorganizing. Essentially, §362(d) requires the single asset real estate debtor to produce an expedited plan of reorganization or to make other arrangements with such creditors to avoid lifting of the stay against the real property.

3. Overview of a Chapter 11 Case

Plan of reorganization A plan proposed under Chapter 11.

The goal of a business filing for Chapter 11 relief is survival. Sometimes we refer to the **rehabilitation of the debtor**, but the reality in most instances is that the Chapter 11 case is an effort by a struggling business to avoid liquidation. Filing the Chapter 11 petition triggers the automatic stay, which gives the debtor breathing room: time to negotiate with creditors and to come up with a **plan of reorganization** to which the creditors will consent. In contrast to a Chapter 13 plan, which can run for no more than five years, the Code does not place a limit on the duration of a Chapter 11 plan of reorganization.

Chapter 11 does not allow a debtor to win court approval of its plan of reorganization as easily as a Chapter 13 debtor. The creditors of the Chapter 11 debtor, both secured and unsecured, must be involved in the plan negotiation process and, in most instances, their approval must be obtained in a formal voting process. So critical is the involvement of creditors in a Chapter 11 case that if the debtor fails to produce a plan that can win sufficient creditor support within the **exclusivity period** granted it by the Code (see Chapter Twenty-Five, Section A), creditors are allowed to propose competing plans that may be approved over the debtor's objection. As part of the plan approval process, the debtor must provide a comprehensive **disclosure statement** explaining in detail its financial dealings, the sources of its financial distress, and how the proposed plan will succeed. Once a plan of reorganization meets the confirmation requirements of the Code and is confirmed by the bankruptcy court, the reorganized debtor will operate its business pursuant to the plan and with continued court monitoring and creditor input. At the conclusion of the plan, the case is closed and the debtor emerges from Chapter 11.

Illustration 23-a: THE STAGES OF A CHAPTER 11 BUSINESS REORGANIZATION PROCEEDING

1. Petition filed (voluntary or involuntary)
   - Automatic stay goes into effect, per §362
   - Debtor operates business as a debtor in possession, per §1108, unless a bankruptcy trustee is appointed prior to plan confirmation, per §1104
2. Creditors' committee appointed by U.S. Trustee, per §1102
3. Preliminary operational motions regarding use of cash collateral; use, sale, or lease of other property; payment of critical prepetition debts; and hiring of professionals
4. The first meeting of creditors
5. Plan negotiation period
   - Motions regarding postpetition financing, executory contracts, and interim compensation
   - Debtor has benefit of 120-day exclusivity period to file plan
   - Property of the estate, per §541, is identified and brought under DIP control using turnover and avoidance powers
6. Disclosure statement and proposed plan filed
   - Hearing on adequacy disclosure statement conducted
   - Disclosure statement approved or disapproved by court
   - Approved disclosure statement and proposed plan distributed to creditors, equity security holders, and U.S. Trustee
7. Solicitation of support for plan
8. Voting on plan
9. Confirmation hearing conducted on plan; objections heard
10. Order of confirmation entered on accepted plan, per §1129(a), or by cramdown over objections, per §1129(b)
11. Discharge of preconfirmation debts for entity debtor upon confirmation and for individual debtor upon completion of plan payments
12. Reorganized debtor operates pursuant to confirmed plan
13. Plan consummated: case closed and debtor emerges from plan

As the old saying goes, "there's many a slip twixt the cup and the lip," and there are multiple steps and many opportunities for failure from the filing of a Chapter 11 petition to the confirmation of a plan and from confirmation to plan consummation. A significant number of Chapter 11 cases fail somewhere along the way and convert to Chapter 7 liquidation. The various stages of a Chapter 11 proceeding are shown in Illustration 23-a, and these will form the basis for our step-by-step study of the business reorganization.

4. The Impact of a Business Filing on Owners, Officers, and Others

Whenever a bankruptcy case is filed for a business entity such as a corporation, limited liability company, or partnership, questions arise concerning the impact of that filing on those who own the debtor business or serve as its officers or directors, not to mention its employees. Are jobs going to be lost? Is compensation going to be reduced? Will benefits be slashed? Will customers, suppliers, or others who have dealt with the debtor business be negatively impacted by the filing? What if the owners or officers of the business have personally guaranteed the debt of the business, a very common occurrence for many businesses? Upon default by the debtor business, those guarantors can expect a demand from the creditors holding the guarantees to demand payment of the entity's debts.

For all these reasons, the bankruptcy filing by a business entity often produces a domino effect. Those negatively impacted by the filing find themselves in financial peril and seek consultation as a result. It is not unusual to see multiple bankruptcy filings, particularly where individuals have personally guaranteed the debt of the entity.

P-H 23-a: Look at Assignment Memorandum #1 in Appendix C. Do you see that the two brothers now operating this business, Charles and Timothy Banowsky, have personally guaranteed the obligation that their business owes to its largest creditor, Capitol City Bank (CCB), which is currently owed $1.5 million? When the corporation files for Chapter 11 reorganization, Charles and Timothy are listed on the Schedule H (see Document #11 in the Banowsky Brothers case file) as co-debtors on that obligation. If the corporation defaults on that obligation, CCB can be expected to pursue both brothers on their guarantees. If Charles and/or Timothy consults with the firm for which you work regarding their options, what kinds of questions should be asked to determine if they should be advised to consider filing a bankruptcy case of their own? Which chapters of the Code might they consider filing under? What does your firm need to know in order to give that advice?

---

5. The "Prepackaged" Chapter 11

Where time and resources allow, a business may be able to negotiate a plan of reorganization with creditors *before* filing the Chapter 11 petition. If the business can win prepetition agreement from debtors for a plan of reorganization, the Chapter 11 petition can be filed, the plan submitted immediately, and confirmation obtained speedily, in the absence of creditor objections. We call such a case a **prepackaged Chapter 11**. A fairly typical Chapter 11 debtor is Banowsky Brothers Furniture, Inc. Let's meet Charles and Timothy Banowsky and become familiar with their family owned business, BBF. Go to Appendix C at this time and read Assignment Memorandum #1.

Prepackaged Chapter 11 A Chapter 11 proceeding in which the plan of reorganization has been drafted and informally approved by creditors prepetition.

P-H 23-b: Based on the information provided in Assignment Memorandum #1 in Appendix C, why will BBF not qualify for treatment as a small business debtor when it files its Chapter 11 petition? Why will it not be governed by the rules regarding a single asset real estate company since it only owns the one piece of real property?

B. Filing a Chapter 11 Case and the "Debtor in Possession" Concept

1. The Petition, Schedules, and Other Documents

A Chapter 11 case is commenced in the same way as a case under any other chapter of the Code, by filing a **voluntary petition** with a bankruptcy court having proper venue (see the BBF Chapter 11 petition, Document 1 in the BBF case file). Though it is unusual, an **involuntary petition** can be filed by creditors who meet the requirements of §303, which we considered in Chapter Fifteen, Section A, in connection with an involuntary Chapter 7 petition.

The filing fee must be paid when the petition is filed and cannot be paid in installments by a corporate debtor. Pursuant to §521 of the Code and Federal Rules of Bankruptcy Procedure (FRBP) 7001, at the same time it files its petition, the entity debtor must also file the items listed in Illustration 23-b.

Pursuant to §1116(1), a debtor who qualifies as a small business debtor must file with the petition its most recent balance sheet, statement of operations, cash-flow statement, and federal income tax return. An individual Chapter 11 debtor must also file the Exhibit D certificate of prepetition credit counseling with his petition, as required by §521(b), along with the OBF 21 Statement of Social Security Number, as required by FRBP 1007(f).

At the time the petition is filed, or within 14 days thereafter, the Chapter 11 *entity* debtor must also file the documents listed in Illustration 23-c.

The *individual* Chapter 11 debtor must file with his petition, or within 14 days thereafter, the various schedules of assets and liabilities including Schedules I and J, the Statement of Financial Affairs, and the other statements and documents discussed in Chapter Fifteen, Section B.

P-H 23-c: Remember that OBF 200 lists all the required schedules, lists, and statements for each chapter under which a debtor may file for bankruptcy relief. Locate OBF 200 for Chapter 11 filers and see if BBF has filed all the required documents to accompany its petition (all official bankruptcy forms are available at www.uscourts.gov/bkforms/index.html).

The time for filing the required schedules and statements that need not accompany the petition can be extended by motion filed with the bankruptcy court, as discussed in Chapter Fifteen, Section C. But for small business cases,

Illustration 23-b: DOCUMENTS THAT MUST BE FILED WITH THE CHAPTER 11 PETITION OF AN ENTITY DEBTOR

- A list of creditors (Document 2 in the BBF case file)
- A corporate resolution authorizing the filing of the petition (Document 3 in the BBF case file) (a partnership will file an appropriate consent or appointment of general partner with authority to file)
- A list of the 20 largest unsecured creditors, supplied using Official Bankruptcy Form (OBF) 4 (Document 4 in the BBF case file)
- Exhibit A to OBF 1 for *publicly traded corporations* only

Illustration 23-c: DOCUMENTS THAT MUST BE FILED WITH THE CHAPTER 11 PETITION OR WITHIN 15 DAYS THEREAFTER BY THE ENTITY DEBTOR

> - The various schedules of assets and liabilities (Documents 5 through 12 in the BBF case file) (excluding Schedules C, I, and J, which are for individual debtors only).
> - The Declaration Under Penalty of Perjury Regarding Debtor's Schedules (Document 13 in the BBF case file).
> - A Statement of Corporate Ownership for entity debtors required by FRBP 7007.1 (Document 14 in the BBF case file).
> - A Statement of Current Income and Expenditures (Document 15 in The BBF case file).
> - A Statement of Financial Affairs (Document 16 in the BBF case file).
> - A Statement Disclosing Compensation Paid or to be Paid to an Attorney (Document 17 in the BBF case file).
> - A List of **equity security holders** of the debtor (Document 18 in The BBF case file). Equity security holders are the shareholders or owners of the debtor corporation. If the debtor is a limited liability company, the equity holders are the owner/members. If the debtor is a partnership, the equity holders are the partners (see §§101(9)(16) and (17)).

Equity security holders The holders of an ownership interest in an entity debtor.

§1116(3) limits the permissive extension period to 30 days after the order for relief "absent extraordinary and compelling circumstances."

2. The Debtor in Possession

A bankruptcy trustee is *not* automatically appointed upon the filing of the Chapter 11 petition, as happens in a Chapter 7 or 13. Instead, the debtor is considered the **debtor in possession (DIP)**, per §1101(1). The debtor, as DIP, retains possession and control of its assets while reorganizing, as well as the right to continue operating the business per §1108 (that section has been so construed by the courts even though it makes no mention of the DIP). Section 1107 of the Code gives the DIP essentially all the rights and powers of a **bankruptcy trustee** in a case (other than the right to compensation), including the turnover and avoidance powers that we considered in Chapter Seventeen, Sections D and E. The DIP can also pursue claims that are property of the estate (Chapter Seventeen, Section B), hire professionals as needed (e.g., attorneys, accountants, or appraisers) (see Chapter Seventeen, Section F) and can object to any claim made by a creditor, just as a trustee could (see Chapter Seventeen, Section A).

Debtor in possession (DIP) The legal status given a debtor filing a Chapter 11 or 12 case.

The DIP operates the business under the close supervision of the U.S. Trustee. The U.S. Trustee may schedule a §1116(2) **initial debtor interview** or other informal meeting with representatives of the DIP to discuss matters related to the case. The DIP usually must file a **property inventory** within 30 days and periodic **operating reports**, just as a trustee would do per §1106(a)(1) and FRBP 2015(a)(3). Reporting requirements for DIPs are often addressed in the **local rules** of the bankruptcy court. The operating reports provided by the DIP will contain a detailed disclosure of all the business operations of the debtor during the period covered (receipts, disbursements, accrued expenses, changes in cash position, changes in inventory, or other assets, etc.). The operating reports will be examined closely by the U.S. Trustee and creditors to see if reorganization seems feasible or whether a motion should be made to convert the case to a Chapter 7 liquidation (see Chapter Twenty-Four, Section C) in order to protect creditors. Creditors who see the DIP wasting its assets or going deeper into debt each reporting period will likely move for conversion of the case to a liquidation in order to stop the bleeding and maximize their return from remaining assets.

The DIP is technically considered an entity separate and apart from the prepetition business. Accordingly, the local rules or the U.S. Trustee will require the DIP to open new bank accounts in the name of the business, specifically adding "Debtor in Possession" to the name of the account.

EXAMPLE

> Prior to filing its Chapter 11 petition, all bank accounts of BBF were in the name of "Banowsky Brothers Furniture, Inc." Immediately after the petition is filed, at the direction of either the local rules or the U.S. Trustee, BBF as DIP will close out all its accounts and reopen them under the name, "Banowsky Brothers Furniture, Inc., Debtor in Possession."

P-H 23-d: It should be obvious at this point, from our discussion of the debtor's role as DIP, that very few businesses can comply with the requirements imposed by the Code on the Chapter 11 debtor without near-constant legal advice. The debtor will continue operating its business postpetition but every "business decision" it makes must now be made in light of its responsibilities as a Chapter 11 DIP. Since there is no trustee, the DIP will need its attorney to undertake any turnover and avoidance actions. In cases involving large corporate debtors, the attorney may actually operate from an office in the debtor's workplace due to his fulltime involvement in the debtor's case.

You can imagine the thorough explanation that debtor's attorneys must give to their clients about how their world will change once the petition is filed. Consider how often various persons operating the business will need to consult with the attorney before making what were, prepetition, routine business decisions. Consider how well the debtor's attorney must understand the client's business in order to provide sound legal advice. How important is it that the debtor's attorney and assisting legal professionals have an adequate financial, accounting, and business background, as well as legal training? How important is it that the debtor's attorney have a good working relationship with the U.S. Trustee? What types of non-legal professional help is the DIP likely to need in order to comply with the reporting and other requirements imposed by the U.S. Trustee? Should the owners of the business expect to devote more or less time to business affairs once they file a Chapter 11 petition?

3. Appointing a Bankruptcy Trustee

In most Chapter 11 cases a bankruptcy trustee is never appointed and the case proceeds with the DIP operating the business under the U.S. Trustee's supervision. But the Bankruptcy Court does have the power to appoint a bankruptcy trustee in a Chapter 11 case. Section 1104 of the Code sets out the grounds upon

Illustration 23-d: GROUNDS FOR APPOINTING A BANKRUPTCY TRUSTEE IN A CHAPTER 11 CASE

> - For cause, including fraud, dishonesty, incompetence, or gross mismanagement of the affairs of the debtor by current management, either before or after the commencement of the case
> - If such appointment is in the interests of creditors, any equity security holders, and other interests of the estate
> - As an alternative to converting the case to a Chapter 7 liquidation or dismissing it when it appears that a trustee might be able to save the reorganization from failing, if grounds exist to convert or dismiss the case under §1112 but the court determines that the appointment of a trustee or an examiner is in the best interests of creditors and the estate

which the court, on request of the U.S. Trustee or a party in interest, can appoint a bankruptcy trustee in the case; those grounds are summarized in Illustration 23-d.

When the bankruptcy court orders a trustee to be appointed in a Chapter 11 case, the U.S. Trustee makes the appointment from the **trustee's panel**, discussed in Chapter Sixteen, Section B. The bankruptcy trustee is authorized by §1108 to operate the debtor's business and will expect to have the debtor's cooperation in doing so. The trustee is authorized by §1106 to perform all the normal duties of a trustee including to:

- Exercise the turnover and avoidance powers;
- Review and dispute claims;
- File any schedules or statements the debtor has not filed;
- File the periodic operating reports;
- File any tax returns the debtor has failed to file;
- Investigate the financial circumstances of the debtor and the conduct of its management in order to make a recommendation on the feasibility of reorganization;
- Formulate a plan of reorganization if the debtor fails to do so;
- Keep the U.S. Trustee, creditors, and the court advised as to all material developments; and
- Make appropriate recommendations to the court.

As an alternative to the appointment of a trustee, the court may appoint an **examiner**, pursuant to §1104(c). An examiner does not assume responsibility for operating the debtor's business or have the powers of a trustee. Instead, the examiner will be charged with making investigations into specific aspects of the debtor's business and reporting back to the court.

Trustee's panel Persons approved by the U.S. Trustee to serve as trustees in Chapter 7 or 11 cases in a district.

Examiner A person appointed by a bankruptcy court to investigate specific aspects of a Chapter 11 debtor's conduct or management of the estate.

C. The Creditors' Committee

Creditors' committee A committee of creditors appointed by the U.S. Trustee in Chapter 11 cases and sometimes in Chapter 7 cases to represent the interests of all creditors.

We mentioned in the overview of a Chapter 11 case, in Section A, that creditors play a critical role in a Chapter 11 reorganization. And we learned in Section B (see Illustration 23-b) that one of the required schedules that the Chapter 11 debtor files is a list of its 20 largest unsecured creditors. (See OBF 4, Document 4 in the BBF case file.) Section 1102(a) of the Code requires that the U.S. Trustee appoint a committee of unsecured creditors "as soon as practicable after the order for relief." Section 1102(b)(1) suggests but does not require that this **creditors' committee**

Illustration 23-e: FUNCTIONS OF THE CREDITORS' COMMITTEE IN A CHAPTER 11 CASE

- To consult with the DIP or trustee concerning the administration of the case
- To investigate the debtor's financial condition and business operations
- To participate in the formulation of the plan of reorganization
- To request the appointment of a trustee, if appropriate
- To keep other creditors not on the committee advised
- To perform "such other services as are in the interest of those represented," per §1103(c)

consist of the seven largest unsecured creditors. That section does require that the members of the committee be "representative of the different kinds of claims."

EXAMPLE

If the debtor owes unsecured lenders, that is a claim class with different interests than unsecured trade creditors or unsecured tort claimants. Each of these classes should be represented on the creditors' committee.

Pursuant to §§1102(b)(3) and 1103, the creditors' committee performs a number of functions, as summarized in Illustration 23-e.

Party in interest Any party having a stake in the outcome of a matter arising in a bankruptcy case.

The creditors' committee is a **party in interest** in the Chapter 11 case, entitled to notice of all proceedings and entitled to be heard by the court on all matters. It may hire an attorney, accountant, or other professional to assist it in its work, subject to court approval per §1103(a). The creditors' committee may be authorized by the bankruptcy court to initiate a turnover or avoidance action if the DIP has refused a demand to do so. Under certain circumstances, it can even propose its own plan of reorganization for the debtor (see Chapter Twenty-Five, Section A).

Section 1102(a) gives the U.S. Trustee discretion to create other committees as it sees fit, including a committee of equity security holders. Sections 101(16) and (17) define an equity security holder as one holding an ownership interest in an entity debtor (a corporation or partnership) or holding a warrant or other right to purchase such an ownership interest. Equity security holders are also parties in interest in a Chapter 11 case, entitled to notice and to be heard. Chapter 11 frequently refers to **claims and interests**, a phrase encompassing not just creditors holding "claims" against the debtor, but owners holding ownership "interests." The creditor hopes to recover all of the debt owed to it in the debtor's reorganization; the owner hopes to maintain or receive the value of his investment in the debtor.

P-H 23-e: Review the U.S. Trustee's notice of appointment of creditors committee in the BBF case (Document 22 in the BBF case file). How many creditors were appointed to the committee? Do they represent more than one class of unsecured creditors? Did the U.S. Trustee appoint more than one committee of creditors?

Pursuant to §1102(a)(3), the court may order that a creditors' committee not be appointed in a small business case, discussed in Section A. You will recall that the nonappointment of such committee is one of the prerequisites for treatment of a Chapter 11 debtor under the small business case rules of the Code.

In a prepackaged bankruptcy case, discussed in Section A, the creditors' committee will have been formed prepetition. FRBP 2007(a) authorizes the court, on motion, to approve that committee's formation and membership ex post facto in order to expedite the reorganization case.

D. ▶ Preliminary Operational Motions in a Chapter 11 Case: First Day Orders

Automatic stay The prohibition on creditors continuing collection efforts against a debtor that arises automatically upon the debtor's filing of a bankruptcy petition.

Property of the estate All property in which the debtor holds a legal or equitable interest at the commencement of a bankruptcy case.

First day orders Practitioner's phrase for orders commonly sought immediately upon filing of a Chapter 11 case.

The days immediately following the filing of a Chapter 11 petition are a critical period for the debtor hoping to successfully reorganize. Once the petition is filed, the debtor continues to operate his business, but now it must do so under the rules of the Code and not just the rules of the marketplace. The filing of the petition triggers the **automatic stay** provision of §362(a) and the §541(a) concept of **property of the estate**. Now that the business has filed for relief, its creditors are momentarily stayed from collection efforts but its property is now technically vested in the bankruptcy estate. Consequently, the DIP cannot do whatever it wants with its property. It is no longer business as usual. The creditors, owners, and the U.S. Trustee are entitled to provide input on how the debtor utilizes its assets in the conduct of its business and the bankruptcy court now has the final say.

In most Chapter 11 cases, the debtor's attorney will file one or more motions on the same day that the petition is filed, seeking court approval of its intent to use or dispose of business assets in an extraordinary manner, or to use cash that is encumbered for any purpose, or to obtain new credit or to hire certain professionals, and so on. So routinely are these types of motions filed with the petition that practitioners sometimes refer to the orders sought on those early motions as **first day orders**. The Code does not *require* that these motions be made on the day the petition is filed or even shortly thereafter, but circumstances usually do. Often the debtor must have court approval for these matters or the business will fail. That is why these **preliminary operational motions** are so critical to the Chapter 11 case. Without court approval of these motions in the very earliest days of the case, the reorganization effort is stillborn.

EXAMPLE

Assume that BBF decides to file a Chapter 11 petition to stop an anticipated repossession of its CAD/CAM systems and production equipment by New Century Automation (NCA). A week before filing, it receives notification from three essential trade creditors that unless their past due bills are all paid in full by cash or cashier's check within one week, they will stop doing business with BBF. If that occurs, BBF will be out of business. BBF files its Chapter 11 petition triggering the §362 automatic stay and delaying NCA's repossession. But BBF still needs to use its cash immediately to satisfy the three critical trade creditors and to pay its employees or it will be out of business anyway. Thus, the preliminary operational motions that the attorney for BBF files along with the petition will be as critical to its survival as stopping the repossession.

Let's look at the most common preliminary operational motions filed in a Chapter 11 case. The Code sections dealing with these motions refer to "the trustee" being authorized to do this or that. But remember that §1107 gives the DIP the powers of a bankruptcy trustee and that, in most Chapter 11 cases, a trustee is never appointed. So we will study these sections on the assumption that they refer to the DIP, as in practical effect they do.

1. The Motion for Authorization to Use Cash Collateral

Section 363 of the Code deals with the DIP's right to *use, sell, or lease property* of the estate post-petition. And, generally speaking, so long as the DIP is using, selling, or leasing assets of the debtor in the **ordinary course of business**, it can do so without court approval. (We will consider the DIP's need to use, sell or lease property in other than the ordinary course of its business in Chapter Twenty-Four, Section D.) However, the Code treats the DIP's use of cash that has been pledged as collateral to a creditor (**cash collateral**) differently than other property. Section 363(c)(2) provides that cash collateral cannot be used by the DIP post-petition even in the ordinary course of its business unless

- The creditor secured in the cash consents to the use or
- The court authorizes the use. (See Document 19 in the BBF case file.)

Cash collateral is defined in §363(a) to mean not just bank notes on hand in a cash register but also cash held in deposit accounts, negotiable instruments (e.g., promissory notes, certificates of deposit, or uncashed checks) and securities, documents of title, or other instruments readily turned into cash and thus called **cash equivalents**. For the cash collateral rules to apply, the cash or cash equivalents must be pledged as collateral. If the cash is unpledged, it is subject to the same §363 rules as other property of the DIP (to be considered in Chapter Twenty-Four, Section D).

Ordinary course of business In general, following the typical usual practices engaged in by a business.

Cash collateral Cash or *cash equivalents* that are part of the property of the estate and which are subject to a security interest in favor of a creditor.

Cash equivalents Instruments easily convertible to cash, such as checks or promissory notes.

EXAMPLE

The master loan that BBF arranged with Capitol City Bank (CCB) in YR-6 required BBF to pledge, not just its real property, but its inventory, accounts receivable, and cash as security for that loan. Thus, CCB is secured in the cash and cash equivalents of BBF. This will include the cash in all BBF bank accounts, any promissory notes it holds, and any uncashed checks it has.

If the creditor secured in the cash the DIP seeks to use post-petition will not consent and the DIP is forced to file a motion seeking authorization from the court to use it, §363(c)(4) obligates the DIP to keep the cash collateral in a separate account from other cash, pending the resolution of the motion.

The primary issue in the DIP's request for authorization to use cash collateral is always **adequate protection** of the secured creditor's interest in the cash. Sections 363(c)(3) and (e) provide that when a motion for authorization to use cash collateral is filed, the court "shall prohibit or condition such use . . . as is necessary to provide adequate protection of such interest." Adequate protection has to do with the secured creditor's right to have the value of the property in which it is secured protected or maintained throughout the case, such that the creditor has the same advantaged position as a secured creditor throughout a case as it had at the beginning. Remember that per §506(a)(1) a secured creditor's

Adequate protection The protection that must be provided by the bankrupt estate to a creditor whose interest in property is threatened by the estate's continued possession and use of the property.

claim is only secured up to the value of the collateral as of the date the petition is filed. That is the value the secured creditor is entitled to have adequately protected if the debtor contemplates doing anything with the property other than turning it over to the creditor.

P-H 23-f: Both the DIP's need to use the cash collateral and the secured creditor's concern about its depletion should be fairly obvious. Consider BBF's position. It needs to use its cash to continue ordering inventory, making furniture, paying its employees, and meeting other obligations in order to stay in business to have any hope of reorganizing. Consider CCB's position. BBF owes it money and agreed that it could have a secured position in all its cash. To the extent this struggling debtor depletes its cash, CCB's secured position is impaired. What questions about the various uses to be made of the cash might the judge have for BBF at the hearing on its motion for authorization to use cash collateral? Will it be concerned about BBF's declining sales over the past few years? Will it be concerned about the salaries it pays its workers? What about the other overhead of BBF? What other concerns might the judge have?

What constitutes adequate protection is not comprehensively defined in the Code but §361 provides that it may be provided by:

- Periodic cash payments to the creditor sufficient to compensate for the decrease in value of the collateral;
- Providing the creditor with a lien on other property sufficient to compensate for the decrease in value of the collateral being used; or
- Granting other such relief as will result in the creditor receiving the indubitable equivalent of its interest in the property.

Floating lien A security interest (lien) that attaches automatically to property of the debtor acquired after the date the security interest was created.

After-acquired property Property acquired by a debtor that automatically becomes subject to a preexisting security interest (lien) of a creditor.

We will consider §361 in more detail in Chapter Twenty-Four, Section D, when we examine motions by the DIP to use other property of the estate outside of the ordinary course of its business. It is sufficient here to note that the most typical adequate protection arrangement made in cash collateral disputes is for the debtor to grant the creditor a security interest in other property as contemplated by §361(2). In many situations, this simply means granting the creditor a security interest in the same kinds of property acquired **postpetition** in which the creditor held a **prepetition** security interest. To understand this, recall that in Chapter Five, Section C, we learned that a security interest in personal property— like cash, inventory, and accounts receivable—is subject to the **floating lien** concept, including **after-acquired property**.

EXAMPLE

The security agreement in which BBF pledged to CCB its inventory, accounts receivable, and cash would have provided that the security interest extend not only to inventory, accounts receivable, and cash on hand at that moment, but also to the same such property as the debtor might acquire in the future.

Section 552(a) of the Code provides, however, that the security interest of a creditor does *not* extend to property acquired by the debtor postpetition. The security interest in after-acquired property is effectively suspended with the filing of the petition and will not attach to that property. So providing adequate protection in a cash collateral dispute often involves nothing more than the DIP offering the creditor a security interest in the same property it acquires postpetition that would have been subject to the original prepetition security agreement but for the bankruptcy filing.

EXAMPLE

> If BBF proposes to grant CCB a security interest in its postpetition inventory and accounts receivable, CCB may consent to that arrangement or, if a motion is necessary, the court may approve that arrangement as adequate protection and authorize the use of cash collateral.

The procedures for motions for the authorization to use cash collateral set forth in FRBP 4001(b) provide that the court is *not* to conduct a final hearing on the motion any earlier than 14 days after the motion is filed and served on the various parties entitled to notice. A delay of that length could be disastrous for a DIP needing to pay employees, order and pay for new materials, and the like. Fortunately, the rules do allow the court to conduct a **preliminary hearing** prior to the expiration of the 14 days and to there authorize the use of "that amount of cash collateral that is necessary to avoid immediate and irreparable harm to the estate pending a final hearing." The typical motion for authorization to use cash collateral will allege such harm and ask for the expedited preliminary hearing (see Document 19 in the BBF case file). If relief is granted at the preliminary hearing, a **final hearing** on the motion will be scheduled for a date more than 14 days after the original motion was filed. Section 363(c)(3) of the Code supplements FRBP 4001(b)(2) by providing that authorization to use cash collateral can be approved at the preliminary hearing "only if there is a reasonable likelihood" that the DIP will prevail at the final hearing on the motion. (Although §363(c)(3) uses the word "trustee" rather than "DIP," remember that per §1107, the DIP has all the rights, title, and power of a bankruptcy trustee in a Chapter 11 case.)

2. The Motion for Authorization to Pay Critical Prepetition Debts Under the "Necessity Doctrine"

The right of a creditor to pursue payment of a prepetition debt is automatically stayed upon the filing of the petition, per §362. Normally, no payment of prepetition debt is required or made in any case under the Code until the stay is lifted for a secured creditor, or property is abandoned to a creditor, or there is a distribution in a Chapter 7, or payments begin under a confirmed plan in a Chapter 13, 12, or 11. And we have learned that interest does not accrue on prepetition unsecured debts awaiting payment and accrues on prepetition secured debts only up the value of the collateral (see Chapter Seventeen, Section A).

But sometimes in a Chapter 11, the DIP needs authorization from the court to go ahead and pay certain **critical prepetition debts** in order to stay in business and make reorganization feasible.

On the date BBF filed its petition, its employees, paid every other week, were in the middle of a two-week pay period and are now owed for that prepetition week. If they are not paid promptly, they may quit and BBF will be out of business. BBF also has two critical vendors threatening to stop doing business with it unless payment is made on their outstanding invoices. If these two vendors stop doing business with BBF, BBF will be unable to continue making furniture. (See BBF's motion in Document 20 in the BBF case file.)

Necessity doctrine The court-made rule that a Chapter 11 debtor may pay certain prepetition debts to critical vendors or essential employees if necessary for the business to survive.

Interestingly, no provision of the Code deals specifically with this problem. But the courts have developed what is known as the **necessity doctrine**, pursuant to which payments of prepetition unsecured debt can be made in a Chapter 11 *if* the DIP can show that the failure to make those payments will imperil the ability of the business to survive and reorganize. Payments of prepetition wages to **essential employees** are the most compelling basis for employing the necessity doctrine. But in recent years, some courts have expanded it to apply to **critical vendors** of the DIP as well. The source of the court's authority to order what is obviously a post-petition preferential payment to certain unsecured creditors to the detriment of the others is uncertain. Some courts rely on a common law doctrine preceding the Code, while others base their rulings on the inherent **equitable powers** of a bankruptcy court arising out of §105(a), which authorizes the court to "issue any order, process, judgment that is necessary or appropriate to carry out the provisions of this title."

P-H 23-g: Look again at BBF's motion for permission to pay prepetition debts (Document 20 in the BBF case file). Why do you think the motion advises the court that none of the employees for whom payment is sought in the motion are insiders of BBF? Might creditors or the creditors' committee be more likely to object to the motion if a portion of the payment went to Charles or Timothy Banowsky or some other member of the Banowsky family? Note that the motion also asks for permission to pay various withholding obligations of BBF associated with the unpaid wages. There may be an objection to allowing payment of those withholding obligations at the beginning of the Chapter 11 case since, alternatively, they could be paid following plan confirmation as administrative expenses entitled to priority under §507(a)(8).

3. The Motion to Hire Professionals

As discussed in Section B, the DIP will need substantial legal and other professional assistance in preparing to file the Chapter 11 case, wading through the preliminary motions, putting together the plan of reorganization, winning its confirmation, and then operating in the plan through consummation. Obtaining court authorization for hiring the attorney who will assist the DIP and other needed professionals, pursuant to authority granted the DIP in §327 and FRBP 2014, is another of those motions made seeking a first day order in a Chapter 11.

We discussed the process for the hiring of professionals in Chapter Seventeen, Section F, and you should review that section at this time. Although FRBP 6003 provides that, absent a showing of **immediate and irreparable harm**, the court cannot grant an application for permission to hire a professional person during the first 21 days following the filing of the petition, most courts, finding the requisite standard met, routinely grant first-day motions seeking this relief at least as to attorneys for the debtor.

4. Preliminary Operational Motions in a Prepackaged Chapter 11

In a prepackaged Chapter 11, the debtor will have worked out arrangements with creditors and other parties and resolved disputes regarding these issues (the debtor's use of cash collateral; the payment of critical prepetition debt; and the hiring of professionals) before filing the petition. The debtor will then file motions asking the court to approve those arrangements on the same day the petition is filed so approval can be obtained quickly, in the absence of objection, and the case can proceed quickly.

CONCLUSION

What we call *first day orders* may not be sought or issued on the very same day that the petition is filed, but they must be sought and resolved during the first few days following the filing in order for the case to move off of square one. Once the case is filed, preliminary operational motions are filed and orders obtained, there is still much for the DIP to do. Business operations must continue under the watchful eye of the creditors' committee, U.S. Trustee, and the court. A feasible plan of reorganization must be put together and successfully confirmed. All this is the subject of the next two chapters.

CHAPTER SUMMARY

Chapter 11 is a business reorganization proceeding used mostly by entity debtors seeking to reorganize their finances as an alternative to liquidation. Chapter 11 allows a debtor to continue to operate as a debtor in possession (DIP) under the protection of the automatic stay and to propose a plan of reorganization, which must be approved by creditors and confirmed by the court. Chapter 11 contains some special rules for the small business debtor and the single asset real estate debtor but otherwise operates similarly for all qualifying debtors. A prepackaged Chapter 11 is one where the debtor's plan of reorganization has already been worked out and agreed to by creditors and is confirmed by the court, in the absence of objection, promptly after the case is commenced.

Upon filing the petition, the Chapter 11 debtor continues operating its business as a DIP. No bankruptcy trustee is appointed unless one or more statutory grounds for appointment exists and a party in interest requests such appointment. A creditors' committee, usually consisting of the seven largest unsecured creditors, is appointed in a Chapter 11 case to work with the DIP, offer input, and to serve as and speak as a representative of all creditors in matters before the court. In most Chapter 11 cases, the DIP will file certain operational motions along with the petition seeking first day orders authorizing the DIP to use the property of the estate in various ways. Such motions may include a motion to use, sell, or lease property in other than the ordinary course of business and a motion to use cash collateral. Both motions may require the DIP to provide adequate protection to secured creditors whose interest in property of the estate may be impaired by the contemplated use of it. Another common first day motion is the motion for permission to pay critical prepetition debts under the necessity doctrine. The DIP may also file motions early in the case to hire needed professionals. A first meeting of creditors is conducted in a Chapter 11.

REVIEW QUESTIONS

1. Who can file for Chapter 11 relief? Explain what is meant by the small business case and the single asset real estate debtor. How are the rules of Chapter 11 different for such debtors?
2. List the various stages of a typical Chapter 11 case.
3. What is a prepackaged Chapter 11? Describe what happens between a debtor and its creditors before the petition is filed in a prepackaged case.
4. List four documents that must be filed with the Chapter 11 petition. Name one schedule that a Chapter 7 or 13 debtor will file that a Chapter 11 debtor will not.
5. Who are equity security holders in a Chapter 11 debtor?
6. What are the grounds for appointing a bankruptcy trustee in a Chapter 11 case?
7. Explain the difference between a bankruptcy trustee and an examiner.
8. Why do we say that the debtor in possession is a different entity from the prepetition business?
9. What changes must a business make once it becomes a debtor in possession?
10. What is the typical makeup of a creditors' committee in a Chapter 11 case?
11. What is the role of a creditor's committee in a Chapter 11 case?
12. What is adequate protection in the context of a motion to use, sell, or lease property or a motion to use cash collateral? When might adequate protection be an issue?
13. How might a Chapter 11 debtor provide adequate protection to a secured creditor?
14. What is the necessity doctrine in the context of a motion to pay critical prepetition debts? Provide examples of such debts.
15. What is the statutory source of the bankruptcy court's inherent powers of equity?

WORDS AND PHRASES TO REMEMBER

administrative expense
adequate protection
after-acquired property
automatic stay
bankruptcy trustee

burden of going forward
burden of production
burden of proof
business reorganization
cash collateral

cash equivalents
creditors' committee
critical prepetition debts
critical vendors
debtor in possession (DIP)
encumbered
entity debtor
equitable powers
equity interests
equity security holders
essential employees
exclusivity period
examiner
first day motions
first day orders
floating lien
immediate and irreparable harm
initial debtor interview
involuntary petition

necessity doctrine
operating reports
ordinary course of business
party in interest
plan of reorganization
preliminary operational motions
prepackaged Chapter 11
property inventory
property of the estate
publicly traded corporation
rehabilitation of the debtor
single asset real estate case
small business case
small business debtor
sound business reasons
superpriority
trustee's panel
use, sell, or lease property
voluntary petition

TO LEARN MORE: A number of TLM activities to accompany this chapter are accessible on the student disc accompanying the text and at the Author Updates link to the text Web site at http://www.aspenparalegaled.com/books/parsons_abcdebt/default.asp.

Chapter Twenty-Four:

 # The Chapter 11 Case: Operating the Business Prior to Plan Approval

We think we know what we're doin'
That don't mean a thing
It's all in the past now
Money changes everything
　　　　　　　　　　　　　—Tom Gray

 ## A. The First Meeting of Creditors in a Chapter 11

Equity security holders The holders of an ownership interest in an entity debtor.

Pursuant to §342 of the Code, upon the filing of the Chapter 11 petition, the bankruptcy court clerk will issue a **notice of commencement of case** to the creditors and the U.S. Trustee using OBF 9F. (See Document 21 in the Banowsky Brothers Furniture, Inc. (BBF) case file.) The notice of commencement will advise of the date scheduled for the §341 **first meeting of creditors**. Section 341(b) authorizes the U.S. Trustee to convene a meeting of **equity security holders** in the debtor (those holding an ownership interest in a debtor entity: shareholders of a debtor corporation, members/owners of a debtor limited liability company, or partners in a debtor partnership) as well. In a prepackaged Chapter 11, where the proposed plan of reorganization has been negotiated and approved prepetition, §341(e) authorizes the court to order that *neither* a meeting of creditors nor of equity security holders be held.

B. Creditor Claims in a Chapter 11

Proof of claim The writing that a creditor submits as evidence of its claim against the estate.

Deeming Code process where certain determinations are deemed made unless a timely objection is filed.

Pursuant to §1111(a) and Federal Rule of Bankruptcy Procedure (FRBP) 3003, a creditor in a Chapter 11 case is *not* required to file a **proof of claim** unless its debt was not listed in the debtor's schedules or was listed there as disputed, contingent, or unliquidated. Instead, Chapter 11 utilizes a unique **deeming** approach, pursuant to which listed claims are *deemed filed* under §1111(a) and, as in all cases under the Code, claims are *deemed allowed* under §502(a) unless an objection is filed. If a creditor required to file a proof of claim does so, then the debtor in possession (DIP) or a party in interest can object to a creditor's claim pursuant to §502, as in other cases (discussed in Chapter Seventeen, Section A).

Equity security holders need not file a **proof of interest**. Instead, FRBP 3003(b)(2) provides that their right to participation in the case as a party in interest, including the right to vote on the plan, is to be established from the list of equity security holders that the debtor files at the beginning of the case. (See Illustration 23-c and Document 18 in the BBF case file.)

C. ▶ Conversion or Dismissal of a Chapter 11 Case

The debtor in a Chapter 11 case has the right to convert the case to a Chapter 7 liquidation at any time under §1112(a), unless

- A trustee has been appointed,
- The case originally was commenced by an involuntary petition, or
- The case was converted to a case under Chapter 11 other than at the debtor's request.

The Chapter 11 debtor does *not* have an automatic right to have the case dismissed. A party in interest may file a motion to dismiss or convert a Chapter 11 case to a Chapter 7 liquidation case "for cause" under §1112(b)(1). Section 1112(b)(4) lists 16 different circumstances constituting cause; those are summarized in Illustration 24-a.

Generally, if cause is established after notice and a hearing, the court must convert or dismiss the case unless it specifically finds that the requested conversion or dismissal is not in the best interest of creditors and the estate. Alternatively, the court may decide that appointment of a Chapter 11 trustee or an examiner is in the best interests of creditors and the estate as authorized by §1104(a)(3).

Illustration 24-a: WHAT CONSTITUTES "CAUSE" TO DISMISS OR CONVERT A CHAPTER 11 CASE TO A CHAPTER 7 LIQUIDATION

- The substantial or continuing diminution of the estate with no likelihood of rehabilitation
- Gross mismanagement of the estate
- Failure to maintain insurance with resulting risk to the estate or the public
- Unauthorized use of cash collateral substantially harmful to a creditor
- Failure to comply with an order of the court
- Unexcused failure to comply with any filing requirement
- Failure to attend the 341 meeting or a Rule 2004 examination without good cause
- Failure to timely provide information or to attend meetings requested by the trustee, if any
- Failure to file tax returns or pay taxes due after the date of the order for relief
- Failure to file a disclosure statement or a plan within the time permitted
- Failure to pay any fees or charges in connection with the Chapter 11
- Revocation of an order confirming a plan
- Inability to effectuate substantial consummation of a confirmed plan
- Material default by the debtor with respect to a confirmed plan
- Termination of a confirmed plan, pursuant to a condition in the plan
- Failure of an individual debtor to pay a domestic support obligation that first becomes due after the filing of the petition

D. ▶ Operational Motions Critical to Formulating a Plan of Reorganization

If the DIP survives the flurry of activity associated with obtaining the **first day orders** considered in Chapter Twenty-Three, operation of the business continues as the debtor prepares its plan of reorganization (see Illustration 23-a). However, there can be quite a delay between the time the petition is filed and the time a plan of reorganization is finally proposed and between the time a plan is proposed and its confirmation. During those delays, the DIP must keep the business operating and stave off motions to dismiss or convert the case to a Chapter 7 liquidation.

There are a number of critical operational motions that frequently arise during this period of the case which may be just as "make or break" as the preliminary operational motions considered in Chapter Twenty-Three. These additional motions may be made before the plan is formally proposed as part of the DIP's ongoing operations or they may be proposed in the plan itself. (And, of course, the motions we considered in Chapter Twenty-Three may be made as part of the ongoing operation of the DIP rather than at the beginning of the case or included in its plan.) Before we look at these additional motions, let's see what decisions BBF has made regarding the future of its business. Go to Appendix C at this time and read Assignment Memorandum #2.

1. The Motion for Authorization to Use, Sell, or Lease Property in Other Than the Ordinary Course of Business

Section 363 of the Code deals with the DIP's (or trustee's if one has been appointed) right to **use, sell, or lease property of the estate** postpetition. With the exception of cash collateral, the special rules for which we considered in Chapter Twenty-Three, Section D, so long as the DIP is using, selling, or leasing its assets in the **ordinary course of business**, it can do so without court approval.

EXAMPLE

> At the time the petition is filed, it is in the ordinary course of business for BBF to continue selling its furniture in the showroom attached to the factory building (see Assignment Memorandum #1 in Appendix C). After its Chapter 11 petition is filed, it can continue to do so without court permission.

However, if the DIP wants to use, sell, or lease the assets *other* than in the ordinary course of business, §363(b)(1) requires that it file a motion for permission to do so. That motion is decided using the "after notice and a hearing" standard.

EXAMPLE

> Assume BBF, instead of continuing to sell its furniture as it has done in the past, wants to sell it in bulk to a retailer so it can begin producing different lines of furniture pursuant to the plan of reorganization it is preparing to propose. Because this is not a sale in the ordinary course of business for BBF, it can proceed only with permission granted by the court after notice and a hearing.

Sometimes there is a dispute regarding whether a proposed use, sale, or lease of property is or is not within the debtor's ordinary course of business.

EXAMPLE

> Assume that immediately after filing its Chapter 11 petition, BBF advertises a 50 percent off sale on all the furniture in its showroom attached to the factory building. Does it need court permission for this sale? A creditor concerned that BBF maximize its receipts on its existing inventory of furniture might argue that this is an extraordinary event requiring court approval because of the steep discount being offered. BBF might counter that it regularly conducts sales offering steep discounts and that this sale is nothing out of the ordinary so court permission is not required.

P-H 24-a: The usual test used to decide whether a proposed sale or other use of the debtor's property is within the ordinary course of the debtor's business is whether the parties in interest should reasonably have foreseen a transaction of the type contemplated, given both the history of the debtor's business practices (the vertical factor) and the normal practices within the industry (the horizontal factor). An informative case concerning the **reasonable foreseeability** test is *In re Dant & Russel, Inc.*, 853 F.2d 700 (9th Cir. 1988). Research the decisions of the bankruptcy, district, and circuit courts in your federal circuit to see if they follow the two-part vertical/horizontal test or employ some other test.

When an intended use, sale, or lease of the debtor's property is found to be outside the ordinary course of its business, the court must decide whether to approve it over an objection. The factors to be considered are

- Whether the proposed use, sale, or lease is on fair and reasonable terms,
- Is in the best interests of the estate, and
- Will not pose an unjustifiable risk to parties in interest.

These factors require factual determinations by the court based on the particular circumstances of the case.

EXAMPLE

> If BBF files a §363(b)(1) motion seeking permission to sell its inventory of furniture in bulk to a retailer in order to begin producing new product lines, the court will have to consider whether such sale is in the best interests of the estate and furthers the goal of reorganization. In the process of making that decision, the court will hear proof regarding the fairness and adequacy of the proposed sale price, the price at which the inventory furniture could be sold in the ordinary course of business, how the proceeds would be applied to the anticipated conversion to new product lines, the impact on creditors, and so forth. Often these operational motions require the court to consider the feasibility of some aspects of a debtor's plan for reorganization before the plan has been formally proposed.

When the DIP files a §363(b)(1) motion seeking permission to sell all or substantially all of the assets of the business, objections are often made that such a proposal should be dealt with in the final, confirmed plan of reorganization

Sub rosa Practitioner's term for an operating motion in a Chapter 11 that is effectively a plan of reorganization and for a plan of reorganization that is effectively a liquidation.

rather than by preplan motion. The argument is that the §363(b)(1) motion is itself a *sub rosa* ("under the rose," connoting secrecy or misdirection) plan that avoids the rigorous disclosure, solicitation, voting, and confirmation process that a plan ordinarily goes through (to be considered in Chapter Twenty-Five). After all, selling all or substantially all the assets of a business would be a fundamental aspect of a business reorganization plan. On the other hand, the open bidding that often results from an approved §363(b)(1) sale may result in a higher return than in a sale through the confirmed plan. Most courts follow the leading case of *In re Lionel Corp.*, 722 F.2d 1063 (2nd Cir. 1983), holding that a sale of all or substantially all of a debtor's assets via §363(b)(1) motion rather than a confirmed plan will be approved only where **sound business reasons** support such a sale, but there are many variations on that rule.

E-C 24-a: When a debtor files a Chapter 11 case with the primary intent of selling all of its assets and ceasing doing business, you might think that an appropriate objection is that the entire proceeding is a *sub rosa* liquidation that should have been filed under Chapter 7. But in fact Chapter 11 does not prohibit liquidation of a debtor as its ultimate plan of reorganization nor does it require a debtor to continue doing business after confirmation of its plan. Many debtor's attorneys choose Chapter 11 for the liquidation of their business clients to avoid the automatic appointment of a Chapter 7 trustee whose fees will be charged against the proceeds of liquidation in a Chapter 7. Using Chapter 11 for liquidation isn't unethical and it may be smart lawyering.

a. The Role of Adequate Protection in Connection with the Motion for Permission to Use, Sell, or Lease Encumbered Property

The right of the DIP to use, sell, or lease property in the ordinary course of its business without court permission under §363 is not affected by the fact that the property involved is encumbered by the lien of a secured creditor (except in the case of cash collateral as discussed in Chapter Twenty-Three, Section D). However, the intended use, sale, or lease of the encumbered property is *always* subject to the secured creditor's right to **adequate protection**, per §§363(e) and 361, whether the planned sale or other use is in the ordinary course of the debtor's business or not.

Adequate protection The right of a secured creditor to have the value of its collateral protected and maintained throughout a bankruptcy case where debtor maintains possession of that collateral postpetition.

Adequate protection involves the secured creditor's right to have the value of the property in which it is secured protected or maintained throughout the case. Since a secured creditor's claim is only secured up to the value of the collateral as of the date the petition is filed per §506(a)(1), it is that value which the secured creditor is entitled to have adequately protected.

EXAMPLE

After it files its petition, BBF continues to "use" the CAD/CAM systems and other production equipment in which NCA holds a security interest. It is using the property in the ordinary course of its business so it need not seek court permission under §363. However, NCA may have an argument that BBF's continued use of the property will result in the impairment of the value of that property and thus the impairment of BCA's secured position. NCA is prepared to prove that on the day the petition is filed, the CAD/CAM systems and production equipment in which it is secured is worth $350,000 but that it is depreciating at $25,000 a year. Thus, if BBF uses the systems and equipment during the term of a multi-year plan, it will have lost substantial value and seriously impair NCA's secured position in it. NCA can demand adequate protection as a condition to BBF's continued use of the property, per §§363(e) and 361.

Note that in the preceding example, the burden will be on the creditor, NCA, to file a motion to bring the adequate protection issue to the court's attention because BBF is planning to use the property in the ordinary course of its business. But if BBF contemplated using the property in other than the ordinary course of its business, then the burden would have been on BBF to file a motion for permission to use it, per §363(b)(1).

What constitutes adequate protection is not defined in the Code but some guidelines as to what it may be are provided in §361. Section 361(1) says that adequate protection may be provided by periodic cash payments to the creditor sufficient to compensate for the decrease in value of the collateral.

EXAMPLE

In the previous example, the court may order that as a condition to the continued use of the CAD/CAM systems and production equipment, BBF pay NCA $25,000 per year, an amount equal to the annual decrease in value of the collateral, which is also the extent to which NCA's secured claim is impaired by BBF's continued use of that collateral.

Section 361(2) says that the adequate protection requirement may be satisfied by the debtor providing the secured creditor with a lien on other property sufficient to compensate for the decrease in value of the collateral being used.

EXAMPLE

The court may order that, as a condition to the continued use of the systems and equipment for a plan of three years duration, BBF grant NCA a security interest in other property valued at $75,000, an amount equal to the annual decrease in value of the collateral, which is also the extent to which NCA's secured claim is impaired by BBF's continued use of the collateral. Of course, that would only be feasible if BBF has property with $75,000 of equity in it that could be pledged to NCA.

Section 361(3) says that adequate protection may be provided by the debtor granting the creditor "such other relief" as will enable the creditor to realize the "indubitable equivalent" of its interest in the pledged property. This is obviously an open-ended provision suggesting that, based on the facts of the case, the parties may work out, or the court may order, a unique solution to the adequate protection dilemma so long as the unquestioned value of the creditor's interest in the property is protected.

EXAMPLE

Charles and Timothy Banowsky may offer to personally guarantee the debt of BBF to NCA, and NCA may accept these personal guarantees as adequate protection. Or, one or both of the brothers may grant NCA a mortgage in

Administrative expense Postpetition expenses incurred in preserving the property of the estate and in administering the estate by the trustee or debtor in possession.

Superpriority A priority granted to the holders of some claims that is superior even to other priority claims.

their personal residences up to the amount of the impairment of the NCA lien in the machinery. Can you think of other solutions the debtor or its owners might propose to adequately protect NCA?

Section 507(b) allows a secured creditor whose adequate protection is ultimately found to be insufficient to claim an **administrative expense** for the amount of that insufficiency and gives that claim a **superpriority** among other allowed administrative expenses. (See Illustration 18-a and the discussion of administrative expenses in Chapter Eighteen, Section B.) However, §361(3) stipulates that "such other relief" must be something *other than* the fact that the creditor may have an administrative claim later for the amount by which the adequate protection being proposed now ultimately proves insufficient

EXAMPLE

Assume that Charles and Timothy Banowsky offer the personal guarantees or mortgages as suggested in the preceding example, but NCA objects on the grounds that the impairment may be greater than what is being projected and the offer does not constitute adequate protection. BBF may want to argue that the judge should go ahead and approve the proposal since NCA will have a §507(b) superpriority administrative expense claim for the amount of any ultimate insufficiency. But §361(3) prohibits that. The adequate protection proposal must be found sufficient on its own terms without regard to the possible §507(b) claim.

The adequate protection dispute can become complicated when the debtor is in arrears to the secured creditor whose property the debtor desires to use, sell or lease postpetition. In that situation it is natural for the creditor to ask that the DIP make up the arrearage or pay the creditor interest on the balance owed as a part of the adequate protection arrangement. However, most bankruptcy courts hold that prepetition arrearages are not a relevant issue in adequate protection decisions and are properly dealt with in the plan itself. And in *United Savings Association of Texas v. Timbers of Inwood Forest Associates, Ltd.*, 484 U.S. 365 (1988), the Supreme Court rejected a creditor's claim for interest payments on an arrearage as an adequate protection remedy based on alleged *lost opportunity* costs.

b. The Role of the Automatic Stay in Connection with the Motion for Permission to Use, Sell, or Lease Encumbered Property

Closely related to the issue of adequate protection when the DIP anticipates the use, sale, or leasing of encumbered property is the secured creditor's right to seek the lifting of the **automatic stay** of §362(a). We examined aspects of the automatic stay and lifting of the stay in Chapter Sixteen, Section E, in connection with a Chapter 7 liquidation; you may want to review that section at this time.

Frequently, a secured creditor's response to the DIP's intention to use, sell, or lease property in which the creditor is secured is a motion to lift the stay, under §362(d). In other words, the creditor not only opposes the DIP's plan to use, sell, or lease the property, it wants the stay lifted so it can repossess or foreclose on the property. Thus, bankruptcy courts frequently have two competing motions before them simultaneously: the DIP's §363(b)(1) motion and the creditor's competing §362(d) motion.

As we learned in Chapter Sixteen, one of the grounds for lifting the automatic stay under §362(d)(1) is lack of adequate protection, which we now know is also a consideration under §363(e) in the court's decision to permit the DIP's use, sale, or lease of the property. The adequate protection issue involves the same general analysis under both §§362(d)(1) and 363(e) such that if the court rejects the DIP's proffered adequate protection needed to satisfy §363(e), it will likely also find a sufficient ground exists to lift the stay as to the collateral under §362(d)(1).

EXAMPLE

> If the court finds that the various proposals of BBF or its owners to provide NCA adequate protection for the impairment of its interest in the CAD/CAM systems and production equipment insufficient, that finding will support both a rejection of BBF's intended use of the property under §363(e) and a lifting of the stay under §362(d)(1). Since losing that property will likely put BBF out of business, winning these operational motions is critical to BBF.

The alternative ground for lifting the automatic stay under §362(d)(2) is that

- The debtor has no equity in the property (more is owed on it than it is worth) and
- The debtor does not need it for an effective reorganization.

Note that both prongs of this test must be established by the creditor to have the stay lifted.

EXAMPLE

> Under §362(d)(2), NCA will be able to show that it is owed $425,000 by BBF and that the property in which it is secured is worth only $350,000. Thus, it can satisfy the first prong of the §362(d)(2) test. But how do you think the court will rule if NCA contends that the CAD/CAM systems and production equipment is not needed by BBF for an effective reorganization? Of course, it could be that BBF in fact is not using and will not need some portion of that property, in which case the stay would likely be lifted as to that portion of the property, perhaps even with BBF's consent. Otherwise, do you see why NCA is more likely to move to lift the stay under §362(d)(1) than under (d)(2)?

For the **single asset real estate debtor**, §362(d)(3) provides generally that the automatic stay will be lifted against the real property that constitutes its primary income-producing asset within 90 days from the entry of the order for relief unless by that time the debtor has either

- Proposed a plan of reorganization with a reasonable possibility of being confirmed or
- Begun making interest payments to the secured creditor based on the value of the secured property at the then-prevailing nondefault contract rate.

Ex parte An appearance before a court seeking relief without notice to other parties.

FRBP 4001(a) governs the procedure for filing a motion to lift stay pursuant to §362(d) or to condition the use, sale, or lease of property by the DIP on adequate protection pursuant to §363(e). That rule provides that either motion can be issued by the court **ex parte** (at the request of one party without the other being present) if the moving creditor alleges that **immediate and irreparable injury, loss, or damage** will occur unless the relief is granted without a hearing. But the order lifting stay issued ex parte will normally be **stayed** (held in abeyance) for 14 days until notice can be given to the DIP and a hearing held.

2. The Motion to Incur Postpetition Debt

Operating a business after the Chapter 11 petition has been filed will typically involve the DIP incurring new or additional debt, either in the form of purchases on credit or the borrowing of funds.

EXAMPLE

> A DIP operating a restaurant will need to order food items every day from suppliers. A debtor in the office supply business will need to order new inventory weekly. BBF has furniture orders yet to be filled and will need to purchase additional materials to fill those orders. If suppliers of any of these DIPs will not sell to them on credit as they ordinarily would, the DIPs may need to borrow money to pay for the needed supplies.

a. Postpetition Unsecured Debt Incurred in the Ordinary Course of Business

Section 364(a) authorizes the DIP to incur unsecured debt postpetition (in the form of a loan or extension of credit) without court approval so long as the debt is incurred in the ordinary course of the debtor's business. It further provides that such debt is to be treated as an administrative expense under §503(b)(1), which receives priority treatment over prepetition unsecured claims (see Illustration 18-a). This serves as an inducement to creditors to provide credit to a risky debtor postpetition but, understandably, it makes existing creditors of the struggling debtor nervous.

EXAMPLE

> In the last example, so long as the purchases of food items by the restaurant, inventory by the office supply business, and manufacturing materials by BBF are done in the ordinary course of those debtors' businesses, they will need no court approval for them. Suppliers who provide such DIPs with postpetition credit have the comfort of knowing their claims will be treated as priority administrative expense in the Chapter 11.

If a DIP has ordinarily done business with its suppliers on credit, continuing to do so will be within its ordinary course of business, even if the terms of credit change.

EXAMPLE

> Assume BBF's suppliers normally sell to it on 30-day credit terms: payment due 30 days after delivery. But after the Chapter 11 petition is filed they are more wary and require payment within ten days after delivery. Such arrangement will still be in the ordinary course of BBF's business because it is still a credit arrangement. No court approval will be needed.

b. Postpetition Unsecured Debt Incurred in Other Than the Ordinary Course of Business

If the DIP needs to incur unsecured debt *other* than in the ordinary course of its business, §364(b) requires that a motion for authorization to incur the debt or obtain credit be filed. The motion is governed by the "after notice and a hearing procedure."

EXAMPLE

Assume BBF's suppliers, who have normally sold to it on credit, now demand cash on delivery so BBF arranges an unsecured line of credit with New Era Capital Alliance (see Assignment Memorandum #2 in Appendix C) to pay the suppliers. BBF will have to file a motion for authorization to obtain that loan, pursuant to §364(b), since that is not the way it has ordinarily done business.

EXAMPLE

If BBF wants to begin purchasing teakwood and rubberwood on credit from the Hong Kong supplier (see Assignment Memorandum #2) prior to confirmation of its plan of reorganization, this postpetition unsecured credit arrangement would be outside its ordinary course of business since it had not previously purchased such wood for its manufacturing process. A motion will be required.

Anytime a motion to obtain court approval of postpetition indebtedness is required, the burden is on the DIP to show the court that the proposed transaction is made on fair and reasonable terms, is in the best interests of the estate, and will not pose an unjustifiable risk to parties in interest.

Postpetition debt incurred in other than the ordinary course of the debtor's business also receives priority treatment as an administrative expense under §503(b)(1). That may be sufficient inducement to the creditor make the loan or extend the credit. But what if a potential creditor concludes it is not a sufficient inducement? Section 364(c)(1) authorizes the court, on motion, to approve a postpetition loan or credit transaction that gives the creditor a **superpriority** position over all other administrative expense claims. Since all postpetition expenses have priority as administrative expenses, this approach may induce the creditor to extend unsecured postpetition credit to the DIP by granting it a first-among-equals priority status as to its claim.

> **Superpriority** A priority granted to the holders of some claims that is superior even to other priority claims.

c. Postpetition Secured Debt

Often potential creditors refuse to extend postpetition loans or credit unless they can receive a security interest in property of the estate. Approving a postpetition debt arrangement involving the granting of a security interest to the creditor *always* requires court approval. Whether the proposed transaction will receive court approval depends in large part on how it is structured. A particular concern is how the proposed post-transaction debt arrangement will impact on prepetition creditors.

Section 316(c) provides that if the DIP is unable to obtain postpetition unsecured debt, the court can approve a secured postpetition debt arrangement in two ways, neither of which will impair the position of fully secured prepetition creditors.

First, the court can approve a transaction giving the postpetition creditor a security interest in property that is not presently encumbered.

EXAMPLE

> Assume BBF requests the court approve a postpetition loan from New Era Capital Alliance but New Era refuses to make the loan unless it is granted a security interest in some property of sufficient value. If BBF can show the court that it is unable to otherwise obtain this loan and it is in a position to grant New Era a security interest in some property not already pledged, the court can approve the transaction.

Second, the court can approve the transaction giving the creditor a **junior security interest** in property that is presently encumbered.

EXAMPLE

> Assume BBF requests the court to approve a postpetition credit arrangement with the Hong Kong supplier but the supplier refuses to extend the credit unless it is granted a security interest in some property. If BBF can show the court that it is unable to otherwise obtain this credit and that the supplier is willing to take a second secured position in the computerized machinery in which New Century Automation (NCA) already holds a prepetition first position, the court can approve the transaction.

Priming lien A senior security interest granted to a creditor as an inducement to provide postpetition loan or credit to a Chapter 11 debtor; superior to a prepetition interest in the same property.

Section 364(d) authorizes the court to approve a postpetition debt arrangement that grants the creditor a secured position senior to that of a prepetition secured creditor. For this reason, a lien granted to a postpetition creditor under §364(d) is sometimes referred to as a **priming lien** because it *primes* (is deemed senior to) prepetition liens and *primes the pump* for the postpetition loan. Granting a priming lien to a postpetition creditor is obviously a dramatic step for a court to take and it is rarely granted. And it can only be granted where

- The DIP is unable to obtain postpetition unsecured debt or credit under one of the means authorized by §364 and
- The secured creditor whose prepetition lien is impaired is given adequate protection for its loss as by being granted an additional lien in other property or cash payments.

A postpetition debt arrangement not specifically addressed in the Code but approved by some courts is one that allows a prepetition creditor—secured or undersecured—to provide postpetition debt or credit to the DIP in exchange for the DIP granting the creditor a security interest covering not only the postpetition indebtedness, but also prepetition indebtedness owed to that creditor.

EXAMPLE

> NCA is a prepetition creditor of BBF. NCA is owed $425,000 and is secured in property worth only $350,000. It is an undersecured creditor on the prepetition debt. If BBF seeks to purchase additional computer systems or equipment from NCA on credit, as part of its postpetition operations, NCA may condition such grant of further credit on BBF giving it a security interest in the goods to be sold to BBF, securing payment of not just the new debt being created but also the prepetition debt to the extent NCA is undersecured in it. Should the court approve that?

Cross-collateralization An arrangement whereby a creditor agrees to extend postpetition credit to a debtor in exchange for which property of the estate is pledged to secure both the postpetition and prepetition claims of the creditor.

Some courts reject such **cross-collateralization** proposals for postpetition debt on the grounds that they are not specifically authorized by §364.

Any proposed postpetition debt arrangement has a potential impact on unsecured and undersecured prepetition creditors because the increased total indebtedness of the debtor threatens to dilute the return to such unsecured creditors in the event of a liquidation. Postpetition debt that involves granting a security interest in property to the postpetition creditor is of special concern to unsecured prepetition creditors because the creditor to whom it is pledged now has a superior claim to it. In deciding whether to approve a motion to incur postpetition debt, the court will consider the impact of the proposed arrangement on unsecured claims in its analysis of whether the proposed transaction is in the overall best interests of the estate and whether it presents an unjustified risk to all parties in interest.

d. Appealing Bankruptcy Court Decisions Regarding Postpetition Debt

It is not unusual for a DIP who is denied authorization of a proposed postpetition credit arrangement by the bankruptcy court to appeal that denial to the district court or the Bankruptcy Appellate Panel (BAP) (see Illustration 13-g) in hopes of having the ruling reversed. It is also not unusual for a party in interest to appeal a bankruptcy court decision approving a proposed postpetition debt arrangement that the party opposes. Such an appeal can pose a real threat to the DIP, who desperately needs that postpetition arrangement to move forward. The bankruptcy judge has discretion at that point to **stay** (stop) the authorized arrangement, pending the outcome of the appeal, or to let the arrangement go forward, notwithstanding the appeal.

Section 364(e) provides that, unless the bankruptcy court stays the approved postpetition debt arrangement pending the appeal, it will be a valid and enforceable arrangement even if the bankruptcy judge's decision to authorize it is reversed or modified on appeal, so long as the creditor extended the new debt proposal in good faith. This provision reflects the Code's recognition of how absolutely critical postpetition debt arrangements can be to reorganizing debtors.

In some Chapter 11 cases, the motion to incur postpetition debt is made at the time the petition is filed and becomes the subject of one of the preliminary first day orders sought by the DIP that we considered in Chapter Twenty-Three, Section D.

EXAMPLE

Assume BBF files its Chapter 11 petition and, on the same day, a motion for authorization to use its cash collateral to pay certain obligations. But assume it has insufficient cash to pay all of those obligations even if that motion is granted. It may also file a motion to incur postpetition debt along with the petition and seek first day orders on both motions.

3. The Motion to Assume, Reject, or Assign Executory Contracts

Executory contract An agreement not yet fully performed by the parties to it.

Every business filing for Chapter 11 reorganization is going to be a party to leases or other **executory contract** (an agreement not yet fully performed by the parties to it). Decisions must be made as to whether the DIP will fulfill its obligations under those contracts by formally *assuming* them as part of the reorganization or will decline to fulfill its obligations under those contracts by formally *rejecting* them. For some contracts the DIP may have a third alternative, to *assign* the contract to another. Section 365 governs the procedure for making this important decision and seeks to balance two competing interests: the right of the DIP to make decisions in its own best interest as a reorganizing entity and the right of the other party to the contract to receive the benefit of the prepetition bargain the DIP made.

EXAMPLE

Assume that BBF at one time had a contract with Columbiana Leasing Company (CLC), pursuant to which it leased showroom space in a strip mall in which to sell its furniture at retail. The contract expired a year before BBF filed its Chapter 11 petition. BBF had paid all rental amounts it owed to CLC, and CLC had made the leased space available to BBF for the term of the lease. By the time BBF files its Chapter 11 petition, this contract has been fully performed by both parties. It is not executory, but executed.

EXAMPLE

Assume that when BBF's lease with CLC expired a year ago, BBF still owed CLC for three months' rent. CLC had continued to make the leased space available to BBF throughout the term of the lease. If BBF has not paid the past-due rent by the time it files its Chapter 11 petition, this is not an executory contract subject to §365 because CLC has fulfilled all its obligations under the contract. BBF has not, however, so BBF is, at the time its petition is filed, in breach of the contract with CLC, and CLC can make a claim as an unsecured creditor in BBF's case.

EXAMPLE

Assume that, six months before BBF's lease with CLC expired, CLC wrongfully evicted BBF, even though BBF was paying rent as it came due and otherwise complying with its obligations under the lease. When BBF files its Chapter 11 petition, this is not an executory contract subject to §365 because BBF fulfilled all its obligations under it until CLC breached it. BBF has a claim against CLC for that breach at the time it files its Chapter 11 case and that claim becomes property of the estate under §541 and can be pursued by BBF in the Chapter 11.

EXAMPLE

In fact, the lease agreement between BBF and CLC is still in effect when BBF files its Chapter 11 petition and has two years left in its term. BBF still has the obligation to lease the space and pay rent at $750 per month. CLC still has the obligation to lease the space to BBF. This is an executory contract subject to §365 because both parties still have duties to perform at the time the petition is filed. BBF must decide whether to assume or reject this contract as part of its reorganization.

Illustration 24-b: TYPES OF EXECUTORY CONTRACTS SUBJECT TO UNIQUE RULES FOR ASSUMPTION OR REJECTION UNDER §365

- Contracts for the lease of space in a shopping center [§§365(b)(3) and (h)(1)(C)]
- Contracts for the lease of aircraft terminals and gates [§§365(c)(4) and (d)(5) through (9)]
- Contracts for the lease of nonresidential real property [§§365(d)(3) and (4)]
- Contracts for the lease of nonconsumer personal property [§365(d)(10)]
- Contracts under which the debtor is the seller of an interest in a timeshare [§§365(h)(2)(i) and (j)]
- Contracts licensing the use of intellectual property [§365(n)]
- Contracts involving a commitment by the debtor to a federal depository institution [§365(o)]

Section 365 is a lengthy, convoluted section of the Code that provides detailed rules for the assumption or rejection of numerous specific types of contracts. Illustration 24-b lists the types of specific contracts that are subject to their own unique rules under §365.

a. The Procedure for Assuming or Rejecting a Contract and the Standards for Approval

Business judgment rule A rule applied by the bankruptcy court to a trustee's (or DIP's) decision to assume or reject an executory contract pursuant to which the court will not interfere with the trustee's decision if it was made in good faith and reflects reasonable business judgment.

In general, and subject to specific requirements for contracts listed in Illustration 24-b, the DIP must file a motion for the court to approve its assumption or rejection of an executory contract. (See Document 23 in the BBF case file.) Bankruptcy courts typically show some deference to a DIP's decision to assume or reject a contract. The test used in most courts in deciding whether to grant the motion to assume or reject is the **business judgment rule**, which means the court will grant the DIP's motion if it appears to have been made in **good faith** and appears to be based on a **reasonable business judgment** that the assumption or rejection is in the best interest of the estate. When the motion seeks to reject a contract, some courts use the **undue burden** test, requiring the DIP to show that it would be unduly burdensome to the estate to have to fulfill its obligations under the contract.

EXAMPLE

BBF has filed a motion to reject the executory contract with CLC (see Document 23 in the BBF case file). In support of the motion to reject, it is prepared to show that its sales of furniture in the space leased from CLC have steadily declined and no longer represent a profitable venture for BBF and that, as part of its anticipated plan of reorganization, it will no longer be making the kind of furniture sold in the leased space. Do you think those arguments will satisfy the best judgment rule? Will they satisfy the undue burden test?

b. The Timing of the Motion to Assume or Reject an Executory Contract

In general, §365 imposes no time limit on a debtor to decide whether to assume or reject an executory contract. In some instances, however, it calls for the **automatic rejection** of a contract if no formal motion to assume or reject is made within a specified time frame.

> Section 365(d)(1) provides that in a Chapter 7 case (the role of §365 in a Chapter 7 liquidation is discussed in more detail below) executory contracts (other than nonresidential real property leases) are automatically deemed rejected by the debtor unless a motion to reject or assume is made within 60 days of the order for relief. Section 365(d)(4) provides that, in any proceeding under the Code, an executory lease of nonresidential real property is deemed automatically rejected if no motion to assume or reject is filed within 120 days after the order for relief or the entry of an order confirming the plan of reorganization, whichever is earlier.

Whether or not a Code provision calls for the automatic rejection of a contract on the expiration of a specified time period, there is almost always a delay between the time the petition is filed and the filing of a motion to assume or reject an executory contract. The petition is often filed in a rushed effort to stop an anticipated foreclosure or repossession and it is only afterwards that the DIP is able to consider its options regarding the assumption or rejection of a contract. Section 365 is largely silent about the responsibilities of the parties to the executory contract during the period between filing and assumption or rejection. Must both parties continue to perform? Must leased property be returned by the debtor to the lessor? Section 365 clarifies this issue in connection with only two kinds of contracts and then only partially. Section 365(d)(3) does require the debtor to "timely perform" its obligations under a *nonresidential lease agreement* from the time the order for relief is entered but gives the debtor 60 days to begin such performance. Section 365(d)(5) obligates a Chapter 11 debtor only (i.e., it does not apply in other cases under the Code) who is a lessee in an *equipment lease agreement* to make all payments that arise after 60 days following the order for relief.

Obligations that the DIP owes to the creditor between the time the petition is filed and the time the contract is ultimately rejected and that are not paid by the debtor as an ordinary business expense under §363 are treated as §503(b) administrative expenses and will receive priority treatment under §507(a)(2) (see Illustration 18-a).

c. Assuming a Contract on Which the Debtor Is in Default

If a DIP is not in default on an executory contract and wishes to assume the obligation as part of its reorganization, the creditor is usually more than happy to agree to the assumption. But if the DIP is in default on its obligations under the contract and still wishes to assume it, the creditor has a right to demand that something be done to **cure the default** as a condition to the assumption. Section 365(b)(1) provides that the debtor seeking to assume an executory contract of which it is in breach must do three things as a condition to approval of the assumption. The DIP must

Cure the default Payment of an arrearage to bring the defaulting party into compliance with its obligations under a contract.

- Cure the past default or give adequate assurance that it will cure;
- Compensate the creditor for any "actual pecuniary loss" resulting from the default or provide adequate assurance that it will compensate the creditor; and
- Provide adequate assurance of future performance under the contract.

Section 365 does not define what *adequate assurance* is in this context, except in the case of *shopping center lease agreements* where the term is defined in detail in §365(b)(3).

> Assume that BBF desires to assume its lease agreement with CLC for the shopping center space but it is in default for not paying the last three months' rent. Assume, too, that CLC can show that because BBF was in arrears on its rent payments to CLC, CLC was late with its own mortgage payment on the shopping center and incurred a $500 late fee. As a condition to assumption, BBF will have to pay CLC the past-due rent to cure the default (or somehow give assurance it will be paid) and pay CLC the $500 pecuniary loss it suffered as a result of BBF's default (or assurance of payment) and provide adequate assurance of future performance.

Where the DIP is in default on an executory contract, the other party may have the right to terminate the contract even if the DIP wishes to assume it by complying with §365(b)(1). Whether the other party can do so depends on the nature of the DIP's default. Some contracts contain a clause specifically authorizing the nondebtor party to declare default and terminate the contract on the grounds of insolvency, financial condition, or filing bankruptcy. Section 365(e)(1) prohibits the enforcement of these so-called **ipso facto clauses** post-petition. However, if the DIP is in material breach of the contract for reasons other than the violation of an ipso facto clause, the nondebtor party can normally declare the contract at an end and reject the proffered assumption. Most courts require the nondebtor party to the contract to file a motion to lift the automatic stay of §362(a) in order to terminate the contract (see *In re Carroll*, 903 F.2d 1266 (9th Cir. 1990)).

d. The Assignment/Delegation of Contract Rights

When one party to a contract transfers his rights under the contract to another he **assigns** those rights. When one party to a contract transfers his duties under the contract to another he **delegates** those duties. (The assignment of contract rights is discussed generally in Chapter Two, Section B) Under the common law of contracts, contractual rights and duties can be freely assigned or delegated, unless

- The contract itself prohibits such assignment or delegation;
- A statute or rule prohibits such assignment or delegation;
- The contract involves the personal performance by the party seeking to delegate his performance to another;
- The contract involves a performance by the party seeking to assign his rights to another that could impact on the duty of the other party to perform; or
- The other party to the contract is a governmental entity.

Section 365(c)(1) provides that unless such "applicable law" prohibits an **assignment** or **delegation**, the DIP can assign its rights or delegate its duties under an executory contract in lieu of assuming or rejecting it. However, §365(f)(2) requires that the person to whom the assignment or delegation is made (the **assignee** or **delegatee**) must provide the other party to the contract with adequate assurance that the assignee/delegate will perform.

EXAMPLE

> Assume that in lieu of rejecting its lease with CLC, BBF proposes to assign its lease of the premises to another furniture manufacturer. This assignment can be approved by the court if the furniture manufacturer to whom the lease is assigned can provide CLC with adequate assurance of performance.

e. The Effect of Nonassumption or Nonassignment Clauses in Contracts

Nonassignment clauses A provision in a contract that prohibits one or both parties from assigning the contract to a third party.

Contracts sometimes contain clauses that specifically prohibit their assumption or assignment. Sections 365(e) and (f) generally provide that such **nonassumption** or **nonassignment clauses** will *not* be given effect in a bankruptcy proceeding.

EXAMPLE

> Assume that BBF proposes to assign its lease agreement with CLC to another furniture manufacturer but the lease agreement itself prohibits such assignment. That nonassignment clause will not be given effect in the Chapter 11.

f. Contracts That Cannot Be Rejected

Section 365(h) provides that a DIP who is the lessor of real property cannot reject that lease, although some of its obligations under the lease agreement can be rejected, such as the obligation to provide maintenance. Sections 365 (h) and (i) impose similar restrictions on the DIP's right to reject a timeshare contract in which the DIP is the seller or an installment land contract where the DIP is the seller. Section 365(n) provides that a DIP cannot reject a contract under which it has licensed another to use its patent, copyright, or other intellectual property.

EXAMPLE

> Assume that one year before filing its Chapter 11 petition, BBF had entered into a contract to sell its manufacturing facility and had signed an installment agreement pursuant to which the buyer was to pay BBF in monthly installments over 20 years. That contract is executory when BBF files its Chapter 11 petition but it cannot reject it.

EXAMPLE

> Assume that one year before filing its Chapter 11 petition, BBF had entered into licensing agreements with three other furniture manufacturers giving them the right, for ten years, to make furniture using a patented carving tool that BBF devised. Those contracts are executory when BBF files its Chapter 11 petition but it cannot reject them.

g. The Limited Right to Reject a Collective Bargaining Agreement

Section 1113 requires that a DIP seeking to reject a **collective bargaining agreement** (CBA) first negotiate with the union representative in an attempt to reach an agreement modifying the CBA, rather than rejecting it outright. If that negotiation fails and the DIP moves to reject the CBA, the court can approve the rejection only if the DIP can show

- That the CBA unduly burdens the estate and
- That the "balance of equities clearly favors rejection."

Section 1114 adopts a similar procedure and test where the DIP seeks to reject or modify a contract involving payment of retirement benefits to company employees. If there is no union representative representing the retired employees affected, the DIP negotiates with a committee of retired employees appointed by the court.

P-H 24-b: There is no better example of the dramatic power of bankruptcy law to alter existing contract rights in a way that impacts the lives of many people than this limited right to reject a collective bargaining agreement between an employer and a duly certified union representative. An excellent article to read to learn more about the modification of collective bargaining agreements in Chapter 11 is *Collective Bargaining Agreements in Corporate Reorganizations*, by Andrew B. Dawson, Am Bankr. L. J. Volume 84, Issue 1 2010. Locate and read that article. Do the courts seem generally receptive or hostile to such proposals? What priority seems to be given to the potential impact on current and retired employees of CBA rejection? Should the Code prohibit rejection of a CBA? Make it more difficult?

P-H 24-c: A recent and highly controversial example of a bankruptcy court approving the modification of a Chapter 11 debtor's contractual obligation to employees is seen in the case of Patriot Coal Corporation, a subsidiary Peabody Coal, the largest coal company in the world. The bankruptcy court for the Eastern District of Missouri (Case #12-51502-659) allowed Patriot to jettison its obligation to pay health care and pension obligations to 22,000 former employees (and spouses) of Peabody Coal, rejecting arguments by current and former employees that Patriot had been created by Peabody for the express purpose of loading it up with the obligations of Peabody so that they could be modified. See the article at www.newrepublic.com/article/113342/judge-approves-peabodypatriot-move-against-retired-coal-miners# and the opinion at http://patriotcaseinformation.com/pdflib/4081_51502.pdf. Do you agree with this decision? Determine if this ruling has been appealed to the district court or beyond and, if so, the current status.

---

h. The Consequences of the Rejection of a Contract by the DIP

If the DIP properly rejects a contract pursuant to §365, the rejection is treated as a prepetition breach, pursuant to §365(g)(1), and the other party to the contract will have an unsecured claim for any prepetition amounts owed by the DIP and other damages resulting from that breach. But that party will have an administrative expense claim as to contractual obligations that only accrued postpetition and were not paid by the DIP. If a debtor assumes an executory contract and then rejects it, the rejection is then treated as a postpetition breach by the estate and, pursuant to §365(g)(2), all damages accruing from the breach are treated as an administrative expense whether prepetition or postpetition.

EXAMPLE

> If the motion of BBF to reject its contract with CLC (Document 23 in the BBF case file) is granted, CLC will have an unsecured claim for damages resulting from the breach, including any prepetition obligations that were not paid. However, any obligations that came due postpetition and that were not paid will receive priority treatment as administrative expenses in the plan of reorganization (Document 25 in the BBF case file).

Abandonment is accomplished by the filing of a notice of intent and is governed by the "after notice and a hearing" procedure.

4. The Motion to Abandon Property of the Estate

As discussed in Chapter Eighteen, Section A, §554 of the Code and FRBP 6007 authorize the trustee to **abandon** any property of the estate that is

- Of inconsequential value to the estate or
- Is burdensome to the estate.

EXAMPLE

> BBF has a lot of old, worn-out saws and other equipment that has no real value and that it should have gotten rid of long ago. This property may be subject to a §554 notice of intent to abandon for that reason. Or assume BBF has a piece of equipment that sprays a particular lacquer finish on some furniture. The lacquer contains a particular chemical closely regulated by the Environmental Protection Agency (EPA) that requires BBF to file quarterly reports of use to the EPA. But in fact, the equipment is not used any longer because neither BBF nor any other furniture maker still uses that lacquer. But as long as BBF owns that equipment, it must file the EPA reports. BBF may file a §554 notice of intent to abandon that equipment as either of inconsequential value or as unduly burdensome to the estate.

5. The Motion for Interim Compensation

By their nature, Chapter 11 cases that survive the preliminary operational motions considered in Chapter Twenty-Three tend to go on for some time and involve a lot of work by the DIP's attorney and other professional persons retained by the DIP or the creditors' committee or by the trustee, if one has been appointed. Consequently, motions for **interim compensation** are common. Section 331 provides that motions for interim compensation can be made not more than once every 120 days after the order for relief, though the court has discretion to permit them more frequently. FRBP 2016 requires that all motions for compensation and reimbursement of expenses be accompanied by a detailed statement of services rendered, time spent, and expenses incurred.

6. Comparison to Operational Motions in a Chapter 7 Business Liquidation

All of the motions we have considered in this section and in Chapter Twenty-Three, Section D, could also be filed in a Chapter 7 liquidation, though they rarely are. As was noted in Chapter Eighteen, Section A, in a Chapter 7 liquidation of an ongoing business, the trustee may in some cases seek permission, pursuant to §721, to continue operating the business postpetition for a while in order to maximize the value of the property of the estate and the ultimate payout to creditors. If the court authorizes the trustee to operate the business as part of its liquidation, then the same concerns about operating a business postpetition may arise in that Chapter 7 as we have considered in these two sections with regard to a Chapter 11.

E. ▶ Gathering the Property of the Estate

Recall that §1107(a) grants the DIP the powers of a bankruptcy trustee. This includes the power to pursue contingent or unliquidated claims that are assets of the estate to judgment (see Chapter Seventeen, Section B), to compel turnover of the debtor's property from third persons and custodians holding it (see Chapter Seventeen, Section D), and to avoid other prepetition transfers of the debtor's property (see Chapter Seventeen, Section E). If the DIP for any reason refuses to pursue such action, a creditor or the creditor's committee can seek permission from the court by motion to pursue it for the benefit of the estate, and the attorney's fees and other expenses incurred may be treated as administrative expenses, pursuant to §§503(b)(3) and (4), and receive priority treatment, per §507(a)(2) (see Illustration 18-a).

EXAMPLE

Assume that just before filing its Chapter 11 petition, BBF declared an unusual $10,000 cash dividend payable to all five shareholders. That transfer might well be recoverable as a fraudulent transfer but the shareholders operating BBF as DIP might be reluctant to sue themselves. One or more creditors might petition the court for authority to file suit for the recovery of those funds for the estate. Of course, such activity by the shareholders of BBF might also cause a creditor to move for the appointment of a trustee in the case for cause (see Illustration 23-d) or to dismiss or convert the case to a Chapter 7 for gross mismanagement (see Illustration 24-a).

CONCLUSION

The ultimate purpose of filing a Chapter 11 case is, of course, to win confirmation of a plan of reorganization. In the next and last chapter we will consider the contents of a Chapter 11 plan and the process by which it is proposed, voted on, and, hopefully, confirmed by the bankruptcy court.

CHAPTER SUMMARY

Claims of creditors whose claims are correctly listed in the debtor's schedules are deemed to have filed a proof of claim and will participate in distributions under the approved plan. Generally, a Chapter 11 debtor can elect to convert its case to a Chapter 7 liquidation. A Chapter 11 case can be dismissed or converted by motion of a party in interest upon a showing of cause. There are a number of operational motions commonly filed in Chapter 11 cases. Postpetition debt may be incurred without court approval if it is incurred in the ordinary course of the DIP's business but otherwise requires court approval obtained by motion using the "after notice and a hearing" procedure.

Postpetition debt is given priority status as an administrative expense. To induce creditors to extend credit to the DIP, the Code authorizes the court to grant the creditor a superpriority position over all other administrative expense claims. Or it can approve a request to give the creditor a security interest on property that is not presently encumbered. Or it can approve the transaction giving the creditor a junior security interest on property that is presently encumbered. It can even approve a proposal to grant a priming lien, giving the postpetition creditor a secured position senior to that of a prepetition secured creditor. Some courts also allow the cross-collateralization of postpetition debt with prepetition debt. The DIP must decide whether to assume, reject, or assign executory contracts and file motions with the court seeking approval of the choice made or rely on the 60-day automatic rejection rule. Most courts show deference to the DIP's choice pursuant to the business judgment rule and others use the undue hardship test in evaluating motions to reject executory contracts.

Contracts on which the DIP is in default cannot be assumed unless the DIP cures the default or provides adequate assurance of cure and future performance. Ipso facto clauses in contracts are not enforceable against the debtor in a Chapter 11 case. The debtor may also assign an executory contract if nonbankruptcy law allows and the assignee provides the nondebtor party to the contract adequate assurance of performance. Nonassignment clauses in contracts are not enforceable against the debtor in a Chapter 11 case. Some contracts cannot be rejected by a Chapter 11 debtor. A DIP seeking to reject a collective bargaining agreement must first negotiate in good faith with the union representative under the agreement. If negotiations fail, the DIP can only reject by showing that the agreement unduly burdens the estate and that the balance of equities clearly favors rejection. When the DIP properly rejects a contract, the rejection is treated as a prepetition breach and the other party will have only an unsecured claim for any prepetition amounts owed by the DIP and other breach damages. That party will have an administrative expense claim only as to contractual unpaid obligations that accrued postpetition.

The DIP may surrender property to secured creditors and abandon such property as being of unduly burdensome or of inconsequential value to the estate. Motions for interim compensation must be accompanied by a detailed statement of services rendered, time spent and expenses incurred. The DIP is empowered to use the powers of a trustee to liquidate claims of the estate, compel turnover of property of the estate, and to avoid prepetition transfers of estate property.

REVIEW QUESTIONS

1. Why do most creditors not need to file proofs of claim in a Chapter 11 case? What is the deeming approach used in Chapter 11? When would a creditor in a Chapter 11 be required to file a proof of claim? What is a proof of interest?

2. When can a Chapter 11 debtor *not* convert the case to a Chapter 7 liquidation without court approval?

3. List as many things as you can recall that constitute cause to dismiss a Chapter 11 case or to convert it to a Chapter 7 liquidation.

4. What is the procedure for obtaining postpetition debt in a Chapter 11 case? Describe the various priorities postpetition debt may enjoy either automatically or by court order including the priming lien and cross-collateralization of debts.

5. Explain the process for appealing a decision of the bankruptcy court approving or not approving a motion to incur postpetition debt. Is a decision of the court granting postpetition debt stayed pending the appeal of the decision?

6. What is an executory contract? What is the business judgment rule? What is the undue hardship rule? What is the 60-day automatic rejection rule? What is required for a DIP to assume a contract on which it is in default?

7. What is an ipso facto clause? Are they enforceable to deny a DIP's request to assume an executory contract? Under the common law, when can a contract not be assigned?

8. What is a nonassignment clause? Are they enforceable to deny a DIP's request to assign an executory contract?

9. List three types of contracts a Chapter 11 debtor cannot reject. Under what circumstances can a DIP reject a collective bargaining agreement?

10. Describe the consequences of the rejection of an executory contract on the claim the nondebtor party to the contract may have against the DIP for breach of contract.

WORDS AND PHRASES TO REMEMBER

abandonment
adequate assurance
assignment/delegation (contract rights)
assume or reject contracts
automatic rejection of contract
business judgment rule
collective bargaining agreement
cross-collateralization
cure the default
deeming
ex parte
equity security holders
executory contract

first meeting of creditors
interim compensation
ipso facto clauses
junior security interest
nonassignment clauses
nonassumption clause
notice of commencement of case
priming lien
proof of claim
proof of interest
sub rosa
superpriority
undue burden test

TO LEARN MORE: A number of TLM activities to accompany this chapter are accessible on the student disc accompanying the text and at the Author Updates link to the text Web site at http://www.aspenparalegaled.com/books/parsons_abcdebt/default.asp.

Chapter Twenty-Five:

The Chapter 11 Case: The Plan of Reorganization and Comparisons with Chapter 9

If I owe you a pound, I have a problem.
But if I owe you a million, the problem is yours.

—*John Maynard Keynes*

A. The Exclusivity Period for Filing a Plan of Reorganization

The Chapter 11 debtor in possession (DIP) may file a proposed plan of reorganization with the petition or at any time thereafter, per §1121(a). Section 1121(b) gives the DIP the exclusive right, during the 120 days following the order for relief, to file a proposed plan. Practitioners call this the **exclusivity period**. If the DIP does file a proposed plan during the exclusivity period, then no competing plan can be filed until 180 days after the petition is filed. This gives the DIP additional time to get its plan confirmed. Both the 120-day and 180-day periods begin to run from the day the order for relief is entered, and the 180-day period is available to the DIP regardless of at what point in the 120-day exclusivity period the DIP proposes its plan.

> **Exclusivity period** The period of time in which a Chapter 11 debtor has the exclusive right to propose a plan of reorganization.

EXAMPLE

If the DIP files its plan 30 days after filing its petition, it will have 150 additional days to obtain confirmation before any other party in interest can file a competing plan. If the DIP files its plan 120 days after filing its petition it will have 60 additional days to obtain confirmation before any other party in interest can file a competing plan.

Section 1122(d)(2) authorizes the court, upon request, to extend the 120-day exclusivity period, but not beyond 18 months, and the 180-day period, but not beyond 20 months.

Exclusivity does not apply if a trustee has been appointed, in which case §1121(c) provides that any party in interest—including the debtor, trustee, creditor, equity security holder, or any committee that has been named—can file a proposed plan. And if the DIP fails to file a proposed plan during the 120-day exclusivity period or cannot get its plan confirmed within the 180 period, then those same parties in interest are free to propose a plan.

The prospect that a creditor might file a competing plan of reorganization if the DIP fails to take advantage of the exclusivity period gives those creditors leverage in negotiating the terms of a plan with the DIP. This leverage is even greater because creditors get to vote to approve or disapprove of the DIP's plan of reorganization as part of the confirmation process (see Section E). The DIP has to formulate its plan knowing that if it cannot propose it in the time allowed or win sufficient creditor approval for its confirmation, an alternative plan may be proposed that is much less advantageous to it. For all these reasons, the plan negotiation period of a Chapter 11 case (see Illustration 22-a) tends to be yet another white-knuckle time for the DIP.

P-H 25-a: By now you should appreciate how pressure-packed a Chapter 11 case can be from the time the decision is made to file, forward. What does this aspect of the business reorganization say about the professional skills needed by attorneys representing the debtor, creditors, or creditors' committees and the legal professionals assisting them? Is this an area for the inexperienced lawyer or paralegal to work without close supervision? What does it say about the importance of communication and negotiating skills? What does it say about the importance of being able to meet numerous deadlines and of beginning work early in order to do so? What does it say about the ability of all the players to perform at a high level under constant pressure?

In the small business case (see Chapter Twenty-Three, Section A), §1121(e) provides for only a single 180-day exclusivity period for the small business DIP to file its plan and mandates that the plan be filed within 300 days after the order for relief. Extension of these time periods is available only if the small business DIP convinces the court by a preponderance of the evidence that a plan likely will be confirmed within a reasonable time, and any extension granted must state a new deadline.

Remember that, in a case involving a single asset real estate DIP (see Chapter Twenty-Three, Section A), §362(d)(3) mandates that the automatic stay will be lifted against the debtor's real property unless, within 90 days following the order for relief, the DIP has filed a plan having a reasonable possibility of being confirmed or has commenced interest payments to the creditor in the real property. If the interest payments have commenced within the 90 days but no plan is filed by the single asset real estate DIP during that period, it will have the benefit of the 120-day and 180-day provisions of §1121(b).

In a prepackaged Chapter 11 case, the plan will typically be filed with the petition.

B. ▶ Content of the Plan of Reorganization

Section 1123 governs the contents of a plan of reorganization. Section 1123(a) contains a number of mandatory plan provisions, while §1123(b) sets out a number of optional plan provisions. We will examine some of the key mandatory and optional provisions here.

1. Classes of Claims and Interests

Classes Designated groupings of creditor claims or equity interests with members of each class receiving equal treatment.

Section 1123(a)(1) requires that the plan place creditors' claims and equity security holder interests into **classes**. Per §1122(a), the claims and interests placed in each class must be **substantially similar**. The Code does not define the phrase *substantially similar* but courts have construed it to refer primarily to the similarity of the *legal rights* arising from the nature of the claim and its priority.

EXAMPLE

Secured and unsecured creditors have different legal rights and must be placed in different classes. A secured creditor holding a first mortgage on real property has different legal rights than a secured creditor holding a junior mortgage and would normally be put in a different class. Creditors secured in realty have different legal rights than those secured in personalty. Holders of priority claims under §507 have different legal rights than those holding non-priority claims. Creditors holding disputed, nonliquid, or contingent claims have different rights than creditors whose claims are not disputed, noncontingent, and liquidated. Unsecured creditors holding trade debt (e.g., suppliers of the debtor) have different legal rights than unsecured creditors holding nontrade debt (e.g., utilities). If a corporation had issued both preferred and common stock, the legal rights of those interest holders are different and they must be placed in separate classes.

Most Chapter 11 plans place each secured claim in its own separate class. Pursuant to §1111(b)(1), an **undersecured claim** may be treated in two different classes: one class for its secured claim up to the value of the collateral, per §506(a)(1), and another class for its unsecured balance.

EXAMPLE

Election of remedies Doctrine requiring a secured creditor to choose between exercising a right of foreclosure on secured property or suing the debtor for a judgment, but disallowing both foreclosure and a suit for deficiency judgment.

New Century Automation (NCA) holds a claim of $425,000 against Banowsky Brothers Furniture, Inc. (BBF), and is secured in the CAD/CAM systems and production equipment valued at only $350,000. It is an undersecured creditor. In the BBF plan (Document 25 in the BBF case file), the secured claim of NCA valued at $350,000, per §506(a)(1), is placed in one class and the unsecured portion of its claim valued at $75,000 is placed in another.

This right of an undersecured creditor to have its claim bifurcated in this way under §1111(b)(1) is present in a Chapter 11 even though under the contract or state law that creditor has no recourse against the debtor for the unsecured portion of its claim. (See the discussion of the **election of remedies** doctrine recognized in some states in Chapter Four, Section D.)

Administrative expenses Postpetition expenses incurred in preserving the property of the estate and in administering the estate by the trustee or debtor in possession.

Creditors holding unique claims can be placed in a class by themselves. And §1122(b) allows for the placing of dissimilar but low-value claims in a single class, if the classification is reasonable and necessary for **administrative convenience**.

EXAMPLE

A plan might lump together in one class all miscellaneous unsecured claims for less than $200.

P-H 25-b: Review the plan of reorganization proposed by BBF (Document 25 in the BBF case file) and identify the various classes of claims and interests it creates. Are these classifications reasonable? Are any subject to challenge as not being based on substantially similar claims or interests? Do you see why the various secured claims are treated in separate classes?

Administrative expenses and other §507 priority claims (see Illustration 17-a) receive specialized treatment in a plan of reorganization. Section 507(a)(2) **administrative expenses** and §507(a)(3) expenses arising out of the **gap period** in an *involuntary case* must be paid in full on the effective date of the plan, per §1129(a)(9)(A). Tax claims holding §507(a)(8) priority must be paid in full within six years of assessment, per §1129(a)(9)(C). Because of the nondiscretionary treatment of such claims, some plan drafters treat them as not subject to classification and simply recite the mandated treatment. But, more typically, §507 priority claims are placed in the first class of claims designated in the plan.

Gap period The period of time between the filing of an *involuntary* petition and entry of the order for relief.

P-H 25-c: Review the treatment of §507 administrative expenses in Article III of the BBF plan of reorganization (Document 25 in the BBF case file). Does Class 1 comply with the requirements of §§507(a)(2) and (8) regarding the payment of administrative expenses and priority tax claims? Do you see why if the court denies the DIP's motion to pay prepetition tax withholding claims associated with unpaid prepetition wages (see discussion in Chapter Twenty-Three, Section D, and P-H 23-f), those claims will receive priority treatment under the plan per §507(a)(8)? Do you understand why the plan makes no specific mention of §507(a)(3) gap operating expenses (see Illustration 18-a)? Recall that if the DIP's motion to reject its contract with Columbiana Leasing Company (CLC) (Document 23 in the BBF case file) is granted, CLC will have an administrative expense claim for the December YR-1 rent that came due postpetition. When will it be paid if the BBF plan is confirmed?

---

2. Impaired Classes and Their Treatment

Section 1123(a)(2) requires that the plan specify all classes of claims and interests that are not **impaired** under the plan. If the plan does not specify a class to be **unimpaired** we assume that it is impaired.

Impaired A class created in a Chapter 11 plan whose claims are not to be paid according to their contractual terms.

Impairment is an important concept in plan approval under Chapter 11 and we will return to it several times in this chapter. Section 1124(1) provides that a claim or interest is unimpaired if the plan does not alter the holder's underlying rights. That means a claim is impaired if the right to payment is altered either because it will not be paid in full or when due.

EXAMPLE

Assume a creditor is owed $1,000, which is due the first day of next January. If the plan calls for that creditor to be paid the full $1,000 on the date the plan is confirmed or next January 1, whichever is sooner, that claim is not impaired. If the plan calls for that creditor to be paid only $750 in full satisfaction of his claim, the claim is impaired because the creditor is receiving less than 100 percent of what is owed. If the plan calls for that creditor to receive $1,000 to be paid in installments over five years, the claim is impaired because of the delay in payment. If the original debt agreement had called for the debtor to make ten payments of $100 each but the plan calls for 20 payments of $50 each, the claim is impaired because the payment schedule is decelerated. If the debt was past due when the petition is filed and the plan calls for it to be paid in full on the date of confirmation, it is still impaired because it is not being paid when due.

However, §1124(2) provides that a claim can still be considered unimpaired if the plan calls for the cure of any default and compensation for any delay in payment.

EXAMPLE

If the debt in the previous example was past due when the petition was filed and the plan calls for it to be paid in full on the date of confirmation together with interest to compensate the creditor for the late payment, the claim is not impaired. If the debt was an installment debt on which the debtor had missed three payments when its petition was filed, and if the plan calls for the payment of the arrearage in full together with interest to compensate for the delay in paying the missed installments, as well as for the payment of future installments as called for in the original contract, the claim is not impaired.

A class of **interests** is impaired if the owners in that class will suffer any diminution of their ownership interests.

EXAMPLE

The plan of reorganization proposed by BBF provides that New Era Capital Alliance will become a shareholder in the corporation holding preferred stock with a priority right to dividends over the holders of common stock (see Articles III and IV of the BBF plan, Document 25 in the BBF case file). This proposal diminishes the ownership interests of the current shareholders and impairs all classes of interests in BBF.

Section 1123(a)(3) requires that the plan explain how every class of impaired claims and interests will be treated. Section 1123(a)(4) requires that all claims or interests within each class must receive the same treatment, whether impaired or unimpaired.

The DIP must be very careful how it defines its classes of claims and interests and how it treats impaired claims. As we will see, if one or more class of claims is impaired in a proposed plan the DIP must win the support of at least one impaired class in order for the plan to be confirmed. Thus, if the plan calls for one or more class of claims to be impaired as most do, the plan will be carefully designed to treat at least one class of impaired claims in a way that does not cause the members of that class to oppose the plan.

Subject to those concerns, the Code does allow the DIP considerable flexibility in fashioning proposals for treatment of claims. Sections 1123(a)(5) and (b) authorize a plan to propose that

- Arrearages be paid in full, in part, or not at all;
- Property be retained by the debtor, abandoned, or transferred to another person or entity;
- Security interests be retained, satisfied, or modified;
- New shares of a corporate debtor be issued or that the corporation merge or consolidate with another;
- Maturity dates on debt be extended or installment payments reduced and extended;
- Unsecured debt be paid in full, in part, or discharged;
- Claims in a particular class be paid from the proceeds of designated property to be sold;
- Members of a class receive a transfer of designated property in satisfaction of their claims; or
- Any other proposal not inconsistent with the Code be allowed.

P-H 25-d: How many of the classes created in the BBF plan of reorganization (Document 25 in the BBF case file) are impaired? Does the plan call for any arrearages to be cured? For property to be abandoned? For leases or other contracts to be rejected? That security interests be retained, satisfied, or modified? That maturity dates be extended? That secured debt be paid in full or part? That unsecured debt be paid in full or in part? That new security interests be issued?

---

3. The Right to Modify a Secured Claim in a Chapter 11

As in a Chapter 13 or Chapter 12 case, a Chapter 11 debtor can propose to treat an allowed secured claim as a **pay through** (or **ride through**), which means the obligation will not be modified and will instead be paid according to the terms of the underlying contract during the term of the plan and beyond. However, §1123(b)(5) allows a plan to **modify the rights** of a secured creditor other than one secured by real property that is the principal residence of an individual Chapter 11 debtor. (You may want to review and compare the discussions of a Chapter 13 and Chapter 12 debtor's right to modify a secured claim in Chapters Twenty-One, Section B, and Twenty-Two, Section G.) This means that

- The plan of an individual Chapter 11 debtor can avoid a lien to the extent necessary to preserve an exemption (recall that entity debtors do not claim exemptions);
- The plan can propose to cure an arrearage on a secured debt during the term of the plan, make all future scheduled payments, and retain the collateral;
- The plan can propose to pay an undersecured creditor the **value** of the collateral and treat the balance as unsecured debt in the plan (though Chapter 11 forbids this cramdown by an individual debtor on real property used as his principal residence, Chapter 11, like Chapter 12, contains no limitation on the cramdown like the 910 day rule and one year rule of §1325(a) applicable in Chapter 13 cases);

- The plan can propose to pay the amount owed a secured creditor in full but lower the amount and extend the term of the installments called for in the contract so long as the present value of the secured creditor's claim is paid during the term of the plan;
- The plan may propose to surrender collateral to the secured creditor, satisfying the secured claim of the creditor and leaving the creditor with, at most, an unsecured claim for the balance owed over the value of the collateral.

Present value Calculation of the current value of property for purposes of determining the value of a secured claim in bankruptcy.

Recall from our discussion of these various ways of modifying a secured claim in a Chapter 13 case (Chapter Twenty-One, Section B) that under §506(a)(1) a creditor is secured up to the value of the collateral at the time the petition is filed. And that value is determined by **replacement cost**, per §506(a)(2) and *Associates Commercial Corp. v. Rash*, 520 U.S. 953 (1997). Recall, too, that the total of the installment payments to a secured creditor in a cramdown to value must be based on a **discounted present value** equal to the value of the collateral, which means the plan payments to the secured creditor must include interest sufficient to compensate the creditor for the delay in receiving the full value of its claim. Recall further that we base that interest rate on a formula based on the then-current **prime rate** with an additional risk premium to be decided by the court based on the circumstances of the case, per *Till v. SCS Credit Corp.*, 541 U.S. 465 (2004). All of this is identical to what we learned was possible in connection with a Chapter 13.

P-H 25-e: Review Chapter Twenty-One, Section B, and the BBF plan of reorganization (Document 25 in the BBF case file). Identify each proposal you see there that modifies a secured claim and be sure you understand the basis for the proposed modification.

Section 1111(b) does provide one twist on the cramdown to value treatment of a secured interest in a Chapter 11 plan, which we will deal with in Section D when we look at voting on and confirming a plan of reorganization.

In those situations where one or more creditors has a perfected security interest in a portion of the property but there is still equity for the estate (i.e., the creditor is oversecured), the plan can propose that the property be the subject of a **sale free and clear of liens**, pursuant to §363(f) and FRBP 6004(c). The secured creditor's right to **credit-bid** at such a sale is assured by §363(k) as discussed in Chapter Eighteen, Section A (see P-Hs 18-a, 18-b and Document 37 in the Carlson Chapter 7 case file).

4. Means of Implementing the Plan

Section 1123(a)(5) requires that the plan explain the means by which the plan will be implemented.

EXAMPLE

Will there be a new infusion of capital? Is a new contract going to produce revenue to fund the plan and save the company? Is new management coming in who might turn the company around? Are cost-cutting measures going to be taken that will produce profitability? Are unprofitable assets or divisions of the company going to be sold or abandoned, which will improve the bottom line? Is a new or modified business plan going to be pursued?

These are the type of questions that must be explained in the plan. As suggested by §1123(b), the plan may also utilize a number of matters we dealt with in Chapter Twenty-Two, Section D, regarding operational motions. It may call for the approval of postpetition credit or loan arrangements or the rejection or assumption of existing contracts not just to stay in business, but as a key element of its reorganization plan.

P-H 25-f: Review the BBF plan of reorganization (Document 25 in the BBF case file). How is the plan to be implemented? What will be the source of new capital? Are assets being disposed of or contracts being rejected as part of the plan?

 C. **The Disclosure Statement**

As we have noted, creditors and equity security holders will vote whether to accept or reject a proposed plan of reorganization. To ensure that those voting understand the plan and how it works, §1125 requires that the DIP first file, and the court approve, a **disclosure statement** (see Document 24 in the BBF case file). FRBP 3016(b) requires that the disclosure statement be filed along with the proposed plan. FRBP 3017(a) then provides that the court must hold a hearing, upon 28 days' notice following the filing of the disclosure statement, to determine whether the disclosure statement should be approved. Section 1125(b) forbids postpetition solicitation for acceptance or rejection of a plan until the court has approved the disclosure statement. In a prepackaged Chapter 11 the solicitation would have occurred prepetition. In the small business case (see Chapter Twenty-Three, Section A), §1125(f) authorizes the court to waive the disclosure statement requirement if it finds that the plan itself provides adequate information.

> **Disclosure statement** A detailed summary of the Chapter 11 debtor's financial and operational history and prospects sufficient to enable holders of claims and interests to make an informed judgment of a proposed plan of reorganization.

The disclosure statement must provide **adequate information** concerning the affairs of the debtor to enable the holder of a claim or interest to make an informed judgment about the plan. Section 1125(a)(1) provides that in determining whether the disclosure statement does provide adequate information, the court is to consider

- The complexity of the case;
- The benefit of additional information to the parties in interest; and
- The cost of providing additional information.

Illustration 25-a summarizes the specific categories of information a disclosure statement should contain.

Once the disclosure statement is filed, the court will issue an order setting a date for the **hearing on the adequacy of the disclosure statement** and giving notice to parties in interest (OBF 12 and Document 26 in the BBF case file). At the hearing, the disclosure statement may be approved as written, modified and approved, or not approved. The plan proponent who fails to win approval of his disclosure statement at the hearing may amend and resubmit it for further hearing. Keep in mind that if the DIP has not filed a plan within the 120-day exclusivity period or has not succeeded in winning confirmation of its plan (not just approval of its disclosure statement) within the 180-day period of

Illustration 25-a: CATEGORIES OF INFORMATION A DISCLOSURE STATEMENT SHOULD CONTAIN

- A detailed summary of the plan
- A detailed description of how the plan will work
- Financial projections for the duration of the plan
- A *liquidation analysis* comparing the plan to the likely results of a Chapter 7 liquidation
- A discussion of the potential material federal tax consequences to the debtor or any successor of the debtor contemplated by the plan and to any hypothetical investor typical of the current holders of claims and interests
- A description of the balloting procedure to be used in voting on the plan

§1121(c)(3), there may be one or more competing disclosure statements and plans being filed and considered for approval by the court. It is unusual, but it is possible for more than one proposed plan to be presented for consideration by those entitled to vote.

EXAMPLE

Assume a DIP proposes a plan 120 days after the order for relief but cannot get its disclosure statement approved before 180 days have run. The DIP may amend and resubmit its disclosure statement, but other plans and disclosure statements may now be submitted for court consideration.

Upon approval of the disclosure statement, the court will issue an order approving the disclosure statement, establishing a deadline for filing acceptances or rejections of the plan, fixing a time for the distribution of ballots to those voting on the plan, and scheduling a date for the confirmation hearing on the plan (OBF 13 and Document 27 in the BBF case file). FRBP 3017(d) requires that the DIP or other plan proponent then provide the U.S. Trustee, creditors, and equity security holders a copy of

- The plan or a court approved summary of the plan;
- The disclosure statement approved by the court;
- Notice of the time within which acceptances and rejections of the plan may be filed; and
- Such other information as the court may direct, including any opinion of the court approving the disclosure statement or a court-approved summary of the opinion.

In addition, the plan proponent must mail to the creditors and equity security holders entitled to vote on the plan

- Notice of the time fixed for filing objections to the plan;
- Notice of the date and time for the hearing on confirmation of the plan;
- A ballot for accepting or rejecting the plan; and
- If appropriate, a designation for the creditors to identify their preference among competing plans.

P-H 25-g: Review the BBF disclosure statement (Document 24 in the BBF case file). Does it contain all of the categories of information listed in Illustration 25-a? Do the contents of the disclosure statement (other than those excluded from the illustration) appear to be complete? If you were a creditor of BBF would you be satisfied with the information contained in the disclosure statement or would you want more? What questions might you have for BBF representatives at the hearing on the adequacy of its disclosure statement?

D. ▶ Solicitation for Support or Opposition and Voting on the Plan

Under §1126(a) both creditors with allowed claims and equity security holders with allowed ownership interests are entitled to vote for or against the proposed plan of reorganization. In Chapter Twenty-Four, Section B, we considered how claims and interests are "deemed" allowed in a Chapter 11 case.

Proponents and opponents of the plan may solicit those entitled to vote. Such solicitation must be done in **good faith**, per §1125. Section 1126(f) provides that if a class of claims or interests is not impaired by the plan, they are **conclusively presumed** to have accepted the plan and their vote need not be solicited. Section 1126(g) provides that if a class of claims or interests is to receive nothing under the plan, it is "deemed not to have accepted" the plan and members of that class need not be solicited.

Good faith Generally, honesty in fact and compliance with the letter and spirit of the Code.

P-H 25-h: Review the proposed plan of BBF (Document 25 in the BBF case file). Are there any classes of claims or interests created in it that need not be solicited?

Each creditor or equity interest in a class created by the plan receives a ballot (OBF 14 and Document 28 in the BBF case file) along with the other materials provided to them after the hearing on the disclosure statement. They must mark the ballot indicating an acceptance or rejection of the plan and return it by the deadline prescribed by the court.

In a vote to approve or reject a Chapter 11 plan, it is the vote of each class of claims and interests that matters, not the vote of any individual member of the class. In other words, each class forms a voting block that itself accepts or rejects the plan. Section 1126(c) provides that a class of claims accepts a plan if

- At least two-thirds of the dollar amount represented in the class votes to approve and
- More than one-half of the creditors in that class vote to approve.

EXAMPLE

If there are 20 unsecured trade creditors in a class, at least 11 must vote to approve the plan, and the dollar amount of claims held by those 11 must represent at least two-thirds of the total dollar amount of all 20 creditors in the class. If both those requirements are satisfied, we say that the class—not just the individual creditors within the class—has voted to approve the plan.

When the class is made up of equity interests, rather than creditors with claims, §1126(d) provides that the class can approve the plan by a vote that represents two-thirds of the dollar amount of the interests represented. There need not be a majority of the number of owners in the class supporting the plan.

EXAMPLE

> If a class of interests includes 20 shareholders in the debtor corporation, one of whom holds 70 percent of the outstanding shares of stock in the corporation, representing 70 percent of the value of all the shares represented, that one shareholder can cause the class to accept or reject the plan even if the 19 others vote the other way.

§1111(b)(2) election The right of an *undersecured creditor* in a Chapter 11 case to demand that the plan treat its claim as secured up to the full amount owed.

Recall that the holder of an undersecured claim is entitled to treatment in two classes under the plan: one for the secured portion of its claim up to the value of the collateral under §506(a)(1) and one for the unsecured portion for the balance per §1111(b)(1). However, under §1111(b)(2) an undersecured creditor can elect to have its claim treated as secured up to the full amount owed. If the undersecured creditor makes this **§1111(b)(2) election**, then §1129(b), which sets forth the requirements for plan confirmation, requires that the plan call for the payment of the entire amount of the claim and not just an amount equal to the value of the collateral, and the plan cannot be confirmed under §1129(a)(7)(B) unless it does so.

EXAMPLE

> Assume a creditor is owed $500,000 and is secured in real property having a current value of $400,000. The plan may call for treating that as a secured claim for $400,000 and an unsecured claim for $100,000. But if this undersecured creditor makes the §1111(b)(2) election, the claim must be treated as a secured claim for the entire amount owed—$500,000. And if the debtor wishes to keep the property securing the debt, the plan must call for the payment of the entire amount owed.

The effect of an undersecured creditor making the §1111(b)(2) election is to defeat the debtor's right to cramdown to value. The most common situation in which a Chapter 11 creditor makes the election is where the value of the collateral is currently depressed but has potential to increase.

EXAMPLE

> Assume the real property in the preceding example is valued at $400,000 due to a depressed real estate market. But the expectation is that in one to two years the market will improve and the property will appreciate to equal or exceed the amount owed. The currently undersecured creditor will consider whether to exercise its §1111(b)(2) option.

You might think that an undersecured creditor would always exercise its §1111(b)(2) election in order to defeat a possible cramdown of its secured claim to value. But that isn't the case at all. There are disadvantages to a creditor exercising this election. First, the debtor may simply surrender the property to the creditor instead of attempting to retain it. If that happens, the creditor now has to deal with disposing of the property at its depressed value and the debtor can treat any arrearage as an unsecured claim anyway. Second, a creditor who makes this election waives the right to vote on the plan as an unsecured creditor, which may be desirable leverage to have over plan approval. But because it elected to have its entire claim treated as secured, it only gets a vote in the secured class where its claim is placed. Third, the creditor making the election waives its right to participate in the distribution to holders of unsecured claims.

P-H 25-i: How has BBF treated the undersecured claim of NCA in its plan? (See Document 25 in the BBF case file.) Did it cramdown that claim? How does the plan treat the secured and unsecured claims of NCA? Should NCA have exercised its §1111(b)(2) election?

E. ▶ Confirmation of the Plan

Confirmation The court's formal approval of a plan of reorganization under Chapter 11.

Cramdown The right to confirm a plan of reorganization despite the opposition of some creditors.

Section 1129 governs the requirements for the court's **confirmation** of the plan of reorganization. There are two alternative methods of confirmation outlined in that section. In general, confirmation under §1129(a) contemplates that all classes of creditors and claims, including any impaired class, have approved the plan. Confirmation under §1129(b), known as **cramdown confirmation**, is used when all impaired classes have not accepted the plan and confirmation is therefore not possible under §1129(a).

1. Section 1129(a) Confirmation

Confirmation under 1129(a) requires much more than approval of the plan by all classes. In fact, there is a laundry list of requirements for confirmation listed in this section but a number of them are very technical and we will consider only the ones that generally come into play.

a. Approval of the Plan by All Classes, Including Any Impaired Classes [§1129(a)(8)]

Recall that unimpaired classes are conclusively presumed to have accepted the plan, per §1126(f), so if there are no impaired classes, this test is met. If any class is to receive nothing, then §1126(g) provides that class is deemed not to have accepted the plan which means that the plan cannot be confirmed under §1129(a) if any class is to be paid nothing. Consequently, the focus of this requirement is on impaired classes and whether all impaired classes have voted to approve the plan.

P-H 25-j: How many impaired classes does the BBF plan create? (See Document 25 in the BBF case file.) Has it designated any class to receive nothing? Consider the proposals contained in the plan from the standpoint of each of the secured creditors. Should they vote to accept or reject the plan? If they vote to reject, should they propose their own plan or seek to force BBF into liquidation? Will any secured creditor come out better in a liquidation than under the plan as proposed? Will any unsecured creditor? (Look at the liquidation analysis in BBF's disclosure statement, Document 24 in the BBF case file, in connection with these last two questions.) If secured or unsecured creditors argue for a more favorable payout to themselves under the plan, what is likely to be BBF's response?

Insiders A person in close relationship with a debtor such that he may be assumed to have superior access to information and be subject to special treatment.

Best interest of creditors test A test for confirmation of a plan of reorganization under Chapter 11 or 13 of the Code, which requires a showing that unsecured creditors will receive at least as much under the plan as they would have received in a Chapter 7 liquidation.

b. Approval by at Least One Impaired Class Discounting Affirmative Votes of Insiders [§1129(a)(10)]

As we just saw, §1129(a)(8) requires that all classes have approved the plan, including any impaired class, so at first blush, this requirement seems inconsistent with that. But this section deals with the possibility that §1129(a)(8) was complied with only because **insiders** of the debtor who were members of an impaired class voted to approve the plan. In that event, even though all classes did in fact vote to approve the plan and §1129(a)(8) is complied with, this section requires a showing that at least one impaired class would have voted to approve without regard to those insider votes.

c. The Best Interests of Dissenting Creditors Test [§1129(a)(7)]

This section requires that the court determine that individual creditors and owners who voted against the plan (even if their entire class approved it) receive or retain as much in the Chapter 11 reorganization as they would have in a Chapter 7 liquidation. Practitioners call this the **best interest of creditors test**, though that phrase is not used in the Code section.

EXAMPLE

> Recall from Illustration 25-a that one part of a disclosure statement is a liquidation analysis, comparing the effect of the proposed plan on creditors with what they would receive in a Chapter 7 liquidation. The requirement of §1129(a)(7) is an extension of that analysis, applied to specific dissenting creditors.

Feasibility test A test for confirmation of a plan of reorganization requiring a showing that the debtor has a reasonable prospect of completing the plan.

d. The Feasibility Test [§1129(a)(11)]

What practitioners call the **feasibility test** requires that the court determine that the plan of reorganization is in fact feasible and is not likely to be followed by liquidation or another reorganization (unless a second reorganization is called for in the plan).

> **P-H 25-k:** What kinds of contingencies does the BBF plan (Document 25 in the BBF case file) depend on? What kinds of proof would the bankruptcy court expect to hear at the confirmation hearing in order to determine the feasibility test of §1129(a)(11)?

e. The Lawfulness and Good Faith Tests [§§1129(a)(1)(2) and (3)]

These three sections together require that the court determine whether both the conduct of the plan proponent in connection with the formulation of the plan and the terms of the plan itself comply with the Code and, further, whether the "plan has been proposed in good faith and not by any means forbidden by law." Referred to generally as the good faith requirement, the court will consider whether the proponent has acted with honesty, integrity, and fairness in connection with the plan's formulation. If the proponent has employed dishonest, abusive, or coercive tactics, the court has the discretion to refuse confirmation.

f. Treatment of §507 Priority Claims [§1129(a)(9)]

Unless the holder of a claim entitled to priority treatment under §507 (see Illustration 18-a) consents to a different treatment, the plan must provide for the following treatment of such priority claims:

- Section 503(b) administrative claims allowed under §507(a)(2) and all "gap claims" arising in an involuntary case allowed under §507(a)(3) must be paid in full as of the effective date of the plan.
- Section 507(a)(8) tax claims must be paid in full in installments over a period not to exceed five years from the date of the order for relief.
- Section 507(a)(1), (4), (5), (6), and (7) claims must be paid in full.

If the classes that include the §§507(a)(1),(4),(5),(6),(7), and (8) priority claims approve the plan, the payments can be made in installments over the term of the plan. If any class including those claims rejects the plan (and confirmation is accomplished by §1129(b) discussed below), they must be paid in full as of the effective date of the plan like the §503(b) priority claims.

P-H 25-l: How many classes of priority claims does the BBF plan (Document 25 in the BBF case file) create? Does its treatment of priority claims comply with §1129(a)(9)?

---

2. Section 1129(b) Confirmation

Most Chapter 11 plans are successfully negotiated so that all classes vote to accept the plan and confirmation is accomplished through §1129(a). Confirmation through §1129(b) becomes necessary only when one or more classes have voted to reject the proposed plan. Even under §1129(b), however, at least one class must have voted to accept the plan because of the requirements of §1129(a)(10) (discussed above), which applies in a §1129(b) confirmation, as well as in a §1129(a) confirmation. In fact, all of the requirements for a §1129(a) confirmation must be satisfied in a §1129(b) confirmation as well except for §1129(a)(8), which requires that all classes have voted to accept the plan. But in addition to those §1129(a) requirements, a confirmation under §1129(b) has its own unique requirements.

Because §1129(b) allows a plan to be confirmed notwithstanding one or more classes having rejected it, practitioners refer to it as a **cramdown confirmation**; the plan is being "crammed down" on the objecting classes. Under a §1129(b) confirmation, we are concerned only with those objecting classes because the other classes have voted to accept the plan. Under §1129(b) a plan can be confirmed by cramdown on an objecting class if

- The requirements of §1129(a) are satisfied, other than §1129(a)(8), including approval by at least one impaired class, per §1129(a)(1);
- The court finds, pursuant to §1129(b)(1), that the plan does not **discriminate unfairly** against the objecting class; and
- The court finds, pursuant to §§1129(b)(1) and (2), that the plan is **fair and equitable** to the objecting class.

a. Approval by One Impaired Class

The lawyer drafting a Chapter 11 plan that will have to be confirmed by §1129(b) cramdown must be careful to create at least one impaired class that will approve the plan. Otherwise, cramdown on the objecting classes is not possible. As a result, the lawyer will be careful to provide sufficient sweeteners in the proposal for that impaired class so that, despite the impairment, its approval is certain.

EXAMPLE

> Recall that in the discussion of classes in Section B, above, we noted that a plan might create a class of unique claims for administrative convenience, such as small, miscellaneous claims under $200. Assume a plan calls for the class containing nonpriority, unsecured trade debt creditors to receive 30 percent of their claims over the life of the plan and that the class is expected to reject the plan. To enable cramdown approval under §1129(b), the plan also creates an impaired class of nonpriority, unsecured claims that includes miscellaneous, small claims under $200 on the basis of administrative convenience and calls for those claims to be paid 100 percent within 60 days following confirmation. This slightly impaired class can be expected to approve the plan, satisfying this requirement of §1129(b) confirmation.

P-H 25-m: Review the BBF plan of reorganization (Document 25 in the BBF case file). Does it appear to have structured an impaired class likely to approve the plan if cramdown confirmation is needed under §1129(b)?

Of course, the plan creating this "likely-to-approve" impaired class must comply with the requirements of Chapter 11 regarding class characteristics, which we considered in Section B, above. And the treatment of the impaired class counted on for approval must pass two remaining tests for §1129(b) confirmation discussed next.

b. The No Unfair Discrimination Requirement of §1129(b)(1)

The class voting to reject a plan is going to be one whose claims are impaired under the plan because classes of unimpaired claims are "conclusively presumed" to have accepted the plan, pursuant to §1126(f). So the plan obviously "discriminates" against an impaired class. The issue under §1129(b)(1) is whether the discriminating impairment is "unfair."

Most courts determine the issue of unfair discrimination by looking at

- How the objecting class is treated relative to other similar classes of claims;

- Whether the motivation for the discriminatory treatment (the impairment) is reasonable or motivated by bad faith or ill will; and
- Whether the discriminatory treatment appears to be reasonably necessary to a successful reorganization.

The question of unfair discrimination is a question of fact to be decided on the facts of each case.

P-H 25-n: You be the judge on this one. Examine the BBF plan (Document 25 in the BBF case file). Assume that any impaired class in the plan might vote to reject it. Based on the plan as an entirety and what you know at this point concerning BBF, does the plan appear to unfairly discriminate against any of the impaired classes? What other information would you want to have in order to make that decision? If you were examining a plan like the one mentioned in the previous example, would you find unfair discrimination in the treatment of the small claims class that is to receive 100 percent payment for administrative convenience when trade creditors are to get only 30 percent?

The resolution of the issue of fair and equitable treatment under §§1129(b)(1) and (2) turns on whether the objecting class is made up of secured or unsecured creditors.

c. The Fair and Equitable Requirement of §§1129(b)(1) and (2) as to Secured Claims

In order to meet the fair and equitable requirement for a cramdown confirmation, the plan must insure that an impaired, secured claim in a class objecting to the plan receives the full amount of the allowed secured claim (and recall that, pursuant to §506(a), the amount of the secured claim is limited to the value of the collateral). The plan can assure that the objecting secured creditor receives the full amount of its secured claim in one of three ways:

- the plan can call for the secured creditor to retain its lien on the property and receive deferred cash payments per §1129(b)(2)(A)(i);
- the plan can call for selling the property free and clear of the lien and grant the creditor a lien on the proceeds of sale up to the value of its secured claim per §1129(b)(2)(A)(ii); or
- the plan can provide the secured creditor with the "indubitable equivalent" of its claim per §1129(b)(2)(A)(iii).

If the claim is undersecured and the creditor exercises the §1111(b)(2) election, then the plan must deal with the claim as discussed in the section above on solicitation for approval or rejection and voting on a plan.

P-H 25-o: In *Radlax Gateway Hotel, LLC v. Amalgamated Bank*, 132 S. Ct. 2065 (2012), the Supreme Court held that a Chapter 11 plan could not be confirmed using the cramdown procedure of §1129(b)(2)(A), where the plan proposed to sell property pledged to an objecting creditor free and clear of the lien per §1129(b)(2)(A)(ii) but denied that creditor the right to credit-bid for the property at the sale. The creditor wanted the right to bid to purchase the property at the sale using the debt it was owed to offset the purchase price, a common practice known as credit-bidding (see discussion in Chapter Eighteen, Section A). The court said that by denying the creditor the right to credit-bid on the pledged property, the plan failed to satisfy the fair and reasonable requirement since §1129(b)(2)(A)(ii) requires that any sale free and clear of liens is subject to §363(k) of the Code, which specifically preserves a creditor's right to credit-bid in a sale free and clear of liens. *Radlax* confirms that a secured creditor cannot be denied the right to credit-bid when the property in which it holds a security interest is sold in a bankruptcy proceeding, whether on motion for sale free and clear of liens or as part of a plan of reorganization.

P-H 25-p: What is meant by providing the creditor with the "indubitable equivalent" of its claim in §1129(b)(2)(A)(iii)? That curious phrase comes from *In re Murel Holding Corporation*, 75 F.2d 941 (2d Cir. 1935), authored by revered Judge Learned Hand. Providing a secured creditor with the indubitable equivalent of its claim usually means surrendering all or a portion of the property to the creditor or providing the creditor with a secured position in other property that is indubitably (by clear and convincing evidence) of the same or greater value. For a good discussion of indubitable equivalence, see *In re Riddle*, 444 B.R. 681, 686 (Bankr. N.D. Ga. 2011).

P-H 25-q: Does the BBF plan (Document 25 in the BBF case file) appear to meet the fair and equitable requirement of §1129(b)(2)? Would it meet that requirement if any of the secured creditors involved exercised the §1111(b)(2) election? How would you alter that plan to make it more likely to satisfy the fair and equitable requirement?

---

d. The Fair and Equitable Requirement of §§1129(b)(1) and (2) as to Unsecured Claims

The fair and equitable requirement can be satisfied as to impaired, unsecured claims in a class objecting to the plan in one of two ways. Section §1129(b)(2)(B)(i) provides that it can be satisfied by the plan paying the full amount of the claims in deferred installments over the term of the plan.

Alternatively, §1129(b)(2)(B)(ii) provides that it can be satisfied if the holders of equity interests in the debtor neither receive anything under the plan nor retain any ownership interest in the reorganized debtor. This second method of satisfying the fair and equitable requirement as to an objecting class of impaired unsecured claims is known as the **absolute priority rule**: If the unsecured claims in the objecting class are not paid in full, then "any claim or interest that is junior" to the claims in the impaired objecting class must receive nothing and retain nothing under the plan. The only interests junior to unsecured claims are the equity interest of the owners, so the effect of this rule is that the owners of the debtor must forfeit their entire ownership interest in the debtor.

Absolute priority rule The principle applicable in Chapter 11 cases that no junior class of claims or interests in a plan of reorganization should receive any distribution until senior classes are paid in full.

EXAMPLE

> Assume BBF proposes a plan in which the class of trade creditors holding unsecured debt are to receive 50 percent of what they are owed. The class is impaired and votes to reject the plan. BBF cannot satisfy the fair and equitable requirement via §1129(b)(2)(B)(i) because the creditors in the objecting impaired class are not receiving 100 percent of their claims over the term of the plan. To satisfy the absolute priority rule of §1129(b)(2)(B)(ii), the plan must provide that all five shareholders in BBF forfeit their entire investment in BBF. They cannot receive any distribution as owners under the plan and they cannot retain an ownership interest in BBF under the plan. The plan would have to call for the passing of ownership to another for no consideration or for the bidding off of the ownership interest with the proceeds going to the corporation, not its prior owners, the Banowsky family.

New value exception An exception to the absolute priority rule in a Chapter 11 case enabling holders of equity interests in a bankrupt debtor to retain their interests even though senior claim holders will not be paid in full.

Most courts recognize an exception to the harsh absolute priority rule. This exception is known as the **new value exception**. Under that exception, if the plan calls for the owners of the debtor to invest new capital in the debtor in cash or property in an amount at least equal to the value of their interests, then the plan can be approved even though the unsecured claims in the objecting class are paid less than full value. But the new capital requirement is strictly construed to include only the contribution of cash or property having actual value. A proposal to provide "services" or "expertise" to the corporation in exchange for stock will not be deemed new value for this purpose.

EXAMPLE

> In a bankruptcy court recognizing the new value exception, the plan could call for the impairment of the objecting class of unsecured creditors by paying them less than 100 percent and for the members of the Banowsky family to contribute new capital to the corporation in exchange for a continuing ownership interest. But the new capital will have to be cash or property having actual value, and the contributions of each family member will have to equal or exceed the value of their interests at the time the Chapter 11 petition was filed.

3. The Confirmation Hearing

These confirmation issues are raised at the **confirmation hearing**. Once the court confirms the plan, an **order of confirmation** is entered based on OBF 15 (Document 29 in the BBF case file).

P-H 25-r: Was the BBF plan confirmed under §1129(a) or §1129(b)?

---

4. The Effect of Plan Confirmation

The terms of a confirmed plan bind the debtor, any successor to the debtor created in the plan, the owners, and all creditors, per §1141(a). Property of the estate immediately **vests** in the **reorganized debtor** upon confirmation, per §1141(b), and is free and clear of all liens, claims, and interests, except as allowed by the confirmed plan per §1141(c).

Discharge Permanent relief from debt pursuant to order of the bankruptcy court.

Section 1141(d)(1) provides that confirmation of a plan operates as a **discharge** of all debts arising before the date of confirmation if the debtor is an entity. The idea is that the debtor now operates solely within the terms of the confirmed plan as to its preconfirmation obligations. However, §1141(d)(3) provides that an *entity* Chapter 11 debtor whose plan calls for effective liquidation of the business and the ceasing of operations will *not* receive a discharge of any debts if any of the grounds set forth in §727(a) for denial of a discharge to a Chapter 7 debtor are present. (See Chapter Eighteen, Section E, and Illustration 18-d.) Moreover, BAPCPA added new §1141(d)(6), which provides that a corporate debtor receives no discharge as to an obligation owed to a government entity for money, property, services, or an extension of credit obtained by fraudulent pretenses or by the use of fraudulent financial statements in violation of §§523(a)(2)(A) or (B). (See Chapter Eighteen, Section D, and Illustration 18-c.)

Section 1141(d)(2) provides that an *individual* Chapter 11 debtor cannot receive a discharge in Chapter 11 from any nondischargeable debt listed in §523 (see Chapter Eighteen, Section D, and Illustration 18-c). BAPCPA added new §1141(d)(5) to make a Chapter 11 discharge for an individual operate much like the discharge received by a Chapter 13 debtor under §§1328(a) and (b): No discharge is received by the individual until completion of the plan payments unless the individual qualifies for a **hardship discharge** (see Chapter Twenty-Two, Section D, and Illustration 22-b).

Notwithstanding the entry of the confirmation order, the bankruptcy court retains authority to issue any other order "necessary to administer the estate" under FRBP 3020(d). This authority includes the postconfirmation determination of objections to claims or adversary proceedings, which must be resolved before a plan can be fully consummated. Sections 1106(a)(7) and 1107(a) of the Code require the reorganized debtor (or trustee if one was appointed) to file periodic reports on the progress made in implementing a plan after confirmation.

5. Postconfirmation Modification of a Chapter 11 Plan

Section 1127(b) provides that at any time after confirmation and before **substantial consummation** of a plan, the reorganized entity debtor can ask the court to modify the plan. Upon the filing of a motion for modification, the court will conduct a hearing on the request and can order a postconfirmation modification of the plan "if circumstances warrant such modification." Under §1127(e), an individual Chapter 11 debtor can seek modification at any time prior to completion of all payments called for in the plan and without regard to whether there has been substantial consummation.

Section 1121(f) provides that the proposed modification of the plan cannot be approved unless it complies with the various requirements of Chapter 11 including the disclosure and approval procedures of §§1121 through 1128. However, §1121(d) provides that any holder of a claim or interest that voted to approve the original plan will be deemed to approve the proposed modification unless they notify the court of a change in their position within the time set by the court to do so.

P-H 25-s: What kinds of postconfirmation events might cause BBF to seek modification of the BBF plan?

---

6. Revocation of an Order of Confirmation

Revocation of an order confirming a plan requires a showing that the order "was procured by fraud," according to §1144, and a motion to revoke an order of confirmation must be made by a party in interest within 180 days after the order is entered. If the court does revoke the order of confirmation, any discharge made effective by the confirmation is revoked.

F. ▶ Postconfirmation Dismissal or Conversion of a Chapter 11 Case

Recall the discussion of the grounds for seeking dismissal of a Chapter 11 case or conversion of the case to a Chapter 7 liquidation in Chapter Twenty-Four, Section C. Several of the grounds for dismissal or conversion we saw in Illustration 24-a involve cause arising after confirmation of the plan, including the revocation of an order of confirmation, the inability to effectuate a substantial consummation of a confirmed plan, or a material default by the debtor with a term of the confirmed plan.

EXAMPLE

> Assume that BBF's plan of reorganization is confirmed but that its new business plan does not produce the income flow projected in its disclosure statement (Document 24 in the BBF case file), so that payments called for under the plan to begin nine months following the date of confirmation never begin. Or assume that the new business plan is successful for a couple of years and then falls apart, causing BBF to default on plan payments. These are the types of occurrences that may give rise to a motion by BBF to modify the plan or to a motion by creditors to dismiss or convert.

G. ▶ Consummation of the Plan of Reorganization

Pursuant to FRBP 3022, when the case has been **fully administered** the court will enter an order closing the case.

H. ▶ The Chapter 9 Adjustment of Debts of a Municipality

Chapter 9 bankruptcy filings are rare. Between 1981 and 2012 there were only 42 Chapter 9 filings nationwide (10 of those, however, were filed between 2008 and 2012, fallout from the Great Recession). Thus most legal professionals working in the bankruptcy field will never encounter a Chapter 9 case, even in a long career. But when they do occur, the cases tend to be significant events on a local and even a statewide or national level.

Chapter 9 is unique in most ways but is probably most analogous to the Chapter 11 case and so we will summarize it here at the end of our consideration of Chapter 11.

1. Purpose and Scope of Chapter 9

Chapter 9 is designed to provide the financially distressed **municipality** temporary relief from its creditors while it develops a **plan for adjustment of debts**. Per §109(c)(1), only a municipality may seek protection under Chapter 9. Section 101(40) of the Code defines a municipality as a "political subdivision or public agency or instrumentality of a state" and that has been construed to include:

- Cities
- Counties
- Townships
- School districts
- Public improvement districts
- Quasi-public bodies such as bridge authorities, highway authorities, and gas authorities

Interestingly, §109(c)(2) requires that a municipality filing for Chapter 9 relief be specifically authorized by the state in which it is located to do so. Section 903 preserves the authority of states to limit or qualify the power of a municipality to file. Conversely, municipalities can only file under Chapter 9; no other provision of the Code is available to them. Thus if a state does not authorize municipalities to file for Chapter 9 relief they must seek such relief under state law or seek special state legislation for relief. Currently, 24 states allow municipalities to file under Chapter 9. Some of those require the municipality to seek specific authorization from the state before filing, and at least one (Iowa) permits filing only if the insolvency is caused by involuntary debt (e.g., a court judgment entered in a liability suit).

P-H 25-t: What is the policy behind Congress's decision to let states decide whether municipal entities can file under Chapter 9? Is it ultimately a policy issue or a constitutional one arising under the 10th Amendment to the Constitution, which reserves to the states a large measure of sovereignty over their internal affairs? The original congressional act seeking to regulate bankruptcy proceedings for municipalities was struck down by the U.S. Supreme Court for 10th Amendment reasons in *Ashton v. Cameron County Water Improvement Dist. No. 1*, 298 U.S. 513, 532 (1936). A subsequent 1937 act was upheld in *United States v. Bekins*, 304 U.S. 27, 54 (1938), and is the source of modern-day Chapter 9.

Additional §109(c) requirements for filing a petition in Chapter 9 require that the municipality be insolvent as that term is defined in §101(32)(C) and that it desires to effect a plan to adjust its debts (i.e., no involuntary filing is allowed) and that it meets at least one of the following criteria:

- It has obtained the agreement of creditors holding at least a majority in amount of the claims of each class that it intends to impair under it Chapter 9 plan;
- It has negotiated in good faith with creditors but failed to obtain the agreement of creditors holding at least a majority in the amount of the claims of each class that the debtor intends to impair under a plan;
- It has been unable to negotiate with creditors because such negotiation is impracticable; or
- It reasonably believes that a creditor may attempt to obtain a preference.

P-H 25-u: Prior to the Great Recession, the largest municipal bankruptcy in American history was the 1994 Chapter 9 filing of Orange County, California, the third most populous county in the State of California and the sixth most populous county in the nation. Triggered by risky investment strategies by the county treasurer who was later indicted and convicted of six felonies, the county was unable to service its debt, sending the national municipal bond market into chaos. You can read a good history of the Orange County bankruptcy at www.ppic.org/content/pubs/op/op_398op.pdf. Fallout from the Great Recession has included several municipal filings, including that by Harrisburg, Pennsylvania, in October 2011; Jefferson County, Alabama, in November 2011; and Stockton, California, in June 2012. Unlike Orange County, these filings were triggered by falling tax revenues over an extended period of time as effects of the Great Recession persisted, juxtaposed against an inability to reduce the cost of government services. Do some research to determine the current status of these three significant municipal filings. Have there been additional filings by major municipalities since mid-2013? Have any municipalities in your state filed in Chapter 9 as a result of the Great Recession?

---

2. Filing the Case and Notice to Creditors

Like proceedings under other chapters of the Code, a Chapter 9 case is initiated by the municipality filing a petition per §301(a) and the commencement of the case constitutes an order for relief in the case per §301(b). The municipality must also file a list of creditors per §924 at the time the petition is filed or within the time ordered by the court per FRBP 1007.

In all other cases under the Code, the clerk of the bankruptcy court where the petition is filed will assign a new filing to a particular judge. However, §921(b) mandates that the chief judge of the court of appeals for the federal circuit in which the filing occurs designates the bankruptcy judge to preside over the case. This provision reflects the political sensitivity of a municipal filing as well as concerns about the experience and qualifications of a judge who would preside over a filing potentially having momentous public consequences.

Notice of the filing must be given by the clerk of the bankruptcy court to the listed creditors as required by §923. In addition, the notice must also be published "at least once a week for three successive weeks in at least one newspaper of general circulation published within the district in which the case is commenced, and in such other newspaper having a general circulation among bond dealers and bondholders as the court designates."

Section 921(c) authorizes the filing of objections to the petition that will typically arise out of the qualifications for a municipality to file (e.g., Is the debtor a true municipality? Is the debtor insolvent? Does the state authorize the filing?). The bankruptcy court can dismiss the Chapter 9 petition if it finds, after notice and a hearing, that the petition was not filed in good faith or that the qualifications for filing are not present. Section 930 authorizes the court to dismiss the petition for cause, which can include:

- Lack of prosecution;
- Unreasonable delay by the debtor found to be prejudicial to creditors;
- Failure to propose or confirm a plan within the time fixed by the court;
- Material default by the debtor under a confirmed plan; or
- Termination of a confirmed plan by reason of the occurrence of a condition specified in the plan.

3. The Automatic Stay and Creditor Claims

The automatic stay of §362 of the Code is applicable in Chapter 9 cases per §901(a). The stay blocks all collection actions against the debtor and its property. Section 922(a) actually expands the scope of the automatic stay in Chapter 9 cases by prohibiting actions against officers and inhabitants of the debtor if the action seeks to enforce a claim against the debtor.

EXAMPLE

> The stay prohibits a creditor from bringing a mandamus action (an action to compel a government officer to perform his duty or to cease from violating it) against an officer of a municipality on account of a prepetition debt. It also prohibits a creditor from bringing an action against a resident of the debtor municipality to enforce a lien on or arising out of taxes or assessments owed to the debtor.

Per §922(d), a Chapter 9 petition does not operate to stay application of pledged special revenues to payment of indebtedness secured by such revenues. Thus, for example, a bond trustee may continue postpetition payments from pledged funds to bondholders without violating the stay.

Section 925 provides that a creditor is required to file a proof of claim in the Chapter 9 case only if that creditor is not listed on the list of creditors filed by the municipality or if the listed claim is shown as disputed, contingent, or unliquidated or if the claim is listed in an incorrect amount.

4. Postpetition Operation of the Debtor Municipality

Chapter 9 does not use the phrase "debtor in possession," but that idea is very much a part of the postpetition procedure in a Chapter 9. The powers of the bankruptcy court to oversee or interfere with the operations of the municipality are extremely limited. No bankruptcy trustee is appointed unless the debtor refuses to pursue a turnover or avoidance action under §§544-545 or 547-550 (discussed in Chapter Seventeen, Sections D and E), in which case the court can appoint a trustee under §926(a) for the limited purpose of pursuing such action. There is no property of the estate concept in a Chapter 9 as there is in other chapters of the Code, thus no estate for the bankruptcy court to administer. Pursuant to §903, the Chapter 9 filing does not limit or impair the power of the state to control or regulate the municipality as by legislation or agency rule.

Section 904 specifically limits the power of the bankruptcy court to interfere with:

- Any of the political or governmental powers of the debtor;
- Any of the property or revenues of the debtor; or
- The debtor's use or enjoyment of any income-producing property unless the debtor consents or the plan so provides.

This makes it clear that the debtor's day-to-day activities are not subject to court approval, the debtor may borrow money without court authority, and the court cannot interfere with the debtor's use of its property and revenues. The case cannot be converted to a liquidation proceeding.

Subject to court approval, the municipality can adjust burdensome contractual relationships under the power to reject executory contracts and unexpired leases like a debtor in Chapter 11. The debtor has the same avoiding powers as debtors in other cases under the Code and disputes arising from such claims will be resolved by the bankruptcy court. Interestingly, a municipality debtor can reject collective bargaining agreements and retiree benefit plans as part of its plan for adjustment of debts without going through the special procedures for approval for such a proposal in Chapter 11 cases.

A municipality can borrow money during a Chapter 9 case as an administrative expense per §901(a). It can obtain credit as it does outside of bankruptcy and the bankruptcy court has no supervisory authority over the amount of debt the municipality incurs in its operation. The debtor municipality can employ professionals without court approval, and the professional fees incurred are reviewed only within the context of plan confirmation.

The U.S. Trustee does not supervise the administration of a Chapter 9 case as that office will in other cases under the Code. No first meeting of creditors is held. A creditor's committee is appointed by the U.S. Trustee and §901(a) gives it most of the same powers it has in a Chapter 11 case pursuant to §1103 including:

- Selecting and authorizing the employment of one or more attorneys, accountants, or other agents to represent the committee;
- Consulting with the debtor concerning administration of the case;
- Investigating the acts, conduct, assets, liabilities, and financial condition of the debtor;
- Participating in the formulation of a plan; and
- Performing such other services as are in the interest of those represented.

Conversely, as will be discussed in more detail below, if certain requirements are met, the debtor's plan is binding on dissenting creditors.

Parties in interest in a Chapter 9 case may include not just creditors but also municipal employees, organizations of employees of the debtor (unions), local residents, nonresident owners of real property, taxpayers, securities firms, local banks, and federal agencies such as the U.S. Department of Treasury and the Securities and Exchange Commission.

5. The Plan for Adjustment of Debts

Section 941 mandates that the debtor municipality file a plan for adjustment of its debts with the petition or at such later time as set by the court. Unlike a Chapter 11, no creditor or other party in interest can file a competing plan.

As already indicated, the municipal debtor has much more flexibility in proposing a Chapter 9 plan than a Chapter 11 debtor does in proposing a plan under that chapter of the Code. A major source of revenue for most municipalities is **municipal bonds**. There are two general types of municipal bonds. A **general obligation bond** (GOB) is backed by the full faith and credit of the issuing municipality and bond buyers can look to all the revenue and assets of the municipality for payment of principal and interest when due. A **special revenue bond** (SRB) is payable out of revenue from a specific public project (e.g., a city parking garage).

The two types of bonds receive different treatment in the Chapter 9 case and in the Chapter 9 plan. GPBs are treated as general debt in the Chapter 9 case. The municipality is not required to make payments of either principal or interest on account of such bonds during the case. The obligations created by GOBs are subject to negotiation and possible restructuring under the plan of adjustment. Per §928, SRBs must remain secured by the specified revenue source and must be serviced during the case so long as revenue is received from the specified source. Holders of special revenue bonds can expect to receive payment on such bonds during the Chapter 9 case if special revenues are available.

Per §926(b), holders of either GOBs or SRBs are exempt from §547 preference liability regarding prepetition payments as are holders of promissory notes issued by the municipality regardless of whether the prepetition payment was made while the debtor was insolvent.

6. Confirmation of a Chapter 9 Plan

The standards for confirmation of a Chapter 9 plan are similar in only some ways to those that apply to confirmation of a Chapter 11 plan. Section 943(b) provides that the bankruptcy court must confirm the Chapter 9 plan if all of the following conditions are met:

- All amounts to be paid by the debtor or by any person for services or expenses in the case or incident to the plan have been fully disclosed and are reasonable;
- The debtor is not prohibited by law from taking any action necessary to carry out the plan;
- Except to the extent that the holder of a particular claim has agreed to a different treatment of such claim, the plan provides that on the effective date of the plan, each holder of a claim of a kind specified in §507(a)(1) will receive on account of such claim cash equal to the allowed amount of such claim;

- Any regulatory or electoral approval necessary under applicable nonbankruptcy law in order to carry out any provision of the plan has been obtained is expressly conditioned on such approval;
- The plan is in the best interests of creditors and is feasible; and
- The plan complies with the provisions of Chapter 9.

The requirement that the plan be in the "best interests of creditors" means something different under Chapter 9 than it does under Chapter 11. As we have seen, in a Chapter 11, a plan is said to be in the "best interest of creditors" if creditors would receive as much under the plan as they would if the debtor were liquidated (§1129(a)(7)(A)(ii)). But there is no liquidation of assets in a Chapter 9 to pay creditors so "best interests of creditors" in the Chapter 9 context is generally interpreted to mean that the plan must be better than other alternatives available to the creditors. See 6 *Collier on Bankruptcy* §943.03(7). The courts generally apply the test to require a reasonable effort by the municipal debtor that is a better alternative for its creditors than dismissal of the case.

Section 943(b)(1) also requires as a condition for confirmation that the plan comply with the provisions of the Code made applicable by §§103(e) and 901(a). The most important of these for purposes of confirming a plan are that §1129(a)(8) requires that the plan has been accepted by each class of claims or interests impaired under the plan (the legal, equitable, or contractual rights of such claims are altered). Unimpaired classes need not accept for the plan to be approved. If any class of impaired claims does not consent, the plan may still be confirmed via §§1129(a)(10) and 1120(b) if at least one impaired class accepts the plan. The plan can be crammed down on other impaired classes if that one impaired class accepts and the court finds that the plan does not unfairly discriminate against nonconsenting impaired classes and is otherwise fair and equitable.

7. Chapter 9 Discharge

Per §944(b), a municipal debtor receives a discharge in Chapter 9 of debts the plan proposes to discharge after:

- Confirmation of the plan;
- Deposit by the debtor of any money or property to be distributed under the plan with the disbursing agent appointed by the court; and
- A determination by the court that securities (e.g., bonds) deposited with the disbursing agent to be distributed under the plan are valid legal obligations of the debtor.

Per §§901(a) and 1144, at any time within 180 days after entry of the confirmation order, the court may, after notice and a hearing, revoke the order of confirmation if the order was procured by fraud.

CONCLUSION

We have now considered a Chapter 11 case from filing to completion and compared it to the rarely used Chapter 9. Ideally, the reorganized debtor emerges from the Chapter 11 revitalized and able to function successfully. For the legal professional, there can be great satisfaction in seeing a business survive instead of fail and knowing that your expertise and hard work made the difference.

CHAPTER SUMMARY

The DIP has the exclusive right to file a proposed plan of reorganization during the 120 days following filing of the petition, and if it does so, no competing plan may be filed until 180 days postpetition. The plan must create classes of creditor and equity claim holders. Those in each class must have substantially similar claims. Undersecured claims may be treated in two different classes: one for secured and one for unsecured. Creditors holding unique claims may be placed in a class by themselves for administrative convenience.

A class of claims or interests is impaired if the plan proposes to alter the underlying rights of the holders. A Chapter 11 plan can propose to modify the rights of a secured creditor other than one holding a mortgage in the residence of an individual debtor to the same extent as allowed in a Chapter 13 case. Non-priority unsecured claims may be modified in whole or part and discharged under the plan. Administrative operating expenses must be paid in full on the effective date of the plan and priority tax claims must be paid within six years of assessment.

To ensure that those voting on the plan understand it, the plan proponent must file a disclosure statement containing adequate information regarding the plan and the debtor. The court conducts a hearing on the adequacy of the disclosure statement. If the disclosure statement is approved by the court, it will issue an order establishing dates for distribution of ballots, setting time limits for voting on the plan, and setting a date for a confirmation hearing. Holders of allowed claims and interests can vote for or against the plan and good faith solicitation of support or opposition to the plan is allowed. Approval of a plan depends on its approval by the classes created by the plan. Approval of the plan by a class requires both approval by at least two-thirds of the dollar amount represented in the class and by more than one-half the creditors in the class. An undersecured creditor may make the §1111(b)(2) election to have its claim treated as secured up to the full amount owed.

A plan may be confirmed by the court in either of two ways. Confirmation under §1129(a) is used where all classes of creditors and claims, including any impaired class, approve the plan including any impaired class and other criteria are satisfied, including the best interests of creditors, good faith, lawfulness and feasibility tests and priority claims are treated as required. Confirmation under §1129(b), cramdown confirmation, used when all impaired classes have not accepted the plan, requires that the various §1129(a) tests be satisfied and that at least one impaired class have approved the plan, that the plan not unfairly discriminate against objecting classes, and that the plan be fair and equitable to objecting classes. The fair and equitable requirement of §1129(b) can be satisfied if the plan proposes to pay the full amount of the objecting claims in deferred installments over the term of the plan or if the plan proposes that equity holders receive nothing under the plan and retain no ownership interest in the reorganized debtor, the absolute priority rule. Some courts mitigate the harsh absolute priority rule with the new value exception.

Once the plan is confirmed, an order of confirmation is entered. The court retains postconfirmation authority to enter any order necessary to administer the case. A plan may be modified upon motion at any time before substantial consummation. An order of confirmation can be revoked upon motion made within 180 days and a showing that confirmation was procured by fraud. A Chapter 11 case can be dismissed or converted to a Chapter 7 liquidation for cause occurring postconfirmation as well. When the Chapter 11 case has been fully administered, the court will enter an order closing the case.

REVIEW QUESTIONS

1. Explain the 120-day exclusivity period of Chapter 11. What is the earliest date that a nondebtor can file a proposed plan? Under what circumstances must nondebtors wait 180 days postpetition to file a proposed plan?
2. Explain the rules for creating classes of claims in a Chapter 11 plan.
3. What does it mean to say that a class of claims or interest is impaired under Chapter 11?
4. What options are available to the DIP for dealing with secured debt in a Chapter 11 plan?
5. List the different kinds of information a disclosure statement should contain.
6. Explain the §1111(b)(2) election available to an undersecured creditor. Why would an undersecured creditor not make this election?
7. Explain the §1129(a) confirmation procedure. Be sure to mention the role of the best interests of creditors, good faith, lawfulness and feasibility tests, and the required treatment of priority claims.
8. Explain the §1129(b) confirmation procedure. Be sure to mention the no unfair discrimination and fair and equitable treatment requirements, including the absolute priority rule and the new value exception to it.
9. Summarize changes that can be made in a Chapter 11 plan or the case itself postconfirmation.
10. Under what circumstances can an order of confirmation in a Chapter 11 case be revoked? What time frames are applicable to a motion to revoke confirmation?

WORDS AND PHRASES TO REMEMBER

absolute priority rule
adequate information
administrative convenience
best interest of creditors test
confirmation hearing
cramdown confirmation
discharge
disclosure statement

discounted present value
election of remedies
exclusivity period
fair and equitable
feasibility test
final decree
general revenue bond
good faith

hardship discharge
hearing on adequacy of disclosure
    statement
impaired
legal rights
liquidation analysis
modification of (Chapter 11) plan
modification of rights
municipal bond
municipality
new value exception
no unfair discrimination test

order of confirmation
pay through
plan for adjustment of debts
present value
reorganized debtor
replacement cost
revocation of confirmation
sale free and clear of liens
special revenue bond
substantially similar
undersecured interest
§1111(b)(2) election

TO LEARN MORE: A number of TLM activities to accompany this chapter are accessible on the student disc accompanying the text and at the Author Updates link to the text Web site at http://www.aspenparalegaled.com/ books/parsons_abcdebt/default.asp.

▶ In Re Marta Rinaldi Carlson Chapter 7 Bankruptcy

ASSIGNMENT MEMORANDUM

TO: Paralegal
FROM: Carolyn A. Thomas, supervising attorney
RE: Marta Rinaldi Carlson
DATE: November 19, YR-1

Marta Rinaldi Carlson is an executive assistant at Tomorrow Today, Inc. (TTI). Marta was one of the original employees of TTI, hired as a secretary to Howard Kine, a computer software genius and TTI shareholder. At Kine's urging, Marta obtained an associate's degree from Capitol City Community College in computer science. She then transferred to Columbiana State University and has been pursuing her bachelor's in software engineering. Marta needs only 20 more semester hours to complete her degree, which she hopes to do in 18 months. Kine told Marta that once she receives that degree, he will recommend that TTI promote her from executive assistant to computer software engineer. Marta makes $34,000 per year at TTI. If she can secure the computer software engineer position, her pay should jump to the mid-50 thousands. But that is at least 18 months away.

Completing her education has been a long, hard road for Marta. At 37, when she began her college work, she had been out of school for 20 years, since completing high school. Now 40, she works full time for TTI so must attend school at night. She has two children: a son, Chris, who is 14, and a daughter, Adela, who is 11. Marta and her husband, Eugene, separated about the time she began college and the divorce became final 20 months ago.

From a financial standpoint, when Marta and Eugene were together, they were a typical middle-class family. They had a house mortgage that was always paid on time, a couple of credit cards on which they carried a little higher balance than they should have, and they rarely put any money into savings. But the bills got paid, vacations got taken, both Marta and Eugene drove late-model cars, purchased with affordable loans, and everybody in the family had all the accoutrements of American middle-class life.

All that changed with the divorce. Six months after the decree became final, Eugene lost his job as an assistant manager of a mid-sized regional retail discount chain when it was bought out by a national concern. The divorce decree required him to pay Marta $2,000 per month in child support and to keep Marta and the kids covered under his health insurance policy. Eugene is now $15,000 in arrears on his child support obligation and unable to provide health insurance coverage. Consequently, Marta pays to have herself and the two children covered under TTI's group policy.

Two months after the divorce, Adela got sick with what Marta thought was an intestinal flu. The 11-year old had bouts of nausea and diarrhea that would last three to four days, resolve, and then recur a week later. The third time it happened, Adela was hospitalized for almost a week. The doctors diagnosed irritable bowel syndrome related to stress from the separation and divorce of Adela's parents. Medication was prescribed but did no good at all. Finally, Marta took her daughter to a gastrointestinal specialist in another city, who diagnosed Giardiasis, a condition caused by a waterborne, intestinal parasite. Though no one can say for sure where the child picked it up, it was probably on a swimming trip with friends to a popular swimming hole at a local lake. By the time the correct diagnosis was made, Adela's condition was serious and she had to undergo surgery to remove a portion of her large intestine, followed by an extended hospitalization. The infection was eventually checked but Adela still has to take very expensive medications and follow a strict diet. She will be under a doctor's watchful care for several years. Between the high deductible on her TTI policy and the limited coverage provided for several of the tests and procedures conducted on Adela, as well as the medications she is taking, Marta has unpaid medical bills totaling more than $60,000 and growing. Eugene remains unemployed and is unable to help financially.

In addition to Adela's health problems, Marta has been faced with responsibility for health care costs associated with her widowed 73-year-old mother, Estell Rinaldi. Six years ago Estell was diagnosed with Alzheimer's. She was able to live in her home for a year after the diagnosis but finally sold the home and went into a nursing facility, Pine Ridge Nursing Home. Although Marta had hoped that the proceeds from her mother's home, in addition to her remaining savings, would be enough to pay for the nursing home care, she was asked by the nursing home to sign a personal guaranty, promising to pay any costs her mother's assets and government assistance did not. She did so without consulting an attorney. A little over a year ago, her mother's assets were depleted and Marta began receiving bills from the nursing home. Her mother finally passed away two months ago, but the accumulated bills from her care, for which Pine Ridge Nursing claims Marta is responsible, total more than $45,000. Marta is disputing that claim against her, contending that when her mother's assets ran out, she advised the nursing home that she would not be able to pay anything and that she was verbally told by the home's administrator that she would not be billed anything on the guaranty because the government would pay all costs from that point on. Pine Ridge has filed suit to collect the indebtedness from Marta. She has answered the complaint denying any liability on the guarantee and alleging, in the alternative, that a portion of the nursing home's claim against her represents sums the government has paid to Pine Ridge.

Eugene's unemployment has caused Marta other further financial problems. Under the divorce decree, he was ordered to assume liability for the accumulated credit card debt of the couple, which totaled more than $40,000 at the time. He made very few payments on the outstanding balance of that debt and Marta is now being dunned for it. With interest and late fees, the total balance owed to two different card providers is more than $50,000.

Marta has had to borrow money to finance her college education. She took out one loan from Columbiana Federal Savings & Loan in the principal amount of $5,000 for her community college expenses and has just begun paying that back. She took out a second loan from Capitol Savings Bank for $10,000 to finance her studies at Columbiana State University. Under the terms of that student loan, repayment will not begin until three months after she graduates. Both student loans are guaranteed by the federal government.

Six years ago, Eugene and Marta bought the house where Marta now lives with her children. They paid $200,000 for it, borrowing $150,000 from Capitol Savings Bank (CSB). The loan was for 30 years at a fixed-rate of interest at 6.5 percent per annum. The monthly payments to CSB, with taxes and insurance, total $965.

Three years ago, Eugene and Marta took out a second mortgage on the house when they borrowed $50,000 from Dreams Come True Finance Company (DCT) to finance a business venture for Eugene that ultimately failed. The DCT loan was for 15 years at 8 percent interest and required monthly payments of $477.

In the divorce, Marta was awarded the house and Eugene quitclaimed his interest in it to her. The divorce decree provided that Marta was to assume responsibility for the remaining mortgage payments to CSB, though Eugene remained on the promissory note to CSB. Eugene was to assume responsibility for the remaining mortgage payments to DCT, though Marta remained liable on that note. Marta knew it would be a stretch for her to make the mortgage payments to CSB on her salary alone, but she decided it was worth the risk in order to keep her children in their home. The current principal balance on the loan from CSB is $142,500; the current principal balance on the loan from DCT, which has been in default for some time now, is $37,500. Marta is two payments behind to CSB and three behind to DCT. A realtor has told Marta that the house has a market value of $255,000. DCT has declared default on its loan and is preparing to foreclose on the home.

Marta is maxed-out on the Capitol City Bank Visa card issued in her own name following the divorce. Her balance on the card is $8,200, on which she manages to make no more than the minimum payment each month. She drives a four-year-old Toyota Camry, which is titled in her name only. The book value of the car is $8,500 and she owes a balance on it of $1,750 to Automotive Financing, Inc. (AFI), which holds a security interest in the car. Her monthly payments to AFI are $210 and she is two payments in arrears at this time. She has no savings except her 401k plan at TTI, which has a current balance of $7,600.

Her 14-year-old son, Chris, has had his own problems since the divorce. His grades have dropped and he's started running with a group of friends Marta is not happy with. Eugene rarely sees either child, electing not to exercise his visitation rights most months. Last month Chris and another juvenile were arrested for malicious destruction of property. Marta had to come up with $500 to pay a lawyer who did manage to keep Chris from being sentenced to a juvenile facility. When Chris began experiencing problems after the divorce, Marta took him to Crisis Counseling Center, which billed her a total of $1,250. Her insurance did not cover the counseling and she has been unable to pay the bill. That debt has been turned over to a collection agency. She is getting two to three phone calls a week from the collection agency asking when the bill will be paid.

Marta's own health has deteriorated since her financial problems began following the divorce. She suffers from chronic indigestion, which she suspects is an ulcer, but she has put off going to a doctor because she just can't afford it.

We are going to file a Chapter 7 bankruptcy for Ms. Carlson. Please contact her and begin gathering the additional information needed for the petition and schedules.

CASE FILE INDEX

[The documents listed in this index for the Chapter 7 bankruptcy case of *In re Marta Rinaldi Carlson* are available on the disc that accompanies the text. The Official Bankruptcy Forms (OBF) seen there were completed using bankruptcy software from Best Case Solutions.]

1. Petition with Exhibit D
2. Application to Pay Fee in Installments
3. Order Granting Application to Pay Fee in Installments
4. List of Creditors
5. Motion for Additional Time to File Schedules, Statement of Affairs, and Other Documents with Notice of Motion
6. Order granting Motion for Additional Time to File Schedules, etc.
7. Schedule A
8. Schedule B
9. Schedule C
10. Schedule D
11. Schedule E
12. Schedule F
13. Schedule G
14. Schedule H
15. Schedule I
16. Schedule J
17. Summary of Schedules
18. Declaration re Schedules
19. Statement of Financial Affairs
20. Debtor's Statement of Intent
21. **A.** OBF 22A Statement of Current Income and Means Test
    B. Alternative OBF 22A Statement of Current Income and Means Test Assuming Above Median Debtor
22. Statement of Social Security Number
23. Statement Disclosing Reasonably Anticipated Changes to Income
24. Statement Disclosing Compensation Paid or to be Paid to Attorney for the Debtor
25. Payment Advices within 60 Days
26. Notice of Commencement of Case
27. Motion for Order of Contempt for Violation of Automatic Stay and for Damages with Notice of Motion
28. Order on Motion for Order of Contempt, etc.
29. Trustee's §704(b)(1) Report
30. Proof of Claim with Exhibit
31. Objection to Claim with Notice of Objection
32. Motion for Permission to Hire Professional and to Approve Fee
33. Order on Motion to Hire Professional, etc.
34. Complaint for Turnover of Property or Money Judgment for Its Value
35. Debtor's Certification of Completion of Postpetition Instructional Course Concerning Personal Financial Management

36. Notice of Intent to Abandon Property with Notice of Motion
37. Motion for Permission to Sell Property Free and Clear of Liens with Notice of Motion
38. Reaffirmation Agreement
39. Discharge of Debtor

▶ In Re Roger H. and Susan J. Matthews Chapter 13 Bankruptcy

Assignment Memorandum

TO: Paralegal
FROM: Carolyn A. Thomas, supervising attorney
RE: Roger H. and Susan J. Matthews
DATE: November 20, YR-1

Roger Matthews is 33 years old and works for City Plumbing Company. Roger has a high school diploma, almost two years of college, and a certificate in plumbing from Columbiana College of Technology. He brings home $2,400 a month based on a gross salary of $36,000 per year. Susan Matthews is 32 years old and works as the librarian for Heart and Soul Academy, a private school in Capitol City for kindergarten through eighth grade. Susan has a bachelor's degree in library science from Columbiana State University. She brings home $1,733 a month based on a gross salary of $26,000 per year.

Roger and Susan have been irresponsible in their credit card spending. They have used six different cards for the last several years and accumulated $35,000 of debt on those cards. Less than $30,000 of the debt was for actual charges, the rest of the balance has built up over the years from interest and fees charged on balances carried over month to month and occasional penalties for late payments.

The Matthews own a home in Capitol City, which they purchased three years ago. A realtor friend told them informally that the home has a current market value of $120,000. There are two mortgages on the property. The first mortgage is in favor of First Bank of Capitol City (FBCC) with a balance of $100,000 on a 30-year note with 27 years remaining. The Matthews pay FBCC $850 per month and are one payment in arrears. The second mortgage is in favor of Capitol Savings Bank (CSB) with a balance of $30,000 on a $35,000 home improvement loan the Matthews took out a year ago (thus the Matthews have no equity in their home). They have 48 months of payments remaining on the second mortgage. The Matthews pay CSB $700 per month on the second mortgage and are current on those payments.

The Matthews own three vehicles. Roger drives a YR-3 Ford Truck F-150 worth $7,500, on which they owe $9,000 to Automotive Financing, Inc. (AFI), which holds a lien on the truck. The Matthews make payments of $360 per month to AFI on the truck. Susan drives a YR-4 Honda Civic worth $8,000, on which they owe $7,500 to Columbiana Federal Savings & Loan (CFSL), which holds a lien on the Civic. The Matthews make payments of $240 per month to CFSL on the Civic. They also own a YR-10 Oldsmobile Intrigue worth $2,000, on which they owe $5,000 to Car World (CW), which holds a lien on the Intrigue. The Matthews make payments to CW of $120 per month on the Intrigue. The Matthews are current on all three car payments but are pretty sure they will surrender the Intrigue to CW since it is an extra vehicle.

Roger and Susan have two daughters: Carrie is 7 years old and her sister, Elizabeth, is 11 months. Medical expenses incurred in connection with Elizabeth's birth are the straw that broke the camel's back for the couple financially. Susan experienced complications with the pregnancy and, although the baby is fine, the unpaid doctor and hospital bills for Susan still total $25,000. Susan was out of work the last three months of YR-2 and January of YR-1 due to her health problems and the baby's birth, which devastated the couple's cash flow. Susan returned to work six months ago but they are too deeply in the hole financially to catch up. Susan's mother is keeping the baby during the day and Carrie after school to spare them child care expenses, but she's not going to be able to do that much longer.

Roger and Susan also borrowed $2,500 from Capitol City Finance Company (CCFC) last year to finance a vacation they couldn't otherwise afford. The couple pledged Roger's plumbing tools and all their furniture to secure the loan from CCFC the balance of which is $2,000. At about the same time, Roger was assessed $1,000 in taxes, penalties, and interest by the IRS as a result of unreported income from YR-2 when he did some independent plumbing work for a local contractor.

I have drawn up the following informal budget for the Matthews, which we will use in fashioning a proposed plan of reorganization for them under Chapter 13.

Monthly prepetition budget for Roger and Susan Matthews:

<u>Net monthly income:</u>

Roger:	$2,400
($3,000 per month minus withholding of $600 in taxes)	
Susan:	$1,733
($2,167 per month minus withholding of $360 in taxes and $74 health insurance premium)	
Total net monthly income	$4,133

Living expenses:

Food		475
Home maintenance		75
Clothing		175
Dry cleaning/laundry		25
Gas/transportation		150
Utilities, phone, and cable		500
Electric & gas	$315	
Water & sewer	$50	
Phones	$70	
Cable & Internet	$65	
Insurance (auto)		60
Medical/dental		100
Charitable contributions		50
Entertainment/recreation		50
Miscellaneous		100
Total living expenses		$1,760

<u>Payments on secured debt:</u>

House payments	1,550
(FBCC $850, one payment behind)	
(CSB $700, current)	
Car payments	720

(AFI for YR-3 Ford Truck $360, current)
(CFSL for YR-4 Honda Civic $240, current)
(C-W for YR-10 Olds $120, current)

Total payments on secured debt $2,270

Total payments on living expenses and secured debt $4,030

Available to pay other debt $103

Debt not being paid:

Credit cards 35,000
Doctor & hospital 25,000
Tax bill from YR-2 1,000
CCFC secured loan 2,000

Total debt not being paid $63,000

CASE FILE INDEX

[The documents listed in this index for the Chapter 13 bankruptcy case of *In re Roger H. and Susan J. Matthews* are available on the disc that accompanies the text. The Official Bankruptcy Forms (OBF) seen there were completed using bankruptcy software from Best Case Solutions.]

1. Petition with Exhibit D
2. List of Creditors
3. Schedule A
4. Schedule B
5. Schedule C
6. Schedule D
7. Schedule E
8. Schedule F
9. Schedule G
10. Schedule H
11. Schedule I
12. Schedule J
13. Summary of Schedules
14. Declaration re Schedules
15. Statement of Financial Affairs
16. A. OBF 22C Statement of Current Monthly Income and Calculation of Commitment Period and Disposable Income
    B. Alternative OBF 22C Statement of Current Monthly Income and Calculation of Commitment Period and Disposable Income Assuming Above Median Debtors
17. Statement of Social Security Number
18. Statement Disclosing Reasonably Anticipated Changes to Income
19. Statement Disclosing Compensation Paid or to be Paid to Attorney for the Debtor
20. Payment Advices within 60 Days
21. Chapter 13 Plan
22. Notice of Commencement of Case
23. Debtor's Certification of Completion of Postpetition Instructional Course Concerning Personal Financial Management
24. Order Confirming Chapter 13 Plan
25. Wage Orders

▶ In Re Banowsky Brothers Furniture, Inc., Chapter 11 Bankruptcy

ASSIGNMENT MEMORANDUM #1

TO: Paralegal
FROM: James W. Forsyth, supervising attorney
RE: Banowsky Brothers Furniture, Inc.
DATE: November 10, YR-1

In 1931, as the Great Depression tightened its grip on America, Philip Banowsky, the grandfather of Charles and Timothy Banowsky, lost his job as local manager of an insurance company in Capitol City and turned to the only other thing he knew: furniture making. He started his business, Banowsky & Son Fine Furniture, in his garage and the handmade wooden furniture he produced not only kept his family fed but also gained a reputation for being very well made and sturdy. When Philip passed away in 1955, his son, Richard, took over the business, which by then had a small factory building next to the family home where it both made and sold furniture to the public. During the years that he operated the business, Richard incorporated the business, expanded the manufacturing facility, and opened three regional stores in leased locations selling Banowsky furniture exclusively. It was while Richard operated the business that Banowsky furniture came to be known for its intricate hand carving. Richard himself was a noted woodcarver, and by the time he retired in 1993, the company employed three other Master Carvers. Over the years, the company has focused on solid wood furniture made from pine, oak, or cherry in natural, stained, or colored finishes. It specializes in sets of furniture for the dining room, bedroom, and study, including entertainment centers, bookcases, and corner pieces.

When Richard's two sons, Charles and Timothy, took over the business in 1993, they changed the name to Banowsky Brothers Furniture, Inc. and expanded the family business further by negotiating contracts with two chain department stores, Sherman Department Store and Maddens Home Furnishings, to carry BBF furniture in their stores. In YR-6 the brothers undertook a major modernization of their factory by doubling the size of the facility and by purchasing computer-operated robot systems for material handling and product finishing. They went to computer-aided design/computer aided manufacturing (CAD/CAM) systems to operate all new routers, panel saws, and other production equipment. The brothers also leased two new regional store locations, for a total of five, in addition to the showroom that is part of the furniture factory building. This YR-6 expansion was funded by a master loan from Capitol City Bank (CCB), which already held a mortgage in the factory property, and the balance owing was refinanced as part of the master loan. The amount of the master loan was $2 million, to be repaid over 25 years. In addition to the mortgage, CCB took a security interest in BBF's inventory, including furniture in process, accounts receivable, and cash, to secure repayment of the loan, the current balance of which is $1.5 million. Both Charles and Timothy have personally guaranteed the debt owed by the business to CCB.

The new computerized systems were purchased from New Century Automation (NCA), which also financed BBF's purchase of new production equipment, including routers, panel saws, and so forth. The total purchase price was $500,000 to be paid over a 12-year term. NCA retained a security interest in the CAD/CAM systems as well as the production equipment to assure repayment. The current balance owed to NCA is $425,000.

All of BBF's other assets—six vehicles, office furniture, fixtures, supplies, and nonproduction equipment—is pledged to Columbiana Federal Savings & Loan, which is owed $175,000.

The Banowsky brothers had hoped that their YR-6 modernization and expansion would accomplish two major goals: to reduce high labor costs in the production of their furniture and, at the same time, increase their cash flow by shortening the production period, thereby expanding the sales outlets for their products. That is not what happened, however. The transition from labor-intensive material handling and furniture production did not go well due to poor training and problems with the systems, which kept them offline for long periods. Additionally, beginning in YR-5, company sales began to flatten out rather than rise, even as raw material prices began to soar. The wood used by the company has always been purchased in the United States which, in recent years, has been a profitable selling point. But the cost of domestic supplies has risen steadily while the competition from foreign furniture makers, who benefit from cheaper sources of wood and far lower labor rates, continues to cut into BBF's sales.

For all these reasons, the gross income of the corporation has fallen steadily over the past several years. Last year the corporation actually operated at a loss and it appears it will do so again this year. BBF is in arrears on its payments to both CCB and NCA. If CCB forecloses on the mortgage or NCA repossesses the CAD/CAM systems and production equipment of BBF, the corporation will be out of business. BBF's unsecured trade debt is badly in arrears and now totals more than $350,000. Two trade creditors have filed lawsuits against BBF to collect the amounts owed to them. Two critical suppliers have put BBF on notice that they will no longer sell to BBF on credit and will demand cash on delivery. BBF has already closed four of its five leased retail locations. The company also has an unpaid corporate income tax to the state in the amount of $27,000.

There are five shareholders in BBF. In addition to Charles and Timothy, who each hold 25 percent of the stock in the corporation, their father and mother, Richard and Virginia Banowsky, each own 20 percent and a sister, Beverly Banowsky Davis, owns the other 10 percent. Richard and Virginia, though no longer involved in the business, depend on the income from the corporation to support themselves in retirement. Things have gotten so bad that Charles and Timothy have not drawn any salary or other compensation from the company in more than a year, and no dividend has been declared or other distribution made to any shareholder since YR-2.

BBF has decided to file for Chapter 11 reorganization. I need your assistance in preparing the petition and schedules. Please contact Charles Banowsky and begin gathering the necessary information.

ASSIGNMENT MEMORANDUM #2

TO: Paralegal
FROM: James W. Forsyth, supervising attorney
RE: Banowsky Brothers Furniture, Inc.
DATE: November 20, YR-1

Charles and Timothy Banowsky have concluded that there is no future for BBF in continuing with the company's traditional furniture business. They believe that the same market trends that have created the current financial emergency for the company (rising prices of domestic wood and foreign competition benefiting from lower material and labor costs) will continue and accelerate. The other owners of the corporation are in agreement. Consequently, they are putting together a plan pursuant to which the company will import teakwood and rubberwood from a supplier in Hong Kong, China, and begin to manufacture various home and office furniture for sale in primarily Asian markets through Furniture Internationale SE (FI), an Italian company based in Milan, Italy.

FI distributes various lines of furniture featuring unique national emblems and characteristics through a network of dealers located in the urban areas of China, Japan, Korea, and other Asian locations. The selling point of the various lines of FI furniture is that they are made of materials preferred by the customers in the targeted markets but reflect the character of foreign exotic places for those customers. The targeted urban markets reflect the explosion of middle class wealth in those markets, particularly China. BBF will supply FI with what will be called the American Patriot Line of furniture for distribution in these markets. Furniture made by BBF will take advantage of its established reputation for high-quality hand carving, which will feature American emblems recognized worldwide such as the stars and stripes of the American flag, the American eagle, the Statue of Liberty, the White House, Mount Vernon, Monticello, the Alamo, etc.

To pursue this new business plan, BBF will no longer use any significant quantity of domestic wood. It will no longer distribute or sell its furniture products domestically. It will be able to utilize most of its current production equipment and systems. It will need to keep the three Master Carvers it currently employs and add as many as three more within the next 12 months. Once the conversion begins, BBF estimates it will be six months before any significant cash flow is received. But FI has been in business for 12 years and its record for producing profits with its other national lines of furniture, based to date on Italian, English, French and Mexican characteristics, has been impressive. FI has assisted BBF in developing this business plan and has helped BBF locate a company, New Era Capital Alliance based in Montreal, Canada, willing to provide venture capital for the undertaking.

These decisions will guide the formulation of our plan of reorganization for BBF, which I hope to have ready to file immediately following the §341 meeting, assuming we obtain the make-or-break first-day orders and prevail on other postpetition operational motions that become necessary. At that point, I will need your assistance in putting together the disclosure statement and plan.

CASE FILE INDEX

[The documents listed in this index for the Chapter 7 bankruptcy case of *In re Banowsky Brothers Furniture, Inc.* are available on the disc that accompanies the text. The Official Bankruptcy forms (OBF) used there were created using bankruptcy software from Best Case Solutions.]

1. Petition
2. List of Creditors
3. Corporate Resolution
4. List of 20 Largest Unsecured Creditors
5. Schedule A
6. Schedule B
7. Schedule D
8. Schedule E
9. Schedule F
10. Schedule G
11. Schedule H
12. Summary of Schedules
13. Declaration re Schedules
14. Corporate Ownership Statement
15. Statement of Current Income and Expenditures
16. Statement of Financial Affairs
17. Statement Disclosing Compensation Paid or to Be Paid to Attorney
18. List of Equity Security Holders
19. Motion for Authorization to Use Cash Collateral with Notice of Motion
20. Motion for Authorization to Pay Prepetition Debts with Notice of Motion
21. Notice of Commencement of Case
22. Notice of Appointment of Creditor's Committee
23. Motion to Reject Executory Contract with Notice of Motion
24. Disclosure Statement
25. Plan of Reorganization
26. Notice of Hearing on Adequacy of Disclosure Statement
27. Order Approving Disclosure Statement, Setting Time for Ballot Distribution, and Confirmation Hearing
28. Ballot
29. Order Confirming Plan

Glossary

All section references are to the Bankruptcy Code. Italicized words refer to other defined terms. The parenthetical at the end of each definition references the chapter(s) where the concept is introduced or receives primary attention.

Abandonment. The trustee's releasing of any claim by the estate to property deemed burdensome or of inconsequential value to the estate per §544 of the Code. See *surrender*. (Ch. Eighteen and Twenty-Four)

Absolute priority rule. The principle applicable in Chapter 11 cases that no junior class of claims or interests in a *plan of reorganization* should receive any distribution until senior classes are paid in full. (Ch. Twenty-Five)

Acceleration clause. A common provision in a promissory note and other installment contracts making all future installments immediately due and payable upon the debtor's default. (Ch. Three)

Acceptance. The decision of the members of a designated class of claims or interests in a Chapter 11 case to approve the proposed *plan of reorganization*. (Ch. Twenty-Five)

Adequate protection. The protection that must be provided by the bankrupt estate to a creditor whose interest in property is threatened by the estate's continued possession and use of the property. Provision of such assurance may be made in various ways per §361 but is recognized by the Code as a condition to the estate's continued possession and use of the property. In the context of the assumption or assignment of an executory contract the debtor or assignee must provide the other party to the contract, called adequate assurance of performance. (Ch. Sixteen, Twenty-Three, and Twenty-Four)

Administrative expenses. Postpetition expenses incurred in preserving the property of the estate and in administering the estate by the trustee or debtor in possession. Governed by §503, such expenses are granted a first priority in estate distribution by §507. (Ch. Eighteen and Twenty-Five)

Adversary proceedings. Certain disputes defined by Bankruptcy Rule 7001 that arise in a bankruptcy case and are resolved by the procedures governing a formal civil lawsuit. Cf. *contested matter*. (Ch. Thirteen)

Affidavit/declaration. A signed statement made under oath subject to penalties of perjury. Often used in connection with applications for *default judgment* in *collection lawsuits*. (Ch. Eight)

After-acquired property. Property acquired by a debtor that automatically becomes subject to a preexisting security interest (lien) of a creditor. See *floating lien* and *future advance*. (Ch. Five and Twenty-Three)

After notice and a hearing. A Code procedure requiring notice to parties in interest of the motion, objection or intended action, but requiring a hearing only if a party in interest requests one. (Ch. Thirteen)

Allowed claim. A creditor's claim that is acknowledged as being owed by the estate under §502. (Ch. Seventeen and Eighteen)

Alternative dispute resolution. Methods of resolving disputes outside of the litigation process (e.g., mediation or arbitration). (Ch. Two and Twelve)

Amortization. The process of calculating payments on an installment note so that each installment payment of principal and interest is equal despite the declining principal balance. (Ch. Three)

Ancillary proceeding. A bankruptcy case filed in a bankruptcy court in the United States that is related to the primary case filed in another country. Governed by new Chapter 15 of the Code. (Ch. Twelve)

Annual percentage rate (APR). The annualized rate of interest charged periodically (e.g., monthly) by lenders on the balance of a debt account such as a credit card balance. (Ch. Three)

Answer. The pleading a defendant must file to a *complaint* filed against him to avoid a *default judgment*. (Ch. Eight)

Antecedent debt. A debt that was existing prior to a transfer from the debtor in satisfaction of the debt. Relevant to *fraudulent transfer* law and a *preferential transfer* under §547 of the Code. (Ch. Nine and Seventeen)

Anti-Assignment Act. A federal statute (41 U.S.C. §15) prohibiting the *assignment* of a contract to which a federal agency is a party without the consent of the agency. (Ch. Two)

Appeal. The process of asking a court of appeals to review the final judgment entered in a trial court for error. (Ch. Ten and Thirteen)

Applicable commitment period. The required duration of a Chapter 13 plan, always running 3–5 years. Determined by the debtor's income as compared to the applicable *state median family income*. (Ch. Twenty)

Arbitration. A form of alternative dispute resolution in which the disputing parties agree that a third-person *arbitrator*, or panel of arbitrators, may hear the dispute informally and render an decision (arbitrator's award). May be binding or non-binding. (Ch. Eight, Nine, and Thirteen)

Arbitrator. One who arbitrates a dispute between others. (Ch. Eight, Nine, and Thirteen)

Article I courts. In the federal court system, courts created by Congress under Article I of the Constitution for some specialized legislative purpose involving resolution of disputes over public rights; do not enjoy plenary Article III powers; judges of these courts do not have lifetime tenure. See *Article III courts, private rights,* and *public rights.* (Ch. Thirteen)

Article III courts. In the federal court system, courts existing under Article III of the Constitution having plenary judicial powers to resolve disputes involving both public and private rights; judges of these courts have lifetime tenure. See *Article I courts, private rights,* and *public rights.* (Ch. Thirteen)

Artisan's lien. The right of one who performs work on the personal property of another to retain possession of the property as security for payment for the work done and to sell the property and apply the proceeds to the amount due. A common law lien in some states; statutory in others. (Ch. Six)

As a matter of law. Something that occurs automatically under existing law without either the consent of the parties involved or court judgment. (Ch. Two)

Asset buyers (or debt buyers). Persons who purchase delinquent or charged-off accounts from creditors for a fraction of the face value of the debt and then seek to collect it themselves or resell to another asset buyer. (Ch. Seven)

Asset protection (self-settled) trust. A trust permitted in a handful of states whereby the settlor can convey his own property into trust and name himself as the beneficiary to receive distributions of principal or interest as proscribed in the trust document, yet prevent his creditors from seizing trust assets not yet distributed. Previously available only as questionable foreign asset protection trusts or offshore trusts. (Ch. Ten)

Assignment. In contract law the transfer of rights under a contract from a party named in the contract to a third party. Often used to refer to the transfer of duties under the contract as well. See *delegation* and *nonassignment clause.* (Ch. Two and Twenty-Four)

Assignment for the benefit of creditors. A state law insolvency procedure involving the assignment of the debtor's property to a trustee empowered to liquidate the property and distribute the proceeds to creditors who are given notice and elect to participate. (Ch. Twelve)

Assumption of executory contract. The election of a bankrupt estate under the Code to assume responsibility for a prepetition *executory contract* such that it becomes the obligation of the estate. See *rejection (of contract).* (Ch. Twenty-Four)

Attachment. The creation of a security interest (lien) in favor of a creditor in property of the debtor. See *perfection.* (Ch. Four and Five)

Automatic perfection. The perfection of a security interest (lien) immediately upon its attachment. (Ch. Five)

Automatic stay. The prohibition on creditors continuing collection efforts against a debtor that arises automatically upon the debtor's filing of a bankruptcy petition per §362 of the Code; enforceable by the contempt powers of the bankruptcy court. Expires automatically on personal property 45 days following the first meeting of creditors in individual Chapter 7 cases unless the debtor *redeems* the property or *reaffirms* the debt. (Ch. Sixteen, Seventeen, and Twenty-Three)

Avoid. To cancel or negate; such as avoiding a lien to preserve an exemption or avoiding a preferential transfer. (Ch. Fifteen, Seventeen, and Twenty-One)

Avoidance power. 1. The trustee's powers under the Code to set aside certain pre-petition transfers of property of the estate. 2. The right of an individual debtor to set aside a lien in property of the estate to the extent it impairs an exemption in that property. See *preference, fraudulent transfer,* and *exempt property.* (Ch. Fifteen, Seventeen, Eighteen, and Twenty-One)

Bad debt. An uncollectible debt. May be written off as a loss. (Ch. Seven and Eight)

Badges of fraud. In the law of fraudulent transfer, certain recognized circumstances from which the inference may fairly be drawn that a transfer was made with intent to defraud creditors. (Ch. Nine and Seventeen)

Bailment. A legal arrangement in which the owner of personal property (bailor) turns possession of that property over to another (bailee), resulting in legal duties owed by the bailee to the bailor and possibly in lien rights in the property in favor of the bailee. (Ch. Six)

Balance sheet test. A test of *insolvency* whereby a debtor's liabilities exceed his assets. (Ch. Nine and Seventeen)

The Bankruptcy Abuse Prevention and Consumer Protection Act of 2005 (BAPCPA). The 2005 statute that amended the Code in numerous ways including introducing the means test for Chapter 7 filers. (Ch. Twelve, Thirteen, Fourteen, and Nineteen)

Bankruptcy Act. The predecessor of the current Bankruptcy Code. Enacted in 1898 and superseded in 1978. See *Bankruptcy Reform Act.* (Ch. Twelve)

Bankruptcy Appellate Panel (BAP). A court made up of bankruptcy judges appointed in some federal circuits to hear the appeal of rulings by other bankruptcy judges in lieu of the District Court. (Ch. Thirteen)

Bankruptcy petition preparer. One who prepares a bankruptcy petition for a fee and who is not an attorney or working under the supervision of an attorney. (Ch. Fifteen)

Bankruptcy referee. Office created under Bankruptcy Act of 1898. Predecessor to the modern bankruptcy judge. (Ch. Twelve and Thirteen)

Bankruptcy Reform Act. The 1978 statute that introduced the current Code. Also the name of the 1994 statute that amended the Code. (Ch. Twelve)

Best interests test. A test for confirmation of a plan of reorganization under Chapter 11 or 13 of the Code which requires a showing that unsecured creditors will receive at least as much under the plan as they would have received in a Chapter 7 liquidation. (Ch. Twenty-One and Twenty-Five)

Bifurcated claim. Description of the treatment of the bankruptcy claim of a secured creditor whose dollar claim exceeds the value of the collateral securing the claim. See *secured debt*. (Ch. Seventeen, Eighteen, and Twenty-One)

Body attachment. An abusive judgment collection tactic pursuant to which the judgment debtor is taken into custody for failure to appear at a postjudgment deposition and held until there is a court hearing or the debtor posts bond. (Ch. Eleven)

Bona fide purchaser for value. One who purchases property in good faith with no actual or constructive knowledge of a defect in title; takes good title to such property. (Ch. Eleven)

Budget and credit counseling agency. An entity approved by the U.S. Trustee to provide prepetition credit counseling or predischarge financial management services to consumer debtors. See *credit counseling agency*. (Ch. Fourteen, Fifteen, and Nineteen)

Bulk Sales Act. Article 6 of the *Uniform Commercial Code* providing a non-bankruptcy procedure for the sale of all or substantially all of the assets of a business outside the ordinary course of business. Repealed in most states. (Ch. Twelve)

Business bankruptcy case. A bankruptcy case in which the debtor is an entity or an individual with primarily business debts. (Ch. Twelve)

Business judgment rule. A rule applied by the bankruptcy court to a *trustee*'s decision to assume or reject an *executory contract* pursuant to which the court will not interfere with the trustee's decision if it was made in good faith and reflects reasonable business judgment. (Ch. Twenty-Four)

Car title loan. Loan in which consumer signs title to his vehicle over to the lender to secure a similar short term loan, often at a predatory rate of interest. (Ch. Three)

Case Management/Electronic Case Files (CM/ECF). The current system for filing documents with a bankruptcy court electronically. Access to case filings available through Public Access to Court Electronic Records (PACER). (Ch. Thirteen)

Cash collateral. Cash or *cash equivalents* that are part of the property of the estate and which are subject to a security interest in favor of a creditor. (Ch. Twenty-Three)

Cash equivalents. Instruments easily convertible to cash, such as checks or promissory notes. (Ch. Twenty-Three)

Chapter 13 plan. A plan proposed by a Chapter 13 debtor. (Ch. Twenty-One and Twenty-Two)

Chapter 20 case. Practitioner's term for a Chapter 13 bankruptcy case filed by a debtor within 4 years of receiving a discharge in a Chapter 7 case (7 + 13 = 20). (Ch. Nineteen)

Choice of law clause. Contract provision designating the law of a particular state to control disputes over the contract. (Ch. Three)

Chose in action. The right to sue on a claim arising under a contract or from a cause of action in tort. (Ch. Two and Five)

Claim. A right to payment that may be secured or unsecured, disputed or undisputed, fixed or contingent, liquidated or unliquidated. (Ch. Seventeen and Eighteen)

Claim bifurcation. The splitting of a claim in bankruptcy between its secured portion equal to the value of the property securing the claim and its unsecured portion. (Ch. Seventeen, Eighteen, and Twenty-One)

Claims bar date. The deadline set for creditors in a case to file proofs of claim. Claims not filed by the bar date may be disallowed or *subordinated* to other claims. (Ch. Seventeen)

Claims docket. A list of claims filed in a bankruptcy case. (Ch. Seventeen)

Classes (of claims or interests). Designated groupings of creditor claims or equity interests with members of each class receiving equal treatment. (Ch. Twenty-One and Twenty-Four)

Co-debtors. Two or more debtors liable for the same debt. Cf. *Joint case.* (Ch. Nineteen)

Co-debtor stay. The Chapter 13 rule that the automatic stay extends to co-debtors of the Chapter 13 debtor. (Ch. Nineteen)

Collateral. The property subject to a consensual or non-consensual security interest (lien). (Ch. Five)

Collateral mortgage obligation. A security instrument created for trading on world markets, the assets of which consist of bundled mortgages. (Ch. Four)

Collection lawsuit. A lawsuit to collect a preexisting debt. (Ch. Eight)

Commercial debt. Debt incurred for business or commercial purposes. Non-*consumer debt*. See *business bankruptcy case*. (Ch. One and Twelve)

Commercially reasonable manner. The standard governing the creditor's sale of repossessed property. What is commercially reasonable depends on the prevailing circumstances surrounding the sale and what is common or usual in the market for goods of that kind. (Ch. Five)

Complaint. 1. The pleading that initiates a civil suit to collect a debt. (Ch. Eight) 2. The pleading that initiates an adversary proceeding in a bankruptcy case per Rule 7003. (Ch. Sixteen)

Composition agreement. A contract made between a debtor and his creditors pursuant to which partial payment is made and accepted in full satisfaction of claims. See *extension agreement*. (Ch. Twelve)

Community property. A form of concurrent ownership between husband and wife in which each spouse is deemed to own an undivided one-half interest in property acquired during the marriage. See *concurrent ownership, joint tenancy, tenancy by the entireties,* and *tenancy in common.* (Ch. Ten)

Concurrent ownership. Ownership of property by two or more persons simultaneously. See *community property, joint tenancy, tenancy by the entireties,* and *tenancy in common.* (Ch. Ten)

Confession to judgment (cognovit or warrant of attorney). A debtor's waiver of the right to contest liability and authorization of the creditor to enter a consent judgment on his behalf. (Ch. Eight)

Confirmation. The court's formal approval of a plan of reorganization under Chapter 11, 12, or 13. See *confirmation hearing*. (Ch. Twenty-Two and Twenty-Five)

Confirmation hearing. The formal hearing conducted by a bankruptcy court to determine whether a proposed plan of reorganization under Chapter 11, 12 or 13 should be confirmed. See *confirmation*. (Ch. Twenty-Two and Twenty-Five)

Consensual lien. A security interest (lien) in property voluntarily granted by a debtor to a creditor in a contract such as a mortgage instrument or security agreement. (Ch. Four and Five)

Consent decree. A final judgment entered by agreement of the parties. (Ch. Nine)

Consolidation. The joining together of two or more bankruptcy cases involving interrelated debtors into one case for joint administration. (Ch. Twelve)

Constitutional jurisdiction. The issue of whether a bankruptcy court, as an Article 1 court, can enter final judgment in disputes traditionally within the province of Article 3 courts. (Ch. Thirteen)

Constructive fraud (presumed fraud). A means of finding fraud based on inference from circumstances rather than proof of actual intent. (Ch. Nine and Seventeen)

Constructive notice. Notice of an event (e.g., a sale) or circumstance (e.g., the identity of the owner of property) that is conclusively presumed from the act of properly filing or recording an appropriate document. To be distinguished from actual notice. (Ch. Five)

Constructive trust. An equitable remedy pursuant to which one who has wrongfully obtained title to or possession of property is deemed to hold that property in trust for the benefit of the true owner. (Ch. Six)

Consumer bankruptcy case. A bankruptcy case in which the debtor is an individual with primarily *consumer debts*. (Ch. Twelve)

Consumer debt. Debt incurred for personal, family or household purposes. (Ch. One, Five, Twelve, and Fourteen)

Consumer Financial Protection Bureau. Federal bureau created in 2010 and charged with developing regulations regarding consumer credit and loan transactions. (Ch. Three and Four)

Contemporaneous exchange for equivalent value. A transaction supported by adequate present consideration. (Ch. Seventeen)

Contempt. Power of a court to declare one subject to the court's order in violation of it. Enforceable by fines, penalties, and incarceration. See *automatic stay*. (Ch. Eleven and Sixteen)

Contested matter. A proceeding arising in a bankruptcy case that is initiated by motion or objection or statement of intent to act. Cf. *adversary proceeding*. (Ch. Sixteen)

Contingent claim. A claim the enforceability of which depends on the happening of an uncertain future event. Also called an unmatured claim. (Ch. Two)

Contract. A legally enforceable agreement. (Ch. Two)

Conversion. 1. The changing of a bankruptcy proceeding under one chapter of the Code to another (e.g., a Chapter 7 converted to a Chapter 13). (Ch. Fifteen and Twenty-Four) 2. The tort of taking or using another's property without consent. (Ch. Seven)

Core proceeding. A proceeding in a bankruptcy case involving the determination of rights under the Code or issues arising in a bankruptcy case as suggested by the list in 28 U.S.C. §157(2). Final orders may be entered by a bankruptcy court in a core proceeding. (Ch. Thirteen)

Co-signer. One who signs a promissory note as a form of security for the lender, making himself primarily liable for the debt of another. (Ch. Four and Nineteen)

Counterclaim. A claim for relief against the plaintiff brought by a defendant in a civil lawsuit. (Ch. Eight)

Cramdown (strip off or strip down). The right of a bankruptcy debtor to reduce the value of some secured claims to the present value of the security. (Ch. Four, Twenty-One, Twenty-Four, and Twenty-Five)

Cramdown confirmation. Confirmation of a Chapter 11 plan of reorganization over the objection of one or more classes. (Ch. Twenty-Five)

Credit-bidding. Also called bidding in, the practice of a creditor secured in property foreclosed on or repossessed bidding the amount owed at the foreclosure/repossession sale and receiving credit for the amount owed against the sales price. In bankruptcy, specifically authorized in 11 U.S.C. §363(k) when property of the estate is sold. (Ch. Four, Eighteen, and Twenty-Five)

Credit Card Accountability, Responsibility and Disclosure Act. Congressional act passed in 2009 imposing new restrictions on credit card issuers. (Chapter Three)

Credit card arrangements (charge card/debit card). A *revolving credit* arrangement where the card holder makes charges against the credit limit using a plastic card and a minimum balance payment is due each month. A variation is the charge card where the entire balance is due and payable each month. Another variation is the debit card where the lender makes an immediate withdrawal of funds from the debit card owner's bank account. (Ch. Three)

Credit counseling agency. A company that provides budget counseling and financial literacy services to debt-strapped individuals or businesses; may also negotiate a debt management plan with creditors of client. See *debt relief agencies* and *budget and credit counseling agency*. (Ch. Three, Fourteen, and Fifteen)

Credit history. The record of an individual's or business' history of paying debts on time. (Ch. Three)

Creditor. One to whom a debt is owed. (Ch. One)

Credit report. A compilation of the debt history and bill-paying record of a borrower. (Ch. Three)

Credit reporting agencies. Companies in the business of compiling credit reports and providing them to creditors and other authorized persons as allowed under the *Fair Credit Reporting Act*. (Ch. Three)

Creditor's bill. An equitable proceeding in which a creditor seeks permission to engage in postjudgment discovery of the debtor's assets, execution on the judgment having not succeeded. (Ch. Eleven)

Creditor's committee. A committee of creditors appointed by the U.S. Trustee in Chapter 11 cases and sometimes in Chapter 7 cases to represent the interests of all creditors. (Ch. Twenty-Three)

Cross-border case. A bankruptcy case involving debtors, assets and creditors in more than one country. Governed by new Chapter 15 of the Code. See *ancillary proceeding*. (Ch. Twelve)

Cross-collateralization. An arrangement whereby a creditor agrees to extend postpetition credit to a debtor in exchange for which property of the estate is pledged to secure both the postpetition and prepetition claims of the creditor. (Ch. Twenty-Four)

Cure. The payment of an arrearage to bring the defaulting party into compliance with its obligations under a contract. (Ch. Twenty-One, Twenty-Two, and Twenty-Four)

Current monthly income. The income of a consumer debtor calculated by averaging the debtor's income from all sources for the six months preceding the filing of the petition. (Ch. Fourteen and Twenty)

Custodian. A person authorized to have possession of a debtor's property for a specific purpose as in a trustee, receiver, or assignee for the benefit of creditors. (Ch. Seventeen)

Debt. Generally, an obligation to pay money. As defined by §101(12), liability on a claim. (Ch. One and Seventeen)

Debt collection companies. Private businesses involved in pre-litigation debt collection activities on behalf of creditors, usually for a percentage of what is collected. (Ch. Seven)

Debt collectors. Under the FDCPA businesses the principal purpose of which is to collect debts owed to consumers and individuals who regularly collect or attempt to collect such debt. (Ch. Seven)

Debt relief agency. Under the Code, one who provides any bankruptcy assistance to an assisted person in return for the payment of money or other valuable consideration. See *credit counseling agency*. (Ch. Fifteen)

Debtor. 1. A person liable for a debt. (Ch. One) 2. A person who files a petition under the Code. (Ch. Twelve)

Debtor in possession. The legal status given a debtor filing a Chapter 11 or 12 case. (Ch. Twenty-Two, Twenty-Four, and Twenty-Five)

Debtor/creditor law. The various laws relating to the rights and obligations existing between the person who owes a *debt,* the *debtor,* and the one to whom the debt is owed, the *creditor.* (Ch. One)

Declaration (or claim) of exemptions. The formal document required to be filed by a judgment debtor in some states in order to successfully exempt property from execution. See *exempt property.* (Ch. Eleven)

Deeming. Code process where certain determinations are deemed made unless a timely objection is filed (e.g., claims deemed allowed absent objection per §502(a)). (Ch. Seventeen and Twenty-Four)

Default judgment. A *final judgment* rendered against a defendant in a civil suit who fails to file an *answer* to the *complaint* or to otherwise defend. Initiated by filing an application for default judgment. (Ch. Eight)

Deficiency (judgment). The amount of a debt that remains owing after the property securing the debt has been liquidated. (Ch. Four and Five)

Delegation. In contract law the transfer of obligations under a contract from a party named in the contract to a third party. See *assignment* and *nonassignment clause.* (Ch. Two and Twenty-Four)

Discharge hearing. The formal hearing conducted by a bankruptcy court to determine whether a debtor is entitled to an order of discharge. See *discharge* and *hardship discharge.* (Ch. Eighteen, Twenty-Two, and Twenty-Five)

Discharge in bankruptcy. Permanent relief from debt pursuant to order of the bankruptcy court. See *non-dischargeable debt* and *exception to discharge.* (Ch. Seventeen, Twenty-Two, and Twenty-Five)

Disclosure statement. A detailed summary of the Chapter 11 debtor's financial and operational history and prospects sufficient to enable holders of claims and interests to make an informed judgment of a proposed plan of reorganization. (Chapter Twenty-Five)

Discovery (formal). 1. In a civil suit the right to submit interrogatories and document requests, take depositions, request a physical or mental examination of an opponent, or to request the opponent make admissions all pursuant to the rules of civil procedure. (Ch. Eight and Thirteen) 2. Also allowed postjudgment in aid of execution. (Ch. Eleven)

Discovery in aid of execution (postjudgment). The right of a judgment creditor to engage in discovery for the purpose of locating assets of the judgment debtor on which to execute. (Ch. Eleven)

Disposable income. 1. The income of a garnishee a statutory percentage of which is subject to garnishment. (Ch. Eleven) 2. The income that a bankruptcy debtor has available to pay creditors after deducting income necessary for the support or maintenance of the debtor and his dependents. (Ch. Fourteen and Twenty)

Distress sale. The sale of property in an emergency or time-pressured context as where a financially strapped debtor sells to raise cash to pay debts or where a secured creditor repossesses collateral and sells it quickly to compensate himself. (Ch. Five)

Distress warrant. See *warrant of distress*.

Distressed goods. Goods sold at a distress sale. (Ch. Five)

Document of title. A formal document evidencing ownership of property (e.g., title to an automobile, farm tractor, or boat). (Ch. Five)

Dodd-Frank Wall Street Reform and Consumer Protection Act of 2010 (the Dodd-Frank Act). Congressional act creating the Consumer Financial Protection Bureau. (Ch. Three and Four)

Domestic support obligation. An obligation to pay alimony, child support or maintenance. (Ch. Eighteen)

Dual tracking. The practice of proceeding with a mortgage foreclosure against a borrower while simultaneously processing the borrower's loan modification application. (Ch. Four)

Due on sale clause. A provision in a mortgage or security agreement providing that if the debtor sells the property pledged as security for repayment without the creditor's consent, a default has occurred and the entire amount due becomes immediately due and payable. (Ch. Four)

Due Process. Fundamental fairness mandated by the Fifth and Fourteenth Amendments to the U.S. Constitution. (Ch. Eight)

Election of remedies. The doctrine recognized in some states requiring a secured creditor to choose between exercising a right of foreclosure on secured property or suing the debtor for a judgment, but disallowing both foreclosure and a suit for deficiency judgment. (Ch. Four)

Electronic vehicle titling (E-Title). System for registering vehicles with the state electronically pursuant to which no paper title issued unless requested. (Ch. Five)

Entity. A corporation, limited liability company, or partnership; in contrast to a natural person. (Ch. Twelve)

Equitable lien (also called common law lien). A lien created by court rulings rather than by statute (e.g., vendor's lien). (Ch. Six and Twenty-One)

Equitable subordination. The inherent power of a bankruptcy court as a court of equity to order that a claim be subordinated to others of the same rank due to inequitable or dishonest conduct of the claimant. (Ch. Seventeen and Eighteen)

Equity. 1. An ownership interest in property unencumbered by any security interest or lien. Also called owner's equity. 2. The body of rules and principles developed historically by courts whereby they are authorizes to provide relief when remedies at law are inadequate. (Ch. Three, Six, Seventeen, Eighteen, and Twenty-One)

Equity of redemption. A mortgagor's right to prevent the sale of real property in foreclosure by paying the entire indebtedness owed prior to the foreclosure sale (see *redemption*). (Ch. Four)

Equity security holder. The holder of an ownership interest in an entity debtor (e.g., shareholder in a corporation, member of a limited liability company or partner in a partnership). (Ch. Twenty-Three)

Escrow account. An account established by a lender in which payments by the borrower are placed until it is time to pay certain obligations such as property taxes or insurance. (Ch. Three)

Estate. 1. All of the property in which a person owns an interest. 2. The estate created by filing a bankruptcy petition per §541. (Ch. Seventeen)

Evidentiary hearing. A court hearing at which sworn testimony is taken and exhibits may be offered. Governed by the Federal Rules of Evidence. (Ch. Sixteen)

Ex parte. An appearance before a court seeking relief without notice to other parties. (Ch. Nine, Thirteen, Sixteen, and Twenty-Three)

Examiner. A person appointed by a bankruptcy court to investigate specific aspects of a Chapter 11 debtor's conduct or management of the estate. (Ch. Twenty-Three)

Exception to discharge. A debt that is not discharged in bankruptcy per §523. (Ch. Eighteen)

Exclusivity period. The period of time in which a Chapter 11 debtor has the exclusive right to propose a plan of reorganization. (Ch. Twenty-Five)

Execution. The satisfaction of a final judgment by the seizure and sale of non-exempt property of the debtor. (Ch. Ten)

Execution grace period. The period of time between entry of a final judgment and the date on which the judgment creditor can begin execution on the judgment. (Ch. Ten)

Execution lien. The claim to property of a debtor on which a judgment creditor has executed (levied). (Ch. Ten)

Executory contract. A contract that has not been fully performed by either party to it. (Ch. Sixteen and Twenty-Four)

Exempt property. 1. Property of a debtor that cannot be seized by a judgment creditor. (Ch. Ten and Eleven) 2. Property of a debtor in bankruptcy that the debtor is allowed to keep and that cannot be made available to his creditors. See *declaration of exemptions* and *wild card exemption*. (Ch. Fifteen, Sixteen, Seventeen, and Eighteen)

Extension agreement. An agreement made by a debtor with his creditors whereby the creditors consent to an extension of time for the debtor to pay. Often reached in conjunction with a *composition agreement*. (Ch. Twelve)

Fair and Accurate Transactions Act of 2003 (FATA). Amended the FCRA to allow consumers to obtain a free copy of their credit report once every 12 months from each of the three national consumer credit reporting companies (Equifax, Experian, and TransUnion). (Ch. Three)

Fair and equitable. A test for cramdown confirmation of a Chapter 11 plan requiring a showing that all classes and claims are treated in a fair and equitable manner. (Ch. Twenty-Five)

Fair Credit Reporting Act (FCRA), 15 U.S.C. §1681, et seq. Federal statute regulating credit reporting agencies and the contents of credit reports, access to them, use of them and correction of errors in them. (Ch. Three)

Fair Debt Collection Practices Act (FDCPA), 15 USC §1601, et seq. Federal statute regulating *debt collectors*. (Ch. Seven)

Fair market value. The estimated price that a willing buyer would pay to a willing seller for the item, neither being under a compulsion to sell and both having reasonable knowledge of the underlying facts. (Ch. Nine, Fifteen, and Seventeen)

Family farmer. A debtor engaged in farming operations and who otherwise meets the requirements to be a debtor under Chapter 12. (Ch. Twelve and Twenty-Two)

Family fisherman. A debtor engaged in a commercial fishing operation and who otherwise meets the requirements to be a debtor under Chapter 12. (Ch. Twelve and Twenty-Two)

Feasibility test. A test for confirmation of a plan of reorganization requiring a showing that the debtor has a reasonable prospect of completing the plan. (Ch. Twenty-Two and Twenty-Five)

Federal Arbitration Act, 9 U.S.C. §1, et. seq. Federal statute governing arbitration in cases affecting interstate commerce or maritime issues. (Ch. Nine and Thirteen)

Federal Rules of Bankruptcy Procedure. The formal rules supplementing the Code and governing proceedings in bankruptcy cases. (Ch. Twelve)

FICO score. A popular credit scoring model developed by Fair Isaac Corporation. (Ch. Three)

Fiduciary capacity (duty). Description of one providing services for another that include a high duty of loyalty, confidentiality, and trust. (Ch. Eighteen)

Fieri facias. See *writ of execution.*

Final judgment. An order or decree entered by a court finally resolving the issues before it. (Ch. Nine)

Financial Fraud Enforcement Task Force. Department of Justice task force created in 2009 to combine resources of 20 federal agencies and work in partnership with state and local agencies to identify, investigate, and prosecute all sorts of financial crimes. (Ch. Four)

Financing statement. A document filed in a designated public office to perfect a security interest in personal property under Article 9 of the UCC. Also called a UCC-1. (Ch. Five and Seventeen)

First day orders. Practitioner's phrase for orders commonly sought immediately upon filing of a Chapter 11 case. (Ch. Twenty-Three)

First meeting of creditors. The meeting of creditors of a bankrupt debtor required by §341 of the Code called by the U.S. Trustee. The debtor may be questioned under oath at the meeting. (Ch. Sixteen)

Floating lien. A security interest (lien) that attaches automatically to property of the debtor acquired after the date the security interest was created. See *after-acquired property* and *future advance.* (Ch. Five and Twenty-Three)

Foreclosure. The process by which the holder of a mortgage in real property takes possession of the property following default by the mortgagor. The property is normally sold and the proceeds applied to the costs of foreclosure and underlying debt. In some cases the property is retained in satisfaction of the debt. A foreclosure may be consensual (power of sale foreclosure) or judicial (court ordered). (Ch. Four and Twenty-One)

Foreign judgment. A final judgment entered in a state other than the state in which it is enforced. See *Uniform Enforcement of Foreign Judgment Act.* (Ch. Eleven)

Fraudulent transfer (or conveyance). A transfer of property by a debtor with actual or constructive intent to defraud his creditors by delaying or hindering their collection efforts. (Ch. Nine and Seventeen)

Fresh start (clean slate). The opportunity provided to a debtor following a discharge in bankruptcy. (Ch. Twelve and Eighteen)

Future advance. A loan or credit extended to a debtor that is subject to a previously created security interest in property of the debtor. (Ch. Five)

Gap period. The Code's description of the period of time between the filing of an involuntary petition and the entry of an order for relief or appointment of a trustee. Claims arising in the gap period are gap claims and have a certain priority under Section 507. (Ch. Eighteen)

Garnishment. A method of executing on a final judgment pursuant to which property of the debtor in the hands of a third person or a debt owed by a third person to the debtor is levied on. (Ch. Nine)

Good faith. Generally, honesty in fact and compliance with the letter and spirit of the Code. (Ch. Sixteen, Twenty-Two, and Twenty-Five)

Grace period. The time between the date a final judgment is entered and the date execution on the judgment can begin. (Ch. Ten)

Guarantor. One who guarantees the debt of another. The guarantor is *secondarily liable* for the debt. (Ch. Four and Nineteen)

Hardship discharge. An early discharge granted at the discretion of the judge in a Chapter 13 or Chapter 11 case. See *discharge*. (Ch. Twenty-Two and Twenty-Five)

Health Care and Education Reconciliation Act of 2010. Federal law establishing the Department of Education's Direct Loan Program for student loans and that program's Income-Based Repayment Program. (Ch. Eighteen and Twenty-Two)

Home equity loan. A loan in which the borrower pledges the *equity* in his home as security for repayment. (Ch. Three)

Homestead exemption. The exemption available to a debtor to protect the equity in his primary residence. (Ch. Ten and Fifteen)

Impaired (class or claims). A class created in a Chapter 11 or Chapter 9 plan whose claims are not to be paid according to their contractual terms. (Ch. Twenty-Five)

Impleader action. A civil lawsuit in which one holding funds that more than one party may be entitled to pays the funds into court and asks the court to designate the appropriate payee. (Ch. Four)

Individual. A natural person, in contrast to an entity. (Ch. Twelve, Fourteen, and Nineteen)

Injunction. A court order directing a party to do or to cease doing something on pain of contempt. (Ch. Three and Nine)

Insider. A person in close relationship with a debtor such that he may be assumed to have superior access to information and be subject to special treatment. Includes relatives of an individual debtor and owners, officers and directors of entity debtors. (Ch. Seventeen and Twenty-Five)

Insolvency. The inability to pay debts as they come due (the *equity test*) or the state of having total liabilities in excess of total assets (the *balance sheet test*). (Ch. Nine and Seventeen)

Installment note (payments). A promissory note calling for payment of the amount owed in periodic (e.g., monthly, quarterly, annually) payments. (Ch. Three)

Intentional fraud. To act (as in the transfer of property) with the actual intent to defraud a creditor. See *badges of fraud* and *constructive fraud*. (Ch. Nine and Seventeen)

Interest. The cost of using another person's money or property. Usually assessed at a percentage of the amount borrowed *per annum*. The interest rate over the term of the loan may be fixed or variable. (Ch. Two, Three, Seventeen, and Twenty-Four)

Interim trustee. A bankruptcy trustee appointed following the order for relief who serves until a permanent trustee is appointed or elected at the first meeting of creditors. (Ch. Sixteen)

Involuntary case petition. A Chapter 7 or 11 case initiated by the creditors of the debtor. (Ch. Fifteen)

Ipso facto clause. A provision in a contract declaring the filing of bankruptcy to be an act of default. (Ch. Twenty-Four)

Joint administration. Where two or more related bankruptcy cases are ordered to be administered by the same trustee to save administrative costs. (Ch. Fifteen)

Joint case (debtors). A single bankruptcy case filed by a married couple. (Ch. Fifteen and Nineteen)

Joint tenancy. A form of joint ownership of property that includes a right of survivorship. (Ch. Ten)

Judgment debtor/creditor. Once a final judgment is entered by a court awarding a money judgment to one party, the party to whom the judgment is awarded is the judgment creditor and the one against whom it is awarded is the judgment debtor. (Ch. Two)

Judgment lien. A judicial lien created on all real property owned by a judgment debtor in the county where the final judgment is recorded or docketed. In some states the lien attaches to personal property of the debtor as well when the judgment is recorded as is a UCC financing statement. (Ch. Nine)

Judgment proof. Condition of a debtor who has no assets that might be seized to satisfy a final judgment. (Ch. Eight)

Judicial lien. Lien obtained by court action, whether judgment, levy, sequestration, or other legal or equitable process or proceeding. (Ch. Eleven and Fifteen)

Judicial lien creditor. Priority status of a creditor in property that has been seized pursuant to a writ of execution to satisfy a judgment in favor of that creditor. (Ch. Fifteen and Twenty-One)

Judicial repossession. A post-default process by which a secured creditor obtains possession of collateral or forecloses on a mortgage by a court order. (Ch. Four and Five)

Jurisdiction. In general, the power of a court to hear and decide a particular case. (Ch. Ten and Thirteen)

Legislative courts. See *Article 1 courts*.

Lender liability. Legal liability of a lender for damages to a borrower arising out of claims for breach of contract, fraud, or breach of fiduciary duty. (Ch. Three)

Levy. Seizing or taking control of a debtor's property pursuant to a lien or writ of execution. (Ch. Six and Eleven)

Liability lawsuit. A civil lawsuit based on claim of liability based on tortious or other wrongful conduct. (Ch. Eight)

Lien. Generally, another word for a security interest. Sometimes used narrowly to refer only to non-consensual secured claims created by law or court order, e.g., mechanic's lien, artisan's lien, judicial lien. (Ch. Four through Six and Fourteen through Twenty-Five)

Lien of levy. The lien existing in favor of a judgment creditor against the property of the judgment debtor seized pursuant to a writ of execution. The judgment creditor then has the status of a *judicial lien* creditor as to such property. (Ch. Eleven)

Lien stripping (or strip down or write down or strip off). Procedure attempted by debtor to reduce lien on property to value of secured claim and retain property with ride through. See *ride through*. (Ch. Eighteen and Twenty-One)

Lienholder/Lienor. The one who holds a lien. (Ch. Six)

Line of credit. A loan in which the borrowed funds are not immediately advanced to the borrower but are put at the disposal of the borrower to draw down on as needed. (Ch. Three)

Liquidated claim (debt). A claim that has been reduced to a dollar amount. See *unliquidated claim*. (Ch. Two)

Liquidated value. The dollar value of property resulting from a forced sale. See *present value*. (Ch. Seventeen)

Liquidation. The sale or other disposition of a debtor's nonexempt assets for the purpose of distribution to his creditors in exchange for a discharge of most unpaid debts. Chapter 7 is a liquidation proceeding. (Ch. Twelve and Fourteen)

***Lis pendens* (L. suit pending).** Public notice that a lawsuit is pending regarding title, possession or other rights to real property. Given by filing or recording notice of pendency in land records for county where the property at issue lies. Understood to create a lien on the realty that will act as a cloud on title until removed. (Ch. Six)

Loan agreement. The contract setting forth the terms of a loan transaction. (Ch. Three)

Loan closing. The meeting at which a loan transaction is finalized. (Ch. Three)

Loan commitment. The lender's statement that the loan is approved and will be issued if and when the rest of the transaction is completed. (Ch. Three)

Local custom and practice. The unwritten way things are done in a particular court. (Ch. Twelve and Sixteen)

Local rules. Supplemental rules of procedure and practice that prevail in a particular court. (Ch. Twelve, Sixteen, and Twenty-Three)

Luxury goods or services. Undefined phrase but includes goods or services not reasonably necessary for the maintenance or support of the debtor or a dependent. Purchases of same within 90 days preceding the petition are presumed fraudulent and non-dischargeable. Presumption rebuttable. (Ch. Eighteen)

Marshalling of assets. Requirement that a judgment creditor executing on property of the judgment debtor seize and exhaust property in a certain order, e.g., all nonexempt personalty before nonexempt realty. (Ch. Eleven)

Materialman's lien. A statutory lien on realty available to a party who has supplied materials for the improvement of the realty. Sometimes called a construction lien. See *mechanic's lien*. (Ch. Six)

Means test. A test for Chapter 7 filers introduced by BAPCPA intended to determine whether the debtor has sufficient *disposable income* to enable the debtor to repay some or all of his debts in a Chapter 13 case. Test raises *presumption of abuse* when debtor's current monthly income exceeds the applicable state *median family income*. Unless rebutted, presumption of abuse mandates dismissal or conversion of case to Chapter 13. (Ch. Fourteen and Twenty)

Mechanic's lien. A statutory lien on realty available to a party who has supplied services or labor for the improvement of the realty. Sometimes called a construction lien. See *materialman's lien*. (Ch. Six)

Median family income. State by state statistics compiled by the U.S. Census Bureau every ten years when a constitutionally mandated census is taken and set out by family size. (Ch. Fourteen and Twenty-One)

Mediation. A form of *alternative dispute resolution* in which an impartial person serving as *mediator* uses back and forth dialogue with the disputing parties to assist them in reaching a settlement. (Ch. Eight and Nine)

Mediator. One who conducts a mediation between disputing parties. (Ch. Eight and Nine)

Miller Act. Federal statute requiring contractors performing public work projects to provide a performance bond guaranteeing the faithful performance of the job and payment of all labor and materials obligations associated with the project. (Ch. Six)

Mortgage. The pledging of liquidation of real property as security for a debt. Created by execution of a document called a mortgage, deed of trust, or security deed. (Ch. Four)

***Ne exeat* (L. let him not go).** A prejudgment writ preventing a party from leaving the court's jurisdiction. Also called a writ of arrest. (Ch. Nine)

Necessity doctrine. The court-made rule that a Chapter 11 debtor may pay certain prepetition debts to critical vendors or essential employees if necessary for the business to survive. (Ch. Twenty-Three)

Negative amortization (NegAm). In an installment contract, the practice of making payments consisting of no principal and less interest than has accrued, resulting in the unpaid interest being added to the principal balance owed notwithstanding the payment. (Ch. Four)

New value exception. An exception to the absolute priority rule in a Chapter 11 case enabling holders of equity interests in a bankrupt debtor to retain their interests even though senior claim holders will not be paid in full. Equity holders must contribute new capital to the debtor at least equal to the value of their interest. (Ch. Twenty-Five)

No-asset case. A Chapter 7 liquidation case in which there are no assets available for distribution to creditors. (Ch. Seventeen and Eighteen)

Nonassignment clause. A provision in a contract that prohibits one or both parties from assigning the contract to a third party. (Ch. Two and Twenty-Four)

Nonattorney bankruptcy petition preparer. Nonattorneys who assists a debtor in preparing petition and schedules for bankruptcy filing. (Ch. Fifteen)

Noncontingent claim. A claim that is not subject to any future contingency. Also called a matured claim. (Ch. Two)

Noncore proceedings. Disputes governed by non-bankruptcy law the outcome of which may affect the administration of a bankruptcy estate. Such disputes fall within the nonexclusive jurisdiction of the bankruptcy court and no final order may be entered on them by the bankruptcy court without the consent of all parties. Absent that consent, such matters are heard by the district court. (Ch. Thirteen)

Non-dischargeable debt. A debt excluded from discharge under §523. (Ch. Eighteen and Twenty-Two)

Nonrecourse secured note. A secured debt for which the debtor has no liability beyond the value of the property securing the debt. No deficiency judgment may be brought after foreclosure or repossession. (Ch. Four)

Notice. Actual or constructive awareness of a fact or event. Often required by statute to be given in writing and/or filed or recorded in a public office (e.g., notice of abstract of lien or notice of intent to levy). (Ch. Six)

Notice and a hearing. Code procedure requiring notice of motion, objection or intended action be given to parties in interest, but requiring a hearing only if a party in interests contests or objects. (Ch. Thirteen)

Notice of intended action. Procedure authorized under the Code for giving parties in interest notice of the intent to take some action (e.g., intent to abandon property). Often joined with notice and a hearing procedure. (Ch. Thirteen)

Novation. The agreement of a creditor to release one debtor from a contract and to look instead to a substituted debtor. (Ch. Two)

***Nulla bona* (L. No goods).** Return made by sheriff on writ of execution when no executable property is found. (Ch. Eleven)

Operating reports. Periodic reports (usually monthly) of business activity required of a debtor in possession in Chapter 11 or 12 cases and of a trustee operating a business as part of a Chapter 7 liquidation. (Ch. Twenty-Three)

Order for relief. The formal beginning of a bankruptcy case. 1. In most districts the filing of a voluntary petition constitutes the order for relief; in others a formal order approving the filing of a voluntary petition. 2. A formal order that is always entered approving the filing of an involuntary petition. (Ch. Sixteen)

Ordinary course of business. In general, following the typical usual practices engaged in by a business. (Ch. Seventeen and Twenty-Four)

Overdraft. The circumstances created when the owner of a checking account authorizes the payment of more funds from his account than he has on deposit in the account. (Ch. Three)

Oversecured debt. A secured debt where the value of the collateral exceeds the amount owed. (Ch. Seventeen and Twenty-One)

Owner's equity. See *equity*.

Partition action. A lawsuit asking a court to segregate or divide the undivided ownership interest of one concurrent owner of property so it can be seized by that owner's creditors. (Ch. Ten)

Party in interest. An important but undefined term in the Code, interpreted generally to refer to any person or entity having a stake in the outcome of a matter arising in a bankruptcy case (e.g., debtor, bankruptcy trustee, U.S. trustee, creditors, and equity security holders). (Ch. Twelve, Thirteen, Fifteen, Sixteen, Nineteen, and Twenty-Three)

Pawn shop loan. A short-term loan taken by a consumer who pledges some kind of personal property as security for repayment and gives pawn lender possession. Loan is made in an amount equal to a reduced value of the property pledged (usually 30–50%) and entitles lender to sell the property for full value if loan is not paid by due date. (Ch. Three)

Payday loan. Variously also called cash advance, check advance, post-dated check loan, deferred deposit check loan or deferred presentment loan; a high interest, short-term loan in which the borrower typically gives the lender a post-dated check for the amount borrowed plus interest and fees. If the amount borrowed is not repaid by the date of the check, the lender will cash it in payment. See *car title loan*. (Ch. Three)

Per annum. Per year. See *interest*. (Ch. Three)

Perfection. Making a security interest in property enforceable against and superior to the rights of other creditors to the property. Normally accomplished by filing or recording required documents in a designated public office or by taking possession of the property. (Ch. Four, Five, and Seventeen)

Personal defenses. A defense to liability unique to the circumstances of the principal debtor and which do not go to the merits of the underlying transaction such as discharge in bankruptcy or lack of capacity due to age or disability. Sureties and guarantors cannot successfully assert personal defenses of the principal debtor as a defense. (Ch. Five)

Personal jurisdiction. The *due process* requirement that a defendant have sufficient minimum contacts with a forum to enable a court in that forum to enter a final order binding on a named defendant. (Ch. Eleven and Thirteen)

Petition. The document filed to initiate a bankruptcy case under the Code. (Ch. Fifteen, Nineteen, and Twenty-Three)

Plan of reorganization. A plan proposed under Chapter 11. Cf. *Chapter 13 plan*. (Ch. Twenty-One, Twenty-Four, and Twenty-five)

Police powers. The authority of state and local governments to regulate behavior and enforce order within their jurisdictions to protect public health, welfare, safety, and morality. (Ch. Five)

Possessory liens. Types statutory or equitable liens that attach to property in the possession of the lien holder (e.g., artisan's lien). Some liens are *nonpossessory* (e.g., *mechanic's* and *materialman's liens; lien lis pendens*). (Ch. Six)

Postjudgment asset discovery. The right of a judgment creditor to discover assets of a judgment debtor subject to execution following entry of the final judgment using interrogatories, document requests, and depositions. (Ch. Eleven)

Postjudgment interest. Statutory interest that runs on a final judgment from the date entered until paid is postjudgment interest. (Ch. Nine)

Postjudgment motions. Motions the losing party may file in the trial court seeking to invalidate or amend a final judgment or a new trial. (Ch. Ten)

Postpetition interest. Interest accruing on claims after debtor files a petition in bankruptcy. (Ch. Seventeen, Twenty-One, and Twenty-Four)

Prayer for relief. The part of a civil *complaint* that states the relief sought from the court. (Ch. Eight)

Preferential transfer. A payment or other transfer of an interest in the debtor's property that results in the creditor receiving the payment or transfer being unfairly advantaged compared to other creditors. May be avoidable pursuant to §547. (Ch. Seventeen)

Prejudgment interest. Interest on an amount owed calculated from due date through date of judgment. Within the trial court's discretion to award. (Ch. Nine)

Prejudgment remedy. Extraordinary relief available to plaintiffs during a civil lawsuit to prevent removal, loss or dissipation of the defendant's property pending final judgment and execution. (Ch. Nine)

Prepackaged Chapter 11. A Chapter 11 proceeding in which the plan of reorganization has been drafted and informally approved by creditors prepetition. (Ch. Twenty-Three)

Prepetition credit counseling. Counseling that an individual debtor must receive from an approved *credit counseling agency* as a qualification for filing for bankruptcy relief. (Ch. Fourteen)

Present value. Calculation of the current value of property for purposes of determining the value of a secured claim in bankruptcy. Normally based on replacement cost of the property considering its age and condition. (Ch. Seventeen, Eighteen, Twenty-One, and Twenty-Five)

Presumption of abuse. The presumption of inappropriate filing of a Chapter 7 case for the debtor who fails the *means test*. The presumption, once raised, must be rebutted by showing *special circumstances* or the case will be dismissed or converted to a case under Chapter 13. (Ch. Fourteen)

Primarily/secondarily liable. One who is primarily liable for the debt of another is liable without regard to whether the lender pursues collection from the other first (e.g., a *co-signer* or *surety*). One who is secondarily liable for the debt of another is liable only if the lender first pursues collection from the other (e.g., a *guarantor*). (Ch. Four)

Prime rate. The interest rate that commercial banks charge their best customers. (Ch. Three and Twenty-One)

Priming lien. A senior security interest granted to a creditor as an inducement to provide postpetition loan or credit to a Chapter 11 debtor and which is superior to a prepetition interest in the same property. (Ch. Twenty-Four)

Priority. 1. The ranking of security interests (liens) in the same property. 2. The ranking of approved claims in a bankruptcy case in the order in which they will be paid. (Ch. Eighteen)

Priority claim. An unsecured claim entitled to a certain order of preferment and payment under §507. (Ch. Eighteen)

Private right of action. The right granted by a regulatory statute for the injured party to being a civil lawsuit for damages apart from governmental regulatory action. (Ch. Seven)

Private rights. Rights existing between private parties arising from state law (e.g., contract and tort law). See *Article I courts*, *Article III courts*, and *public rights*. (Ch. Thirteen)

Proceeds. Money or property received in exchange for an asset. (Ch. Five)

Professional. A person retained by the estate with the permission of the bankruptcy court to provide services for estate administration (e.g., appraiser, surveyor, realtor, auctioneer, accountant, or attorney). (Ch. Seventeen)

Promissory note. A contract containing an enforceable promise by one person (the maker or payor) to pay another person (the payee) a certain sum of money, the principal. The note may be payable installments (an installment note) or in full on a fixed date in the future (a balloon note). The note may be secured by property of the debtor or unsecured. (Ch. Three)

Proof of claim. The writing that a creditor submits as evidence of its claim against the estate. (Ch. Seventeen)

Property of the estate. All property in which the debtor holds a legal or equitable interest at the commencement of a bankruptcy case per §541. In a Chapter 13 case, property acquired by the debtor postpetition is included as well per §1306. (Ch. Seventeen, Nineteen, and Twenty-Four)

Public Access to Court Electronic Records (PACER). See *Case Management/Electronic Case Files*. (Ch. Thirteen)

Public rights. Rights arising between parties as a result of specific government regulation. See *Article I courts*, *Article III courts*, and *private rights*. (Ch. Thirteen)

Punitive damages. Damages intended to punish the wrongdoer in order to deter similar conduct in the future. (Ch. Three and Sixteen)

Purchase money mortgage. A mortgage held by the seller rather than a third-party lender. A form of self-financing by seller. (Ch. Four)

Purchase money security interest (PMSI). A security interest in personal property created by loaning or extending credit to a debtor for the express purpose of purchasing the property. When the property is consumer goods, the PMSI is automatically perfected. (Ch. Five, Seventeen, Eighteen, and Twenty-One)

Reaffirmation agreement. The bankruptcy debtor's agreement with a creditor to pay the creditor a debt that could have been discharged in bankruptcy. (Ch. Eighteen)

Reasonably equivalent value. Its absence is one of the tests to see if a transfer of property is constructively fraudulent as to creditors of the transferor under the Uniform Fraudulent Transfer Act and under §548 of the Code. Determined primarily by fair market value of the property at the time of the transfer. (Ch. Nine and Seventeen)

Receivership. Proceeding in which a person is appointed to take control of a debtor's property and manage it under court supervision. (Ch. Twelve)

Recording statute. The state law controlling how mortgages are perfected thus determining the priority among mortgages or liens on the property. States have variously, race-notice, pure notice or pure race recording statutes. (Ch. Four)

Redemption. 1. In non-bankruptcy law, a debtor's right to buy back property that has been repossessed or foreclosed on. Not available in all states. See *equity of redemption*. (Ch. Four and Five) 2. The right of a Chapter 7 *individual consumer debtor* under §722 of the Code to buy back *consumer property* that has either been claimed as *exempt* by the debtor or abandoned by the trustee by paying the creditor holding a *dischargeable debt* secured by that property *present value* of the property. (Ch. Eighteen)

Referral jurisdiction. A description of the subject matter jurisdiction of U.S. bankruptcy courts, which depends on referral from the U.S. district courts. (Ch. Thirteen)

Regular income. Income from any legal source, earned or unearned, sufficient to make performance of a Chapter 13 plan feasible. (Ch. Nineteen and Twenty)

Rejection (of contract). The bankruptcy estate's optional repudiation of an executory contract with the result that the debtor has no remaining obligations under it and the other party has an unsecured claim for prepetition obligations. (Ch. Twenty-Four)

Related proceedings. See *noncore proceedings.*

Relation-back. The retrospective effect given to some liens giving them priority from a date prior to their perfection. (Ch. Six)

Removal (jurisdiction). The transfer of bankruptcy proceedings from the U.S. district court to the bankruptcy court. (Ch. Thirteen)

Rent-to-own agreement. A contract in which the buyer leases the property until the final payment at which time the seller/lessee conveys title to him. (Ch. Three)

Reorganization proceeding. The rearrangement of a debtor's finances under a court-approved plan as an alternative to liquidation. Cases under Chapters 11, 12, and 13 are reorganization proceedings. Cf. *liquidation* and *straight bankruptcy.* (Ch. Twelve, Nineteen, and Twenty-Three)

Replevin. A civil action for the recovery or provisional possession of specific personal property. (Ch. Nine)

Revolving credit. A credit arrangement whereby funds are borrowed only when the borrower chooses up to the limits of the approved credit limits. (Ch. Three)

Ride through (or pay through or pay and ride). Where a debtor retains possession of pledged collateral through a bankruptcy case by continuing to make payments to the secured creditor. (Ch. Eighteen, Twenty-One, and Twenty-Five)

Right to redeem. See *redemption.*

Rule 2004 examination. The examination under oath as in a deposition of any person in connection with any matter related to a bankruptcy case. (Ch. Sixteen)

Safe harbor provision. A provision in a statute or regulation that exempts a person from liability for certain conduct. (Ch. Three and Sixteen)

Sale free and clear of liens. The sale of property of the estate that is subject to a secured claim to enable the bankruptcy estate to realize the equity in the property in excess of that claim. Per §363, the sale may be authorized over the creditor's objection. (Ch. Eighteen, Twenty-One, and Twenty-Five)

Secured debt (secured claim/secured creditor). A debt the payment of which is secured by real or personal property giving the secured creditor recourse against the property in the event of a default. See *bifurcated claim* and *unsecured debt.* (Ch. Four, Five, Seventeen, Eighteen, and Twenty-One)

Security agreement. A contract creating a security interest. (Ch. Five)

Security interest. A property interest granted by a debtor to a creditor in property of the debtor authorizing the creditor to seize and sell the pledged property to satisfy the debt obligation in the event of a default. (Ch. Three, Four, and Five)

Self-help repossession. The right of a secured creditor granted under a security agreement or mortgage instrument to repossess collateral or foreclose on a mortgage without a court order. See *judicial repossession*. (Ch. Four and Five)

Separation of powers. The constitutional doctrine forbidding any one of the three branches of government from assuming powers granted by the Constitution to another branch. See *constitutional jurisdiction*. (Ch. Thirteen)

Sequestration. See *attachment*.

Setoff. The principle that when two people owe each other a debt, the debts may cancel each other out except to the extent one debt exceeds the other. (Ch. Seventeen)

Sheriff's sale. The sale by public auction or private sale of property of a debtor levied on pursuant to a writ of execution. (Ch. Eleven)

Single asset real estate debtor. A Chapter 11 debtor whose primary business is the operation of a single piece of income producing property and which derives substantially all of its income from that property. (Ch. Twenty-Three)

Slow pay motion. A motion made by a judgment debtor seeking court permission to pay a judgment in installments less than the amount that would be withheld by a lawful garnishment. (Ch. Eleven)

Small business debtor. A Chapter 11 debtor engaged in commercial or business activities which has aggregate non-contingent liquidated debts not exceeding $2 million and who elects to have its case treated as a small business case for expedited administration. (Ch. Twenty-Three)

Special circumstances. Unique financial circumstances of a Chapter 7 debtor involving additional expenses or adjustments of *current monthly income* for which there is no reasonable alternative which may be sufficient to rebut the *presumption of abuse*. (Ch. Fourteen)

Spendthrift trust. A trust arrangement that prohibits alienation of trust property the effect of which is to protect the property from dissipation by the beneficiary or seizure by creditors of the beneficiary. (Ch. Ten and Seventeen)

Standard of review. The standard utilized by higher courts in reviewing decisions of the bankruptcy court; normally such decision will not be revered unless clearly erroneous. (Ch. Thirteen)

Standing trustee. A person appointed by the U.S. Trustee to serve as trustee in all Chapter 12 and 13 cases filed in the district. Cf. *trustee panel*. (Ch. Nineteen)

Statement of intent. Form required of individual debtor in bankruptcy indicating debtor's intent to surrender property pledged as collateral, redeem it, or to reaffirm underlying debt secured by such property. (Ch. Fifteen, Sixteen, and Eighteen)

Statutes of limitation. Statutory time limitations placed on the right to bring a lawsuit. (Ch. Eight and Seventeen)

Statutory lien. A lien created by statute rather than by contract or court order. (Ch. Six and Seventeen)

Stay. See *automatic stay, co-debtor stay,* and *stay bond.*

Stay (supersedeas or appeal) bond. A bond in the form of cash, property or surety contract sufficient to cover the amount of a judgment plus accrued interests during the appeal posted by a party seeking to stay execution as a condition to obtaining such stay. (Ch. Ten)

Stay of execution. A halt or freeze on the judgment creditor's right to execute on a final judgment. (Ch. Ten)

Straight bankruptcy. A Chapter 7 liquidation proceeding. (Ch. Twelve and Fourteen)

Strip off/strip down/write down. The act of reducing the balance owed to a secured creditor to the value or equity available to the creditor in the collateral securing the debt, including stripping off the lien entirely where there is no equity for the creditor in the property. See *cramdown.* (Ch. Eighteen and Twenty-One)

Strong-arm clause. Practitioner's phrase for the trustee's avoidance powers under §544 of the Code. (Ch. Seventeen)

Sub rosa **(L. under the rose).** Practitioner's term for an operating motion in a Chapter 11 that is effectively a plan of reorganization and for a plan of reorganization that is effectively a liquidation. (Ch. Twenty-Three)

Subject matter jurisdiction. A court's power to hear and decide certain types of cases. (Ch. Eleven and Thirteen)

Subordination. The treatment of a claim in a less favored way than others either by consent of the creditor or by court order as a matter of equity as where the creditor has filed a claim after the *claims bar date* or has acted dishonestly or in bad faith to the detriment of junior claim holders. See *equitable subordination.* (Ch. Seventeen)

Subpoena. A formal order issued by the clerk of a court directing a person named therein to appear and give testimony or produce documents at a deposition or trial. (Ch. Eleven)

Substantial abuse. The abuse of the letter and or spirit of Chapter 7 justifying the dismissal of the case. (Ch. Fourteen)

Substantial completion. The date that construction on real property is substantially done. Triggers applicable time limitations for filing mechanic's and materialman's liens. (Ch. Six)

Superpriority. A priority granted to the holders of some claims that is superior even to other priority claims. For example, 1) the priority some states grant tax liens in the debtor's property (Ch. Six); and 2) in bankruptcy, the priority over administrative expenses that can be granted to creditor in exchange for giving postpetition credit to the estate pursuant to §364). (Ch. Twenty-Three and Twenty-Four)

Surety (agreement or bond). A contract pursuant to which a surety makes itself primarily liable to a named principal for a debt owed to the principal by a named obligee. (Ch. Four)

Surrender (property). The act of relinquishing property to another (e.g., the debtor surrendering secured property to the secured creditor). (Ch. Fifteen, Eighteen, and Twenty-One)

Tenancy by the entireties. A form of concurrent ownership of property between a husband and wife where each has a right of survivorship. See *concurrent ownership, joint tenancy,* and *tenancy in common.* (Ch. Ten)

Tenancy in common. A form of concurrent ownership in which each owner has an undivided interest in the property; no right of survivorship. See *concurrent ownership, community property tenancy by the entireties,* and *joint tenancy.* (Ch. Ten)

Till tap. The direct seizure of cash from the cash register of a business pursuant to a writ of execution. (Ch. Eleven)

Time is of the essence clause. A provision in a contract meaning that the parties agree that all time deadlines set out in the contract will be strictly enforced. (Ch. Three)

Title 11. The Bankruptcy Code. (Ch. Twelve)

Troubled Asset Relief Program (TARP). Congressional act approved in late 2008 authorizing the U.S. Department of the Treasury to spend up to $700 billion to purchase or insure troubled assets of endangered banks and other financial companies. (Ch. Four)

Trust. A legal arrangement where the owner of property (trustor, grantor, or settler) conveys property (trust principal or res) into the hands of a *trustee* charged with holding and administering the property for the benefit of named beneficiaries. (Ch. Ten)

Trustee. 1) In the context of a mortgage, the person to whom a power of sale foreclosure is transferred by the mortgagor for the benefit of the lender; 2) in the context of an express or constructive trust, the person to whom the trust property is conveyed to hold title for the benefit of the trust beneficiary; and 3) under the Code, the individual appointed by the U.S. Trustee (or elected by creditors in a

Chapter 7 case) who is charged with administering the bankruptcy estate; the bankruptcy trustee. (Ch. Four, Six, Ten, Thirteen, Sixteen, Seventeen, Nineteen, and Twenty-Three)

Trustee panel. Persons approved by the U.S. Trustee to serve as trustees in Chapter 7 or 11 cases in a district. Cases are normally assigned to panel members on a rotating basis. (Ch. Sixteen)

Turnover. The surrender of estate property to the trustee by the debtor or other person. (Ch. Seventeen)

Undersecured debt (claim/creditor). A secured debt where the value of the collateral is less than the amount of the debt. See *secured debt* and *unsecured debt*. (Ch. Seventeen, Eighteen, and Twenty-One)

Undue hardship. Test for discharge of student loan obligation in bankruptcy. (Ch. Eighteen)

Unfair discrimination. In a plan of reorganization, the unjustified different treatment of similar claims. (Ch. Twenty-Five)

Unfair or deceptive act or practice. Prohibited conduct by debt collectors under the FDCPA. (Ch. Seven)

Uniform Arbitration Act. Uniform statute enacted in approximately 35 states setting forth procedures governing arbitration proceedings. (Ch. Nine and Thirteen)

Uniform Commercial Code (UCC). A uniform code adopted in whole or part in all states covering contracts for the sale or lease of goods, negotiable instruments, security interests in personal property and other commercial transactions. (Ch. Five and Seventeen)

Uniform Enforcement of Foreign Judgment Act. State statute regulating the enforcement in one state of a final judgment entered in another. (Ch. Eleven)

Uniform Fraudulent Transfer Act of 1984 (UFTA). The more current uniform act regulating the recovery of fraudulent transfers. In effect in most states. (Ch. Nine)

Unimpaired (class of claims or interests). See *impaired (class or claims)*.

Unliquidated claim (debt). A claim that has not been reduced to a dollar amount. (Ch. Two)

Unsecured debt (claim/creditor). A debt enforceable only against the bare promise of a debtor to pay and not secured by any property of the debtor or guaranty of a third party. (Ch. Nine, Seventeen, and Eighteen)

U.S. Trustee. Appointed official in federal districts responsible for appointment and supervision of bankruptcy trustees and general oversight of bankruptcy cases in that district. (Ch. Thirteen)

Usury. Charging an illegal rate of interest for a loan. (Ch. Three)

Validation notice. Required language in communication from a debt collector governed by the FDCPA to a debtor regarding the debtor's right to demand verification of the debt. (Ch. Seven)

Vendor's lien (or mortgage lien). An equitable lien afforded to sellers of real property on the real property sold even in the absence of a mortgage. (Ch. Six)

Venue. The appropriate bankruptcy court in which a particular case should be filed. (Ch. Fifteen)

Voluntary case. A bankruptcy case initiated by the debtor. (Ch. Fifteen)

Wage earner plan. Informal and inaccurate name for a Chapter 13 plan. (Ch. Nineteen)

Wage order. A court order in a Chapter 13 case directing the employer of the debtor to pay a certain amount of the debtor's wages to the Standing Trustee to fund the plan. (Ch. Twenty-One)

Warrant of distress. A court order authorizing a landlord to seize property of the tenant to satisfy amount due but unpaid under the lease agreement. (Ch. Six)

Wild card exemption. Practitioner's phrase for §522(d)(5) allowing an individual debtor a general exemption in any property up to a stated value. (Ch. Fifteen)

Workout. 1. A negotiated arrangement done outside of bankruptcy under which a debtor and his creditors agree to terms of payment. Also called a composition and extension. (Ch. Twelve) 2. A negotiated settlement of the terms of a plan of reorganization in a reorganization case. (Ch. Twenty-One)

Writ. A court order directing an official, such as a sheriff, to take some action (e.g. to levy an execution). (Ch. Eleven)

Writ of attachment (or sequestration). A prejudgment court order directed to an official such as the county sheriff directing the official to seize property of a defendant and to hold the same pending outcome of the litigation. (Ch. Nine)

Writ of execution. A court order directed to an official such as the county sheriff directing the official to seize property of a debtor and to liquidate it for the benefit of a creditor. See *fieri facias*. (Ch. Eleven)

Writ of garnishment. A court order directing a person in possession of the property of a debtor (e.g., an employer) to deliver that property to the clerk of the court for payment to a creditor. (Ch. Eleven)

Writ of possession. A court order directing an official such as a sheriff to take possession of property from the one currently in custody of it for the benefit of another with a superior right to it. (Ch. Five)

100 percent plan. A Chapter 13 plan in which unsecured claims are paid in full. (Ch. Twenty-One)

§1111(b)(2) election. The right of an undersecured creditor in a Chapter 11 case to demand that the plan treat its claim as secured up to the full amount owed. (Ch. Twenty-Five)

1,215-day rule. Rule applicable to claiming the homestead exemption in bankruptcy providing that if the debtor has not owned his principal residence for more than 1,215 days preceding the filing of the petition he cannot exempt more than $155,675 of equity in it (as of April 1, 2013) regardless of any applicable state homestead exemption law. (Ch. Fifteen)

Table of Cases

Index